JOHN GAY
DRAMATIC WORKS

JOHN GAY

Dramatic Works

EDITED BY
JOHN FULLER

VOLUME I

CLARENDON PRESS · OXFORD
1983

Oxford University Press, Walton Street, Oxford OX2 6DP

London Glasgow New York Toronto
Delhi Bombay Calcutta Madras Karachi
Kuala Lumpur Singapore Hong Kong Tokyo
Nairobi Dar es Salaam Cape Town
Melbourne Auckland
and associated companies in
Beirut Berlin Ibadan Mexico City Nicosia

Oxford is a trade mark of Oxford University Press

Published in the United States
by Oxford University Press, New York

British Library Cataloguing in Publication Data

Gay, John
John Gay: dramatic works.—(Oxford English texts)
1. English drama
I. Fuller, John
822'.5   PR3473.A4
ISBN 0-19-812701-4

Library of Congress Cataloging in Publication Data

Gay, John, 1685–1732.
John Gay, dramatic works.
(Oxford English texts)
I. Fuller, John. II. Title.
PR3473.A4 1982   822'.5   81-18973
ISBN 0-19-812701-4   AACR2

Set by Eta Services (Typesetters) Ltd.,
Printed in Great Britain by
Thomson Litho Ltd.
East Kilbride, Scotland

PREFACE

NINE days before the opening of Gay's most popular play, the publisher Lintot made an announcement that 'Mr Gay's Dramatick Performances are preparing for the press' (see *The St. James's Evening Post*, 20 January 1728). His proposal was a reasonable one, for although Gay's most recent play, *The Captives* (1724), had been published by Tonson, Lintot owned the copyright of the five earlier ones. Nobody seemed to be predicting the phenomenal success of *The Beggar's Opera*, but it was an unusual enough work for the astute Lintot to have got wind of it. A collection of Gay's dramatic works would have been timely. The proposal, however, came to nothing. Gay sold his copyright in *The Beggar's Opera* and the *Fables* to Tonson and Watts on 6 February. The ballad operas were in fact printed by Watts and the two posthumous prose comedies by Astley. There was no complete collection of the drama until the plays, ballad operas, and *Acis and Galatea* were gathered together for Jeffery's six-volume edition of the *Works* (1795), and there has been no complete collection since then.

The object of this edition is to provide such a collection. The text is accompanied by a textual apparatus recording press variants; a commentary including explanatory notes and discussion of textual problems; and a critical introduction, in which, however, I have been as much concerned with circumstances of production and reception, or with details of background and interpretation, as with actual criticism of the plays. I have not included the music of *Acis and Galatea*, of the overture to *The Beggar's Opera*, of the songs in the ballad operas, nor of the surviving settings of songs in the comedies, as being beyond the brief of a reader's edition.

My copy-text is in nearly every case the first edition, into which I have introduced from the English editions of Gay's lifetime all the probably authorial variant readings. In the textual notes at the foot of each page I have indicated all departures from the copy-text, together with the variants of the early editions. In the case of *The Beggar's Opera* I have not recorded all the typographical errors introduced and corrected during the press run, and I have not incorporated into the Prologue to *Three Hours after Marriage* the minor revisions made by Pope for the fourth volume of *Miscellanies* (1742), because although Pope's responsibility for the Prologue has been generally accepted, I have preferred to print it in the form in which Gay would have known it at his death.

Spelling is not normalized and I have also refrained from inserting additional stage-directions (though I have omitted the occasional indication of the end of acts). I have, however, silently expanded and regularized the names of characters in the text, in speech-prefixes and in stage-directions as a convenience to the reader. I have also expanded in the stage-directions other contractions due to exigencies of space in the original text. I have also renumbered the Airs in *The Beggar's Opera*, and not distinguished between capitals and small capitals in scene numbers. There is no regularizing of the text in such accidental characteristics as capitalization or italicization, except in a few cases which can be interpreted as compositorial errors, and these have been noted. I am very much aware of inconsistencies of spelling and form (for instance, in *The Wife of Bath*: *Heighday*, *Heigh Day*, *Heigh day*, and *Hey-day*) and of style (for instance, in the stage-directions: irregular use of introductory capitals, square brackets, and italics). These inconsistencies may be due either to Gay's MSS or to the practice of different compositors, but in a large number of cases it is not possible to decide which, and I have preferred to interfere with my copy-texts as little as possible. I have emended punctuation only where it would appear to be erroneous or to impede understanding. I have not recorded such typographical characteristics as the long *s*, swash letters, marks of punctuation set in italics, capitalized initial words of opening speeches, printer's ornaments, ornamental initials or decorative rule.

I have preferred to give the texts in the form in which they were first printed, as they would thus seem likely to conform more closely to the original MSS. In the case of eight of the plays, the first edition actually is the single authoritative text. The revision of *The Wife of Bath* is extensive enough to justify the printing of both versions. My decision to take the text of

The What D'Ye Call It from the first edition of 1715, rather than from *Poems on Several Occasions* (1720; 2nd edn., 1731) is based on the following considerations: (*a*) 1720 was set from 1715, and is therefore likely to be no closer in spelling and punctuation to the original MS; (*b*) 1731 does not appear to have been carefully proofed by Gay; (*c*) the infrequent capitalization, style of speech-prefixes, etc., of 1720 represent the particular practice of a quarto edition; and (*d*) the substantive variants of 1720 and 1731 likely to be of authority are few, and are easily introduced into the text. D. F. Foxon argues in his unpublished Lyell Lectures, 'Pope and the early Eighteenth-century Book-trade' (1975), that Gay experimented with the extensive use of lower-case in the third edition of *The What D'Ye Call It* (1716) and in editions of other works at about that time, and that editors should therefore respect its accidentals. There is no consistent change in Gay's policy, however, and his ultimate intentions are not clear. I have therefore preserved the accidentals of my copy-texts. Except for *The Wife of Bath*, Gay made few revisions of significance in any of his plays. I discuss the claims of the Dublin five-act version of *Three Hours after Marriage* in my Commentary (p. 436). I have elsewhere, incidentally, ignored Dublin editions (and pirated editions) as of no authority. The text of *Acis and Galatea* is, for particular reasons discussed in the Commentary, somewhat eclectic. The demand for *The Beggar's Opera* allowed alterations to the formes to be made almost continuously during the printing of the early editions, but few of the resulting variants are crucial and do not materially affect the decision to use the earliest impression as copy-text. *The Distress'd Wife* similarly exists in states revealing reset, uncorrected, and corrected formes, but the resulting textual variants are minor indeed. Other bibliographical and textual matters relating to the particular plays are discussed in the Commentary, which also explains the sigla and gives the collation and other details of the editions published in Gay's lifetime, or, in the case of the posthumous plays, the first and closely related editions.

A debt to earlier writers on Gay will be evident, but I am particularly grateful for the invaluable researches of G. C. Faber, W. H. Irving, W. E. Schultz, and George Sherburn.

Various editions of *Three Hours after Marriage* and of *The Beggar's Opera* have appeared while I have been working on Gay, and all have proved extremely useful. The staffs of the libraries mentioned herein have been most helpful. I gladly record my thanks to them; to Norman Davis, Ian Donaldson, Roger Lonsdale, Ann Mitchell, the late Dermot Morrah, David Profumo, and Alice Walker, who have supplied me with information; and to Leofranc Holford-Strevens, for his many improvements to the accuracy and usefulness of the commentary. The late Herbert Davis and the late F. W. Bateson provided much-valued advice and encouragement in the work's early stages, and I remember with special gratitude my introduction to Gay twenty years ago under the stimulating guidance of John Bayley.

JOHN FULLER

Oxford,
September 1979.

CONTENTS

VOLUME I

VOLUME II

ABBREVIATIONS

THIS is a list of works sometimes cited in abbreviated form; of libraries, institutions, and periodicals; and of abbreviations used in the textual footnotes. The place of publication of books, here and elsewhere in the edition, is London, unless otherwise stated.

Ault and Butt	Alexander Pope, *Minor Poems*, ed. Norman Ault and John Butt (1954).
Avery	*The London Stage, 1660–1800: A Calendar of Plays, &c.*, Part 2: 1700–29, ed. Emmett L. Avery (2 vols., Carbondale, Ill., 1960).
Bailey	*English Dialect Words of the Eighteenth Century as shown in the 'Universal Etymological Dictionary' of Nathaniel Bailey*, ed. William E. A. Axon (1883).
Baker	*Biographia Dramatica, or A Companion to the Playhouse*, compiled by David E. Baker, Isaac Reed, and Stephen Jones (1812–13).
Barnstaple	The North Devon Athenaeum, Barnstaple.
BL	The British Library.
Bodley	The Bodleian Library, Oxford.
Breval	[John Durant Breval], *The Confederates* (1717).
Bronson	Bertrand H. Bronson, 'The Beggar's Opera' in *Studies in the Comic* (University of California Publications in English, vol. 8, no. 2, 1941), 197–231.
Canting Crew	B. E., *A new Dictionary of . . . the canting Crew* (1690).
Cooke	William Cooke, *Memoirs of Charles Macklin Comedian with the Dramatic Characters, Manners, Anecdotes, &c. of the Age in which he lived* (1804).
Dean	Winton Dean, *Handel's Dramatic Oratorios and Masques* (1959).
Dearing	John Gay, *Poetry and Prose*, ed. Vinton A. Dearing, with the assistance of Charles E. Beckwith (2 vols., Oxford, 1974).

DNB	*The Dictionary of National Biography.*
Drub	['Timothy Drub'], *A Letter to Mr. John Gay, concerning His late Farce, Entituled, A Comedy* (1717).
Dunciad (B)	Alexander Pope, *The Dunciad, In Four Books* (1743).
EC	*The Works of Alexander Pope*, ed. W. Elwin and W. J. Courthope (10 vols., 1871–89).
ELH	*English Literary History.*
Early Career	George Sherburn, *The Early Career of Alexander Pope* (Oxford, 1934).
Faber	*The Poetical Works of John Gay*, ed. G. C. Faber (Oxford, 1926).
Gaye	Phoebe Fenwick Gaye, *John Gay. His place in the Eighteenth Century* (1938).
Genest	John Genest, *Some Account of the English Stage from the Restoration in 1660 to 1830* (Bath, 1832).
Grose	Francis Grose, *A Classical Dictionary of the Vulgar Tongue*, ed. Eric Partridge (1931).
Harrington Smith	*Three Hours after Marriage*, ed. John Harrington Smith (Los Angeles, 1961).
Hooker	*The Critical Works of John Dennis*, ed. Edward Niles Hooker (two vols., Baltimore, 1939, 1943).
Houghton	Houghton Library, Harvard.
Howson	Gerald Howson, *Thief-Taker General: The Rise and Fall of Jonathan Wild* (1970).
Irving	W. H. Irving, *John Gay, Favorite of the Wits* (Durham, NC, 1940).
JEGP	*Journal of English and Germanic Philology.*
Journal to Stella	Jonathan Swift, *Journal to Stella*, ed. Harold Williams (2 vols., Oxford, 1948).
Kerby-Miller	*The Memoirs of Martinus Scriblerus*, ed. Charles Kerby-Miller (New Haven, Conn., 1950).
Key	In context, one of the following: *A Complete Key to the last New Farce, The What D'Ye Call It* (1715); *A Key to the New Comedy; call'd Three Hours after Marriage* in *A Supplement to the Works of Alexander Pope, Esq.* (Dublin,

1758), p. 207; *A Compleat Key to the Beggar's Opera* (originally in the *Craftsman* for 17 February 1728) in Christopher Bullock, *A Woman's Revenge; or, A Match in Newgate* (2nd edn., 1728).

Letters	*The Letters of John Gay*, ed. C. F. Burgess (Oxford, 1966).
Lewis	*The Beggar's Opera*, ed. Peter Elfed Lewis (Edinburgh, 1973).
Linc	Lincoln College Library, Oxford.
Magd	Magdalen College Library, Oxford.
MLR	*Modern Language Review.*
Morton and Peterson	*Three Hours after Marriage*, ed. Richard Morton and William M. Peterson (Painesville, Ohio, 1961).
Motteux	[Miguel de Cervantes Saavedra], *The History of the renown'd Don Quixote de la Mancha* (P. Motteux, 1700–3).
MP	*Modern Philology.*
N & Q	*Notes and Queries.*
New Light	Norman Ault, *New Light on Pope* (1949).
Nichols	John Nichols, *Literary Anecdotes of the Eighteenth Century* (9 vols., 1812–15).
Nicoll	Allardyce Nicoll, *A History of English Drama 1660–1900*, vol. 2: Early Eighteenth Century Drama (3rd edn., Cambridge, 1952).
Noble	*Twentieth Century Interpretations of The Beggar's Opera*, ed. Yvonne Noble (Englewood Cliffs, NJ, 1975).
OED	*Oxford English Dictionary.*
Parker	E. Parker, Philomath, *A Complete Key to the New Farce, call'd Three Hours after Marriage* (1717).
PBSA	*Papers of the Bibliographical Society of America.*
Pearce	Charles E. Pearce, *'Polly Peachum', being the story of Lavinia Fenton (Duchess of Bolton) and 'The Beggar's Opera'* (1913).
PMA	*Proceedings of the Musical Association.*
PMLA	*Publications of the Modern Language Association of America.*

PQ	*Philological Quarterly.*
PRO	Public Record Office.
RES	*Review of English Studies.*
Scouten	*The London Stage, 1660–1800*, Part 3: 1729–47, ed. A. H. Scouten (Carbondale, Ill., 1961).
Schultz	William Eben Schultz, *Gay's Beggar's Opera, its Content, History and Influence* (New Haven, Conn., 1923).
Sherburn	*The Correspondence of Alexander Pope*, ed. George Sherburn (5 vols., Oxford, 1956).
SP	*Studies in Philology.*
Spence	Joseph Spence, *Observations, Anecdotes, and Characters of Books and Men*, ed. James M. Osborn (2 vols., Oxford, 1966).
Stone	*The London Stage, 1660–1800*, Part 4: 1747–76, ed. George Winchester Stone, Jr. (Carbondale, Ill., 1962).
Strype	John Stow, *A Survey of the Cities of London and Westminster*, rev. John Strype *et al.* (1720). (Bound in parts with separate pagination.)
Suffolk Corr.	*Letters to and from Henrietta, Countess of Suffolk, and her second husband, the Hon. George Berkeley; from 1712 to 1767*, [ed. J. W. Croker] (two vols., 1824).
Swift Corr.	*The Correspondence of Jonathan Swift*, ed. Harold Williams (5 vols., Oxford, 1963–5).
Tillotson	Alexander Pope, *The Rape of the Lock and Other Poems*, ed. Geoffrey Tillotson (1940).
TLS	*Times Literary Supplement.*
Trevelyan	G. M. Trevelyan, *England under Queen Anne* (3 vols., 1930).
Trin	Trinity College Library, Cambridge.
V & A	Dyce and Forster Auxiliary Collection, Victoria and Albert Museum.
Wit and Mirth	*Wit and Mirth: or, Pills to Purge Melancholy*, ed. Thomas D'Urfey (6 vols., 1719–20).
Worc	Worcester College Library, Oxford.

The following abbreviations are used in the textual notes:

~	The exact form of word cited.
∧	Absence of punctuation.
del	(After siglum) a deleted reading in the MS.
om	(Before siglum) omitted in that text.
var	(After siglum) some copies of that edition or impression.
sd	Stage direction or other silent line of text.

INTRODUCTION

> Thus far our Riots with Success are crown'd,
> Have found no stop, or what they found o'ercame.

These first two lines of Gay's first play are a parody of the
opening lines of Dryden's *Tyrannick Love*, lending an absurd
swagger to the small triumphs of the town rowdy who utters
them; the final couplet of his last published play solemnly
asserts:

> The Drift of Plays, by *Aristotle*'s Rules,
> Is, what you've seen—Exposing Knaves and Fools.

Both these plays are short farces, yet the contrast of tone that I
have suggested is wholly characteristic of Gay's development
from impertinent mock-heroics and imaginative absurdity to
an aggrieved righteousness and confident moral self-
justification. But Gay's best work does fall within the last
quarter of his career, and his pen was active up to his death:
we cannot call him a failure as a dramatist. It was, however,
an uncertain career, with the profitable direction not always
clearly taken and mistakes too often repeated. For this reason
he is usually remembered only as the author of *The Beggar's
Opera*, and his other plays are, by and large, neither
performed nor much read. This is a great pity, since several of
these plays are first-class and help to establish Gay at the
forefront of the characteristic writers of his age.

His career as a playwright spans the twenty years between
the War of the Spanish Succession and the supremacy of
Walpole; between, roughly, the last of Restoration comedy in
Vanbrugh, Farquhar, or Steele, and the last of Augustan
comedy in Fielding; between the collapse of wit into
sentiment, and the collapse of satire into censored silence.
Determined from the beginning to strike out on his own, Gay
let his taste for grotesque invention and colloquial realism lead
him to such dramatists as Wilson, Shadwell, or D'Urfey, to
the burlesque of Buckingham, even to Shakespeare, rather
than to the current artificialities of the sentimentalists, Cibber

and Mrs Centlivre. As a poet, Gay had begun in the tradition of William King, Tom Brown, or John Philips. His dramatic work similarly reflects the satirical bent of a young man with a natural delight in oddity and inconsequence, an observant eye and a genuine fondness for the simple life. These qualities, among the most attractive in Augustan literature, well qualified him for his membership of the Scriblerus Club, perhaps the most important single influence on Gay's drama. The resulting Scriblerian plays, *The What D'Ye Call It* and *Three Hours after Marriage*, are much the best of his earlier work. Pope, Swift, and Arbuthnot were sympathetic and stimulating friends, able to direct Gay's attention to the most serviceable targets of pretentiousness and folly, and to encourage by understanding and example his own delicately ironical moral sense. We would not disagree with Cowper's view that they were 'the most celebrated association of clever fellows this country every saw'.[1]

After an uncharacteristic excursion into tragedy, Gay achieved a happy balance of social criticism and literary burlesque in the work of his maturity. He seems to have done most among playwrights of the first half of the century to show in which direction the intellectual drama could profitably tend, even though the work of his natural successor, Fielding, was abbreviated by the Licensing Act of 1737 and diverted into the novel, a theatre of ideas doomed by Whig hypersensitivity. Like Pope, Gay 'stoop'd to Truth', but his growing preoccupation with sexual mores and with political corruption may seem at times a poor exchange for the imaginative riches of Scriblerian farce and burlesque. However, I am sure that we owe much of the slyness and epigrammatic poise of the ballad-operas to this preoccupation. The probability that it springs from Gay's own disappointed search for preferment, and from his *odi et amo* movement in Court circles, does not invalidate the seriousness of his criticism of government patronage or fashionable life, even where it acquires a monotony not fully relieved by dramatic inventiveness, as is perhaps the case with *The Distress'd Wife*.

It will become evident that my opinion of the posthumous plays by no means so unfavourable as to cast doubt on Gay's having played his full part in the superior works of collaboration. Scriblerus was largely a catalyst, and the responsibility of Pope or Arbuthnot for the best in Gay's early farces (or even the ballad-operas) has been exaggerated. When Pope brought part of *The What D'Ye Call It* to the players in his own handwriting, Cibber jumped to the conclusion that has haunted critics ever since: 'After this, seeing a knife with the name of J. Gay upon it, [he asked] "What, does Mr. Pope make knives, too?"' (Spence, i. 103). We have to remember that this became an habitual stand taken by Pope's enemies. Addison and his friends, for instance, persisted in regarding Gay as one of Pope's docile 'élèves' (Spence, i. 62) and there were others who assiduously ascribed the most biting satire of *The Beggar's Opera* to Pope or Swift. No one was more aware of the injustice of all this than Pope, who was often at pains to reverse the process of misattribution. Indeed, there are several occasions in his letters where out of generosity or deception he gives Gay the whole credit even against our better knowledge. This is why the critical pendulum should not swing too far the other way. I would not wish to suggest that Pope or Arbuthnot would have been quite at sea without Gay's dramatic talents: this is as patently unfair as the first, and commoner, theory. There is much, for example, in the bizarre dialogue of Pope's *The Narrative of Dr. Robert Norris* to match the brilliant humour of *Three Hours after Marriage*. All this I hope to make clear in discussing the individual works.

Gay's first play, *The Mohocks*, was not only carefully researched but highly topical, probably written in rather less than three weeks. In it Gay makes fun of a current scare, the factual basis of which is now somewhat elusive, but for that reason no less relevant to an appreciation of the play, and a very interesting example in itself of Gay's method of exalting and fantasizing reality, a method brought to perfection in the mock-tragic press-ganging and horse-stealing of *The What D'Ye Call It* or the tea-table manners of the prostitutes in *The Beggar's Opera*. Gay's play was published on 10 April 1712. Only a month before, the Mohocks were hot news. 'Did I tell you', wrote Swift to Stella on 8 March, 'of a race of Rakes calld the Mohacks that play the devil about this Town every Night, slitt peoples noses, & beat them &c.' The next day Henry Davenant 'was telling us at Court how he was sett upon by the Mohacks; and how they ran his Chair thro with a Sword' and a rumour had it that Thomas Burnet, youngest son of the Bishop of Salisbury, was one of the gang.[2] It turned out, though, that Davenant had merely been assailed by a drunk, and the Mohocks' connections in high places were not particularly credible. Swift was disinclined to believe reports that the Mohocks had designs on his own life, yet the *Journal to Stella* is full of his fear of walking home late at night: 'the Dogs will cost me at least a Crown a Week in Chairs' (ii. 525). Remembering the Roaring Boys, Tityre-tues, Bugles, Hectors, Scourers, and Nickers who preceded the Mohocks, we must allow that social conditions made such night rowdyism inevitable, and the violence does seem to have been real, if exaggerated. Swift was not being over-timorous in keeping to his sedan-chair; but nor, on the other hand, was his scepticism about the political implications of the Mohocks misplaced.

Both parties made political capital out of the incidents. The Whigs accused the Tories of being unable to keep the peace (in the *Observator*, 15 March 1712, for example) and the Tories were inclined to blame the disturbances on Whigs seeking to make propaganda against the government. On the night of Tuesday 11 March a large number of arrests was supposedly made, with among those arrested such well-known men as Lord Hinchinbroke and Sir Mark Cole.[3] There were even stories of a plot of Marlborough and Prince Eugene to seize the Tower, set fire to London, and murder Lord Oxford, but these were invented by a Jacobite spy, Plunket, and were not believed by the Ministry.[4] On Wednesday 12 March the press was full of the Mohocks. 'Grubstreet Papers about them fly like Lightning', wrote Swift to Stella (ii. 511). Among these were the *True List*, the broadside *The Town-Rakes: or, The Frolicks of the Mohocks or Hawkubites*, and the *Spectator* no. 324, the last providing Gay with some of the details of his play (see, in my Commentary, the notes to the Dramatis Personae, ii. 33, ii. 180 sd and iii. 37). On 16 March Swift gave an account to Stella of an attack on old Lady Winchelsea's maid (ii. 515) and on the following day the Queen issued a Proclamation, offering £100 reward for information leading to an arrest.[5] A contemporary attributed to Gay a broadside published on 18 March called *An Argument Proving from History*,

Reason, and Scripture, That the Present Mohocks and Hawkubites are the Gog and Magog mention'd in the Revelations, etc., a pastiche of fanatical Camisard prophecy and diatribe.[6] Another pamphlet which might have had some influence on Gay's play is *The Mohocks: A Poem, in Miltonic Verse: Address'd to the Spectator* (1712).[7]

One may presume that about this time Gay began to write his farce, but the dating of the Dedication 'April, 1' does not, of course, necessarily imply that it was quite finished by then. The players refused it, and it was published on 15 April. Swift had written on 22 March: 'Our Mohocks are all vanisht' (*Journal to Stella*, ii. 522), but Sir Roger de Coverley attended the theatre a few days later elaborately guarded (in the *Spectator* no. 335, on 25 March), and on the day after that Swift admitted: 'Our Mohawks go on still' (ii. 524). The scare, however, was passing. The Whigs defended themselves with some assurance against the Tory rumours in the *Medley* of 28 March, and by 8 April Budgell was able to write in the *Spectator* no. 347 of the 'late Panick Fear', and that 'very many begin to doubt whether indeed there were ever any such Society of Men'. This became the official Whig view (in, for example, Oldmixon's *History of England*, 1735, iii. 494) and is no doubt nearest to the truth which the impartial and inventive imagination of Gay has perhaps done most to obscure. As William Maitland wrote: 'it does not appear, that ever any Person was detected of any of the said Crimes; and notwithstanding I made all the Inquiry imaginable, in those places where the Offences were said to have been chiefly committed, I never could learn of any one Person having received the least Hurt upon that Account' (*History and Survey of London*, 1756, i. 510).

The play is thus geared as closely as possible to the events it describes. Even so, Gay must have wasted some time before publication trying to get it accepted at the playhouse and then fitting it out with a neat and original 'Prologue. To be Spoken by the Publisher' and an ironical Dedication to John Dennis, boasting of the play's neo-classical perfection. We have seen how current Mohock literature gave Gay some ideas, but Gay's conception of his subject is already characteristically his own. To show a harmless fop accused of being a

Mohock is no doubt a Whiggish gesture, and the Mohocks themselves claim at the end that 'We are Gentleman, Sirs, 'twas only an innocent Frolick' (iii. 159). But for most of the play their masquerade is serious enough, and the real point is surely that Gay needs the Mohocks to exist, to speak like fallen angels or Hamlet's ghost and leave the ground ·'covered with Noses—as thick as 'tis with Hail-stones after a Storm' (ii. 43). The 'nose', of course, can be a phallic euphemism. There is a good deal of suggestive fear for the nose in this play, while the final indignity proposed by the Mohocks is actually castration (ii. 160) and its curious, though logical, female equivalent:

Poor *John Mopstaff*'s Wife was like to come to damage by them—for they took her up by the Heels and turn'd her quite inside out—the poor Woman, they say, will ne'er be good for any thing more—honest *John* can hardly find the Head from the Tail of her. (ii. 63).

Their association with prostitutes (mentioned by the *Spectator* no. 324) seems to be another aspect of their dangerous and exclusive virility. Peg's and Jenny's politeness to the Mohocks when they are freed at ii. 149 ('Your humble Servant, Mr. *Mirmidon*' etc.) anticipates the exeunt of the prostitutes in *The Beggar's Opera*, II. vi, a sophistication of the underworld typical of Gay, and pertinent here. *The Mohocks* is perhaps nearer in atmosphere to *The Beggar's Opera* than is any other play of Gay's, though actual points of resemblance are few. One might compare the song at i. 69 with Air XIX of *The Beggar's Opera*, and Jenny's speech at ii. 183 is a hint of the kind of moral inversion that lies behind the later work: 'Pox on't, Mr. *Mirmidon*—'tis as dangerous for us to use a Watchman ill, as for a Stage-Coachman to be uncivil to an High-way Man', in which the insinuation about authority has the characteristic Gay reverberation. In Gay's world a Macheath is heroic only because his sophistication has inverted his real role as the actual clothes-changing in *The Mohocks* cannot do. The roisterers are already impossibly elevated, above even the superb privileged carelessness of the highwayman Macheath. And of course the paralysed Watch are the very opposite of sophisticated.

The fondness of the Mohocks for ritual is turned to good

account by Gay to supply connotations of other contemporary bogeys. They boast of more women than the 'Grand Seignior's' seraglio (i. 86) and talk of a 'Janizary' (ii. 189); one of them is a 'Grand Vizier' (iii. 34), and their Emperor wears a crescent moon on his forehead (ii. 180 sd). Remembering the power of the Ottoman Empire at this time, it is no wonder that Joan Cloudy exclaims: 'The Laird keep us, say I, from the Great *Turk*, and from Popery!' (iii. 124). The Mohocks were probably, after all, only well-to-do bullies, but Gay turns them into sinister epic villains ('*Horrid* and *Tremendous*' according to the Dedication) whose discomfiture in the comic reversal of the slight but shapely plot is all the more absurd for their initial menace grandly suggested by the parody of Dryden's Maximin:

> Thus far our Riots with Success are crown'd,
> Have found no stop, or what they found o'ercame;
> In vain th' embattell'd Watch in deep array,
> Against our Rage oppose their lifted Poles;
> Through Poles we rush triumphant, Watchman rolls
> On Watchman; while their Lanthorns kick'd aloft
> Like blazing Stars, illumine all the Air.

The miniature satanic bullying of this metropolitan War in Heaven is delightful: this is mock-heroic with a purpose.

The watch, on the other hand, are neo-Shakespearean clowns through and through: after the roles have been exchanged it is not surprising that feeble watchmen make feeble Mohocks. But though they may verbally remind us of Dogberry or Falstaff or Bottom at almost every line, the bite has gone. They are as fine imitations as the period could produce, but they have been inevitably scaled down to the comfortable pantomime of Norris and Penkethman, the comedians for whom the main parts were written. As a foil to the Mohocks they could hardly be bettered. Their world is one in which women are fully in control. The husband's sexual potency becomes a mere matter of domestic economy (iii. 126), while its threatened loss is feared in terms of the woman being deprived of her 'only comfort' (ii. 165). Characters are uncompromisingly frank about the assumed inequality of their sexual appetites: 'What two Women! why

a Woman with common Modesty in her Demands would not
have desired above two Men' (iii. 54). It is easy to understand
the heroic proportions of the Mohocks' roistering: Gay is here
ironically confronting two extremes of the male sexual
character.

Gay's second play, *The Wife of Bath*, was accepted by the
players for performance after *Cato*, and seems to have suffered
a little from being acted in its shadow. 'Cato was not so much
the wonder of Rome, itself, in his days', wrote Pope to Caryll
on 30 April 1713, 'as he is of Britain in ours' (Sherburn, ii.
174). As the run of Addison's play lengthened, Gay must have
feared that his would not get performed at all. On 23 April he
wrote to Maurice Johnson: 'my Play comes on, on the 5ᵗʰ of
May; it was put off upon account of Cato; so that you may
easily imagine I by this time begin to be a little sensible of the
approaching Danger.'[8] The play was not actually put on until
12 May, and then was performed only twice. Irving (p. 82)
says that the play ran for three nights, and is followed by
Burgess in his edition of the *Letters* (p. 3), but according to
Avery, though it was announced for 14 May, performance
was deferred. Sixteen years later, Gay automatically referred
to it as a 'damned play' (*Letters*, p. 86).

Conditions were not entirely unfavourable. Two years
earlier Gay had praised Steele in *The Present State of Wit*, and
in 1713 Steele asked him to write a couple of *Guardians*,
printed four of his poems in his *Poetical Miscellanies*, and on 8
May gave *The Wife of Bath* a comforting puff during that
awkward waiting period:

I had just given my Orders for the Press when my Friend Mrs.
Bicknell made me a Visit. She came to desire I would show her the
Wardrobe of the *Lizard*'s (where the various Habits of the Ancestors
of that Illustrious Family are preserved) in order to furnish her with
a proper Dress for the *Wife of Bath*. Upon Sight of the little Ruffs,
she snatched one of them from the Pin, clapt it round her Neck, and
turning briskly towards me, repeated a Speech out of her Part in the
Comedy of that Name. If the rest of the Actors enter into their
several Parts with the same Spirit, the humorous Characters of this
Play cannot but appear excellent on the Theatre: For very good
Judges have informed me, that the Author has drawn them with
great Propriety, and an exact Observation of their Manners.
(*Guardian* no. 50).

Pope may have supplied the Epilogue (see my Commentary, pp. 412 ff), and on 12 May Lintot bought the copyright for £25, a distinct advance over the £2. 10s. paid for *The Mohocks* (Nichols, viii. 296). There was thus no lack of sympathetic interest in the play, and Gay must have been really disappointed in its failure.

It was not that his subject was unpromising: he was something of an expert on popular customs and beliefs, as he was to demonstrate with a charming abundance in 'Thursday' of *The Shepherd's Week* and in some of his Prioresque tales. Witch-hunting and ghost-hunting were a legitimate pursuit of the virtuosi in the age of Glanvill (since to prove the existence of immaterial substances was to refute Hobbes and forestall any charges of atheism that might be made against experimental science) while astrology and even alchemy were not yet discredited.[9] Gay largely restricts the scope of his satirical subject here, however, to Myrtilla's resistance and Chaucer's wooing stratagems. The jokes are comparatively incidental and fairly mild, as when, for instance, Chaucer asks the old astrologer for a disguise and is equally provided with the astrologer's own, false, beard (IV. 43). It might with justice be said, then, that supernatural credulity, while figuring in the plot, is not an intrinsic enough part of it to become a sufficient object of satire, and Gay's attitude, good-humoured and even indulgent, is hardly sharp enough.

The real failure was no doubt one of structure and organization. Irving (p. 79) suggests that the interest is continually divided between Florinda's elopement with Merit, and Chaucer's wooing of the reluctant Myrtilla. But it is not true to say that the 'second group of characters do not appear until the fourth scene of Act II', and Irving does not, I think, give enough credit to the neat deployment of the linking characters: Doggrell, the snobbish poet designed by Franklyn for Florinda; and the eponymous Alison, who turns Doggrell's interest in Myrtilla first to her own and then to Myrtilla's maid's account, herself in the end marrying Franklyn. This is hardly a 'broken-backed' plot on paper. What does get a little out of hand is the scene-by-scene continuity, the managing of exits and entrances, the minor actions and motivations.

During 1729, with notable, if misguided, industry and perseverance, Gay almost entirely rewrote the play. It was still not a success, but he had clearly tried to do two things: to give it a greater organic unity, and to excise much of the derivative exuberance of style. In the second version, Myrtilla and Florinda are old school friends who change clothes to allow Florinda to escape, and it is this rather than Doggrell's clumsily prepared snobbery that sets him in pursuit of Myrtilla. The mechanics of time and place are much more smoothly managed. Myrtilla is less antagonistic towards Sir Harry (Chaucer). Plowden (Franklyn) refuses his blessing to Florinda and has no intention of marrying Alison, who in this version has already been tricked out of marrying Doggrell. But this gain in realism, with its sparer dialogue, is accompanied by a loss of the essential atmosphere of the original.

This atmosphere was, of course, something of a mélange. One might call it (remembering Steele's preview) Chaucer in ruffs, for Gay had no very clear idea of period and there is more than one moment in the play when the 'Inn, lying in the Road between London and Canterbury' might be mistaken for the Boar's Head Tavern. Swift hinted as much on 20 November 1729, replying to Gay's news of his proposed revision: 'I have heard of the Wife of Bath, I think in Shakespear, if you wrote one it is out of my head' (*Swift Corr.*, iii. 360). How far this friendly irony about the play's Shakespearean borrowings stimulated Gay in his revision, one cannot say, for Swift's words have even been taken to reveal his ignorance of Shakespeare, and many of his less obviously avuncular counsels have this apparent remoteness. Gay's Chaucer is the Chaucer of ribaldry, with jokes about friars in confessionals, amorous widows, and bed-tricks. As Pope was to complain in 'The First Epistle of the Second Book of Horace':

> Authors, like Coins, grow dear as they grow old;
> It is the rust we value, not the gold.
> Chaucer's worst ribaldry is learn'd by rote.[10]

To associate this penny-ballad tradition of the Wife of Bath with the more dramatically accessible world of Elizabethan comedy was perfectly natural, and it is in the scenes which in

1730 Gay felt obliged to omit or tone down that one can best
see the influence: in the mirror-scene with its *Macbeth*-like
incantations (IV. 187); the scene where Merit disguises himself
as a drawer (II. 327); or the scene where Antony and William,
like Dogberry or the gravediggers in *Hamlet*, quibble clown-
ishly on legalistic points (II. 41). Omitted, too, are many of the
verses and songs. One particularly misses the spirited
D'Urfeyesque 'There was a Swain full fair'.

In 1713 Gay lavished on the style, with its impulsive
proverbializing and perhaps over-deliberately racy texture,
the attention which in 1730 he found better deployed in
trying to inject a more dramatically convincing evolution of
plot. This led him to be barer, if less rhetorical, in the
revision. Gain and loss may be judged by comparing almost
any passage, say the first entry of Myrtilla's lover:

<table>
<tr><td>

(1713)

Chaucer. What, turn'd Pilgrim, my Dear,
—and must Love give Place to Religion,—
[*Kisses her.*] Have I no Hopes but by
turning Fryar, and calling my Love Con-
tinence and Mortification—I was very
luckily a Day or two since informed of
Lady *Myrtilla*'s Resolution—

Busie. Oh, dear Sir, pray how long have
you been return'd from your Travels?

Chaucer. But just arriv'd—Absence, Mrs.
Busie, has not been able to deface the
Impressions of Love,—and still the Lady
Myrtilla reigns in my Bosom, haunts my
waking Thoughts, and is ever present in
my Dreams.—I think, I talk, I write of
nothing but her.

</td><td>

(1730)

Sir *Harry.* What!
turn'd pilgrim, my
Girl!

I was very luckily a
day or two ago in-
form'd of *Myrtilla*'s
resolution.

Busy. But, dear Sir
Harry, how long have
you been return'd
from your travels?

Sir *Harry*. But a
very few days; and
as much in love as
ever. My passion was
beyond the cure of
absence, and I could
like no woman, but
as she more or less
put me in mind of
Myrtilla.

</td></tr>
</table>

Busie. I am afraid, Mr. *Chaucer*, your Case will be just the same as the Boys in the Fable,—you have talked of Love Artillery, Flames, Eyes, and Darts, so long in Jest, that it will be very difficult to gain belief, now you are in Earnest.

Chaucer. But pray, Child, is Devotion or Discontent the Cause of her Retirement? —For Mad-houses and Nunneries are as much inhabited by disappointed Lovers as Devotees—and I fear, should a Cloyster be her Choice, the other would soon be my Fate.

Busy. Her heart is fortified by superstition; the stars oppose you, and the planets fight against you: In short, she hath nothing weak about her but her inclination.

Sir *Harry.* Am I quite forgot, Mrs. *Busy?*

It may be admitted that in their second speeches in this scene, Chaucer and Sir Harry talk in the language of the seventeenth-century romance and the eighteenth-century novel respectively, but this could only represent an advance if the play itself were maturer in conception: Chaucer as a Queen Anne gallant, however odd an idea, is still preferable, and demands a touch of flamboyance in the style. One misses in the later version, too, the figurative habit of 1713: the boys crying wolf; and the notion of the spurned lover taking orders, with its delicious corollary that one could be a 'Devotee' of a madhouse as well as of a nunnery. Or compare Alison's vivid speech in 1713 on spirits (III. 86) with her slightly acid mock-affectation in 1730 (III. vi. 19):

Frighten'd! quotha—No, no, Madam,—I have, thanks to Experience, seen Spirits of all Shapes, and all Countries—Why, a *Jerusalem* Spirit is no more like an *English* Spirit than a Hog is like a Rhinoceros.—I have been Witness of all the Devil's Frolicks—Idad, to my certain Knowledge, he makes nothing of unfurnishing a Kitchen to entertain himself with a Country-Dance of Dishes and Platters; many be the times and often, he has rattled my Curtains, and made the Bed shake under me, when I have not had the comfort of a Bedfellow; many a dark Night have I seen the Headless Horse, and have had the Honour to Converse with the Queen of the Fairies. (1713)

To be sure, Madam, I never saw any thing worse than myself in all my life. Frighten'd, said you? Alack-a-day, all my skittish days are over. When I was young, indeed, like other young girls, I thought fear very becoming; and I had then, Madam, tho' I say it, a very genteel scream. (1730).

The earlier dismissal comes of experience (summarizing pages of *Saducismus Triumphatus*); the later self-deprecation seems too involved for the character, though the idea of a 'genteel scream' is pure Gay. The later humour is often more concise and sophisticated in this way, but the earlier colour is an essential aspect of the youthful dramatist, who, for instance, if he is to make his characters swear at all, seems to make them swear with all the variety he can muster: a casual inspection produces *i'faith, s'bud, s'buddikins, 'slife, i'dad, bless me, 'slid, s'diggers, fie, i'facking, ods-my-life, slidikins, i'fackins, s'heartlikins, i'troth, harrow and alas, by St. Thomas of Kent, ah Benedicite, alack and well-a-day, legerdemain and necromancy, Gad a-mercy, by my fay* and *by my troth*. In the final scene alone, Alison addresses Franklyn as *old Chronicle, Shaver, old Nicodemus, old Jereboam, old Touchwood, my Heart of Oak, old Boy, my lusty Nestor, old Greybeard, Chicken*, and *my old Hero*. It is as if Gay wished his language to create the sense of abundance of life often cramped by the stiffer actualities of character and action. The style often betrays the 'pudding-like quality' that Bonamy Dobrée observed in Shadwell,[11] a kind of native festivity ill-suited to the formal demands of wit. Not that the 1713 version is without its share of Gay's particular form of insane logic, as in the girl who reflects: 'Methinks one's natural Inclination would induce one to try Matrimony once,—purely for the sake of Novelty' (I. 163). Indeed, the humour in general is not without a characteristic cutting edge behind the garrulity, and more of it might well have been preserved. The natural ease and epigrammatism of his mature dramatic style in the period of the ballad-operas is, to my mind, an unsure advance in the revision over the first vigour and awkwardness, for this was not, and never could be, a comedy of manners; and only gusto and rhetoric could successfully begin to disguise its lack of one of Gay's redeeming skills, imaginative metamorphosis and farce.

The What D'Ye Call It, produced on 23 February 1715, was Gay's most successful play next to *The Beggar's Opera*. He was paid £16. 2s. 6d. for the copyright (Nichols, viii. 296) and Pope said that he made 'about 100 ll. of this farce' (Sherburn, i. 283). It was frequently revived, and a translation into French appeared in the second volume of C. P. Patu's *Choix de petites pièces du théâtre anglais* (Paris, 1756). Although it was the first of his dramatic works to endear itself to the theatre-going public, it is also the first to present serious difficulties of authorship. Pope may have inspired the Dedication of *The Mohocks* or even penned an Epilogue for *The Wife of Bath*, but the substance of those plays was Gay's own. Now Scriblerus had come into being in the autumn of 1713, and in a happy atmosphere of enthusiastic collaboration, Arbuthnot, Swift, Gay, Parnell, and Pope set about their wholesale parody of all kinds of cultural and scientific pedantry and pretentiousness. Gay might be considered 'too young'[12] for such intellectual frolics, but he caught the spirit in his mock-naturalist 'Alphabetical Catalogue of Names, Plants, Flowers, Fruits, Birds, Beasts, Insects, and other material things mentioned in these Pastorals' appended to *The Shepherd's Week* (published in April 1714), itself a minor weapon in Pope's current disengagement from Button's.[13] These shifts of allegiance are doubly responsible for the minor notoriety of *The What D'Ye Call it*, for Scriblerus naturally demanded a parody of the tragic poets, and the alienated Buttonians, perhaps sensitive to the impending *Iliad* and anxious to discredit him, saw only Pope as responsible. When Addison and Philips were parodied in it, Steele (Governor of Drury Lane since the accession of George I) staunchly declared that 'the farce should not have been acted if he had been in town' (Sherburn, i. 287) and Philips seems likely to have stimulated some of the pamphlet attacks on the play (see my Commentary, p. 420). But Rowe was parodied too, and did not appear to mind: the play cast its net sufficiently wide (Shakespeare, Dryden, Southerne, Otway, Lee, Banks, Congreve) to have drowned the isolated voices of dissent. Dennis, indirectly attacked in the Preface, assumed slightingly that the play was Pope's. The authors of the *Key*[14] refer to Gay and Pope, perhaps more accurately but no less impolitely, as 'lovely Yoak-mates, Joint Fathers of a poor Jest', and admit that 'where the maggot first grew, or to what refin'd Head it owes its Original, is kept, as it ought to be, a great Secret'. Nonetheless, 'a certain tall, well-dress'd Modern of great Gravity and much Politeness', who has been identified as Philips, is quoted as saying of Pope: 'But this malevolent Critick fights, like little Teucer, behind the Shield of impenetrable Stupidity',[15] a comparison made more than once with reference to Pope's so-called literary cowardice. Broome repeats the charge, writing to Fenton about Pope's role in the composition of *The Beggar's Opera* (Sherburn, ii. 489). This view of the relationship was to be much strengthened by Pope's and Arbuthnot's reticence about owning their part in *Three Hours after Marriage* (see Breval, *The Confederates*, 1717, i) and was no doubt irritating to Gay. Even worse, and fully intended to annoy, was feigned sympathy for Gay's predicament, like Welsted's:

> 'Midst this vain tribe, that aid thy setting ray,
> The Muse shall view, but spare, ill-fated Gay:
> Poor Gay, who loses most when most he wins,
> And gives his foes his fame, and bears their sins:
> Who, more by fortune than by nature curs'd,
> Yields his best pieces, and must own thy worst.[16]

Gay protested good-humouredly about his scapegoat role in the Advertisement to *Trivia* in 1716: 'The criticks ... allowed me an honour hitherto only shown to better writers: That of denying me to be the author of my own works.' Pope, too, incidentally, in giving an account of the reception of *The What D'Ye Call It* to Caryll on 3 March 1715 wrote that Gay had 'wrought all the above said wonders' (Sherburn, ii. 283) but this remark has something of an air of friendly generosity and pride in a protégé.

In fact, there is every reason to believe that Pope's enemies were correct in noting his hand in the play. Arbuthnot wrote to Swift on 26 June 1714: 'Pope has been collecting high flights of poetry, which are very good; they are to be solemn nonsense' (*Swift Corr.*, ii. 43). These are the fragments which were to illustrate Pope's *ΠΕΡΙ ΒΑΘΟΥΣ*, published in 1728, but it is conceivable (and critics have presumed it) that some of them found their way into *The What D'Ye Call It*. These were by no means necessarily the starting point. The skeleton (and some detail) of the play seem to be provided by *The Shepherd's Week*: the seducing squire and the girl who doesn't want to stab herself because that is how pigs die, for instance, the parody of Philips, or the use of the ninepence as a love token. The rural setting and sympathies must surely be Gay's. When Gay wrote to Parnell on 29 January 1715, however, his reference to the play as a collaboration was casual but unambiguous: 'among us we have just finish'd a Farce in Rhime, of one Act, which is now ready for Stage. 'tis upon the design I formerly have mention'd to you of a Country Gentleman's having a play acted by his Tenants. that you see something of the nature of it I have transcrib'd a speech of an Aunt to a Bench of Justices for saving her nephew from being Press'd' (*Letters*, p. 17). It is almost impossible now to point with any sort of certainty to what might be Pope's, but the interested reader is directed, in my Commentary, to the following notes: Introductory Scene l. 81, I. i. 71, I. i. 94 ff, I. iv. 8 sd, II. iv. 30, II. v. 4, II. v. 6, and II. viii. 22. Cowper's assertion that Swift and Arbuthnot collaborated in the song ''Twas when the Seas were roaring', though possibly made on reasonable evidence (Cowper's aunt was a friend of Pope's) is not very likely, since Swift, as Irving (p. 117) points out, had been in Ireland since August or September 1714. In the letter to Parnell quoted above, however, Gay goes on to say: 'I see Mr Harcourt often & Dr Arbuthnot', and Arbuthnot may be not entirely unconnected with the ghost's song at I. iv. 16 ff (see my Commentary). Kerby-Miller (p. 43) writes: 'It is not unlikely that all the Scriblerians had a finger in the play in its early stage. . . . The motive for producing it promptly under Gay's name was an obvious and powerful one—Gay needed the money.' But Parnell, for one, needed to be reminded of even the basic idea, which Gay had 'formerly . . . mention'd' to him. It does not look as though he could have contributed.

Whatever his share in the play, Pope showed a lively interest in its reception. He described its success to Caryll in a letter of 3 March:

The farce has occasioned many different speculations in the town, some looked upon it as a mere jest upon the tragic poets, others as a satire upon the late war. Mr Cromwell hearing none of the words and seeing the action to be tragical, was much astonished to find the audience laugh; and says the Prince and Princess must doubtless be under no less amazement on the same account. Several Templars and others of the more vociferous kind of critics, went with a resolution to hiss, and confessed they were forced to laugh so much that they forgot the design they came with. The Court in general has in a very particular manner come into the jest, and the three first nights (notwithstanding two of them were Court nights) were distinguished by very full audiences of the first quality. The common people of the pit and gallery received it at first with great gravity and sedateness, some few with tears; but after the third day they also took the hint, and have ever since been very loud in their clapps.[17]

The What D'Ye Call It is in the tradition of *The Rehearsal* in its extensive parody of the tragic drama of the time, but as the *Key* pointed out, Buckingham '*has laid his Finger on the proper Subjects of Ridicule, such as,* ill-contriv'd Plots, unnatural Connections, silly Peripetia's, unreasonable Machinery, affected Stile, extravagant Rants *and* Nonsense, *and in particular the* arbitrary Pedantry *of one over-grown Writer*' whereas *The What D'Ye Call It* '*has but very little of this good Design, and seems rather to be a Banter on the solemn stile of Tragedy in general*' (fol. A3). The distinction is true enough, and perhaps significant of the age. Gay would have considered tragedy the highest kind of dramatic art, as Pope considered the epic the highest kind of poetry, and he would have found the same difficulty in accommodating his desired subject-matter to the still-current Renaissance modes as Pope did, since these no longer well enough served the concern of many Augustan writers for a serious literature of ideas, or for the details and morality of the common life. In the age of the periodical essay, the novel, or the ballad opera, or even of the newspaper or the pantomime, tragedy and epic find fewer and fewer footholds. Stage comedy and the comic epic (the novel) do indeed flourish, but often through the nervous invigoration of burlesque; and it is burlesque of a high order that informs the best works of the Scriblerians, alone or in collaboration.

We should not mistake the irreverent or grotesque humour for triviality. Pope's *ΠΕΡΙ ΒΑΘΟΥΣ*, for instance, as he said himself, 'though written in so ludicrous a way, may be very well worth reading seriously as an art of rhetoric' (Spence, p. 57). Thus his collection of high flights of poetry is really more than 'solemn nonsense': it is an investigation into the forms of poetic language desirable in an age wary of all rhetorical cant, when pretension is so often pretentiousness. Gay, I think, means what he says, too, when he proposes that '*the Sentiments of Princes and Clowns have not in reality that difference which they seem to have: their Thoughts are almost the same, and they only differ as the same Thought is attended with a Meanness or Pomp of Diction*' (The Preface, l. 38). Such remarks are woven into a critical apologia brilliantly designed to confound the neo-classicism of a Dennis with mock logic, impeccable Greek and French authorities, and a relentlessly circular argument, but the whole feel of the play supports the essential irony of their context: an aunt, for instance, who is said to be introduced in imitation of the nurses of the ancients, nonetheless functions as an indignant exposer of the savage indignities of the Game Acts (i. i. 33 ff.). Just as Pope half-consciously betrays his literary distance from Homer or Milton in investigating the social milieu and behaviour of Belinda and the Baron, so Gay really rejects the modes of Seneca or Dryden in portraying the sufferings of Kitty and Filbert: but they both do this by parody. *The What D'Ye Call It* is Gay's *Rape of the Lock*.

Swift was later to tease Gay that he could not 'distinguish Rye from Barly, or an Oak from a crab-tree' (*Swift Corr.*, iv. 16), but Gay's interest in the country is clear from *Rural Sports* (1713) and *The Shepherd's Week* (1714): *The What D'Ye Call It* is in his most subtle vein of bucolic realism. It is true that the melodramatic action tends to set the feeling at a distance (which accounts for the puzzlement of the deaf Cromwell) but Gay's humorous and observant eye usually brings it back into focus. Kitty may rave like a distracted heroine of Otway, but her pastoral delirium is quaint and practical:

> Bagpipes in Butter, Flocks in fleecy Fountains,
> Churns, Sheep-hooks, Seas of Milk, and honey Mountains.
> (ii. viii. 84).

Again, Peascod may be given the death-scene speeches of a betrayed conspirator out of Otway or Addison, but his career

of crime has consisted of robbing orchards and playing
ninepins during the sermon, and his remorse is so excessive
that he bursts into tears over the very title-page of the 'good
Book' he is given to pray in:

> Lend me thy Handkercher—*The Pilgrim's Pro*— [*Reads and weeps.*
> (I cannot see for Tears) *Pro—Progress*—Oh!
> —*The Pilgrim's Progress—Eighth—Edi-ti-on*
> *Lon-don—Prin-ted—for—Ni-cho-las Bod-ding-ton:*
> *With new Ad-di-tions never made before.*
> —Oh! 'tis so moving, I can read no more.   (ii. i. 23).

Much of the vigorous life of this play thus lies in the assumed
detail of rural life, not only butter-making and Bunyan
(already a second Bible in cottage homes), but Pope-burning,
pig-watching and poaching; begging soldiers, tippling JPs,
and corrupt churchwardens. In this firmly and delicately
realized setting, Gay has lodged as much criticism of social
injustice as one's belief in the characters can bear; one's sense
of genuine outrage is almost matched and contained by the
play's fine poise of sentiment.

It is hardly, apropos of Pope's letter quoted above, 'a satire
upon the late war', but Gay's treatment of military pillaging
or the much-abused Recruiting Acts would accord with Tory
criticism of the conduct of the war. Gay had expressed relief
after Utrecht in terms that were perhaps to suggest the further
possibilities of the press-gang as a subject:

> So forth I far'd to Court with speed,
> Of Soldier's Drum withouten Dreed;
> For Peace allays the Shepherd's Fear
> Of wearing Cap of Granadier.[18]

The fear was real enough, for at one stage special protection
had to be given to harvest-labourers, many of them having
been impressed, or in hiding for fear of imprisonment.[19]
Desertion was easy, since there were no barracks, and if
Peascod had had five pounds he might have bribed his way
out of the firing squad, but there must still have been some
ugly scenes. Fortescue (p. 567) reports that the whole town of
Exminster once turned out with flails and pitchforks against
an officer who claimed a deserter. It is Gay's fun to make
Peascod distribute his possessions among his friends like

Banks's Mary Queen of Scots, but his predicament is given real substance: the guns are 'well ramm'd' and he 'must be dead by Ten'. The arrival of the reprieve and the arrest of the recruiting sergeant satisfy the simplest demands of poetic justice. Similarly, we are meant to smile when Dorcas, who has falsely accused Filbert of getting her with child and is the cause of his conscription, defends herself with the inevitable sentiment from Guarini (i. i. 94 ff.). But Gay's introduction of the ghost of an unmarried mother, whipped till she miscarried, though a grotesque parody of Shakespeare, is horrific enough; and when Dorcas reveals that she has been bribed by the real father, the Squire, we are left uneasy. The revelation is, after all, close to the theme of the whole play.

The steward has found that his daughter, Kitty, is pregnant by his master's son, Squire Thomas, and so he uses a play-trick to get them married. In the play within the play the pair are given roles relevant to their real lives. Squire Thomas, as Filbert, sees in Dorcas's explanation of her seduction what his own money and power could allow him to do, but this course of action he is encouraged to reject. Filbert's being impressed and its false cause do not deter Kitty. She even proposes to follow him, like Polly Oliver, and when they are parted she contemplates suicide. Again, I think this suggests a situation which her 'real life' rejection by Squire Thomas might bring about. Sir Roger, too, plays himself, sentencing Filbert for the very crime of which as his son he is really guilty. A production of the play would make apparent the effect of this casting upon Squire Thomas, for it does seem to have an effect. At the dénouement, while his father storms out in a passion, he merely accepts the situation, with as much vagueness as good grace to be sure, but without demur. The virtuous course has been presented to him, giving him good reason (in addition to the play-trick) for genial submission: he seems less the 'booby Squire' we were led to expect, certainly very different from Gay's most vivid portrayal of the landed boor, in his eclogue 'The Birth of the Squire' (Dearing, i. 231). The steward's Christmas theatricals may be seen, then, as more than a mere trick: they are a form of social therapy designed to demonstrate the powers of love and fidelity implicit in rural life, a message finely sharpened by Gay's mock-heroic treatment.

Gay's talent for absurdity was more fully exercised by his next play, *Three Hours after Marriage*, first performed on 16 January 1717 and published on 21 January by Lintot, who paid £43. 2s. 6d. for the copyright (Nichols, viii. 296). This thoroughly Scriblerian farce (Gay called it a comedy) of the old virtuoso, his young wife, his playwright niece and the seduction wager, is a carefully organized work, full of intellectual jokes, *double entendres*, and near-surrealism. It ran for seven nights to full houses, but encountered such a 'tide of malice and party' that its revivals were few, and until this century it was often neglected or maligned by editors and critics.[20]

The malice was largely, it seems, of the same sort that had stimulated the lone voices raised against *The What D'Ye Call It*: malice against Pope from the Buttonian wits,[21] and from Curll, who had published the *Court Poems* and been given his emetic the year before;[22] malice from Dennis, satirized in the play as 'Sir Tremendous Longinus';[23] and from friends of John Woodward, satirized in the play as 'Dr. Fossile'.[24] It was the same old story of Gay as an innocent Ajax shielding a malevolent Teucer. Breval makes Pope soliloquize as a stage villain:

> Thus in the *Zenith* of my Vogue I reign,
> And bless th'Abundance of my fertile Vein;
> My pointed Satire aim alike at All,
> (Foe to Mankind) and scatter round my Gall:
> With poyson'd Quill, I keep the World in Awe,
> And from My Self my own THERSITES draw.
> This very Night, with Modern Strokes of Wit,
> I charm the *Boxes*, and divert the *Pit*;
> Safe from the Cudgel, stand secure of Praise;
> Mine is the Credit, be the Danger GAY's.
>
> (*The Confederates*, i)

Breval is referring to Gay's brush with Cibber behind the scenes after the latter had mocked the play in an ad-lib during a revival of *The Rehearsal*.[25] This and other legendary matter, such as stage mishaps and financial aid from the Maids of Honour, complicates any account of the impact of the play. Not least among the factors in its reception was the Collier-like outcry against its obscenity, and a curious prejudice against the introduction of a mummy and a crocodile as the ultimate disguises of the competing gallants: these were closely connected, since many of the pamphlet attacks focus on *doubles entendres* arising out of the masquerade. Blackmore dwells upon the play's obscenity, as do Parker, Drub, Welsted, and Giles Jacob in his Preface to *The Rape of the Smock* (1717). Harrington Smith (p. 6) identifies a two-page quotation in Drub from Jeremy Collier, and even suggests that Drub might be Collier himself. Gay was particularly indignant at this much-exaggerated line of attack, and he wrote a pamphlet pretending to find similar innuendoes in the work of Addison and Steele. Pope, probably with justice, persuaded him not to publish this *tu quoque* (Spence, p. 104).

The extent of the opposition and the industry of the interpreters may seem to us somewhat misplaced, but Pope's enemies must have been disappointed in finding so little to get their teeth into, and they therefore seem to have made it their business to stir up as much trouble as possible. Burnet had voiced the general anticipation before the play was produced: 'Pope is coming out with a Play, in which everyone of our modern Poets are ridiculed.'[26] But this was nowhere near the truth. Apart from Phoebe Clinket, who even now cannot be clearly identified, the only poet ridiculed is a 'poor dog' of a pastoralist who seems to be Lady Mary Wortley Montagu (see my note to II. 48 in the Commentary). The significant point is Burnet's assumption about Pope's authorship: it was to set the tone of the attack.

We have rather more authority for treating *Three Hours after Marriage* as a collaboration then we had for *The What D'Ye Call it*. For one thing, Gay publicly acknowledged in the Advertisement 'the Assistance I have receiv'd in this Piece from two of my Friends; who, tho' they will not allow me the Honour of having their Names join'd with mine, cannot deprive me of the Pleasure of making this Acknowledgement'. Identification of these friends as Pope and Arbuthnot was, of course, quickly made: first, apparently, by *The Drury-Lane Monster* on 22 January, the day following publication. But the collaboration runs deeply, and it is impossible to be certain about individual responsibilities. A glance at the drafts of the 'Double Mistress' episode of *The Memoirs of Martinus Scriblerus*, transcribed by Kerby-Miller, suggests the methods of work that would need to be uncovered, and this could hardly be done from the printed text alone. The original draft of the *Memoirs* episode is in Arbuthnot's handwriting. The heavy corrections in Pope's hand shorten the passage and clarify and sharpen the style. Kerby-Miller (pp. 297–9) argues that the episode, which forms Chapters XIV and XV of the *Memoirs*, was written shortly after *Three Hours after Marriage*. The play and the *Memoirs* share certain material such as fluxion, monstrous twins, a glass trumpet, the bird porphyrion, mantegers, and the diet of the parents of an unborn child (see my Commentary). General satire on Woodward is common to them both. It has been suggested that it was Arbuthnot who chose to make Woodward the hero, and who looked after the medical and antiquarian jargon. This is a fairly safe guess, but even so its validity is based on regarding such things as specialities. We might on these grounds be forced, for instance, to refer to Gay's friend William Fortescue for the legal terminology in the last scene. Warton said he was responsible for *Stradling versus Stiles* (*EC*, x. 430) and he would no doubt have been available for consultation on any other Scriblerian matters. There is no real evidence, however, to connect him with *Three Hours after Marriage*, and in any case many of Gay's plays contain detailed satire on the law. Pope has been held responsible for Phoebe Clinket and Sir Tremendous, and it is true that some slender stylistic and other analogies with his work may be found in these scenes (see in my Commentary the notes to I. 124, 173, 268, 310, 312, and 324) but to make Arbuthnot the author of the Fossile scenes and Pope the author of the sub-plot leaves Gay doing very little except holding the pen. In his first scene, Breval makes Pope say to Arbuthnot:

> Know, Caledonian, Thine's a simple Part,
> Scarce any thing but some Quack-Terms of Art,
> Hard Words, and Quibbles; but 'tis I that sting,
> And on the Stage th'*Ægyptian Lovers* bring;
> Miss *Phoebe*, *Plotwell*, *Townley*, all are Mine,
> And Sir *Tremendous*:—*Fossile*'s only Thine.

This view was accepted by the editor of Gay's plays in the Abbey Classics series (1923). He omitted 'this justly abused piece' on the grounds that 'the authors of the greater part were Pope and Arbuthnot'. All this is too much the Buttonian line to remain entirely credible even in the heavily qualified form in which it most often appears (for example, in Morton and Peterson, p. x). Pope is usually held responsible for the Prologue, also, on evidence which is made clear in my Commentary (see also Ault and Butt, p. 179). The only authoritative word about the collaboration, however, is found in a letter of Gay to Pope, the source of which is William Ayre's *Memoirs of the Life and Writings of Mr. Pope* (1745), but which Sherburn thinks 'may well be genuine' (i. 388):

Too late I see, and confess myself mistaken, in Relation to the Comedy, yet I do not think had I follow'd your Advice, and only introduc'd the *Mummy*, that the Absence of the *Crocodile* had sav'd it. I can't help laughing myself, (though the Vulgar do not consider that it was design'd to look very ridiculous) to think how the poor Monster and Mummy were dash'd at their Reception, and when the Cry was loudest, thought that if the Thing had been wrote by another, I should have deem'd the Town in some Measure mistaken, and as to your Apprehension that this may do us future Injury, do not think it; the Doctor has a more valuable Name than can be hurt by any Thing of this Nature, and yours is doubly safe; I will (if any Shame there be) take it all to myself, as indeed I ought, the Motion being first mine, and never heartily approv'd of by you. (*Letters*, p. 31).

It is interesting to see behind this deference and modesty an underlying assumption that his original conception was in itself valid: he seems inclined to blame the audience, and is content to accept responsibility. As the only document on the subject of any of the triumvirs it is significant in showing Gay in mature and calm control, and, above all, aesthetically in the right.

The play, then, was received with some interest, and was revived in 1737, 1746, and at Bath in 1765. Because of the opposition, however, it seems to have been deprived of the natural success it deserved. The seven nights of its first run were for a long time considered by critics to be not incompatible with failure. Indeed, Clinket remarks in the play itself: 'Suppose this Play acts but Six Nights, his next may play Twenty' (i. 521), where six nights is considered a small number. This is true enough, considering that *The What D'Ye Call It* had received thirty-five performances already by the opening night of *Three Hours after Marriage*, but as George Sherburn was at pains to point out in his article, the seven nights were interrupted only by a Sunday: it was the largest number of consecutive performances that season at Drury Lane, and there is every reason to believe that the play would have had earlier and more frequent revivals if it had not been for the quarrel with Cibber, or possible pressure put upon Steele or the actor-managers. The first production seems to have been at once successful (if riotous) and abrupt, but the quarrel with Cibber did not break out until 20 February, so the run could not, therefore, have been terminated on that score.

We may piece together the first four performances from three different contemporary accounts, two of which appear to be without bias, and none of which is necessarily far from the truth. These are Breval's *The Confederates*, and two pieces appended to the reprint of the play in *A Supplement to the Works of Alexander Pope, Esq.* (Printed for W. Whitestone, Dublin, 1758): *A Key to the New Comedy; Call'd, Three Hours after Marriage, Written by a Person of Distinction in London, To His Friend in the County of Cornwal* (Dedication: 'To Sir H. M.') and *A Letter, giving an Account of the Origin of the Quarrel between Cibber, Pope, and Gay* ('wrote by a person who is still alive, and tho' a woman, intimate with the poets of this century, and consequently with most of the theatrical persons worthy notice'). The authenticity of these documents is undoubted, but see pp. 436 ff. for a discussion of the value of this Dublin edition. The author of the 1758 *Key* (p. 210) had caught the anticipatory excitement, and went along to Drury Lane on the opening night, but could not get in: 'every door that was opened to me, diffus'd more heat than a baker's oven, or the mouth of a glass-house'. Breval (scene i) lets Gay give his account of the first night's audience:

> Betimes, the better to conceal my Face,
> In th'*Eighteen-Penny Row* I chose a Place;
> Whence, unobserv'd, I might attend the *Play*,
> And the loud Criticks of the *Pit* survey.
> So vast a Throng took up the spacious Round,

Scarce for a Mouse, or *You, had Room been found; [*To Pope.
Heroes and Templars here were mix'd with Wits,
There Bawds and Strumpets, with a Group of Cits;
Rang'd in each Box were seen th'Angelick Fair,
Whose Footmen had since *Two* been posted there.
Round me I gaz'd with Wonder and Delight,
And wish'd that this had been the *Poet*'s *Night*.

ARBUTHNOTT.
    It promis'd well.

GAY.
    It did; but mark the End:
    What boots a *Croud*, unless that *Croud*'s your Friend?
    The *Prologue* finish'd, in the Doctor came,
    And with him, Hand in Hand, th'intriguing Dame.
    Silent a while th'attentive *Many* sate,
    The Men were hush'd, the Women ceas'd their Chat:
    But soon a Murmur in the *Pit* began,
    And thence all round the *Theatre* it ran;
    The noise increasing as along it mov'd,
    Grew loud at last, and to a *Hiss* improv'd.

The triumvirate take the play as damned, and the rest of
Breval's action involves the reluctance of Oldfield, Bicknell,
and Cibber to continue unless they are paid handsomely.
Then a purse of gold arrives from the Court Ladies, the Misses
Griffin, Bellendine and Lepell, and the play is saved. Parker
makes a note of this gift, and he even mentions the amount
(four hundred guineas) but these are the only authorities for
the affair. Breval notes in his third scene that in return for this
favour Pope will 'record their Names' in his *Court Ballad*
(published on 31 January). The tradition thus connecting the
Ballad with the play was finally killed by Ault (*New Light*, p.
179). The *Ballad* was written before 18 January (see Ault and
Butt, p. 183) but there is nothing to show that it was written
after the 16th, and not a hint of a reference to the play. These
lines from Pope's 'The Sixth Epistle of the First Book of
Horace Imitated' (1738):

> His Wealth brave Timon gloriously confounds;
> Ask'd for a groat, he gives a hundred pounds;
> Or if three Ladies like a luckless Play,
> Takes the whole House upon the Poet's day.   (85–8).

might conceivably refer to the incident, but John Butt, in his edition of the *Imitations of Horace*, p. 242 n, does not mention it, and notes only Warton's conjecture that the play was Young's *Busiris*, and Malone's that it was Breval's *Plot*. The gift is by no means impossible, for in December 1716 Pope wrote 'Gay dines daily with the Maids of honour' (Sherburn, i. 379). Their friendship was genuine.

If the play had been really damned, no amount of bribing or packing the house (as Breval also suggests) could have prolonged it for a week. The reception was obviously very mixed, as the author of the 1758 *Key* (p. 210) suggests in his account of what happened the next morning: 'I strolled to several coffee-houses, where I knew the wits and criticks met like surgeons, to dissect the body of any new piece; but I found more opinions among them, than there are sectaries in the world: So I resolv'd to venture a sweating the next evening, and be my own judge.' His account of the second night dramatically presents the conflict of taste and opinion, but without much detail:

When I came to the Theatre, I found it crowded as the night before, but fortunately got a seat in the boxes among some of my acquaintance. Wilk's spoke the prologue with his usual vivacity and applause! but he had no sooner ended, and thrown the fool's cap on the stage, but the storm began, and the criticks musick of cat-calls join'd in the chorus.—The play was acted like a ship tost in a tempest; yet notwithstanding, through those clouds of confusion and uproar, I, as one of the neutral powers, could discover a great many passages that gave me much satisfaction; and while the inimitable Oldfield was speaking the epilogue ... the storm subsided—And to speak poetically, my friend—
    The billows seem'd to slumber on the shore.
But when the play was given out for the third night, (tho' the benefit of the author was not mention'd) the roar burst out again, like sudden thunder from two meeting clouds; but I with pleasure observ'd, the roar of applause overcame and triumph'd. (p. 210).

He went again on this third night, and had a quite different report: 'I went the third night to the pit, where I saw the comedy perform'd to a numerous and polite audience with general applause! as for my own particular part, I was extremely delighted' (p. 211). The house may have been packed for the author's benefit, but it is more likely merely that the critics felt they had done their worst, and had retired to pen their keys and diatribes. It is also possible that some hasty bowdlerizing took place, for Drub (p. 8) remarks: 'the Players have made you full amends for not observing the *Stage-Rules* in the Representation. For, *Sir,* they left out a considerable load of Obscenity and Prophaness, which tho' you were not ashamed to print, they had so much Modesty as not to speak.' The authoress of the *Letter* (p. 220) describes how on the fourth night Penkethman, with the tail of his crocodile costume, knocked down Mrs Hunt (playing Sarsnet) 'flat upon her back, where she discovered more linnen than other habilements, and, more skin and flesh than linnen' and then himself got stuck in the mummy's open case. She elaborates the mishap ('This scene took more than half an hour in the action') but her account of its enthusiastic reception and the good-natured clamour on the fifth night for it to be deliberately repeated (which it was not) is a sign of the friendliness of the ensuing audiences.

The creative association of the Tory wits at this time was a formative influence of the greatest importance for Gay. The Scriblerus Club itself ceased to meet as early as the summer of 1714 (*Early Career*, p. 78). The departure of Swift and Parnell to Ireland, and the fall of Oxford and Bolingbroke, meant that in the following summer only the triumvirate were left together in London. But the gradual disbanding of Scriblerus thereafter set Gay on his own feet. In the ballad-operas we do indeed find burlesque and innovation, but everything is finely shaped by his own maturer poise, his growing concern with paradoxical moral judgment, his political disillusion and deepening sentiment and wit. In other words he finds his true dramatic voice. In the farces of 1712 to 1717, his youthful exuberance is more obviously experimental, and his development shows him profiting from the intellectual stimulus of Pope, Swift, and Arbuthnot. Gay's deft sense of dramatic form is already in evidence in *The Mohocks*, but he liked to have 'hints', he needed ideas: and *Three Hours after Marriage* is a farce of ideas as well as of situation. It cannot claim the fundamental innocence of *The Mohocks* or *The What D'Ye Call It*, where clowns predominate. By contrast, Fossile's sharpness of character and gloomy predicament are analogous in some ways to those of Morose in Jonson's *The Silent Woman*, which Gay may have seen on 3 March 1715, during the run of *The What D'Ye Call It*, or on 25 January 1716, when he may have been in London for the publication of *Trivia* on the following day. The casting may have been influenced by this resemblance (see my Commentary, p. 438) and the result seems to encourage a robust Jonsonian sophistication contrasting with the miniature neo-Shakespearean worlds of the earlier plays. The sustained comic invention, the appropriate[27] and carefully-plotted metaphor, the Ovidian[28] or Old Testament imagery and the adherence to the unities, put it on a different level altogether of power and assurance. It offers itself as the peak of Gay's early dramatic achievement.

Three Hours after Marriage falls between the different political eras of *The History of John Bull* and *The Beggar's Opera*, and has little of the sublime sense of cultural outrage of *The Dunciad*; but its playfulness is characteristic of the authors of these works, and its objects of fun are also serious bêtes noires: the slovenly bluestocking, the quack doctor, the irascible critic, the credulous antiquarian, and the quibbling JP. These are all self-deceiving characters: Phoebe Clinket does not keep house, but disrupts it with all the riff-raff of the playhouse, her head full of impossible drama and half-digested Descartes, her hair stuck with pens; Dr Fossile has visions of grandeur as a Baconian scientist and medical man, but his collection includes such rubbish as the 'jelly' of meteors and a fragment of Seth's pillar, his medical theories are Hermetic and he dabbles in magical potions and alchemy ('I deal not in impossibilities. I search only for the grand Elixir'); Sir Tremendous has nothing good to say about Shakespeare, Jonson, Otway, Etherege, or Dryden, and in all respects is in complete conflict with the taste of the town, which he professes to influence; while Possum's legal skills lead only to his friend being saddled with a bastard that is obviously not his.

These, then, are the unwitting destroyers of all the social values they are meant to represent: art, domestic peace, medicine, learning, criticism, and law. The play is a satirical vision of folly and anarchy, and only the outrageous self-assurance of the characters imposes some sort of acceptable order upon the action. This is probably true of most farces, and *Three Hours after Marriage* has been shown to derive in a number of minor characteristics from contemporary examples of the genre (see my Commentary), but there is a particular kind of persistence in, say, Townley's explanation of Plotwell's letter (I. 248) or the mistaking of Clinket's dramatic 'offspring' for the infant actually wailing on the stage (III. 460) that bestows upon these incidents the rare beauty of insane but inevitable logic. It is a mad household indeed, ruled by the twin votaries of Apollo, and invaded by brilliantly resourceful rakes. Pope, by the way, had already noted that Apollo is patron of poetry and of medicine in the Epistle Dedicatory to *A Key to the Lock*, and there had been a doctor with a poetical niece in Aphra Behn's *The Emperor of the Moon* (1687), but there is something wholly appropriate and original in the relationship of Fossile and Clinket.

It takes two to make a marriage, even one that lasts for only three hours, and Townley's and Fossile's reasons for marrying are, in combination, about the most disastrous one could think of. What future could be predicted for a city prostitute on the make, and a society doctor and antiquarian anxious to disinherit a mad niece? The sexual disproportion alone has classic possibilities. It is against this chaotic collision of motive that the seduction wager operates, engendering both Townley's fatal dalliance with her past beaux, and Fossile's phlegmatic but resourceful jealousy. The climax sees the unexpected fulfilment of their subconscious wishes: Fossile, who fears her sexual demands and has already significantly referred to her as 'thou best of my Curiosities' (I. 26), finally, with some relief, locks her into his museum; where she is immediately gratified by the grotesque erotic display of the 'Egyptian lovers', the mummy and the crocodile.

But Townley had no need to make a serious choice between Plotwell and Underplot, for the play belongs to the literature of cuckoldom, and we are aware that our interest properly resides with the character really affected by the masquerade: Fossile. The rivals' most convincing efforts are taxed by his early suspicions and vigilance ('Were my Wife as Chaste as *Lucretia*, who knows what an unlucky Minute may bring forth') but the vigilance relaxes into despair, and the despair into resignation: the beaux are packed off to the bear garden, and Townley is finally unmasked. At the end of the play Fossile is, in all senses, left holding the baby. Our sympathies are surely with him in his final and touchingly generous stoicism:

What signifies whether a Man beget his Child or not? How ridiculous is the Act it self, said the great Emperor *Antoninus*! I now look upon my self as a *Roman* Citizen; It is better that the Father should adopt the Child, than that the Wife should adopt the Father.

After the *cause célèbre* of *Three Hours after Marriage*, a play written with the stimulation and assistance of literary friends who knew how to draw out his talents, Gay seems once again to have been left to his own dramatic devices and, perhaps, to have lost his sense of direction. Between that Scriblerian farce and *The Beggar's Opera* eleven years later lie only a masque, two unsuccessful tragedies (one never acted), and the lost revision of a version by Thomas Wright of Molière's *Les Femmes Savantes*. Gay's urge to try his hand at tragedy is understandable, but on the whole the gods did not smile at the result. One factor may be the possibly lingering hostility of Cibber. In February 1720 Cibber was directed to produce *Dione* (see my Commentary, p. 455) but it was never performed. Then Gay rewrote Wright's *Female Virtuosoes* (1692) as *No Fools Like Wits* for performance at Lincoln's Inn Fields on 10 January 1721, intending to expose Cibber's plagiarism from the same play in his *The Refusal*.[29] It is significant that in 1721 there were no performances of *The What D'Ye Call It*, although it had previously been in the repertoire at Drury Lane every year since its first performance: it is as though Cibber could not bear to put it on, popular as it was. *No Fools Like Wits* has not survived. Curll, in his strategically timed reprint of Wright, gives us our only hint of what it was like: 'the Reviver ... to honour *Moliere*, has blended the *Miser* [note: L'Avare, *de Moliere*] and the *Generous Man* [note: Chrisalus in *Les Femmes Scavantes*] to form a New Character, but such a one as can only be called *Monstrum & Horrendum*.'[30] In 1722 performances of *The What D'Ye Call It* resumed, and *The Captives* was produced at Drury Lane on

15 January 1724. Cibber refused *The Beggar's Opera* for Drury
Lane, and we may suspect that he played a minor role in the
suppression of its sequel, *Polly* (see p. 54). However, evidence
of this lingering feud will not explain why Gay turned
momentarily from burlesque, nor why the consummate mock-
pastoralism of *The Shepherd's Week* and the psychological
realism of his poem 'The Toilette' should have been so closely
followed by the pastoral entertainment *Acis and Galatea* and
the pastoral tragedy *Dione*.

There is no record of a performance of *Acis and Galatea*
before 26 March 1731, when Rochetti sang Acis at Lincoln's
Inn Fields, although excerpted songs had been appearing in
print since 1722. It was composed by Handel for the Duke of
Chandos (or Earl of Carnarvon, as he then was) in 1718,[31]
and a performance at that date in the grand saloon of Canons,
'a magnificent apartment with a wonderful ceiling, painted
by Bellucci, which was supported by marble columns',[32] may
be presumed. The attribution of the words to Gay was first
made in an edition of the libretto published in 1739. Gay
himself never acknowledged it, and there seems to be no
authority for Irving's statement (p. 283) that the poet
supervised the Rochetti performance. Moreover, we have no
evidence that Gay had anything to do with the Arne
production of 17 May 1732, and the 1732 libretto issued in
connection with that production could hardly, with its
mislineation and verbal errors, have been prepared or
overseen by him, although this is the edition commonly used
as copy-text. Handel's own first public production of *Acis and
Galatea* did not take place until after Gay's death, for the
production of 10 June 1732 was in fact of his Neapolitan
serenata *Aci, Galatea e Polifemo*, composed in 1708, with the
addition of a chorus and an aria in English which there is no
reason to think that Gay had provided.[33] Handel was content
to make use of this macaronic version until December 1739
when, deprived of Italian singers for that season, he revived
the Canons version.

Gay may possibly have met Handel through his old school
friend Aaron Hill. Handel came to England in the winter of
1710, and his opera *Rinaldo*, with a libretto by Hill, was
produced in 1711 at a time when Gay was working for Hill's

journal *The British Apollo*. It is perhaps more likely that Gay first encountered Handel at Burlington's house in Piccadilly. Handel stayed there in 1713 during performances of *Teseo*, and visited frequently until he went to Canons as *Kapellmeister* in 1718. Handel is said to have provided the music for ''Twas when the Seas were roaring' in *The What D'Ye Call It* in 1715 (but see my Commentary, p. 433) and Gay's vignette of the composer at Burlington's in *Trivia*, ii. 497–500, was published on 26 January 1716:

> There *Hendel* strikes the strings, the melting strain
> Transports the soul, and thrills through ev'ry vein;
> There oft' I enter (but with cleaner shoes)
> For *Burlington*'s belov'd by ev'ry Muse.

Closer collaboration between the muses was probably stimulated by a number of pastoral masques in English produced between 1715 and 1718. Dean (p. 157) goes so far as to suggest that John Hughes's *Apollo and Daphne*, set by Pepusch and produced at Drury Lane in January 1716, was the actual model for *Acis and Galatea*, and he adduces some verbal resemblances. A more immediate literary source for Gay, however, was Dryden's translation of the story of Acis, Polyphemus and Galatea from the thirteenth book of Ovid's *Metamorphoses*, reprinted in Garth's Ovid of 1717. Pope's and Gay's contributions to this volume had already stimulated their interest (the Ovidian imagery in *Three Hours after Marriage* has been noted) so that it is not surprising that a mythological episode suitable for a pastoral entertainment should also have been found in Ovid. It has been suggested that 'O ruddier than the Cherry!' owes a debt to Theocritus,[34] but clearly it is only the bare notion of Polyphemus' love-sick complaint in the eleventh idyll that can lie behind the Cyclops' celebrated song to Galatea in Gay. Theocritus' Polyphemus is a rather different character, a figure of pathos due to be outwitted by Ulysses. This prophetic irony colours the whole mood of the Greek idyll. Gay on the other hand is happy to make use of the comic vigour of Ovid's Polyphemus, and his debt is made all the more striking by a large number of borrowings from Dryden's translation (see my Commentary, pp. 453–4).

In addition to the presence in the text of half-digested fragments of Dryden's Ovid, there are two passages which many critics have taken to be written by Pope because of their close resemblance to known lines of his (ii. 80–2) while the song 'Would you gain the tender Creature', not present in Handel's autograph MS and published in John Hughes's *Poems on Several Occasions* (1735), i. 145, would appear to have been provided by Hughes at an unknown date, though before 1722. These facts, together with Gay's silence about his authorship, has led to the libretto being considered as in some degree a collaboration. Its date of composition, in the year following the memorably scandalous *Three Hours after Marriage*, would inevitably lead someone to ascribe it to the Scriblerian triumvirate, and sure enough, the Preface to *Omnipotence, A Sacred Oratorio* (1774) claims that *Acis and Galatea* was translated from the Italian 'by Mr Pope, Dr Arbuthnot, and Mr Gay' and that they were also responsible for the libretto of the oratorio *Esther*. *Esther* was written by Samuel Humphreys out of the text of the Canons version known as *Hamon and Mordecai*. Irving (p. 184) accepted Gay's part in it, but there seems to be no further evidence (see Dean, pp. 197–8). The claim in *Omnipotence* can hardly be reliable, for *Acis and Galatea* is not, of course, a translation. We may take it that with the exception of the one aria by Hughes, the libretto is essentially the work of Gay, and we have no means of knowing why he did not provide that aria himself, when Handel discovered that it was needed.

Acis and Galatea may not have been acted in 1718, for the Arne production was described as 'being the first Time it ever was performed in a Theatrical Way'. It seems likely that this claim, however, was made in order to distinguish it from the Rochetti production of the previous year. The opportunity for action is not great, and today it is usually only performed in concert halls. In this it looks forward, of course, to the mature Handelian oratorio, whereas contemporary examples, with greater use of spectacle or comedy, more clearly recall the earlier English masque. *Acis and Galatea* is a musical work, and the reader of this volume will therefore approach the libretto with circumspection. The text alone cannot convey the emotional atmosphere, and was never intended to, even though we may in a reading notice amusing or significant contrasts which might not be so evident in performance. For instance, Acis in love has neglected one of the shepherd's traditional functions as poet ('No more thy tuneful Pipe we hear') whereas the absurd Polyphemus in love is moved to it for the first time ('Bring me a hundred Reeds of decent growth, / To make a Pipe for my capacious Mouth'), an irony in fact underlined by Handel in his use of the sopranino recorder in the setting of Polyphemus' following love song. 'O ruddier than the Cherry!'

Gay contrasts the delicate commitment of Acis with the sensual appetite of Polyphemus, but suggests that both forms of love are a 'rage' that may provide temporary happiness or not as the case may be, but are bound in the end to lead to ruin or oblivion ('Wretched Lovers ...'). He ironically contrasts the harmless happiness-in-nature of the nymphs and swains with the treacherous erotic 'happiness' of the lovers, into which the arrival of the giant breaks like a reminder of estrangement or death. Galatea in particular feels the oppressiveness of her own sexual desire, a feeling which underlines her horror at being the object of Polyphemus' love, for this looks like turning her into a real victim.

A timely emendation in Handel's autograph MS (whether by Handel or Gay himself) turned the giant's 'saucy' love into 'hideous' love: the theme does require the comedy of Polyphemus to contain at some point a serious suggestion of awesome sexual excess, so that Acis after his murder may be purified of all sensual contamination, his heart's blood turned into a timeless crystal fountain, and sexuality itself be exorcized by this outwitting of its most extreme embodiment. Acis as a river flows away from the mountain (Polyphemus traditionally represents Mount Etna) and seeks the sea (Galatea is a Sicilian sea-nymph). The Ovidian mythology, and the older geographical ætiology lurking within it, propose significant symbols of fidelity apotheosized and tumescent rage defeated. Gay's libretto provides a graceful and charming realization of these symbols.

Encouraged by the evident artistic success of this work for Handel, Gay turned next to pastoral tragedy. *Dione* was ready for acting in February 1720, but despite a directive from the

Lord Chamberlain that it was to be produced after Hughes's *The Siege of Damascus* (Drury Lane, 17 February) the play has never been performed. Gay's disappointment was alleviated only by the opportunity to give it pride of place in the handsomely printed *Poems on Several Occasions* which appeared in July of the same year. Johann Friedrich Lampe's operatic version was produced at the Haymarket on 23 February 1733, less than three months after Gay's death. According to Scouten (i. 273) the author of the libretto is unknown, but the published text reveals that the plot and recitative are taken from Gay's *Dione*, with songs added.[35] *Dione* was translated into German by Johann G. P. Müchler, and may be found in *Schäferdichte. Aus dem Englisch- Französisch- und Italiänischen übersetzt* (1759).

Dr Johnson's celebrated dismissal of *Dione* has remained unchallenged. 'A Pastoral of an hundred lines may be endured', he wrote in the concluding paragraph of his *Life of Gay*, 'but who will hear of sheep and goats, and myrtle-bowers and purling rivulets, through five acts?' Warton, however, unlike Johnson, wished to distinguish it from earlier pastoral drama: '*Dione* has not rescued us from the imputation of having no pastoral-comedy that can be compared, in the smallest degree, to the Aminta or Pastor Fido.'[38] Both Johnson and Warton have in different ways blurred Gay's intentions here. He departs from the predictable Italian models and (as we see from the Prologue) is conscious of the risk. He is certainly not producing a 'pastoral-comedy', nor is he merely avoiding a happy ending. His protagonists are not shepherds (even the episode from Cervantes supplies him only with a scholar playing at being one) and the action has little to do with the customs or superstitions of the country. Gay is aware that he has chosen an unusual environment for such a tragic conflict as he presents, without 'trumpet's clangor' or any sort of 'pomp or show', but it does of course provide him with a traditional arena for an investigation into the rival claims of natural law and social convention in matters of love. We remember, too, that in most Renaissance pastorals the characters tend to be visitors to the pastoral setting, and if we would have expected Gay (like Fletcher before him) to have more of the supernatural than Guarini or Tasso, then it may be answered that Gay is concerned here only with the psychology of extreme erotic emotions and their reflection in a stylized environment. Machinery of any kind, even of plot, is minimal.

Gay's most significant debts are to Shakespeare and to Cervantes. The relationship of Dione/Alexis with Parthenia evokes echoes of that of Viola/Cesario with Olivia or of Rosalind/Ganymede with Phebe (and is to be ludicrously remembered in grenadier-Polly's scenes with Jenny Diver in *Polly*). The episode of Chrysostom's hopeless love for Marcella in *Don Quixote* (see my Commentary, p. 456) serves to establish quite powerfully the role of Parthenia as an unwilling Belinda of the woods. She despairs of her unusual attractiveness because in the Arcadian context her refusal to grant her favours looks like intolerable smugness. When 'Shepherds explain their wish without offence, / Nor blush the nymphs;—for Love is innocence' (iii. iii. 17–18), chastity becomes an untenable position. Gay is, as so often, concerned with the oppressive requirements and obligations of sexuality.

His suffering heroine is possibly of less interest than this, although the play's considerable descriptive and metaphorical energy is expended mostly upon her predicament. It is hard now to be moved by the gothic landscapes or oppressive images of death. Indeed, when at v. ii. 77 ff. Dione reviews the means of suicide at her disposal (like Phyllis in one of the epistles of Ovid) we can hardly help remembering Gay's earlier burlesques of the situation in 'Wednesday' of *The Shepherd's Week* and in *The What D'Ye Call it*. Dione is a serious prospective suicide only by virtue of the assertions of Gay's imagery, though doubtless he assumed that it was because she possessed a more refined sensibility than Sparabella or Kitty Carrot. The conventions demand that her escape from the prospect of an arranged marriage into 'horrid caverns of despair' shall, when aggravated by her true lover's defection, issue in quantities of purple gore. So be it. The reader's consolation lies in incidental details and felicities that a poet of Gay's quality could hardly have avoided if he had tried. These are usually of things observed, like the descriptions of hare-coursing, the downy peach that feeds the black snail, or the rising of the moon at the beginning of Act V. His victims insistently compare themselves to birds. Evander is like a lured lark or caged linnet (II. ii. 9) or is caught like a finch on a limed twig (II. v. 89). Dione is like a turtle-dove who has lost her mate (I. i. 89) or a young linnet in a storm (II. iv. 3). These assertions of their plight bear witness of Gay's carefully plotted imagery, but do not embody sufficiently established emotions nor indicate any really felt awareness of the cruelty of fate or circumstance. The poetry rarely rises above this kind of decorative pathos, and lacks the lyric grace of the songs in the ballad-operas where similar metaphor is used much more successfully.

Gay's next tragedy returned to the conventional tragic themes of the period—conspiracy, loyalty, illicit passion, self-sacrifice—and wove them into a neater if still unexciting plot. The result had greater dramatic success, but there is evidence that Gay had to exert himself in other ways to attain it. *The Captives* was put on at Drury Lane on 15 January 1724 and was acted for seven nights, a respectable run. Fenton, however, heard a rumour that Gay 'gave thirty guineas to have it acted the fifth night' (Sherburn, ii. 216), presumably in order to secure a second author's benefit on the sixth night. Tots of brandy were distributed to the waiting footmen in the boxes on the opening night[37] and the Princess of Wales, who had allowed Gay to dedicate the play to her, was encouragingly present. Edward Young stated in a letter to Lady Mary Wortley Montagu that *The Captives* brought Gay 'above £1000'[38] but it hardly seems likely that this, if true, was the result of income from production and publication alone, and a Royal gift may be suspected. Fenton writes decisively that 'Gay's play had no success' (Sherburn, ii. 216); *Pasquin* no. 105, 4 February 1724, though praising the play, shows that it was not much liked and 'seems to have miscarry'd'; while Elizabeth Harrison's adulatory *Letter to Mr John Gay, on his Tragedy, call'd, The Captives* (21 January 1724) admits on the first page that it was 'much criticis'd'. The presumption of a number of critics that it went into two editions seems unfounded. One is forced to admit that its reception, therefore, was mixed.

In January 1724, the Turks were again in Persia: contemporary newspapers provide clear evidence that the setting was topical. However, Gay was merely reverting to an exoticism long popular on the Augustan stage, and *The Captives* is similar in many ways to earlier Persian tragedies such as Banks's *Cyrus the Great* (1696), Rowe's *The Ambitious Step-mother* (1700) or Theobald's *The Persian Princess* (1707). Although Fenton's statement to Broome that the story was Gay's own invention is probably true (Sherburn, ii. 215), it is possible to trace the influence of other writers and of stage tradition on certain of the characters and situations.

Astarbe reminds Adina Forsgren of Cleopatra or Lady Macbeth.[39] Although the first scene of the play is written with more than a nod in the direction of *Macbeth* and *Julius Caesar*, Astarbe herself seems to me more likely to have been modelled on Nourmahal in Dryden's *Aureng-Zebe* (as is Rowe's Artemisa in *The Ambitious Step-mother*). The character of Cylene may have been suggested by Dryden's Indamora, who is a captive Persian queen, while the old Emperor's love for Indamora in *Aureng-Zebe* in many ways parallels Astarbe's love for Sophernes. It is interesting to see that these resemblances were reinforced by the casting of the parts. On 11 December 1721 and again on 11 March 1723, *Aureng-Zebe* was revived at Drury Lane and advertised as 'Not Acted these Ten Years' (Avery, ii. 651). On both occasions Nourmahal was played by Mrs Porter (who also played Astarbe) and Indamora by Mrs Oldfield (who also played Cylene). It may even be that the revival had some direct influence on Gay's treatment of these characters, and that he himself had positive ideas about the casting.

A further suggestion has been made by Viola Papetti: 'Forse *The Captives* non sarebbe stata scritta se poco tempo prima Gay non si fosse trovato a passare le acque a Bath con l'ammirato e amato amico Congreve. Si tratta infatti di una imitazione della tragedia congreviana *The Mourning Bride* (1697), che aveva reso di moda quegli scenari sepolcrali, per cui Gay attirerà su di sé l'ilare parodia del Fielding.'[40] Dungeon scenes are, of course, legion in plays of this kind (compare, for example, the visit of Amestris to Artaban in Act III of *The Persian Princess*) but the suggestion has some point when we recollect the friendship between Congreve and Gay, and the influence discernible in *The Distress'd Wife*. Among the resemblances we may particularly note the captive queen Zara's ruse to free Alphonso by asking that her mutes shall be allowed to visit him in prison in order to strangle him, a device which may well have suggested Cylene's similar offer to execute Sophernes in *The Captives*, III. x.

The most striking debt, however, is to Southerne's *Oroonoko*. The nobility of Oroonoko in captivity and the friendly sympathy of Blanford provide quite clearly the principal source for the scene between Sophernes and Orbasius in *The Captives*, I. v (for details, see my Commentary, p. 460). Oroonoko's reunion with Imoinda, his driving away of the attacking Indians in Act II, and the readiness of the slaves to revolt, also find echoes in Gay's play. The connection between Southerne's Prince of Angola and Gay's Persian Prince would have been underlined by the fact that although Boheme seems to have played Oroonoko more frequently, it was Booth who played the part at Drury Lane on 21 September 1723 and 3 February 1724 (Avery, ii. 737, 758) and it was Booth who played Sophernes. The resemblance was noted in *Pasquin* no. 105, 4 February 1724 (the day after the second of these performances of *Oroonoko*), which claimed moreover that if the resemblance was deliberate, then 'I think he has much surpass'd his Original'.

All these echoes serve only to remind the reader that *The Captives* does not rise above the modest achievement of its genre, establishing without real passion the usual view that passion itself is more powerful than status and may overcome both the security of rank and the limitations of adversity. *Pasquin* admired Gay's sententiousness, but sententiousness alone cannot raise the pity which his Prologue claims is tragedy's first function.

It seems that no one who saw the play was to reflect (as they were all too likely to do four years later at *The Beggar's Opera*) upon a possible political significance of *The Captives*. The false accusation of Sophernes as being implicated in the conspiracy upon the King's life bears some resemblance to the arrest of Atterbury on the charge of treasonable correspondence with the Pretender. We now know that Atterbury was indeed involved in a Jacobite conspiracy, but the evidence at the time was flimsy and he was exiled in the summer of 1723 only after a bill of pains and penalties had been passed by the House of Lords.[41] A number of Gay's friends were close to Atterbury (Pope was a witness at his trial) and they seem to have been as convinced of his innocence as the stoical nobility of Gay's Sophernes may suggest. Most of the evidence collected by Walpole depended upon the efforts of Government decipherers whose mysterious calculations must have seemed very like the manipulation of dreams and rumours by the Median priests (see in my Commentary the note to i. v. 9). There is, too, something metaphorically apt in representing the Tories in opposition as captive Persians, ready to be manipulated by the real conspirator, the disinherited Hydarnes, who like an exiled Stuart is ready to return from banishment to avenge his 'house'. We may note, too, that Atterbury's wife had recently died, and that the particular opposition of the odious Araxes may represent the single-minded prosecution of the energetic Walpole, 'Author of all I suffer', according to Atterbury.[42]

It is strange that the pro-government *Pasquin* found no hint of such political nuances in *The Captives* and indeed went out of its way to praise it. We have to remember, however, the royal interest in this play and the firm treatment of the doomed Hydarnes, who as an exiled conspirator himself would be likely to lay a false scent. There had been allusions to the Atterbury case on the stage[43] but it was no longer quite such a fresh issue, and it was not until 1726 that the literary opposition to Walpole became at all coherent or identifiable.[44] *Pasquin* could afford its generosity to a work that seemed loyal enough.

The play engages, too, in a Shakespearean definition of mercy which is suitably ambiguous. The uncompromising vindictiveness of Astarbe (for example, at iii. viii. 10 ff.) was intended to lead to one of the principal conflicts of the play's climax, Phraortes' unwitting vow to execute Cylene before the facts of the case are revealed to him. Our expectation of a happy outcome in tragedy of the period deprives this moment of real tension, but there is no denying the reality of Gay's feelings about the royal prerogative in general. Orbasius's speech at iii. i. 17 ff., for instance, has a genuine ring: though Sophernes is innocent, it may still please the

King to pardon him. If Bolingbroke could be pardoned and
allowed to return from exile, so could Atterbury.

Gay's next play happily returned to the kind of burlesque
he had already brilliantly exploited in *The What D'Ye Call It*,
substituting a metropolitan for a rustic milieu. The pastoral
origins of *The Beggar's Opera* (produced at Lincoln's Inn Fields
on 29 January 1728) are not perhaps wholly obvious, but the
first hint does go back a dozen years earlier to the time when
the pastoral controversy was still alive and Gay was ready to
poke fun at writers inept at literary decorum. Swift wrote to
Pope on 30 August 1716 that Gay might try his hand at a set
of Quaker pastorals (which he did) and went on to remark: 'I
believe further, the personal ridicule is not exhausted; and
that a porter, foot-man, or chair-man's pastoral might do
well. Or what think you of a Newgate pastoral, among the
whores and thieves there?' (*Swift Corr.*, ii. 215). When Gay
saved this idea up for a comedy and mentioned to Swift that
he had begun work on it, the latter was, surprisingly, not
much impressed (Spence, i. 107). Gay, however, persisted. He
no doubt felt that even if purely formal or stylistic burlesque
was somewhat played out, the dramatic possibilities inherent
in the mock-genre were not. He seems to have borrowed some
of *The What D'Ye Call It*'s most absurdly touching scenes in
the initial shaping of his plot. Once again we have a criminal
awaiting execution and behaving like a tragic hero. Again
there is the prolonged and elevated emotional parting of a
pair of socially insignificant lovers. Again there is a reprieve,
and the visible stage-managing of the play within the play by
its author.

One of the literary allusions in the earlier work, the rivalry
of Kitty and Dorcas evoking that of Statira and Roxana for
Alexander the Great in Lee's *The Rival Queens*, is taken up
again in the rivalry of Polly and Lucy for Macheath's
affections (a situation seized upon by Hogarth in his famous
engraving of III. xi. as the quintessence of the plot). Such an
allusion is a happy one for *The Beggar's Opera*, conceived as it
partly was as burlesque of the Italian opera: Handel's
Alessandro, produced on 5 May 1726, had been specially
written for Faustina Bordoni's London debut and was
designed to show off her and Cuzzoni's talents to contrasted

advantage. As Bronson (pp. 209 ff) points out, this opera has some general resemblance to *The Beggar's Opera* in Alessandro's vacillation between Rossane and Lisaura, and in their own discussion of their mutual unhappiness. At any rate, Macheath clearly impressed himself upon Swift as a kind of raffish Alexander the Great; too late, on 28 Marcy 1728, he wrote to Gay with a suggestion quite in the required spirit of literary parody: 'I wish Mackheath when he was going to be hang'd had imitated Alexdr the great when he was dying. I would have had his fellow rogues, desire his commands about a Successor, and he to answer, let it be the most worthy: &c' (*Swift Corr.*, iii. 276).

Earlier hints may have been supplied by Pope, since much of the play was written at his house, but in general one receives the impression that Gay maintained the habit of independence acquired during the writing of his tragedies. Pope in fact denied collaboration beyond the altering of an expression here and there (Spence, i. 57). It was Gay, after all, who was addicted to city pleasures and who may have actually had the contacts in the underworld necessary to paint convincing portraits of highwayman, pickpocket, fence, and gaoler. The affairs of the most notorious criminals of the age were, of course, no secret to the public at large, being already the subject of ballads, popular biographies, or stage mimes. Gay himself had written 'Newgate's Garland', a ballad about Joseph ('Blueskin') Blake's attempt to cut Jonathan Wild's throat when on trial at the Old Bailey. It was sung in the third scene of Thurmond's mime *Harlequin Sheppard* (1724) which celebrated Jack Sheppard's sensational escape from Newgate prison. Sheppard was treated as a hero by the crowds when he was finally hanged (compare *The Beggar's Opera*, i. xii). It was the activities of gangsters like Blake, Sheppard, and Wild in the early 1720s that must have turned Gay's mind to the underworld as a subject for *The Beggar's Opera*: Sheppard and Wild were direct models for Macheath and Peachum, while Lockit appears to have been conceived as an amalgam of Charles Hitchen (Under City-Marshal) and Spurling, the Newgate turnkey.[45] An anecdote in *The Flying-Post* for 11 January 1729 suggests that Gay, meeting Wild by chance in a Windsor hotel, pretended to be a thief himself and thereby managed to extract a great deal of useful information from 'the genuine Peachum'.[46] If we are inclined to treat such gossip with circumspection, it is at least true that Gay himself wrote of going to Newgate 'to finish my scenes the more correctly' (*Letters*, p. 69). The play was finished by 22 October 1727, and was shown to Congreve and to Voltaire.[47]

Gay's friends were not confident of the play's success, but he pressed on with it. He was smarting under his recent failure to obtain a decent position at Court after attempting to win favour with such works as *The Captives* and the *Fables*, and was in just the right mood to persevere with a work which seemed to everyone to be a doubtful novelty. He could later congratulate himself that he had (in contrast to *The Captives*, perhaps) 'push'd through this precarious Affair without servility or flattery' (*Letters*, p. 70). Cibber turned the play down for Drury Lane, perhaps not entirely for personal reasons (see above, p. 31, for Gay's relations with Cibber in the aftermath of *Three Hours after Marriage*). The Duke of Queensberry remarked, when shown the play: 'This is a very odd thing, Gay; I am satisfied that it is either a very good thing, or a very bad thing', echoing Congreve who had said that 'it would either take greatly, or be damned confoundedly'. The view was to a degree shared by John Rich, manager of Lincoln's Inn Fields, who ultimately produced it.[48]

In the event it did take greatly. It is Gay's most celebrated play, and more has been written about it than about the rest of his work put together. I cannot pretend to deal with it more than cursorily in this context, and the interested reader is directed to Schultz's detailed account. Undoubtedly its great success was due to its novel use of songs sung to popular airs which Gay chose himself,[49] fitting to them lyrics which meaningfully elaborated upon the themes of the play. Gay had used songs in his plays before, but never so extensively. There was ample precedent for the use of popular tunes of the day in dramatic works. Thomas Duffet's 'Epilogue in the manner of Macbeth', added to a burlesque of Settle's *The Empress of Morocco* (1673), does so. *The Rehearsal* (1672) uses broadside ballads, and Gay admired D'Urfey's *Wonders in the Sun* (1706). Perhaps his principal model was, however, the *comédie en vaudeville* of the Théâtre de la Foire in Paris, where from the 1690s ballads to familiar tunes had been used to parody the operas of Lully and others.[50] Originally no accompaniment to the songs was intended, until Rich suggested it on the second last rehearsal and the Duchess of Queensberry insisted upon it.[51] At this stage the composer Pepusch was brought in to arrange the tunes, and to provide an overture. Pepusch was in his early sixties at the time, a respected composer and used to working in the theatre. Gay no doubt admired his *Apollo and Daphne* (1716), to words by Hughes, since his own libretto for *Acis and Galatea* owes much to it.

It is not known whether Handel, already a friend and collaborator of Gay's, had been approached first. It seems, on the face of it, hardly likely that he could have worked with much enjoyment on an enterprise designed in some measure to make fun of the very kind of entertainment he was most concerned with in these years. And yet Gay's parody of Italian opera is not as central to the play as has sometimes been supposed, and may represent comparatively late thoughts in his conception of the piece. The principal parodic elements are openly discussed in the Beggar's framing scenes,[52] and it is to the framing device that the title draws attention. Similarly, some aspects of musical burlesque found in the Overture and in some of the songs would be entirely due to the musical arrangement, known to be a last-minute matter. In many cases where the characters, incidents, or structure of the play itself seem to owe something to *Alessandro* or to other Italian operas, there is a sufficient source in the ordinary tragic stage of the period, which of course Gay was well-used to mocking (but see Bronson, pp. 212 ff.). If he felt that his own tragedies had been less than successful, he would have had an idea of what to blame. The new music was a threat to tragedy, finding an easy (and predominantly female) ear, as the Epilogue to *The Captives* ruefully observes:

All Ladies love the play that moves the most.
Ev'n in this house I've known some tender fair,
Touch'd with meer sense alone, confess a tear.
But the soft voice of an *Italian* wether,

Makes them all languish three whole hours together.
And where's the wonder? Plays, like Mass, are sung,
(Religious *Drama*)!—in an unknown tongue.   (16–22).

This sentiment is echoed by Lady Ninny in *The Rehearsal at Goatham*, v. 89. A little earlier Gay had extended the cultural damage to the whole of classical literature: 'People have now forgot Homer, and Virgil & Caesar, or at least they have lost their ranks, for in London and Westminster in all polite conversation's Senesino is daily voted to be the greatest man that ever liv'd' (*Letters*, p. 43). Senesino was, of course, a castrato. Macheath's bountiful sexuality restores the heroic status quo: at least in this sense Macheath is a 'great man'. We must judge the extent of operatic parody by what we can find in the text: in this connection it is interesting to note that Bronson, who is the most detailed commentator in this respect, does not think that the play is a serious attack on Italian opera (p. 216) and the absence of satire upon extravagant devices of staging or upon incomprehensible libretti would support the view. Certainly the burlesque is neither extensive nor ill-natured, and Handel bore no grudge, even though the tearaway success of *The Beggar's Opera* meant a loss of audience for the 'outlandish' opera.[53] The *Somerset House Gazette* records a rather dry exchange between Pepusch and Handel:

P: I hope, sir, you do not include me amongst those who did injustice to your talents.

H: Nod at all, nod at all, God forbid! I am a great admirer of the airs of 'The Beggar's Opera' andt every professional gendtleman must do his best for to live.

Gay had indeed done his best this time, and was able to repair the ravages of the South Sea Bubble, earning £693. 13*s.* 6*d.* from the production alone.[54] The familiar joke that the play had made Rich gay and Gay rich was coined by *The Craftsman* no. 83 as early as 3 February. By 12 February all the boxes had been booked to the twenty-fifth night, and even the author himself was proud of his ability to obtain tickets (*Daily Journal*, 12 February; *Letters*, p. 70). The play ran for an unprecedented sixty-two nights, Gay's portrait was engraved, the actress playing the part of Polly became the toast of the town despite being inaudible[55] and ran away with the Duke of Bolton. The circumstances of the play's reception and popularity are well-known. It inaugurated a vogue for the ballad-opera which lasted for eight years, and was a direct influence upon the German *Singspiele* of the 1750s. The proceeds enabled Rich to set about building Covent Garden.

The immediate success of the play owed much to its musical charm and to the character of Polly (as Boswell's story of the first audience's response to Air XII suggests) but its role as a *cause célèbre* was undoubtedly due to its social and political satire. 'Does W—— think you intended an affront to him in your opera.' wrote Swift on 26 February 1728. 'Pray God he may' (*Swift Corr.*, iii. 267). Despite the fact that the play is by no means a *pièce à clef*, he may be thought to have had good enough reason. Gay first establishes taxation as a form of highway robbery in the allusion to Walpole at I. iii. 28 as 'Robin of Bagshot, alias Gorgon, alias Bluff Bob, alias Carbuncle, alias Bob Booty', reinforcing the point by making Macheath the highwayman his hero ('by this Character every Body will understand *One*, who makes it his Business arbitrarily to *levy* and *collect* Money on the People for his *own Use*, and of which he always dreads to give *any Account*').[56] Macheath's embarrassment at the rival claims of Polly and Lucy was taken to glance at Walpole's relationship with Lady Walpole and with his mistress, Molly Skerret, and the *Key* later points out the sobriquet of 'Great Man' as another significant link. Yet Gay pulls this particular punch by first of all presenting Peachum, the thief-catcher and fence, at the centre of a web of self-aggrandizement and multiple deception that had an immediate and much stronger political impact, underlined by his first song ('*And the Statesman, because he's so great, | Thinks his Trade as honest as mine*'). Peachum was based upon Jonathan Wild, and the equation Wild = Walpole had already been established by *Mist's Weekly Journal*, 12 and 19 June 1725. The *Key* (p. 72) says that Peachum and Lockit can be linked as Walpole and his brother-in-law Townshend, a relationship apparently supported by the quarrel at II. x. At this point, however, the parallels become unclear. It is Lockit (played by Jack Hall, 'a very *corpulent, bulky* Man') who according to this theory is labelled the '*prime Minister* of

Newgate': Peachum was played by John Hippisley as 'a *little,
awkward slovenly* Fellow'. Moreover, as Schultz points out (p.
371), the famous quarrel at Cleveland Court between
Walpole and Townshend is misdated by Cooke when he gives
an account of it in his *Memoirs of Macklin*, p. 57, and could not
therefore have been a model for the Peachum/Lockit quarrel,
even though earlier quarrels may have been. The author of
the *Key* prefers to think that Macheath, 'who hath also a *goodly
Presence*, and hath a tolerable *Bronze* upon his Face' (p. 73),
represents Walpole. In this way the political parallels subtly
shift, offering a slightly different perspective from each
viewpoint. A recent article even claims Macheath as George
II and Lucy as the Countess of Suffolk.[57] If Mrs Howard were
indeed in Gay's mind at the time, it would be much more
likely to be as the agent of his disappointed hopes of Court
preferment. Such disappointment (he had refused the by no
means totally ignominious appointment of Gentleman-Usher
to the Princess Louisa the previous October, an appropriate
office for a poet who had just written his *Fables* for another
royal child) might well have been what directed his attention
to Walpole, however, who believed that Gay had once
libelled him, had reported as much to the Queen,[58] and was
no doubt responsible for the supposed meagreness of the office.
Gay's friends were already aligned behind Bolingbroke and
the Dawley group against Walpole: the success of *The Beggar's
Opera* left no doubt that Gay was of their company. Walpole
himself encored and applauded Air XXX when the first-night
audience obviously felt that it was directed against him, and
took no action against the play (Cooke, p. 53). This was a
statesmanlike quick-wittedness worthy of Bolingbroke's turning of *Cato* to the Tory account fifteen years before (Sherburn,
i. 175). Gay himself lost his Whitehall lodgings, originally
granted to him by the Earl of Lincoln, and even found his
letters being read by the post office, but was otherwise not
unduly persecuted: his position as Lottery Commissioner, for
instance, continued from 1722 to 1731. However, stage
attacks on Walpole's administration intensified in the years
after *The Beggar's Opera*, and Gay's sequel, *Polly*, was not
allowed to be performed.

There is a sense in which the burlesque tragedy of *The What*

D'Ye Call It is wholly appropriate. When the steward of a
country house comes to put on a play which he has
presumably written himself he will want it to sound as
sublime as Lee or Banks, even though the only serious events
that he knows anything at all about are of purely local
significance: poaching, conscription, and unwanted preg-
nancies. Similarly, when a beggar comes to write an opera
(to celebrate the marriage of two ballad-singers) he knows
nothing of Alexander the Great, but everything about the
criminals who rule the underworld he inhabits. The wedded
pair would have wanted to hear ballads, naturally, and this
accounts for the novelty of Gay's extensive use of ballad tunes,
but they would also have wanted an opera about the leaders
of organized crime to whom they very likely themselves owed
allegiance:

> Let not the ballad-singer's shrilling strain
> Amid the swarm thy list'ning ear detain:
> Guard well thy pocket; for these *Syrens* stand
> To aid the labours of the diving hand;
> Confed'rate in the cheat, they draw the throng,
> And cambrick handkerchiefs reward the song.[59]

It is thus that Brecht made use of mendicant beggars in *Die
Dreigroschenoper*, lending a further social realism to the
Edwardian Soho which was his particular version of Gay's
underworld.[60] Benjamin Britten's adaptation also introduced
beggars, but softened their criminal function.[61]

However, Gay's Beggar is not only a representative of this
underworld, as his very first words show: 'If Poverty be a
Title to Poetry, I am sure No-body can dispute mine'. The
claim is proverbial, but Gay intends to suggest that since most
poets are incompetent they will make no money out of their
work. The Beggar is 'really' therefore (as indeed he is openly
in the Introduction to *Polly*) simply a poet, and a bad one,
since he is incompetent in handling genres. The same point
was more elaborately made by Pope in *The Dunciad*: the Cave
of Poverty and Poetry is a place where, among other lapses of
decorum, 'Tragedy and Comedy embrace' (i. 69) and where,
therefore, the Beggar's notion of presenting an opera about
criminals would appear quite acceptable. In the correct world
it is not, and that is why he is a beggar.

Gay's 'modern' Preface to *The What D'Ye Call It* proposed that '*the Sentiments of Princes and Clowns have not in reality that difference which they seem to have*'. A recipe for literary disaster if taken seriously, this notion is the very backbone of the social satire in *The Beggar's Opera*. 'Through the whole Piece', claims the Beggar in the penultimate scene, 'you may observe such a similitude of Manners in high and low Life, that it is difficult to determine whether (in the fashionable Vices) the fine Gentlemen imitate the Gentlemen of the Road, or the Gentlemen of the Road the fine Gentlemen.' Gay had been musing on this identity for some time. In 1717 he (or possibly Pope) presented Cadogan as a parvenu and a cut-purse in *Horace, Epod. IV, Imitated By Sir James Baker, Kt. To Lord Cad—n*, and in August 1723 he wrote to Mrs Howard: 'I cannot indeed wonder that the Talents requisite for a great Statesman are so scarce in the world since so many of those who possess them are every month cut off in the prime of their Age at the Old-Baily' (*Letters*, p. 45). Kerby-Miller (p. 287) notes a probable hint for *The Beggar's Opera* in Chapter xii of *The Memoirs of Martinus Scriblerus*: 'He did not doubt likewise to find the same resemblance in Highway-men and Conquerors', and Gay may also have remembered his early farce *The Mohocks*, where the town rowdies comport themselves like epic heroes and the whores have unusually polite manners. When, in *The Beggar's Opera*, the highwaymen, prostitutes, and fences speak and act like politicians, court ladies, and lawyers, their ambiguous social position yields infinite variations on the kind of moral inversion which Gay wishes to explore.

The qualities which an opera might be expected to take seriously (love, ambition, loyalty) are continually undermined by the paradoxical assumptions of characters who wear their criminality with an air of gracefulness, fashion, or practicality. Peachum, who has a vast organization for the reception of stolen property, and yet who also makes money by informing on the thieves whose talents he employs, justifies his moral position by comparing it with that of a lawyer: 'Like me too he acts in a double Capacity, both against Rogues and for 'em; for 'tis but fitting that we should protect and encourage Cheats, since we live by them' (i. i. 10). All our moral expectations are therefore reversed in

Peachum's world. And yet the closeness to the puritanical and hypocritical bourgeois ethic remains, and is credible enough to give his paradoxes the full sting of moral satire. His long speech at I. iv. 75, for instance, exposes a father's economic interest in his daughter as ingeniously as possible without being downright macabre. Peachum is running a family business, but we are reminded that any family is a business of a kind, and the rationale of social pimping provides a solid basis for a number of good jokes about marriage in the following scenes (for example, at I. viii. 12: 'Married! . . . Do you think your Mother and I should have liv'd comfortably so long together, if ever we had been married?'). Polly, who has married for love, will not care that a highwayman might treat her just as badly as a Lord. She is well versed in the romances that Macheath has been lending her, and these tell her that 'none of the great Heroes were ever false in Love' (I. xiii. 16). With Polly played straight, the burlesque of pathetic tragedy and victimization becomes a rather more equilibrist exercise than in the case of Kitty and Filbert, so that while we can see very well that she is being used to burlesque sentimentalism, she remains at the same time a true creature of sentiment, and her love for Macheath is indeed genuine. With her predicament at once amusing and moving us, one of the most absurdly touching scenes in the play is when her rival Lucy Lockit decides that she is simply not happy enough to deserve to be poisoned. The very precariousness of happiness is one of the important thematic under-currents of the play ('A Moment of time may make us unhappy for-ever': II. xv. 30) so to grasp it boldly in the face of calculated opposition becomes really heroic. Polly's love is one of the very few reliable ideals in a world of particularly unreliable concrete things (like missing property or double-dealing employers) so that our feelings are taxed when her lofty emotion is bestowed upon a robber and multiple bigamist whom most other characters in the play wish at one time or another to betray.

Gay makes sure, then, that we are attracted to Macheath as well, and does so by lending him an aristocratic swagger that contrasts favourably with the dogged book-keeping of Peachum (for an extended discussion of the subtle social implications of this contrast, see Chapter VI of William

Empson's *Some Versions of Pastoral*, 1935, the best criticism that the play has had). Our assent to the Player's objections to Macheath's being hanged in the penultimate scene is an assent assiduously worked towards. It goes beyond a burlesque of the happy endings of operas, although the happy ending was a particularly vulnerable development in serious drama in the eighteenth century, and it was one which Brecht was still eager to satirize when producing his version of the opera almost exactly two hundred years later. It is appropriate, perhaps, where the victim is not the villain, but has been manipulated by the real villains of the piece. One of the reasons, no doubt, for the undercurrent of moral protest about the play throughout the eighteenth century, from Justice Fielding and others like him, was the attractiveness of Macheath, though as Dr Johnson remarks in his *Life of Gay*: 'It is not possible for anyone to imagine that he may rob with safety because he sees Macheath reprieved upon the stage.'[62] The amoral hero was not new, of course. A contemporary portrait of the actor Thomas Walker as Macheath describes the character as 'a second Dorimant' and emphasizes those manly qualities which appeal to the ladies.[63] *Memoirs . . . of Captain Mackheath* (cited by Schultz, p. 232) underlines in more detail this debt to Etherege, and is perhaps worth quoting at some length:

The Dramatick Writer has indeed dress'd him out to Advantage, he stands erect the first Piece in the Canvas, and has gained much popular Applause; he has made him the Lover and the Warrior, he is the Darling of the Fair, and the Glory of the thievish Heroes who surround him: He is a perfect, polite, modern fine Gentleman, and *Dorimant* in Sir *Fopling*, though a Person of equal Morals, is not a more accomplish'd Rake. He commits his Robberies with an Air of Authority and Gallantry, the common People mistake his Vice for Virtues; and those who are not in his Gang, applaud him.

It was thus clearly a mistake in a production in 1777 to introduce a scene in which Macheath is sent to the hulks for three years, even though, as we understand from Gay's own sequel, transportation is the result of the Player's and the Beggar's intervention. Macheath's charm must seem sufficient to show him rising buoyantly above any of the conventional demands of justice. Once really transported, the authority and gallantry of the rake are utterly destroyed. This is clear enough from *Polly*, where Macheath is discovered living ignominiously in disguise in the West Indies with only one prostitute. He even betrays his gang. This is not behaviour worthy of a hero, and in his sequel Gay was able, without any risk of rebuke from 'the taste of the town', to kill him off and marry Polly to the Noble Savage, Cawwawkee.

But a moral outcome of this kind was not to protect the sequel from Government interference. At the end of November 1728 it was reported that 'two eminent Actors of the said House [the theatre in Lincoln's Inn Fields] have lately attended his Majesty with a Second Part of the Beggar's Opera in order for his Majesty's Approbation'.[64] It would appear from Gay's Preface to *Polly* that this visit merely established the prohibition of the play's rehearsal until the Lord Chamberlain should have had the opportunity to read it (see also *Letters*, p. 78). The Duke of Grafton was out of town at this time. Gay took a copy of the play to him personally on 7 December, and the news of its suppression reached him on 12 December. The Lord Chamberlain traditionally had authority over the stage, even though this authority was not often exercised. His shadow as censor was felt, however, if ironically. Pope, writing to Caryll in March 1715, noted with comic truculence: 'Yet is there not a proclamation issued forth for the burning of Homer and the Pope by the common hangman; nor is the *Whatd'yecall-it* yet silenced by the Lord Chamberlain' (Sherburn, i. 287). Silence, however, is in this case what was requested. Walpole, according to Lord Hervey, 'resolved rather than suffer himself to be produced for thirty nights together upon the stage in the person of a highwayman, to make use of his friend the Duke of Grafton's authority as Lord Chamberlain to put a stop to the representation of it'.[65] Accordingly, the play was forbidden to be acted, 'without any particular Reasons being alledged'.[66]

Polly, as it was eventually published, appears to be no more, indeed perhaps rather less, slanted against Walpole than its predecessor. There is a great deal of general political satire, it is true, but nothing quite so invidious as in *The Beggar's Opera*. Walpole may well have been affected by rumour about the play. The popularity of *The Beggar's Opera* had led Gay's friends to use it as a weapon against the Government. It appeared that much the same was being done with its sequel by his enemies, at a time when it had been neither performed nor published. A leading article in the form of a letter significantly signed 'Hilarius' appeared in the *Craftsman* no. 135, 1 February 1729, giving several instances of unwarranted gossip about the contents of it:

They spread a Report through every Part of the Town that the *Sequel to the Beggar's Opera* was a most insolent and seditious Libel; that the Character of *Mackheath* was drawn for one of the *greatest* and *most virtuous Men* in the Kingdom; that This was too plain, in the *former Part*; but that, in the *Second*, He is *transported*; turns *Pyrate*; becomes *Treasurer* in a certain Island abroad; proves corrupt; and is sacrific'd to the Resentment of an *injured People*. Happening to step into a Coffee-house, near St. *James's*, some time ago, I found a certain Gentleman, famous for his Corinthian Face, who was giving the Company an Account to this Purpose.[67]

Gay intended to refute such gossip by printing his play (or so the Preface claims) and in doing so gave up 'all present views of profit which might accrue from the stage' (Vol. II, p. 70). But the suppression had turned him into 'a publick person a little Sacheverel' (*Swift Corr.*, iii. 325) and as it turned out he made upward of £1,200 from this edition, published on 25 March 1729 at his own expense: this was far more than he could have hoped for from a stage production (Spence, i. 108). Subscribers paid a guinea each, and the Duchess of Marlborough gave £100 for one copy (*Letters*, pp. 79–80). The edition of 10,500 copies sold well at first, even though it was priced as high as 6*s.*, but within three weeks Gay was advertising that he was forced to dispose of his impression at a great loss (2*s.* 6*d.* a copy).[68] The reason for this was no doubt the large number of pirated editions of the work, against the publishers of which Gay was granted an injunction in the Court of Chancery on 12 June 1729.[69]

Gay's Preface and his letter to Swift of 2 December 1728 (*Letters*, p. 78) make it clear that *Polly* was largely written 'in the view of taking care of myself' during the five or six months he spent at Bath during the summer of 1728, although some of the songs may have been written at Middleton Stoney, with the Duchess of Queensberry helping him out with rhymes. The Duchess also reports that Pulteney may have suggested the idea of a sequel:

the Duchess told me, that on Gay's being accused of immorality in the end of yᵉ Beggars Opera, some Nobleman (I really think Lord Bath but I am not certain) said 'Why Gay you have only *transported* him pursue him, & bring him to punishment—' & see says she '*I* was punished because Macheath was to be hanged; & Gay's morality vindicated—I told the L.ᵈ Chamberlain *I thanked him*—it saved me trouble & Curtisies.[70]

This punishment was the result of her perfectly natural commitment to the play which led her to be active in seeking subscriptions to Gay's edition even in the King's Drawing-room, and for this she was forbidden the Court. The Duke also took this opportunity to resign his office as Admiral of Scotland, a move that he had however been contemplating previously.[71] At the time of publication, the room next to the Duchess's dining-room in her London house was full of the printed sheets as two men from Bowyer's did the collating and binding (*Letters*, p. 80). Her survival until the first production, by Colman, on 19 June 1777, seems a touching reward for her loyalty and concern: she heard the play with delight and joined in all the songs herself.[72] She attended this production more than once, and died very shortly afterwards.

Polly takes up the Polly Oliver theme which surfaced briefly in *The What D'Ye Call It*, 1. i. 73. Macheath has been transported to the West Indies and Matt's promise in *The Beggar's Opera*, III. xiv. 16, to shop Lockit and Peachum has evidently been carried out. At any rate, with her father hanged, Polly is free to leave England in search of her husband. Macheath is disguised as a negro, Morano, his identity known only to Jenny Diver, whom he has married. Since Polly does not discover the secret until after Macheath has been led away to execution, there is little opportunity for real dramatic tension here, and the irony is not much exploited. Interest is instead divided between Polly's scenes with the Ducats and her scenes with the Indians. The former lack the satirical bite of *The Beggar's Opera* and the latter introduce a new gravity and piety of sentiment in his attack on a corrupt society, a tone not present in *The Beggar's Opera*. Gay used memories of the Houyhnhnms and of Oroonoko for his portrayal of Cawwawkee. The aboriginal Arrowauks or Arawaks (whence the Prince's name probably derives) had in fact been exterminated in 1655, and such an alliance between colonists and Indians as forms the basis of the armed conflict in the play seems historically unlikely. However, Gay's portrayal of the buccaneers (all transported sharpers, drawers, and pimps) restores some of the low-life atmosphere that he had made his own convincing province. When Pope talked to Gay about the possibility of writing 'American pastorals' some moral notions may have lingered in his mind; he may even have obtained some local information from Pope's nephew, John Rackett, who was a trader in the West Indies;[73] but whatever is still vital in the play owes most to the heroi-comic metaphors of *The Beggar's Opera*.

Thus it is that two old women may exhibit a stoical endurance at the clearly not unpleasing prospect of being ravished (i. xii. 34) and a gang of pirates propose to carve up the New World between them (ii. ii. 137: 'Death, Sir,—I shall not part with *Mexico* so easily'). In cases like these the high-mindedness is inappropriate with just that dry poise of Gay's that takes the point beyond satire into the ridiculous. By contrast, Ducat is a throwback to the humours of *The Mohocks* and *The Wife of Bath*, and his wife a prototype of the jealous viragos of later plays, such as Theaspe or Lady Willit. In these early scenes a sexual/political metaphor is substituted for the criminal/political metaphor of *The Beggar's Opera*, and this is a sign of a new direction in Gay's work. Polly herself cannot carry the play, but moves with candour and charm *en travestie* through the various scenes she links, a Shakespearean heroine in conception, without any saving wit. Macheath at least retains his self-confidence (iii. xi. 58: '*Alexander* the great was more successful. That's all') but he is in fact less of a mock-Alexander than a mock-Antony, as Hacker's words about Jenny at ii. ii. 98 ('She's an arrant *Cleopatra*') openly suggest.[74] In context his presumptuousness lacks charm (for example at iii. vii. 23, when he continues to demand ransom even when Cawwawkee has escaped) and his death is ignominious.

Perhaps, as the *Flying-Post* predicted, *Polly* achieved a

unique off-stage popularity: 'As 'tis not allowed to be acted, we shall have it in Miniature in a thousand little Circles, over a Bottle, as soon as our merry Fellows have got some of the Songs by heart, which they are now very studiously humming over.'[75] But Gay naturally wished to see a play of his in the theatre again, and he may have turned to his sixteen-year-old comedy *The Wife of Bath* at this point as an innocuous means of persuading Rich that his work was not always political dynamite (see *Letters*, p. 86: 'The ridicule turns upon Supe[rsti]tion, & I have avoided the very words Bribery & corruption'). It was heavily rewritten, and put on at Lincoln's Inn Fields on 19 January 1730. I have already compared the two versions (see above, p. 10). Gay no doubt wished to improve the early work, but there may have been financial reasons for producing a technically new play. Lintot had already paid £25 for the copyright of the 1713 version, but he was ready to pay £75 for the new one (Nichols, viii. 296), publishing it in both octavo and quarto on 3 February. Gay wrote to Swift on 3 March: 'My old vamp'd Play got me no money, for it had no success' (*Letters*, p. 88). He was now becoming used to large financial rewards for his plays, of course, and is here somewhat understating what was a passable income from a revival of this kind: in addition to the £75 from Lintot he received £56. 6d. from the playhouse receipts on the author's benefit night (Scouten, i. 32). It could hardly be said to have been a success, however. A typical reaction came from the *Universal Spectator, and Weekly Journal*, 24 January 1730: 'Gay's Wife of Bath, alter'd, a Comedy, lately acted at Lincoln's-Inn Play-House, did not Run so much as was expected, therefore People think Mr. Gay was not the sole Author of *The Beggar's Opera*; and they go so far as to say, The first Song in that Performance was Dr. Swift's.' Despite its unpopularity, the play was translated into German. See Brockmann, *Die Witwe von Kecskemet* (Vienna, 1788).

Gay was naturally anxious for the success of his third ballad-opera, *Achilles*, produced posthumously at Covent Garden on 10 February 1733 and published on 1 March.[76] I take it that the work is in no serious sense incomplete, despite the slightness of plot and the fact that it is only about two-thirds as long as *Polly* and even one-seventh shorter than *The Beggar's Opera*. Burnet's *Achilles Dissected* claims that it is a fragment which Gay would have lengthened to five acts, and that Gay's friends supplied many of the songs. The same points are made in an article in *The Daily Courant*, 16 February 1733:

> Mr. *Gay* could not *deviate* into so much *Dulness*. He had the Plan given him, but unhappily died, the Play unfinished, and the Songs not wrote. But rather than the Scheme should fail, the Patriot became the Poet—Sir *W*. the Esquire, the Satyrist, and his Grace, held their Consultations, Nor could it be unpleasant to hear a *discarded Courtier* humming out—Joan's *Placket is rent and tore* then
>
> > *Reputation hack'd and cut*
> > *Can never be mended again*
>
> While a noble Lady with a *natural Simplicity of Thoughts*, recollects—
>
> > *My a Dilding, my a Dolding,*
> > *Lilly bright and shine*
>
> The *Scot* insists in eternizing the Memory of his *Cat*; while the *little Satyrist* tags the Verse, and *points* the Song.

If the point were true, it would be natural to suppose Arbuthnot or Pope to be collaborators, but the disaffected Queensberrys are dragged in out of malice, and for the rest it shows up the article as merely a pro-government writer's gleeful opportunity to involve opposition leaders like Bolingbroke, Wyndham, and Pulteney in what seemed to be a negligible and ineffective political lampoon. There is no corroborating evidence. Burnet's further claim, that the 'Prologue. Written by Mr. *GAY*' is in fact by Pope, has been accepted by Ault (see my Commentary, Vol. II, p. 390). If this is correct, then Pope pretends to find the play a daring novelty, showing '*the Heroes of old* Greece . . . *In a Comic Piece*'. There was some recent precedent, however, for travesty of this sort. Mottley and Cooke's *Penelope* (1728) presents Ulysses as an English sergeant and Penelope as the landlady of an alehouse. Though this play is written in couplets, it does contain songs. Forrest's *Momus Turn'd Fabulist, or Vulcan's Wedding* (1729) has an Olympian cast and is written in prose, with, moreover, some similarities of tone to *Achilles*. But Gay's is naturally a more distinguished performance than these, even if it is one of his dramatically least striking works. One reason is the consistency and ingenuity of the cultural transference. There is a minimum of vulgarity and every opportunity for observed domestic satire. F. W. Bateson was surely right when he found it to be not a burlesque, but 'more properly a modernization of the same kind as Mr. Shaw's *Caesar and Cleopatra*'.[77]

Gay's principal source seems to have been Statius, but the story also appears in Bion and Ovid. One of the few odes of Horace to provoke anything more than the most factual of marginal glosses in his annotated copy of Mattaire's Horace (1715)[78] was I. viii, *Ad Lydiam*, in which the rebuke to Sybaris culminates in a comparison of him with Achilles:

> quid latet, ut marinae
> filium dicunt Thetidis sub lacrimosa Troiae
> funera, ne virilis
> cultus in caedem et Lycias proriperet catervas?

Gay's Achilles, it emerges, it not so afraid, but is disguised as a girl at the court of Lycomedes simply to please his mother, the goddess Thetis, who knows 'that odious Siege of *Troy* wou'd be the Death of thee' (I. i. 11). His discovery by Ulysses provides the predictable conclusion to the fable, and he leaves gladly for the Trojan war after putting the seal of marriage on his affair with Deidamia. The latter's predicament (oddly for Gay, who enjoyed parting his heroines from their lovers) is not fully developed. There were ample hints in Statius (for instance, *Achilleis* i. 939: 'o timor! abripitur miserae permissus Achilles') for elaborating upon the cruelty of her abandonment. Gay is evidently much more interested in the efforts of Lycomedes and his pimping minister Diphilus to woo Achilles, and in the consequent jealousy of Theaspe. These scenes allow him to investigate 'the whole matrimonial Rhetorick' (II. x. 39) of female abuse, wheedling and recrimination, something that he was already well practised in, and which in Lady Willit and Lady Bustle he was to bring to its forceful extreme. Gay's years as a spa-haunting bachelor, observing with horror the marital persecution of the well-to-do, had obviously paid off.

Burnet was anxious to discredit the play, but found nothing

political in it beyond the situation of 'a monarch engrossed by his Prime Minister'. *The Daily Courant* claimed that its 'secret History' was unintelligible. Gay seems (whether willingly or not) to have abandoned political satire, for if Burnet's suggestion had any real truth we would no doubt be able to find in Diphilus some more tangible resemblance to Walpole.

Achilles had a modest success, and was given nineteen performances in the first season. The Prince of Wales attended on the second night, the play having met with general applause from a distinguished audience at its opening.[79] A *Life of Achilles*, particularly designed to enlighten audiences, was put out by Roberts, and there was some predictable sniping from papers like *The Daily Courant* (12 and 16 February) and *The Auditor* (16 February). It was the sort of reception to be expected of a minor work by a popular author only two months dead. If the Prologue was right in playing up its novelty, one can only conclude that the novelty was not sufficiently exploited. Swift had no doubt that *Achilles* belonged essentially to an exhausted vein, and wrote as much to Pope on 30 March 1733: 'It hath been printed here [Dublin], and I am grieved to say, it is a very poor performance. I have often Chid Mr Gay for not varying his Schemes, but still adhering to those that he had exhausted' (*Swift Corr.*, iv. 133). Pope, however, thought it 'of his very best manner' (Sherburn, iii. 337).

Indeed, Gay had made the most of his success in creating a new genre, but he was obviously at the time of his death on 4 December 1732 ready to try other things. Besides *Achilles*, he left two comedies, *The Distress'd Wife* and *The Rehearsal at Goatham*, 'finished . . . and intended for the Stage before his Death' according to a notice advertising the second edition of *The Distress'd Wife* in the preliminaries of *The Rehearsal at Goatham*. These do show Gay trying his hand at something new, a sober comedy of manners and a Fieldingesque farce *à clef*, both rather more socially observant and politically disillusioned than previous work. *The Distress'd Wife* was performed on 5 May 1734, but not published until May 1743, and *The Rehearsal at Goatham*, never acted, did not reach publication until April 1754. These delays are not easy to explain.

Gay's sisters inherited his property, but they wisely allowed the Duke of Queensberry to take charge of his papers and the committing of posthumous works to the press. Where responsibility for publication actually lay, and whether it was motivated by literary, financial, or other considerations, does not appear to be known. Gay's friends were concerned for his reputation, and did not want to see anything they considered unworthy of him in print. Pope seems to have been satisfied with the Duke's handling of *Achilles* (Sherburn, iii. 337, 347), but Swift was not so sure:

As to our poor friend, I think the D. of Qu. hath acted a very noble & generous part. But before he did it, I wish there had been so much cunning used as to have let the Sisters know, that he expected they would let him dispose of Mr Gay's Writings as himself, and other friends should advise, and I heartily wish His Grace had entirely Stifled that Comedy if it were possible, than do an injury to our friend's reputation only to get a hundred or two pounds to a couple of (perhaps) insignificant women. . . . I think it is incumbent upon you to see that nothing more be publish'd of his that will lessen his reputation, for the sake of adding a few pence to his Sisters, who have already got so much by his death. (*Swift Corr.*, iv. 133)

In reply, Pope reassured Swift that 'our poor friend's papers are partly in my hands, and for as much as is so, I will take care to suppress things unworthy of him' (Sherburn, iii. 365). But Swift was really worried, and answered:

I am sorry for the scituation of Mr Gay's papers. You do not exert your self as much as I could wish in this affair; I had rather the two Sisters were hanged than see his works swelled by any loss of credit to his memory: I would be glad to see his valuable works printed by themselves, those which ought not to be seen burned immediatly, and the others that have gone abroad printed separately like Opuscula, or rather be stifled & forgotten. . . . I shall write to the Dutchess who hath lately honoured me with a very friendly letter, and I will tell her my opinion freely about our friend's papers. (*Swift Corr.*, iv. 153).

Thus it may have been pressure from Pope and Swift that kept the second volume of *Fables*, *The Distress'd Wife* and *The Rehearsal at Goatham* so long in manuscript: these were all advertised as printed with Queensberry's permission. But it is difficult to see the Duke merely holding on to them until

Gay's friends no longer cared, or were ill or dead. He may, of course, have waited in each case for a politically opportune moment (with the Walpole lampoon of *The Rehearsal at Goatham* left longest of all) or publication may have been teased out of him by the needy and maligned sisters. It is just possible that the MS of *The Rehearsal at Goatham* had been lent by the Duchess to her brother, Lord Cornbury (a man with literary interests), rediscovered among his papers after his death in 1753 and published in the following year. Gay himself admired Lord Cornbury, who was one of his pall-bearers (*Letters*, p. 121).

More important is the question of the actual dates of composition. *The Rehearsal at Goatham* must, as I shall show, have been written after the suppression of *Polly*; and *The Distress'd Wife*, with its pervasive tone of disgust with Court life and scorn of place-hunting, seems to belong to the same period. Both plays were said to be, and appear to be, finished and ready for the stage, but there is no evidence to place them either before or after *Achilles* in order of composition, since Gay does not mention his 'Scheme to raise my finances by doing something for the Stage' of 16 May 1732 by name (*Letters*, p. 122). They may have been written before, and *Achilles* preferred for production because it was a ballad-opera; or they may have been written afterwards, with negotiations for *Achilles* held up because of the *Polly* fiasco. It is impossible to say. *The Rehearsal at Goatham* is not such an angry little squib that it must have immediately followed the events it allegorizes, and 1730 seems a reasonable date for it. Cibber's appointment as laureate was announced in November (see below, p. 68), while Irving (p. 280) reports that 'Faulkner, the Dublin printer, claims that, in 1730, Swift wrote two acts of a comedy which he sent to Gay to finish. This was called, says he, *The Players' Rehearsal*, and all trace of it has been lost'. Gay's farce has only one act, and concerns puppets, not players, and an attempted performance, not a rehearsal. Nevertheless, the genre is the same, and some of the fatuous remarks and anecdotes of the aldermen's wives, elaborate and irrelevant to the main action, sound like a small-town version of the *Polite Conversation*, though without the essential jargon. Lady Bustle's card game at v. 61 also appears to put in an appearance in Swift. Compare his 'The Journal of a Modern Lady' (1729), 50–3:

> 'But, was it not confounded hard?
> 'Well, if I ever touch a Card:
> 'Four *Mattadores*, and lose *Codill*!
> 'Depend upon't, I never will.'

Gay was busy with the revised version of *The Wife of Bath* until early in 1730, but from March to December there was a long and happy period with the Queensberrys at Amesbury in which one may imagine the play written, perhaps for private performance. A letter from Lady Westmorland to Lady Denbigh of 3 April 1748 mentions the Duchess of Queensberry building a stage and having plays acted.[80] There is every likelihood of her having done this before.

The Distress'd Wife is a comedy of manners with some resemblance to the work of Congreve, and it shows Gay experimenting with psychologically exact character portrayal in a way he had never quite done before. It has perhaps something of that quality which John Loftis senses in Fielding or Popple tending towards the novel;[81] the formal demands of plot are curiously minimal, and the social orientation and motivation of the characters is presented with a grave and deliberate concern for realism and moral rectitude which is refreshing. It concerns the efforts of a country gentleman to reclaim his wife from a life of spendthrift triviality in their West End house. This he can only bring about (on the advice of his merchant uncle) by a show of moral strength that reduces her to near-hysteria. Her specific plan to get them permanently established in London (by trading his niece in marriage for a place for him at Court) is finally foiled by the niece's announcement that she is already married. The wife is hauled back to the country unreformed: it seems to require the activities of a corrupt steward to supply the urgency needed to get the family away from London and the danger of financial ruin.

Sir Thomas and Lady Willit are thus emblematic of Gay's vision of an England at once seduced and revolted by Walpole's power. They represent the traditional landed economy standing bemused between the world of fashion, flattery, and the scramble for political advancement on the one hand, and the world of solid mercantile virtue on the other. They find themselves having to choose between Court and City, between corruption and commerce, between Lord Courtlove and Uncle Barter: the drama seems at once personal and national.

Although Sir Thomas is off-stage for much of the time, this is essentially his problem. One of the play's weaknesses, indeed, is the superficial presentation of Lady Willit: she is drawn entirely in one key of narrow obstinacy and cruelty, persecuting servants and dependent relations alike, refusing to see that it is natural for tradesmen to present their bills, and living only for her own immediate pleasure. Her harangues and intrigues, however, provide a vivid foreground to Sir Thomas's struggle for responsibility and integrity, a struggle set in motion not only by his steward's defaulting and his dwindling credit in town, but also (and this is less convincingly presented) by his jealousy of Lady Willit's supposed affair with the coxcomb Pert. In all this he is aided by the counsels of Barter, who, acting as a kind of chorus, stimulates his nephew to action, reforms Lord Courtlove and establishes the moral norm.

Barter is almost too sober a spokesman for Gay's new-found sympathies. More attractive here are the dependent niece and cousin, Sprightly and Friendless. Sprightly can't take Lord Courtlove seriously, even when he is proposing to her:

What signifies my Consent?—After Marriage I can act without your Consent, as you act without mine before.—That's a most enormous Perriwig, my Lord; o'my Conscience, 'twould load an Ass, and cover Head, Ears and all. (III. iii. 12).

Her pleasant assurance and good sense are complemented by the more wistful virtues of Friendless, an *ingénue* who writes shrewd letters to the country housekeeper, plays cribbage with the maid and is continually subjected to the indignities of Lady Willit. Friendless's eventual marriage to Courtlove smacks a little too much of Busy's marriage to Doggrell in *The Wife of Bath* to please us, but her presence in the play is a reminder of Gay's sympathy for the under-privileged: the scene where she is frisked by the suspicious Lady Willit (II.

viii) is particularly well-observed and detailed. Her despairing cry on refusing to be bribed by Lord Courtlove: 'Which of us two thinks the other the most contemptible?' (IV. viii. 47) might also be a motto for the play, with its unresolved conflict between prudence and pleasure, between reason and extravagance. Indeed, the very word *reasonable* (it occurs over twenty times in the play) acquires an ironical ambiguity, for it can mean both 'rational' and 'may be reasoned with', and these are very different things: Lady Willit at her most irrational will try to reason her way into or out of anything, so that her husband seems to her therefore 'unreasonable' not through departing from reason, but through refusing to be persuaded out of it.

With surprisingly little contemporary reaction to the play surviving, James Thomson's critique, in his letter to Elizabeth Young of 28 September 1743,[82] is worth reproducing for the touch of primitivism and sensibility in its response to Gay's anatomy of West End society:

I would have sent you the Distressed Wife before now, but I had mislaid it and only found it again yesterday. The Perusal of it gave me more Disgust than Pleasure, it presents so vile and perhaps so natural a Picture of a Town-Life. There are no Animals in the whole Creation that Pass their Time so idly, and in my Opinion so miserably, as they who compose what they call the Gay World do. With Regard to them it is Virtue to be a Misanthrope; and instead of the gay they should be called the gayly-wretched World. It is a World not of God's making, but a true Limbo of Vanity, made up of ridiculous shocking Phantoms of Folly, Affectation, and Vice. One Hour of virtuous Retirement, consecrated to Love Friendship and the Study of Nature, is worth an Age of it. I would have it an Article in the Litany—And from the dull, tiresome, vain, tattling, impertinent, unfeeling, and utterly worthless gay World, good God deliver me! The Design of the Play is very good, to satirize this Life so unworthy of a reasonable Creature, but I dont think it so well executed. Barter is the best Character in it; but there are few such citizens as he: they are still more vile, by their Imitation of the Luxuries of this End of the Town. S.ᵗ Thomas Willit is a weak man, and if he had a Heart could not possibly bestow it upon such a Woman as his Lady. For Her, she is detestable, and past all Reformation. Besides her Affectations are drawn so monstrous, they are not the Affectations of a Woman of Sense and Wit but of a Fool. Miss Sprightly's Wit is affected, and has not that amiable Softness and gentle Character which ought to recommend the Sprightliness of your Sex. And poor Miss Friendless how came the Author too to be so little her Friend, as to make her a matrimonial Prostitute to the most foolish of all foolish Lords. I expected, from her sensible and serious Turn, that she would have disdained the Proposal, and rather lived in a Cottage with some Person she loved. Pardon these Criticisms on a Play you seemed to like; but I like several Things in it as much as you, and am greatly pleased with the honest Intention and Moral of the Piece.

On 27 April 1771, an adaptation of *The Distress'd Wife* called *The Modern Wife* was mounted by George Colman at Covent Garden.[83] In the 1770s Gay's reputation was particularly high. Colman was also to adapt *Achilles* (1773) and *Polly* (1777), and *The Distress'd Wife* was again prepared for production in 1777 (this time with its original title) but was not performed.[84] *The Modern Wife* is an interesting version of the play. It was never printed, but a MS is preserved in the Larpent Collection in the Huntington Library (MS Larpent 321). I think it reveals by its alterations what were in fact the strengths of the original. Courtlove has been split into Lord Gloss (a coxcomb) and Southell (a confidant of Sir Thomas). Courtlove was over-grave and pompous, it is true, 'a formal pedant in politics', but he was open to Barter's wise words, and his marriage to Friendless was meant to be acceptable. Gloss is merely a 'part', foppish where Courtlove was not, and full of duplicity and talk (though not without amiability and wit). His wooing of Miss Newland (Sprightly) is a blind: all he really wants is a mistress. Nor is he trying to get Sir Thomas a place.

The main action now involves the plan of Southell to test Lady Willit by lending money and making advances to her, all with her husband's connivance. Sir Thomas's being given a more active and intimate confidant in addition to Gresham (Barter) alters the whole scheme of the play, for it doubly focuses attention on Southell, both on his trial of Lady Willit and on his alliance with Miss Newland. Friendless has gone, and Pert, Forward, and Flutter have been telescoped into Lord Gloss, so that most of the underlying conflict of Country and Town has gone. Lady Willit's temptation is sheer melodrama, and her reform inevitable:

Lad. W. I have undone Your Fortune, and have brought even your life into Danger—the Horror of my situation strikes full upon me, And I no longer want Your friendly Admonition to waken me to a sense of the Mischief I have occasion'd, or the happiness I have for ever lost.

Sir T. I am transported to see the present state of her mind (aside) (p. 84).

One might compare it with Mrs Centlivre's *The Basset Table* (1705), v. i, where Lady Reveller is reclaimed by a similar stratagem. Perhaps Colman had this in mind. What is significant is the wholly predictable sentimentalizing of Gay's moral point, and the blurring of his sharply observed and distinguished characters. In Gay, as I have tried to suggest, Sprightly and Friendless illustrate an attractive principle of life: reading romances, being untidy, quizzical, irreverent, and marrying Cousin Harry. In Colman, Miss Newland is reduced to the same smug moral plane as the reformed Lady Willit. His Gresham, too, is much more avuncular and matchmaking than Gay's Barter, and is significantly unable to convert Gloss to a more critical view of Court life. Colman was an expert play-doctor, and he no doubt tightened the dramatic structure of *The Distress'd Wife*, but only at the expense of Gay's subtle and uncompromising realism.

The Rehearsal at Goatham continues a theme of *The Distress'd Wife* that 'if Family Disputes were to be made publick, of all States, the State of Matrimony must be the most ridiculous' (i. i. 20). The captiousness of the aldermen at a harmless puppet-play leads them unwittingly to reveal all their marital secrets, embarrass their wives, and get hooted from the room. They also, however, expose their political corruption, and thus their discomfiture becomes a cartoon of the precariousness and sensitivity of those in power. This may be wishful thinking on Gay's part, perhaps, but it is a healthy enough piece of therapy, reminiscent of *The What D'ye Call It* in its treatment of the relationship between drama and real life. Irving (p. 303) styled it 'by all odds the least important of the posthumous plays', and I would not quarrel with this estimate.

However, the piece has an historical importance as a combination of anti-Walpole satire with partial allegory of the suppression of *Polly*, and is essential in any account of Gay's reaction to the events of the autumn of 1728, when the sequel to *The Beggar's Opera* was kept from the stage.

The Craftsman, with which Gay was associated, was full of rumours that Cibber had something to do with the suppression (see above, p. 54). Cibber, who had refused *The Beggar's Opera* for Drury Lane, had certainly little to lose by making trouble. Though Gay's part in the Cibber quarrel seems to have been at once more violent and more ephemeral than Pope's, there could, even at this date, have been little love lost between them. Cibber's appointment to the laureateship, announced in November 1730, must have strengthened any suspicion Gay might have had that he had ingratiated himself with the Government in some way: the appointment was at the disposal of the very Court official who had been instrumental in banning *Polly* from the playhouse, the Lord Chamberlain. Though no particular reasons were officially given for the banning, the cause was perfectly well known. Walpole had not enjoyed his portrayal as a highwayman, and did not look forward to his portrayal as a pirate.

Governmental hypersensitivity is fully reflected in *The Rehearsal at Goatham*. The play is based on the incident of Peter and his puppet show from *Don Quixote* (see my Commentary, Vol. II, p. 394). This is preceded in the novel by the story of the two aldermen who go to look for a lost ass, and merely discover their own skill in braying, an escapade which is ridiculed by a neighbouring town. It is from the latter incident that Gay derives the true basis of his play—the rival towns of Goatham and Assborough, and the aldermen who are to make such fools of themselves at Peter's puppet show. The point is that they consider themselves libelled by his perfectly harmless play of *Melisendra* (just as Gay imagined the government to have done) and cause it to be prohibited (as the government had ordered *Polly* to be). Peter is suspected of being a secret emissary from the rival corporation of Assborough, sent to make fools of them all. Here are the main outlines of the allegory: the two corporations are the Whig government and the Tory opposition, and Peter is Gay himself, remarking characteristically at the end of the play: 'There is nothing to be done here; they have the Power, and we must submit—So to-morrow we'll leave the Town'. The chief alderman, Sir Headstrong Bustle, appears to be a typical Walpole figure, who can exclaim: 'To what End hath a Man Riches and Power, if he cannot crush the Wretches who have the Insolence to expose the Ways by which he got them!' (ix. 14). The aldermen's wives politely differ over precedence, their husbands appearing to have been only recently knighted (v. 3). This would seem to be a hit against the proliferation of titles distributed as political rewards. 'Sir Bluestring' himself was the first commoner to be made a Knight of the Garter (on 26 June 1726) since 1660.

What makes the play interesting are Gay's firm indications of the reasons for much of the aldermen's captiousness: they have been approached and warned beforehand by Jack Oaf, a writer, and his friend Will Gosling, whose uncle, Cackle, would be done out of business by Peter's show. Cackle and Broach (who is sponsoring Peter) keep rival inns in Goatham, the *Swan* and the *Dragon*. Here we have an obvious reference to the two main theatres in London at the time, Drury Lane and Lincoln's Inn Fields. Indeed, Broach is easily identifiable as John Rich, the licensee of Lincoln's Inn Fields, who did so well out of *The Beggar's Opera*. Broach is significantly said to be already in a 'good thriving Way of Business' at the beginning of the play (i. 16).

Opposed to Broach, as we have seen, is Oaf, intent on getting the puppet-show suppressed. That this character is intended to represent Cibber I hope will soon be made apparent. He is one of 'the favourite Wits of our top Men' and is 'so comically profane upon all Occasions, that he makes them all titter and laugh 'till they are ready to burst' (ii. 10). He is given a very Cibberian imperiousness, as when he remarks: 'To suffer *Peter* to come into the Town at all; was not Usage that I expected from the Corporation. After the Theatrical Entertainments I have writ, and I may say without Vanity, writ up to their Tastes.—I think the Town ow'd me so much, as not to suffer any Interlopers in a Dramatic Way' (i. 74). In the early part of the play some indications of the suggestive way the part could be played are provided by some

noticeably foppish expressions, 'rot me', 'pox take me', 'Faith
and Troth', and 'by Jupiter', used only by Oaf. That Cibber's
best-acted roles were fops, and that consequently he was
regarded as one in private life, is well known.[85] Further, both
Oaf and Gosling are shown to be 'so well acquainted with the
Manner and Stile of our Writers, that they no sooner hear an
Author's Name, but they decide upon the Performance' (vii.
27). Oaf, in fact, is extensively shown to be guilty of that very
behaviour of which Cibber is accused in the 'Hilarius' letter in
the *Craftsman* (quoted above, p. 54):

> *Broach.* I know there are idle Reports about Master *Peter* and his
> Shew.—But have you seen it, Mr *Oaf*? Have you read it, Mr
> *Gosling*?
> *Oaf.* I cannot say that.
> *Gosling.* But we know enough of the Thing in general.
> *Oaf.* There are Things quoted.
> *Gosling.* Passages, very obnoxious Passages.   (ii. 53)

Oaf can be summed up dramatically, perhaps, by Betty
Broach's remark: 'The Splutter *Jack Oaf* makes, is the Envy
and Rancour of an Author; that's all' (iii. 8).

Many absurdly innocent passages are found offensive by Sir
Headstrong Bustle and the rest. The aldermen's interjections
significantly remind us of the 'Hilarius' letter, too, where the
writer says that Gay, 'upon reading his Play to a certain
Gentleman, when he came to that Part, where one of the *Crew*
offers, upon some Occasion, to *wager a Gallon*—He was
happily interrupted with this Rebuke *Hold, Sir; no Reflections, I
beg of you, upon Sir CHARLES WAGER and the GALLEONS*'.[86]
Sir Headstrong's insistence that he is the Moor (x. 199) may,
too, refer to Macheath's disguise in *Polly* as Morano, 'a Negro
villain'. The aldermen's sensitivity leads them to a nonsensical
extreme which is typical of Gay. Pickle remarks that the hero
meets 'accidentally with some of his own . . . Neighbours' (x.
221), at which the aldermen, deciding that they are all
'Neighbours to some body or other', stop the performance.

Whatever the truth about Cibber's part in the suppression
of *Polly*, it will probably never be fully known. It does seem
likely, even so, that Gay himself had a suspicion that Cibber
had something to do with it. In *The Rehearsal at Goatham* the

bulk of the ridicule is naturally put upon the government, however, and despite the traces of bitterness, Gay is largely able to laugh at their high-handedness. This geniality is never far from the surface, even in the posthumous plays. He thus manages to find a place in *The Rehearsal at Goatham* for the traditional dance of the afterpiece, that in *The Mohocks* or *The What D'Ye Call It* perhaps more appropriately celebrates social harmony or relief at the resolved conflict.

But here we can see once more the road that Gay has travelled: the early social criticism and relaxed playfulness make room for narrower resentments and more sophisticated writing. This is not the whole story, of course, but it does colour the picture which emerges. The nature of his attack shifts, and I believe we are unwilling to pay the same attention to the monstrous Astarbe, Lady Willit, or Sir Headstrong Bustle that we were to the suffering Cloudy, Kitty, or Fossile: the early plays contain within their parody or buffoonery serious social and cultural indictments, but in them Gay's irony is subtle and defensive and therefore all the more insidious. At his best, Gay can unite these strands in his work: we are properly and creatively outraged by Polyphemus or Peachum, and are just faintly unnerved by the sympathy evoked for Polly and Macheath. And this is due to the overriding comic vision in which hero and villain are alike united.

NOTES

1. *The Correspondence of William Cowper*, ed. Thomas Wright (1904), ii. 92.
2. Jonathan Swift, *Journal to Stella*, ed. Harold Williams (Oxford, 1948), ii. 508–9.
3. See *A True List of the Names of the Mohocks and Hawkubites Who were Apprehended and Taken on Monday night, Tuesday, and this Morning* which Swift said was 'all a Lye' (*Journal to Stella*, ii. 511). News of similar arrests was still circulating a month later. See *A Full and true Account of the Apprehending and Taking of the L—d W— P—t, a notorious Mohock, &c*, advertised in the *Supplement* no. 703, 9–12 April 1712. The 'arrests' were all embarrassing to the Whigs. Other pamphlets appearing in 1712 include *The Church of England's vision; or, Dr. Richardson's dream, &c* (single sheet folio printed for J. Williams in Holborn) and *Who plot best? the Whigs or the Tories . . . in a letter to Mr. Ferguson* (21 pp.).
4. See Swift, *History of the Four Last Years of the Queen* in *Prose Works*, ed. Herbert Davis, vii. 26–7, and G. M. Trevelyan, *England under Queen Anne* (1934), iii. 203 n.
5. See the *London Gazette* no. 4979, 15–18 March 1712. There is a copy of this Proclamation at Harvard (Houghton 15461. 556 PF).
6. The broadside was published by Lintot and advertised in his *Miscellany* (May, 1712). The British Library copy (816 m. 19. 73) is ascribed, in a contemporary

hand, to Gay, and the broadside was reprinted, with minor changes, as 'A Wonderful Prophecy' in the second volume of the Pope-Swift *Miscellanies* (1727). Oldmixon, in the *Medley* of 28 March 1712, evidently thought William Wagstaffe wrote the broadside, but Gay's authorship is generally accepted (see Irving, p. 65). Omitted from the reprint were the verses 'From *Mohock* and from *Hawkubite*' which Faber (p. 211) has no doubt were written by Gay. Dearing prints the *Miscellanies* version with circumstance.

7. For other verse about the Mohocks, see D'Urfey, *Wit and Mirth*, vi. 336, and *The Huzza* (see Irving, p. 66). See also Gay's *Trivia*, iii. 326, and Prior's *Alma*, iii. 230–9.

8. *Letters*, p. 3. In the MS (Houghton 50 M–128 F) '5ᵗʰ' appears to have been altered from '6ᵗʰ'. See also John Nichols, 'Antiquities in Lincolnshire', *Bibliotheca Topographica Britannica* (1790), iii, p. xxii.

9. See R. F. Jones, 'The Background of the Attack on Science in the Age of Pope', *Pope and His Contemporaries: Essays Presented to George Sherburn* (Oxford, 1949), 96–113.

10. Gay is less guilty of this view of Chaucer than some of his contemporaries, but see the sexual allusions in his notes to *The Shepherd's Week*, 'Monday', 79, and 'Wednesday', 89, (Dearing, i. 99, 107), his 'An Answer to the Sompner's Prologue of Chaucer' (Dearing, i. 198) and Pope's allusion to the last couplet of the unfinished Cook's Tale in a letter to Gay of 24 December 1712 (Sherburn, i. 169). For Pope's and Gay's interest in Chaucer at this time, see my Commentary, p. 412.

11. See *Restoration Comedy, 1660–1720* (Oxford, 1924), p. 117.

12. Swift to Arbuthnot, 3 July 1714 (*Swift Corr.*, ii. 46).

13. See *Early Career*, pp. 114 ff., for the background.

14. For a discussion of the authorship of the *Key*, see my Commentary, p. 418.

15. *Key*, fols. A4ᵃ, A2ᵇ, A3ᵃ.

16. Leonard Welsted, 'One Epistle to Mr. A. Pope' (1730) in *Works*, ed. John Nichols (1787), p. 193.

17. Sherburn, i. 282–3. Cromwell was deaf, and the Prince and Princess of Wales knew little English. Some of the play's success was no doubt due to this Court interest. With Swift's and Oxford's help, Gay had been chosen to assist Clarendon in his mission to Hanover in the previous year, and on Pope's advice had published the successful *A Letter to a Lady, occasioned by the Arrival of Her Royal Highness the Princess of Wales*. He was conscious of the value of cultivating Court acquaintance.

18. Prologue to *The Shepherd's Week*, 45–8. See also Gay's 'To my ingenious and worthy Friend W[illiam] L[owndes] Esq' (1717), 55–7.

19. See Sir John Fortescue, *A History of the British Army* (1899), p. 566.

20. See the letter from Pope to Parnell (Sherburn, i. 395). For a general account of the play's history, see George Sherburn, 'The Fortunes and Misfortunes of *Three Hours after Marriage*', *MP*, xxiv (1926), 91–109. So far as I know, the play was not even printed between 1807 (*Supplementary Volume to the Works of Alexander Pope, Esq.*) and 1961 (the editions of Morton and Peterson, and Harrington Smith).

21. Most of the pamphlets in this category were issued under the imprint of James Roberts. See *The Drury-Lane Monster*, a broadside published on 22 January; 'Timothy Drub', *A Letter to Mr. John Gay, concerning his Late Farce, Entituled, A Comedy*, published just before 1 March, a work patronizing to Gay in the most irritating manner; and Leonard Welsted, *Palaemon to Caelia, at Bath; or the Triumvirate*, published on 7 March. See also *A Satyr on the Present Times*, sold by J. Morphew and published on 23 January, and the Prologue of Charles Johnson's *The Sultaness*, produced on 25 February.

22. John Durant Breval was a Curll author. See his *The Confederates, a Farce* (Printed for R. Burleigh), published on 30 March. If it was felt, as George Sherburn suggests, that Phoebe Clinket was Mrs Centlivre (see my Commentary, p. 440) this might be an added spur to replies from Curll. See also my Commentary, p. 447 (the note to ii. 48).

23. Dennis did not write directly against the play, but chose the occasion to issue his *Remarks upon Mr Pope's Translation of Homer* on 28 February. Some of his savage *A True Character of Mr. Pope and his Writings*, originally published by Curll in 1716, reappeared in the *Weekly Journal; or British Gazetteer* for 9 February, and (according to George Sherburn in 'Fortunes and Misfortunes': the Bodleian and British Library copies do not contain it) appended to E. Parker, Philomath', *A Complete Key to the New Farce, &c* (Printed and Sold by E. Berrington), published on 2 February. Parker had poked good-humoured fun at Pope in the previous year in *Mr. Joanidion Fielding His True and Faithful Acount of the Strange and miraculous Comet which was Seen by the Mufti of Constantinople*. See *Early Career*, pp. 182–3.

24. Parker comes to Woodward's defence, and contradicts Arbuthnot with some antiquarian authorities. Sir Richard Blackmore, a friend of Woodward, attacked the play in the Preface to his *Essays on Several Subjects*, published on 26 March. Woodward, it may be noted, was Steele's personal physician, and any move to stifle the play might well have found favour with the governor of Drury Lane.

25. An account of this incident in the context of Pope's long quarrel with Cibber is given in *New Light*, pp. 298 ff. The authorities are the 1758 *Letter*, p. 218 (see above, p. 25), and the letter from Montagu Bacon to James Montagu in George Paston, *Mr. Pope* (1909), i. 197. Both write of a threat from Pope and a consequent scuffle between Gay and Cibber. The accounts differ slightly, and what actually happened is obscure. Neither was much hurt. The *Letter* places Pope's threat on the third, and Gay's attack on the fourth, evening of the revival (i.e. 20 and 23 February. Harrington Smith unfortunately misreads Avery here, and tries to make the night of Gay's attack 21 March. This leads him to doubt the *Letter*, since Drub, published just before 1 March, also writes of the incident). Cibber's own account (*A Letter from Mr. Cibber, to Mr Pope*, 1742, pp. 18–19) does not mention Gay's part in all this, while 'A Congratulatory Poem; Inscribed to Mr. Gay, on his Valour and Success behind Drury-Lane Scenes', appended to Breval, does not mention Pope's.

26. *Letters of Thomas Burnet to George Duckett*, ed. D. Nichol Smith (1914), p. 119.

27. Including, for example, the nautically figurative descriptions of Jack Capstone. Compare the Shipman in *The Wife of Bath* (1730). This was a form of characterisation by jargon that Gay particularly enjoyed.

28. See Morton and Peterson, pp. xi–xiii, for a perceptive analysis of the Ovid references. Pope and Gay contributed to Book IX of Garth's *Metamorphoses*, published in August 1717.

29. See Mottley, *Complete List of all the English Dramatic Poets* (1747), and Avery, ii. 608.

30. From the prefatory letter in the second edition, dated 'Feb 15, 1720/21'.

31. The long controversy over the date of composition is resolved by the discovery of a copy bearing this date in the collection of the Earl of Malmesbury. See Terence Best's letter in the *Musical Times* no. 1547, cxiii (1972), 43.

32. According to R. A. Streatfeild, *Handel, Canons and the Duke of Chandos* (1916), p. 21.

33. The chorus ('Smiling Venus Queen of Love') and the aria ('Love ever vanquishing') end the second part of the 1732 macaronic *Acis and Galatea*. 'Love ever vanquishing' had appeared in *A Collection of Choice English Songs* (1731),

published by Walsh. An emended version of 'Smiling Venus Queen of Love' is bound in with Handel's autograph score of the Canons version in the British Library (RM 20. a. 2).

34. R. T. Kerlin, *Theocritus in English Literature* (Lynchburg, Va., 1910), p. 59.
35. *Dione. An opera as it is acting at the New-Theatre in the Hay-Market. Set to Musick by Mr Lampe* (Printed for Mechell and Chrichley, 1733).
36. Joseph Warton, *Essay on the Genius and Writings of Pope* (5th edn., 1806), ii. 245 n.
37. *The Briton* for 22 January 1724 mentions 'this *Hottentot* custom' as something fairly new.
38. *The Correspondence of Edward Young, 1683–1765,* ed. Henry Pettit (Oxford, 1971), p. 25.
39. *John Gay, Poet 'of a lower order'* (Stockholm, 1964), i. 170 n.
40. *John Gay o dell'eroicomico* (Rome, 1971), p. 119.
41. See G. V. Bennett, *The Tory Crisis in Church and State 1688–1730: The career of Francis Atterbury Bishop of Rochester* (Oxford, 1975).
42. Quoted by Henry Beeching, *Francis Atterbury* (1909), p. 306.
43. These had, however, been plays with such political implications from the Whig point of view. In Ambrose Philips's *Humfrey, Duke of Gloucester* (1723), Cibber had played the corrupt Bishop of Winchester, Beaufort: "'tis the Curse of busy, ambitious Churchmen, / Ever to plot; and, Never, to succeed!' (III. ii). See *Pasquin* no. 15, 6 March 1723, which finds that 'under this character he has couch'd an *Allegory*'. Political capital was also made out of Aaron Hill's *Henry V* (5 December 1723). See *Pasquin* nos. 88, 3 December 1723, and 102, 20 December 1723.
44. See Bertrand A. Goldgar, *Walpole and the Wits: The Relation of Politics to Literature, 1722–1742* (Lincoln, Nebraska, 1976), ch. 2.
45. See Gerald Howson, *Thief-Taker General: The Rise and Fall of Jonathan Wild* (1970), p. 284. Spurling's niece married Jonathan Wild. For a note on Wild, see my Commentary, Vol. II, p. 377.
46. First noticed by James R. Sutherland, *TLS,* 25 April 1935, p. 272. The anecdote is reprinted in J. V. Guerinot and R. D. Jilg, *The Beggar's Opera* (Hamden, Conn., 1976), p. 46, where the editors date the meeting as 1 August 1724. Gay of course also had the benefit of a long tradition of rogue literature, ranging at least from Richard Brome's *A Jovial Crew, or the Merry Beggars* (1641) to *The Prison Breaker, or The Adventures of John Sheppard* (1725). For a few parallels in these and other works, see Schultz, pp. 167–73.
47. See Spence, i. 107 and Archibald Ballantyne, *Voltaire's Visit to England* (1893), pp. 105–6.
48. Boswell, *Life of Johnson* (1775), ed. G. B. Hill (Oxford, 1934), ii. 368; Spence, i. 107; Benjamin Victor, *The History of the Theatres of London and Dublin* (1761), ii. 153–4.
49. According to G. A. Aitken, *The Life and Works of Dr. John Arbuthnot* (Oxford, 1892), p. 120 n., Gay had some help from Arbuthnot's daughter, Anne.
50. Guerinot and Jilg (op. cit., p. 7) reprint the first scene of *Le Tableau du Mariage,* a *comédie en vaudeville* performed in London during May 1726, pointing out some significant stylistic similarities to *The Beggar's Opera.*
51. Cooke, *Memoirs of Macklin,* p. 60.
52. Similes, prison scenes, the Cuzzoni/Faustina quarrel, and recitative in the Introduction; happy endings in III. xvi.
53. See Gay's letters to Swift of 15 February and 20 March 1728 (*Letters,* pp. 70–3) and Pope's note to *The Dunciad,* iii. 326.
54. Figures from Rich's Account-book. See *N & Q,* i (1850), 178–9.
55. See Vedder M. Gilbert, *N & Q,* cxcviii (1953), 337–9.

56. 'A Compleat Key to the Beggar's Opera' (originally in the *Craftsman* for 17 February 1728) in Christopher Bullock, *A Woman's Revenge; or, A Match in Newgate* (2nd edn., 1728), p. 72.
57. See C. F. Burgess, 'Political satire: John Gay's *The Beggar's Opera*', *Midwest Quarterly*, vi (1965), 265–76.
58. *Suffolk Corr.*, i. 400, ii. 47.
59. *Trivia*, iii. 77–82. See also 'There was a Jovial Beggar' (*Wit and Mirth*, iii. 266), stanza 6: 'Seven Years I begg'd / For my old Master *Wild*'.
60. Produced in 1928. See Bertolt Brecht, *Gesammelte Werke* (Frankfurt, 1967), vol. 2.
61. See Britten's vocal score, Hawkes & Son, 1949, p. [v]: 'The production of this new version sprang from a hint given in the original Prologue to the play, which stated that the opera had previously been performed in the beggar's "great room at Saint Giles", to celebrate the marriage of two ballad-singers. Accordingly the producer and the composer planned to stage the opera in this "great room", which they imagined as a laundry frequented by beggars, who worked there in return for food and warmth.'
62. The initial move was made by the Rev. Thomas Herring in a sermon preached during March 1728 at Lincoln's Inn Chapel. Some contemporary points of view may be traced in *Mist's Weekly Journal*, 2 March 1728 ('certain People . . . attribute the Frequency of the late Robberies to the success of the Beggar's Opera'); in letters to the *London Journal* for 30 March and 20 April 1728; in *Memoirs Concerning the Life and Manners of Captain Mackheath*, published on 14 May 1728; and in *Thievery A-la-Mode: or the Fatal Encouragement*, published in June 1728. For Fielding's opposition, see the *Gentleman's Magazine* for September 1773. The whole question is fully discussed in Schultz, ch. xxi.
63. The print is in the Gabrielle Enthoven Collection, Victoria and Albert Museum.
64. *Applebee's Original Weekly Journal*, 30 November 1728.
65. *Memoirs*, ed. R. Sedgwick (2nd edn., 1952), p. 52.
66. *Craftsman* no. 128, 14 December 1728. See also the Preface to *Polly*, Vol. II, p. 68.
67. i.e. Cibber, who in *Love in a Riddle* had played Philautus, 'A Conceited Corinthian Courtier'. Cf. 'An Epigram' in *Fog's Weekly Journal*, 8 February 1729. Reports of the banning of Gay's play were significantly juxtaposed with those of the reception of Cibber's *Love in a Riddle* in the *Craftsman* no. 128, 14 December 1728, and no. 132, 11 January 1729. The *Craftsman's* campaign against Cibber continued in nos. 140, 8 March; 143, 29 March; 145, 12 April; and 153, 7 June 1729. The accusation against Ciber was made elsewhere (e.g. in *The Life of Mr. James Quin*, 1766, p. 39) and Cibber felt it necessary to deny it in his *Apology* (ed. R. W. Lowe, 1889, i. 246–7). See above, p. 31 and pp. 68–70, and also my article 'Cibber, *The Rehearsal at Goatham*, and the Suppression of *Polly*', *RES*, NS xiii (1962), 125–34.
68. See *The Flying-Post: or, Weekly Medley*, 12 April 1729, and *The Whitehall Evening-Post* no. 1653, 12–15 April 1729. The first edition was advertised as 'Now Re-published' at 1s in 1754 on fol. A2ᵃ of *The Rehearsal at Goatham*.
69. See Charles Viner, *A General Abridgment of Law and Equity*, iv. 279. For an account of the piracy, see James R. Sutherland, '"Polly" Among the Pirates', *MLR* xxxvii (1942), 291–303.
70. L. W. Conolly, 'Anna Margaretta Larpent, The Duchess of Queensberry and Gay's *Polly* in 1777', *PQ* li (1972), 955–7.
71. The account is in Hervey's *Memoirs*. See also *The Autobiography and Correspondence of Mary Granville, Mrs Delany* (1861), i. 193, and Gay's letter to Swift of 18 March 1729 (*Letters*, p. 79).
72. Conolly, *op. cit.*
73. Spence, i. 151, 47; Sherburn, ii. 246, iii. 339, iv. 168–9.

74. A few parallels with *All for Love* are examined in relation to the theme of the choice of Hercules by Joan Hildreth Owen, '*Polly* and the Choice of Virtue', *Bulletin of the New York Public Library*, lxxvii (1974), 393–406.
75. *The Flying-Post: or, Weekly Medley*, 12 April 1729.
76. See *Letters*, pp. 124, 127, 131, and the Prologue, possibly by Pope.
77. *English Comic Drama 1700–1750* (1929), p. 98.
78. 'The design of this Ode is to reproach Lydia that she suffers Sybaris to be near her in ~~Woman's Apparell~~ Actions of Effimanacy' (V & A Forster Collection 4226).
79. *B. Berington's Evening Post*, 13 February 1733; *Craftsman* no. 346. 17 February 1733; *The Bee: or, Universal Weekly Pamphlet*, 17 February 1733.
80. See *Historical MSS Commission*, 8th R., Pt. 1, Sect. iii, p. 569a.
81. See *The Politics of Drama in Augustan England* (Oxford, 1963), pp. 152–3.
82. Douglas Grant, *James Thomson: Poet of 'The Seasons'* (1951), p. 292.
83. See Baker, *Biographia Dramatica*, iii. 54, and Genest, v. 310.
84. The production was scheduled for 15 May 1777 (see Dougald MacMillan, *Catalogue of the Larpent Plays in the Huntington Library*, San Marino, Cal., 1939, p. 73).
85. See R. H. Barker, *Mr. Cibber of Drury Lane* (New York, 1939), p. 32; the unpublished B. Litt. thesis (Oxford, 1954) by W. M. Peterson, 'Colley Cibber as a Comic Dramatist', pp. 8 ff; and Pope, *Dunciad* (B), i. 109–10.
86. *Craftsman* no. 135, 1 February 1729. Sir Charles Wager was one of the lords commissioners of the Admiralty. In February 1727 he was sent with a fleet to reinforce the garrison at Gibraltar. One of his tasks was to prevent the Spanish treasure ships from reaching Cádiz, but early in March, much to his disgust, some vessels from Havana succeeded in slipping past him.

THE

MOHOCKS.

A

Tragi-Comical Farce.

As it was Acted near the

Watch-house in *Covent-Garden*.

BY

Her MAJESTY's Servants.

*Quo, quo, scelesti, ruitis? aut cur dexteris
Aptantur enses conditi?*   Hor.

TO Mr. *D****.

SIR,

THERE are several Reasons which induce me to lay this Work at Your Feet: The Subject of it is *Horrid* and *Tremendous*, and the whole Piece written according to the exactest Rules of Dramatick Poetry, as I have with great care collected them from several of your elaborate Dissertations.

The World will easily perceive that the Plot of it is form'd upon that of *Appius* and *Virginia*, which Model, indeed, I have in great measure follow'd throughout the whole Conduct of the Play.

10 The Action is plain and simple, the Time not above an hour and three quarters, and the Scene shifted but twice in the whole *Drama*: I am apt to flatter my self that those two Transitions are extremely natural and easie; being only out of the Tavern into the Watch-house, and, *vice versâ*, out of the Watch-house into the Tavern.

I am informed that several of these Scenes have already received your Approbation in your elegant Retreat in the Country; where, I have the Pleasure to learn, that you are laying out your Time in such Rhapsodies and Speculations as cannot but be beneficial to the Commonwealth of Letters.

20 As we look upon you to have the Monopoly of *English* Criticism in your Head, we hope you will very shortly chastise the Insolence of the *Spectator*, who has lately had the *Audaciousness* to show that there are more Beauties than Faults in a Modern Writer.

I am not at all concern'd at this *Tragedy's* being rejected by the Players, when I consider how many of your immortal Compositions have met with no better Reception.

I am proud to answer the malicious World in this Case, with that memorable Saying which was formerly apply'd to *Scaliger*, *I had rather be in the Wrong with the ingenious Mr.* D***, *than in the Right with*
30 *any body else.*

I am, Sir, with great Respect and Gratitude,

Your most oblig'd,
most obedient,
most humble,
and most devoted Servant,

London, April, 1.   W. B.

THE PROLOGUE.

To be Spoken by the Publisher.

This Farce, if the kind Players had thought fit,
With Action had supply'd its want of Wit.
Oh Readers! had you seen the Mohocks *rage,*
And frighted Watchmen tremble on the Stage;
Had you but seen our Mighty Emperor *stalk;*
And heard in Cloudy *honest* Dicky *talk,*
Seen Pinkethman *in strutting* Prig *appear,*
And 'midst of Danger wisely lead the Rear,
It might have pleas'd; for now-a-days the Joke
Rises or falls as with Grimace *'tis spoke.*   10
As matters stand; there's but this only way,
T' applaud our disappointed Author's Play:
Let all those Hands that would have clapp'd, combine
To take the whole Impression off from mine.
That's a sure way to raise the Poet's Name:
A New Edition gains immortal Fame.

Dramatis Personæ.

The Emperor of the *Mohocks*.
Abaddon,
Moloch,
Whisker,
Mirmidon, } *Mohocks.*
Cannibal,
Gogmagog,
Constable Prig.
Peter Cloudy,
Starlight,
Frost,
Windy, } *Watchmen.*
Moonshine,
Bleak,
Gentle, *a Beau.*
Joan Cloudy, Cloudy's *Wife.*
Justice Wiseman.
Justice Kindle.
Justice Scruple.
Peg Firebrand, } *Whores.*
Jenny Cracker,

Other Watchmen.

Moloch] Molock *12*   Firebrand] Fireband *12*

SCENE I.

A Tavern.

The Emperor of the Mohocks *sitting in State*, Mohocks *attending him.*

   Abaddon. THUS far our Riots with Success are crown'd,
Have found no stop, or what they found o'ercame;
In vain th'embattell'd Watch in deep array,
Against our Rage oppose their lifted Poles;
Through Poles we rush triumphant, Watchman rolls
On Watchman; while their Lanthorns kick'd aloft
Like blazing Stars, illumine all the Air.
   Moloch. Such Acts as these have made our Fame immortal,
And wide through all *Britannia*'s distant Towns,
The Name of *Mohock* ev'ry Tongue employs;   10
While each fond Mother at the Sound grows pale
And trembles for her absent Son—
   Whisker. Let's lose no longer time in idle Talk,
Which might be better spent in new Exploits.
Most mighty Emperor, a Noble Youth,
Fir'd with our Deeds to glorious Emulation,
Desires Admittance—
   Emperor. Go, Introduce him:
But search with care th' Intentions of his Heart,
See he be not a superficial Sinner,   20
That talks of Mischiefs which he ne'er perform'd:
Those are mean Villains, and unworthy us.
   Mirmidon. I'll answer for him, for I've known him long,
Know him a Subject worthy such a Prince;
Sashes and Casements felt his early Rage,
H' has twisted Knockers, broken Drawers Heads,
And never flinch'd his Glass, or baulk'd his Wench.
But see he comes—

Enter New Mohock.

New Mohock. Great Potentate, who leadst the *Mohock*
    Squadrons
30 To nightly Expeditions, whose dread Nod
Gives Law to those, lawless to all besides:
To thee I come—to serve beneath thy Banner.
Mischief has long lain dormant in my Bosom
Like smother'd Fire, which now shall blaze abroad
In glorious Enterprize—
    Emperor. Bravely resolv'd—henceforth thy Name
Be *Cannibal*—like them, devour Mankind.
But come—Night wears apace—begin the Rites.
               [*They all take Hands in a Circle and Kneel.*
    Gogmagog. By all the Elements, and all the Powers,
40 Celestial, nay Terrestrial, and Infernal;
By *Acheron*, and the black Streams of *Styx*,
An Oath irrevocable to *Jove* himself,
We swear true Fealty, and firm Allegiance
To our most High and Mighty Emperor.
    All. We Swear.
    Gogmagog. That we'll to Virtue bear invet'rate Hate,
Renounce Humanity, defie Religion;
That Villany, and all outragious Crimes
Shall ever be our Glory and our Pleasure.
50   *All.* We Swear.
    Gogmagog. Let all Hell's Curses light upon his Head,
That dares to violate this solemn Oath;
May Pains and Aches cramp his rotten Bones;
May constant Impotence attend his Lust;
May the dull Slave be bigotted to Virtue;
And tread no more the pleasing Paths of Vice,
And then at last die a mean whining Penitent.
    All. This Curse involve us all.
    Emperor. 'Tis well—   [*The* Emperor *stands in the midst of*
                       them, and speaks this Speech.
60 Now bring the generous Bowl—Come—pledge me all—
Rouse up your Souls with this Celestial Nectar.
What gain'd the *Macedonian* Youth the World?
'Twas Wine. What rais'd the Soul of *Catiline*
To such brave, unparallell'd Ambition?

Wine, Potent, heav'nly Juice, Immortal Wine.
Slothful awhile inglorious Mortals lay,
But Wine to Noble Action led the Way;
Wine conquers all things—all must Wine obey.

[*Drinks.*

A SONG

[The *Mohocks* stand in a Circle, with the Glasses in
their Hands.

>   *Come fill up the Glass,*
>   *Round, round, let it pass,*   70
>   *'Till our Reason be lost in our Wine:*
>   *Leave Conscience's Rules*
>   *To Women and Fools,*
>   *This only can make us divine.*

Chorus. *Then a* Mohock, *a* Mohock *I'll be,*
>   *No Laws shall restrain*
>   *Our Libertine Reign,*
>   *We'll riot, drink on, and be free.*   [All Drink.

>   *We will scower the Town,*
>   *Knock the Constable down,*   80
>   *Put the Watch and the Beadle to flight:*
>   *We'll force all we meet*
>   *To kneel down at our Feet,*
>   *And own this great Prince of the Night.*

Chorus. *Then a* Mohock, *a* Mohock, *&c.*   [All Drink.

>   *The Grand Seignior shall own*
>   *His Seraglio outdone,*
>   *For all Womankind is our booty;*
>   *No Condition we spare*
>   *Be they Brown, Black or Fair*   90
>   *We make them fall down, and do Duty.*

Chorus.   *Then a* Mohock, *a* Mohock *I'll be,*
    No Laws shall restrain
    Our Libertine Reign,
    We'll riot, drink on, and be free.   [All Drink.
                                           [Exeunt.

SCENE II.

The Street before the Watch-house.

Moonshine. Lookye, Brother Watchman, you are a Man of
Learning and can read the News.
   Windy. Why, Neighbour, for that matter as a Body may
say, Mr. Constable is a great Man, a great Man, Neighbour,
and fair Words cost nothing—But as I was saying, *Peter Cloudy*
there is ready with his Verses.
   Frost. Ay, ay, *Peter's* Verses may be seen pasted up in every
Barber's Shop in the Parish; *Peter* shall be our Spokesman to
induce our New Mr. Constable.
                    Enter Constable.
10 Come, *Cloudy,* begin.
   Cloudy. *O Magistrate, thou art, as I may say,*
So Great by Night, as is Queen Anne *by Day,*
And what greater Power can any where be seen?
For you do represent the Person of the Queen.
The greatest Judge in England *cannot do,*
Or execute more greater things than you.
God save you, Master Constable, we pray,
Who are your honest Watch-men Night and Day.
   Constable. Well said, *Peter*—but heark ye, my Lads, we are
20 like to have hot work on't to Night—the *Mohocks* without
doubt will be abroad.
   Starlight. Oh, Master Constable, bloody-minded Fellows!
that have broke more Windows than the great Storm, and are
more mischievous than a Press-gang.
   Cloudy. You may take my word for it, Mr. Constable—
Sufferers may have leave to complain—my Head and Ribs
have been thwack'd over and over again like a Flock-bed by
them.

Constable. Why, they say that they slit Noses, cut and slash all they meet with, poach Folks in the Calves of the Legs, and   30 disturb us and our Officers in our lawful Authority—I charge you all, knock down upon Suspicion—that we may not be forced to cut Capers against our Wills—pox of such Dancing Masters, say I, that will make a Man Dance without a Fiddle.

Starlight. They make no more of our Poles than so many Straws; let me tell you, Sir, that I have seen them do such things that would make a Man's Hair stand on end—let me see—ay—to-morrow Night, 'twill be three Nights ago—when I was going my round—I met about five or six and thirty of these *Mohocks*—by the same token 'twas a very windy   40 Morning—they all had Swords as broad as Butchers Cleavers, and hack'd and hew'd down all before them—I saw—as I am a Man of credit, in the Neighbourhood—all the Ground covered with Noses—as thick as 'tis with Hail-stones after a Storm.

Constable. So—between Whores and *Mohocks*, we shall not have a Man left with a handle to his Face—Heav'n keep us, say I—and preserve that Member from danger—for a Man of Reputation would never be able to show his Nose after such an Affront.   50

Frost. Ha, ha, ha—but that is nothing to what I have seen—I saw them hook a Man as cleverly as a Fisher-man would a great Fish—and play him up and down from *Charing-Cross* to *Temple Bar*—they cut off his Ears, and eat them up, and then gave him a swinging Slash in the Arm—told him that bleeding was good for a fright, and so turn'd him loose.

Constable. And where was you all the while?

Frost. I blow'd out my Candle, and lay snug in the corner of a Bulk.

Starlight. Poh—poh!—that's nothing at all—I saw them   60 cut off a Fellow's Legs, and if the poor Man had not run hard for it, they had cut off his Head into the bargain.

Cloudy. Poor *John Mopstaff's* Wife was like to come to damage by them—for they took her up by the Heels and turn'd her quite inside out—the poor Woman, they say, will ne'er be good for any thing more—honest *John* can hardly find the Head from the Tail of her.

Windy. Hark! hark! what Noise is that?—oh the *Mohocks*—

the *Mohocks*—oh—*Will, Harry, Gregory, Peter, George, Thomas,*
70 to your Poles—quickly—ay—there—stand to it—stand to it.
                                    [*Pushing them forwards.*
Constable. Where?—where are they?—ay, Gentlemen—
stand to it.   [*Pushing them forwards.*
Starlight. Oh—there they come—oh—yonder is one with a
Face like a Lion—the *Guildhall* Giant is a meer Dwarf to him.
Cloudy. Where, where?—oh—keep your Ranks, Brothers—
hark!
Starlight. Nothing but Fancy, Neighbours, all's well, only a
shadow, only a shadow; but if they had come—
All. Ay, if they had come—
                    [*All with their Poles lifted up and advancing.*
80 *Bleak.* We would have—hark—keep your Ranks, *Peter,*—
stand to them, Boys. [*Pushing 'em.*] Nothing, nothing,
Neighbours.
Cloudy. I'm afraid these plaguy suspexions are fore-runners
of them; but if they had come—
Constable. Ope thy Lanthorn, *Peter.*
                    [*The Constable speaks lighting his Pipe.*
The *Mohocks*—are but Men—and—we be Men as well as they
be—and—a Man—is a Man, Neighbours—now—you be the
Watch—and I—am the Constable—they may—mayhap—
venture upon a single stragling Watchman—but we—are a
90 Garrison—a Garrison, Brothers.
Bleak. Ay, Mr. Constable, and we'll all stand by you with
our Lives and Fortunes.
Constable. A *Mohock*—Brothers—a *Mohock*, I say, will no
more come near a Watch-house than a Whore—Here—we
are unattackable—but we be—not only to be upon the
Defensive—Brothers—I mean, to defend the Watch-house—
but upon the Offensive—I mean, to offend—destroy—knock
down—take up—and—commit—and bring *Mohocks* to
Justice.—Therefore, Neighbours,—as our Duty requires us—I
100 order the greatest Party of you to go—through all the
several—Streets—Lanes and Alleys—to endeavour—to
seize—and apprehend the *Mohocks*—if you apprehend them—
d'ye hear—bring them hither before me—But if—they apprehend you—d'ye hear—then—you need not come—The

Justices are now sitting—and have ordered all the *Mohocks* that we shall take, to be immediately brought before them.

            [*They all go out, but the Constable and six Watchmen.*

Cloudy. Mr. Constable—d'ye see, Mr. Constable, here is this Pole, Mr. Constable—I'll engage that this Pole—Mr. Constable, if it takes a *Mohock* in the right Place—it shall knock him down as flat as a Flounder, Mr. Constable—Pole is 110 the word, Sir—I, one Night, Mr. Constable, clap'd my Back against the Watch-house, and kept nine *Mohocks*, with their Swords drawn, at Poles length, broke three of their Heads, knock'd down four, and trim'd the Jackets of the other six.

Bleak. I, for my part, remember the ancient *Mohocks* of King *Charles* his Days; I was a young Man then; now times are alter'd with me—some of the greatest Men of the Kingdom were *Mohocks*, yet for all that we did not care a Fig for them.

Constable. There have been *Mohocks* in all Reigns and in all Ages, but, thank Heav'n, there have been Constables too, 120 with heart and hand to suppress them—though a Constable be a Civil Magistrate, yet upon great occasions he is allow'd to take up Arms; and there is not a Man among you that shall step a Step farther than my self.   [*A noise of the* Mohocks.

Windy. Mr. Constable stands in the front.

                [*Pushing one another forwards.*

Frost. A brave Man! a gallant Man! I warrant him.

Constable. Hold, hold, Gentlemen, let us do all things in order—Do you advance, Gentlemen, d'ye see, and while you advance I'll lead up the Rear.

           Enter the Mohocks *singing.*

>   '*Tis Wine and a Whore,*   130
>   *That we* Mohocks *adore,*
> *We'll drink 'till our senses we quench;*
>   *When the Liquor is in,*
>   *We're heighten'd for sin;*
>   *Then heigh! for a brisk jolly Wench.*
>   *Fa, la, la, la.*

Abbadon. Hola! the Watch, down—down with them; oh, the Devil, down with your Poles and Dogs—upon your Knees—worship the *Mohocks* and be damn'd to you.

    [*The Watch throw down their Poles and fall on their Knees.*

140   *Starlight*. Oh for Pity's sake, Gentlemen, I've a Wife and
four Children.
      Moloch. Rot your Wife and Children, make Fricassees of
them, Sirrah, and invite the Devil to Supper.
      Whisker. And I'll cut off the Noses of all these Rascals to
garnish the Dish.
      Mirmidon. Heighday—what, *Peg Firebrand* in Limbo?
      [*Looking towards two Wenches which the Watch have in Custody.*
      Gogmagog. Come,   you   Scoundrel   there—unhand   the
Doxies—upon your Knees, you Dog, and receive Sentence.
      Peg. Your humble Servant, Mr. *Mirmidon*.
150   *Jenny*. Who thought to have found Mr. *Gogmagog* here!
      Peg. Pox of these destroyers of Game—and Mr. *Moloch* too!
Mr. *Moloch* I am your humble Servant.
      Cannibal. Come, I'll sacrifice this Rascals's Ears to you, *Peg*.
      Emperor. The Constable is my Prisoner—hark ye, Sirrah,
are you married?
      Constable. Yes, an please your Honour.
      Emperor. Then you are a Cuckold, Coxcomb.
      Constable. Yes—an—an—an—please—you—your Worship.
      [*Trembling for fear.*
      Abbadon. This Dog's Face Phiz is scarce worth the spoiling.
160 Come, Sirrah, I'll save your Wife the charge of more
Children, and make you cry a dark cloudy Morning like an
Italian.
      Cloudy. Oh pray your Honour, good your Honour, my Ears
or my Nose is wholly at your Worship's Service; but pray,
good, dear loving Sir, don't let poor *Gillian* lose her only
Comfort.
      Moloch. Come, let's dispatch, cut, slash, and mangle, and
pursue more noble Game.
      Emperor. Hold, hold, for once we'll have a merry frolick.
170 Since we have the Constable and Watch in our Power, we will
divest our self of our Imperial Dignity, make them *Mohocks*,
and our selves Constable and Watchmen.
      All. Agreed, agreed—come strip, Sirrah, strip Sirrah.
      Emperor. Ay, ay, come, come, Sirrah, let us put the Lion's
Skin upon the Ass.
      Constable. Yes, Sir, yes; oh pray, Sir, I'll be an Ass or any
thing—but pray your Honour let me be an Ass with Ears.

Starlight. Little does my poor Wife at home think what a pitiful taking her Husband is in—Poor Soul—she is sound asleep—and thinks nought of all this. [*Aside.* 180

[*The Emperor changes Cloaths with the Constable, and places a Patch like an half Moon in his Forehead; the other* Mohocks *strip the Watchmen and take their Poles and Lanthorns.*

Mirmidon. Come, strip this Scoundrel, *Jenny,* and plague the Rogue now thou hast got him in thy power.

Jenny. Pox on't, Mr. *Mirmidon*—'tis as dangerous for us to use a Watchman ill, as for a Stage-Coachman to be uncivil to an High-way Man; for our Trade forces us to travel the Streets all the Year round—Remember, Sirrah, you owe me an Escape without a Fee to the Constable.

Peg. And me.

Whisker. Why, the Dog looks as terrible as a Janizary.

Cloudy. Oh Law, Sir, I'm a poor quiet harmless Fellow, and 190 no Janzary—*Peter Cloudy* by Name—I'm known all the Neighbourhood over, and can bring several good creditable Housekeepers to vouch for my Honesty.

Cannibal. The next Man that speaks a Word forfeits an Ear; and for the second fault, a Nose—

Cloudy. Let me see, oh, ay, I was afraid he had took him off as a Mountebank draws a Tooth—with a Touch.

[*Feeling his Nose. Aside.*

Cannibal. Silence in the Court—while our most mighty Emperor sits in Judgment.

Emperor. You *Cannibal,* you *Abbadon,* with *Whisker* and the 200 rest of you, bring all you meet before me.

Enter Gentle.

Moloch. Heigh-day, here's a Fellow got into the Trammels already; come, you Sir, before the Constable—on, on.

[*They seize* Gentle.

Gentle. Pray, Gentlemen, treat a Man of Fashion with more Civility.

Cannibal. Damme Sir—you are a *Mohock.*

Gentle. I vow and protest Gentlemen. I just now came from my Lady *Pride*'s in the City, from playing at Ombre, and had there been a Coach or a Chair to be found, I had not walk'd a-foot. 210

203 sd *seize*] size 12

Abbadon. Before the Constable—come, come, before the Constable.

Gentle. Be civil, I beg you, Gentlemen, disengage your Poles from my full Bottom—and I'll wait upon you.

Emperor. Hearkye, Fellow, you seem very suspicious, you have a downcast hanging look.

Gentle. A languishing Air, you mean, Sir.

Emperor. Give an Account of your self, Fellow, whence come you? whither are you going? What is your business
220 abroad at this time of Night?—take his Sword from him there, lest he should have some evil design against the Queen's Officer.

Gentle. I am a Gentleman, Sir.

Emperor. A doubtful, a shuffling Answer! we need no further proof that he is a *Mohock*—commit him.

Gentle. 'Tis a strange thing that the vulgar cannot distinguish the Gentleman—pray Sir, may I ask you one Question—have you ever seen a *Mohock*? has he that softness in his Look? that sweetness of delivery in his Discourse? believe me, Sir,
230 there is a certain *Je ne scay quoi* in my manner that shows my Conversation to have lain altogether among the politer part of the World.

Emperor. Look ye, Sir, your Manners in talking *Latin* before her Majesty's Officer, show you to be an ill-designing Person.

Gentle. Ha, ha, ha, very merry, as I hope to be caress'd. *Latin* and *French* sound alike in the Ears of the vulgar—*Je ne scay quoi* is a *French* Phrase much in vogue at the Court end of the Town, ha, ha, ha.

Emperor. Meer Prevarication! to the Round-house with
240 him—a *Mohock* without dispute—here's Evidence against you, Friend, downright Evidence against you.

Moloch. With these very Eyes, Mr. Constable, I saw him in a dark Alley, where one could not see ones Hand, slit a Cinder Wenches Nose, because she would not yield to his Brutality.

Gentle. Is there any thing in my Appearance that shows a *Goust* for a Cinder Wench? Improbable! downright falsity!— this Usage, Sir, will make me complain to some higher Power of your illegal Proceedings.

Emperor. What! dispute my Authority! bind him, and see

212 Constable.] ∼∧ *12*   220 Night?] ∼∧ *12*

you guard him strictly. 250

Gentle. Pray—Gentlemen—indeed—I vow—Gentlemen—
you daub my Ruffles; let not your Lanthorns come nigh my
Cloaths—bless me! my Perriwig!—hold, hold, I vow and
protest upon the word of a Gentleman, that I am a civil
Person—fogh! the stench of the Lanthorns confounds me—
Have a care what you do Mr. Constable, for I shall find
redress.

Emperor. Bind him, bind him, I value not his Threats.
Mohocks are thus to be treated, where and whenever they shall
be taken. [*They bind Gentle.* 260
     Enter Joan Cloudy.

Gogmagog. Come on, Woman, before the Constable—Here
is a Stragler that is just now fallen into my Hands, Mr.
Constable.

Joan. Where is *Peter?*—What, is *Peter* going his rounds? I'm
Peter's Wife, Mr. Constable—an please your Worship—and
am come to take a Pot with him, and take care of him this
cold Weather. What, is not *Peter* among you? What! is not
Peter come back from his rounds?—*Peter*, Mr. Constable, an
please your Worship, is a diligent Man in his Office—I have
been in Bed this two hours, and was so strangely a-dream'd of 270
the *Mohocks* that I could not rest, but must come and see
him—alas! alas! these are strange hazardous Times! I was a-
dream'd methought that the *Mohocks*—

Emperor. Hold, hold, Woman, are you drunk with Mild,
Stale, or Stout?

Cloudy. Heav'n grant that I may not be made a Cuckold
before my own Face—What a plague made her stirring?
            [*Aside*.

Joan. Drunk, Mr. Constable, Drunk! whether you know it
or no, though I am a poor Woman, I am a sober Woman—I
work for what I get, and I thank no body for a 280
Maintenance.—Drunk! tell your Wife of being Drunk with
Mild, Stale, and Stout—would *Peter* was here, he should not
hear his Wife affronted after this manner.

Emperor. I'll take care and Tongue-tye you, Woman.

Joan. To be Tongue-tyed is fit for nothing but Lyars and
Swearers. I'll speak the Truth and shame the Devil. Though a

Constable be to keep Peace and Quietness, yet the greatest
Constable in *England* shall not make me hold my Tongue,
when there is occasion for speaking. My Husband is a Watch-
290 man, *Peter Cloudy* by Name, a good House-keeper, though he
be a poor Man.—Why these are all strange Faces, methinks.
Where is *Peter*, Friend? oh Law! oh Dear! this ugly Dream
runs in my Head most strangely!—[*Spies* Peter.] Oh Gracious!
what's this our *Peter?* why *Peter?*—sure I be'nt out of my
Dream yet—why, *Peter*, I say, *Peter!*　　　　　　[*Bawls.*
　　　　　　　　　　　　　　　[Peter *shakes his Head.*
　　Gogmagog. Ay, why there now, good Woman, while you
thought he was upon the Watch, he was about a *Mohocking*—
Why he is a *Mohock*, good Woman.
　　Joan. Oh good Lord!
300　　*Whisker.* Here—we took him in company with these two
Wenches.
　　Joan. What, and Constable *Prig* a *Mohock* too! and honest
Harry Starlight!
　　Cannibal. Mohocks all, good Woman, every Soul of them.
　　Joan. Why *Peter*, *Peter*, Mr. *Prig*, *Harry Starlight!* what are
you all dumb? [*Cloudy shakes his Head.*] Oh, you ungracious
Rogue! you ungodly Wretch! what, must you have your
Wenches, Sirrah, while your poor Children at home—ay, and
your poor Wife, nay your honest, true and careful Wife, are
310 ready to starve. Why, *Peter*, I say, fye upon't, what, hadst thee
no more Wit to be a *Mohock* too?　　[*Cloudy shakes his Head.*
　　Joan. Why! you notorious Rogue, won't you answer your
poor Wife?　　　　　　　　　　　[*Cloudy shakes his Head.*
　　Joan. Alack, alack! do I live to see this with my own Eyes?
oh, *Peter*, *Peter!* an old Fool of all Fools is the worst—a
Hawkubite! a Rogue! I hope, I shall see thee at the Gallows for
this, Blockhead! What, you there with your hairy Bush upon
your Head, I suppose are the Ring-leader of them, I'll
Hawkubite you, Sirrah.　　　　　　　　　　[*To* Gentle.
320　　*Gentle.* I vow and protest, Madam, you do me the greatest
Injustice in the World, I am a Gentleman of Honour, but at
present labour under the Misfortune of being suspected.
　　Emperor. Come, come, Woman, don't be troublesome, we
can see through your Designs; you are a Female *Mohock*, I

perceive—and under that Denomination I order you to be apprehended.

Joan. I, a Female *Mohock*! a Female Jesuit as soon—

Emperor. Bind her, bind her.

Joan. But my Tongue shall still be at Liberty; he must have good Luck, ifackins, that ties a Woman's Tongue. Why, *Peter*, 330 Sirrah, all this comes of your ungracious Tricks, you *Hawkubite* Rogue.

Emperor. Heigh-day! what's here— [*Takes a Paper out of the Constable's Pocket.*] a Warrant for the apprehending us *Mohocks!* I find the Justices are sitting in all the several Quarters of the Town this Night to examine them; what think you, my Heroes—shall we improve the Jest? carry the Scoundrels before some Justices of a Ward where they are unknown, and so make them commit their own Officers instead of us.   340

All. A Merry Frolick! with all our Hearts.

Emperor. We'll immediately carry them before the Justices of the next Ward, commit the Rascals to the Round-house, and so finish the Night's Adventure.

Whisker. Come, come, to the Justices—to the Justices.

Emperor. Leave this Fellow, and this Female *Mohock* till our Return; bind them Back to Back, and there will be no fear of *Peter's* being Jealous.   [*They bind them.*

Gentle. I beg you, Gentlemen; this Posture is so like Man and Wife, that a Man of Mode may be perfectly ashamed 350 of it.

Joan. Go you *Hawkubite* Rogue, you ungracious Wretch!

Gentle. Figurative Matrimony, as I hope to be caress'd; one pulls one way, and the other the other.

[*They bolt* Gentle *and* Joan *into the Watch-house, and Exeunt.*

SCENE III.

A Tavern.

The Justices sitting.

Scruple. What says the Statute Book, Brother *Wiseman*, in relation to these kind of Enormities? I am informed that there

were *Mohocks* in Queen *Elizabeth*'s Days. Have you search'd
all the Statutes of her Reign for an Act in relation to this
Affair?

Kindle. What occasion for all these doubts, Mr. Justice
Scruple? for where the Law is silent, there, our Will is the
Law—If we have no Precedents of *Mohocks*—come, Mr.
Justice *Scruple*, my hearty Service to you—if we have no
10 Precedents, I say, of any *Mohocks*—my hearty Service to you
again, Mr. Justice—yet *Mohocks* inclusively are comprehended in disorderly Persons, and disturbers of her Majesty's
Peace, and as such, I say, they may and ought to be
committed.

Scruple. But we must refer to the Statute Books upon all
Occasions—The Statute Books must be our guide in all
Cases—and where the Statutes will not come within our
Cases—we must make our Cases come within the Statute's
Cases—That's the Method of all judicious practising Lawyers,
20 Brothers.

Wiseman. Let us act Justice, and be guided by Reason.

Kindle. What has Reason to do with Law, Brother
Wiseman? if we follow the Law, we must judge according to
the Letter of the Law.

Scruple. You are in the Right, Brother *Kindle*—Reason and
Law have been at variance in our Courts these many Years—
a mis-spell'd Word, or a Quibble will baffle the most
convincing Argument in the World; and therefore if we are
guided—Mr. Justice *Wiseman*, my hearty respects to you—if
30 we are guided, I say, in any measure by the Law, 'tis my
Opinion, that we must keep strictly to the Letter of the Law.

Enter the Mohocks, *Constable and Watchmen.*

Emperor. An please your Worship we have brought some
Mohocks before your Honours; This, an please your Honours,
is the Emperor, and this his Grand Vizier, and all the rest are
Princes of the Blood.

Abaddon. I, my own self, an please your Honours, saw this
very self-same Fellow here, tip the Lyon upon five several of
her Majesty's true-born Subjects, and afterwards slit all their
Noses.

40 *Moloch.* This Fellow here—is a Dancing-Master—an please
your Worships, he pricks Passengers in the Calves of the Legs

to make them show their Agility.

Whisker. And this Terrible-look'd Fellow, and please your Honours, is their Master Cooper, his Office is to Barrel up old Women—all the rest of them have their proper Employments.

Wiseman. Where, and how were they taken?

Cannibal. In an Attack upon the Watch-house—after an obstinate fight of about an hour and an half we made them all Prisoners.

Starlight. The Devil is a most confounded Lyar!   [*Aside.* 50

Emperor. We took this *Mohock*, Mr. Justices in an actual Assault to ravish these two Women—oh—he's a Devilish Fellow for a Wench—the Rogue has no Conscience with him—no more Conscience than a Woman—what two Women! why a Woman with common Modesty in her Demands would not have desired above two Men—what, two Women at once!

Peg. He gagg'd me, and please your Worships; then drew his Sword, and threaten'd to kill me, if I did not—

Jenny. And if the Watchman had not come just in the 60 Nick—

Cloudy. If I lose both my Tongues and my Ears—I must and will speak—And please your Worships, I am an honest Watchman—*Peter Cloudy*—

Whisker. What are you, Sirrah—what are you—such a Word more—   [*Aside to him.*
                    [*The* Mohocks *prick* Cloudy *behind.*

Cloudy. I am—oh—yes—I am—oh—I am a *Mohock* an please your Worships—a Watchman I mean—and this is Mr. Constable *Prig*—oh no—I beg your Worship's Pardon, he is— oh no—oh no—he is not—   70

Gogmagog. Come, come, confess—   [*Aside to* Cloudy.

Cloudy. Yes, he is—Emperor of the *Mohocks*, an please ye—

Kindle. I perceive that you are a prevaricating shuffling Rogue—commit him, commit him—when a Man talks backwards and forwards—I have done with him.

Cloudy. Oh, Dear Mr. Justice—indeed—oh pray sweet, loving, good, kind Mr. Justice—I have been a Watchman, these twenty Years.

Moloch. What's that you say, Rascal?   [*Aside to* Cloudy.

80   *Cloudy*. A *Mohock* these twenty Years, an please your Honours.

     Kindle. Commit them—commit them—we need no further Proof—Impudent—Impudent—Rogue—pretend to be the Queen's Officer!—I'll hear no more—away—away with them.

     Scruple. But hold, Brother *Kindle*—though the Case is plain in Relation to this Fellow—yet we must not punish the Guilty with the Innocent—

     Kindle. The Innocent with the Guilty, you would say, 90 Brother—they are all of a Gang—all Rogues alike—away—away with them.

     Wiseman. Do you confess what is alledg'd against you by these honest Watchmen, Friends? you are accused of being a Riotous sort of Creatures called *Mohocks*—Answer to your Charge—are you Guilty or not Guilty?—

                                [*The* Mohocks *prick them behind.*

     All. Not Guilty—an please your Worship—Oh yes, yes—Guilty—Guilty—Guilty.

     Kindle. What need we examine further?

     Cloudy. But as to the Ravishing—Mr. Justices—oh me!— 100 Yes I will speak [*Aside to the* Mohocks.] as I was saying, Mr. Justices, as to the Ravishing—I know nothing of that matter—oh, oh! yes, yes—I did Ravish—I did Ravish them—an please your Worships.

     Kindle. A most Impudent Rogue—the Fellow has a confounded Ravishing Look—Heav'n preserve our Wives and Daughters—away, away—they are dangerous Persons—commit them.

        [*As they are carrying them out, Enter the other Party of*   *Watch—with* Joan Cloudy *and Beau* Gentle.

     1 *Watchman*. An please your Worships—we found this Gentleman here, and Woman here, joyn'd together in a very 110 odd Posture.

     Kindle. As how—Friend, as how?

     1 *Watchman*. Why they were tyed together—back to back—an please your Worships.

     Wiseman. A very odd Posture—Brother *Scruple*—a very odd Posture.

Joan. But Mr. Justices—Oh you ungracious Wretch! Mr. Justices—you are Justices of the Peace, and I hope your Worshipful Honours will do me Justice—Look, how the sneaking Rogue looks upon me now!

Scruple. Proceed, Woman, to the Matter in Hand.   120

Joan. Why, an please your Worshipful Honours, to make short of my story—this great Boobily Lubber here—it seems, while I thought he was upon the Watch, went about a *Mohocking*—The Laird keep us, say I, from the Great *Turk*, and from Popery! but to make short of my Story, Mr. Justices,—this Slave here, this *Hawkubite* Rogue, throws away upon two Wenches in one Night, [*Weeping.*] what with good Huswifery would have satisfied his poor Wife for a Fortnight;—can you deny this, Sirrah, can you deny it?—but to make short of my Story, an please your worshipful Honours;   130 when I came to the Watch-house, thinking to find him in his Office, I found him [*Weeping.*] taken up for a *Mohock*.

Emperor. Faith, 'tis high time for us to sneak off.   [*Aside.*

[*The* Mohocks *are going.*

Wiseman. Hold—hold!—let us examine further into these Affairs.

2 *Watchman.* Why, *Harry*—how cometh thee in this Pickle?

[*Aside to* Starlight.

Gentle. These Gentlemen, Sirs, treat all alike without the least Distinction—one would rather fall into the Hands of the *Mohocks*, than suffer the Barbarities of these ill-bred sort of Creatures.   140

Cloudy. Why they are all *Mohocks*—an please your worshipful Honours—they unconstabled the Constable.

Starlight. And unwatch'd the Watch—an please your Honours.

Cloudy. Ay—faith—I don't value your Staring—it shall all out—fath—now I have got all my Friends about me. [*Aside to the* Mohocks.] They stript us—an please your worshipful Honours—made us *Mohocks*, and themselves Constable and Watch.

Kindle. Very strange—Brother *Scruple*—very strange.   150

Cloudy. This is Mr. Constable *Prig*, an please your Honours.

Starlight. And I am *Harry Starlight*, an please ye.

137 These] ~, 12

Joan. And is not my *Peter* a *Mohock* then!—art not thee a *Hawkubite, Peter?*—are not these thy Wenches?—oh, *Peter!*
> [*Hugging him.*

All the Watch. These are all our Brother Watchmen,—we'll vouch for them—an please your Worships.

Wiseman. A plain case, Brothers,—Oh, then you are the *Mohocks*, it seems, Gentlemen.

160 *All the Mohocks.* We are Gentlemen, Sirs, 'twas only an innocent Frolick.

Wiseman. Frolicks for Brutes and not for Men.— Watchmen, seize your Prisoners.

Cloudy. Heark ye, Sir—are you a *Mohock*—or are you not a *Mohock*—[*Takes away the Dagger, with which they prick'd him.*] Come, come, give up your Poles and your Lanthorns—hold up your Head, Friend—Mr. *Hannibal* I think they call him— oh—I find you have Ears to lose—I was afraid the Pillory had been before-hands with me—come strip.
> [*The Watchmen strip the* Mohocks.

Joan. Oh *Peter! Peter!* and art not thee a *Mohock* then, 170 *Peter?*

Gentle. Have I been a Captive of the *Mohocks?*—well—I vow, 'tis mighty happy, that I have preserv'd all my Features entire for the Ladies.

Emperor. Pray, Gentlemen, give us our Liberty.

All the Mohocks. We'll ask Pardon.

Emperor. Treat us like Gentlemen.

Wiseman. Let them be brought before us by ten a Clock— You may assure your selves, Gentlemen—these Proceedings of yours shall be punished with the utmost Severity.
> [*Exeunt Justices.*

180 *All the Mohocks.* We'll submit, ask Pardon, or do any thing.

Constable. Come,—let's call up the Musick that is below, and rejoice for our happy Deliverance—Let us show the Emperor here, that we can Dance without his Instructions.

All. Agreed.

A Dance of Watchmen.

Constable. *This is the Day—the joyful Night indeed In which* Great Britain's *Sons from the* Mo-hocks *are freed.*

Our Wives and Daughters they may walk the Street,
Nor Mohock *now, nor* Hawkubite *shall meet.*
Mohock *and* Hawkubite, *both one and all,*
Shall from this very Night date their Down—fall. 190

THE EPILOGUE,

Design'd to be spoken by the Person who should have play'd
Joan Cloudy.

WHAT woful things do we poor Folks endure,
To keep our Spouses to our selves secure?
We Wives—(of one and all this may be said,)
Ne'er think our Husbands safe,—but when in Bed.
But now, to quit the Wife—How would it please ye,
Could you dissolve the Marriage Noose as easie.
Marriage would then no more entail for Life,
And Coquets venture on the Name *of Wife:*
What Woman would not!—if this Scheme would do,
10 *Just for a Frolick—take a Spouse or two.*
Ye Criticks that are scatter'd o'er the Pit,
And stare and gape to catch descending Wit,
Meer Mohocks, *that on harmless Authors prey,*
And damn for want of Sense a Modern Play,
I vow 'tis hard.—Yet if it must be so,
I still must ask one Favour e'er I go.
If you condemn him, grant him a Reprieve,
Three days of Grace to the young Sinner give,
And then—if his sad Downfal does delight ye,
20 *As witness of his* Exit *I invite ye.*

FINIS.

THE
WIFE of BATH.
A
COMEDY.

————Magicis sanos avertere Sacris
Experiar Sensus.　　　　Virg.

PROLOGUE.

Spoken by Mrs. *Mountfort.*

Iғ *ancient Poets thought the* Prologue *fit,*
To Sport away superfluous Starts of Wit;
Why should we Moderns lavish ours away,
And to supply the Prologue *starve the* Play?
Thus Plays *of late, like Marriages in Fashion,*
Have nothing good besides the Preparation.
How shall we do to help our Author out,
Who both for Play *and Prologue is in doubt?*
He draws his Characters from Chaucer's *Days,*
On which our Grandsires are profuse of Praise;
When all Mankind,—(if we'll believe Tradition,)
Jogg'd on in settled Conjugal Fruition:
Then, as Old Wives with serious Nod will tell us,
The wise contented Husband ne'er was Jealous;
The youthful Bride no sep'rate Trading drives,
Ev'n Citizens could—satisfie their Wives.
The cautious Virgin, ignorant of Man,
No Glances threw, nor exercis'd the Fan,
Found Love a Stranger to her easie Breast,
And 'till the Wedding Night—enjoy'd her Rest.
No gilded Chariot drew the Ladies Eyes,
Ensnar'd their Hearts, and bore away the Prize;
Then the strict Father no hard Bargains drove
For Jointures—all their Settlement was—Love.
Believe all this who will,—for let me die!
They knew the World as well as You and I.
Lovers would Then,—as Now-a-days, forswear,
Seize the soft Moment, and surprise the Fair,
And many a modest, knowing Bride was led,
With artful Blushes to the Nuptial Bed.
Our Author hath from former Ages shown,
Some ancient Frailties which are still our own;

Prologue 16 *Citizens*] *Citizen 13*

The Wife of Bath *in our weak Wives we find,*
And Superstition runs through all the Kind;
We but repeat our Grandsires Actions o'er,
And copy Follies which were theirs before.

36 *copy*] *Copy 13*

EPILOGUE.

Spoken by Mrs. *BICKNELL.*

The Toil of Wedlock five Times bravely past,
You'll say, 'twas cruel to be baulk'd at last.
Grown old in Cupid's Camp—*long vers'd in Arms,*
I from my Youth have known the Pow'r of Charms:
Was I to single Combat ever slow?
Did I e'er turn my Back upon the Foe?
Is this the Way old Service is rewarded,
And must the joyless Widow be discarded?
Stint me not, Love—But while I yet survive,
10 *Throw in another Comfort to the Five.*
Bless me!—When I reflect on former Days!
Youth can make Conquests sev'ral thousand Ways;
I danc'd, I sung, I smil'd,—I look'd demure,
And caught each Lover with a diff'rent Lure:
In frequent Wedlock join'd, was Women still,
And bow'd subservient Husbands to my Will.
If Reason governs Man's superior Mind,
A ready Cunning prompts the Female Kind.
Then learn from me—So, Hymen *bless your Lives,*
20 *Preserve the just Prerogative of Wives;*
Know to command each Look, each Tear, each Smile,
With Eyes, and Face, and Tongue, and Heart beguile:
Ev'n he that loves in Search of Game to roam,
By feign'd Reprizals may be kept at Home.
When-ever Heav'n was pleas'd to take my Spouse,
I never pin'd on Thought of former Vows;
'Tis true, I sigh'd, I wept, I sobb'd at first,
And tore my Hair—as decent Widows—must:
But soon another Husband dry'd mine Eyes;
30 *My Life, my Dear!—supply'd the Place of Sighs:*
Amidst continual Love I've relish'd Life,
A forward Maid, and a triumphant Wife.

Epilogue 28 *must*] *Must 13*   30 *supply'd*] *Supply'd 13*

Then grant, O Cupid, *this my latest Pray'r*
If no kind Husband will relieve my Care;
Since Inclination yet out-lives my Face,
At least indulge me with a Coup de Grace.

Dramatis Personæ.

MEN.

Chaucer.	Mr. *Wilks.*
Doggrell.	Mr. *Pack.*
Franklyn, *a Rich Yeoman of* Kent.	Mr. *Penkethman.*
Doublechin, *a Monk.*	Mr. *Bullock*, Sen.
Merit *in Love with* Florinda.	Mr. *Bullock*, Jun.
Astrolabe, *an Astrologer.*	Mr. *Ryan.*
Antony, } *Servants to* Franklyn.	Mr. *Norris.*
William, }	Mr. *Lee.*
A Drawer.	Mr. *Spillar.*

WOMEN.

Myrtilla, *a Lady of Quality.*	Mrs. *Porter.*
Florinda, Franklyn's *Daughter.*	Mrs. *Mountfort.*
Alison, *the Wife of* Bath.	Mrs. *Bicknell.*
Busie, Myrtilla's *Woman.*	Mrs. *Saunders.*

SCENE an Inn, lying in the Road between London *and* Canterbury.

Time from Nine at Night, to Nine in the Morning.

ACT I. SCENE I.

SCENE *A large Hall.*

Enter Franklyn *and* Doggrell.

Franklyn. FLORINDA, poor Rogue, little thinks she shall lye in Wedding-Sheets to Morrow.—Never fear, Boy, I'll answer for the Girl's Inclinations.

Doggrell. Her beauty is, I must confess, most exquisitely Charming, and her Fortune will allow of no Exceptions; but you know her Extraction, Sir—

Franklyn. What—though I did marry my Servant-Maid, I have pretty good Assurances my Daughter is of my own begetting;—and, in troth, a stanch Country Gentleman, and an honest, plain, downright *Kentish* Damsel, may raise as good 10 a Breed as a Lady and a *Valet de Chambre*, though her Lord have Faith and Fondness enough to own himself the Father.

Doggrell. But in the Eye of the World, Sir, a Family is corrupted by an Alliance with the Vulgar—What a scurvy Figure will my Marriage make in a Genealogical Table, to be recorded in this manner;—*Francis O'Ogrelle*, Esq; married *Florinda*, Daughter of *Amos Franklyn*, by *Dorothy Turnbroach* his Kitchen-Wench—faugh—

Franklyn. Why,—how now, *Frank?*—*D'Ogrelle*,—Do-puppy, I think,—thy Grandfather's Name was *Doggrell*, and thy 20 Father's Name was *Doggrell*. Look you, Sir,—and when my daughter loses the Name of *Franklyn*, she shall be called no otherwise than *Florinda Doggrell*, d'ye see.

Doggrell. Not so passionate, Sir, I beseech you,—the Fault in former Centuries lay in the Orthography and Pronunciation.—My name is originally of *French* Extraction, and is written with a *D*, and an Apostrophe—as much as to say, *De Ogrelle*, which was the antique Residence of my Ancestors.

30   *Franklyn.* Come, come, *Frank*, this is not a time of Day to dispute of Families—we are now got about the Mid-way to *Canterbury*, and within twelve Miles of my House.

Enter Merit.

Merit. Excuse my Freedom, Gentlemen,—I am about to engage my self in an Affair of Consequence, and beg you would oblige me in being Witnesses of the Contract.

Franklyn. A Mortgage or a Conveyance of some part of thy Patrimony, I suppose; how much *per Cent.* do you give in these ticklish Times with good Security?

Merit. Mine, Sir, is only a Conveyance of my Person—and
40 knowing the Inconstancy of Female Love, I would not willingly, methinks, have so serious an Affair as Matrimony depend long upon a Woman's Pleasure.

Franklyn. Very right, Sir,—a good Sailor always lays hold of the first fair Wind, and a judicious Lover never stays for a second Consent.

Merit. Come on then, Old Gentleman.

Franklyn. Here *Frank* is an Example for you,—a brisk, jolly, handsome young Fellow, that plunges into Matrimony with a Resolution.—Pray, Sir, may I presume to know your
50 Mistress's Pedigree?

Merit. If you would judge of her Descent by her Conversation, *Pallas* was her mother; if by her Beauty, *Venus.*

Franklyn. But who was it, Friend, that begot her?

Merit. That is a Point we must leave to the Mother's Determination.

Franklyn. Is she of this Country, Sir?

Merit. In short, Sir,—she is a plain, simple *Kentish* Yeoman's Daughter—she has Virtue without Formality—all the good Breeding of the Court with the Country Simplicity—
60 Beauty without Vanity, and Wit without Affectation.

Doggrell. But a Family, Sir, would add a Lustre to these Endowments; and these Qualities appear very awkward in a Woman of mean Extraction.

Merit. Virtue, Sir, becomes all alike, and there's no true Nobility without it.

Franklyn. Well said, i'faith,—What say you to that Mr. *Doggrell*, with your *D'Ogrelles*, Pedigrees, Family Tables, and Extractions?

Doggrell. You expose me, Sir,—*D'Ogrelle* is my Name,—and was I not under some Restraint by my Father's Will, your Behaviour would make me quit all Pretentions to your Daughter.

Franklyn. Never insist then upon Pedigrees, *Frank.*—A single Tree in my Wood, I'll maintain it, is worth all the Genealogical Trees in the Universe;—come, *Frank*, let us go and be Witnesses of his happy Conjunction:—And to Morrow, Sir, I shall desire you would make one at the Wedding of this Gentleman with my Daughter.

Merit. You do me too much Honour, Sir.

Franklyn. You must know, Sir, that we came thus far with the *Canterbury* Pilgrims,—certainly the most diverting Company that ever travell'd the Road—and my House lying in the Way, I design to invite them all to the Wedding to Morrow.

Doggrell. And there is a Nun of Quality, I am told, hath just now joyned them.

Franklyn. The Wife of *Bath* is enough to make any Mortal split his Sides. She is as frolicksome as a young Wench in the Month of *May*, plays at Romps with the Pilgrims all round, throws out as many quaint Jokes as an *Oxford* Scholar;—and, in short, exerts herself so facetiously, that she is the Mirth of the whole Company.

Doggrell. But the Support of the Society is Mr. *Chaucer*—he is a Gentleman of such inexhaustible good Sense, Breeding, and Civility, that since I have had the Happiness to converse with him, he hath honour'd some of my Productions with his Approbation.

Franklyn. Hold, hold, *Doggrell*,—if once thou dost let loose thy Tongue upon the Topick of Poetry, we shall quickly be bewilder'd upon the Muses Promontory.—Ah Boy!—to morrow Night it will be thy Turn.—Come, Sir, we are now ready to wait on you.   [*Exeunt.*

     Enter Myrtilla *in a Nun's Habit,* Alison *and* Busie.

Alison. A Nun at these Years, and with so much Beauty!—fye, fye, Madam;—Nunneries and Hospitals had originally the same Institution;—they are only for the maimed, and those that are worn out in the Service; and shall a Lady that hath all her five Senses to Perfection, with the Bloom of Youth

on her Cheeks, and Sprightliness in her Eyes, hide all those
Charms in a Cloyster?—Lookye, my Dear, if you are for
110 Confinement—I would by all means advise you to a
Husband.

Myrtilla. When 'tis allotted by the Stars, that a Person shall
always remain in the State of Virginity, 'tis but common
Prudence to retire from the World.

Alison. Were it my Case, by my troth, I should beg the
Stars Pardon.—Besides, I do not think it in the Power of all
the Stars in the Firmament to influence so ticklish a thing as a
Woman's Inclination.

Myrtilla. But all the Astrologers that I ever was so unhappy
120 as to consult, seem to hint at the same Thing.

Alison. An Astrologer's Prediction, like an Oracle, is not to
be unravel'd 'till after the Event.—And do but once, Honey,
pitch upon a Husband—and the Planets, I'll pass my Word
for it, shall very readily give their Consent.

Myrtilla. Besides, I have try'd three Midsummer-Eves
successively; and there hath not been so much as the Shadow
of a Man.

Alison. What signifies the Shadow, when your Ladyship
hath Youth and Beauty enough at any time to command the
130 Substance?

Myrtilla. But it is my Resolution to retire.

Busie. And mine—if you stick to your Resolution, to quit
your Service—for, may I never be kiss'd—if I can perceive
that I have the least bit of Nun's Flesh about me.   [*Aside.*

Alison. Let me look on your Hand, Honey,—I have as good
an Insight into Palmistry, though I say it my self, as the best
of them all.—The Learned vary—Come, come, Madam,
never despair.

Myrtilla. My Fortune is already determined.

140   *Alison.* Bow your Hand a little more—[*Looking on her Hand.*]
there, there, enough—ods-my-life, a downright Miracle of a
Hand—Matrimony without Crosses, and a most delicate
Table—and a Brace, i'facking, of as proper handsome
Husbands as ever ask'd a Lady the Question.

Busie. Let us see what my Hand promises—come, come, a
Husband is every Woman's Concern.

Myrtilla. Nay, now I recollect, a Fortune-teller some time since told me the very same Thing.

Alison. And that Mole there, beneath the tip of your Right-Ear, is a most shrewd Sign—no, I won't tell you where there 150 is another.—Ah Madam, Madam.

Busie. Ay—this must be one here—with two little things branching out; for that is an infallible Mark of a Husband.

Alison. You search in the wrong Place, Child.

Busie. Well—I'm satisfied of this—if there is never a one appears in my Hand,—I'm sure there is one in my Heart.

Alison. Lookye here, my Dear, Thanks to my lucky Planets,—I have made a Shift to dispatch five already—and welcome the sixth say I,—one, two, three, four, five,—and here is another little tiny thing; and if it will not reach to a 160 Husband, my Life for it—my good Conduct shall make it stretch to a hopeful Gallant.

Myrtilla. Methinks one's natural Inclination would induce one to try Matrimony once,—purely for the sake of Novelty— but Destiny cannot be avoided.

Alison. Destiny, Honey, is lodg'd in never a Conjurer's Tongue in Christendom—and a Fig, say I, for that Conjurer that doth not consult a Lady's Disposition, her Age, her Complexion, and the natural Bent of her Temper.

Myrtilla. But Matrimony, perhaps, may be the more severe 170 Penance.

Alison. Most Husbands—I have experienc'd them, Madam,—are tame quiet sort of Animals.—'Tis the Wife's own Fault if ever she gives up the Reins of Government—and for Jealousie, I'd advise you to my Remedy, seem to be more jealous of him.—I watch'd his Waters for him;—would he, an old Niggard, have had ever the less Light for letting a Neighbour light a Candle at his Lanthorn?

Myrtilla. But you know we promise Obedience—and is not the Husband the Lord, the Head of his Wife? 180

Alison. They claim the Title, Chicken, but, ods-my-life, we always dispute the Power;—and Women, like the Rudders of Ships, always govern their Heads.

Myrtilla. You give one mighty good Encouragement, Madam.

149 your] our *13*

Alison. I was ever from my Cradle a Friend to the Mathematicks, Madam: Why, one that pewkingly dies a Maid, loses the End of Creation, and, in short, leaves the World without having ever tasted the true Refreshments of
190 Life.

Myrtilla. But are you sure that these Marks signifie Husbands?

Alison. Am I sure that I ever knew the Comforts of one?— Why, one of 'em, as I hope for his Fellow, is at least six Foot high.

Busie. Nay, mine is a very long one too—
                                          [*Looking on her Hand.*

Alison. 'Tis a strange Thing, that our *English* Ladies should be so backward in coming to Knowledge—Why, an *Italian* Girl thinks at Twelve, meditates at Thirteen, ripens into
200 Perception at Fourteen—and here we shall have an awkward *English* Bride want Advice on her Wedding-day, though she is not married 'till Five and twenty.—Go, make haste to Bed: Child, think of the Fortune that I have told you, and dream of a Husband.   [*Exit.*

Myrtilla. You remember, *Busie,* I flung two Husbands at the last Fortune-Book.

Busie. Yes, Madam.

Myrtilla. And I dreamt of a strange Gentleman, when I slept about a Week since with the Bride-Cake under my
210 Pillow.

Busie. If Dreaming would have supply'd one with a Sweetheart, I am sure I had not been unprovided at this Time of Day.   [*Aside.*

Myrtilla. What is the Clock?

Busie. Almost ten, Madam.

Myrtilla. You remember, I suppose, this is St. *Agnes's* Night, and that I resolve to try the Experiment of the Dumb-Cake.   [*Exit.*

                    Enter Chaucer.

Chaucer. What, turn'd Pilgrim, my Dear,—and must Love
220 give Place to Religion,—[*Kisses her.*] Have I no Hopes but by turning Fryar, and calling my Love Continence and Mortification—I was very luckily a Day or two since informed of Lady *Myrtilla's* Resolution—

Busie. Oh, dear Sir, pray how long have you been return'd from your Travels?

Chaucer. But just arriv'd—Absence, Mrs. *Busie*, has not been able to deface the Impressions of Love,—and still the Lady *Myrtilla* reigns in my Bosom, haunts my waking Thoughts, and is ever present in my Dreams.—I think, I talk, I write of nothing but her. 230

Busie. I am afraid, Mr. *Chaucer*, your Case will be just the same as the Boys in the Fable,—you have talked of Love Artillery, Flames, Eyes, and Darts, so long in Jest, that it will be very difficult to gain Belief, now you are in Earnest.

Chaucer. But pray, Child, is Devotion or Discontent the Cause of her Retirement?—For Mad-houses and Nunneries are as much inhabited by disappointed Lovers as Devotees— and I fear, should a Cloyster be her Choice, the other would soon be my Fate.

Busie. Very probably, Sir, for you'll have a double Pretence 240 to it—as you are a Wit too.

Chaucer. You are smart, Mrs. *Busie*—But is there no Hopes to divert her from this voluntary Banishment?—Has she any Symptoms of Love?—Does she talk incoherently, sigh often, or read Romances?

Busie. There are Methods which perhaps might have some Influence upon her;—but Confidents, Sir, must not divulge Secrets.

Chaucer. Say'st thou so, my dear Girl?—And I am come so opportunely to thy Relief—when thou hast so uneasie a thing 250 as a Secret in thy Possession.

Busie. A Secret, Sir, is as safe in a Woman's keeping, as a Lady's Reputation in a Man's—But pray, Dear Mr. *Chaucer*, don't ask me.

Chaucer. Would you have your Lady lost purely upon a Punctilio?—I know, my Dear, you have conquer'd your Sex, and have the knack of Secrecy—but a Secret of this Consequence—   [*Gives her Gold.*

Busie. It is of Consequence, I confess.—You know, Sir, my Lady is as Superstitious as an ignorant Abbot,—her Humour 260 by Day depends upon her Dreams by Night, spilling of Salt throws her into the Vapours,—half the Week is lost upon account of unlucky Days—and she has an entire Confidence

in Astrologers—'tis those Wretches that have past the severe
Sentence of Virginity on her.

Chaucer. And so she designs to sacrifice all the Pleasures of
Life to their Ignorance.

Busie. And for fear she should change her Mind, which you
know we are pretty much given to, she has resolv'd to put it
270 out of her own Power, by retiring into a Cloyster—but she just
now was a little wavering.

Chaucer. Have the Dictates of Nature then at last over-
byass'd her Superstition?

Busie. You must know, Sir, the Wife of *Bath* just now made
her a Visit,—and meerly ridicul'd her out of her Project.—
She consulted her Hand, and very agreeably contradicted all
her former Fortune by a Promise of two Husbands.

Chaucer. Which the Lady I presume seems fond of
believing.

280 *Busie.* Yes, O my Conscience—and fond of having too—
with the Permission of the Planets—this being St. *Agnes* Night,
she hath provided the Dumb-Cake, and performs the
Ceremony, in order, if 'tis possible, to get a glympse of
Matrimony.

Chaucer. The most lucky Incident in the World.—Now
have I the Opportunity to make my Approaches by way of
her Superstition, I can never fail of Conquest—This Night,
pretty Creature, I'll play the Apparition.

Busie. Just my Thought, I vow—this Key of her Closet, I
290 suppose, may be of some Service—for that Body of yours will
scarce be able to enter a Chink, or pass through a Key-hole—
remember the Hour,—and make haste to your Post, Sir.

[Exeunt severally.

Enter Franklyn, Doggrell, Doublechin *and* Alison.

Alison. One Wedding, the Proverb says, begets another:
What think you, old Heart of Oak, shall Experience supply
the want of Youth?—come, let you and I for once verifie the
old Saying—give me thy Hand, Old Boy.

Franklyn. Hold, hold, Dame, Marry in haste and repent at
leisure—There is a Proverb for your Proverb.

Doublechin. But Matrimony is not like common Crimes,
300 Mr. *Franklyn*—for the most tedious Repentance can never
hope for Absolution.

Franklyn. We are too Old now-a-days to pretend to those things.

Alison. Slidikins!—Old, old!—pray do not measure my Corn with your Bushel, old dry Bones—this Person of mine—I would have you to know, like a Medlar—grows the sweeter for its Age, Old Gray-beard.

Enter Merit.

Merit. Shall I prevail with you, Sir, to do the Office of a Father upon this Occasion?

Franklyn. With all my Heart, Sir.   310

Alison. Hah, hah, young Stripling, are you our bold Adventurer?—A little of my Advice, Younker, would do you no harm, I believe,—soft and fair,—take Care of your Constitution.—Matrimony is a lasting Entertainment—[*Exit* Merit.] This is very hard upon your Order, Father *Doublechin*,—meer Tantalization—to see Matrimony so often before your Eyes, yet never to have it in your Power to taste it—But stolen Fruit, stolen Fruit—ah Father *Doublechin*.

Enter Merit *leading* Florinda, *she starts back in Surprise.*

Florinda. Ha!—my Father!—I am undone.   [*Aside.*

Franklyn. Florinda! hurry durry—what is the Matter 320 now?— Death! this is all Trick and Banter.   [*Aside.*

Merit. My too much Care hath betray'd me.   [*Aside.*

Alison. Hey-day! what, are we all knock'd in the Head at once?—Come, you Hoary-Pate there, deliver up your Charge—and you Mr. Sanctity, make haste and do your Office,—young Folks are impatient.

Franklyn. What Wind, in the Name of Fury, blew you hither, Wench.

Florinda. Oh, Sir,—had not you thus timely interpos'd, I had been utterly lost.   330

Franklyn. By your Leave, Sir, [*To* Merit] This, *Frank*, is my Daughter [*Gives her to* Doggrell.] How, Girl?—What, without your Father's Consent?—But I hope, the Rogue hath not begun at the fag end of the Ceremony.

Alison. Look ye, Shaver, we will sometime or other enjoy our own Choice,—and if we cannot procure it in a Husband, i'fackins, we will make it up in a Gallant—How, in the Name of *Cupid*, can you baulk so handsome a young Fellow?—Come hither, Stripling,—show your Shapes and walk gracefully:—

340 See, how portly he plants himself—ah Rogue!

Franklyn. Heark ye, Fellow, what Pretensions had you to seduce my Child,—hah?

Merit. Your Daughter, Sir, is still in your own Disposal—and I only made use of this Device to ask your Consent.

Franklyn. A very pretty Excuse!—Old Birds are not caught with Chaff, Friend.—You are a fine hoity toity Thing, I perceive,—I'll warrant, I secure you, Madam, from any further Excursions.

Florinda. He stole me, Sir, threaten'd me,—and would have
350 forc'd me to his Arms.—And what, alas! can a weak Woman do?

Merit. What does she drive at by all this?—How easie she seems under this Disappointment!—ah Woman, Woman!

[*Aside.*

Franklyn. Well, Child, however—since he has set agog your Inclinations, you shall not want a Husband.—This worthy Gentleman is of my providing.—Let us have no Hums nor Haws, nor fiddle-faddle Consideration.—Come, Father *Doublechin*, and you there, Mr. *Kidnapper*, now 'tis your Turn to be Witness.

360 *Doggrell.* Let us first, Sir, be assur'd that the Lady has not dispos'd of her self—perhaps we may now be invading another Gentleman's Property.

Franklyn. Has a Thief a Property in stoln Goods, because he hath them in Possession?

Florinda. My Duty, Sir, obliges me to comply with your Commands,—but, pray Sir, grant me some small time to recover my Fright—my Spirits are so disorder'd that I cannot support my self.   [*Faints.*

Franklyn. What, I'll warrant,—the terrible Shape of Father
370 put you in this Consternation, Hussy.

Alison. Poor Girl, poor Girl! here, Child—drink a little of my Cordial, a little of my Cordial, [*Drinks her self.*] this is the Life and Soul of a Traveller.

> *Then who would not be a Bride,*   [*Sings.*
> *Then who would not be a Bride,*
> *For the sweetest Kiss,*

342 hah?] ~. 13

> *Is not half of her Bliss :*
> *This all will say,—who have try'd.*

Franklyn. A Husband is the best Physick for her—and
though, like all other Doses, it may seem nauseous at first, yet 380
I'll warrant she'll like the Operation—Come, come, marry
her, Boy, and write thy own *Epitalmium.*

Doggrell. Epithalamium, Sir.

Alison. What, marry her to a Poet! the gingle of Love in a
Copy of Verses will never answer a Wife's Expectation.—
Besides, Poverty is the meer Bane of Love.

Franklyn. But Mr. *Doggrell,* they tell me, writes only for his
Diversion, nay, he pays the Bookseller for printing his
Works,—and writes the most like a Gentleman of any Man on
this side *Parnassus.*   390

Doggrell. Your Father, Madam, does me too much
Honour,—but no Poet ever celebrates his Wife—the word
Wife, methinks, has as ill a Sound in Poetry as in the Mouth
of a Husband.

Franklyn. Heark ye, you Woman-stealer,—you had best
withdraw, lest I let loose my Indignation upon you, and send
you to the Gallows, to give Mr. *Doggrell* here a Subject for an
Elegy.

Doggrell. D'Ogrelle,—I beseech you, Sir.

Merit. Sure this is the most malicious Adventure that ever 400
cross'd an unfortunate Lover.   [*Aside. Exit.*

Doublechin. After Supper, you may command me, Sir; for if
you can live upon Love, good People, 'tis what one of my
Substance cannot so easily subsist upon.

Franklyn. Well,—compose your self, Girl; Mr. *Doggrell,* she
is your Charge.

Doggrell. Madam,—   [*Leading her off.*
> *To your Relief your ardent Lover flies.*
> *Ah! those attractive Lips, and dear deluding Eyes!*
>   [*Exeunt.*

ACT II. SCENE I.

SCENE *Continues.*

Enter Doggrell *and* Florinda.

Doggrell. I v o w, Madam, to consider your Beauty and Pedigree together, you are just like a Rose grafted on a Thorn.—That was a most egregious wrong Step of your Father's.

Florinda. My Father, 'tis true, with all the Inconsideration of Youth, married meerly for Love,—an Action, I must own, unbecoming a Gentleman.

Doggrell. The chief End of Matrimony, I conceive, is the Support of a Family, and the Encrease of an Estate—but so many Graces, Madam,—so many Charms!—will overballance a small Defect of Genealogy.

Florinda. Then I have the Misfortune, Sir, to be so extreamly like my Mother, that upon all Occasions my Presence gives a Hint to Reflection.—Now, will I work him into a Dislike of me by seeming to strike in with his Humour. [*Aside.*

Doggrell. An Unhappiness, indeed, Madam,—Love generally proves an edg'd Tool to an old Man's Fingers.

Florinda. This Error of my Father will make me in every respect submit my self to his Pleasure, to avoid the like Inconvenience my self.

Doggrell. Let me die, if she does not seem fond of me. [*Aside.*

Florinda. To convince you, Sir, that I scorn to act dishonourably with a Gentleman of your Merit—I ought to acquaint you with another Disgrace, that a Slip of one of my Ancestors entail'd upon the Family;—but should my Father know—

Doggrell. Nay, Madam, I am as secret as a Confessor—as I am a Man of Honour.

Florinda. My great great Grandfather, Sir,—

Doggrell. What of him, Madam?

Florinda. Was—hanged—Sir.

Doggrell. Hang'd!—and I will follow his Example sooner than Marry into a Family made up of Knaves and Fools. [*Aside.*

Florinda. I intreat you, Sir, ask me no further—It is mighty hard, methinks, that an Ancestor's Failings should devolve upon his Posterity.

Doggrell. So that, Madam, your Father's Indiscretion will grace my Coat with a Spit—and your great great Grandfather's Slip, as your Ladyship terms it, blazon my 'Scutcheon with a Gallows. Ha, ha, ha.

40

Enter Antony *and* William *at a distance*.

Antony. Look-ye there,—yonder she is, i'faith—softly, softly *William*,—swop upon en at once, knack en dawn, and I will secure young Mistress.

William. But what shall we do with the plaguy Toad when we have caught en,—Is it not a hanging Matter, *Antony?* thee understand'st the Law to be sure, who canst read the Statue Book, and draw out Leases for Maaster—S'bud, 'tis a rare thing to be Lorned.

Antony. We must first and foremost enquire, whether or no a Dafter be Goods and Chattels, *William*—in the next place, d'ye see, whether or no, She stole He, or He stole She;—but according to the best of my Reading, it seems plainly to be a Ravishment—but stay, let us catch en first,—lay hold of his Pitch-frog *William*—for all these swaggering Blades Courage lyes within-side the Scabbard.

50

William. Hoh, hoh, Sir,—as flat as a Flounder, by *George*,— [*Trips up* Doggrell's *Heels*.] A cord, a Cord, *Antony*,—look ye, Sir, we kill Foxes for making bold with our Geese, and hang Dogs for choaking our Sheep—and i'faith, I'll make thee an Example to all Fortune-stealers.—What, is Maaster's only Chick a Bit for your Chaps, Sirrah?

60

Doggrell. Pray, Gentlemen,—my Mony is at your Service; but I entreat you, Gentlemen, spare my Life for that Fair Lady's Repose,—may I be informed of the Occasion of this Assault?—or are you Officers of the Law,—at whose Suit, Gentlemen?

Antony. Look-ye, *William*, I find it plainly to be a Hanging Matter, d'ye see,—for look-ye, d'ye see,—thoff stealing of a Woman should be no Felony, we can Indict en for stealing the Rigging and Appurtenances, d'ye see, as in the first place, *William*,—*Item*, For stealing of Mistress's Head-Geer, with all the dangling Ribbons, Lace, *&c.* thereunto belonging; a Silk

70

Gown and Petticoat, and all Mistress's wearing Apparel, d'ye see; for thoff a Jury, perhaps, would not bring in the bare Woman above the value of ten Pence,—yet the Cloathing, *William*.

William. Always reckon'd the chiefest Part of a Woman— as plain as a Pike-staff, as clear as the Sun, *Antony*.

Florinda. Pray, treat the Gentleman with more Civility,—
80 what brought you hither, *Antony?*

Antony. Oh, Mistress, Mistress! you left the whole House at Home in a most pitiful taking—for my own Part, I had rather have lost the best Weather of all the Flock, than such a Mishap should have happen'd to the Family.

William. To be plain with you, Forsooth, a Woman costs a hugeous deal the rearing, and we could never have answered such a Loss to Maaster, Forsooth.

Doggrell. Upon my Honour, Gentlemen.

Florinda. They are my Father's Servants, Sir,—you are in
90 no danger—But I shall not endeavour wholly to undeceive them, since their Care in confining him may possibly set me at Liberty.   [*Aside*.

Doggrell. Downright Barbarity, I vow!

William. 'Sbud, chez believe 'tis Ravishment in good earnest, now,—for young Mistress excuses en hugeous feelingly;—but how shall we order Maters? I think 'twill be the safest Way to hang up the Prisoner to rights, to save the labour of Carriage.

Doggrell. I vow Gentlemen,—I beg you—you mistake the
100 Person,—I was never, upon my Honour, concern'd in seducing the young Lady—The Rusticity of these Mortals, Madam, leads them into innumerable Absurdities.

William. Never talk to us of your Nummeribble Absuddeties, nor speak your Pedlars-*French*, d'ye see,—to juggle young Mistress out of our Clutches again, d'ye see,— there, there, bind en a little tighter, *Antony*.

Antony. I cannot well tell whether we can answer Hanging of en, or no, but suppose, *William*, we let en have the Honour of dying the Death of a Gentleman, and we kill en in a
110 Duel,—I have heard say, that is but Manslaughter, if the worst come to the worst.—Hah, hah!

[*Makes Passes at a distance*.

Doggrell. As I am a Man of Honour, I was no way concern'd: I appeal to the Fair Lady, there.

Florinda. Have a care, *Antony*, this Gentleman makes his Applications to me, with the Approbation of my Father.

Antony. Do thou guard the Prisoners, d'ye see,—Here is a Justice, they say, below in the Inn—we had best ask his Worship's Opinion before we Kill en outrights, d'ye see.

> [*Going to shut them into a Closet together.*

William. Oh, oh, gracious, hold, hold,—let us never Pen them in together—Why—'Slife Man, that is the main Way to 120 become Accessaries our selves.

Antony. Why, odsmylife, Mistress,—do but let Maaster know that your Mouth begins to Water after Man, and my Life of it he will never starve the Cause.

> *Enter* Franklyn *and* Doublechin.

William. Oh dear, Maaster, Maaster, we were all like to come to a most lamentable Mishap—Young Mistress, forsooth—slidikins, I am overjoy'd to see you,—'sbud, who thought to have found your Worship's good Grace here—but as I was saying, Young Mistress, forsooth, took it in her Head to run astray, and Fath, was stole—or else laid the Moveable 130 in the Thief's Way, forsooth.

Antony. Oh, Sir, oh dear Sir, the House at home is in a most piteous taking,—we rose all the whole Parish, as a Body may say, and sent all the Labourers abroad, *East, West, North,* and *South.*

Franklyn. Hold, hold *Antony*—I know of my Daughter's Proceedings.

Antony. See how the Plaguy Toad looks—Here is a Maaster's Honour here for you now, Mr. *Brazenface.*

Franklyn. You are under a Mistake, *Antony*—Unbind the 140 Gentleman—but however, I cannot but commend your Diligence,—I hope *Frank*, you will excuse the Ignorance of these Fellows.

William. Under a Mistake, *Antony*,—under a Mistake.— do'st hear?

Antony. Ay—under a Mistake, under a Mistake.

> [*Exeunt* Antony *and* William.

Franklyn. Well, Damsel, are your Spirits in Tune yet,—and how stand your Inclinations affected, honest *Frank?* Only give

the Word Boy,—and Father *Doublechin* shall secure you in a
150 more pleasing Bondage—I will warrant my Girl shall do her
Duty—What say you Damsel?—Come Father *Doublechin*, you
should never let Love or a good Dinner cool, for want of your
Assistance.

Doggrell. Matrimony throws one at once off from the
Conversation of the *Beau Monde*—a Husband among them is
neither allow'd to be handsome, well bred, or witty.—he loses
all his former *Politesse* with his Liberty—but then again my
undervaluing my Family lays me open to Satyr; and when the
Ladies are out of Hope their Tongues are under no restraint.
[*Aside.*

160 *Franklyn.* Why *Frank*—what still shill I shall I—Is this
owing to your Behaviour Mrs. Contradiction; Come, Hussy,
show what a dutiful Wife you will make by your Obedience to
your Father.

Florinda. I am entirely at your Disposal, Sir—I may now
safely venture to consent without running the risque of his
Compliance.   [*Aside.*

Franklyn. Here is a glorious Girl for you, *Frank*—Come
Father *Doublechin*, all Parties are now agreed.

Doggrell. I must confess, Sir, the Lady's Merits are beyond
170 all Dispute—but your dishonourable Proceedings, Sir, have
put a stop to the Progress of my Amour.

Franklyn. My dishonourable Proceedings, *Frank!*—

Doggrell. I am not to be imposed upon, Sir, in a thing that
so nearly concerns my Posterity.

Franklyn. What, still upon the old String?—ah, *Frank*,
Frank, that Love can never be sincere that raises so many
Objections.

Doggrell. Think of your Great Grand-father, Sir—

Franklyn. He was a Gentleman every Inch of him; marry'd
180 into the Family of Sir *Thomas Pedigree*—and I will warrant
you, he could trace out his Genealogy for two or three
hundred Years beyond the Conquest.

Doggrell. When I find my self once impos'd upon, I always
distrust the same Person in his whole Proceedings.—Who was
your great Grand-father's Physician, Sir, during his last
Sickness?

Franklyn. Come, come *Frank*, never endeavour to perplex the Matter.—These Poets talk so allegorically, there is no understanding them.—We never had one of our Generation prescrib'd to Death—nor spoil'd the Breed of our Family with Bolusses, Pills and Purges;—we never had any Physician belonging to our House but Nature, nor any Distemper but Age. 190

Doggrell. 'Tis more honourable to die by the Hands of the Physician than the Hangman, Sir.

Franklyn. True, *Frank*, you may plead the Custom of the World for it.—but dying is dying,—and I believe dead Men make but small difference between Poison and a Halter.— Here Father *Doublechin*, I join them together—Now do you clap on the Matrimonial Yoke. 200

Doggrell. Sir, I return the Present;—The Lady is too deserving of me,—and so corrupt a Family.

Franklyn. Oh these wicked Weeds Poetry and Genealogy have quite over-grown poor *Frank's* Understanding—Thou a Poet!

Doggrell. Did not I check my Anger by the Dictates of Philosophy, I should let loose my Resentment—but, however, Sir, to let you see that I scorn to be a Bubble,—I cannot help showing you that I am acquainted with the secret History of your Family, Sir,—I know, that your Worship made an Alliance with a Lady of the Kitchen,—and that your great Grandfather, Sir, made his Exit on the Gallows.—You are my Guardian, 'tis true, Sir, and have my Fortune in your Possession, but not in your Disposal. 210

Franklyn. Heigh day!—What, in a Passion, *Frank?* baulk my Daughter, and belye my Ancestors? Come, come, come, Girl. [*Exeunt* Franklyn, Doublechin *and* Florinda
Enter Alison.

Alison. Well, honest Heart,—my bonny Champion,— beware Head, old Boy,—for i'faith I design to throw the Stocking—pure rosie Cheeks, ruby Lips, and a rolling Eye!— a most glorious Girl! worth a Man's pawning his Liberty. 220

Doggrell. The Match is entirely her Father's Proposal, Madam, not my Inclinations.

Alison. 'Tis only People of ordinary Fashion that now-a-

days marry for Love.—Your Men of Quality, I know, marry
one, and love another, but i'dad—'tis a most confounded
expensive way,—'tis this occasions so many Divorces, and
separate Beds,—and lays the Charge of Keeping on a Family.

Doggrell. Oh the charming Nun!—Your Interest, Madam,
230 might assist a desponding Lover, and at the same time relieve
a most beautiful Lady from Confinement.

Alison. Very hard upon the young Lady, I vow,—
disappoint her Lover, and afterwards leave her in the lurch!
Drive the Ox from the Manger without ever designing to taste
the Hay! and what,—I'll warrant,—young Spindle-shanks—
you take me for an O—ld Woman now,—that hath lost all
Relish; only fit to set young Folks together, and think of times
past.

Doggrell. I beg your Pardon, Madam,—your Complexion,
240 'tis true, seems a little to confute your airy Temper—I vow,
Madam, you have a World of Vivacity.

Alison. What! make me undergo the Fatigue!—without
Hope of sharing the Diversion.

Doggrell. I beg your Pardon, Madam,—you might command me in an Office of the like Nature.

Alison. Say'st thou so, my Lad?—Wilt thou do a good Turn
for receiving one?—I have a few Wrinkles, 'tis true, con-
tracted in my Virginity and Widow-hood—But Matrimony
would soon smooth and polish my Countenance again.—
250 believe me, Sir,—there is not a greater Impairer of Beauty,
than the Longing of a Virgin, and the tedious Expectation of
a Widow.—Why, who wears worse than your old Maid, Sir?

Doggrell. You speak with a wonderful deal of Judgment,
Madam.—I am informed she is a Lady of Quality—will you
oblige me, Madam, so far as to convey my Sighs to the fair
Lady, and do me the friendly Office of a *Zephyr*.

Alison. Poor Fellow!—thou thinkest to make me only
Auxiliary—but i'faith, I'll lay ten to one, I'll make my self
Principal in the end.   [*Aside.*
260 *Doggrell.* A *Billet*, Madam.

Alison. Send her a Kiss, Boy,—there is some Savour in such
a Present, and it brings some Benefit to the Bearer too.

Doggrel. Nay, Madam,—I shall tell her in the Epistle that I desire to kiss her fair Hands.

Alison. That is meer throwing away a Kiss;—come, come, Stripling, Ladies know that the Lips were made for kissing.

Doggrell. You must know, Madam, that I dedicate my vacant Hours to the Muses; and always write to the Ladies in Verse.—The Sentiments of Love glide so smoothly into a Lady's Heart, set off with the Ornaments of Poetry—that 270 before they are acquainted with the Person, they are in Love with the Poet.

Alison. But the Kiss,—Mr. *D'Ogrelle.*

Doggrell. 'Tis at your Service, Madam,—but we never send so rude a Present to the Ladies.   [*Kisses her.*

Alison. Ah!—again, my bonny Hero,—I shall now speak most pathetically in thy Commendation. [*Kisses him.*] Never fear, my Lad, I owe *Cupid* some good Turns for past Services,—I'll bring you together,—and my Life for it, she'll never be able to resist so charming a Gentleman.   280

Doggrell. You are mighty obliging, Madam,—Beauty warms the Poet's Imagination, and Love is the very Food of Wit.—I have known a Gentleman, that could not read a Couplet with juster Emphasis than a Parish Clerk, write very prettily upon his Mistress's Eyes.—I have at least celebrated above fifty Ladies *pour passer le temps*, which I call Love *Ouvertures.*—A Lady of Quality cannot pull off a Glove, and display a beautiful little Finger, but it immediately flows into a Sonnet—a Lady's Dress, a random Glance, or a new Suit of Ribbons, are Occasions that inspire a Man of the least 290 Gallantry with the brightest turns of Fancy.

Alison. A sure way, Sir, to attack the whole Sex at once.— and that Man must take very bad Aim, who shoots amongst a whole Flock and brings off none of the Game.

Doggrell. Oh Charming Nun!

Alison. Come on then,—young *Ovid.*—Out with it— Extempore now.

Doggrell. Oh charming *Nun of Noble Race*—no, no,—hold, *of noble Line.*—But an Affair of this Nature requires more serious Application—So Madam, I shall beg leave to retire a 300 Moment or two to adjust my Thoughts with more regularity.

[*Exit.*

Alison. A handsome young Fellow, with little Wit and a

good Stock of Vanity. Why what then! He hath a good
comfortable Proverb of his Side, and have at him—i'faith—I,
a Match-maker, quotha—no, I thank my Stars, I am not as
yet of so cold a Constitution to look on with Indifference—a
Match-maker, i'dad, in other Terms, is nothing else but a
lawful Pimp.   [*Exit.*

Enter Merit.

Merit. Accuse me! promise Obedience!—throw her self
310 under her Father's Protection!—all my Hopes are grounded
on her Sex, for Nature teaches them Dissimulation—A
Woman often smiles on the Man she hates, and frowns on him
she loves.

Drawer. Coming, coming, Sir.

Enter a Drawer.

Merit. Hold, hold, Sirrah,—where do you carry that Wine?

Drawer. Coming, coming, Gentlemen,—into the *Dragon*,
Sir,—I'll bring your Honour a Pint of the same
immediately—Coming, coming, Sir—Score a Quart of Sack
in the *Dragon*—below there.

320 *Merit.* Here's Mony for you, Sirrah.   [*Gives him Mony.*

Drawer. Coming, coming—I humbly thank your Honour,
your Honour may take my Word for the Matter—*Betty* is as
tight and wholesome a Girl as any in all the Neighbourhood.
You shall treat with her your self—Coming, coming,
Gentlemen.

Merit. How readily the Rogue answers in his Profession—
Betty may to Night oblige another Customer, I want none of
your pimping Tricks, Sirrah, only lend me your Apron and
Cap, tarry in the next Room, and let me serve the Company
330 where you were going.

Drawer. With all my Heart, Sir, here's my Apron—make
haste, Sir, or ten to one you'll have your Head broke for my
delay.

Merit. Come, come, the Cap, the Cap.   [*Knocking heard.*

Drawer. Coming, coming, Sir—plague of your
Impatience—a damn'd Cholerick old Chuff, I'll warrant ye;
he has a most confounded passionate Knock; there is nothing
discovers a Man's Temper more than his manner in
knocking—Coming, coming, Sir—A fine Gentleman, I see,
340 will upon occasion make a good smart sort of a Drawer,—

Here, here nimbly, and away.

Merit. Why don't you bawl, Sirrah? D'ye hear? bawl you
Dog—come, come, the Wine, and the Glasses.

Drawer. Coming, coming, Sir—there, there, away, away.
                                    [*Gives him the Bottle and Glasses.*

Merit. Coming, coming, Gentlemen.   [*Exit.*

Drawer. 'Tis a sad Life that we Gentlemen Drawers must
submit to, we are meer Spaniels, brought under Command by
the Discipline of the Cane—the smart Fellows at our Expence
give the first Proofs of their Courage, and we very often stand
the Spleen of a losing Gamester—A Drawer may be said to be   350
thoroughly qualified, when he can lie with a good Grace,
Pimp dextrously, be scoundrell'd without grumbling, and
bear a beating with Patience.   [*Exit.*

SCENE *draws, and discovers* Franklyn's *Apartment.* Franklyn,
   Florinda *and* Doublechin; *to them enter* Merit, *as the Drawer.*

Merit. Coming, coming, Sir.

Franklyn. No Attendance to be had here! no Attendance!

Merit. A choice Flower—your Worship—as rich a Pipe as
ever was brought from the *Canaries*, broach'd on purpose for
your Honour, meer Amber.   [*Pouring out Sack.*

Franklyn. I'll amber you, you Dog you, you Villain, you
Rascal; what, must we tarry here all Night, you Scoundrel, to   360
wait your Pleasure? Let me go, Father, that I may thresh the
Dog into better Manners. Make a Gentleman wait your
Pleasure, Sirrah!—but hold, I had best let him alone, for who
knows but the Dog may Poison me in my Sack.

Merit. I only staid—your Honour—to broach a fresh Pipe.
I'll warrant the Wine pleases your Worship.

Doublechin. Keep your Temper, Mr. *Franklyn*,—the Lad
speaks well—keep your Temper—come, come, a Glass will
reconcile Matters, and make us all Friends—fill about, Boy.

Franklyn. A Rogue, a Dog, a downright wenching House by   370
the Attendance! Sirrah, I could find in my Heart—

Doublechin. Never lye at his Mercy, Mr. *Franklyn*—he may
Poison you—who knows—he may—ay, he may Poison you—
[*Drinks.*] I vow, a most delicious Flavour—fill the angry

Gentleman a Glass, Sirrah, the other Glass, my Lad, and then I'll venture to pass my Judgment—Come, Sir, my Service to you—here's your Daughter's Inclinations. [*Drinks.*] Come, come, Sir, drink and be easie.

Franklyn. Look ye, Father, your drinking after that ex-
380 travagant Rate is the ready way to lighten the Bottle, but not my Afflictions.

Florinda. How every Dress becomes him!   [*Aside.*

Franklyn. As you say, Father, the Wine passes [*Drinks*] neat and clean off the Palate.—Go, Sirrah, fill the Girl there a Glass—never fear, Child—[Doublechin *holds* Merit.] I'll warrant, *Frank* will come to at last,—but who can suffer all these Affronts?—Baulk my Daughter, and abuse my Family?

Doublechin. Why, you Relapse, Sir,—Here, you *Hic &
Ubique*, fill t'other Glass to Mr. *Franklyn*—this, Sir, will inspire
390 you with good Humour—come, Sir, here is to your Daughter's happy Conjunction.   [*Drinks.*

Franklyn. Pox on it, as long as the Bottle holds, we shall have nothing but the Glass and your Lips in Conjunction— Stay, hold, Father, spare the Wine and your Compliments a little, I beg you.—Sirrah, did not I order you to fill to my Daughter?

Merit. Oh, my *Florinda!* may I hope you are Constant? How could you quit me with so much Disdain! and fly with Pleasure to my Rival's Arms?   [*Aside to* Florinda.
400 *Florinda.* You wrong me, Sir, I am and ever will be constant. I feign'd Obedience, and looked with Indifference on you, only to avoid Suspicion.

Franklyn. Heigh Day! what is to be done here!

Florinda. See the Sheets are well aired, d'ye hear me. [*To* Merit *aloud.*] I think, Sir, you are apt to take cold on the Road.   [*To* Franklyn

Franklyn. Set down the Bottle, Rogue, and about your Business,—but Father *Doublechin*, let me tell you, these Objections of Mr. *Doggrell* look shrewdly suspicious.—Tax my
410 Family with the Gallows, a Rogue! a downright Poetical Fiction.

Florinda. My seeming Fondness towards him, chills his Love—A Lover that makes an easie Conquest despises his Victory.   [*To* Merit.

Franklyn. What a Vengeance, now we have as much Plague to get rid of You, as we had to bring You hither—And the Dog hath the Impudence to be in close Conference with my Daughter!

Merit. Shall I order the Chamberlain to call your Worship in the Morning—all the Rooms are ready—You, Sir, I think lye in the *Mairmaid*, you in the *Dolphin*, and your Ladyship—   420

Franklyn. Hold Sirrah, her Ladyship shall be disposed of as I think fit—Fetch me the Key of her Apartment, d'ye hear.— I'll allow of no such private Caballing—About your Business, Sirrah.

Doublechin. Come, wash off the Remains of your peevish Humour with a Glass of Sack, Sir—See here Sir, the very look of it brightens a Man's Countenance.—Come Madam, here is a Health to your Lover.   [*Drinks.*

Merit. My Master, Sir, has three Pipes of this same Wine,   430
neat as it came over, of the true natural Flavour, without the least Adulteration—I'll watch every Motion, and be always ready, my dearest Creature, to fly to your Relief.

[*To Florinda.*

Florinda. The first favourable Opportunity you may expect me.   [*To* Merit.

Franklyn. See the Impudence of this Rogue.—What still there, Sirrah; away, carry the remainder of the Bottle into my Daughter's Chamber—I'll conduct her thither.

Merit. Coming, coming, Gentlemen.   [*Exit.*

Franklyn. An impudent Coxcomb—Come Daughter, to   440
Night you are under my Protection, to Morrow you shall be under your Husband's Protection—While the Steed is safe, is the time to secure the Door—*Frank*, you will find, upon a Night's Consideration, will be convinced of his Folly.—To morrow Morning, Father.

Doublechin. I'll attend you, Sir.

Florinda. *Since Marriage binds us fast in lasting Bands,*
     Love that unites our Hearts, shall join our Hands.

[Aside.
[*Exeunt.*

ACT III. SCENE I.

SCENE *Lady* Myrtilla's *Apartment.*

The SCENE *draws and discovers* Myrtilla *leaning on a Table, set off with a Cake and a Bottle of Wine:* Busie *is seated at a distant part of the Stage. To them enters* Chaucer, *places himself at the Table, he eats; and drinks to* Myrtilla, *who continues in silence; he afterwards makes Love to her by Signs, she still remains in the same Posture;* Chaucer *at last being no longer able to contain himself, rises from the Table and advances towards her with the profoundest Respect, and Kneeling at her Feet thus accosts her in a Tragic Strain.*

Chaucer. SINCE *the kind Stars to mutual Love constrain,*
Why should the Tongue conceal our secret Pain?
Was it for this, inexorable Fair,
Your Magick drew me through the distant Air?
Tho' some curst Charm your wonted Speech denies,
At least shed Pity from those radiant Eyes,
And look me into Hope.—

In short, Madam, you see Destiny will have it so; and we have nothing else to do but submit.—Come, come, Madam,
10 let us delay no Time, the Yoke of Matrimony sets best upon Young Shoulders.—Since the Tongue is upon the reserve, let us make use of the Lovers Language, and interpret by the Eyes;

We from the Ladies Eyes our Fate may learn,
And in those Glasses Love or Hate discern.

What, both your Tongue and Eyes under Command?—let me die if I do not think you the only Lady in Christendom that hath either of them in her Power.—I vow, Madam, you have an exquisite pretty Hand—so finely turn'd—
[*He offers to take her by the Hand, she shrieks and runs out of the Room.*
20   *Busie.* Go, you unthinking Creature, you—you forgot you was a Spirit.
Chaucer. That is true, as you say, Child—my Love is not so Spiritual as it should be—but Pox on't, the Flesh has so much Interest in this whimsical Passion, that it will be medling, spite of one's Teeth.

Busie. Why, you should not have spoken one Syllable, much less have offer'd to touch her.

Chaucer. We Lovers are generally guilty of most egregious Blunders—How could any Mortal think to gain upon a Woman by Silence? for the Man that talks much among them, is always esteem'd pretty Conversation. 30

Busie. Hark! what Noise is that? as I am alive, all the whole House is alarmed; we are utterly undone, Mr. *Chaucer*; you will lose your Mistress, I shall lose my Service, and my Lady will lose her Reputation.—What shall we do? where will you hide your self?

Chaucer. Lookye, Mrs. *Busie*, though we have unhappily involved our selves in this difficulty, we will not give up the Cause—A good steady Assurance may still carry on the Deceit—for my part, I'll play the Apparition in my *Exit*, and 40 vanish—Do you try, for once, whether a Woman can feign Fear as well as Sorrow,—look Astonisht, and say you neither saw nor heard any thing, but observed the Candle burn Blue, and smelt Brimstone most intolerably—Superstition, my Dear, is very Credulous. [*Exit* Chaucer.

Enter Myrtilla *and* Alison.

Myrtilla. Oh, dear Madam, I was so extreamly Frighten'd—Your good Nature, I hope, will excuse this Disturbance.

Alison. What is the Matter, Precious, has Love committed Burglary, and broke into thy Chamber?—Ah Rogue!—He is 50 a sly Young Thief, and very seldom comes honestly by his Possessions.

Myrtilla. Hold—ah!—there he is—

Alison. What—where, where is he?

Myrtilla. I beg your Pardon Madam,—it hath made so deep an Impression on me, that Fancy recalls my Fears.

Alison. Do you see now, my Dear? these are some of the Scarecrows that attend Virginity; just my Case when I was a Maid, as I hope for a Help-mate; why, I lived upon Fancy, and my whole Life was made up of Inconsistences. I sighed 60 for I could not tell what, was wondrous fanciful in my Dreams, and was not a little whimsical too when I was Awake.

Myrtilla. Busie.

Busie. Madam.

Myrtilla. Where do you run?—where are you?—why do you leave me?—there is more Vexation with these Creatures—I vow, 'tis intolerable.

Busie. I imagined, by your Ladyship's Looks, that you was
70 taken with an Hysterick Fit, or surprised by the Vapours—but when I heard you Shriek so lamentably—bless me!—I thought I should have sunk in the Place.

Myrtilla. You saw him, I suppose, *Busie.*

Busie. What, Madam?

Myrtilla. The Apparition.

Busie. I neither saw nor heard any thing—but was frighted to that degree—

Myrtilla. 'Tis mighty strange.

Busie. The Candle, I perceived, appear'd more than
80 ordinary blueish, and I was almost suffocated with Brimstone.

Alison. The very downright Symptoms of a Spirit!—a Spirit as certainly attacks your Nostrils with the Fumes of Sulphur, as a Beau with a Digestion of a Civet.—I think I do smell it,—Yes, yes, I do smell it.

Myrtilla. You seem to be frighten'd.

Alison. Frighten'd! quotha—No, no, Madam,—I have, thanks to Experience, seen Spirits of all Shapes, and all Countries—Why, a *Jerusalem* Spirit is no more like an *English* Spirit than a Hog is like a Rhinoceros.—I have been Witness
90 of all the Devil's Frolicks—Idad, to my certain Knowledge, he makes nothing of unfurnishing a Kitchen to entertain himself with a Country-Dance of Dishes and Platters; many be the times and often, he has rattled my Curtains, and made the Bed shake under me, when I have not had the comfort of a Bedfellow; many a dark Night have I seen the Headless Horse, and have had the Honour to Converse with the Queen of the Fairies. [*Looking towards the Table.*] Hah, hah, Damsel! Cake and a Bottle!—Heighday!—and St. *Agnes*'s Night too!—are you thereabouts, Girl—'Twas a Ghost I perceive of
100 your own raising, my Dear, ha, ha, ha.

Myrtilla. Your contradicting my former Fortune, Madam, drew me in to commit this new piece of Folly.

Alison. Come Honey,—here is his Health,—with all my Heart.

> *The Maiden and the Batchelor,*   [Sings.
>   *Pardie—are simple Elves,*
> *And 'till they grow to Man and Wife,*
>   *Know nothing of themselves.*

> *Then since we're each others by Nature design'd*
>   *Let's unite, and our Knowledge improve;*   110
> *Here's a Health to the Lass that is passively kind,*
>   *And the Youth that is active in Love.*   [Drinks.

—S'heartlikins, Madam, the very Expectation has embellished your Phisiognomy; then what may we not hope from the Possession?—Tell me now, Honey, did not his Appearance make the Blood shoot through your Veins, *and tickle your Heart's Root?*

Myrtilla. The Gentleman, I confess ingenuously, is the most my Aversion of all the whole Sex; and I cannot imagine how the Fellow can have the Impudence to make his Applications 120 so much above his Condition.

Busie. The Gentleman, Madam, may, perhaps, ballance those Defects by some other extraordinary Qualities.

Myrtilla. I tell you, I hate the Fellow mortally—This Impertinence does not become you, Mistress Pert.

Alison. Just the quaint Whim of the whole Sex, by St. *Thomas* of *Kent,*—always to reject the Thing that offers itself, and be ever hankering after and craving for the Thing that is denied them.

Myrtilla. Sure I am destined to Misfortune,—why had I 130 not retired, and never revived this tormenting Fellow in my Imagination?

Alison. Why, what are your Objections now, Chicken: Is he Old, Forsooth?

Myrtilla. No.

Alison. Then have at him, i'faith, my Sweeting.—Youth is a Sauce that will make almost any Husband go down.—Ah *Benedicite!* Youth—Golden Days, and Love in abundance;— the Spring of Life, and *Cupid*'s Harvest!—Here is a Constitution, Madam, that wears like the never-fading 140 Lawrel, that even flourishes in the very Winter of Age.—My Conscience, 'tis very hard that you should not know the true Uses of Youth, 'till 'tis out of your Power to enjoy it.

Myrtilla. Do you believe, Madam, that I must inevitably submit my self to this Fortune?—

Alison. Here are two Husbands you see [*Looking on her Hand.*] marry to rights—make haste and love this same to Death, to make room for the second.—come, come, Child, he is handsome that handsome does, and there is no judging of a
150 Husband without Trial.—We can never know a Horse's Paces by his Shapes.

Myrtilla. But perhaps, my Fancy may have impos'd upon me, and this whole Scene may be all Delusion.

Alison. Try the Trick over again, Madam,—a second view of him I suppose would convince you,—here is in the Inn one of the most expert Cunning-men that ever drew Circle.—ah, he is a most rare Fellow for consulting the Planets.—Lookye, Bird, if you find him of the same Opinion, you must even stick by the Bargain, I think, and marry as soon as you can.
160 *Myrtilla.* I'll follow your Advice, Madam.—in the Morning consult the Doctor, and take proper Measures accordingly—   [*Exeunt* Myrtilla, Busie *and* Alison.

SCENE *The Hall.*

Enter Doggrell, *to him enter* Alison.

Alison. Ha, Ha! old *Crambo,*—the Lady is thine own, Boy, i'faith.

Doggrell. With what Air did she receive the Sonnet, Madam?—Did you mark the Rise and Fall of her Passions at every Pause? for I may without Vanity affirm, that I have a World of the *Tendresse* in my Performances.

Alison. 'Slidikins! She receiv'd it, my Lad, with all the
170 Exstasie that a Criminal receives a Reprieve.—Bless us all, had you but seen her, Man;—why 'twas a perfect Charm.— The very first Couplet made Love twinkle in her Eyes, the next gave her a languishing Air,—but as she read on, she was in a downright Rapture.—as I hope for Indulgence, I never saw a Poet repeat his own Verses with more Admiration than she express'd at every Line.

Doggrell. Did not her Passion, Madam, excite her Curiosity, and draw her in to ask some Questions relating to my Person or Condition?

Alison. Since we have made this Breach in her Heart, my 180
Lad, there is now no fear of gaining the Citadel.—Come,
come, a Woman's Love is not so easily quenched neither—
'Slidikins, the Poet knew our Temper to a Hair, that said—

> *Women's Love is like Wild-fire*
> *The more it burneth the more it doth desire.*

Doggrell. But every little Circumstance adds to a Lover's
Satisfaction;—did she ask no Questions at all, Madam?
Alison. Ah Rogue! didst thou but know all, thou wouldst
envy thy own Sonnet.—As soon as she had read it, she lifted
up her Eyes in Admiration, clapt it close to her precious 190
Lips—and—kiss'd it—thus—[*Kisses him.*] again, and again, as
eagerly, I warrant you.—Harrow and alas, when I was of her
Years, I could love too by the Force of Imagination.
Doggrell. An old Woman's Kisses, to my Taste, are like the
Embraces of a Drunkard.—But did not her Ladyship request
my Name or Character? Or was she only in Love with the
Compliment, without examining into the Author of it?
Alison. Why, she asked at least a hundred Questions in a
Breath, and I told her—ah *Benedicite*, what did I not tell
her?—Ods'my Life, I was almost in Love with my own 200
Description—I said your Shape was of a most curious Turn—
Doggrell. You are mighty obliging, Madam.
Alison. That the Vivacity of your Wit sparkled in your
Eyes.
Doggrell. You were too liberal, Madam, in my
Commendation.
Alison. That your good Nature extended to all Mankind
but the Wits—upon whom, as you are one of the Fraternity,
you was oblig'd to exercise your Spleen.
Doggrell. Most extreamly complaisant, Madam,—a mighty 210
Fine *Encomium*, I vow.—But did not you heighten my
Character, Madam, with an Account of my Family, which,
modestly speaking, is of as great Antiquity as the best Quality
in the Universe.
Alison. 'Slid, I told her every thing. But harkye, young
Madrigal, let us see, I pray you, how do you mean to carry on
your Approaches now.—Come, come, Lad, your Youth with
my Experience will go a great way.

Doggrell. The Quality, Madam, claim just Distance and
220 *decorum*, and a Courtship in Form.—I'll approach her with
Veneration, and lay my Heart at her Feet with the profoundest Submission.

Alison. Wrong, all wrong, Youngster—Why, a Lady will
hold out a regular Courtship, purely upon a Punctilio of
Honour.—S'diggers, one of her Temper, like a Widow, must
be carry'd by Storm.—Never stand upon Decency and
Cringes, Boy, pour a Volley of Love at once upon her
Ladyship at the first Onset—and my Life for the Matter, she
will soon come to Capitulation.

230 *Doggrell.* But her Ladyship, perhaps, from so rash an
Attempt will be apt to conclude, that for want of good Sense,
I was forced in the vulgar way of the World to call in
Impudence to my Assistance.

Alison. Ah Boy! there is not so winning a Card to be play'd
as Assurance.—S'heartlikins, a young Fellow with this
Rhetorick will make a palpable Absurdity pass among the
Females for a current Piece of Wit, will convert ill Manners
into a Jest, and laugh downright Rudeness into a Piece of
Gallantry.

240 *Doggrell.* But, Madam, may I be so happy as to hope for an
Interview, will her Ladyship condescend to afford me the
sweet Melody of her Conversation?—but I fear my natural
Bashfulness, Madam—

Alison. Pish! a fig for Bashfulness, say I.—Raise your
Courage with a Glass of Wine, my Lad,—this secret Hour of
the Night favours you—Lady *Myrtilla* will expect you here
this Instant—Go, Boy, brighten thy Understanding, and
return with Vigour to the Place of Assignation.—

Doggrell. May my Love, Madam, be Ship-wrack'd on the
250 Quicksands of Inconstancy, if I know how to return this
Obligation.

Alison. I vow, Mr. *D'Ogrelle*, you are a wonderful pretty
Gentleman.

Doggrell. You betray your Judgment mightily, Madam,—
ha, ha, ha!

Alison. Courage then, my young Hero,—come, come, my
Presence shall never spoil your Proceedings in your Amour—
I'll leave you together.

Doggrell. I'll retire for a Moment or two, to whet the Edge of my Wit with your Prescription, Madam, just study a few 260 fine things to open the Conference. Madam, your Civilities extend beyond Measure. I am your most obedient, humble Servant. [*Exeunt severally*.

Enter Chaucer *and* Busie.

Chaucer. Well, my pretty Rogue, and what says Lady *Myrtilla?*

Busie. She hates you.

Chaucer. Does she so? Why then, I think, she must even fling her self into Matrimony, like the Ladies that marry for a Jointure, and run the risque of loving.—Well, my little Engineer, you must direct my Approaches, who best know the 270 weakest part of the Fortress.

Busie. She interprets the whole Affair most maliciously, and that which we would have her believe the Will of the Fates, she throws wholly upon the Strength of her Imagination. She distrusts her own Senses, and hath prevailed with her self, that the whole Scene was meer Delusion.

Chaucer. Pox on it, why was I such a Fool as to be in Love? But, Mrs. *Busie*, is she positively resolved against me?

Busie. I thought you were too well acquainted with our Sex to dread a Woman's Resolutions, and especially in Love 280 Affairs.—However, Sir, we are not yet quite Desperate.—My Lady was informed of a Fortune-teller now in the Inn, whom she fully designs to consult in the Morning, and if she can suit his Description to your Person, 'tis my Opinion, you may still be the happy Man.

Chaucer. Say'st thou so, my dear Girl,—then, faith, it shall go hard but I'll be before-hand with her, and make my Appearance once again without the help of Magick.

Busie. I vow, and protest, Sir, my Lady's Love is a meer false Appetite; she seems as if she always had a good Stomach, 290 yet will never fall to, when there is a good Dish set before her.—Make but Doctor *Astrolabe* your Friend, Mr. *Chaucer*, and you may assure your self of my Lady's Compliance.

Chaucer. Well, my Dear, I thank thee for all thy good Offices, and wish thee a good Night. [*Kisses her*.

Busie. Oh, fie, Sir,—I shall rob my Lady—ha, ha, ha, of her Property.

Chaucer. I only stay my Stomach, Child, since Lady
Myrtilla has thought fit to defer the Entertainment—Good
300 Night, my Dear.   [*Exeunt severally.*
        Enter Alison *in a Nun's Habit, she lifts up her Veil, and walks*
                              about the Stage.
    Alison. What is bred in the Bone, I find, will never out of
the Flesh—*Alack, and well-a-day!—that ever Love was Sin.*—Say
I,—Inclination, I perceive, does not only float in youthful
Veins.—A fine World, truly! to banter us out of the Comforts
of Life, and persuade us out of the most pleasing of our
Senses! no, i'fackins, I shall not, at this time of Day, let the
World be Judge of my Constitution, which i'troth has worn
out two Brace and a half of brave jolly Husbands already;—
yet I still dare venture on t'other matrimonial Voyage—But
310 hold, I must now suit my Conversation to the Formality of my
Habit.
                        Enter Doggrell.
    Doggrell. Fair Lady, show your self a generous Conqueror;
and since I am taken Captive by your Charms, and bound in
the Golden Chains of your Beauty, throw me not into the
Dungeon of Disdain, but rather confine me in the pleasing
Mansions of your Bosom; where my Heart will glory in its
Captivity, and despise the less Substantial Joys of Liberty.
    Alison. These fine things might ensnare a Heart disposed to
Love, but you are sensible, Sir, I have already devoted mine
320 to another Service.—You Men of Wit are general Lovers of
the whole Sex, and think to try the Strength of every Lady's
Resolutions at the small Expence of a Sonnet.—Come, Sir,—I
know Poets and Knights Errant can never subsist without a
Mistress—for Love is as well a Spur to Wit as Valour.—
    Doggrell. You are the Center of my Love, Madam, which
like my Poetry is founded on the Basis of Eternity; we are, it
must be acknowledged, Madam, like Knights Errant devoted
to the Service of the Fair, but still, like them, we have but one
Peerless Beauty, one bright Star of Angelical Vertues, where
330 we pay Adoration.—A more alert Behaviour is the only Lure
to make her stoop to my Addresses. [*Aside.*] Let me die,
Madam, if I don't think you a very pretty Creature.
    Alison. Do you so, Sir?
    Doggrell. Come, Madam, let this malicious Cloud no longer

Eclipse the Sun-shine of your Beauty—[*Offers to lift up her Veil.*] Ah those Eyes!

Alison. Desist, I beg you; these Liberties do not become you, Sir.

Doggrell. I vow and protest, Madam, you are most ex-treamly Beautiful—Look ye, Madam,—I quarter as many 340 Coats as any Gentleman whatever: My Estate is by no means despicable; as for my Person, and other intrinsick Merits, I leave them to the Mercy of your Ladyship's Judgment.

Alison. I must confess, I entertain a good Opinion of you, Sir, and think you very deserving.

Doggrell. Your Ladyship does me too much Honour—but what think you, Madam,—could you like me for a Husband?

Alison. A very blunt Question!

Doggrell. But a very sincere one, Madam.

Alison. You railly very severely, Sir. 350

Doggrell. No, I vow and protest, Madam,—by these dear yeilding Lips, I swear, [*Kisses her.*] by your bright Eyes,—that Odorous balmy Breath, and by the Bloom that smiles upon your Cheeks, by those white Teeth, that grace your pretty Mouth, like rows of Oriental Pearl—

Alison. Let me die, if I have ever a one in my Head, but what I am obliged to the Operator for—Ah Imagination!— true is the Proverb i'fackins—All Cats are gray, when Light is away.   [*Aside.*

Doggrell. Nay, by all your Charms, I swear, I'll dedicate 360 my self entire to your Service, will sacrifice my Liberty to Matrimony, and—

Alison. Hold, Sir—make no further Protestations—perform what you have already promised, and no Lady whose Thoughts are bent that way can dislike you for a Husband.

Doggrell. Nay, even my Muse, Madam, shall be subservient to your Commands.—I'll turn my Panegyric into Satyr; and your Resentment shall have the Pleasure to see all those Ladies lampoon'd, that I formerly celebrated.

Alison. We Women, Sir, naturally fly to extreams—but 370 methinks from a Nunnery to a Husband is too great a Transition—but I must beg your Pardon, it grows late.

Doggrell. Will your Ladyship grant me the Honour of your Hand; and shall I be so happy, Madam, as to conduct you to your Apartment?

Alison. I fear you will be rude, Sir; and how shall I, that dare not trust my self abroad in the World, with safety venture a young handsome Gentleman in my Bed-chamber?

Doggrell. You may confide in my Behaviour, Madam, I
380 shall presume to take no Liberties but will be agreeable.

Alison. *Beauty, like Colour, owes it self to Light;*
For Youth and Age boast equal Charms by Night;
And we can still please ev'ry Sense—but Sight. [Aside.

[Exeunt, Doggrell *leading* Alison.

ACT IV. SCENE I.

scene *Doctor* Astrolabe's *Chamber.*

Enter Chaucer *to* Astrolabe.

Astrolabe. I beg, Sir, you would not intrude upon my Studies; I am at present unravelling a great Lady's Nativity; and cannot as yet attend your Questions.

Chaucer. My Affair, Sir, requires Dispatch—lookye, Doctor, here are three broad Peices for you, I suppose these will disentangle you a Moment or two.

Astrolabe. I am willing to oblige as far as lyes in the Circumference of my Power, and especially a Person that appears and speaks so much like a Gentleman as your self—
10 Propose your Question, and if it lyes within the compass of lawful Art.—

Chaucer. My Case, Doctor, is not in the common Road. I do not want to be assured of the Happiness of Life, or the Health of an absent Friend; I neither desire to have a Thief described, nor a Philter for a Mistress:—'Tis true, I have lost a Heart, but the Marks of the dear Thief are too strongly imprinted on it already.

Astrolabe. I perceive, Sir, that the Design of your Visit is purely to vilifie the Science, and to cast Aspersions on the
20 honourable Professors.

Chaucer. You mistake me,—lookye, Sir, to make you a true Judge of my Affair, I ought to acquaint you, that I am in

Love with a Lady that is extreamly Superstitious, who having heard of your Fame, designs to consult you this Morning in relation to her Marriage.—Now, that we may play the surest Card, I shall only desire the Favour of your Habit, and the conveniency of your Apartment, to treat with her in my own Person.

Astrolabe. This would be mere prostituting the Science.— But to show you, Sir, that my Function does not straiten my 30 Civilities, upon Promise of Secrecy, I shall comply with your Demands.

Chaucer. You may safely repose in me, Sir, [*Gives him Gold.*] I shall not disparage the Science, I have all the twelve Signs by Heart; my Memory is pretty well stocked with Terms of Art, and I can talk unintelligibly.

Astrolabe. You are pleas'd to make free with the Profession, Sir,—This, Sir, is my Hieroglyphical Cap, [*Puts his Cap on* Chaucer's *Head.*] and this, Sir, is the Mystical Wand—[*Gives* Chaucer *his Wand.*] under Covert of these Necromantical 40 Vestments, you may approach the Fair without the least Danger of a Discovery.   [Chaucer *puts on* Astrolabe's *Habit.*

Chaucer. But Pox on't, though, Doctor, methinks I look a little too young for a Conjurer; a Beard and a Pair of Whiskers would undoubtedly give a good magical Air to my Countenance, and add a kind of awful Solemnity to my Pronunciation.—Come, prithee Doctor, you cannot sure be without such a Convenience.

Astrolabe. Why, Sir, that's true, Sir—look ye, Sir—you have given me your Honour to act with me like a Gentleman; 50 and rather than you shall be at a Loss for so necessary an Ornament, I will divest my own Chin of its Longævity. [*Takes off his Beard.*] I am a young Fellow you see, Sir, that have made use of my Fortune, and run my self Head and Ears in Debt: I was forced to take up this Way of Livelihood, to endeavour to retrieve my Condition, and skreen my self from the Bailiffs. If I can serve you in any other Respect, you may command me, but for the present give me leave to attend you in this Masquerade, as your Servant; perhaps I may be necessary.   60

Chaucer. So much Frankness and good Nature surprizes me.

Astrolabe. I consider'd that judicial Astrology, as the World

goes, was at best but an Amusement, and set up at a small
Expence—that there was nothing requisite to give it Credit;
but a solemn unintelligible *Jargon*, and an awful Appearance.

Chaucer. Appearance, Sir, bears away the Bell, almost in
every thing—What composes a fine Gentleman? but Dress.—
A Scholar is owing to superficial Terms; the Lawyer amuses
you with a Medley of Law-Terms and a Face of Importance—
70 and if you go to the precise Teacher, 'tis ten to one you will
find all his Religion lye in his Cloak and Band.

Astrolabe. To your Post, Sir; the Lady appears.

Enter Myrtilla *and* Busie.

Myrtilla. Is your Name Doctor *Astrolabe*, Sir?

Chaucer. Yes, Madam, my Name is—Doc-tor *As-tro-labe.*—
Ger-ma-ny has the Honour of my Birth, and *Scorpio* was
Ascendant at my Nativity.—I am, Madam,—not only the
seventh Son, but the Son of the seventh Son.—The occult
Sciences have been my Study from the Cradle;—I have, my
Lady,—by the Way, you see I can give you a Sketch of my
80 Proficiency,—and show you that I am not unacquainted with
your Quality.

Busie. As I live, the Doctor is in the right of it.

Myrtilla. Pray, cease your Impertinence, and be silent.

Chaucer. I have, as I was saying, made practicable, and by
great Labour and Application, brought to Perfection the
Green and Hermetical Dragon;—'Twas owing to my in-
defatigable Searches, that the Female Fern-Seed was brought
to light.—And if I can rely on some of the most plain
Phænomena's of Art, the Philosophers Stone will not lye long
90 undiscover'd.—My Head, Madam, is a meer *Microcosm,*—or,
if you please, like the Concave of the Heavens, lined with
Planets, and powder'd with the Constellations.—Perhaps,
before I fall directly on the Matter in hand, it will not be
unnecessary to acquaint you with some of the Sciences that
lye within the Circle of my Profession. *Astrology, Astronomy,*
Physick, Metaphysicks, Palmistry, Chiromancy, Physiognomy, Botany,
Opticks, Catopticks, Diopticks, Necromancy, Divination, and
Algebra.—with several others, which at this time would be too
tedious to recount.—Your Business, Madam, is inscrib'd in
100 your Fore-head; and the Fates decree you Happiness.—

though I must acquaint you, you seem to embrace it with Reluctance.

Myrtilla. I suppose, Doctor, since you say you are acquainted with my Quality,—you are not a Stranger to my Name.

Chaucer. Your Name, Madam,—if my Art fails me not,— Let me see—begins—ay—its first Letter is an—M—and a Y seems to me to be the following Vowel,—if you will have me proceed, I will go quite through all the three Syllables of it.

Busie. Myr-till-a [*Spelling.*] just three Syllables, and no 110 more,—that is certain.

Myrtilla. Let not your Tongue, I charge you, blab thus out of Season. [*To* Busie.] But Doctor, my Business, I pray you?

Chaucer. Your Business, Madam,—as the Celestial Globe informs me,—lyes in *Gemini*,—that is to say, the House of Marriage.

Myrtilla. It may be so, Sir—Then I am marry'd, I presume, Doctor.—

Chaucer. No, Madam.—Nor would be so, if your own Inclinations took place.—The Gentleman, that at this time 120 seems your Aversion—will—make you happy.

Busie. Nay, now 'tis a plain Case.

Myrtilla. Will you never have done your tittle-tattle? [*To* Busie.] Has the Gentleman, I pray, Doctor, that promises so much Happiness ever made his Applications to me?

Chaucer. You beheld him,—even with your own Eyes,—last Night at an unseasonable Hour,—and it will not be long— many Hours, I mean, 'till he honours himself with another Visit.—Credit my Prognostications,—and use him respectfully,—Hate, I find, is not his Portion—Love in the 130 End will turn the Ballance.

Enter Alison.

Astrolabe. Pray Woman, don't be so troublesome,—I tell you, the Doctor is engag'd.—and cannot attend your Business at present.

Alison. O'my Conscience, great Folks keep a Cargo of impertinent Servants about them, to defend them from Visitants.—if ones Business leads one to dance Attendance after Quality, our Message, forsooth, must be deliver'd at the Door-Passage, and there, like a Watch Word through a

140 Camp, it must flye through at least half a Dozen Skips before it can reach my Lord's Ears—and now, forsooth, the World is come to a fine pass truly, that we must make Application to the Conjurer's Imp, in our way to the Conjurer.

Chaucer. Let the Woman have her way—

Alison. Why, how now, Doctor?—do not you remember your old Acquaintance?—harrow and alas!—I believe, I am mistaken,—you are none of Doctor *Astrolabe*, I perceive.

Chaucer. Yes, Madam, I am Doctor *Astrolabe*—the *Camelion*, throughout all his Colours, still retains the Name of a 150 *Camelion*, and so am I my self, Madam, the same, throughout all my Metamorphoses—we always, Madam, suit our Shape to the Nature of the Study we are intent upon.

Alison. Oh, I crave your Mercy, good Doctor.—Well Madam, has the Doctor satisfy'd our Curiosity?

Chaucer. That your Ladyship may be ascertain'd that I do not deal in Uncertainties, I can give you Ocular Demonstration of my Infallibility.—The Looking-glass you see there, is my Necromantic Mirror,—wherein I represent Past, Present, and to Come.—A Thief starts up in it in the 160 twinkling of an Eye;—and a Lady may here behold her Lover's Picture without being obliged to the Painter—What say you, Madam, would you command my Art to this further Operation?

Alison. 'Sdiggers, a pretty Question for a Conjurer indeed!—raise him in your Glass, Doctor, as soon as you please, I'll warrant you, she will be beforehand with you in her Imagination.

Myrtilla. I presume, Sir, there is no Danger in the Operation.

170 *Chaucer.* None—not in the least, Madam.—I must request the Absence of those Ladies.—The Affair only relates to you, Madam.

Alison. Nay,—prithee Doctor.

Chaucer. Lookye, Ladies, we can upon no Account run counter to the Established Method of Art.

Alison. I'dad, I perceive that Conjurers, as well as Physicians and Confessors, love to have the Ladies under private Examination.—Good Luck attend you, my Dear.

Busie. May every thing succeed according to your

Ladyship's Wishes. [*Exeunt* Alison *and* Busie. 180

Chaucer. Situate your self, my Lady, exactly in this Point of View,—in the Centre of the Circle that I now describe—nor once presume to turn your Head either to the Right or Left.— I am afraid I shall have a difficult Task to keep a pretty Lady from giving her self Airs, when there is a Looking-glass in view.—Be cautious, and fear nothing.

Thrice I wave my Wand around,
And Consecrate this Spot of Ground.
Zutphin, and Zephin,—ye that Reign
Far beyond the Northern Main.
Quickly, quickly take your Flight,
And leave the dark Abyss of Night;
Hither, hither, gently fly,
Ye milder Spirits of the Sky,
Let now my Science be your Care,
And bring her Lover to the Fair.

He puts off the Conjurer's Cap and Beard, and puts on his Hat, &c. and peeps over her Shoulder, as 190 she looks in the Glass.

Myrtilla. Hah!
Chaucer. Hold, hold, Madam,—stand firm, guard your Footsteps, and let the Center be still covered with the soles of Female Feet. 200

Swiftly, swiftly haste away,
And my inverted Wand obey:
Let no hurly-burly rise;
Nor Storms the Face of Heav'n disguise;
Let the Winds in silence lye,
Nor dreadful Lightnings streak the Sky;
Let Thunder sleep, and Calmness reign,
In Fire, in Air, in Earth, and Main,
Lightly skim the tops of Mountains,
Nor blast the Corn, nor taint the Fountains,
Swiftly, swiftly haste away,
And my inverted Wand obey.

He puts on his Disguise again.

210

The Charm is finished,—Well, Madam, has my Art convinced your Incredulity?
Myrtilla. Is Matrimony then to be inflicted on me as a Penance, and am I unfortunate by Necessity?
Chaucer. Believe me, Madam, so many Hours as you defend

your self from Marriage, so many happy ones you strike out of the Register of Life.—Your Love, I foresee, as in common
220 Cases, is not to be trifled away in a tedious Courtship; but is reserved, as an inexhaustible Treasure, to sweeten the Matrimonial Condition.

Myrtilla. The Gentleman, I must confess, has a World of valuable Qualifications; and since, I find I must—I shall endeavour, in his next Application, to treat him with more Humanity.

Chaucer. Your Resolution, I assure you, is founded on Prudence, and establish'd on Wisdom: Cherish the first Motives of his Love, and lay hold on *Hymen*'s kind
230 Invitation.—The Gentleman I pronounce very deserving:— His Heart, I foresee, is the Seat of Constancy, and his Love is as lasting as honourable.

Myrtilla. Well, Sir, I believe I shall show that I entertain a good Opinion of the Doctor, by submitting my self to his Pre-scriptions.   [*Exit* Myrtilla.

Astrolabe. Well, Sir, they are at last all very fairly dismissed.—Your Adventure, Sir, is accompanied with the utmost of my good Wishes.

Chaucer. I am at a loss to make you Returns for so much
240 good Nature—for this Fee, Sir, you are obliged to the Lady's Superstition, [*Gives him what he had before received of* Myrtilla.] and I hope my Success will soon put it in my Power, some way or other, to retrieve your Fortune.   [*Exeunt.*

SCENE The Hall.

Enter Franklyn, Doggrell, and Doublechin.

Franklyn. Why, *Frank*, Man, I thought a Person of thy reading had known, that a young giddy Girl will make a World of Doubles, to lead her Lover into a Fault.—An inconsiderate Gipsy!—What, throw Dirt upon her Ancestors!

Doggrell. Do not, Sir, without further Evidence, entertain the Suggestions of your Jealousie, nor censure the Lady of an
250 Indiscretion which had its Birth in your own Fancy.

Franklyn. Give me leave to tell you, *Frank*, I know,—and you shall receive immediate Satisfaction from her own Recantation.

Doggrell. An Affair requires my Attendance for a Moment or two.—I must beg your Pardon, Gentlemen.

[*Exit* Doggrell.

Doublechin. Oh Sleep, Sleep!—The Chamberlain thought fit last Night to conduct me over the Stable; and what, with the noise of the Horses, and the Carriers bawling Conversation, I was forced, very much against the Grain, to employ the whole Night in Meditation. 260

Franklyn. Poor Father, I pity you.—But let us see you now deny your self a Nap by way of Mortification. Watching is enough to founder your Devotion, that is certain; for Eating, Drinking, and Sleeping, are the three main Props of the Order.—But lookye Father, d'ye see, the Case stands thus now;—my Daughter *Florry* does not lay *Frank*'s Love to Heart, so much as she should do.

Doublechin. Ay, it may be so. [*Nodding.*

Franklyn. Nay, but Father, let us give Nature a fillip with t'other Toast and Sack—Hah, hah, Old *Dominic*,—what say 270 you, Father, would not a Bottle, or a Female Confession, draw your Attention now?—Now you must know, I came to this Conclusion—

Doublechin. Very good.— [*Nodding.*

Franklyn. To this Conclusion—I say. [*Bawls in his Ear.*

Doublechin. Yes, yes, Sir, I understand the Conclusion, Sir.

Franklyn. Now has his Reverential Drowsiness dreamt over all my Thoughts, and waked just at the Conclusion of them— See Hoy there. [*Hollows.*

Doublechin. Well Sir, well Sir,—I hear you—you may go 280 on.

Franklyn. My *Florry*, as I was saying, not setting a true Value on *Frank*'s Love, has rais'd this Scandal on her great Grandfather of her own Invention, purely to disgust *Frank* in his Proceedings.

Doublechin. To disgust *Frank* in his Proceedings.—Right, you say well, I hear you well enough,—proceed Sir.

Franklyn. Now granting this, Sir,—though we allow the Fellow stole her last Night, we may with good Reason conclude she was an Accomplice in the Theft. 290

Doublechin. Yes, an Accomplice in the Theft.—I mind you Sir,—well, and what then?

Franklyn. Now, what would you advise me to do in this Case?—Why, lookye, Sir, I have considered, that while the Ceremony of Matrimony is in Agitation, the Man and Wife must of Necessity be of one Mind. Now, I would have you go preach up Obedience to my Daughter; whilst I new moddel *Frank* for a Husband: and just as we have drawn them both in for their Consent, you shall Nick them slabdash with the

300 Ceremony.

Doublechin. Slabdash with the ceremony—Yes, Sir,—very well,—then I am it seems to exhort her to Filial Duty.

Franklyn. Right, Father—That was spoken now like a Man with both Eyes open.

Doublechin. You may rely on my pious Endeavours, Sir.

Franklyn. This Key, Father, is the only Security I have of her Duty—and this—putting Confidence in the Strength of your Virtue,—I deliver into your Possession.

[*Exeunt severally.*

Enter Myrtilla *and* Busie.

Myrtilla. The Doctor's Mirror has made so strange an

310 Impression on me, that I cannot so much as endeavour to remove the Fellow from my Thoughts:—I, this time, discovered something so mightily agreeable in him as struck me insensibly.—I vow, *Busie*, my Temper of a sudden is most unaccountably changed;—Dress again begins to be my Care, and the Thoughts of a Convent are grown perfectly distastful—Do these Ribbons, *Busie*, suit my Complexion?

Busie. They are most wonderfully becoming, Madam.

Myrtilla. I begin to be sensible that those young Ladies, who protect their Modesty in a Nunnery, lay themselves

320 extreamly open to Censure, and betray their secret Inclinations. They deny themselves the Conversation of Mankind, just as a young Fellow that is infected with Play shuns a Gaming-House; upon no account, but because they are conscious they cannot resist the Temptation.—Is Mr. *Chaucer*, d'ye hear, *Busie*, returned from his Travels?

Busie. Since I found him not worth your Ladyship's Regard, I never thought him worth my Enquiry.—But I some time since was accidentally informed, that he was expected;— Is Mr. *Chaucer* then the happy Man at last, Madam, to whom

330 we are obliged for this Deliverance?

Myrtilla. The Doctor just now promised that He would make his Addresses in Person;—and if this third Circumstance should agree with the last Night's and this Morning's Experiment, I fear my Resolutions would not be strong enough to deny him; I vow, I cannot tell what ails me,—methinks, he grows more and more agreeable insensibly.—Hah!

Enter Chaucer.

Chaucer. Sure I dream still, or has Fortune thrown me at once on all my Hopes?—May I presume, Madam, to give Credit to my Eyes, and call your Name—*Myrtilla.*   [*Sighs.*   340

Myrtilla. You are not mistaken, Mr. *Chaucer.*

Chaucer. Then I must own my self your Ladyship's Convert; and am now convinced that the Presages of Dreams are not to be ridicul'd—I last Night, Madam, had the Honour to see you; nor did my Dreams deny me admission to your Person;—I spoke, I beg'd, I intreated:—You still was silent,—I afterwards aspired to touch your Hand, you hastily snatched it from me.—But then, Madam, the Morning entertained me with a more agreeable Dream;—methought you seemed with a kind Smile to call me to you;—at the   350 charming Voice I awaked in Extasie,—and Morning Dreams, I learnt from your Ladyship's Observation, are most to be rely'd upon.

Myrtilla. I confess, I am mightily surprised to see you at this Juncture—Destiny, I think, seems to throw you in my way in spite of my Inclinations—as you are a Stranger, Sir, you now claim my Civility; and I give you leave to Credit your Morning's Amusement.

Chaucer. 'Tis Love, Madam, that hath bless'd me with this Interview, and I must unload my Heart, and confess my   360 Passion, though I run the risque of your Displeasure.

Myrtilla. Your Passion certainly must be very violent, that could support it self under so long an Absence—As often as a Traveller changes his Climate, he lets out his Heart to a new Mistress; and you must think me a very credulous Creature to perswade my self you have been constant all this time.

Chaucer. Faith, Madam, I don't think that either Sex ought to value themselves much upon that Quality—but for Constancy, as it passes at present, my Heart is a *Non-*

370 *pareille;*—and as well turned for a Husband as any reasonable
Woman can require.

Myrtilla. Now granting I should put such Confidence in
you, Sir,—really, you have surprised me in a mighty good
Humour;—you must know, Sir, the Whim led me to consult a
Fortuneteller this Morning, who has extreamly diverted me.

Chaucer. I am glad to find, Madam, you were so agreeably
entertained.

Myrtilla. The Doctor has laid some Obligations on you, Sir,
and appeared very Zealous in your Interest, I'll assure you:
380 He engaged for your Constancy, promised me Happiness, and
a World of fine Things; if I thought convenient to follow his
Prescriptions—ha, ha, ha.

Chaucer. My Passion, Madam, is too serious an Affair to be
trifled withal—If Delay separates us once again—

Myrtilla. Why—I hope, Sir, you are not about making
another *Tour*.

Chaucer. I don't know, Madam—just as Inclination leads
me;—my Passions, I must confess, are a little predominant;
and if they should command me to *France* or *Italy* again: I am
390 afraid my Good-nature would not be able to deny them—and
then, Madam, I'll warrant, I shall be compared to the Winds
that made me dance over the Waves; I shall be as faithless as
the Sea, and as unmerciful as the Billows—when, in reality,
my Sails were only filled with the Gales of your Ladyship's
Inconstancy.

Myrtilla. Well, Sir,—to deal then ingenuously with you;—I
would advise you to cast Anchor: And if the Winds are lodged
in my Power, you shall wait long enough 'till I oblige you
with a fair Gale.

400 *Chaucer.* And will your Ladyship at last condescend to make
me Happy?

Myrtilla. The Fates, it seems, design it so, Sir; ha, ha, ha.
Enter Doggrell.

Doggrell. Fair Lady, I beg your Pardon—Mr. *Chaucer*, a
Word with you.

Chaucer. Nay, prithee,—you see I am engaged—I hope,
your Civility, Sir, will not break in upon a Lady's private
Conversation.

Doggrell. I presume, the Lady will indulge me for a

Moment, since it is an Affair of Consequence.—Madam, shall
I beg the Honour to deprive Mr. *Chaucer* of a Minute or two of 410
your most agreeable Conversation?

Myrtilla. The Gentleman is at his own Liberty, Sir—A
formal Coxcomb!   [*Aside.*

Chaucer. Some other time, Sir, I will wait on you; an
Opportunity with the Ladies must never be neglected—Sir, I
am your humble Servant—Well—Madam—

Doggrell. The Lady's Good-nature will excuse my
Rudeness, Sir.

Chaucer. Pox on it,—these Fellows stick as close to a Man as
a Cast Mistress; there is no dismissing them without present 420
Satisfaction, [*Aside.*] Well—Sir—

Doggrell. I beg your Pardon, Madam, for this small Breach
of Decorum;—but I will return you Mr. *Chaucer* with all
imaginable Expedition—[*Exit* Myrtilla] You must know,
Sir,—that I last Night ran through the whole Exercise of
Love:—I was captivated, I courted, and won the Fair;—
Oh—the most charming Angel!—then the wittiest Creature,
that ever flirted a Fan! and the most engaging Shape and
Mien!—meer Imagination elevates me into an Ecstasie.

Chaucer. Well, Sir,—and what is all this to me, I pray you? 430

Doggrell. I beg your Pardon, Sir, I meant you no Affront.

Chaucer. To Abridge your Story—I suppose,—you are
married.—

Doggrell. A Secret, I know, Sir, is safely lodg'd in the
Cabinet of your Discretion.—Yes, Sir,—the Lady im-
mediately took fire—and on the Spot treated me like a
Gentleman.—I marry'd her last Night upon Honour; and now
am going to give her Personal Security, and sign the Lease for
Life.

Chaucer. Really, Sir, I am in no respect capable of keeping 440
a Secret of this Nature;—so, Sir, your humble Servant.

Doggrell. Nay, prithee, Mr. *Chaucer*—but I should first of all
have acquainted you that she fell a Victim to my Poetry.—
And now, Sir, to maintain my Conquest, I have levy'd a
Stanza or two to bring down upon her Ladyship, which I
shall beg leave, Sir, to submit to the Candor of your
Judgment.

Chaucer. Some other time, you may command me, Sir.

Doggrell. Now, Sir,—no, Now,—Dear Sir,—I long to have
450 your Sentiments on the Ode.—See, Sir—'tis upon a Fair
Lady's making me happy. [*Gives him a Paper.*] Your reading
the Lines, Sir, will do them a world of Justice.

Chaucer. Reads very carelesly.]

STANZAS, upon a Fair Lady making me Happy.

> *Ye Gods! did Jove e'er taste such Charms,*
> *When prest in fair* Alcmena's *Arms,*
> *O ye Immortal Pow'rs!*
> *For He in all his triple Night,*
> *Did ne'er enjoy such soft Delight,*
> *As I in half a one of yours.*

460 Very fine, Sir—very fine—[*Reading on.*] *Oh Ecstasie! what*—

Doggrell. Hold, hold, Sir,—Mark the Harmony, Sir;—and
the easie Cadence that falls through the whole Stanza.

> *Ye Gods! did* Jove *e'er taste such Charms,*
> *When prest, &c.*

> [*Repeats with Affectation, and beats Time, while*
> Chaucer *appears very uneasie.*

—I defie the *Italian* to run more soft.—See, Sir,—the first Hint
is perfectly Pindarick!—but observe, Sir, as most Poets mount
into Sublimity at the close of a Poem; I leave the common
Road,—and start into the Heavens at the very first flight.—*Ye
Gods!*—now my breaking out into—*O ye immortal Powers*,
470 brings the Scene of Action in view,—and the Poet seems to be
at that instant clasp'd into the Embraces of his charming fair
One—now mind—the easie flowing Softness of the following
Lines,

> *For He in all his triple Night*, &c.

That *triple* is one of the most happy Epithets—*Virgil* himself
might not blush to have been the Author of it.

Chaucer. Such Harmony, Sir, can never fail of chiming the
Lady into a second Trance.—But the Beauties lie so near the
Surface that there is no room for a Critick's Discoveries—So,
480 Sir, your humble Servant.

Doggrell. The next Stanza—I beseech you, Dear Mr.

Chaucer.

Chaucer. But the Incivility to the Lady, Sir—

Doggrell. Will give a Gentleman of your Capacity an Opportunity of exerting his Wit.

Chaucer. In my own Defence then.   [*Aside*.

> *Oh Ecstasie! what Wit can tell,*
> *Those Charms that lie beneath your Veil*
>   *Those Lightnings of your Eye?*
> *No longer then your Beauty shroud,*   490
> *Nor place the Sun behind a Cloud,*
>   *For ah! fair Nun, I faint, I die.*

—A Nun, Sir!

Doggrell. A Secret, Sir, touch'd at one end flies through the whole, like a Train of Gun-powder—You must know then, that there is a Lady of Quality who upon some Disgust with the World, was about sheltering her Virtue in a Nunnery; I made my Addresses to her, and vanquish'd her with as much ease as I write a Couplet;—but least the Lady should take a Whim to recede from her Engagements, I last Night took 500 Possession before the Writings were sign'd.

Chaucer. Last Night, Sir?

Doggrell. Yes, Sir,—She conceal'd her Blushes with her Veil; nor would Consent to make me totally Happy 'till the Consummation.

Chaucer. Her Virgin Modesty, I find, would not permit her to Sin, but under Covert. How happy was this Coxcomb's Presence to frighten me from the Snare—The Muses then hereafter shall still be my Mistress; nor shall one Lady pretend to engross what with good Husbandry will oblige so 510 many.   [*Aside*.

Doggrell. Let me die if he is not repeating my Lines in a perfect Rapture! See how good Poetry strikes a Man of Genius.   [*Aside*.

[*He advances to* Chaucer.] But Mr. *Chaucer*, pray what think you of the last Stanza? That Admiration of her concealed Beauties, shows wonderfully the Vivacity of the Poet's Imagination—Now for my fair Nun, Sir. You will excuse me, Mr. *Chaucer*, since you know the Occasion.—

          Enter Myrtilla.

520 So, Sir, your most obedient humble Servant. Fair Lady, yours
most obediently. [*Exit* Doggrell.

Myrtilla. The Gentleman, Sir, has entertained you with a
mighty long Conference; I am glad you were so well
diverted—Poetry, I presume.

Chaucer. Yes, Madam, the Gentleman has received some
Favours from his Mistress; and his Gratitude, it seems, hath
led him to express himself in Rhime.

Myrtilla. Love naturally flows into Poetry. I admire, Sir,
that your Muse was never so obliging as to throw away a few
530 tender things upon the Lady to whom you are so generous as
to bestow your Heart.

Chaucer. Really, Madam, I never write Elegy; my Muse
does not delight in Sighs and Complaints—nor loves to
bemoan Absence and Inconstancy—Don't you think,
Madam, that Gentleman has a very happy Talent of Writing?

Myrtilla. Both the Gentleman and his Writings are
Strangers to me,—the Fates you see, Sir, have given you
Hopes; and suppose now I should confirm their Decree,
would not your Muse be so Complaisant as to acknowledge
540 the Favour?

Chaucer. Methinks his Lines have a peculiar Softness in
them; so easie, and so tender, that, like the *Syrens*, they at once
charm and betray—they can disarm a Lady's Virtue, and lay
her Modestly asleep, while they keep her inclinations awake.
Stop your Ears, Madam, he is a dangerous Fellow.

Myrtilla. This Caution is useless, Sir, since I am entirely a
Stranger to the Gentleman—but you see, I dare trust my self
in the sound of your Poetry, Sir,—if I should be captivated, I
know you are generous enough to treat your Prisoner with
550 Honour.

Chaucer. Excuse me, Madam, I am not disposed to write at
present.

Myrtilla. Turns from him.] *Busie*, What ails the Fellow to
treat me with so much Indifference? His Love is a meer Ague,
and the cold Fit hath now seized on him—I'll again
endeavour to hate him: And if I am decreed at last to
Sacrifice my self to one whose Love dwindles into that cold
term Civility, I will only involve the latter Scene of my Life in
Matrimonial Penitence. [*Exeunt* Myrtilla *and* Busie.

Chaucer. I lov'd her, I must confess, while I believ'd her 560
Virtuous; but I will exert my Reason, and disdain to make
my self a Husband to skreen a Woman's Frailties from
Censure—Love avaunt, and welcome Liberty.

> *Now Blithe and Debonnaire, I'll relish Life,*
> *Nor sour it with that lasting Evil—Wife:*
> *My Love at random through the Sex shall fly,*
> *And Treach'rous Vows allure them to comply:*
> *I'll artfully each tender Fair subdue,*
> *And, like themselves, for half an hour be true.*

ACT V. SCENE I.

SCENE *the Hall.*

Enter Busie *to* Chaucer.

Busie. O H, dear Mr. *Chaucer*, my Lady is retired in the most
grievous fret—go, go, I am perfectly ashamed of you—You a
Poet! and want Assurance?

Chaucer. Look ye, my Dear, to speak my Sentiments freely:
I would always have Love and Matrimony walk Hand in
Hand; and Lady *Myrtilla* shall have both the Stars and my
leave to dignifie that Gentleman with the Title of Husband,
whom she last Night made happy with her Person.

Busie. Then the Riddle is at last explained—Hath that
Coxcomb's Folly boasted of Favours from my Lady, and was 10
you so easie of belief, to distrust her Honour? His Vanity, Sir,
hath both imposed upon himself and you: For last Night,
missing my Lady's Nuns Habit—I found the Wife of *Bath*'s
laid in its Room—my Curiosity prevail'd with me to search
her Pockets, where I found this Letter, which, I presume, will
satisfie you to whom the Gentleman owed those mighty
Favours.   [*Gives him a Letter.*

Chaucer. His Hand, and Style—I'll swear;—

Busie. O' my Conscience, I fear she will never be reconcil'd
to you,—you was as cold and unmannerly as a morose 20
Husband; and those Symptoms in an humble Servant, Mr.
Chaucer, let me tell you, give a Lady too just Occasion for

Resentment.

Chaucer. Scandal finds an easie Passage to the Heart; and what we fear we very readily believe.

Busie. See what a Dance Jealousie leads a Man—beware of this same Passion in Matrimony, Sir,—for then it will be a plaguy troublesome Companion.

Chaucer. This Mistake then, I perceive, is purely owing to a
30 Gamesome Frolick of the Wife of *Bath*, who hath diverted her self at the Expence of your Lady's Honour—Look ye, my Dear, suppose now I could point you out a convenient Husband,—would the Present be agreeable?

Busie. Really, Sir, I have not Vanity enough to set me out for a Coquet.—Humble Servants now-a-days are not to be trifled withal—and should I neglect a good Offer, I fear the Fate of an old Maid would too late convince me of my Folly.

Chaucer. Well—what think you then, my Dear, of Mr. *Doggrell* your self?—He is a Man of an Estate, which you
40 know, Child, is the best of Sauce for so constant a Dish as Matrimony;—The Wife of *Bath* hath engag'd him to give her Nuptial Security for her last Night's Favour;—he will immediately fly to the Habit—now if that is in your Possession, make but your self the Nun, and you may commence Wife as soon as you please.—The Dark, or a Veil, creates you as good a Lady as any in the Universe.

Busie. Well; it pleases me wonderfully, indeed it does—I'll about it instantly; for I have secured the old Lady from taking t'other Trip in Masquerade;—But now to your Affair, Sir,—
50 go, and throw your self at my Lady's Feet; touch again upon the String of Love, while her Passions are in a Ferment, nor give her present Resentment Time to settle into a fix'd Aversion.—Hold, Sir,—here she comes—I must fly—for I durst not be seen with you.   [*Exit*.

Enter Myrtilla.

Chaucer. I vow, Madam, you treated me barbarously—here I have been ever since in Contemplation of your Beauties— wandring over your Perfections, ransacking the Skies for Metaphors, and culling the Goddesses for Similies;—while you most maliciously withdrew the Original, and left me to
60 finish the Picture purely by the Height of Imagination.

Myrtilla. Oh dear, Mr. *Chaucer*,—do—repeat me the

Verses, and you will oblige me infinitely.

Chaucer. Really, Madam, I have quite forgot them.

Myrtilla. Nay, I long to hear them—the Verses and the Subject are, I suppose, both treated alike,—soon forgotten;— I swear I shall never forgive you, if you will not indulge me in this Particular.

Chaucer. Pox on it, I have brought my self into a fine Dilemma.—have I never a lucky Thought about me?—yes, faith,—this does.   [*Aside.* 70

I.

Daphne, *a coy and foolish Dame*,
    Flew from Apollo's *Charms*,
Had he confess'd in Verse his Flame,
    She had flown into his Arms.

II.

Whenever Orpheus *touch'd the Lyre*,
    Or sung melodious Airs,
He made the very Stones admire,
    And tam'd the fiercest Bears.

III.

Are Ladies Hearts more hard than Stone,
    Are Wolves and Bears less fierce?   80
Then, prithee, Nymph, no longer frown,
    But own the Pow'r of Verse.

Myrtilla. Mighty pretty! wonderful gallant!

Chaucer. Well, Madam, has Poetry soften'd your Passions? And will your Love at last condescend to shake Hands with Destiny?—consider, Madam, 'tis only in your Power to delay it.

Myrtilla. It would be far more generous, I confess, to make my Love a Present;—and methinks I would not wear out your Love in Expectation neither,—you have my Leave, Sir, to 90 continue your Addresses.

Chaucer. Come, Madam, let your Heart accompany your Hand, [*takes her by the Hand.*] and double the Value of the Gift, by putting me in present Possession.

Myrtilla. It would be in vain to be obstinate.

Chaucer. Let *Hymen* then, Madam, join our Hands; let us be complaisant to the Fates for our Fortune, and readily embrace the Happiness the Stars have allotted us.

Myrtilla. You see, Sir, I am not at my own Disposal.

100 *Chaucer.* From this Instant then I date my Happiness.

Myrtilla. If it is decreed, Sir—

Chaucer. Come on then, my charming Fair—

> *Marriage, the chiefest Good that Mortals know,*
> *Doubles our Joy, while it divides our Woe:*
> *What anxious Cares can then our Bliss controul,*
> *When Heav'n assents, and Love unites our Soul?*

SCENE Florinda's *Apartment.*

Enter Doublechin *to* Florinda.

Doublechin. I come, by your Father's Orders, to inculcate—into you—the Doctrine of Obedience—Watching and Cares,—and Sack, will most certainly wear out this 110 Constitution of mine.—Sleep—perhaps, Madam,—may weaken the Force of my Arguments—but—though, Madam,—I am a little drowsie in showing you your Duty—I hope, you will be vigilant in performing it—Mr. *Doggrell,* Madam,—has most excellent Capacities—for an Husband;—and I do not in the least Question—but you have as excellent Capacities for a Wife.

Florinda. Well, Sir,—my Father's Pleasure, pray?

Doublechin. In brief—Madam,—to be as short as possible—[*Nods.*]—not to trouble you with Circumlocutions.—[*Nods.*] 120 but fall directly on the Matter in Hand—I vow, Madam,—Drowsiness has almost broke the Thread of my Story—pray, Madam,—what is your Will and Pleasure, I beseech you?

Florinda. To be inform'd of my Father's Commands, Sir.

Doublechin. Your Father, out of his great Wisdom, and worldly Policy,—has thought fit to make choice of Mr. *Doggrell* for your Husband:—And you have, it seems,—endeavoured to cool the Heat of the Gentleman's Passion,—by throwing Scandal upon your Ancestors—we allow—you—Madam, to Sacrifice as many living Reputations as you think

fit—but Calumny on the Dead, methinks does not lye within 130
the Province of Female Conversation.

Florinda. Come, Father, enliven your Understanding a
little—Come, Sir, here is Mr. *Doggrell's* Health, and to the
glorious and unspotted Memory of my Ancestors, [*Drinks.*]
your Judgment must tell you, Sir, that Love is an Appetite
that will not be regulated by another's Palate—you that have
been so long conversant with Female Confessions, cannot be
ignorant of the frequent Combats of Love and filial Duty.—
But you will pledge me, Sir.   [Doublechin *drinks.*

Doublechin. Sleep will not give me leave to behold your 140
Eloquence in its utmost Perfection—the Beauty of the Speaker
gives a wonderful Grace to Elocution—and those pretty Lips
of yours, Child, must have a mighty persuasive Faculty.

Florinda. Come, Father, sprightly Liquor, sprightly
Reason—What, refuse to pledge a Woman?—See how it
smiles upon you, Sir.

Doublechin. It must be very hard with a Man, when neither
Sack nor a pretty Lady can keep him awake—but Sleep,
Madam, is very often an unmannerly and unsociable
Companion to the Ladies; but now, Madam—I have three 150
Arguments to convince you of the Duty of filial Obedience—
and the first is this—   [*Drinks.*

Florinda. Right Sir,—I agree with you,—the whole Stress of
the Argument, I plainly perceive, lyes in the Words *Filial* and
Obedience—but your Glass, Father—come, Sir,—will you not
give me leave to pledge you!—   [Doublechin *drinks.*

Doublechin. Methinks, Madam,—the Glass has a very quick
Circulation—But now, Madam, the second Thing I shall urge
is—that a Daughter being not a Free Agent—

Florinda. Not a free Agent!—How, Father,—what, compli- 160
ment the Sex with Slavery?—marry a Woman to her
Aversion, and give her a Mortification for Life?—Our
Fortunes are very often bestow'd on us, with too severe
Conditions—Can a Father convert a sottish morose Husband
into an obliging well-bred Companion? Can he put a Churle
in good Humour, or make a Brute in love with Honour, and
Virtue? Can a Father unite separate Beds, and dissuade a
loose base Fellow from a Mistress?

Doublechin. Right, Madam—right [*Nods.*] But methinks,

170 Madam, you are a little in the wrong too—for—Womens Arguments are generally superficial—and we often assent out of Complaisance—I protest, Madam, the Vows of our Order begin to sit a little uneasie on me—Give me a Kiss,—and wake me, my Dear—

Florinda. I would not, for the World, have my Beauty be accessary to the mis-leading Ecclesiastical Chastity—Fie, Father, fie! I am concerned for you; practise Mortification.— See here Father,—What, give Love the Preference to Wine?—Come, Sir, let my Health give new Spirit to the 180 Liquor.—

Doublechin. I would not have you though, Madam, mis-construe this Behaviour of mine, neither.—I am not fudled, Madam, [*Drinks.*] I must beg your Pardon a Moment or two,—the Musick of your Voice, I swear, Madam hath quite charmed my Senses into a Lethargy—When you find my Argumentative Faculty grow upon me, do you see—pray be so kind as to wake me.   [*Sleeps.*

Florinda. The Wings of Love shall soon bear me to my charming *Merit.*—Just out of one Cage into another;—but in 190 Matrimony we are like Turtles, and make Confinement pleasant with an agreeable Companion;—Sound a-sleep! Come, Father, deliver up your Charge— [*Takes the Key out of his Hand.*] Oh, Sir—your most humble Servant—but stay,—a Disguise would secure my Escape, and therefore I must request Sir, you would oblige me with your Habit. [*Gently pulls off his Habit.*] Oh, dear Sir, most wonderful complaisant!—Come, my Hood shall defend your bald Pate from the Inclemencies of the Air. [*Puts her Hood on his Head.*] And

200   *Love like an Apparition's unconfin'd,*
    And scorns a Leading-String though young and blind;
    Woman by Nature all Restraint disdains;
    And she that wears will chuse the Nuptial Chains.   [*Exit.*

SCENE *Changes to the Hall.*

Enter Doggrell *meeting* Alison.

v. 195 me] we *13*

Alison. Ha, ha, Stripling! The Rogue's Dimples there betray his Success.—With what Air did she receive you?—Did not you observe Love flush into her Cheeks, and peep through her pretty sparkling Eyes?—Did she sigh out never a Scrap of thy Poetry? No Squeeze by the Hand, or a gentle Tap with her Fan?—i'dad I knew she would fall a Sacrifice to the Muses.   210

Doggrell. Ah, Madam,—the most lovely of her Sex! kind, tender and obliging!—to find her pretty Lips the very Fountain of Wit, threw me in a perfect Extasie;—Harmony dwells in her Voice, and *Zephyrs* wanton in her Breath;—*Venus* sits in her Features, and her Mein confesses a *Juno*—Oh Raptures and Paradise!

Alison. Was you thereabouts, my Man of Might,—'twas I advis'd you, my Lad, to bask it in the Sun-shine of her Eyes—did not I tell you, that the Lips were the readiest Way to the Heart?—a rare Pupil i'fackins!—Her Breath sweet as balmy   220
Zephyrs! 'Slidikins,—I begin to think my self young again—[*Aside.*] Well, but did you carrry your Point?

Doggrell. Ah, Madam, infinitely beyond Expectation—She was immediately captivated with my Person, in Love with my Family, and, as I live, downright enamour'd with my Poetry.

Alison. Well perform'd, i'faith.

Doggrell. Her Love, Madam,—I am convinced,—is more sincere than the Turtle's,—more Pathetick and transporting than the Sparrows—and as immutable—as my own.

Alison. But Heark'ye now, you ought to pursue the   230
Conquest,—S'diggers, I just now left her, and she sends this Message to you; that nothing but a small Indisposition should have hindred this Morning's Assignation: That half an Hour hence, she will make the Garden the Scene of Love.—Here is a smart Girl for you—true as Steel, and as taking as Tinder;—ah Boy, 'tis my very Life and Soul to be the Harbinger of *Cupid.*—the Garden,—Ah, my dear Chicken, mind the Garden,—then consummate your Vows, and sign the Contract;—and call *Hymen* to witness the Bond—Women may change, and 'tis good to have Security in these Cases.   240

Doggrell. Ah, Madam; Security!—I have all the Security of a Husband.—Her Hand, her Heart, nay all her charming

242 Heart,] ～＾ *13*

Person. I started, Madam, with Vigour into the Race, and reached the Goal of Love the first Heat.—Methinks, I have flown into *Elysium* in a Dream,—ah, *Myrtilla*, lovely *Myrtilla*!—no more shall fleeting Fancy raise her Shadow, nor grasp a Cloud for a Celestial Queen.

Alison. The Garden, ah, Rogue the Garden!—the Garden is a most inviting Place: 'S'diggers, I never think of a Garden,
250 but presently some of my youthful Excursions pop into my Memory.—Ods'my Life, why a Damsel hath not the Heart to say you a Negative *No*, in an Arbour, Man.—Don't you remember the old Song, Boy?

Doggrell. No, I protest.—Pray, Madam, will you oblige me with it.

I.

Alison. *There was a Swain full fair,*   [Sings.
        Was tripping it over the Grass,
    And there he spy'd with her Nut-brown Hair,
      A Pretty tight Country Lass.
260   *Fair Damsel, says he,*
          With an Air brisk and free,
      Come let us each other know;
        She blush'd in his Face,
        And reply'd with a Grace,
    Pray forbear, Sir,—no, no, no, no.

II.

      The Lad being bolder grown,
      Endeavour'd to steal a Kiss,
    She cry'd, Pish!—let me alone,
      But held up her Nose for the Bliss.
270   *And when he begun,*
          She would never have done,

---

256 *was a*] *was an an* S MM H   257 *tripping it*] *triping itt* S   257 *Grass,*] ~ ;
MM   258 *And*] *&* S   258 *spy'd*] ~ , *MM* H   258 *Nut-brown*] *Nutbrown* S
259 *Lass.*] ~ , S; ~ : H   260 *Damsel*] *damsell* S   260 *says*] *said* H   261
With] *w^th* S   261 *Air*] *aire* S   261 *and free,*] *MM* H; ~ ^ 13; *& free,* S   262
Come] ~ , *MM*   262 *let*] *lett* S   262 *know;*] ~ , S; ~ : MM H   264 *And*] *&* S
265 *Sir,*] S^r S; ~ ; *MM* H   266 *Lad*] *lad,* H   267 *Kiss,*] *kiss;* H   268
cry'd Pish!] *cryd Pish* S; ~ ^ *MM* H   268 *alone,*] *a lone,* S; ~ ; *MM*; ~ ! H   269
Bliss.] *bliss,* S; ~ : *MM*; *bliss;* H   271 *would*] *wou'd* S MM H

But unto his Lips she did grow,
Near smother'd to Death,
As soon as she'ad Breath,
She stammer'd out, no, no, no, no.

III.

Come, come, says he, pretty Maid,
Let's walk to yon' private Grove,
Cupid always delights in the cooling Shade,
There I'll read thee a Lesson of Love.
She mends her Pace,   280
And hastes to the Place,
But if her Love Lecture you'd know;
Let a bashful young Muse,
Plead the Maiden's Excuse,
And answer you,—no, no, no, no.

Doggrell. Wonderfully entertaining I vow—but her Ladyship's *No* would stand her in no stead at present.—May I confide in you, Madam?—For my Marriage is as yet a Secret to Mankind.

Alison. Marriage?—Why, sure 'tis not come to that pass 290 already.

Doggrell. We last Night, Madam, mutually exchang'd our Vows.—And this Morning I met her, by Assignation; lovely as *Aurora*, led her to the Priest; and have by his solemn Assistance chang'd the beautiful Nun into a Bride.

Alison. S'diggers!—but you are not in Earnest, I hope.

Doggrell. Yes, Madam; 'tis unquestionably true.—The Lady *Myrtilla*, is now, at this present Instant, the lawful Wife of *Francis D'ogrelle*, Esq;—and I flatter my self that her Interest at Court will soon be able to Honour her Husband 300 with a Title suitable to the Dignity of his Ancestry.

272 *grow*,] ~ ; *MM*; ~ : *H*   274 *As soon*] *Assoon S MM H*   274 *she'ad*] *she'd MM*   275 *out, no, no, no, no*] *out no no no no S*; *out No, no, no, no MM*; *out, No, no, no, no H*   276 *Come, come, says he*,] *Come come says he S*   277 *Let's*] *Lett's S* 277 *yon'*] ~~*S MM H*   277 *Grove*,] ~ ; *MM*   278 *always*] *allways S*   278 *the*] *y^t S*   278 *Shade*,] *S MM H*; ~~ *13*   279 *There*] *S MM H*; ~, *13*   279 *Love.*] ~, *S*; ~ : *MM*; *love*; *H*   281 *hastes*] *hast S*   281 *Place*,] ~ : *MM H* 282 *Love Lecture*] *Lecture S MM H*   282 *know*;] ~, *S MM H*   283 *bashful*] *bashfull S* 284 *Maiden's*] *maidens S*   285 *you,—no, no, no, no*] *you no no no no S*; *you No, no, no, no MM*; *you, No, no, no, no H*

Alison. Then, it seems,—I have been playing a pretty Game all this while.—To let a young forward Baggage here make me her Bait to fish for a Husband!—'twas a little Unchristian-like too, methinks, to take the advantage of an old Woman.—But Slidikins,—when there is a handsom young Fellow in the Case,—Self is the Word, and we spare neither Friend nor Foe.   [*Aside.*

Doggrell. The good Offices, Madam, that you have done 310 me in my late Matrimonial Negotiations make me Request that you would honour my Nuptials with your entertaining Company.—But hold, here comes my Guardian.—Be secret, I beseech you, Madam, and let us not forestall the Jest.—Now will he nauseate my Taste with the Smell of the Kitchin, after I have supt upon Quality.

Enter Franklyn.

Franklyn. The Girl is a Wag, *Frank*—a meer Wag; and invented the Story purely to exercise thy Love.—Come, come, marry her, Boy, and make haste and get Sons and Daughters.—She looks like a rare Breeder, *Frank*.

320   *Alison.* Gad a-mercy, my bonny *Franklyn*.—Give me thy Hand, old Chronicle: The Rogue has got the very Air of an old Sinner. Ah Shaver, we were merry Grigs in times past, by my fay.

Franklyn. Let us mind my Daughter first of all—young Folks Appetites are keen. You are ready I see, *Frank*,—my Daughter shall make her Entrance presently,—and then—*Frank*.

Doggrell. Now dare not I make a Discovery of my Marriage, 'till my Lady be present to support me against this 330 old Rogue's Insolence.   [*Aside.*

Franklyn. Methinks tho',—Father *Doublechin* is a little tedious in his Conferences.—*Florinda, Florinda.*—What a Vengeance, does no Body answer there?

Alison. S'heartlikins,—We shall have rare Work upon the Anvil by and by.   [*Aside.*

Franklyn. Florry—Florinda, why, how now? What is here to be done? No body within there? [*Listens.*] Nothing stirring?

Alison. Then, by my Troth,—there is no Danger of your Daughter, old *Nicodemus.*

340   *Franklyn.* But I do not like these silent Sort of Matrimonial

Disputes—What, a plague on you all,—if you don't open the Door immediately—I'll rattle it down about your Ears.

                            [*He bounces at the Door.*

Enter Doublechin *with a Hood on his Head; gaping, as just come from Sleep.*

Doublechin. Yaw, yaw.   [*Gapes.*

Franklyn. Why heigh-day—What is—yaw—the meaning of all this? Pox, where is my Daughter?—   [*Runs into the Room.*

Doggrell. Father *Doublechin* found it convenient to indulge himself with the Sweets of Repose, after the Fatigue of instructing a young Lady, that is all,—ha, ha, ha.

                    Re-enter Franklyn.

Franklyn. Why, Plague, Thunder and Combustion! Where is my Daughter, I say?—Look'ye Father,—none of your Jokes 350 I beseech you.

Doggrell. As a Trophy of his Conquest,—do you see, Sir?— He has adorn'd his Head with some of your Daughter's Favours, ha, ha, ha.

Alison. But hark you,—Old *Jereboam*; never give Way to Passion, Man.—S'bud;—Was the Girl my Concern—he should give an Account of his private Behaviour.—Bring them Face to Face, and s'buddikins, if Guilt should chance to flash in my Damsel's Countenance,—I would do no better nor no worse, but immediately qualifie his Reverence for a 360 Chaunter—i'fackins, I would—

Franklyn. Where is my Girl? My Girl, I say.

Doggrell. Nay, now, Sir—you discompose your self; be calm, I beg you.

Franklyn. Why, heigh day.—What, is the Fellow dumb?— Speak, or by *Hercules*—this Cane shall presently find you a Tongue, Sirrah.   [*Strikes* Doublechin.

Doggrell. Let me die—this is palpable Incivility.—I beseech you, Sir, keep your Passion within the Bounds of *Decorum.*
                                  370

Doublechin. Why Sir, why Sir,—One need be an *Argus* to keep Guard on a Woman.—Now, you must know, Sir, after I had—reason'd her into Reason—I, I,—

Franklyn. Well, and what then?

Doublechin. Why I fell asleep—yaw—and then, Sir—

Franklyn. What then, Sir—What then, Sir?

Doublechin. By my Order, I know nothing further.—I was, after that, all in the Dark.

Franklyn. By *Jove*, this is all a Contrivance; a
380 Combination,—Furies! I am trick'd, [*Runs stamping about the Stage, and beats them all.*] Why, what in the Name of Thunder,—you are all Rogues alike.—Confounded Rogues, treacherous pilfering Rogues.

Doggrell. Oh dear Sir,—'tis only your Age, old Fellow, that protects you in these Liberties.

Franklyn. Why, Sirrah, if nothing else touches you, Decency, Rascal; Decency should teach you, like the Widow, to shed a Tear or two.—And you, there, Doctor Paunch, what Sleep upon Duty, and wink at my Daughter's Escape?

[Franklyn *walks about talking to himself.*
390 *Alison*. Look in my Face, old Touchwood.

Franklyn. Well, and what then?

Alison. Have not I a bonny Complexion, my Heart of Oak? dost thou not trace the Remains of Beauty through every Feature?—Look again, Man,—view me all over, old Boy—Slidikins, my Face is like an ancient Medal—Antiquity does but add to its Value;—What say you, my Lad, are you for t'other Bout of Matrimony, t'other trip to the Temple of *Hymen?* Hang Sorrow,—what you have lost in a Daughter, Man, make up in a Wife.

400 *Franklyn*. 'Sbuddikins, I'll alarm all the Country but I'll get Intelligence of my Girl—for who knows but this covetous Rogue may have enticed her to Sacrifice her Fortune to a Monastry?—Ah, they have ruined many a poor foolish Girl to enrich the Brotherhood.

Alison. I advise you to a Wife my lusty *Nestor*; and at the same time that I prescribe you the Medicine, I offer my self in Person for the Remedy—What think you, old Gray-beard, dare you venture on a Girl of my Vivacity?

Doggrell. This, I vow, is just like taking advantage of a
410 Widow's Tears for her first Husband, by surprising of her into a Consent to a second.

Alison. 'Sdiggers,—dare you interrupt my Amour, i'faith, out pops your Marriage, and the old Fellow's Anger shall strike you dead like a Thunderbolt—Lookye, Sir, your Daughter hath disposed of her self, you see, and in short, this

complaisant Gentleman has been led by the Nose by Love,
and—

Doggrell. Nay, pray Madam,—faith Madam,—'tis downright uncivil—let me die,—but you shall not—was my Lady
present, she would protect me from his Insults—Pax then, if I   420
cannot prevail with you—indulge your Spleen, and discharge
the Secret—I'll hum a Tune, and receive the Storm with all
the Patience of an ancient Philosopher.

Alison. In short, this same Gentleman hath disposed of
himself in Marriage; and 'Slidikins, we will marry in spite,
and get Heirs in defiance of Age and the World—We will,
Chicken.

Franklyn. Married!—the Devil he is—to my Daughter, I
hope.

Alison. No, no,—Love hath made another Choice for   430
him;—and for your Daughter, my Mind give me most
plaguily, that the sly Rogue that invited you to the Wedding
last Night, hath not had the Civility to invite you a second
time.

Franklyn. Death! a meer train of Misfortunes!—what, both
of them obstinate wilfull Puppies,—Why *Frank, Frank*, you did
not think your self a fit Present for my Daughter, it seems; but
idad, I have your Love Ammunition in my Hands, Coxcomb,
and you shall whistle for your Fortune 'till the Law forces me
to surrender it.   440

Doggrell. Fa, la, la, la.   [*Sings.*

Franklyn. Why, you ungenerous Rogue you, why Sirrah,
answer me.

Doggrell. Fa, la, la, la.   [*Sings.*

Franklyn. Why, was this now, *Frank*, acted like a Gentleman?   [*Calmly.*

Doggrell. *Fair Amaryllis in a pleasant Grove,*
          For her dear Boy a flow'ry Garland wove.

Franklyn. Why, what a Vengeance, are all the Folks mad or
bewitch'd? have you, Sirrah, stole a Marriage without the   450
consent of your Guardian, or not?

Alison. Revenge your self by your own Marriage, old Boy,
and baulk all their Contrivances.

Franklyn. Pox, and that is the ready way to have the
Revenge light on my own Head too;—Why *Frank* now,

prithee now, *Frank*, do not be inspired at present, but give a
Man a rational Answer.

Doggrell. *For* Damon *stay'd;—*Damon *the Loveliest Swain;*

Franklyn. Bred up a Child under my own Wing, as a Body
460 may say—

Doggrell. *And she the fairest Nymph of all the Plain.*

Franklyn. Mad! stark staring Mad!—Why *Frank*, Sirrah.

Doggrell. *Thus she complains, while all the Feather'd Throng,*

Franklyn. Death, and Confusion!

Doggrell. *And Silence, list'ned to the mournful Song.*

Franklyn. A Man of your Amorous Constitution *Frank*, can
Breakfast upon a Smile, Dine upon a Kiss, and Sup upon—
Pox, Mony would but make Love Mercenary.

Doggrell. Hold, hold Sir,—I am Married, I confess,—but
470 both Quality and Fortune accompany the Lady.—She hath a
Purse that shall vindicate my Right, and make you restore
what you detain by Fraud and Injustice;—But stay, yonder
she comes; the most accomplished Bride that ever bless'd
Mortality.—Youth, Beauty, Fortune, and—Quality.

Enter Busie *in a Nun's Habit.*

This is my Lady, Sir.   [*Presents her to* Franklyn.

Franklyn. And what then, Sir?

Doggrell. Why, then Sir, 'tis my Lady,—that's all.—An
unmannerly Brute! [*Aside.*] Madam, this Blessing I owe to
your Generosity—My Right Honourable Bride, Madam.

[*To* Alison.

480   *Alison.* Why, Heighday! *Legerdemain* and *Necromancy!—*
Why, Mrs *Busie!*—art thou Married in earnest, my dear Girl?
Odsmylife, I wish thee Joy Child, with all my Heart and Soul.

[*Kisses her.*

Doggrell. Nay, pray Madam,—this Familiarity gives
Quality distaste—Distance and Decorum support their
Grandeur,—Ceremony keeps them out of the Vulgar Method
of Conversation.—They are not pester'd with the nauseous
Freedoms of Friendship, nor subject to the forward Liberties
of Good-nature.—Pray, Madam, regulate your Behaviour,
and remember she is a Woman of Quality.

490   *Alison.* Ha, ha, ha,—or the Woman of a Woman of
Quality, Sir.

Doggrell. What do you mean, Madam?

Alison. That your Generosity, my Son of *Parnassus*, hath lay'd hold of the Maid instead of the Lady.

Busie. Mr. *D'Ogrelle*'s Passion was not sway'd by sordid Interest;—Love was the only Motive of his Choice; and a mutual Duty to each other shall make our Lives glide on with Serenity; and show Matrimony in its utmost Perfection.

Doggrell. What have I done!

Franklyn. Hah, hah, *Frank*,—my Daughter cannot be set in 500 competition with Youth, Beauty, Fortune—and Quality—She hath a Purse, *Frank*, yes, yes, she hath a Purse, for vindicating a Husband's Right, I don't in the least question, ha, ha, ha.

Doggrell. Faith, Love hath not dealt by me like a Gentleman, to Reward a Man of Honour thus.—Oh most egregious Error! Embarras'd with a Chamber maid, when I bid fair for a Countess!

Franklyn. Dal te ral, tal lal.   [*Sings.*

Doggrell. Irretrievable Loss! flung my self out of the *Beau Monde*, to be entertained with Bone-Lace, and whipping of 510 Muslin.

Franklyn. Dal te ral, te ral.   [*Sings.*

Doggrell. I vow, this is most insupportable—What is your Name, Madam? Have you any Family to make me Satisfaction?

Busie. *Busie*, Sir.

Franklyn. The *Busie*'s of *Yorkshire*, Sir,—as noble a Family as any in Christendom; she bears for her Coat, three Needles proper, with a Thimble *Argent* for her Crest—ha, ha, ha, tal deral.   [*Sings.* 520

Alison. Her Great Grandfather was killed at the Battle of *Cressy;* and her Great Uncle, in the Fifty Ninth degree, was Groom of the Privy Stool to *William* the Conqueror—ha, ha, ha—

      Enter Merit *and* Florinda.

Merit. Sir, I come to beg your Pardon, and your Blessing.

Franklyn. Apply your self to your Mother there, Hussy— idad I will marry on purpose to get Heirs to disinherit thee, Gipsie.

Doublechin. Vindicate my Honour, I beseech you, Madam;—here my Honesty hath been called in Question, my 530 Continency censured, and my Virtue is at stake.

Florinda. Why, look ye, Sir,—then this was the Case;—
Love, by the help of a Bottle of Sack, charmed my honest
Father here to Sleep, to assist his constant Votary, which is
your dutiful Daughter—Now you must know, Sir, to secure
my Escape, my obliging Father's Cowle and Vestments were
somewhat necessary: And so, Sir, under Ecclesiastical Covert
I retired to my Lover.

Alison. Ah, Rogue!—ifackins, I like a Lad that pushes an
540 Amour to an Extremity; that will not drop it for a
Disappointment, but enjoys the Toil of an Intrigue. [*To
Merit.*] But hark you, old Boy, we are to match up it seems.—
Give me thy Hand then, old *Nestor*—I will defie the World to
shew another such like Couple, in the decline of their Age.
Ours is a meer *Italian* Autumn, that even excells the Spring in
its variety of Beauty.

Enter Chaucer *and* Myrtilla.

Hah! hah! Don *Chaucer* and the Lady *Myrtilla!*—The
Pilgrim's here have made *Hymen*'s the Shrine of their
Devotion, instead of St. *Thomas*'s.—I hope, Madam, you will
550 approve of Mrs. *Busie*'s choice: She hath quitted your
Ladyship's Service, and serves for the future under Mr.
Doggrell—my Daughter-in-law here, is a Volunteer under this
Gentleman's Banner—and a random Glance of mine, for-
sooth, has captivated my old Hero here.

Chaucer. Ladies and Gentlemen I wish you all Joy.

Doggrell. Ah, Mr. *Chaucer*, Love Counter-plotted me; and I
dare swear, hath now taken his Revenge on me, for my former
Cruelty to the Ladies—This Creature here—

Chaucer. Nay, Sir, pray treat her like a Gentlewoman: Her
560 Family is, without dispute, of as great Antiquity as any in
England.

Doggrell. Then, Madam, I fly into your Arms: You want
no Accomplishment but Fortune, and that, Madam, you
command by your Alliance with me.

Chaucer. Destiny has at last crowned my Wishes with the
Lady *Myrtilla*, and I come now to invite the good Company to
celebrate the Wedding.

Alison. Your Ladyship married!

Myrtilla. The Fates have so ordained it, you see, Madam.

570 *Alison.* We wish your Ladyship Joy.

Doggrell. Mr. *Chaucer*, I vow this is mighty strange; but I heartily Congratulate you. My Ambition, Madam, aspired to your Ladyship; but my Fortune, Madam, threw me more upon a level. May your Days, Mr. *Chaucer*, flow on with Pleasure; may your Nights be crowned with Joy; may no Cares intrude, and your Matrimonial State be one constant Calm. Soften my Fate, Madam, and for the future call my lovely Bride here, your Ladyship's Companion.

Chaucer. We will all turn Mediators, and reconcile Differences at a more convenient Opportunity. In the mean 580 time let us lovingly take Hands, and agree in a Dance; come, I'll lead it up.

A DANCE.

Chaucer.

> *She who by Rules of Superstition goes,* ⎫
> *Upon her self does rig'rous Laws impose;* ⎬
> *While Fancy gives or takes away Repose.* ⎭
> *Yet why should I this female Whim deride,*
> *Since to her Stars I owe my beauteous Bride?*
> *Through the whole Sex this Pious Humour runs,*
> *Were there no Men, all Women would be Nuns.*

FINIS.

THE
WHAT D'YE CALL IT:
A
Tragi-Comi-Pastoral
FARCE.

—*Spirat Tragicum satis, & feliciter audet.*
Hor.

——*Locus est & pluribus Umbris.*
Hor.

THE PREFACE.

As I am the first who have introduced this Kind of Dramatick Entertainment upon the Stage, I think it absolutely necessary to say something by way of Preface, not only to shew the Nature of it, but to answer some Objections that have been already rais'd against it by the graver sort of Wits, and other interested People.

We have often had Tragi-Comedies upon the English *Theatre with Success: but in that sort of Composition the Tragedy and Comedy are in distinct Scenes, and may be easily separated from each other. But the whole Art of the* Tragi-Comi-Pastoral Farce *lies in interweaving the several Kinds of* 10 *the Drama with each other, so that they cannot be distinguish'd or separated.*

The Objections that are rais'd against it as a Tragedy, *are as follow.*

First, As to the Plot, they deny it to be Tragical, because its Catastrophe is a Wedding, which hath ever been accounted Comical.

Secondly, As to the Characters; that those of a Justice of Peace, *a* Parish-Clark, *and an* Embryo's Ghost, *are very improper to the Dignity of Tragedy, and were never introduc'd by the Antients.*

Thirdly, They say the Sentiments are not Tragical, because they are those of the lowest Country People.

Lastly, They will not allow the Moral to be proper for Tragedy, because 20 *the End of Tragedy being to show human Life in its Distresses, Imperfections and Infirmities, thereby to soften the Mind of Man from its natural Obduracy and Haughtiness, the Moral ought to have the same Tendency; but this Moral, they say, seems entirely calculated to flatter the Audience in their Vanity and Self-conceitedness.*

You all have Sense enough to find it out.

To the First Objection I answer, that it is still a disputable Point, even among the best Criticks, whether a Tragedy may not have a happy Catastrophe; *that the French Authors are of this Opinion, appears from most of their Modern Tragedies.*

30 *In answer to the Second Objection, I cannot affirm, that any of the Antients have either a* Justice of Peace, *a* Parish-Clark, *or an* Embryo Ghost *in their Tragedies; yet whoever will look into* Sophocles, Euripides, *or* Seneca, *will find that they greatly affected to introduce* Nurses *in all their Pieces, which every one must grant to be an inferior Character to a Justice of*

Peace; in imitation of which also, I have introduced a Grandmother and an Aunt.

To the third Objection, which is the Meanness of the Sentiments, I answer that the Sentiments of Princes and Clowns have not in reality that difference which they seem to have: their Thoughts are almost the same, and they only differ as the same Thought is attended with a Meanness of Pomp of Diction, 40 or receive a different Light from the Circumstances each Character is conversant with. But these Criticks have forgot the Precept of their Master Horace, *who tells them,*

      —Tragicus plerumque dolet sermone pedestri.

In answer to the Objection against the Moral, I have only this to alledge, That the Moral of this Piece is conceal'd; and Morals that are couch'd so as to exercise the Judgments of the Audience, have not been disapprov'd by the best Criticks*. And I would have those that object against it as a Piece of Flattery, consider, that there is such a Figure as the Irony.

The Objections against it as a Comedy *are,*   50

First, They object to the Plot, that it throws the Characters into the deepest Circumstances of Distress: *Inferiors trampled upon by the Tyranny of Power, a Soldier to be shot for Desertion, and an innocent Maid in the utmost Despair.*

Secondly, That Ghosts are introduced, which move Terror, a Passion not proper to be moved in Comedy.

Thirdly, They will not allow the Sentiments to be Comical, because they are such as naturally flow from the deep Distresses abovementioned. *The Speech of a dying Man, and his last Advice to his Child, are what one could not reasonably expect should raise the Mirth of an Audience.*   60

First, That the Plot is comical, I argue from the Peripætia *and the* Catastrophe. Peascod's *Change of Fortune upon the Reprieve's being produced,* Kitty's *Distress ending in the Discharge of her Sweetheart, and the Wedding, are all Incidents that are truly Comical.*

To the Second Objection I answer, That Ghosts have not been omitted in *the Antient Comedy;* Aristophanes *having laid the Scene of his* Βάτραχοι *among the Shades; and* Plautus *has introduc'd a* Lar familiaris *in his Prologue to the* Aulularia, *which tho' not actually a Ghost, is very little better.*

As to the Third Objection, That the Sentiments are not Comical, I answer, 70 *That the Ghosts are the only Characters which are objected to as improper for*

---

    * See Bossu's *Chapter* of concealed Sentences.

37 *Objection,*] *20 31*; ~ ; *15 16 25*   37 *answer*] *20 31*; ~ , *15 16 25*   42 *with*] *20 31*; in *15 16 25*   62 *Reprieve's*] reprieves *20*   67 familiaris] ~ , *15 16 25* 68 *Ghost,*] ~ ; *20*

Comedy, which I have already proved to be justly introduced, as following the Manner of the old Comedy; but as they allow that the Sentiments naturally flow from the Characters, those of the Justice, Clowns, &c. *which are indisputably Comical Characters, must be Comical. For the Sentiments being convey'd in Number and Rhime, I have the Authority of the best Modern* French *Comedies.*

The only Objection against it as a Pastoral *falls upon the Characters, which they say are partly* Pastoral, *and partly not so. They insist* 80 *particularly, that a Sergeant of Granadiers is not a Pastoral Character, and that the others are so far from being in the State of Innocence, that the Clowns are Whoremasters, and the Damsels with Child.*

To this I reply, that Virgil *talks of Soldiers among his Shepherds.*

Impius hæc tam culta Novalia miles habebit.

And the Character of the Sergeant is drawn according to the Epithet of Virgil, Impius Miles, *which may be seen in that Speech of his,*

You Dog, die like a Soldier—and be damn'd.

For, in short, a Soldier *to a Swain is but just the same thing that a* Wolf *is to his Flocks, and as naturally talk'd of or introduc'd. As for the rest of the* 90 *Characters, I can only say I have copied Nature, making the Youths Amorous before Wedlock, and the Damsels Complying and Fruitful. Those that are the most conversant in the Country are the best Judges of this sort of Nature.*

Lastly, They object against it as a Farce,

First, Because the Irregularity of the Plot should answer to the Extravagance of the Characters, which they say this Piece wants, and therefore is no Farce.

Secondly, They deny the Characters to be Farcical, because they are actually in Nature.

Thirdly, If it was a true Farce, *the Sentiments ought to be strain'd, to* 100 *bear a proportional Irregularity with the Plot and Characters.*

To the First I answer, That the Farcical Scene of the Ghosts is introduced without any Coherence with the rest of the Piece, might be entirely left out, and would not be allowed in a regular Comedy. There are indeed a great Number of Dramatick Entertainments, where are Scenes of this Kind; but those Pieces in reality are not Comedies, *but* five Act Farces.

Secondly, Let the Criticks consider only the Nature of Farce, that it is made up of Absurdities and Incongruities, and that those Pieces which have these Qualities in the greatest Degree are the most Farces; and they will allow this to be so from the Characters, and particularly from that of the speaking Ghost

101 answer,] ~^ 31   101 Farcical] ~, 31   103 a great Number] 20 31; great
Numbers 15 16 25   105 five Act] five-act 25   108 Degree] ~, 16 25

of an Embryo, *in the Conclusion of the first Act. I have, 'tis true,* 110
Aristophanes' *Authority for things of this sort in Comedy, who hath
introduced a* Chorus of Frogs, *and made them talk in the following manner:*

Βρεκεκεκὲξ, κοὰξ, κοάξ,
Βρεκεκεκὲξ, κοὰξ, κοάξ,
Λιμναῖα κρηνῶν τέκνα, &c.

Mr. D'Urfey *of our own Nation has given all the Fowls of the Air the
Faculty of Speech equal with the Parrot. Swans and Elbow-Chairs in the
Opera of* Dioclesian *have danc'd upon the* English *Stage with good Success.*
Shakespear *hath some Characters of this sort, as a* speaking Wall, *and*
Moonshine*. *The former he designed to introduce (as he tells us himself)* 120
with something rough cast about him, *and the latter comes in with a
Lanthorn and Candle; which in my Opinion are Characters that make a good
Figure in the Modern Farce.*

*Thirdly, The Sentiments are truly of the Farce Kind, as they are the
Sentiments of the meanest Clowns convey'd in the Pomp of Numbers and
Rhime; which is certainly forc'd and out of Nature, and therefore Farcical.*

*After all I have said, I would have these Criticks only consider, when they
object against it as a Tragedy, that I design'd it something of a Comedy;
when they cavil at it as a Comedy, that I had partly a View to Pastoral; when
they attack it as a Pastoral, that my Endeavours were in some degree to write a* 130
*Farce; and when they would destroy its Character as a Farce, that my Design
was a Tragi-Comi-Pastoral: I believe when they consider this, they will
all agree, that I have happily enough executed what I purpos'd, which is all I
contend for. Yet that I might avoid the Cavils and Misinterpretations of severe
Criticks, I have not call'd it a Tragedy, Comedy, Pastoral, or Farce, but left the
Name entirely undetermin'd in the doubtful Appellation of* the What d'ye call
it, *which Name I thought unexceptionable; but I added to it a* Tragi-Comi-
Pastoral Farce, *as it comprized all those several Kinds of the* Drama.

*The Judicious Reader will easily perceive, that the Unities are kept as in
the most perfect Pieces, that the Scenes are unbroken, and Poetical Justice* 140
strictly observ'd; the Ghost of the Embryo *and the* Parish-Girl *are entire
new Characters. I might enlarge further upon the Conduct of the particular
Scenes, and of the Piece in general, but shall only say, that the Success this
Piece has met with upon the Stage, gives encouragement to our Dramatick
Writers to follow its Model; and evidently demonstrates that this sort of*
Drama *is no less fit for the Theatre than those they have succeeded in.*

* *See his* Midsummer Night's Dream.

110 *have,*] ~^ 20 31   111 Aristophanes'] Aristophanes's 25 31   113, 114
Βρεκεκεκὲξ] Βρεκεκεκέξ 16 25   113, 114 Κοάξ] κοὰξ all editions   115 Λιμναῖα
κρηνῶν] 31 ;   Λιμναῖα κρῆνῶν   15 20 ; Διμναῖα κρηνῶν 16 ; Διμναῖα κρηνῶν 25   122
Opinion] 20 31 ; ~, 15 16 25   126 Rhime] rhyme 20 31   132 believe] 20 31 ; ~,
15 16 25   141 Parish-Girl] Parish Girl 16 25 ; Parish-Girle 20 31

Dramatis Personæ.

MEN.

Sir *Roger*	Mr. *Miller.*
Sir *Humphry*	Mr. *Cross.*
Justice *Statute*	Mr. *Shepherd.*
Squire *Thomas*, Sir *Roger*'s Son, *alias, Thomas* } Filbert	Mr. *Johnson.*
Jonas Dock, alias *Timothy Peascod*	Mr. *Penkethman.*
Peter Nettle, the Sergeant	Mr. *Norris.*
Steward to Sir *Roger*	Mr. *Quin.*
Constable	Mr. *Penroy.*
Corporal	Mr. *Weller.*
Stave, a Parish-Clark.	
The Ghost of a Child unborn	Mr. *Norris* Jun.
Countrymen, Ghosts, and Soldiers.	

WOMEN.

Kitty, the Steward's Daughter, alias *Kitty* } Carrot	Mrs. *Bicknell.*
Dorcas, *Peascod*'s Sister	Mrs. *Willis* Sen.
Joyce, *Peascod*'s Daughter left upon the Parish	Miss *Younger.*
Aunt	Mrs. *Baker.*
Grandmother.	

alias,] ~^ *31*   Jun] Junior *20 31*   Sen] Senior *20 31*   Aunt] ~. *31*

SCENE, *A Country Justice's Hall, adorn'd with Scutcheons and Stag's Horns.*

Enter Steward, Squire, Kitty, Dock, *and others in Country Habits.*

Steward. So, you are ready in your Parts, and in your Dress too, I see; your own best Cloaths do the Business. Sure never was Play and Actors so suited. Come, range your selves before me, Women on the Right, and Men on the Left. Squire *Thomas*, you make a good Figure.

[*The Actors range themselves.*

Squire *Thomas.* Ay, thanks to *Barnaby's* Sunday Cloaths; but call me *Thomas Filbert*, as I am in the Play.

Steward. Chear up, Daughter, and make *Kitty Carrot* the shining Part: Squire *Thomas* is to be in Love with you to Night, Girl.   10

Kitty. Ay, I have felt Squire *Thomas's* Love to my Cost. I have little Stomach to play, in the Condition he hath put me into.   [*Aside.*

Steward. Jonas Dock, dost thou remember thy Name?

Dock. My Name? *Jo—Jo—Jonas.* No—that was the Name my Godfathers gave me. My Play Name is *Timothy Pea— Pea—Peascod*; ay, *Peascod*—and am to be shot for a Deserter.—

Steward. And you, *Dolly?*

Dolly. An't please ye, I am *Dorcas, Peascod's* Sister, and am to be with Child, as it were.   20

1*st Countryman.* And I am to take her up, as it were—I am the Constable.

2*d Countryman.* And I am to see *Tim* shot, as it were—I am the Corporal.

Steward. But what is become of our Sergeant?

Dorcas. Why *Peter Nettle*, *Peter*, *Peter*.

[*Enter* Nettle.]

Nettle. These Stockings of *Susan's* cost a woundy deal of

pains the pulling on: But what's a Sergeant without red
Stockings?

30   *Dock.* I'll dress thee, *Peter*, I'll dress thee. Here, stand still, I
must twist thy Neckcloth; I would make thee hold up thy
Head, and have a ruddy Complexion; but prithee don't look
black in the Face, Man. [*Rolling his Neckcloth.*] Thou must
look fierce and dreadful. [*Making Whiskers with a burnt Cork.*]
But what shall we do for a Grenadier's Cap?

     Steward. Fetch the Leathern Bucket that hangs in the
Bellfry; that is curiously painted before, and will make a
Figure.

     Nettle. No, no, I have what's worth twenty on't: The
40   Pope's Mitre, that my Master Sir *Roger* seiz'd, when they
would have burnt him at our Market Town.

     Steward. So, now let every body withdraw, and prepare to
begin the Play.

[Exeunt Actors.]

My Daughter debauched! and by that Booby Squire! Well,
perhaps the Conduct of this Play may retrieve her Folly, and
preserve her Reputation. Poor Girl! I cannot forget thy Tears.

[Enter Sir Roger.]

     Sir *Roger.* Look ye, Steward, don't tell me you can't bring
them in. I will have a Ghost; nay, I will have a Competence
of Ghosts. What, shall our Neighbours think we are not able
50   to make a Ghost? A Play without a Ghost is like, is like,—i'gad
it is like nothing.

     Steward. Sir, be satisfied; you shall have Ghosts.

     Sir *Roger.* And is the Play as I order'd it, both a Tragedy
and a Comedy? I would have it a Pastoral too: and if you
could make it a Farce, so much the better—and what if you
crown'd all with a Spice of your Opera? You know my
Neighbours never saw a Play before; and d'ye see, I would
shew them all sorts of Plays under one.

     Steward. Sir *Roger*, it is contrived for that very purpose.

[Enter two Justices.]

60   Sir *Roger.* Neighbours, you are welcome. Is not this
Steward of mine a pure ingenious Fellow now, to make such a

---

32 prithee] pr'ythee *31*   33 *Rolling*] *20 31*; *Twisting 15 16 25*   33 *Neckcloth.*]
~^ *16 25*   34 *burnt Cork*] *20 31*; *Cork 15 16 25*   37 Bellfry] belfry *20 31*
42 every] ev'ry *20 31*   46 Girl] girle *20 31*   50 i'gad] *20 31*; igad *15 16 25*

Play for us these *Christmas* Holidays. [*Exit Steward bowing.*]—A
rare Headpiece! He has it here, i'faith. [*Pointing to his own
Head.*] But indeed, I gave him the Hint.—To see now what
Contrivance some Folks have! We have so fitted the Parts to
my Tenants, that ev'ry man talks in his own way!—and then
we have made just three Justices in the Play, to be play'd by
us three Justices of the *Quorum.*

    1*st Justice.* Zooks!—so it is;—main Ingenious.—And can
we sit and smoke at the same time as we act?   70

    Sir *Roger.* Ay, ay—we have but three or four Words to
say,—and may drink and be good Company in Peace and
Silence all the while after.

    2*d Justice.* But how shall we know when we are to say these
same Words?

    Sir *Roger.* This shall be the Signal—when I set down the
Tankard, then speak you, Sir *Humphry,*—and when Sir
Humphry sets down the Tankard, speak you, Squire *Statute.*

    1*st Justice.* Ah, Sir *Roger,* you are old Dog at these things.

    2*d Justice.* To be sure.   80

    Sir *Roger.* Why Neighbours, you know, Experience,
Experience—I remember your *Harts* and your *Bettertons*—But
then to see your *Othello*, Neighbours,—how he would rave and
roar, about a foolish flower'd Handkerchief!—and then he
would groul so manfully,—and he would put out the Light,
and put the Light out so cleverly! but hush—the Prologue,
the Prologue.

        [*They seat themselves with much Ceremony at the Table, on
           which are Pipes and Tobacco, and a large Silver
                        Tankard.*

---

   63 i'faith] *20 31*; i faith *15 16 25*   64 Hint.] ‿⌃ *16*   79 old] an old *31*
83 then to] to *20 31*

THE PROLOGUE,

Spoken by Mr. *Pinkethman*.

The Entertainment of this Night—or Day,
This Something, or this Nothing of a Play,
Which strives to please all Palates at a time,
With Ghosts and Men, Songs, Dances, Prose and Rhime,
This Comick Story, or this Tragick Jest,
May make you laugh, or cry, as you like best;
May exercise your Good, or your Ill-nature,
Move with Distress, or tickle you with Satyr.
All must be pleas'd too with their Parts, we think:
10 *Our Maids have Sweethearts, and their Worships drink.*
Criticks, we know, by antient Rules may maul it;
But sure Gallants must like—the What d'ye call it.

Prologue 3 *time,*] ~ . *16*　　4 *Rhime,*] ~~ *20 31*　　5 *Comick*] *comic 20 31*
5 *Tragick*] *tragic 20 31*　　11 *antient*] *ancient 20 31*

ACT I. SCENE I.

Sir ROGER, *Sir* HUMPHRY, *Justice* STATUTE, CONSTABLE, FILBERT, SERGEANT, KITTY, DORCAS, GRANDMOTHER, AUNT.

Sir ROGER.

HERE, *Thomas Filbert*, answer to your Name,
Dorcas hath sworn to you she owes her Shame:
Or wed her strait, or else you're sent afar,
To serve his Gracious Majesty in War.

FILBERT.

'Tis false, 'tis false—I scorn thy odious Touch.
> [*Pushing* Dorcas *from him.*

DORCAS.

When their turn's serv'd, all Men will do as much.

KITTY.

Ah, good your Worships, ease a wretched Maid.
To the right Father let the Child be laid.
Art thou not perjur'd?—Mark his harmless Look.
How canst thou, *Dorcas*, kiss the Bible Book?   10
Hast thou no Conscience, dost not fear *Old Nick?*
Sure sure the Ground will ope, and take thee Quick.

SERGEANT.

Zooks! never wed, 'tis safer much to roam;
For what is War abroad to War at home?
Who wou'd not sooner bravely risque his Life;
For what's a Cannon to a scolding Wife?

FILBERT.

Well, if I must, I must,—I hate the Wench,
I'll bear a Musquet then against the *French*.
From Door to Door I'd sooner whine and beg,
Both Arms shot off, and on a wooden Leg,   20

i. i. 7 Ah] *20 31*; Oh *15 16 25*   17 must,—] must—*20 31*

Than marry such a Trapes—No, no, I'll not:
—Thou wilt too late repent, when I am shot.
But, *Kitty*, why dost cry?

GRANDMOTHER.

            Stay, Justice, stay:
Ah, little did I think to see this Day!
Must Grandson *Filbert* to the Wars be prest?
Alack! I knew him when he suck'd the Breast,
Taught him his Catechism, the Fescue held,
And join'd his Letters, when the Bantling Spell'd.
His loving Mother left him to my Care.
30 Fine Child, as like his Dad as he could stare!
Come *Candlemas*, nine Years ago she dy'd,
And now lies buried by the Yew-tree's side.

AUNT.

O Tyrant Justices! have you forgot
How my poor Brother was in *Flanders* shot?
You press'd my Brother—he shall walk in White,
He shall—and shake your Curtain ev'ry Night.
What though a paultry Hare he rashly kill'd,
That cross'd the Furrows while he plough'd the Field?
You sent him o'er the Hills and far away; ⎫
40 Left his old Mother to the Parish Pay, ⎬
With whom he shar'd his Ten Pence ev'ry Day. ⎭
Wat kill'd a Bird, was from his Farm turn'd out;
You took the Law of *Thomas* for a Trout:
You ruin'd my poor Uncle at the Sizes,
And made him pay nine Pounds for *Nisiprises*.
Now will you press my harmless Nephew too?
Ah, what has Conscience with the Rich to do!
                [*Sir* Roger *takes up the Tankard.*
—Though in my Hand no Silver Tankard shine,
Nor my dry Lip be dy'd with Claret Wine,
Yet I can sleep in Peace—

Sir ROGER.   [*After having drunk.*

50   Woman, forbear.

Sir HUMPHRY.   [*Drinking.*

29 Care.] ~, *16 25*   42 *Wat*] Ralph *16 25*   45 made] wade *31*   49 be]
20 31; is *15 16 25*   50 Woman,] *20 31*; ~^ *15 16 25*   51 sd [*Drinking*] ^~ *20*

The Man's within the Act—

    Justice STATUTE.   [*Drinking also.*
     The Law is clear.

     SERGEANT.
Haste, let their Worships Orders be obey'd.

     KITTY   [*Kneeling.*
Behold how low you have reduc'd a Maid.
Thus to your Worships on my Knees I sue,
(A Posture never known but in the Pew)
If we can Money for our Taxes find,
Take that—but ah! our Sweethearts leave behind.
To Trade so barb'rous he was never bred,
The Blood of Vermine all the Blood he shed:
How should he, harmless Youth, how should he then   60
Who kill'd but Poulcats, learn to murder Men?

     DORCAS.
O *Thomas*, *Thomas!* hazard not thy Life;
By all that's good, I'll make a loving Wife:
I'll prove a true Pains-taker Day and Night,
I'll spin and card, and keep our Children tight.
I can knit Stockings, you can thatch a Barn;
If you earn Ten-pence, I my Groat can earn.
How shall I weep to hear this Infant cry?
     [*Her Hand on her Belly.*
He'll have no Father—and no Husband I.

     KITTY.
Hold, *Thomas*, hold, nor hear that shameless Witch: 70
I can sow Plain-work, I can darn and stitch;
I can bear sultry Days and frosty Weather;
Yes, yes, my *Thomas*, we will go together;
Beyond the Seas together will we go,
In Camps together, as at Harvest, glow.
This Arm shall be a Bolster for thy Head,
I'll fetch clean Straw to make my Soldier's Bed;
There, while thou sleep'st, my Apron o'er thee hold,
Or with it patch thy Tent against the Cold.
Pigs in hard Rains I've watch'd, and shall I do   80
That for the Pigs, I would not bear for you?

   71 sow] sew *25*   72 Weather;] *20 31*; ∼ : *15 16 25*

FILBERT.

Oh, *Kitty*, *Kitty*, canst thou quit the Rake,
And leave these Meadows for thy Sweetheart's sake?
Canst thou so many gallant Soldiers see,
And Captains and Lieutenants slight for me?
Say, canst thou hear the Guns, and never shake,
Nor start at Oaths that make a Christian quake?
Canst thou bear Hunger, canst thou march and toil
A long long Way, a thousand thousand Mile?
90 And when thy *Tom*'s blown up, or shot away,
Then—canst thou starve?—they'll cheat thee of my Pay.

Sir ROGER.   [*Drinking.*

Take out that Wench—

Sir HUMPHRY.   [*Drinking.*

But give her Pennance meet.

Justice STATUTE.   [*Drinking also.*

I'll see her stand—next Sunday—in a Sheet.

DORCAS.

Ah! why does Nature give us so much Cause
To make kind-hearted Lasses break the Laws?
Why should hard Laws kind-hearted Lasses bind,
When too soft Nature draws us after Kind?

SCENE II.

Sir ROGER, *Sir* HUMPHRY, *Justice* STATUTE, FILBERT,
SERGEANT,   KITTY,   GRANDMOTHER,   AUNT,
SOLDIER.

SOLDIER.

Sergeant, the Captain to your Quarters sent;
To ev'ry Alehouse in the Town I went.
Our Corp'ral now has the Deserter found;
The Men are all drawn out, the Pris'ner bound.

SERGEANT.   [*To* Filbert.

Come, Soldier, come—

KITTY.

Ah! take me, take me too.

91 Then—] ~^ *20 31*   91 they'll] *20 31*; they'l *15 16 25*
1. ii. 2 Alehouse] ale-house *20 31*

GRANDMOTHER.
Stay, forward Wench;—

AUNT.
What would the Creature do?
This Week thy Mother means to wash and brew.

KITTY.
Brew then she may her self, or wash, or bake;
I'd leave ten Mothers for one Sweetheart's sake.
O Justice most unjust!

FILBERT.
O Tyranny!   10

KITTY.
How can I part?

FILBERT.
Alas! and how can I?

KITTY.
O rueful Day!

FILBERT.
Rueful indeed, I trow.

KITTY.
O Woeful Day!

FILBERT.
A Day indeed of Woe!

KITTY.
When Gentlefolks their Sweethearts leave behind,
They can write Letters, and say something kind;
But how shall *Filbert* unto me endite,
When neither I can read, nor he can write?
  Yet, Justices, permit us e'er we part
To break this Ninepence, as you've broke our Heart.

FILBERT.   [*Breaking the Ninepence.*
As this divides, thus are we torn in twain.   20

KITTY.   [*Joining the Pieces.*
And as this meets, thus may we meet again.
  [*She is drawn away on one Side of the Stage by* Aunt *and*
                                             Grandmother.

6 do?] ~ ; 25   8 wash,] ~ ~ 20 31   18 *no para 16 25*

Yet one Look more—

> FILBERT.
> [*Haul'd off on the other Side by the Sergeant.*
> One more e'er yet we go.

> KITTY.

To part is Death.

> FILBERT.
> 'Tis Death to part.

> KITTY.
>   Ah!

> FILBERT.
>   Oh!

SCENE III.

Sir ROGER, *Sir* HUMPHRY, *Justice* STATUTE, *and*
CONSTABLE.

> Sir ROGER.   [*Drinking.*

See, Constable, that ev'ry one withdraw.

> Sir HUMPHRY.   [*Drinking.*

We've Business—

> Justice STATUTE.   [*Drinking also.*
> To discuss a Point of Law.

SCENE IV.

Sir ROGER, *Sir* HUMPHRY, *Justice* STATUTE.

> *They seem in earnest Discourse.*

> Sir ROGER.

I say the Press-Act plainly makes it out.

> Sir HUMPHRY.

Doubtless, Sir *Roger.*

> Justice STATUTE.

23 Death.] ⁓ˆ *16 25*
I. iii. 1 See,] ⁓ˆ *31*
I. iv. sd *They . . . Discourse.*] *20 31*; [*They . . . Discourse.*] *15 16 25*   2 *Roger.*] ⁓ˆ
16 25

Brother, without doubt.
A Ghost rises.

1*st* G H O S T.

I'm *Jeffry Cackle.*—You my Death shall rue;
For I was press'd by you, by you, by you.

[*Pointing to the Justices.*

Another Ghost rises.

2*d* G H O S T.

I'm *Smut* the Farrier.—You my Death shall rue;
For I was press'd by you, by you, by you.

A Woman's Ghost rises.

3*d* G H O S T.

I'm *Bess* that hang'd my self for *Smut* so true;
So owe my Death to you, to you, to you.

A Ghost of an Embryo rises.

4*th* G H O S T.

I was begot before my Mother married,
Who whipt by you, of me poor Child miscarried.   10

Another Woman's Ghost rises.

5*th* G H O S T.

Its Mother I, whom you whipt black and blue;
Both owe our Deaths to you, to you, to you.

All Ghosts shake their Heads.

Sir R O G E R.

Why do you shake your Mealy Heads at me?
You cannot say I did it—

B O T H J U S T I C E S.
No—nor we.

1*st* G H O S T.
All Three.

2*d* G H O S T.
All Three.

3*d* G H O S T.
All Three.

3 rue;] ~~ 25   6 press'd] *20 31*; prest *15 16 25*   8 sd *Embryo*] *embrio 16 25*
12 sd *All . . . Heads.*] *20 31*; [*All . . . Heads.*] *15 16 25*   12 sd *Ghosts*] *the ghosts 16 25*
15 [1*st* . . . .] Three.] ~~ *20 31*   15 [2*d* . . . .] Three.] ~~ *31*   15 [3*d* . . . .] Three.]
~~ *20 31*

4*th* GHOST.
All Three.

5*th* GHOST.
All Three.

A SONG sung dismally by a GHOST.

Ye Goblins and Fairys,
With Frisks and Vagarys,
Ye Fairys and Goblins,
With Hoppings and Hoblings,
   Come all, come all
To Sir Roger's *great Hall.*

All Fairys and Goblins,
All Goblins and Fairys,
With Hoppings and Hoblings,
With Frisks and Vagarys.

CHORUS.

Sing, Goblins and Fairys,
Sing, Fairys and Goblins,
With Frisks and Vagarys,
And Hoppings and Hoblings.

[*The Ghosts dance round the Justices, who go off in a*
Fright, and the Ghosts vanish.

ACT II. SCENE I.

A Field.

TIMOTHY PEASCOD *bound;* CORPORAL, SOLDIERS, *and*
COUNTRYMEN.

CORPORAL.

STAND off there, Countrymen; and you, the Guard,
Keep close your Pris'ner—see that all's prepar'd.
Prime all your Firelocks—fasten well the Stake.

---

15 [4*th* . . . .] Three.] ~⁀ 20 31   16 *Fairys,*] ~⁀ 25   19 *Hoblings*] hobblings
20 31   20 *all*] ~, 25   23, 28 *Hoblings*] hobblings 20 31

PEASCOD.

'Tis too much, too much Trouble for my sake.
O Fellow-Soldiers, Countrymen and Friends,
Be warn'd by me to shun untimely Ends:
For Evil Courses am I brought to Shame,
And from my Soul I do repent the same.
Oft my kind *Grannam* told me—*Tim*, take warning,
Be good—and say thy Pray'rs—and mind thy Learning.   10
But I, sad Wretch, went on from Crime to Crime;
I play'd at Nine-pins first in Sermon time:
I rob'd the Parson's Orchard next; and then
(For which I pray Forgiveness) stole—a Hen.
When I was press'd, I told them the first Day
I wanted Heart to fight, so ran away;
                   [*Attempts to run off, but is prevented.*
For which behold I die. 'Tis a plain Case,
'Twas all a Judgment for my Want of Grace.
        [*The Soldiers prime, with their Muskets towards him.*
—Hold, hold, my Friends; nay, hold, hold, hold, I pray;
They may go off—and I have more to say.   20

I. COUNTRYMAN.

Come, 'tis no time to talk.

II. COUNTRYMAN.

                Repent thine Ill,
And Pray in this good Book.   [*Gives him a Book.*

PEASCOD.

           I will, I will.
Lend me thy Handkercher—*The Pilgrim's Pro*—
                   [*Reads and weeps.*

(I cannot see for Tears) *Pro*—*Progress*—Oh!
—*The Pilgrim's Progress*—*Eighth*—*Edi-ti-on*
Lon-don—*Prin-ted*—*for*—*Ni-cho-las Bod-ding-ton:*
With new Ad-di-tions never made before.
—Oh! 'tis so moving, I can read no more.
                    [*Drops the Book.*

II. i. 13 rob'd] robb'd *25*   19 —Hold] ⌃~ *20 31*   25 —The] ⌃~ *20 31*
25 *Pilgrim's Progress*] *Pil-grim's Pro-gress 16 25*   25 *Edi-ti-on*] *e-di-ti-on 16 25*
27 *Ad-di-tions*] *ad-di-ti-ons 16*   27 *never*] *ne-ver 16 25*   27 before.] be-fore, *16 25*
28 —Oh] ⌃~ *20 31*

SCENE II.

PEASCOD, CORPORAL, SOLDIERS, COUNTRYMEN,
SERGEANT, FILBERT.

SERGEANT.

What Whining's this?—Boys, see your Guns well ramm'd.
You Dog, die like a Soldier—and be damn'd.

FILBERT.

My Friend in Ropes!

PEASCOD.

              I should not thus be bound,
If I had Means, and could but raise five Pound.
The cruel Corp'ral whisper'd in my Ear,
Five Pounds, if rightly tipt, would set me clear.

FILBERT.

Here—*Peascod*, take my Pouch—'tis all I own.
(For what is Means and Life when *Kitty*'s gone!)
'Tis my Press Money—can this Silver fail?
10 'Tis all, except one Sixpence spent in Ale.
This had a Ring for *Kitty*'s Finger bought,
Kitty on me had by that Token thought.
But for thy Life, poor *Tim*, if this can do't;
Take it, with all my Soul—thou'rt welcome to't.

                   [*Offers him his Purse.*

I. COUNTRYMAN.

And take my Fourteen Pence—

II. COUNTRYMAN.

                And my Cramp-ring.
Would, for thy sake, it were a better Thing.

III. COUNTRYMAN.

And Master Sergeant, take my Box of Copper.

IV. COUNTRYMAN.

And my Wife's Thimble.

V. COUNTRYMAN.

             And this 'Bacco-stopper.

II. ii. 1 ramm'd.] ~^ *15*
20 31; ~^ *15 16 25*   9 Press Money] press-money *20 31*   10 all,]

SERGEANT.
No Bribes. Take back your Things—I'll have them not.

PEASCOD.
Oh! must I die?

CHORUS *of* COUNTRYMEN.
Oh! must poor *Tim* be shot! 20

PEASCOD.
But let me kiss thee first— [*Embracing* Filbert.

SCENE III.

PEASCOD, CORPORAL, SOLDIERS, COUNTRYMEN, SERGEANT, FILBERT, DORCAS.

DORCAS.
Ah, Brother *Tim*,
Why these close Hugs? I owe my Shame to him.
He scorns me now, he leaves me in the Lurch;
In a white Sheet poor I must stand at Church.
O marry me—[*To* Filbert.] Thy Sister is with child.
[*To* Tim.
And he, 'twas he my tender Heart beguil'd.

PEASCOD.
Could'st thou do this? couldst thou—
[*In anger to* Filbert.

SERGEANT.
Draw out the Men:
Quick to the Stake; you must be dead by Ten.

DORCAS.
Be dead! must *Tim* be dead?

PEASCOD.
He must—he must.

DORCAS.
Ah! I shall sink downright; my Heart will burst. 10
—Hold, Sergeant, hold—yet e'er you sing the Psalms,
Ah! let me ease my Conscience of its Qualms.

19 Bribes. Take] bribes, take *16 25*
II. iii. 1 *Tim*,] ~. *31* 8 you] he *31* 9 dead?] ~! *20 31* 11 e'er]
ere *31* 12 Ah!] ~^ *31*

O Brother, Brother! *Filbert* still is true.
I fouly wrong'd him—do, forgive me, do.   [*To* Filbert.
The Squire betray'd me; nay,—and what is worse,
Brib'd me with two Gold Guineas in this Purse,
To swear the Child to *Filbert.*

PEASCOD.

What a *Jew*

My Sister is!—Do, *Tom*, forgive her, do.   [*To* Filbert.

FILBERT.   [*Kisses* Dorcas.

But see thy base-born Child, thy Babe of Shame,
20 Who left by thee, upon our Parish came;
Comes for thy Blessing.

SCENE IV.

PEASCOD,   CORPORAL,   SOLDIERS,   COUNTRYMEN,
SERGEANT, FILBERT, DORCAS, JOYCE.

PEASCOD.

Oh! my Sins of Youth!

Why on the Haycock didst thou tempt me, *Ruth*?
O save me, Sergeant;—how shall I comply?
I love my Daughter so—I cannot die.

JOYCE.

Must Father die! and I be left forlorn?
A lack a day! that ever *Joyce* was born!
No Grandsire in his Arms e'er dandled me,
And no fond Mother danc'd me on her Knee.
They said, if ever Father got his Pay,
10 I should have Two-pence ev'ry Market-day.

PEASCOD.

Poor Child; hang Sorrow, and cast Care behind thee,
The Parish by this Badge is bound to find thee.
[*Pointing to the Badge on her Arm.*

    14 fouly] foully *16 25*   18 sd Dorcas.] ~^ *16 20 25 31*   20 came;] ~ : *25*
21 Blessing.] ~^ *20 31*

    II. iv. 3 Sergeant;] ~^ *31*   5 forlorn?] ~! *25*   10 Market-day] market
day *20 31*

JOYCE.

The Parish finds indeed—but our Church-Wardens
Feast on the Silver, and give us the Farthings.
Then my School-Mistress, like a Vixen *Turk*,
Maintains her lazy Husband by our Work:
Many long tedious Days I've Worsted spun;
She grudg'd me Victuals when my Task was done.
Heav'n send me a good Service! for I now
Am big enough to wash, or milk a Cow.   20

PEASCOD.

O that I had by Charity been bred!
I then had been much better taught—than fed.
Instead of keeping Nets against the Law,
I might have learnt Accounts, and sung *Sol-fa*.
Farewell, my Child; spin on, and mind thy Book,
And send thee store of Grace therein to look.
Take Warning by thy shameless Aunt; lest thou
Shouldst o'er thy Bastard weep—as I do now.
Mark my last Words—an honest Living get;
Beware of Papishes, and learn to knit.   30

[Dorcas *leads out* Joyce *sobbing and crying.*

SCENE V.

PEASCOD,   CORPORAL,   SOLDIERS,   COUNTRYMEN,
SERGEANT, FILBERT.

FILBERT.

Let's drink before we part—for Sorrow's dry.
To *Tim*'s safe Passage.

[*Takes out a Brandy-bottle, and drinks.*

I. COUNTRYMAN.
I'll drink too.

II. COUNTRYMAN.
And I.

PEASCOD.

Stay, let me pledge—'tis my last earthly liquor.   [*Drinks.*
—When I am dead—you'll bind my Grave with Wicker.
[*They lead him to the Stake.*

I. COUNTRYMAN.

He was a special Ploughman—   [*Sighing.*

II. COUNTRYMAN.
Harrow'd well!

III. COUNTRYMAN.

And at our Maypole ever bore the Bell!

PEASCOD.

Say, is it fitting in this very Field,
Where I so oft have reap'd, so oft have till'd;
This Field, where from my Youth I've been a Carter,
I, in this Field, should die for a Deserter?

FILBERT.

'Tis hard, 'tis wond'rous hard!

SERGEANT.
Zooks, here's a Pother.
Strip him; I'd stay no longer for my Brother.

PEASCOD.
[*Distributing his Things among his Friends.*
Take you my 'Bacco Box—my Neckcloth, you.
To our kind Vicar send this Bottle-Skrew.
But wear these Breeches, *Tom*; they're quite bran-new.

FILBERT.

Farewell—

I. COUNTRYMAN.
B'ye, *Tim*.

II. COUNTRYMAN.
B'ye, *Tim*.

III. COUNTRYMAN.
Adieu.

4 dead—] ~‿^ *20 31*   6 Maypole] may-pole *31*   11 wond'rous] wondrous
20 31   13 'Bacco Box] 'bacco-box *20 31*   16 sd *Leave*] *20 31*; *Leaves 15 16 25*

IV. COUNTRYMAN.

Adieu.

[They all take their Leave of Peascod *by shaking Hands with him.*

SCENE VI.

PEASCOD, CORPORAL, SOLDIERS, COUNTRYMEN, SERGEANT, FILBERT, *to them a* SOLDIER *in great haste.*

SOLDIER.

Hold—why so furious, Sergeant? by your Leave,
Untye the Pris'ner—See, here's a Reprieve.   *[Shows a Paper.*

CHORUS *of* COUNTRYMEN.   *[Huzzaing.*

A Reprieve, a Reprieve, a Reprieve!

[Peascod is unty'd, and embraces his Friends.

SCENE VII.

PEASCOD, CORPORAL, SOLDIERS, COUNTRYMEN, SERGEANT, FILBERT, CONSTABLE.

CONSTABLE.

Friends, reprehend him, reprehend him there.

SERGEANT.

For what?

CONSTABLE.

For stealing Gaffer *Gap*'s gray Mare.

[They seize the Sergeant.

PEASCOD.

Why, heark ye, heark ye, Friend; you'll go to Pot.
Would you be rather hang'd—hah!—hang'd or shot?

SERGEANT.

Nay, hold, hold, hold—

PEASCOD.

Not if you were my Brother.
Why, Friend, should you not hang as well's Another?

II. vi. 3 Reprieve!] ~. *15 16 25*
II. vii. 5 Brother.] ~, *16 25*

CONSTABLE.

Thus said Sir *John*—the Law must take its course;
'Tis Law that he may 'scape who steals a Horse.
But (said Sir *John*) the Statutes all declare,
10 The Man shall sure be hang'd—that steals a Mare.

PEASCOD.   [To the Sergeant.

Ay—right—he shall be hang'd that steals a Mare.
He shall be hang'd—that's certain; and good Cause.
A rare good Sentence this—how is't?—the Laws
No—not the Laws—the Statutes all declare,
The Man that steals a Mare shall sure—be—hang'd,
No, no—he shall be hang'd that steals a Mare.
[Exit Sergeant guarded, Countrymen, &c. huzzaing
after him.

SCENE VIII.

KITTY *with her Hair loose*, GRANDMOTHER, AUNT, HAYMAKERS, CHORUS *of* SIGHS *and* GROANS.

KITTY.

Dear happy Fields, farewell; ye Flocks, and you
Sweet Meadows, glitt'ring with the pearly Dew:
And thou, my Rake, Companion of my Cares,
Giv'n by my Mother in my younger Years:
With thee the Toils of full eight Springs I've known,
'Tis to thy Help I owe this Hat and Gown;
On thee I've lean'd, forgetful of my Work,
While *Tom* gaz'd on me, propt upon his Fork:
Farewell, farewell; for all thy Task is o'er,
10 *Kitty* shall want thy Service now no more.
[Flings away the Rake.

CHORUS of Sighs and Groans.

Ah—O!—Sure never was the like before!

KITTY.

Happy the Maid, whose Sweetheart never hears

15 hang'd,] ~˄ *15var 16 25*
II. viii. sd KITTY] ~, *20 31*   1 farewell] farewel *16 25*   2 glitt'ring]
glittering *16 25*   5 I've] *16 20 31*; have *15 25*   7 I've] I *20 31*
9 Farewell, farewell] *20 31*; farewel, farewel *15 16 25*   11 O!—] O!˄ *25*

The Soldier's Drum, nor Writ of Justice fears.
Our Bans thrice bid! and for our Wedding Day
My Kerchief bought! then press'd, then forc'd away!

CHORUS of Sighs and Groans.

Ah! O! poor Soul! alack! and well a day!

KITTY.

You, *Bess*, still reap with *Harry* by your Side;
You, *Jenny*, shall next *Sunday* be a Bride:
But I forlorn!—This Ballad shews my Care;

     [*Gives* Susan *a Ballad.*

Take this sad Ballad, which I bought at Fair: 20
Susan can sing—do you the Burthen bear.

A BALLAD.

1.

'TWAS *when the Seas were roaring*
With hollow Blasts of Wind;
A Damsel lay deploring,
All on a Rock reclin'd.
Wide o'er the rolling Billows
She cast a wistful Look;
Her Head was crown'd with Willows
That tremble o'er the Brook.

2.

Twelve Months are gone and over,   30
And nine long tedious Days.
Why didst thou, vent'rous Lover,
Why didst thou trust the Seas?
Cease, cease, thou cruel Ocean,
And let my Lover rest;

13 Soldier's] soldiers *16 25*   15 press'd,] *16 20 25 31*; ~~ *15*   22 *roaring*]
~, S1 S2 MM   23 *Wind*;] ~, S1, S2 M H MM   24 *deploring*,] ~~ S1 S2 M
25 *reclin'd*.] ~, S1, S2; ~; M H MM   26 *rolling*] rowling S1 S2 M H; *roaring* MP
26 *Billows*] ~, S1 H MM; billow S2   27 *wistful*] wishfull S1 S2; wishful M H
MP MM   27 *Look*;] ~, S1 S2 H   28 *Willows*] ~, S1 S2 M E MP MM
29 *tremble*] Trembl'd S1 S2; trembled M MM   29 *o'er*] o're S1 S2   29 *Brook*.] ~, S2
30 *are*] were S1 S2 M H MM   30 *gone*] gon S2   31 *Days*.] ~, S1 S2 H; ~; M MM
32 *vent'rous*] ventrous S1 S2 H   33 *Seas*?] ~, S1 S2; ~. H   34 *cease*,] ~~ S1
S2 M H MP MM   34 *thou*] then S1 S2 H MM; then, M   34 *cruel*] cruell S1 S2
35 *let*] lett S2   35 *rest*;] ~, S1 S2; ~: 20 MM *31*; ~. H

Ah! what's thy troubled Motion
  To that within my Breast?

3.

The Merchant, rob'd of Pleasure,
  Sees Tempests in Despair;
But what's the Loss of Treasure
  To losing of my Dear?
Should you some Coast be laid on
  Where Gold and Di'monds grow,
You'd find a richer Maiden,
  But none that loves you so.

4.

How can they say that Nature
  Has nothing made in vain;
Why then beneath the Water
  Should hideous Rocks remain?
No Eyes the Rocks discover,
  That lurk beneath the Deep,
To wreck the wand'ring Lover,
  And leave the Maid to weep.

5.

All melancholy lying,
  Thus wail'd she for her Dear;
Repay'd each Blast with Sighing,
  Each Billow with a Tear;

40

50

36 *Ah!*] ~^ *S1 S2*; ~, *M*   36 *Motion*] ~, *M MM*   37 *Breast?*] ~. *S1 S2 H*
38 *Merchant,*] ~^ *S1 S2 M 16 E 25 MP*   38 *rob'd*] *robb'd M E H 25 MP MM*
38 *Pleasure*] *Treasure H MM*   39 *Sees*] *Views S1 S2 M H*   39 *Despair*] *Dispair*
S1 S2   40 *Treasure*] ~, *S1 S2 M H MM*   41 *Losing*] *looseing S1 S2*
41 *Dear?*] ~^ *S1 S2*   42 *Should*] *Shou'd H MM*   42 *on*] ~, *S1 S2 M MM*
43 *Di'monds*] *Diamonds S1 S2 M H MM*   43 *grow,*] ~; *MM*   45 *But none*] *Not*
one MP   46 *say*] ~, *M*   47 *vain;*] ~, *S1 H*; ~^ *S2*; ~? *E MP*
48 *Water*] *watter S2*   49 *Should*] *Does S1 S2 M; Do H MM*   49 *hideous*] *hiddeous*
S1 S2   49 *remain?* ~, *S1 S2*; ~ : *H*   50 *the*] *those H MM*   50 *discover,*] ~^ *MP*
51 *Deep,*] ~; *MM*   52 *wreck*] *wrack S1 S2*   52 *wand'ring*] *wandring S1 S2*
53 *Maid*] *made H*   stanza number 5] *IV 20*   54 *Melancholy*] *Mellancholly*
S1 S2   54 *lying,*] ~^ *S1 S2*; ~; *E*   55 *wail'd*] *wailed S2*   55 *Dear;*] ~, *S1 S2 H*
56 *Repay'd*] *Repaid S1 S2 M H MM*   56 *Sighing*] ~, *S1 S2*   57 *Tear;*] ~^ *S1*;
~, *S2*; ~. *M*; ~ : *H MM*

> When o'er the white Wave stooping
> His floating Corpse she spy'd;
> Then like a Lilly drooping,   60
> She bow'd her Head, and dy'd.

KITTY.

Why in this World should wretched *Kitty* stay?
What if these Hands should make my self away?
I could not sure do otherways than well.
A Maid so true's too innocent for Hell.
But hearkye, *Cis*—   [*Whispers and gives her a Penknife.*

AUNT.

          I'll do't—'tis but to try
If the poor Soul can have the Heart to die.
                    [*Aside to the* Haymakers.
Thus then I strike—but turn thy Head aside.

KITTY.

'Tis shameless sure to fall as Pigs have dy'd.
No—take this Cord—   [*Gives her a Cord.*

AUNT.

          With this thou shalt be sped.   70
          [*Putting the Noose round her Neck.*

KITTY.

But Curs are hang'd.

AUNT.

          Christians should die in bed.

KITTY.

Then lead me thither; there I'll moan and weep,
And close these weary Eyes in Death.

AUNT.

                    —or Sleep.   [*Aside.*

KITTY.

When I am cold, and stretch'd upon my Bier,
My restless Sprite shall walk at Midnight here:

---

58 *When*] ~, 20   58 *o'er*] *o're S1 S2*   58 *Wave*] *Waves S1 S2 M MM*   58 *stooping*] ~, *S1 S2 M 20 MM*   59 *Corpse*] *Corps S1 S2 M H MM*   59 *spy'd*] *spied S2*
60 *Then*] ~, *MM*   61 *Head,*] ~^ *S1 S2 H MM*   61 *dy'd*] *dyed S2*
64 *well.*] ~, *25*   73 *Death.*—] *death. 20 31*   74 *Bier,*] ~^ *20*

Here shall I walk—for 'twas beneath yon Tree
Filbert first said he lov'd—lov'd only me.

[Kitty *faints*.

GRANDMOTHER.

She swoons, poor Soul—help, *Dolly*.

AUNT.

She's in Fits.

Bring Water, Water, Water.   [*Screaming*.

GRANDMOTHER.

Fetch her Wits.

[*They throw Water upon her*.

KITTY.

80 Hah!—I am turn'd a Stream—look all below;
It flows, and flows, and will for ever flow.
The Meads are all afloat—the Haycocks swim.
Hah! who comes here?—my *Filbert*! drown not him.
Bagpipes in Butter, Flocks in fleecy Fountains,
Churns, Sheep-hooks, Seas of Milk, and honey Mountains.

SCENE IX.

KITTY, GRANDMOTHER, AUNT, HAYMAKERS, FILBERT.

KITTY.

It is his Ghost—or is it he indeed?
Wert thou not sent to War? hah, dost thou bleed?
No—'tis my *Filbert*.

FILBERT.   [*Embracing her*.

Yes, 'tis he, 'tis he.
Dorcas confess'd; the Justice set me free.
I'm thine again.

KITTY.

I thine—

FILBERT.

Our Fears are fled.
Come, let's to Church, to Church.

82 swim.] ~, *16 25*   83 here?] ~ ! *20 31*
II. ix. sd HAYMAKERS,] *20 31*; HAYMAKERS, CHORUS *of* SIGHS *and* GROANS,
15 16 25   5 thine—] ~^ *16 25*

KITTY.

To wed.

FILBERT.

To Bed.

CHORUS *of* HAYMAKERS.
A Wedding, a Bedding; a Wedding, a Bedding.

[*Exeunt all the Actors.*

Sir *Roger.* Ay, now for the Wedding. Where's he that plays
the Parson. Now, Neighbours, you shall see what was never
shewn upon the *London* Stage.—Why, heigh day! what's our
Play at a stand?

Enter a Countryman.

Countryman. So, please your Worship, I should have play'd
the Parson, but our Curate would not lend his Gown, for he
says it is a Profanation.

Sir *Roger.* What a scrupulous Whim is this? an innocent
thing! believe me, an innocent thing.

[*The Justices assent by Nods and Signs.*

Enter Stave *the Parish-Clark.*

Stave. Master Doctor saith he hath two and twenty good 10
Reasons against it from the Fathers, and he is come himself to
utter them unto your Worship.

Sir *Roger.* What, shall our Play be spoil'd? I'll have none of
his Reasons—call in Mr. *Inference.*

Stave *goes out, and re-enters.*

Stave. Sir, he saith he never greatly affected Stage Plays.

Within. Stave, Stave, Stave.

Sir *Roger.* Tell him that I say—

Within. Stave, Stave.

Sir *Roger.* What, shall the Curate controul me? Have not I
the Presentation? Tell him that I will not have my Play 20
spoil'd; nay, that he shall marry the Couple himself—I say he
shall.

Stave *goes out, and re-enters.*

Stave. The Steward hath perswaded him to join their

Final scene 1 Ay,] ~^ *25*   9 me,] *20 31*; ~^ *15 16 25*   9 sd *Parish-Clark*]
Parish-clerk 31   13 What,] *20 31*; ~^ *15 16 25*   15 Stage Plays] stage-plays *25*
19 What,] *20 31*; ~^ *15 16 25*   21 say] ~ , *20 31*   23 perswaded] persuaded
25 31

Hands in the Parlour within—but he saith he will not, and cannot in Conscience consent to expose his Character before neighbouring Gentlemen; neither will he enter into your Worship's Hall; for he calleth it a Stage *pro tempore*.

Sir *Humphry*. Very likely: The good Man may have Reason.

30 Justice *Statute*. In troth, we must in some sort comply with the scrupulous tender conscienc'd Doctor.

Sir *Roger*. Why, what's a Play without a Marriage? and what is a Marriage, if one sees nothing of it? Let him have his Humour—but set the Doors wipe open, that we may see how all goes on.   [*Exit* Stave.

[*Sir* Roger *at the Door pointing.*

So natural! d'ye see now, Neighbours? the Ring, i'faith. To have and to hold! right again—well play'd, Doctor; well play'd, Son *Thomas*. Come, come, I'm satisfy'd—now for the Fiddles and Dances.

Enter Steward, *Squire* Thomas, Kitty, Stave, &c.

40 *Steward*. Sir *Roger*, you are very merry.

> So come a Reck'ning when the Banquet's o'er,
> The dreadful Reck'ning, and Men smile no more.

I wish you Joy of your Play, and of your Daughter. I had no way but this to repair the Injury your Son had done my Child—She shall study to deserve your Favour.

[*Presenting* Kitty *to Sir* Roger.

Sir *Roger*. Married! how married! can the Marriage of *Filbert* and *Carrot* have any thing to do with my Son?

Steward. But the Marriage of *Thomas* and *Katherine* may, Sir *Roger*.

50 Sir *Roger*. What a plague, am I trick'd then? I must have a Stage Play, with a Pox!

Sir *Humphry*. If this Speech be in the Play, remember the Tankard, Sir *Roger*.

Squire *Thomas*. Zooks, these Stage Plays are plaguy dangerous Things—but I am no such Fool neither, but I know this was all your Contrivance.

36 Ring,] ~ᵔ *20 31*   36 i' faith. To] *31*; i-faith—to *15 25*; i faith—to *16*; i-faith.
To *20*   38 *Thomas.*] ~, *25*   42 *Reck'ning,*] ~ ; *16 25*   46 married!] ~ ;
16 25   48 *Katherine*] *20 31*; Katharine *15 16 25*   54 Stage Plays] stage-plays *25*

Justice *Statute*. Ay, Sir *Roger*, you told us it was you that gave him the Hint.

Sir *Roger*. Why Blockhead! Puppy! had you no more Wit than to say the Ceremony? he should only have married you 60 in Rhime, Fool.

Squire *Thomas*. Why, what did I know, ha? but so it is— and since Murder will out, as the Saying is; look ye Father, I was under some sort of a Promise too, d'ye see—so much for that—If I be a Husband, I be a Husband, there's an End on't.—sure I must have been married some time or other.

> [*Sir* Roger *walks up and down fretting, and goes out in a Passion.*

Sir *Humphry*. In troth, it was in some sort my Opinion before; it is good in Law.

Justice *Statute*. Good in Law, good in Law—but hold, we must not lose the Dance.   70

A DANCE.

EPILOGUE.

STAVE.
Our Stage Play has a Moral—and no doubt
You all have Sense enough to find it out.

FINIS.

62 know,] *20 31*; ~^ *15 16 25*   66 sd *fretting,*] ~^ *25*
Epilogue 1 *Stage Play*] *stage-play 25*
FINIS.] *om 20 31*

Three Hours after Marriage.

A

COMEDY.

Rumpatur, quisquis rumpitur invidia.
MART.

Advertisement.

IT may be necessary to acquaint the Reader, that this Play is printed exactly as it is acted; for, tho' the Players in Compliance with the Taste of the Town, broke it into five Parts in the Representation; yet, as the Action pauses, and the Stage is left vacant but three times, so it properly consists but of three Acts, like the *Spanish* Comedies.

I must farther own the Assistance I have receiv'd in this Piece from two of my Friends; who, tho' they will not allow me the Honour of having their Names join'd with mine, cannot deprive me of the Pleasure of making this Acknowledgment.

John Gay.

Advertisement 2   for, tho' . . . Comedies] *om 58*

PROLOGUE.

AUTHORS are judg'd by strange capricious Rules,
The Great Ones are thought mad, the Small Ones Fools.
Yet sure the Best are most severely fated,
For Fools are only laugh'd at, Wits are hated.
Blockheads with Reason Men of Sense abhor;
But Fool 'gainst Fool, is barb'rous civil War.
Why on all Authors then should Criticks fall?
Since some have writ, and shewn no Wit at all.
Condemn a Play of theirs, and they evade it,
Cry, damn not us, but damn the French *that made it;*   10
By running Goods, these graceless Owlers gain,
Theirs are the Rules of France, *the Plots of* Spain:
But Wit, like Wine, from happier Climates brought,
Dash'd by these Rogues, turns English *common Draught:*
They pall Moliere's *and* Lopez *sprightly strain,*
And teach dull Harlequins *to grin in vain.*
How shall our Author hope a gentle Fate,
Who dares most impudently—not translate.
It had been civil in these ticklish Times,
To fetch his Fools and Knaves from foreign Climes;   2ʊ
Spaniard *and* French *abuse to the World's End,*
But spare old England, *lest you hurt a Friend.*
If any Fool is by our Satyr bit,
Let him hiss loud, to show you all—he's hit.
Poets make Characters as Salesmen *Cloaths,*
We take no Measure of your Fops and Beaus;
But here all Sizes and all Shapes ye meet,
And fit your selves—like Chaps in Monmouth-street.
　Gallants look here, this *Fool's-Cap *has an Air—*
Goodly and smart,—with Ears of Issachar.   30
Let no One Man engross it, or confine:

　　　* Shews a Cap with Ears.

PROLOGUE.] PROLOGUE. / Spoke by Mr. WILKS. *58*　　　　　Prologue *5*
Reason] ~ , *17var*　　6 *Fool,*] ~^*58*　　10 *that*] *who M*　　17 *gentle*] *gentler M*
21 Spaniard] *Spaniards 58*　　21 End,] ~^ *58*　　23 *our*] *your 58*　　25 *Characters*]
Chrracters 17var　　26 *Beaus;*] ~.*58*　　27 *ye*] *you M*　　29 *Fool's-Cap*] *fool's*
cap 58　　31 *Man*] *Fool 17var M*

A common Blessing! now 'tis yours, now mine.
But Poets in all Ages, had the Care
To keep this Cap, for such as will, to wear;
Our Author has it now, for ev'ry Wit
Of Course resign'd it to the next that writ:
And thus upon the Stage 'tis fairly † thrown,
Let him that takes it, wear it as his own.

                    † Flings down the Cap, and *Exit*.

    32 *yours*] *your's 58*   37n Cap,] ~^ *58*   38 *as*] *for 58*

Dramatis Personæ.

MEN.

Fossile,		Mr. *Johnson.*
Possum,	} Doctors.	Mr. *Norris.*
Nautilus,		Mr. *Lee.*
Ptisan, Apothecary.		Mr. *Miller.*
Plotwell,		Mr. *Cibber.*
Underplot,		Mr. *Pinkethman,*
Sir *Tremendous,*		Mr. *Bowman.*
First Player,		Mr. *Walker.*
Second Player,		Mr. *Quin.*
Sailor,		Mr. *Bickerstaff.*

Footmen, Servants, &c.

WOMEN.

Mrs. *Townley,*	Mrs. *Oldfield.*
Mrs. *Phœbe Clinket,*	Mrs. *Bicknell.*
Sarsnet,	Mrs. *Hunt.*
Prue,	Mrs. *Willis.*

SCENE, A Room in *Fossile*'s House.

TIME, The same which is taken up in the Representation.

Johnson.] *58*; ~, *17*   *Norris*] *Corey 58*   *Lee*] *Cross 58*   Apothecary.]
58; ~, *17*   *Miller*] *Wright 58*   *Walker*] *Diggs 58*   *Quin*] *Watson 58*
Sailor,] ~. *17 58*   *Townley*] *58*; *Townly 17*   *Bicknell*] *Bicknet 58*
SCENE. . . . Representation.] *om 17var 58*

ACT I.

Enter Fossile, *leading* Townley.

Fossile. WELCOME, my Bride, into the Habitation of thy Husband. The Scruples of the Parson—

Townley. And the Fatigue of the Ceremony—

Fossile. Are at last well over.

Townley. These Blank Licences are wonderful commodious.—The Clergy have a noble Command, in being Rangers of the Park of Matrimony; produce but a Warrant, and they deliver a Lady into your Possession: but I have no Quarrel with them, since they have put me into so good Hands.

Fossile. I now proclaim a solemn Suspension of Arms between Medicine and Diseases. Let Distempers suspend their malignant Influence, and Powders, Pills, and Potions their Operations. Be this Day sacred to my Love. I had rather hold this Hand of thine, than a Dutchess by the Pulse.

Townley. And I this, than a Hand of Matadores.

Fossile. Who knows but your Relations may dispute my Title to your Person? Come, my Dear, the Seal of the Matrimonial Bond is Consummation.

Townley. Alas! what will become of me!

Fossile. Why are thy Eyes fix'd on the Ground? why so slow? and why this Trembling?

Townley. Ah! heedless Creature that I was, to quit all my Relations, and trust myself alone in the Hands of a strange Man!

Fossile. Courage, thou best of my Curiosities. Know that in Husband, is comprehended all Relations; in me thou seest a fond Father.

Townley. Old enough, o'my Conscience. [*Aside.*

Fossile. You may, you must trust yourself with me.

Townley. Do with me as you please: Yet sure you cannot so

soon forget the Office of the Church. Marriage is not to be undertaken wantonly, like Brute Beasts. If you will transgress, the Sin be upon your own Head.

Fossile. Great indeed is thy Virtue, and laudable is thy Modesty. Thou art a Virgin, and I a Philosopher: But learn, that no Animal Action, *quatenus animal*, is unbecoming of either of us. But hold! where am I going? Prithee, my Dear, of what Age art thou?

Townley. Almost Three and Twenty.   40

Fossile. And I almost at my grand Climacterick. What Occasion have I for a Double-Night at these Years? She may be an *Alcmena*, but alas! I am no Thunderer.   [*Aside.*

Townley. You seem somewhat disturb'd; I hope you are well, Mr. *Fossile.*

Fossile. What Business have I in the Bed-chamber, when the Symptoms of Age are upon me? Yet hold, this is the famous Corroborative of *Crollius*; in this Vial are included Sons and Daughters. Oh, for a Draught of the *Aqua Magnanimitatis* for a Vehicle! fifty Drops of *Liquid Laudanum* for her   50 Dose would but just put us upon a *Par*. *Laudanum* would settle the present Ataxy of her Animal Spirits, and prevent her being too watchful.   [*Aside.*

Enter a Servant.

Servant. Sir your Pistachoe-Porridge is ready.   [*Exit.*

Fossile. Now I think of it, my Dear; *Venus*, which is in the first Degree of *Capricorn*, does not culminate till Ten; an Hour, if Astrology is not fallible, successful in Generation.

Townley. I am all Obedience, Sir.

Fossile. How shall I reward thee for so much Goodness? Let our Wedding as yet be a Secret in the Family. In the mean   60 time I'll introduce my Niece *Phœbe Clinket* to your Acquaintance: But alas, the poor Girl has a Procidence of the Pineal Gland, which has occasioned a Rupture in her Understanding. I took her into my House to regulate my Oeconomy; but instead of Puddings, she makes Pastorals; or when she should be raising Paste, is raising some Ghost in a new Tragedy. In short, my House is haunted by all the underling Players, broken Booksellers, half-voic'd Singing-Masters, and disabled Dancing-Masters in Town. In a former Will I had left her my Estate; but I now resolve that Heirs of   70 my own Begetting shall inherit. Yonder she comes in her usual Occupation. Let us mark her a while.

Enter Clinket, *and her Maid bearing a Writing-Desk on her Back.* Clinket *Writing, her Head-dress stain'd with Ink, and Pens stuck in her Hair.*

Maid. I had as good carry a Raree-Show about the Street. Oh! how my Back akes!

Clinket. What are the Labours of the Back to those of the Brain? thou Scandal to the Muses. I have now lost a Thought worth a Folio, by thy Impertinence.

Maid. Have not I got a Crick in my Back already, that will make me good for nothing, with lifting your great Books?

80   *Clinket.* Folio's, call them, and not great Books, thou Monster of Impropriety: But have Patience, and I will remember the three Gallery-Tickets I promis'd thee at my New Tragedy.

Maid. I shall never get my Head-Cloaths Clear-starch'd at this rate.

Clinket. Thou Destroyer of Learning, thou worse than a Book-worm; thou hast put me beyond all Patience. Remember how my Lyrick Ode bound about a Tallow-Candle; thy wrapping up Snuff in an Epigram; nay, the

90   unworthy Usage of my Hymn to *Apollo*, filthy Creature! Read me the last Lines I writ upon the *Déluge*, and take care to pronounce them as I taught you.

Maid.   *Swell'd with a Dropsy, sickly Nature lies,*
        And melting in a Diabetes, dies.

                    [*Reads with an affected Tone.*

Clinket. Still without Cadence!

Maid. Swell'd with a Dropsy—

Clinket. Hold. I conceive—

        The roaring Seas o'er the tall Woods have broke,
        And Whales now perch upon the sturdy Oak.

100 Roaring? Stay. Rumbling, roaring, rustling. no; raging Seas.   [*Writing.*

        The raging Seas o'er the tall Woods have broke,
        Now perch, thou Whale, upon the sturdy Oak.

Sturdy Oak? No; steady, strong, strapping, stiff. Stiff? No, stiff is too short.

        `I. 91 Déluge] Déluge 17`

Fossile *and* Townley *come forward.*
What Feast for Fish! Oh too luxurious Treat!
When hungry Dolphins feed on Butchers Meat.

Fossile. Niece, why Niece, Niece! Oh, *Melpomene,* thou
Goddess of Tragedy, suspend thy Influence for a Moment,
and suffer my Niece to give me a rational Answer. This Lady   110
is a Friend of mine; her present Circumstances oblige her to
take Sanctuary in my House; treat her with the utmost
Civility. Let the Tea-Table be made ready.

Clinket. Madam, excuse this Absence of Mind; my animal
Spirits had deserted the Avenues of my Senses, and retired to
the Recesses of the Brain, to contemplate a beautiful Idea. I
could not force the vagrant Creatures back again into their
Posts, to move those Parts of the Body that express Civility.

Townley. A rare Affected Creature this! If I mistake not,
Flattery will make her an useful Tool for my Purpose. [*Aside.*   120
                         [*Exeunt* Townley, Clinket, *and* Maid.

Fossile. Her Jewels, her Strong Box, and all her Things left
behind! If her Uncle should discover her Marriage, he may
lay an Embargo upon her Goods.—I'll send for them.

Enter a Boy with a Letter.

Boy. This is the Ho-ho-house.
Fossile. Child, whom dost thou want?
Boy. Mistress *Townley*'s Ma-ma-maid.
Fossile. What is your Business?
Boy. A L-l-letter.
Fossile. Who sent this Letter?
Boy. O-o-one.   130
Fossile. Give it me, Child. An honest Boy. Give it me, and
I'll deliver it my self. A very honest Boy.
Boy. So.   [*Exit Boy.*
Fossile. There are now no more Secrets between us. Man
and Wife are One.

Madam, Either I mistake the Encouragement I have had, or I am to
be happy to-Night. I hope the same Person will compleat her good
Offices: I stand to Articles. The Ring is a fine one; and I shall have
the Pleasure of putting it on the first time.

This from your impatient, R. P.   140

In the name of Beelzebub, what is this? *Encouragement! Happy to-Night! same Person! good Offices!* Whom hast thou married, poor *Fossile?* Couldst thou not divert thyself still with the Spoils of Quarries and Coal-pits, thy Serpents and thy Salamanders, but thou must have a living Monster too! 'Sdeath! what a Jest shall I be to our Club! Is there no Rope among my Curiosities? Shall I turn her out of doors, and proclaim my Infamy; or lock her up, and bear my Misfortunes? Lock her up! Impossible. One may shut up 150 Volatile Spirits, pen up the Air, confine Bears, Lyons and Tygers, nay, keep even your Gold: But a Wanton Wife who can keep?

Enter Townley.

Townley. Mrs. *Clinket*'s Play is to be read this Morning at the Tea-table: Will you come and Divert your self, Sir?

Fossile. No: I want to be Alone.

Townley. I hope my Company is not Troublesome already. I am as yet a Bride; not a Wife. [*Sighs.*] What means this sudden Change? [*Aside.*] Consider, Mr. *Fossile*, you want your Natural Rest: The Bed would Refresh you. Let me sit by you.

160 *Fossile.* My Head akes, and the Bed always makes it worse.

Townley. Is it hereabouts?   [*Rubs his Temples.*

Fossile. Too sure.   [*Turns from her.*

Townley. Why so Fretful, Mr. *Fossile?*

Fossile. No; I'll dissemble my Passion, and pump her. [*Aside.*] Excess of Joy, my Dear, for my good Fortune overcomes me. I am somewhat Vertiginous, I can hardly stand.

Townley. I hope I was ordain'd for thy Support.

Fossile. My Disorder now begins to dissipate: It was only a 170 little Flatulency, occasion'd by something hard of Digestion. But pray, my Dear, did your Uncle shut you up so close from the Conversation of Mankind?

Townley. *Sarsnet* and *Shock* were my only Company.

Fossile. A very prudent Young-woman this *Sarsnet*; she was undoubtedly a good and faithful Friend in your Solitude.

Townley. When it was her Interest; but I made no Intimacies with my Chamber-Maid.

Fossile. But was there no Lover offer'd his Service to a Lady in Distress?

Townley. Tongue, be upon thy Guard: These Questions 180
must be design'd to trap me. [*Aside*.] A Woman of my
Condition can't well escape Importunity.

Fossile. What was the Name of that disagreeable Fellow,
who, you told me, teaz'd you so?

Townley. His Name? I think he had a thousand Names. In
one Letter he was *Myrtillo*, in another *Corydon*, *Alexis*, and I
don't know what.

> Enter Sarsnet *in Haste to her Mistress: He
> runs and embraces her with great Earnestness.*

Fossile. Dear Mrs. *Sarsnet*, how am I obliged to thee for thy
Services; thou hast made me happy beyond Expression.—I
shall find another Letter upon her.   [*Aside*. 190

> [*He gets his Hand into* Sarsnet's *Pocket, as searching for a
> Letter.*

> [*Whenever* Sarsnet *goes to whisper her Mistress, he gets
> between them.*

> Enter Ptisan.

Ptisan. Mrs. *Colloquintida* complains still of a Dejection of
Appetite; she says that the Genevre is too cold for her
Stomach.

Fossile. Give her a Quieting Draught; but let us not
interrupt one another. Good Mr. *Ptisan*, we are upon Business.

> [Fossile *gets between* Sarsnet *and* Townley.

Ptisan. The Colonel's Spitting is quite suppress'd.

Fossile. Give him a Quieting Draught. Come to Morrow,
Mr. *Ptisan*; I can see no body till then.

Ptisan. Lady *Varnish* finds no Benefit of the Waters, for the
Pimple on the tip of her Nose still continues.   200

Fossile. Give her a Quieting Draught.

Ptisan. Mrs. *Prudentia*'s Tympany grows bigger and bigger.
What, no Pearl Cordial! must I quiet them all?

Fossile. Give them all Quieting Draughts, I say, or Blister
them all, as you please. Your Servant Mr. *Ptisan*.

Ptisan. But then Lady *Giddy*'s Vapours. She calls her
Chamber-maids Nymphs; for she fansies herself *Diana*, and
her Husband *Acteon*.

Fossile. I can attend no Patient till to Morrow. Give her a
Quieting Draught, I say.   210

[*Whenever* Fossile *goes to conduct* Ptisan *to the Door,* Sarsnet *and* Townley *attempt to Whisper;* Fossile *gets between them, and* Ptisan *takes that Opportunity of coming back.*

Ptisan. Then, Sir, there is Miss *Chitty* of the Boarding-School has taken in no natural Sustenance for this Week, but a Halfpeny-worth of Charcoal, and one of her Mittins.

Fossile. Sarsnet, do you wait on Mr. *Ptisan* to the Door. To Morrow let my Patients know I'll visit round.

[*A Knocking at the Door.*

Ptisan. Oh, Sir; here is a Servant of the Countess of *Hippokekoana.* The Emetick has overwrought, and she is in Convulsions.

Fossile. This is unfortunate. Then I must go. Mr. *Ptisan,* my
220　Dear has some Business with me in Private. Retire into my Closet a Moment, and divert your self with the Pictures. There lies your Way, Madam.　　　　　　　[*To* Sarsnet.

[*Exit* Townley *at one Door, and* Sarsnet *at the other.*

Mr. *Ptisan,* pray do you run before, and tell them I am just coming. [*Exit* Ptisan.] All my Distresses come on the Neck of one another. Should this Fellow get to my Bride before I have Bedded her, in a Collection of Cuckolds, what a Rarity should I make! What shall I do? I'll lock her up. Lock up my Bride? My Peace and my Honour demand it, and it shall be so. [*Locks the Door.*] Thomas, Thomas!

Enter Footman.

230　I dreamt last Night I was robb'd. The Town is over-run with Rogues. Who knows but the Rascal that sent the Letter may be now in the House? [*Aside.*] Look up the Chimney, search all the dark Closets, the Coal-hole, the Flower-pots, and forget not the empty But in the Cellar. Keep a strict Watch at the Door, and let no body in till my Return.

[*Exit Footman. A Noise at the Closet-Door.*

(*Within.*) Who's there?—I'm lock'd in. Murder! Fire!

Fossile. Dear Madam, I beg your Pardon.

[*Unlocks the Door. Enter* Townley.]

'Tis well you call'd. I am so apt to lock this Door; an Action meerly mechanical, not spontaneous.

240　*Townley.* Your Conduct, Mr. *Fossile,* for this Quarter of an

Hour has been somewhat mysterious. It has suggested to me what I almost blush to name; your locking me up, confirms this Suspicion. Pray speak plainly, what has caused this Alteration?   [Fossile *shews her the Letter.*
Is this all?   [*Gives him the Letter back.*

Fossile. [reads]. *Either I mistake the Encouragement I have had.* What Encouragement?

Townley. From my Uncle,—if I must be your Interpreter.

Fossile. *Or I am to be happy to Night.*

Townley. To be Married.—If there can be Happiness in 250 that State.

Fossile. *I hope the same Person.*

Townley. Parson. Only a Word mis-spell'd.—Here's Jealousy for you!

Fossile. *Will compleat her good Offices.* A She-Parson, I find!

Townley. He is a *Welshman.* and the *Welsh* always say *Her* instead of His.

Fossile. *I stand to Articles.*

Townley. Of Jointure.

Fossile. *The Ring is a fine one, and I shall have the Pleasure of* 260 *putting it on my self.*

Townley. Who should put on the Wedding-Ring but the Bridegroom?

Fossile. I beseech thee, pardon thy dear Husband. Love and Jealousy are often Companions, and Excess of both had quite obnubilated the Eyes of my Understanding.

Townley. Barbarous Man! I could forgive thee, if thou hadst poison'd my Father, debauch'd my Sister, kill'd my Lap-Dog; but to murder my Reputation!   [*Weeps.*

Fossile. Nay, I bessech thee, forgive me.   [*Kneels.* 270

Townley. I do: But upon Condition your jealous Fit never returns. To a Jealous Man a Whisper is Evidence, and a Dream Demonstration. A civil Letter makes him thoughtful, an innocent Visit mad. I shall try you, Mr. *Fossile*; for don't think I'll be deny'd Company.

Fossile. Nay, prithee, my Dear; I own I have abused thee. But lest my Marriage, and this simple Story should take Air in the Neighbourhood, to Morrow we will retire into the Country together, till the Secret is blown over. I am call'd to

246 [reads.]] (reads) *17*   278 Neighbourhood] Neigbourhood *17*

280 a Patient. In less than half an Hour I'll be with you again my
Dear.   [*Exit* Fossile.

    Townley. *Plotwell*'s Letter had like to have ruin'd me. 'Twas
a neglect in me, not to intrust him with the Secret of my
Marriage. A Jealous Bridegroom! Every Poison has its
Antidote; as Credulity is the Cause, so it shall be the Cure of
his Jealousy. To Morrow I must be spirited away into the
Country; I'll immediately let *Plotwell* know of my Distress:
and this little Time with Opportunity, even on his Wedding-
Day, shall finish him a compleat Husband. Intrigue assist me!
290 and I'll act a Revenge that might have been worthy the most
celebrated Wife in *Boccace*.

               Enter Plotwell *and* Clinket.

Hah! *Plotwell!* which way got he hither? I must caution him
to be upon his Guard.

    Plotwell. Madam, I am agreeably surpriz'd to find you
here.

    Townley. Me, Sir? you are certainly mistaken, for I don't
remember I ever saw you before.

    Plotwell. Madam, I beg your Pardon. How like a Truth
sounds a Lye from the Tongue of a fine Woman.   [*Aside.*
300   *Clinket.* This, Madam, is Mr. *Plotwell*; a Gentleman who is
so infinitely obliging, as to introduce my Play on the Theatre,
by fathering the unworthy Issue of my Muse, at the reading it
this Morning.

    Plotwell. I should be proud, Madam, to be a real Father to
any of your Productions.

    Clinket. Mighty Just. Ha, ha, ha. You know, Mr. *Plotwell*,
that both a Parrot and a Player can utter human Sounds, but
we allow neither of them to be a Judge of Wit. Yet some of
those People have had the Assurance to deny almost all my
310 Performances the Privilege of being Acted. Ah! what a *Goût de
travers* rules the Understandings of the Illiterate!

    Plotwell. There are some, Madam, that nauseate the smell
of a Rose.

    [*Whenever* Plotwell *and* Townley *endeavour to talk, she inter-
      rupts them.*

    Clinket. If this Piece be not rais'd to the Sublime, let me
henceforth be stigmatiz'd as a Reptile in the Dust of

281 *Exit* Fossile] Exit *Fossile 17*   311 Understandings] understanding *58*

Mediocrity. I am persuaded, Sir, your adopted Child will do you no Dishonour.

Townley. Pray, Madam, what is the Subject?

Clinket. Oh! beyond every Thing. So adapted for tragical Machines! So proper to excite the Passions! Not in the least 320 encumber'd with Episodes! The *Vray-semblance* and the *Miraculous* are linkt together with such Propriety!

Townley. But the Subject, Madam?

Clinket. The *Universal Deluge.* I chose that of *Deucalion* and *Pyrrha*, because neither our Stage nor Actors are hallow'd enough for Sacred Story.

Plotwell. But, Madam—   [*To* Townley.

Clinket. What just occasion for noble Description! These Players are exceeding Dilatory.—In the mean time, Sir, shall I be obliged to you and this Lady for a Rehearsal of a Scene 330 that I have been just touching up with some lively Strokes.

Townley. I dare assure you, Madam, it will be a Pleasure to us both. I'll take this occasion to inform you of my present Circumstances.   [*To* Plotwell.

Clinket. Imagine *Deucalion* and *Pyrrha* in their Boat. They pass by a Promontory, where stands Prince *Hæmon* a former Lover of *Pyrrha*'s, ready to be swallowed up by the devouring Flood. She presses her Husband to take him into the Boat. Your Part, Sir, is *Hæmon*; the Lady personates *Pyrrha*; and I represent *Deucalion.* To you, Sir,   340

[*Gives* Plotwell *the Manuscript.*

Plotwell. What ho, there Sculler!   [*reads.*

Townley.   Hæmon!

Plotwell.   *Yes, 'tis* Hæmon!

Townley. Thou seest me now sail'd from my former Lodgings,
Beneath a Husband's Ark; yet fain I would reward
Thy proffer'd Love. But Hæmon, *ah, I fear*
To Morrow's Eve will hide me in the Country.

Clinket. Not a Syllable in the Part! Wrong, all wrong!

Plotwell. Through all the Town, with diligent Enquiries,
I sought my Pyrrha—   350

Clinket. Beyond all Patience! the Part, Sir, lies before you; you are never to perplex the *Drama* with Speeches *Extempore.*

Plotwell. Madam, 'tis what the top-Players often do.

330 a Rehearsal] the ~ *58*

Townley. Though Love denies, Compassion bids me save thee.
                                        [*Plotwell kisses her.*
   Clinket. Fye Mr. *Plotwell*; this is against all the Decorum of
the Stage; I will no more allow the Libertinism of Lip-
Embraces than the Barbarity of Killing on the Stage. Your
best Tragedians, like the Ladys of Quality in a Visit, never
turn beyond the back-part of the Cheek to a Salute, as thus
360 Mr. *Plotwell.*   [*Kisses* Plotwell.
   Plotwell. I don't find in *Aristotle* any Precept against
Kissing.
   Clinket. Yet I would not stand upon the brink of an
Indecorum.
   Plotwell. True, Madam, the finishing Stroke of Love and
Revenge should never shock the Eyes of an Audience. But I
look upon a Kiss in a Comedy to be upon a Par with a Box on
the Ear in Tragedy, which is frequently given and taken by
your best Authors.
370   *Clinket.* Mighty just! for a Lady can no more put up a Kiss
than a Gentleman a Box on the Ear. Take my Muse, Sir, into
your Protection [*gives him her Play*] the Players I see are here.
Your personating the Author will infallibly introduce my Play
on the Stage, and spite of their Prejudice, make the Theatre
ring with Applause, and teach even that injudicious *Canaille*
to know their own Interest.
              Enter Sir Tremendous *with two Players.*
   Plotwell. Gentlemen, This Lady who Smiles on my
Performances, has permitted me to introduce you and my
Tragedy to her Tea-Table.
380   *Clinket.* Gentlemen, you do me Honour.
   1st Player. Suffer us, Sir, to recommend to your
Acquaintance, the famous Sir *Tremendous*, the greatest Critick
of our Age.
   Plotwell. Sir *Tremendous*, I rejoice at your Presence; though
no Lady that has an Antipathy, so sweats at a Cat, as some
Authors at a Critick. Sir *Tremendous*, Madam, is a Gentleman
who can instruct the Town to dislike what has pleased them,

     358 Ladys] ladies *58*   360 Plotwell] *Plotwell 17*   368 in] in a *58*
371 Take] ~, *17*   376 sd *Enter . . . Players.*] *Exit.* ACT II. PLOTWELL,
TOWNLEY, CLINKET, with Sir TREMENDOUS and two Players, discovered
seated round a Table. *58*   385 Cat,] ~^ *58*

and to be pleased with what they disliked.

Sir *Tremendous*. Alas! what signifies one good Palate when the Taste of the whole Town is viciated. There is not in all this *Sodom* of Ignorance Ten righteous Criticks, who do not judge things backward. 390

Clinket. I perfectly agree with Sir *Tremendous*: Your modern Tragedies are such egregious Stuff, they neither move Terror nor Pity.

Plotwell. Yes, Madam, the Pity of the Audience on the First Night, and the Terror of the Author for the Third. Sir *Tremendous*'s Plays indeed have rais'd a sublimer Passion, Astonishment.

Clinket. I perceive here will be a Wit-Combat between these Beaux-Esprits. *Prue*, be sure you set down all the Similes. 400

Prue *retires to the back part of the Stage with Pen and Ink*.

Sir *Tremendous*. The Subjects of most modern Plays are as ill chosen as—

Plotwell. The Patrons of their Dedications.

[Clinket *makes Signs to* Prue.

Sir *Tremendous*. Their Plots as shallow—

Plotwell. As those of bad Poets against new Plays.

Sir *Tremendous*. Their Episodes as little of a Peice to the main Action, as—

Clinket. A black Gown with a Pink-colour'd Peticoat. Mark that *Prue*. [*Aside*. 410

Sir *Tremendous*. Their Sentiments are so very delicate—

Plotwell. That like whipt Syllabub they are lost before they are tasted.

Sir *Tremendous*. Their Diction so low, that—that—

Plotwell. Why, that their Friends are forced to call it Simplicity.

1*st Player*. Sir, to the Play if you please.

2*d Player*. We have a Rehearsal this Morning.

Sir *Tremendous*. And then their Thefts are so open—

Plotwell. That the very *French* Taylors can discover them. 420

Sir *Tremendous*. O what Felony from the Ancients! What Petty-Larcenry from the Moderns! There is the famous

407 Peice] piece *58*   409 Peticoat] petticoat *58*   422 Petty-Larcenry] petty larceny *58*

Iphigenia of *Racine*, he stole his *Agamemnon* from *Seneca*, who stole it from *Euripides*, who stole it from *Homer*, who stole it from all the Ancients before him. In short there is nothing so execrable as our most taking Tragedys.

 1st Player. O! but the immortal *Shakespear*, Sir.

 Sir *Tremendous.* He had no Judgment.

 2d Player. The famous *Ben. Johnson!*

430 *Clinket.* Dry.

 1st Player. The tender *Otway!*

 Sir *Tremendous.* Incorrect.

 2d Player. Etheridge!

 Clinket. Meer Chit-chat.

 1st Player. Dryden!

 Sir *Tremendous.* Nothing but a Knack of Versifying.

 Clinket. Ah! dear Sir *Tremendous*, there is that *Delicatesse* in your Sentiments!

 Sir *Tremendous.* Ah Madam! there is that Justness in your

440 Notions!

 Clinket. I am so charm'd with your manly Penetration!

 Sir *Tremendous.* I with your profound Capacity!

 Clinket. That I am not able—

 Sir *Tremendous.* That it is impossible—

 Clinket. To conceive—

 Sir *Tremendous.* To express—

 Clinket. With what Delight I embrace—

 Sir *Tremendous.* With that Pleasure I enter into—

 Clinket. Your Ideas, most learned Sir *Tremendous!*

450| Sir *Tremendous.* Your Sentiments, most divine Mrs. *Clinket.*

 2d Player. The Play, for Heaven's Sake, the Play.

    [*A Tea Table brought in.*]

 Clinket. This finish'd *Drama* is too good for an Age like this.

 Plotwell. The universal Deluge, or the Tragedy of *Deucalion* and *Pyrrha*.   [*reads.*

 Clinket. Mr. *Plotwell*, I will not be deny'd the Pleasure of reading it, you will pardon me.

 1st Player. The Deluge! the Subject seems to be too *recherché*.

423 *Iphigenia*] Ephigenia *58* 426 Tragedys] tragedies *58* 427 *Shakespear*] Shakespeare *58* 427 Sir.] ~, *17* 441 so] so much *58* 454 *reads.*] ~, *17*

Clinket. A Subject untouch'd either by Ancients or
Moderns, in which are Terror and Pity in perfection.   460

1st Player. The Stage will never bear it. Can you suppose,
Sir, that a Box of Ladies will sit Three Hours to see a rainy
Day, and a Sculler in a Storm? Make your best of it, I know it
can be nothing else.

2d Player. If you please, Madam, let us hear how it opens.

Clinket. [reads.] *The Scene opens, and discovers the Heavens
cloudy. A prodigious Shower of Rain, at a distance appears the Top of
the Mountain* Parnassus, *all the Fields beneath are over-flowed, there
are seen Cattle and Men swimming. The Tops of Steeples rise above
the Flood, with Men and Women perching on their Weather-cocks—*   470

Sir *Tremendous*. Begging your Pardon, Sir, I believe it can
be proved, that Weather-cocks are of a modern Invention.
Besides, if Stones were dissolved, as a late Philosopher hath
proved, how could Steeples stand?

Plotwell. I don't insist upon Trifles. Strike it out.

Clinket. Strike it out! consider what you do. In this they
strike at the very Foundation of the *Drama*. Don't almost all
the Persons of your Second Act start out of Stones that
Deucalion and *Pyrrha* threw behind them? This Cavil is levell'd
at the whole System of the Reparation of human Race.   480

1st Player. Then the Shower is absurd.

Clinket. Why should not this Gentleman rain, as well as
other Authors snow and thunder?—[reads.] *Enter* Deucalion
in a sort of Waterman's Habit, leading his Wife Pyrrha *to a Boat—*
Her first Distress is about her going back to fetch a Casket of
Jewels. Mind, how he imitates your great Authors. The first
Speech has all the Fire of *Lee*.

>   *Tho' Heav'n wrings all the Sponges of the Sky,*
>   *And pours down Clouds, at once each Cloud a Sea.*
>   *Not the Spring-Tides—*   490

Sir *Tremendous*. There were no Spring-Tides in the
Mediterranean, and consequently *Deucalion* could not make that
Simile.

Clinket. A Man of *Deucalion*'s Quality might have travelled beyond the *Mediterranean*, and so your Objection is
answered. Observe, Sir *Tremendous*, the Tenderness of *Otway*,

---

461 it. Can] *58*; it, can *17*   467 *Rain, at*] rain. At *58*   468 Parnassus,]
~ ; *58*   468 *over-flowed,*] ~ ; *58*

in this Answer of *Pyrrha*.

> *Why do the Stays*
> *Taper my Waste, but for thy circling Arms?*

500   Sir *Tremendous*. Ah! *Anachronisms!* Stays are a modern Habit, and the whole Scene is monstrous, and against the Rules of Tragedy.

Plotwell. I submit Sir,—out with it.

Clinket. Were the Play mine, you should gash my Flesh, mangle my Face, any thing sooner than scratch my Play.

Plotwell. Blot and insert wherever you please—I submit my self to your Judgment.

> *Plotwell* rises, and discourses apart with *Townley*.

Sir *Tremendous*. Madam, Nonsence and I have been at variance from my Cradle, it sets my Understanding on Edge.

510   *2d Player*. Indeed, Madam, with Submission, and I think I have some Experience of the Stage, this Play will hardly take.

Clinket. The worst Lines of it would be sufficiently clapt, if it had been writ by a known Author, or recommended by one.

Sir *Tremendous*. Between you and I Madam, who understand better things, this Gentleman knows nothing of Poetry.

1st Player. The Gentleman may be an honest Man, but he is a damn'd Writer, and it neither can take, nor ought to take.

Sir *Tremendous*. If you are the Gentleman's Friend, and value his Reputation, advise him to burn it.

520   *Clinket*. What Struggles has an unknown Author to vanquish Prejudice! Suppose this Play acts but Six Nights, his next may play Twenty. Encourage a young Author, I know it will be your Interest.

2d Player. I would sooner give Five Hundred Pounds than bring some Plays on the Stage; an Audience little considers whether 'tis the Author or the Actor that is hiss'd, our Character suffers.

1st Player. Damn our Character—We shall lose Money by it.

530   *Clinket*. I'le deposite a Sum my self upon the Success of it. Well, since it is to be play'd—I will prevail upon him to strike out some few things.—Take the Play, Sir *Tremendous*.

> Sir Tremendous *reads in a muttering Tone*.

Sir *Tremendous*. Absurd to the last Degree [*strikes out.*] palpable Nonsense! [*strikes out.*]

Clinket. What all those Lines! spare those for a Lady's Sake, for those indeed, I gave him.

Sir *Tremendous.* Such Stuff! [*strikes out.*] abominable! [*strikes out.*] most execrable!

1*st Player.* This Thought must out.

2*d Player.* Madam, with Submission, this Metaphor.   540

1*st Player.* This whole Speech.

Sir *Tremendous.* The Fable!

Clinket. To you I answer—

1*st Player.* The Characters!

Clinket. To you I answer—

Sir *Tremendous.* The Diction!

Clinket. And to you—Ah, hold, hold—I'm butcher'd, I'm massacred. For Mercy's Sake! murder, murder! ah! [*faints.*

Enter Fossile *peeping at the Door.*

Fossile. My House turn'd to a Stage! and my Bride playing her Part too! what will become of me? but I'le know the   550
Bottom of all this. [*aside.*] I am surprised to see so many Patients here so early. What is your Distemper, Sir?

1*st Player.* The Cholick, Sir, by a Surfeit of green Tea and damn'd Verses.

Fossile. Your Pulse is very high, Madam. [*to* Townley.] You sympathize, I perceive, for yours is somewhat feverish. [*to* Plotwell.] But I believe I shall be able to put off the Fit for this time. And as for you, Neice, you have got the poetical Itch, and are possess'd with Nine Devils, your Nine Muses; and thus I commit them and their Works to the Flames.   560

[*Takes up a Heap of Papers, and flings them into the Fire.*]

Clinket. Ah! I am an undone Woman.

Plotwell. Has he burnt any Bank-Bills, or a new *Mechlen* Head-Dress?

Clinket. My Works! my Works!

1*st Player.* Has he destroy'd the Writings of an Estate, or your Billet-doux?

Clinket. A Pindarick Ode! five Similes! and half an Epilogue!

2*d Player.* Has he thrown a new Fan, or your Pearl Necklace into the Flames?   570

Clinket. Worse, worse! The tag of the Acts of a new Comedy! a Prologue sent by a Person of Quality! three Copies of recommendatory Verses! and two Greek Mottos!

Fossile. Gentlemen, if you please to walk out.

2d Player. You shall have our positive Answer concerning your Tragedy, Madam, in an hour or two.

                [*Exit Sir* Tremendous, Plotwell *and* Players.

Fossile. Though this Affair looks but ill; yet I will not be over-rash: What says *Libanius? a false Accusation often recoils upon the Accuser*; and I have suffer'd already by too great
580 Precipitation.   [*Exit* Fossile.

               Enter Sarsnet.

Townley. A narrow Escape, *Sarsnet! Plotwell*'s Letter was intercepted and read by my Husband.

Sarsnet. I tremble every Joint of me. How came you off?

Townley. Invention flow'd, I Ly'd, he Believ'd. True Wife, true Husband!

Sarsnet. I have often warn'd you, Madam, against this Superfluity of Gallants; you ought at least to have clear'd all Mortgages upon your Person before you Leas'd it out for Life. Then, besides *Plotwell*, you are every moment in danger of
590 *Underplot*, who attends on *Plotwell* like his Shadow; he is unlucky enough to stumble upon your Husband, and then I'm sure his Shatterbrains would undo us at once.

Townley. Thy Wit and Industry *Sarsnet* must help me out. To day is Mine, to morrow is my Husbands.

Sarsnet. But some speedy Method must be thought of, to prevent your Letters from falling into his Hands.

Townley. I can put no confidence in my Landlady Mrs. *Chambers*, since our Quarrel at Parting. So I have given Orders to her Maid to direct all Letters and Messages hither,
600 and I have placed my own trusty Servant *Hugh* at the Door to receive them—but see, yonder comes my Husband, I'll retire to my Closet.   [*Exit* Townley *and* Sarsnet.

               Enter Fossile.

Fossile. O Marriage, thou bitterest of Potions, and thou strongest of Astringents! This *Plotwell* that I found talking

---

576 sd *Exit Sir* Tremendous, Plotwell *and* Players] Exit *Sir Tremendous, Plotwell* and *Players 17*   578 *Libanius*] Lybanius *58*   580 Fossile] *Fossile 17*   580 sd Sarsnet] *Sarsnet 17*   602 Townley *and* Sarsnet] *Townly* and *Sarsnet 17*

with her must certainly be the Person that sent the Letter. But
if I have a *Bristol* Stone put upon me instead of a Diamond,
why should I by Experiments spoil its Lustre? She is
Handsome, that is certain. Could I but keep her to my self for
the Future! Cuckoldom is an acute Case, it is quickly over;
when it takes Place, it admits of no Remedy but Palliatives.— 610
Be it how it will, while my Marriage is a Secret—

Within. Bless the noble Doctor *Fossile* and his honourable
Lady. The City Musick are come to Wish him much Joy of his
Marriage.   [*A flourish of Fiddles.*

Fossile. Joy and Marriage, never were two Words so
coupled!

Within. Much Happiness attend the learned Doctor *Fossile*
and his worthy and virtuous Lady. The Drums and Trumpets
of his Majesty's Guards are come to Salute him—

[*A flourish of Drums and Trumpets.*

Fossile. Ah *Fossile*! wretched *Fossile*! into what State hast 620
thou brought thy self! thy Disgrace proclaim'd by Beat of
Drum! new Married men are treated like those bit by a
Tarantula, both must have Musick: But where are the Notes
that can expell a Wife!   [*Exit.*

ACT II.

Enter Fossile *in a Footman's Cloaths.*

Fossile. A Special Dog; this Footman of my Wife's! as
mercenary as the Porter of a First Minister! why should she
place him as a Centinel at my Door? unquestionably, to carry
on her intrigues. Why did I Bribe him to Lend me his Livery?
to discover those intriegues. And now, O wretched *Fossile*, thou
hast debas'd thyself into the low Character of a Footman.
What then? Gods and Demi-gods have assum'd viler shapes:
They, to make a Cuckold; I, to prove myself one. Why then
should my Metamorphosis be more shameful, when my
purpose is more honest?   10

[*Knocking at the Door, enter Footman.*]

Footman. Ay, this is her Livery. Friend, give this to your
Mistress.   [*Gives a Letter to* Fossile *and Exit.*

624 [*Exit*] Exit 17
ACT II] ACT III *58*

Fossile. [reads.] *Madam, You have Jilted me. What I gave you cost me dear; what you might have given me, would have cost you nothing. You shall use my next Present with more respect. I Presented you a fine Snuff-Box, you gave it to that Coxcomb* Underplot, *and* Underplot *gave it to my Wife. Judge of my Surprise.*

Freeman.

A fine circulation of a Snuff-Box! in time I shall have the
20 rarest of my Shells set off with Gold Hinges, to make Presents
to all the Fops about Town. My *Conchæ Veneris*; and perhaps,
even my *Nautilus.*

A Knocking at the Door. Enter an Old Woman.

Old Woman. Can I speak with your good Mistress, Honest
Friend?

Fossile. No, She's busy.

Old Woman. Madam *Wyburn* presents her Service and has
sent this Letter.   [*Exit.*

Fossile. [reads.] *Being taken up with waiting upon Merchants Ladys this morning, I have sent to acquaint you my dear sweet Mrs.*
30 Townley, *that the Alderman agrees to every thing but putting away his Wife, which he says is not Decent at that end of the Town. He desires a Meeting this Evening.*

Postscript.
He does not like the Grocer's Wife at all.

Bless me! what a libidinous Age we Live in! neither his own
Wife! nor the Grocer's Wife! will People like Nobody's Wife
but mine!

[*Knocking at the Door. Enter Footman, gives a Letter and Exit.*]
[*Enter another Footman, gives a Letter, and Exit.*]

Fossile. [reads.] *Sincerely Madam, I cannot spare that Summ; especially in Monthly payments. My good Friend and Neighbour*
40 Pinch, *a quiet, sober Man, is content to go a third part, only for Leave to Visit upon Sabbath days.*

Habakkuk Plumb.

Well, Frugality is laudable even in Iniquity! Now for this
other.

Opens the Second Letter.

Fossile. [reads.] *Madam, I can't make you Rich, but I can make you Immortal.*

Verses on Mrs. Susanna Townley, *in the front Box dress'd in Green.*
    In You the Beautys of the Spring are seen,
    Your Cheeks are Roses, and your Dress is Green.
A poor Dog of a Poet! I fear him not.   50
    Enter a ragged Fellow with a Letter.
Footman. My Master is at present under a Cloud—He begs
you will deliver this Letter to your Lady.   [*Exit.*
Fossile. [reads.] *I am reduced by your Favours to ask the thing I
formerly deny'd; that you would entertain me as a Husband, who can
no longer keep you as a Mistress.*

                             Charles Bat.

Why did I part with this Fellow? This was a Proposal indeed,
to make both me and himself happy at once! He shall have
her, and a Twelve-month's Fees into the Bargain. Where shall
I find him?—Why was the Mistress of all Mankind unknown 60
to thee alone? Why is Nature so dark in our greatest
Concerns? Why are there no external Symptoms of
Defloration, nor any Pathognomick of the Loss of Virginity
but a big Belly? Why has not Lewdness it's Tokens like the
Plague? Why must a Man know Rain by the aking of his
Corns, and have no prognostick of what is of infinitely greater
Moment, Cuckoldome? Or if there are any Marks of Chastity,
why is the Enquiry allowed only to *Jews,* and deny'd to
Christians? O *Townley, Townley!* once to me the fragrant Rose;
now Aloes, Wormwood and Snake-root! but I must not be 70
seen.

       As Townley *and* Sarsnet *enter,* Fossile *sneaks off.*
Townley. Sarsnet, we are betray'd. I have discovered my
Husband posted at the Door in *Hugh's* Livery, he has
intercepted all my Letters. I immediately writ this, which is
the only thing that can bring us off. Run this Moment to
Plotwell, get him to copy it, and send it directed to me by his
own Servant with the utmost Expedition. He is now at the
Chocolate-House in the next Street.
Sarsnet. I fly Madam; but how will you disengage your self
from the Affair with *Underplot?*   80

      64 Why] ~, *17*   68 *Jews*] Turks and Jews *58*

Townley. Leave it to me. Though he wants Sense, he's handsome, and I like the Fellow; and if he is lucky enough to come in my Husband's Absence.—But prithee *Sarsnet* make haste.

[*Exit* Townley *and* Sarsnet, *upon which* Fossile *re-enters,
to him* Underplot.

Underplot. Hearke'e, Friend. I never talk with one of your Coat, but I first tip him.

Fossile. Behold the Lucre of a Pimp! between the Pox abroad, and my Plague at home, I find a Man may never want Fees. [*aside.*] Your Honour's Commands, I pray. I long 90 to serve you.

Underplot. Ah, Boy! thou hast a rare Mistress for Vails. Come, I know thou art a sly Dog; Can'st thou introduce me to her for a Moment's Conversation?

Fossile. Impossible.

Underplot. What, still impossible?   [*Gives more Money.*

Fossile. Still impossible.

Underplot. Poh, Pox. But prithee, Friend, by the by; is there any thing in this Report that she is marry'd to the Doctor here?

100 *Fossile.* I am afraid there is something in it.

Underplot. What a Spirit does a Jealous Husband give to an Intrigue! Pray, is he not a most egregious silly Animal?

Fossile. Not exceeding wise indeed.

Underplot. Rich?

Fossile. He has Money.

Underplot. That will save the Expence of her Gallants. Old?

Fossile. Ay, too old, Heaven knows.

Underplot. How came it into the Puppy's Head to marry?

Fossile. By the Instigation of Satan.

110 *Underplot.* I'll help the old Fool to an Heir.

Fossile. No doubt on't. If the whole Town can do it, he will not want one.

Underplot. Come, prithee deal freely with me. Has *Plotwell* been here since the Wedding?

Fossile. He has! too sure: [*aside.*] He's a dangerous Rival to you; if you have a mind to succeed, keep a strict Watch upon him, that he may not get admittance before you.

Underplot. Well. Since thou hast shown thy self so much my
Friend, I'll let thee into a Secret. *Plotwell* and I no sooner
heard of the Wedding, but we made a Bett of a Hundred 120
Guineas, who should dub the Doctor first. Remember, you go
twenty Pieces with me.

Fossile. But here is some Body coming. Away, you are sure
of my Interest.   [*Exit* Underplot.

Fossile. This was well judg'd. I have a small Territory
coveted by two rival Potentates. It is profound Policy to make
them watch one the other, and so keep the Balance of Power in
my own Hands. Certainly nothing so improves one's Politicks,
as to have a Coquet to one's Wife.

Enter a Footman with a Letter.

Footman. This is for your Lady. Deliver it safe into her own 130
Hands.   [*Exit Footman.*

Fossile. [reads.] *Know, cruel Woman, I have discover'd the Secret
of your Marriage; you shall have all the Plague of a jealous Husband,
without the Pleasure of giving him Cause. I have this Morning
counterfeited Billets-doux and Letters from Bawds; nay, I have sent
Pimps; some of which, I hope, are fallen into your old Coxcomb's
Hands. If you deny me the Pleasure of tipping him a real Cuckold, at
least I'll have the Resentment to make him an imaginary one. Know,
that this is not the hundredth part of the Revenge that shall be executed
upon thee, by*
                                               R. P. 140

Townley. [*Peeping.*] So. The Letter works as I would have it.
                                                    [*Aside.*

Fossile. How true is that saying of the Philosopher! *We only
know, that we know nothing.* The Eruption of those Horns which
seem'd to make so strong a push is now suppress'd. Is the
Mystery of all these Letters nothing but the Revenge of a
disappointed Lover? The Hand and Seal are just the same
with the *Welchman's* that I intercepted a while ago. Truly,
these *Welch* are a hot revengeful People. My Wife may be
Virtuous; she may not. Prevention is the safest Method with
Diseases and Intrigues. Women are wanton, Husbands weak, 150
Bawds busy, Opportunities dangerous, Gallants eager; therefore it behoves honest Men to be watchful. But here comes my
Wife, I must hide my self; for should I be detected, she might

124 Underplot] *Underplot 17*   132 [reads] ⁓ *reads 17*

have a just Cause of complaint for my impertinent Curiosity.
[*Exit* Fossile.

Enter Townley; *and to her* Sarsnet *at the other Door.*

Sarsnet. Your Orders, Madam, have been executed to a tittle, and I hope with Success.

Townley. Extreamly well. Just as we could have wish'd. But I can't forgive that Rascal *Hugh.* To turn him away would be dangerous. We will rather take the Advantage of the
160 Confidence my Husband has in him. Leave the Husband to me, and do you Discipline the Footman. Such early Curiosity must be crush'd in the bud. *Hugh, Hugh, Hugh.* [*calls aloud, and rings*] What is become of the Rogue?

[Townley *runs in, and drags out* Fossile *changing his Cloaths with* Hugh.

Why Sirrah! must one call all Day for you?   [*Cuffs him.*

Sarsnet. A Rogue in Disguise, got in to rob the House! Thieves, Thieves.

Enter Clinket, Prue *with the writing Desk, and Servants.*

Fossile. St. St—no Noise. Prithee, Dearee, look upon me. See, see, thy own dear Husband. It is I.

Townley. What an unfortunate Woman am I! Could not
170 you pass one Day without an Intrigue? and with a Cookwench too! for you could put on a Livery for no other end. You wicked Man.

Sarsnet. His Coldness, Madam, is now no longer a Mystery. Filthy Monster! wer't not thou provided with my Mistress as a Remedy for thy rampant Unchastity?

Townley. Was all your Indifference to me for this! you Brute you.   [*Weeps.*

Fossile. Nay, Prithee, Dearee, judge not rashly. My Character is establish'd in the World. There lives not a more
180 sober, chast, and virtuous Person than Doctor *Fossile.*

Townley. Then why this Disguise?

Fossile. Since it must come out; ha, ha, ha, only a frolick on my Wedding Day between *Hugh* and I. We had a mind to exhibit a little Mummery.

Clinket. What joy arises in my Soul! to see my Uncle in a Dramatick Character! since your Humour led you to the *Drama,* Uncle, why would you not consult a relative Muse in

154 sd Fossile] *Fossile 17*   165 A] This is not Hugh, madam; a *58*

your own Family? I have always used you as my Physician; and why should not you use me as your Poet?

Fossile. Prithee, Dear, leave me a Moment. This is a Scandal to my Gravity. I'll be with you, as my self, immediately.   [*Exeunt omnes, except* Fossile *and* Hugh.

As they are changing Habits, Fossile *says*,
As a mark of my Confidence in thee, I leave thee Guardian of my House while I go my rounds. Let none in but Patients; wan, sickly Fellows, no Person in the least degree of bodily Strength.

Hugh. Worthy Doctor, You may rely upon my Honour.
[*Exit* Fossile.
I have betray'd my Mistress. My Conscience flies in my Face, and I can ease it no way but by betraying my Master.
[*Knocking at the Door.*
This is not the Doctor; but he is dress'd like him, and that shall be my Excuse.
[*He lets* Plotwell *in,* Townley *meets him, they Embrace.*

Townley. Hugh, Go, wait at the Door.   [*Exit* Hugh.

Plotwell. This Disguise gives Spirit to my Intrigue. Certainly I am the first Person that ever enjoy'd a Bride without the scandal of Matrimony.

Townley. I have a different relish, Mr. *Plotwell*, for now I can't abide you, you are so like my Husband.

Plotwell. Underplot, I defy thee. I have laid the Wager, and now I hold the Stakes.

Townley. Opportunity, Mr. *Plotwell*, has been the downfall of much Virtue.   [*As he is leading her off, enter* Hugh.

Hugh. Ah Madam! the Doctor! the Doctor!   [*Exit* Hugh.

Plotwell. Fear nothing. I'll stand it. I have my Part ready.
[*Exit* Townley.

Enter Fossile.

Fossile. I promis'd Lady *Longfort* my Eagle-stone. The poor Lady is like to miscarry, and 'tis well I thought on't. Hah! who is here! I do not like the Aspect of the Fellow. But I will not be over censorious.

[*They make many bows and cringes in advancing to each
other.*

Plotwell. Illustrissime Domine, huc adveni—

214 Longfort] Langfort 58

*Fossile. Illustrissime Domine—non usus sum loquere Latinam—*If
220 you cannot speak *English,* we can have no lingual
Conversation.

Plotwell. I can speak a little *Englise.* I have great deal
heard of de Fame of de great Luminary of all Arts and
Sciences, de illustrious Doctor *Fossile.* I would make commu-
tation (what do you call it) I would exchange some of my
tings for some of his tings.

Fossile. Pray, Sir, what University are you of?

Plotwell. De famous University of *Cracow* in *Polonia minor.* I
have cur'd de King of *Sweden* of de Wound. My Name be
230 Doctor *Cornelius Lubomirski.*

Fossile. Your *Lubomirskis* are a great Family. But what
Arcana are you Master of, Sir?

Plotwell. [*Shows a large Snuff-box.*] See dere, Sir, dat Box de
Snuff.

Fossile. Snuff-box.

Plotwell. Right. Snuff-box. Dat be de very true Gold.

Fossile. What of that?

Plotwell. Vat of dat? me make dat Gold my own self, of de
Lead of de great Church of *Cracow.*

240 *Fossile.* By what Operations?

Plotwell. By Calcination; Reverberation; Purification;
Sublimation; Amalgamation; Precipitation; Volitilization.

Fossile. Have a care what you assert. The Volitilization of
Gold is not an obvious Process. It is by great elegance of
Speech called, *fortitudo fortitudinis fortissima.*

Plotwell. I need not acquaint de illustrious Doctor *Fossile,*
dat all de Metals be but unripe Gold.

Fossile. Spoken like a Philosopher. And therefore there
should be an Act of Parliament against digging of Lead
250 Mines, as against felling young Timber. But inform me, Sir,
what might be your *menstruum,* Snow-water, or May-dew?

Plotwell. Snow-Vater.

Fossile. Right. Snow is the universal Pickle of Nature for
the preservation of her Productions in the hyemal Season.

Plotwell. If you will go your self, and not trust de Servant,

219 *Latinam*] *Latinum 58*   222 speak] speak but *58*   222 I have] Me ave *58*
232 of, Sir?] of? Sir. *17*   239 *Cracow*] *Crawcow 58*   242 Amalgamation] *58;*
Amalgumation *17*

to fetch some of de right *Thames* Sand dat be below de Bridge, I will show you de naked *Diana* in your Study, before I go hence.

Fossile. Perhaps you might. I am not at present dispos'd for Experiments.   260

Plotwell. This Bite wont take to send him out of the Way, I'll change my Subject. [*aside.*] Do you deal in Longitudes, Sir?

Fossile. I deal not in impossibilities. I search only for the grand Elixir.

Plotwell. Vat do you tink of de new Metode of Fluxion?

Fossile. I know no other but by *Mercury.*

Plotwell. Ha, ha. Me mean de Fluxion of de Quantity.

Fossile. The greatest Quantity I ever knew, was three Quarts a Day.   270

Plotwell. Be dere any secret in the Hydrology, Zoology, Minerology, Hydraulicks, Acausticks, Pneumaticks, Logarithmatechny, dat you do want de Explanation of?

Fossile. This is all out of my Way. Do you know of any Hermaphrodites, monstrous Twins, Antidiluvian Shells, Bones, and Vegetables?

Plotwell. Vat tink you of an Antidiluvian Knife, Spoon, and Fork, with the Mark of *Tubal Cain* in *Hebrew*, dug out of de Mine of *Babylon?*

Fossile. Of what Dimensions, I pray, Sir?   280

Plotwell. De Spoon be bigger dan de modern Ladle; de Fork, like de great Fire-fork; and de Knife, like de Cleaver.

Fossile. Bless me! this shows the Stature and Magnitude of those Antidiluvians!

Plotwell. To make you convinc'd that I tell not de lie, dey are in de *Turkey* Ship at *Vapping*, just going to be dispos'd of. Me would go there vid you, but de Business vil not let me.

Fossile. An extraordinary Man this! I'll examine him further. [*Aside.*] How could your Country lose so great a Man as you?   290

Plotwell. Dat be de Secret. But because me vil have de fair Correspondence with de illustrious Doctor *Fossile*, me vil not deny dat *Orpheus* and me had near run de same Fate, for different Reason. I was hunted out of my Country by de

278 de] the *58*

general Insurrection of de Women.

Fossile. How so pray?

Plotwell. Because me have prepare a certain Liquor which discover whether a Woman be a Virgin or no.

Fossile. A curious Discovery! have you any of it still?

300 *Plotwell.* Dere it is, Sir. It be commonly called de *Lapis Lydius Virginitatis*, or Touchstone of Virginity.

[*Gives him a Vial.*

Fossile. It has the smell of your common Hart's-horn. But all your Volatile Spirits have a near resemblance.

Plotwell. Right, Sir. De Distillation be made from the *Hippomanes* of a young Mare. When a deflower'd Virgin take ten Drops, she will Faint and Sneeze, and de large red Spot will appear upon de Cheek; which me call de spot of Infamy. All de young Bridegroom make de experiment. De Archbishop did make Obligation to de Nun to take it every 310 ninth Month. And I fly for the hurlyburly it make.

Enter Hugh.

Hugh. Sir, here is a Patient in a Chair.

Fossile. Doctor *Lubomirski*, let me conduct you into my Study, where we will farther discuss the wonderful Virtues of this Liquor. Tell the Patient I will attend him this Instant.

[*Exeunt* Plotwell *and* Fossile.

Enter Underplot *in a Chair like a sick Man.*

Hugh. The Doctor will wait upon you immediately.

[*Exit* Hugh.

Underplot. I dogg'd *Plotwell* to this Door in a Doctor's Habit. If he has admittance as a Doctor, why not I as a Patient? Now for a lucky Decision of our Wager! If I can't succeed myself, I will at least spoil his Intrigue.

Enter Fossile.

320 *Underplot.* Ah! ah! have you no Place. Ah! where can I repose a little? I was taken suddenly. Ah! ah! 'tis happy I was near the House of an eminent Physician.

Fossile. Rest your self upon that Couch.

Underplot. If I lay a few Minutes cover'd up warm in a Bed, I believe I might recover.

[Fossile *feels his Pulse.* Plotwell *peeps.*

Plotwell. Underplot in disguise! I'll be his Doctor, and cure him of these Frolicks.   [*aside.*

Fossile. What are your Symptoms, Sir? a very tempestuous Pulse, I profess!

Underplot. Violent Head-ach, ah! ah!   330

Fossile. All this proceeds from the Fumes of the Kitchen, the Stomachick Digester wants reparation for the better Concoction of your Aliment: But, Sir; is your Pain pungitive, tensive, gravitive, or pulsatory?

Underplot. All together, ah!

Fossile. Impossible Sir, but I have an eminent Physician now in the House, he shall consult. Doctor *Lubomirski*, here is a Person in a most violent *Cephalalgy*, a terrible Case!

Enter Plotwell.

Fossile. Feel his Pulse. [Plotwell *feels it.*] You feel it Sir, strong, hard and labouring.   340

Plotwell. Great Plenitude, Sir.

Fossile. Feel his Belly, Sir; a great Tension and Heat of the Abdomen—A hearty Man, his Muscles are torose; how soon are the strongest humbled by Diseases! Let us retire, and consult.

Enter Sarsnet *in hast.*

Sarsnet. My Mistress approves your design, bear it out bravely, perhaps I shall have a sudden opportunity of conveying you into her Bed-chamber, counterfeit a fainting Fit, and rely upon me.   [*Exit.*

Underplot. As yet I find I am undiscover'd by *Plotwell*; 350 neither is his Intrigue in such forwardness as mine, though he made a fair push for it before me.   [*aside.*

[Fossile *and* Plotwell *come forward.*

Fossile. I am entirely for a Glister.

Plotwell. My Opinion is for de strong Vomit.

Fossile. Bleed him.

Plotwell. Make de Scarrification, give me de Lancet, me will do it myself, and after dat will put de Blister to de Sole of de Feet.

Fossile. Your dolor proceeds from a frigid *intemperies* of the Brain, a strong Disease! the Enemy has invaded the very 360 Citadel of your Microcosm, the Magazine of your vital

341 Sir.] ~, *17*

Functions; he has sate down before it; yet there seems to be a good Garrison of vital Spirits, and we don't question to be able to defend it.

Plotwell. Ve will cannonade de Enemy wid Pills, bombard him wid de Bolus, blow him up with Volatiles, fill up de Trenches wid de large Inundation of Apozems, and dislodge him wid de Stink-pot; let de Apothecary bring up de Artillery of Medicine immediately.

370 *Fossile.* True, we might unload the Stomach by gentle Emeticks, and the Intestines by Clysters stimulative, carminative, and emollient, with strong Hydroticks, quiet the spasms of the Viscera by Paregoricks, draw off the stagnant Blood by deep Scarrifications, and depurate its Fæculencies by Volatiles; after this, let there be numerous Blisters and potential Cauteries—I consult my Patient's ease; I am against much Physick— he Faints, he is Apoplectick, bleed him this Moment.

Plotwell. Hoy, de Servant dere, make hast, bring de Pan of
380 hot Coals; or de red hot Iron to make application to de Temples.

Enter Hugh.

Hugh. Here's the Poker red hot from the Fire.

Plotwell. Very vell, make de burn dere, exactly dere.
[*putting the Poker near his Head.*

Underplot. Hold, hold, am I to be murder'd? [*starts up.*] I know you, *Plotwell*, and was I not oblig'd by Honour and Friendship, I'd expose you to the Doctor. [*aside to* Plotwell.

Plotwell. Very Lunatick, Mad, fetch de Cord to make de tie upon de Leg and de Arm, take off thirty Ounces of Blood, and den plunge him into de cold Bath.

390 *Fossile.* Your Judgment, Doctor *Lubomirski*, is excellent, I will call my Servants to assist us.

Underplot. Hearke'e, old Put; I came to take your Advice, and not that *French* Son of a Whore's Scarrifications; and so plague take you both. [*Exeunt* Underplot *and* Hugh.

Fossile. Doctor *Lubomirski*, this Vial that you have intrusted

---

362 sate] set *58*   365 wid] with *58*   366 de Trenches] the ~ *58*
368 Apothecary] apotecary *58*   381 sd Hugh] *Hugh 17*   383 vell] well *58*
387 fetch] fetch me *58*   394 *Exeunt. . . .* Hugh.] *Exit . . . Hugh.* ACT IV.
Enter Dr. FOSSILE, and PLOTWELL. *58*

in my custody, shall be with Acknowledgement return'd after
a few Experiments; I must crave your indulgence, Diseases,
you know, Sir, are impertinent, and will tie themselves to no
Hours, poor Lady *Hippokekoana*!

Plotwell. Ah Sir! I beg your pardon, if you make visit to de 400
Patient, me will divert myself in your Study till you make
return.

Fossile. That cannot be, I have a Lady just coming to
consult me in a case of Secrecy.

Plotwell. Have you not de Wife? Me will make
Conversation wid de Ladies till you come.

Fossile. They see no Company in the Morning, they are all
in *déshabillé*; most learned Doctor *Lubomirski*, your humble
Servant.

Plotwell. Most illustrious Doctor *Fossile*, me be, with de 410
profoundest Adoration.

Fossile. With the greatest Admiration

Plotwell. Your most humble

Fossile. Most obedient Servant.

Plotwell. Ah, Monsieur, point de Ceremonie.

[*Exit* Plotwell.

Fossile. Hugh. [*Enter* Hugh.] Bring me a Pint of Sack; let
your Mistress know I want to see her. Take care that her
Orders be obey'd, and that her Trunks and Boxes be
immediately brought hither. *Sarsnet* will give you Directions.

[*Exit* Hugh. Fossile *sits down on a Couch.*

Ah *Fossile*! if the Cares of two Hours of a married Life have so 420
reduc'd thee, how long can'st thou hold out! To watch a Wife
all Day, and have her wake thee all Night! 'twill never do.
The Fatigue of three Feavers, six Small-poxes, and five Great
ones, is nothing to that of one Wife. Now for my Touchstone;
I will try it upon her presently. If she bear it to-day—I am
afraid she will bear it to-morrow too.

Enter Hugh *with a Bottle of Sack, and after*
him Townley. Hugh *gives the Bottle and Glass*
to Fossile, *and exit.*

Sit down by me, my Dear, I was going to refresh my self with a glass of Canary. You look pale. It will do you good.

Townley. Faugh. Wine in the Morning!

[Fossile *Drinks, and fills again, and drops some of the*
Liquor into the Glass;

430 What is the meaning of this? Am I to be Poyson'd! [*Aside.*

Fossile. You must drink it. Sack is Sacred to *Hymen*; of it is
made the Nuptial Posset.

Townley. Don't press me, Mr. *Fossile*, I nauseate it. It smells
strangely. There is something in it.

Fossile. An ill Symptom! She can't bear the Smell. [*Aside.*]
Pray, my Dear, oblige me.

Townley. I'm for none of your Slops. I'll fill my self.

Fossile. I must own, I have put some restorative Drops in it,
which are excellent. I may drink it safely. [*Aside.*] [*Drinks.*]
440 The next Glass I prepare for you.

[*Fills, and pours some Drops in.*

[Townley *Drinks.* Fossile *runs behind to Support her;*
then pores upon her Cheek, and touches it with his Finger.

Townley. Your Insolence is insupportable. 'Twas but this
Moment you suspected my Virtue; and now my Complexion.
Put on your Spectacles. No Red was ever laid upon these
Cheeks. I'll fly thee, and die a Maid, rather than live under
the same Roof with Jealousy and Caprice.

Fossile. O thou spotless Innocence! I cannot refrain Tears
of Joy. Forgive me, and I'll tell thee all. These Drops have
been a Secret in our Family for many Years. They are call'd
the *Touchstone of Virginity.* The Males administer it to the
450 Brides on their Wedding-Day; and by its Virtue have
ascertain'd the Honour of the *Fossiles* from Generation to
Generation. There are Family Customs, which it is almost
impious to neglect.

Townley. Had you married a Person of doubtful
Reputation—But me, Mr. *Fossile!*

Fossile. I did not indeed suspect thee. But my Mother
obliged me to this Experiment with her dying Words—My
Wife is chaste: And to preserve her so, 'tis necessary that I
have none but chaste Servants about her. I'll make the
460 Experiment on all my Female Domesticks. [*Aside.*] I will now,
my Dear, in thy Presence, put all my Family to the Trial.
Here! bid my Niece, and all the Maid-Servants come before

me.   [*Calling out.*
              [*Enter* Clinket, Prue, *and Servants.*]
Give Ear, all ye Virgins: We make Proclamation in the
Name of the Chaste *Diana*, being resolv'd to make a Solemn
Essay of the Virtue, Virginity, and Chastity of all within our
Walls. We therefore Advise, Warn and Precaution all
Spinsters, who know themselves Blemish'd, not on any
Pretence whatsoever to Taste these our Drops, which will
manifest their Shame to the World by visible Tokens.   470

Clinket. I abominate all Kind of Drops. They interrupt the
Series of Idea's. But have they any Power over the Virgin's
Dreams, Thoughts, and private Meditations?

Fossile. No. They do not affect the *motus Primo-primi*, or
Intentions; only Actualities, Niece.

Clinket. Then give it me. I can drink as freely of it, as of the
Waters of *Helicon*. My Love was always *Platonick*.   [*Drinks.*

Fossile. Yet I have known a *Platonick* Lady lodge at a
Midwife's.   [Fossile *offers it round.*

First Woman. I never take Physick.   480

Fossile. That's one. Stand there. My Niece professes her self
a *Platonick.* You are rather a *Cartesian.*

Clinket. Ah dear Uncle! How do the *Platonicks* and
Cartesians differ?

Fossile. The *Platonicks* are for Idea's, the *Cartesians* for
Matter and Motion.

Townley. Mr. *Fossile*, you are too severe.

Second Woman. I am not a-dry.   [*Curtsies.*

Fossile. There's Two. Stand there.

Prue. My Mistress can Answer for me. She has taken it.   490

Fossile. She has. But however stand there, among the
Cartesians.

Third Woman. My Innocence would protect me, though I
trod over red-hot Iron. Give me a Brimmer.

              [*She takes a Mouthful, and spits it out again.*]

Fossile. 'Twas a presumptuous Thing to Gargle with it: But
however, Madam, if you please—walk among the *Cartesians.*

                        [*Two young Wenches run away.*

Clinket. Prue, follow me. I have just found a Rhime for my
Pindarick.   [*They all sneak off.*

Fossile. All gone! What no more Ladies here? No more

500 Ladies! [*looking to the Audience*,] O that I had but a Boarding-School, or a Middle-Gallery!

    Enter Sarsnet, *follow'd by Two Porters bearing*
      a Chest.

Set down the Things here: There is no Occasion for carrying them up Stairs, since they are to be sent into the Countrey to-Morrow.   [*Exeunt Porters.*

What have I done? My Marriage, these confounded Whimsies, and Doctor *Lubomirski*, have made me quite forget poor Lady *Hippokekoana*. She was in Convulsions, and I am afraid dead by this Time.   [*Exit* Fossile.

 Sarsnet. I have brought you a Present, Madam, make good
510 Use of it. So I leave you together.   [*Exit* Sarsnet.

    [Townley *opens the Chest:* Plotwell, *who was cover'd*
      with a Gown and Petticoat, gets out.

 Townley. Never was any Thing so lucky. The Doctor is just this Minute gone to a Patient.

 Plotwell. I tempt Dangers enough in your Service. I am almost crippled in this Chest-Adventure. Oh my Knees! Prithee, my Dear, lead me to a Bed where I may stretch my self out.   [*Leading her off.*

    Enter Sarsnet.

 Sarsnet. Oh Madam! yonder is the Doctor in deep Discourse with *Underplot*: I fear he has dogg'd me, and betray'd us. They are both coming back together.

    [*Exit* Sarsnet.

520 *Plotwell.* I'll shrink snug into my Shell again.

 Townley. That he may directly pop upon you. The Trunk will be the first Place he will examine. Have you no Presence of Mind? You fit for an Intrigue!

 Plotwell. What shall I do?

 Townley. Fear not, you shall be Invisible on this very Spot.

 Plotwell. What do you mean? He's just at the Door. You intend to discover me.

 Townley. Mistrust me not: You shall walk out before his Face at that very Door, though he bring in a Hundred Spies,
530 and not one of them shall perceive you.

 Plotwell. Don't trifle. Are you Mad? [*Knocking at the Door.*] Nay, now 'tis too late.

Townley. Arm thy self with Flounces, and fortify thy self with Whalebone; enter beneath the *Cupolo* of this Petticoat.

Plotwell. The best Security in the World! an Old Fellow has seldom any Thing to do beneath that Circumference.

Townley. No more. But under it immediately.

[Plotwell *gets under it*.

Thus *Venus*, when approaching Foes assail,
Shields her *Æneas* with a Silken Veil.

Enter Fossile.

Townley. O my Dear, you come opportunely. How do you 540 like my Fancy in this new Petticoat? There is something in it so odd!

Fossile. You have another in your Chest much odder. I want to see that.

Townley. How jaunty the Flounces!

Fossile. Ay, 'tis plain she would lure me from the Chest; there I shall find him. [*Aside*.

Townley. The Lace! the Fringe!

Fossile. All this is nothing to the embroider'd Sattin. Prithee, my Dear, give me the Key. 550

Townley. Sure never was any Thing so prettily disposed. Observe but the Air of it: So *Dégagé!* But the lining is so charming.

[*She walks to the Door, and* Fossile *to the Trunk*. Plotwell *kisses her out of the top of the Petticoat, and then goes off*.]

[*As* Fossile *is cautiously opening the Trunk with his Sword drawn*, Townley *comes up to him*.]

What more of your Frolicks, Mr. *Fossile*? What Time of the Moon is this?

Fossile. This *Underplot* is a confounded Villain, he would make me jealous of an honest civil Gentleman, only for an Opportunity to Cuckold me himself. [*Aside*.] Come, my Dear, forget all that is past. I know—I have prov'd thee Virtuous.

[*Exeunt*.

---

537 sd *gets*] goes *58*   552 *Dégagé*] Degageé *17*   559 Virtuous. [*Exeunt*. ACT III] virtuous. But prithee, love, leave me a moment; I expect some Egyptian rarities. [*Exeunt severally*. ACT V *58*

ACT III.

Enter Fossile *with a Vial in his Hand.*

Fossile. THIS is all we have for the flying Dragon so celebrated by Antiquity. A cheap Purchase! It cost me but Fifteen Guineas. But the *Jew* made it up in the Butterfly and the Spider.

Enter Two Porters bearing a Mummy.

Oh! here's my Mummy. Set him down. I am in Haste. Tell Captain *Bantam*, I'll talk with him at the Coffee-House.

[*Exeunt Porters.*

Enter Two Porters bearing an Alligator.

A most stupendous Animal! set him down.

[*Exeunt Porters.*

Poor Lady *Hippokekoana*'s Convulsions! I believe there is a Fatality in it, that I can never get to her. Who can I trust my
10 House to in my Absence? Were my Wife as Chaste as *Lucretia*, who knows what an unlucky Minute may bring forth! In Cuckoldom, the Art of Attack is prodigiously improved beyond the Art of Defence. So far it is manifest, *Underplot* has a Design upon my Honour. For the Ease of my Mind, I will lock up my Wife in this my *Musæum*, 'till my Return.

Enter Townley.

You will find something here, my Dear, to divert your self.

Townley. I hate the Sight of these strange Creatures; but since I am Mr. *Fossile*'s Wife, I shall endeavour to conquer my Aversion.

20 *Fossile.* Thou may'st safely be here to Day, my Dear; to Morrow thou should'st no more enter this Room than a *Pest-house*. 'Tis dangerous for Women that are Impregnated. But poor Lady *Hippokekoana* suffers all this while.

[*Exit* Fossile *with a Key in his Hand.*

Townley. Since he has lock'd me in, to be even with him, I'll bolt him out.

[Plotwell, *dress'd like a* Mummy, *comes forward.*

Plotwell. Thus trav'ling far from his *Egyptian* Tomb,
　　　Thy *Antony* salutes his *Cleopatra*.

Townley. Thus *Cleopatra*, in desiring Arms.

III. 15 sd Townley.] TOWNLEY, and SARSNET *58*

Receives her *Antony*—
But prithee dear pickled *Hieroglyphick*, who so suddenly 30
could assist thee with this Shape?

Plotwell. The Play-house can dress Mummies, Bears, Lions,
Crocodiles, and all the Monsters of *Lybia*. My Arms, Madam,
are ready to break their Past-board Prison to embrace you.

Townley. Not so hasty. Stay till the jealous Fool is out of
Sight.

Plotwell. Our ill Stars, and the Devil, have brought him
back so often—

Townley. He can never parry this Blow, nor grow jealous of
his *Mummy*. A *Mummy* is his intimate Friend. 40

Plotwell. And a Man cannot easily be Cuckolded by any
Body else.

Townley. Here may'st thou remain the Ornament of his
Study, and the Support of his Old Age. Thou shalt divert his
Company, and be a Father to his Children. I will bring thee
Legs of Pullets, Remnants of Tarts, and Fragments of Disserts.
Thou shalt be fed like *Bell* and the *Dragon*.

Plotwell. But Madam; before you entertain me as your
Mummy in Ordinary, you ought to be acquainted with my
Abilities to discharge that Office. Let me slip off this Habit of 50
Death, you shall find I have some Symptoms of Life.—Thus
Jove within the Milk-white Swan compress'd his *Leda*.

[Underplot *in the* Alligator *crawls forward,*
then rises up and embraces her.]

Underplot. Thus *Jove* within the *Serpent*'s scaly Folds,
Twin'd round the *Macedonian* Queen.

Townley. Ah! [*shrieks.*

Plotwell. Fear not, Madam. This is my evil Genius *Underplot*
that still haunts me. How the Devil got you here?

Underplot. Why should not the Play-house lend me a
Crocodile as well as you a *Mummy*?

Townley. How unlucky is this! [*Aside.*] Nay, I don't know 60
but I may have Twenty Lovers in this Collection. You
Snakes, Sharks, Monkeys, and Mantegers, speak, and put in
your Claim before it is too late.

Underplot. Mr. *Mummy*, your Humble Servant; the Lady is
pre-engag'd.

Plotwell. Pray, Mr. *Crocodile*, let the Lady make her own

Choice.

Underplot. Crocodile as I am, I must be treated with common Humanity. You can't, Madam, disown the Message you sent
70 me.

Townley. Well! Ye Pair of *Egyptian* Lovers, agree this Matter between you, and I will acquit my self like a Person of Honour to you both.

Plotwell. Madam! If I don't love you above all your Sex, may I be banish'd the Studies of Virtuoso's; and smoak'd like *Dutch* Beef in a Chimney—

Underplot. If I don't love you more than that Stale Mummy, may I never more be proclaim'd at a Show of Monsters, by the Sound of a Glass-Trumpet.

80 *Plotwell.* May I be sent to *'Pothecary's Hall*, and beat up into *Venice-Treacle* for the Fleet and the Army, if this Heart—

Underplot. May I be stuff'd with Straw, and given to a Mountebank, if this Soul—

Plotwell. Madam, I am a Human Creature. Taste my Balsamick Kiss.

Underplot. A Lover in Swadling-Clouts! What is his Kiss, to my Embrace?

Plotwell. Look upon me, Madam. See how I am embroider'd with Hieroglyphicks.

90| *Underplot.* Consider my beautiful Row of Teeth.

Plotwell. My Balmy Breath.

Underplot. The strong Joints of my Back.

Plotwell. My erect Stature.

Underplot. My long Tail.

Townley. Such a Contest of Beauty! How shall I decide it?

Plotwell. Take me out of my Shell, Madam, and I'll make you a Present of the Kernel.

Underplot. Then I must be upon a Level with him, and be uncrocodil'd.

100 *Townley.* Keep both of you your Shapes, and we are in no Fear of a Surprize from the Doctor: If you uncase, his Presence would undo us. Sure never was any Thing so unlucky—I hear his Footsteps; quickly to your Posts.

      [Mummy *and* Crocodile *run to their Places.*
   [*Enter* Fossile, *Dr.* Nautilus, *and Dr.* Possum.]

Nautilus. Much Joy to the Learned Dr. *Fossile.* To have a

Mummy, an *Alligator*, and a *Wife*, all in one Day, is too great
Happiness for Mortal Man!

Possum. This an *Alligator!* Alack a Day, Brother *Nautilus*,
this is a meer Lizard, an Eft, a Shrimp to mine.

Nautilus. How improving would it be to the Female
Understanding, if the Closets of the Ladies were Furnish'd, or, 110
as I may say, Ornamented and Embellish'd with preserv'd
Butterflies, and beautiful Shells, instead of *China* Jars, and
absurd *Indian* Pictures.

Townley. Now for a Stratagem to bring off my unsuccessful
Pair of Gallants.   [*Aside.*
                                              [*Exit* Townley.

Fossile. Ah, Dr. *Nautilus*, how have I languish'd for your
Feather of the Bird *Porphyrion*!

Nautilus. But your Dart of the *Mantichora*!

Fossile. Your Haft of an Antediluvian Trowel, unquestionably the Tool of one of the *Babel* Masons!   120

Nautilus. What's that to your Fragment of *Seth*'s Pillar?

Possum. Gentlemen. I affirm I have a greater Curiosity
than all of them. I have an entire Leaf of *Noah*'s Journal
aboard the Ark, that was hewn out of a Porphyry Pillar in
Palmyra.   [Fossile *opens the Case of the* Mummy.

Nautilus. By the Formation of the Muscular Parts of the
Visage, I conjecture that this Mummy is Male.

Possum. Male, Brother! I am sorry to observe your
Ignorance of the Symetry of a Human Body. Do but observe
the Projection of the Hip; besides, the Bloom upon the Face; 130
'tis a Female beyond all Contradiction.

Fossile. Let us have no rash Dispute, Brothers; but proceed
methodically—Behold the Vanity of Mankind! [*pointing to the*
Mummy.] Some *Ptolemy* perhaps!—

Nautilus. Who by his Pyramid and Pickle thought to secure
to himself Death Immortal.

Fossile. His Pyramid, alas! is now but a Wainscot Cafe.

Possum. And his Pickle can scarce raise him to the Dignity
of a Collar of Brawn.

Fossile. Pardon me, Dr. *Possum*: The *Musæum* of the 140
Curious is a lasting Monument. And I think it no
Degradation to a dead Person of Quality, to bear the Rank of

an Anatomy in the Learned World.

Nautilus. By your Favour, Dr. *Possum*, a Collar of Brawn! I affirm, he is better to be taken inwardly than a Collar of Brawn.

Fossile. An Excellent Medicine! He is hot in the first Degree, and exceeding powerful in some Diseases of Women.

Nautilus. Right, Dr. *Fossile*; for your *Asphaltion*.

150 *Possum.* Pice-*Asphaltus*, by your leave.

Nautilus. By your leave, Doctor *Possum*, I say *Asphaltion*.

Possum. And I positively say, *Pice-Asphaltus*.

Nautilus. If you had read *Dioscorides* or *Pliny*—

Possum. I have read *Dioscorides*. And I do affirm *Pice-Asphaltus*.

Fossile. Be calm, Gentlemen. Both of you handle this Argument with great Learning, Judgment and Perspicuity. For the present, I beseech you to Concord, and turn your Speculations on my *Alligator*.

160 *Possum.* The Skin is impenetrable even to a Sword.

Nautilus. Dr. *Possum*, I will show you the contrary.

[*Draws his Sword.*

Possum. In the mean time I will try the Mummy with this Knife, on the Point of which you shall smell the Pitch, and be convinc'd that it is the *Pice-Asphaltus*. [*Takes up a Rusty Knife.*

Fossile. Hold, Sir: You will not only deface my Mummy, but spoil my *Roman* Sacrificing Knife.

Enter Townley.

Townley. I must lure them from this Experiment, or we are discover'd.   [*Aside.*

[*She looks through a Telescope.*

What do I see! Most prodigious! A Star as broad as the Moon 170 in the Day-time!   [*The Doctors go to her.*

Possum. Only a *Halo* about the Sun, I suppose.

Nautilus. Your Suppositions, Doctor, seem to be groundless. Let me make my Observation.

[*Nautilus and* Possum *struggle to look first.*

Townley. Now for your Escape:

[*To* Plotwell *and* Underplot.

[*They run to the Door, but find it lock'd.*]

Underplot. What an unlucky Dog I am!

152 Pice-Asphaltus] Pice Asphaltus 17   154 Pice-Asphaltus] Pice-Alsphaltus 17

Townley. Quick. Back to your Posts. Don't move, and rely upon me. I have still another Artifice.

[*They run back to their Places.*

[*Exit* Townley.

Nautilus. I can espy no Celestial Body but the Sun.

Possum. Brother *Nautilus*, your Eyes are somewhat dim; your Sight is not fit for *Astronomical Observations.*   180

Fossile. Is the Focus of the Glass right? Hold Gentlemen, I see it; about the Bigness of *Jupiter.*

Nautilus. No Phenomenon offers it self to my Speculation.

Possum. Point over yonder Chimney. Directly *South.*

Nautilus. Thitherward, begging your Pardon, Dr. *Possum*, I affirm to be the *North.*

Fossile. East.

Possum. South.

Nautilus. North. Alas! What an ignorant Thing is Vanity! I was just making a Reflection on the Ignorance of my Brother   190 *Possum*, in the Nature of the *Crocodile.*

Possum. First, Brother *Nautilus*, convince your self of the Composition of the *Mummy.*

Nautilus. I will insure your *Alligator* from any Damage. His Skin I affirm once more to be impenetrable. [*Draws his sword.*

Possum. I will not deface any Hieroglyphick.

[*Goes to the* Mummy *with the Knife.*

Fossile. I never oppose a luciferous Experiment. It is the beaten Highway to Truth.

[Plotwell *and* Underplot *leap from their
Places; the Doctors are frighted.*]

Possum. Speak, I conjure thee. Art thou the Ghost of some murder'd *Egyptian* Monarch?   200

Nautilus. A rational Question to a *Mummy*! But this Monster can be no less than the Devil himself, for *Crocodiles* don't walk.

Enter Townley *and* Clinket.

[Townley *whispers* Clinket.

Fossile. Gentlemen, wonder at Nothing within these Walls; for ever since I was Married, Nothing has happen'd to me in the common Course of Human Life.

Clinket. Madam, without a Compliment, you have a fine Imagination. The Masquerade of the *Mummy* and *Crocodile* is

extreamly just; I would not rob you of the Merit of the
210 Invention, Yet since you make me the Compliment, I shall be
proud to take the whole Contrivance of this Masquerade upon
my self. [*To* Townley.] Sir, be acquainted with my
Masqueraders.   [*To* Fossile.

Fossile. Thou Female Imp of *Apollo*, more mischievous than
Circe, who fed Gentlemen of the Army in a *Hog*'s-*Stye*! What
mean you by these Gambols? This *Mummy*, this *Crocodile*?

Clinket. Only a little Mummery, Uncle.

Fossile. What an ouragious Conceit is this! Had you
contented your self with the *Metamorphosis* of *Jupiter*, our Skill
220 in the Classicks might have prevented our Terror.

Clinket. I glory in the Fertility of my Invention the more,
that it is beyond the Imagination of a Pagan Deity. Besides, it
is form'd upon the *Vray-Semblance*; for I knew you had a
Mummy and a *Crocodile* to be brought home.

Fossile. Dr. *Nautilus* is an infirm tender Gentleman; I wish
the sudden Concussion of his Animal Spirits may not kindle
him into a Fever. I my self, I must confess, have an extreme
Palpitation.

Clinket. Dear Uncle, be pacified. We are both of us the
230 Votaries of our great Master *Apollo*. To you he has assigned
the Art of Healing: Me he has taught to Sing; Why then
should we jangle in our Kindred Faculties?

Fossile. *Apollo*, for ought I know, may be a very fine Person;
but this I am sure of, that the Skill he has given all his
Physicians is not sufficient to cure the Madness of his Poets.

Possum. Hark ye, Brother *Fossile*! Your *Crocodile* has proved
a Human Creature, I wish your Wife may not prove a
Crocodile.

Nautilus. Hark ye, Brother *Fossile*! Your *Mummy*, as you
240 were saying, seemeth to be hot in the first Degree, and is
powerful in some Diseases of Women.

                                              [*Exit* Nautilus *and* Possum.

Fossile. You Diabolical Performers of my Niece's
Masquerade, will it please you to follow those Gentlemen?

Clinket. Nay, Sir, you shall see them Dance first.

Fossile. Dance! the Devil! bring me hither a Spit, a Fire-
Fork, I'll try whether the Monsters are impenetrable or no.

212 Sir,] *58*; ~⌃ *17*   223 knew] know *58*   234 sure] very sure *58*

Plotwell. I hope, Sir, you will not expose us to the Fury of the Mob, since we came here upon so courteous a Design.

Fossile. Good Courteous Mr. *Mummy*, without more Ceremony, will it please you to retire to your subterraneous 250 Habitation. And you, Mr. *Crocodile*, about your Business this Moment, or you shall change your *Nile* for the next Horse-Pond.

Clinket. Spare my *Masqueraders*.

Underplot. Let it never be said that the Famous Dr. *Fossile*, so renowned for his Charity to Monsters, should violate the Laws of Hospitality, and turn a poor *Alligator* naked into the Street.

Fossile. Deposite your *Exuviæ* then, and assume your Human Shape. 260

Underplot. For that, I must beg your Excuse. A Gentleman would not chuse to be known in these Frolicks.

Fossile. Then out of my Doors. Here, Footmen, out with him; out, thou Hypocrite, of an *Alligator*.

[*Underplot is turn'd out.*

Sir, the Respect I have for Catacombs and Pyramids, will not protect you. [*A Noise of Mob within.*

Enter Prue.

Prue. Sir, Sir, lock your Doors, or else all your Monsters will run Home again to the *Indies*. Your *Crocodile* yonder has made his Escape; If he get but to *Somerset Water-Gate*, he is 270 gone for ever. [*Exit* Prue.

Enter a Footman.

Footman. The Herbwoman swore she knew him to be the Devil, for she had met him one dark Night in St. *Pulchre*'s Church-Yard; Then the Monster call'd a Coach, methought with the Voice of a Christian; but a Sailor that came by said he might be a *Crocodile* for all that, for *Crocodiles* could cry like Children, and was for killing him outright, for they were good to eat in *Egypt*; but the Constable cry'd, Take him alive, for what if he be an *Egyptian*, he is still the King's Subject.

[*Exit* Footman.
[*A Noise of Mob within.*

Enter Prue.

Prue. Then he was hurry'd away by the Mob. A Bull-dog ran away with Six Joints of his Tail, and the Claw of his near 280

Foot before: At last by good Fortune, to save his Life, he fell in with the *Hockley in the Hole* Bull and Bear; the Master claim'd him for his Monster, and so he is now attended by a vast Mob, very solemnly marching to *Hockley in the Hole*, with the Bear in his Front, the Bull in his Rear, and a Monkey upon each Shoulder.

Townley. Mr. *Mummy*, you had best draw the Curtains of your Chair, or the Mob's Respect for the Dead will scarce protect you.   [*Exit* Plotwell *in a Chair.*

290   *Clinket.* My Concern for him obliges me to go see that he gets off safe, lest any further Mischief befall the Persons of our Masque.   [*Exit* Clinket.

Fossile. Sweetly, *Horace. Nunquam satis*, and so forth. A Man can never be too cautious. Madam, sit down by me. Pray how long is it since you and I have been married?

Townley. Near Three Hours, Sir.

Fossile. And what Anxieties has this Time produc'd! The dangers of Divorce! Calumniatory Letters! lewd Fellows introduced by my Niece! groundless Jealousies on both Sides!

300   even thy Virginity put to the Touchstone! but this last Danger I plung'd thee in my self; to leave thee in the Room with Two such robust young Fellows.

Townley. Ay, with Two young Fellows! but, my Dear, I know you did it ignorantly.

Fossile. This is the first blest Minute of Repose that I have enjoy'd in Matrimony. Dost thou know the Reason, my Dear, why I have chosen thee of all Womankind?

Townley. My Face perhaps.

Fossile. No.

310   *Townley.* My Wit?

Fossile. No.

Townley. My Virtue and good Humour?

Fossile. No. But for the natural Conformity of our Constitutions. Because thou art hot and moist in the Third Degree, and I my self cold and dry in the First.

Townley. And so Nature has coupled us like the Elements.

Fossile. Thou hast nothing to do but to submit thy Constitution to my Regimen.

Townley. You shall find me obedient in all Things.

291 befall] befalls *58*

Fossile. It is strange, yet certain, that the Intellects of the 320
Infant depend upon the Suppers of the Parents. Diet must be
prescrib'd.

Townley. So the Wit of one's Posterity is determin'd by the
Choice of one's Cook.

Fossile. Right. You may observe how *French* Cooks, with
their high *Ragousts*, have contaminated our plain *English*
Understandings. Our Supper to Night is extracted from the
best Authors. How delightful is this Minute of Tranquility!
my Soul is at Ease. How happy shalt thou make me! thou
shalt bring me the finest Boy!   [*A knocking at the Door.* 330
No Mortal shall enter these Doors this Day. [*Knocking
again.*] Oh, it must be the News of poor Lady *Hippokekoana*'s
Death. Poor Woman! such is the Condition of Life, some die,
and some are Born, and I shall now make some Reparation
for the Mortality of my Patients by the Fecundity of my Wife.
My Dear, thou shalt bring me the finest Boy!

Enter Footman.

Footman. Sir, here's a Seaman from *Deptford* must needs
speak with you.

Fossile. Let him come in. One of my Retale *Indian*
Merchants, I suppose, that always brings me some odd Thing. 340

Enter Sailor *with a Child.*
What hast thou brought me, Friend, a young Drill?

Sailor. Look ye d'ye see, Master, you know best whether a
Monkey begot him.

Fossile. A meer Human Child!

Townley. Thy Carelesness, *Sarsnet*, has expos'd me, I am
lost and ruin'd. O Heav'n! Heav'n? No, Impudence assist me.

[*Aside.*

Fossile. Is the Child monstrous? Or dost thou bring him
here to take Physick?

Sailor. I care not what he takes; so you take him.

Fossile. What does the Fellow mean?   350

Sailor. Fellow me no Fellows. My Name is *Jack Capstone* of
Deptford, and are not you the Man that has the Raree-Show of
Oyster-shells and Pebble-stones?

Fossile. What if I am?

Sailor. Why, then my Invoice is right, I must leave my

Cargo here.

    Townley. Miserable Woman that I am! how shall I support this Sight! thy Bastard brought into thy Family as soon as thy Bride!

360   *Fossile.* Patience, Patience, I beseech you. Indeed I have no Posterity.

    Townley. You lascivious Brute you.

    Fossile. Passion is but the tempestuous Cloud that obscures Reason; be calm and I'll convince you. Friend, how come you to bring the Infant hither?

    Sailor. My Wife, poor Woman, could give him Suck no longer, for she died Yesterday Morning. There's a long Account, Master. It was hard to trace him to the Fountain-Head, I steer'd my Course from Lane to Lane, I spoke to 370 Twenty Old Women, and at last was directed to a Ribbon-Shop in *Covent-Garden*, and they sent me hither, and so take the Bantling and pay me his Clearings. [*Offers him the Child.*

    Fossile. I shall find Law for you, Sirrah. Call my Neighbour *Possum*, he is a Justice of Peace, as well as a Physician.

    Townley. Call the Man back. If you have committed one Folly, don't expose your self by a Second.

    Sailor. The Gentlewoman says well. Come, Master, we all know that there is no Boarding a pretty Wench, without Charges one way or other; you are a Doctor, Master, and 380 have no Surgeons Bills to pay; and so can the better afford it.

    Townley. Rather than you should bring a Scandal on your Character, I will submit to be a kind Mother-in-Law.

            Enter Justice Possum, *and Clark.*

    Fossile. Mr. Justice *Possum*, for now I must so call you, not Brother *Possum*; here is a troublesome Fellow with a Child, which he would leave in my House.

    Possum. Another Man's Child? He cannot in Law.

    Fossile. It seemeth to me to be a Child unlawfully begotten.

    Possum. A Bastard! who does he lay it to?

    Fossile. To our Family.

390   *Possum.* Your Family, *quatenus* a Family, being a Body Collective cannot get a Bastard. Is this Child a Bastard, honest Friend?

    Sailor. I was neither by when his Mother was Stow'd, nor when she was Unladen; Whether he belong to a fair Trader, or be Run Goods, I cannot tell: In short, here I was sent, and here I will leave him.

Possum. Dost thou know his Mother, Friend?

Sailor. I am no Midwife, Master; I did not see him Born.

Possum. You had best put up this Matter, Doctor. A Man of your Years, when he has been wanton, cannot be too 400 cautious.

Fossile. This is all from the Purpose. I was married this Morning at Seven; let any Man in the least acquainted with the Powers of Nature, judge whether that Human Creature could be conceived and brought to Maturity in one Forenoon.

Possum. This is but Talk, Dr. *Fossile.* It is well for you, though I say it, that you have fallen into the Hands of a Person, who has study'd the *Civil* and *Canon-Law* in the Point of Bastardy. The Child is either yours or not yours.

Fossile. My Child, Mr. Justice! 410

Possum. Look ye, Dr. *Fossile*, you confound Filiation with Legitimation. Lawyers are of Opinion, that Filiation is necessary to Legitimation, but not *è contra.*   [*The Child cries.*

Fossile. I would not starve any of my own Species, get the Infant some Water-Pap. But Mr. Justice—

Possum. The Proofs, I say, Doctor, of Filiation are Five. Nomination enunciatively pronounc'd, strong Presumptions, and circumstantial Proofs—

Fossile. What is all this to me? I tell you, I know nothing of the Child. 420

Possum. Signs of Paternal Piety, Similitude of Features, and Commerce with the Mother. And first of the first, Nomination. Has the Doctor ever been heard to call the Infant, Son?

Townley. He has call'd him Child, since he came into this Room. You have indeed, Mr. *Fossile.*

Possum. Bring hither the Doctor's great Bible.—Let us examine in the Blank Leaf whether he be enroll'd among the rest of his Children.

Fossile. I tell you, I never had any Children. I shall grow 430 distracted, I shall—

Possum. But did you give any Orders against registring the Child by the Name of *Fossile*?

Fossile. How was it possible!

Possum. Set down that, Clark. He did not prohibit the Registring the Child in his own Name. We our selves have observed one Sign of Fatherly Tenderness; Clark, set down the Water-Pap he order'd just now. Come we now—

Fossile. What a Jargon is this!

440 *Possum.* Come we now, I say, to that which the Lawyers call *magnum naturæ Argumentum,* Similitude of Features. Bring hither the Child, Friend; Dr. *Fossile,* look upon me. The unequal Circle of the Infant's Face, somewhat resembles the Inequality of the Circumference of your Countenance; He has also the Vituline or Calf-like Concavity of the Profile of your Visage.

Fossile. Pish.

Possum. And he is somewhat Beetle-brow'd, and his Nose will rise with time to an equal Prominence with the Doctor's.

450 *Townley.* Indeed he has somewhat of your Nose, Mr. *Fossile.*

Fossile. Ridiculous!

Townley. The Child is comely.

Possum. Consider the large Aperture of his Mouth.

Sailor. Nay, the Tokens are plain enough. I have the Fellow of him at home; but my Wife told me Two Days ago, that this with the Wall-Eye, and Splay-Foot belong'd to you, Sir.   [Prue *runs a-cross the Stage with a Letter, which* Fossile
snatches from her.

Fossile. Whither are you going so fast, Hussy? I will examine every thing within these Walls. [*Exit* Prue.] [*Reads.*

460 For *Richard Plotwell,* Esq; This Letter unravels the whole Affair: As she is an unfortunate Relation of mine, I must beg you would act with Discretion.   [*Gives* Possum *the Letter.*

Possum. [*Reads.*] *Sir, the Child which you father'd is return'd back upon my Hands. Your* Drury-Lane *Friends have treated me with such Rudeness, that they told me in plain Terms I should be Damn'd. How unfortunate soever my Offspring is, I hope you at least will defend the Reputation of the unhappy*   Phœbe Clinket.

—As you say, Doctor, the Case is but too plain; every Circumstance hits.

Enter Clinket.

470 *Clinket.* 'Tis very uncivil, Sir, to break open one's Letters.

438 now—] may—*58*   463 [Reads.]] Reads. *17*   467 Phoebe] Phaebe *17*
468 but too] too *58*

Fossile. Would I had not; and that the Contents of it had been a Secret to me and all Mankind for ever. Wretched Creature, to what a miserable Condition has thy Poetry reduced Thee!

Clinket. I am not in the least mortified with the Accident. I know it has happen'd to many of the most famous Daughters of *Apollo*; and to my self several times.

Fossile. I am Thunderstruck at her Impudence! Several Times?

Clinket. I have had one return'd upon my Hands every 480 Winter for these Five Years past. I may, perhaps, be excell'd by others in Judgment and Correctness of Manners, but for Fertility and Readiness of Conception, I will yield to nobody.

Fossile. Bless me, whence had she this luxuriant Constitution?

Possum. Patience, Sir. Perhaps the Lady may be Married.

Townley. 'Tis infamous, Mr. *Fossile*, to keep her in your House; yet though you turn her out of Doors, use her with some Humanity; I will take care of the Child.

Clinket. I can find no *Dénouement* of all this Conversation. 490 Where is the Crime, I pray, of writing a Tragedy? I sent it to *Drury-Lane* House to be Acted; and here it is return'd by the wrong *Goust* of the Actors.

Possum. This Incident has somewhat embarassed us. But what mean you here, Madam, by this Expression? Your Offspring.

Clinket. My Tragedy, the Offspring of my Brain. One of His Majesty's Justices of Peace, and not understand the use of the Metaphor!

Possum. Doctor, you have used much Artifice, and many 500 Demurrers; but the Child must lye at your Door at last. Friend, speak plain what thou knowest of this Matter.

Fossile. Let me relate my Story. This Morning, I married this Lady, and brought her from her Lodgings, at Mrs. *Chambers*'s, in *King-Street, Covent-Garden.*

Sailor. Mrs. *Chambers*! To that Place I was directed, where liv'd the Maid that put the Bantling out to be Nurs'd by my Wife for her Lady; and who she was, 'tis none of our Business

490 *Dénouement*] Denoüement 17   493 *Goust*] gout 58   498 Peace] the peace 58

to enquire.

510   *Possum.* Dost thou know the Name of this Maid?

Sailor. Let me consider—*Lutestring.*

Fossile. Sarsnet, thou meanest.

Sailor. Sarsnet, that's right.

Townley. I'll turn her out of my House this Moment. Filthy Creature!

Possum. The Evidence is plain. You have Cohabitation with the Mother, Doctor, *Currat Lex.* And you must keep the Child.

Fossile. Your Decree is unjust, Sir, and I'll seek my Remedy
520   at Law. As I never was espoused, I never had Carnal Knowledge of any Woman; and my Wife, Mrs. *Susanna Townley,* is a pure Virgin at this Hour for me.

Possum. Susanna Townley! *Susanna Townley*! Look how runs the Warrant you drew up this Morning.

> [*Clark gives him a Paper.*

Madam, a Word in private with you. [*Whispers her.*] Doctor, my Lord Chief Justice has some Business with this Lady.

Fossile. My Lord Chief Justice Business with my Wife!

Possum. To be plain with you, Doctor *Fossile,* you have for
530   these three Hours entertain'd another Man's Wife. Her Husband, Lieutenant *Bengall,* is just return'd from the *Indies,* and this Morning took out a Warrant from me for an Elopement; it will be more for your Credit to part with her privately, than suffer her publickly to be carry'd off by a Tipstaff.

Fossile. Surprizing have been the Events of this Day; but this, the strangest of all, settles my future Repose. Let her go— I have not dishonoured the Bed of Lieutenant *Bengall*—Hark ye Friend! Do you follow her with that Badge of her Infamy.

540   *Possum.* By your Favour, Doctor, I never reverse my Judgment. The Child is yours: For it cannot belong to a Man who has been three Years absent in the *East-Indies.* Leave the Child.

Sailor. I find you are out of Humour, Master. So I'll call to-morrow for his Clearings.

[*Sailor lays down the Child, and Exit with*
Possum, Clark, *and* Townley.]

Clinket. Uncle, by this Day's Adventure, every one has got
something. Lieutenant *Bengall* has got his Wife again. You a
fine Child; and I a Plot for a Comedy; and I'll this Moment
set about it. [*Exit* Clinket.

Fossile. What must be, must be. [*Takes up the Child.*] *Fossile* 550
thou didst want Posterity: Here behold thou hast it. A Wife
thou didst not want; Thou hast none. But thou art caressing a
Child that is not thy own. What then? A Thousand, and a
Thousand Husbands are doing the same Thing this very
Instant; and the Knowledge of Truth is desirable, and makes
thy Case the better. What signifies whether a Man beget his
Child or not? How ridiculous is the Act it self, said the great
Emperor *Antoninus*! I now look upon my self as a *Roman*
Citizen; It is better that the Father should adopt the Child,
than that the Wife should adopt the Father. [*Exit* Fossile. 560

545 sd *Exit*] Exit *17*

EPILOGUE.

Spoken by Mrs. *Oldfield.*

THE ancient Epilogue, *as Criticks write,*
Was, clap your Hands, excuse us, and good-night.
The modern always was a kind Essay
To reconcile the Audience to the Play:
More polish'd we, of late have learnt to fly
At Parties, Treaties, Nations, Ministry.
Our Author more genteelly leaves these Brawls
To Coffee-houses, *and to* Coblers *Stalls.*
His very Monsters are of sweet Condition;
None but the Crocodile'*s a Politician;*
He reaps the Blessings of his double Nature,
And, Trimmer *like, can live on Land or Water:*
Yet this same Monster should be kindly treated,
He lik'd a Lady's Flesh—but not to eat it.
   As for my other Spark, my fav'rite Mummy,
His Feats were such, smart Youths! as might become ye;
Dead as he seem'd, he had sure Signs of Life;
His Hieroglyphicks pleas'd the Doctor's Wife.
   Whom can our well-bred Poetess displease?
She writ like Quality—with wondrous ease:
All her Offence was harmless want of Wit;
Is that a Crime?—ye Powers, preserve the Pit!
   My Doctor too, to give the Devil his due,
When ev'ry Creature did his Spouse pursue,
(Men sound and living, bury'd Flesh, dry'd Fish)
Was e'en as civil as a Wife could wish.
Yet he was somewhat saucy with his Vial;
What, put young Maids to that unnat'ral Trial!
So hard a Test! why, if you needs will make it,
Faith, let us marry first—and then we'll take it.
   Who could be angry, though like Fossile *teaz'd?*
Consider, in three Hours, the Man was eas'd.

10

20

30

How many of you are for Life beguil'd,
And keep as well the Mother, as the Child!
None but a Tar *could be so tender-hearted,*
To claim a Wife that had been three Years parted;
Would you do this, my Friends?—believe me, never:
When modishly you part—you part for ever.
  Join then your Voices, be the Play excus'd
For once, though no one living is abus'd;   40
To that bright Circle which commands our Duties,
To you superior Eighteen-penny Beauties,
To the lac'd Hat and Cockard of the Pit, ⎫
To All, in one Word, we our Cause submit, ⎬
Who think Good-breeding is a-kin to Wit. ⎭

FINIS.

41 *which*] *that* 58

ACIS and *GALATEA*.

A
SERENATA:
OR
PASTORAL ENTERTAINMENT.

THE ARGUMENT.

ACIS *was the Son of* Faunus, *and the Nymph* Symethis. *He loved and was beloved of the Nymph* Galatea, *Daughter to* Nereus, *the Son of* Oceanus *and* Tethys. Acis *was allowed to be the handsomest Youth of all* Sicily; *he was happy in his Amours with* Galatea, *till* Polyphemus *the Cyclop, Son of* Neptune, *fell in love with her, who surprising 'em together, with a Piece of a Rock overwhelmed* Acis. Galatea, *by her Persuasion, gained her Father* Nereus's *Consent to change him into a River. The Story at large is mentioned in* Ovid's Metamorphoses, *Lib.* XIII.

THE ARGUMENT. . . . *Lib.* XIII.] *om 39*

Dramatis Personæ.

MEN.

Acis.	Mr. *Mountier.*
Polyphemus.	Mr. *Waltz.*
Damon.	Mrs. *Mason.*

WOMEN.

Galatea.	Miss *Arne.*

Chorus of Shepherds, and Shepherdesses.

Names of singers om 39

THE FIRST PART.

CHORUS.

O the Pleasure of the Plains!
Happy Nymphs and happy Swains,
Harmless, Merry, Free, and Gay,
Dance and sport the Hours away.

For us the Zephyr blows;
For us distils the Dew;
For us unfolds the Rose,
And flow'rs display their Hue.

For us the Winters rain;
For us the Summers shine;
Spring swells for us the Grain,
And Autumn bleeds the Vine.

O the, &c.

Enter GALATEA.

RECITATIVO.

Galatea. Ye verdant Plains, and woody Mountains,
Purling Streams, and bubbling Fountains,
Ye painted Glories of the Field,
Vain are the Pleasures which ye yield;
Too thin the shadow of the Grove,
Too faint the Gales to cool my Love.

AIR.

Hush, ye pretty warbling Quire;
Your thrilling Strains,

THE FIRST PART] *39*; ACT I *32*   1. 1 *Pleasure*] MS *32*; *Pleasures 39*
1 *Plains!*] *39*; ~, *32*   3 *Harmless, Merry*] MS *32*; *Merry, Harmless 39*   5 *blows*;]
39; ~, *32*   6 *Dew*;] *39*; ~, *32*   8 *flow'rs*] *39*; flowrs *MS*; *Flowers 32*   8 *Hue.*]
39; ~, *32*   9 *For us the Winters . . . Vine.*] for us unfolds the Rose / and sweet the
Air perfume / for us the apple glows, / for us the peaches bloom. *MSdel*   9 *rain*;]
39; ~, *32*   10 *shine*;] *39*; ~, *32*   12 *Vine*] Wine *MS 39*   14 Plains,] *39*;
~^*32*   16 Field,] *39*; ~ ; *32*   17 yield;] *39*; ~, *32*   19 Gales] *39*; ~, *32*
19 Love.] *39*; ~, *32*   20 *Quire*;] ~^ *MS*; ~, *32*; *Choir*; *39*

             Awake my Pains,
        And kindle fierce Desire.
Cease your Song, and take your Flight;
Bring back my Acis to my Sight.

       Hush ye, &c.   [Exit.

         Enter ACIS.

          AIR.

Where shall I seek the charming Fair?
Direct the way, kind Genius of the Mountains.
   O tell me, if you saw my Dear!
Seeks she the Groves, or bathes in Crystal Fountains?   30
   Where, &c.

         Enter DAMON.

       RECITATIVO.

Damon. Stay, Shepherd, stay,
See how thy Flocks in yonder Valley stray.
   What means this melancholy Air?
   No more thy tuneful Pipe we hear.

          AIR.

     Shepherd, what art thou pursuing?
     Heedless, running to thy Ruin.
     Share our Joy, our Pleasure share.
   Leave thy Passion 'till to-morrow,
   Let the Day be free from Sorrow,   40
     Free from Love, and free from Care.

     Shepherd, &c.

         ACIS.

       RECITATIVO.

Acis. Lo here, my Love; turn, *Galatea,*
     Hither turn thy Eyes,
See, at thy Feet the longing *Acis* lies.

23 *fierce*] MS *39*; *soft 32*   24 *Flight;*] ~ , *39*   27 *Fair?*] *39*; ~ , *32*
28 *Mountains.*] *39*; ~ , *32*   29 *me,*] *39*; ~ˆ *32*   29 *Dear!*] *39*; ~ , *32*
30 *bathes*] *39*; *Bathes 32*   37 *Heedless,*] *39*; ~ˆ *32*   37 *Ruin.*] *39*; ~ˆ MS; *ruin-*
ing; 32   38 *Joy*] *mirth* MSdel   38 *share.*] *39*; ~ , *32*   39 *'till*] *39*; ˆ~ *32*
40 *the*] MS *39*; *this 32*   41 *Love,*] *39*; ~ˆ *32*   43 *Love;*] *39*; ~ , *32*
44 *thy*] MS *39*; *thine 32*   45 *longing*] MS *39*; *loving 32*

AIR.

Love in her Eyes sits playing,
And sheds delicious Death;
Love in her Lips is straying,
And warbling in her Breath.

50
Love on her Breast sits panting,
And swells with soft Desire;
No Grace, no Charm is wanting
To set the Heart a-fire.

Love in, &c.

Enter GALATEA.

RECITATIVO.

Galatea. O didst thou know the Pains of absent Love,
Acis would ne'er from *Galatea* rove.

AIR.

As when the Dove,
Laments her Love,
All on the naked Spray;
60
When he returns,
No more she mourns,
But loves the live-long Day.
Billing, cooing,
Panting, wooing,
Melting Murmurs fill the Grove,
Melting Murmurs lasting love.

As when, &c.   [Exeunt.

Enter ACIS, *and* GALATEA.

DUETTO.

Both. *Happy, happy, happy We!*
Galatea. *What Joys I feel!*
70
Acis. *What Charms I see!*
Galatea. *Of all Youths, thou dearest Boy;*

---

47 *Death;*] ～ : *39*   48 *is*] MS *39*; *sits* 32   49 *warbling*] MS *39*; *warbles* 32
50 *on*] MS *32*; *in* *39*   50 *panting*] painting MS   51 *Desire;*] *39*; ～, *32*
52 *wanting*] *39*; ～, *32*   53 *a-fire*] *39*; a fire MS; on Fire 32   59 *Spray;*] *39*; ～, *32*
68 *Happy . . . We!*] MS *39*; *Happy, happy Pair,* | *Happy, happy we,* 32   69 *feel!*] *39*;
～. *32*   70 *see!*] *39*; ～. *32*   71 *Boy;*] *39*; ～, *32*

Acis. *Of all Nymphs, thou brightest Fair.*
Both. *Thou all my Bliss,*
      Thou all my Joy.

CHORUS.

Happy, happy, happy We, &c.   [Exeunt.
The End of the First Part.

THE SECOND PART.
Enter SHEPHERDS.

CHORUS.

Wretched Lovers, Fate has past
This sad Decree, no Joy shall last:
Wretched Lovers, quit your Dream,
Behold the Monster, Polypheme.
See what ample Strides he takes,
The Mountain nods, the Forest shakes,
The Waves run frighted to the Shores;
Hark, how the thund'ring Giant roars.

POLYPHEMUS.
RECITATIVO.

Polyphemus. I rage, I melt, I burn,
The feeble God has stab'd me to the Heart.   10
Thou trusty Pine, Prop of my Godlike Steps,
I lay thee by.
Bring me a hundred Reeds of decent growth,
To make a Pipe for my capacious Mouth;
In soft enchanting Accents let me breathe
Sweet *Galatea*'s Beauty, and my Love.

AIR.

O ruddier than the Cherry!
O sweeter than the Berry!

---

72 *Nymphs,*] *39*; ~~*32*   73 *Thou all*] *MS 39*; *Thou art all 32*   75 *Happy* . . .
&c] *39*; *om MS 32*
   The SECOND PART] *39*; ACT II *32*; *no indication of break in MS*   II. 2 *last*:]
39; ~, *32*   5 *See*] ~, *39*   7 *Shores*;] *39*; ~. *32*   8 *Hark*,] *39*; ~! *32*
13 *a hundred*] *39*; *a hunderd MS*; *an hundred 32*   14 *Mouth*;] *39*; ~. *32*
15 *breathe*] *39*; ~, *32*   17 *Cherry*!] *39*; ~, *32*   18 *Berry*!] *39*; ~, *32*

O Nymph, more bright
20   *Than Moonshine Night!*
Like Kidlings blithe and merry.

Ripe as the melting Cluster,
No Lilly has such Lustre;
Yet hard to tame,
As raging Flame,
And fierce as Storms that bluster.

O ruddier, &c.

POLYPHEMUS.

RECITATIVO.

Polyphemus. Whither, Fairest, art thou running?
Still my warm Embraces shunning?

GALATEA.

30   *Galatea.* The Lion calls not to his Prey,
Nor bids the Wolf the Lambkin stay.

POLYPHEMUS.

ARIOSO.

Polyphemus. Thee, *Polyphemus*, great as *Jove*,
Calls to Empire and to Love,
To his Palace in the Rock,
To his Dairy, to his Flock,
To the Grape of purple Hue,
To the Plumb of Glossy Blue;
Wildings which expecting stand,
Proud to be gather'd by thy Hand.
40   *Galatea.* Of Infant Limbs to make my Food,
And swill full Draughts of Humane Blood!
Go, Monster, bid some other Guest;
I loath the Host, I loath the Feast.   [*Exit.*

POLYPHEMUS.

19 *Nymph,*] *39;* ∼∼ *32*   20 *Night!*] *39;* ∼, *32*   21 *blithe*] MS *39; blith 32*
23 *Lustre;*] *39;* ∼, *32*   29 shunning?] MS *39;* ∼. *32*   37 Blue;] *39;* ∼, *32*
38 Wildings . . . expecting] to strawberrys that waiting *MSdel*   38 Wildings] Wald-
ings *39*   39 thy] the *MS*   41 Blood!] ∼ ; *39*   42 Guest;] ∼, *39*
43 I loath the Feast] *MS 39;* and loath the Feast *32*

AIR.

Polyphemus. *Cease to Beauty to be suing,*
   Ever-whining Love disdaining,
   Let the Brave, their Aims pursuing,
   Still be conqu'ring, not complaining.
  Cease to, &c.

DAMON.

AIR.

Damon. *Would you gain the tender Creature,*
   Softly, gently, kindly treat her;   50
   Suff'ring is the Lover's Part.
   Beauty by Constraint possessing,
   You enjoy but half the Blessing,
   Lifeless Charms, without the Heart.
  Would you, &c. [Exeunt *Polyphemus* and *Damon.*

Enter ACIS.

RECITATIVO.

Acis. His hideous Love provokes my Rage,
Weak as I am, I must engage;
Inspir'd with thy victorious Charms,
The God of Love will lend his Arms.

AIR.

 Love sounds the Alarms, and Fear is a flying;   60
 When Beauty's the Prize, what Mortal fears dying?
 In Defence of my Treasure I bleed at each Vein;
 Without her no Pleasure, for Life is a Pain.

 Love sounds, &c.

DAMON.

44 *Cease. . . . Cease to,* &c] om *39* 44 *Cease . . . complaining.*] who would bear a woman's toying / who would be a whining lover / force her if she's worth enjoying / she'll forgive you when tis over *MSdel*; cease to sue the scornfull beauty / whining lover still desdaining / women mocking humble duty / laugh to see the strong complaining *MSdel* 45 *Ever-whining*] *MS*; *Ever whining, 32* 49 *Would . . . . Heart*] om *MS* 49 *Would*] *39*; wou'd *32* 49 *Creature,*] *39*; ~? *32* 50 *her;*] ~, *39* 51 *Part.*] *39*; ~: *32* 52 *Constraint*] *39*; ~, *32* 56 hideous] saucy *MSdel* 58 with] *MS 39*; by *32* 60 *Alarms*] *MS 39*; *Alarm 32* 60 *and*] pale *MSdel* 60 *flying;*] ~, *39* 62 *I*] *MS 39*; *I'll 32* 62 *Vein;*] ~, *39* 63 *her*] *39*; ~, *32* 64 sd DAMON.] *39*; ACT III. / *Enter* ACIS *in a melancholy Posture,* DAMON / *following him. 32*; *no indication of break in MS*

AIR.

Consider, fond Shepherd, how fleeting's the Pleasure
That flatters our Hope in pursuit of the Fair;
The Joys that attend it, by Moments we measure,
But Life is too little to measure our Care.

Consider, &c.

Enter GALATEA.

RECITATIVO.

70   *Galatea.* Cease, O cease, thou gentle Youth,
Trust my Constancy and Truth.
Trust my Truth and Pow'rs above,
The Pow'rs propitious still to Love.

AIR.

Acis *and* Galatea. *The Flocks shall leave the Mountains,*
The Woods the Turtle-Dove;
The Nymphs forsake the Fountains,
Ere I forsake my Love.

Enter POLYPHEMUS.

Polyphemus. *Torture, Fury, Rage, Despair,*
I cannot, cannot bear.
80 Acis *and* Galatea. *Not Show'rs to Larks so pleasing,*
Nor Sunshine to the Bee;
Not Sleep to Toil so easing,
As these dear Smiles to me.   [Exit *Acis.*
Polyphemus. *Fly swift, thou massy ruin, fly;*
Die, presumptuous Acis, die.
[*Polyphemus* kills *Acis* with a great Stone which he
gathers from a Rock.

Enter ACIS, *supported by* SHEPHERDS.

RECITATIVO.

Acis. Help, *Galatea,* help ye Parent Gods,
And take me dying to your deep Abodes.

65 *Pleasure*] *39*; ~, *32*   66 *Hope*] *MS 39; Hopes 32*   70 *cease,*] *39*; ~ ! *32*
71 *Truth.*] *39*; ~ ; *32*   74 *Mountains*] fountain *MSdel*   75 *Woods*] *Floods MS*
32 39; this emendation first made in a Dublin libretto of *1741*   75 *Turtle-Dove;*] *39*; ~ , *32*
79 *cannot,*] *MS 39*; cannot, no, *I 32*   82 *Not*] *MS 39; No 32*   84 *swift*] flye *MSdel*
84 *fly;*] *39*; ~ , *32*   85 *Die, presumptuous*] *MS 39; Presumptuous 32*   86 Help,]
39; ~^ *32*   86 ye] *MS 39*; the *32*

CHORUS of Shepherds and Shepherdesses.

Mourn, all ye Muses, weep, all ye Swains;
Tune, tune your Reeds to doleful Strains;
Groans, Cries, and Howlings fill the neighb'ring Shore; 90
Ah! the gentle Acis *is no more.*

GALATEA.

Galatea. Must I my *Acis* still bemoan,
Inglorious, crush'd beneath that Stone?

CHORUS.

Cease, Galatea, *cease to grieve,*
Bewail not whom thou can'st relieve.

GALATEA.

Galatea. Must the lovely charming Youth
Die for his Constancy and Truth?

CHORUS.

Cease, Galatea, *cease to grieve,*
Bewail not whom thou can'st relieve.
Call forth thy Pow'r, employ thy Art, 100
The Goddess soon can heal the Smart.

GALATEA.

Galatea. Say, what Comfort can you find,
For dark Despair o'er-clouds my Mind? [*Exit.*

CHORUS.

To Kindred Gods the Youth return,
Through verdant Plains to roll his Urn.

Enter GALATEA.

RECITATIVO.

Galatea. 'Tis done, thus I exert my Pow'r Divine,
Be thou immortal, tho' thou art not mine.

---

88 *Mourn, all ye*] MS *39*; *Mourn all the 32*   88 *weep, all ye*] MS *39*; *weep all the 32*
88 *Swains;*] *39*; ~, *32*   89 *Tune, tune*] *39*; *Tune 32*   90 *Howlings*] *39*; ~, *32*
90 *Shore;*] ~, *39*   91 *Ah! the*] MS *39*; *The 32*   92 Must ... Stone?] om *39*
94 CHORUS.] *39 gives 94–5, 98–101 and 104–5 to Damon*   96 Must ... Truth?]
om *39*   98 *to grieve*] MS *32*; *thy Grief 39*   101 *the*] MS *32*; *thy 39*
102 Say ... Mind?] om *39*   105 *verdant*] *distant MSdel*

AIR.

Heart, the Seat of soft Delight,
Be thou now a Fountain bright;
110   *Purple be no more, thou Blood,*
Glide thou like a crystal Flood.
Rock, thy hollow Womb disclose;
The bubling Fountain, lo, it flows;
Through the Plains he joys to rove,
Murm'ring still his gentle Love.

CHORUS.

Galatea, *dry thy Tears,*
Acis *now a God appears;*
See how he rears him from his Bed!
See the Wreath that binds his Head!

120   *Hail, thou gentle murm'ring Stream!*
Shepherds Pleasure, Muses Theme!
Through the Plain still joy to rove,
Murm'ring still thy gentle Love!

FINIS.

109 *bright;*] ~ : *39*   110 *more, thou*] MS *39; more thy 32*   111 *Flood.*] *39;*
~ ; *32*   112 *Rock . . . flows;*] MS *39;* om *32*   116 *dry thy Tears*] cease thy fears
MSdel   120 *Stream!*] *39;* ~, *32*   121 *Theme!*] *39;* ~, *32*   123 *Love!*] ~. *32*

DIONE.

A
Pastoral Tragedy.

——Sunt numina amanti,
Sævit et injustâ lege relicta Venus.
Tibull. Eleg. 5. Lib. I.

PROLOGUE.

There was a time (Oh were those days renew'd!)
Ere tyrant laws had woman's will subdu'd;
Then nature rul'd, and love, devoid of art,
Spoke the consenting language of the heart.
Love uncontroul'd! insipid, poor delight!
'Tis the restraint that whets our appetite.
Behold the beasts who range the forests free,
Behold the birds who fly from tree to tree;
In their amours see nature's power appear!
10   And do they love? Yes—One month in the year.
Were these the pleasures of the golden reign?
And did free nature thus instruct the swain?
I envy not, ye nymphs, your am'rous bowers:
Such harmless swains!—I'm ev'n content with ours.
But yet there's something in these sylvan scenes
That tells our fancy what the lover means;
Name but the mossy bank, and moon-light grove,
Is there a heart that does not beat with love?
        To night we treat you with such country fare,
20   Then for your lover's sake our author spare.
He draws no *Hemskirk* boors, or home-bred clowns,
But the soft shepherds of *Arcadia*'s downs.
        When *Paris* on the three his judgment pass'd;
I hope, you'll own the shepherd show'd his taste:
And *Jove*, all know, was a good judge of beauty,
Who made the nymph *Calisto* break her duty;
Then was the country nymph no awkward thing.
See what strange revolutions time can bring!
        Yet still methinks our author's fate I dread.
30   Were it not safer beaten paths to tread
Of Tragedy; than o'er wide heaths to stray,
And seeking strange adventures lose his way?
No trumpet's clangor makes his Heroine start,

PROLOGUE.] *Printed separately in 20 and 31 and subtitled "Design'd for the Pastoral Tragedy of* DIONE." Prologue 2 Ere] *31*; E'er *20* 23 pass'd] *31*; past *20* 27 awkward] aukward *31*

And tears the soldier from her bleeding heart;
He, foolish bard! nor pomp nor show regards.
Without the witness of a hundred guards
His Lovers sigh their vows.—if sleep should take ye,
He has no battel, no loud drum to wake ye.
What, no such shifts? there's danger in't, 'tis true;
Yet spare him, as he gives you something new.   40

Dramatis Personæ.

MEN.

Evander under the name of *Lycidas.*
Cleanthes.
Shepherds.

WOMEN.

Dione under the name of *Alexis.*
Parthenia.
Laura.

Scene *ARCADIA.*

ACT I. SCENE I.

A Plain, at the foot of a steep craggy mountain.

DIONE. LAURA.

LAURA.

WHY dost thou fly me? stay, unhappy fair,
Seek not these horrid caverns of despair;
To trace thy steps the midnight air I bore,
Trod the brown desert, and unshelter'd moor:
Three times the lark has sung his matin lay,
And rose on dewy wing to meet the day,
Since first I found thee, stretch'd in pensive mood,
Where laurels border *Ladon*'s silver flood.

DIONE.

O let my soul with grateful thanks o'erflow!
'Tis to thy hand my daily life I owe.   10
Like the weak lamb you rais'd me from the plain,
Too faint to bear bleak winds and beating rain;
Each day I share thy bowl and clean repast,
Each night thy roof defends the chilly blast.
But vain is all thy friendship, vain thy care:
Forget a wretch abandon'd to despair.

LAURA.

Despair will fly thee, when thou shalt impart
The fatal secret that torments thy heart;
Disclose thy sorrows to my faithful ear,
Instruct these eyes to give thee tear for tear.   20
Love, love's the cause; our forests speak thy flame,
The rocks have learnt to sigh *Evander*'s name.
If faultring shame thy bashful tongue restrain,
If thou hast look'd, and blush'd, and sigh'd in vain;

i. i. 22 The] *31*; And *20*

Say, in what grove thy lovely shepherd strays,
Tell me what mountains warble with his lays;
Thither I'll speed me, and with moving art
Draw soft confessions from his melting heart.

DIONE.

Thy gen'rous care has touch'd my secret woe;
30 Love bids these scalding tears incessant flow,
Ill-fated love! O, say, ye sylvan maids,
Who range wide forests and sequestered shades,
Say where *Evander* bled, point out the ground
That yet is purple with the savage wound,
Yonder he lies; I hear the bird of prey;
High o'er those cliffs the raven wings his way;
Hark, how he croaks! he scents the murder near.
O may no greedy beak his visage tear!
Shield him, ye *Cupids*; strip the *Paphian* grove,
40 And strow unfading myrtle o'er my love!
Down, heaving heart.

LAURA.
The mournful tale disclose.

DIONE.

Let not my tears intrude on thy repose.
Yet if thy friendship still the cause request;
I'll speak; though sorrow rend my lab'ring breast.
Know then, fair shepherdess; no honest swain
Taught me the duties of the peaceful plain;
Unus'd to sweet content, no flocks I keep,
Nor browzing goats that overhand the steep.
Born where *Orchomenos*' proud turrets shine,
50 I trace my birth from long illustrious line.
Why was I train'd amidst *Arcadia*'s Court?
Love ever revells in that gay resort.
Whene'er *Evander* past, my smitten heart
Heav'd frequent sighs, and felt unusual smart.
Ah! hadst thou seen with what sweet grace he mov'd!
Yet why that wish? for *Laura* then had lov'd.

LAURA.
Distrust me not; thy secret wrongs impart.

37 Hark,] ∼∧ *31*　　50 line.] ∼∧ *31*　　52 revells] revels *31*

DIONE.

Forgive the sallies of a breaking heart.
Evander's sighs his mutual flame confest,
The growing passion labour'd in his breast;   60
To me he came; my heart with rapture sprung,
To see the blushes, when his faultring tongue
First said, I love. My eyes consent reveal,
And plighted vows our faithful passion seal.
Where's now the lovely youth? he's lost, he's slain,
And the pale corse lies breathless on the plain!

LAURA.

Are thus the hopes of constant lovers paid?
If thus—ye Powers, from love defend the maid!

DIONE.

Now have twelve mornings warm'd the purple east,
Since my dear hunter rous'd the tusky beast;   70
Swift flew the foaming monster through the wood,
Swift as the wind, his eager steps pursu'd:
'Twas then the savage turn'd; then fell the youth,
And his dear blood distain'd the barb'rous tooth.

LAURA.

Was there none near? no ready succour found?
Nor healing herb to stanch the spouting wound?

DIONE.

In vain through pathless woods the hunters crost,
And sought with anxious eye their master lost;
In vain their frequent hollows eccho'd shrill,
And his lov'd name was sent from hill to hill;   80
Evander hears you not. He's lost, he's slain,
And the pale corse lies breathless on the plain.

LAURA.

Has yet no clown (who, wandring from the way,
Beats ev'ry bush to raise the lamb astray)
Observ'd the fatal spot?

DIONE.
O, if ye pass
Where purple murder dies the wither'd grass,

76 stanch] staunch *31*   77 through] *31*; thro' *20*

With pious finger gently close his eyes,
And let his grave with decent verdure rise.   [*Weeps.*

LAURA.

Behold the turtle who has lost her mate;
90 Awhile with drooping wing she mourns his fate,
Sullen, awhile she seeks the darkest grove,
And cooing meditates the murder'd dove:
But time the rueful image wears away,
Again she's chear'd, again she seeks the day.
Spare then thy beauty, and no longer pine.

DIONE.

Yet sure some turtle's love has equall'd mine,
Who, when the hawk has snatch'd her mate away,
Has never known the glad return of day.
When my fond father saw my faded eye,
100 And on my livid cheek the roses dye;
When catching sighs my wasted bosom mov'd,
My looks, my sighs confirm'd him that I lov'd.
He knew not that *Evander* was my flame,
Evander dead! my passion still the same!
He came, he threaten'd; with paternal sway
Cleanthes nam'd and fix'd the nuptial day:
O cruel kindness! too severely prest!
I scorn his honours, and his wealth detest.

LAURA.

How vain is force! Love ne'er can be compell'd.

DIONE.

110 Though bound by duty, yet my heart rebell'd.
One night, when sleep had hush'd all busy spys,
And the pale moon had journey'd half the skies;
Softly I rose and drest; with silent tread,
Unbarr'd the gates; and to these mountains fled.
Here let me sooth the melancholy hours!
Close me, ye woods, within your twilight bow'rs!

102 My looks, my sighs] *31*; The certain signs *20*   105 He came. . . . detest.]
31; Now he with threats asserts paternal sway, / With rich *Cleanthes* names my nuptial
day; / *Cleanthes* long his ardent vows had prest; / But I his honours and his wealth
detest. *20*

Where my calm soul may settled sorrow know,
And no *Cleanthes* interrupt my woe
             [*Melancholy musick is heard at a distance.*
With importuning love.—On yonder plain
Advances slow a melancholy train;   120
Black Cypress boughs their drooping heads adorn.

LAURA.
Alas! *Menalcas* to his grave is born.
Behold the victim of *Parthenia*'s pride!
He saw, he sigh'd, he lov'd was scorn'd and dy'd.

DIONE.
Where dwells this beauteous tyrant of the plains?
Where may I see her?

LAURA.
         Ask the sighing swains.
They best can speak the conquests of her eyes,
Whoever sees her, loves; who loves her, dies.

DIONE.
Perhaps untimely fate her flame hath crost,
And she, like me, hath her *Evander* lost.   130
How my soul pitys her!

LAURA.
          If pity move
Your generous bosom, pity those who love.
There late arriv'd among our sylvan race
A stranger shepherd, who with lonely pace
Visits those mountain pines at dawn of day,
Where oft' *Parthenia* takes her early way
To rouse the chace; mad with his am'rous pain,
He stops and raves; then sullen walks again.
Parthenia's name is born by passing gales,
And talking hills repeat it to the dales.   140
Come, let us from this vale of sorrow go,
Nor let the mournful scene prolong thy woe.   [*Exeunt.*

119 love.] ∽⌃ *31*   129, 130 hath] *31*; has *20*

*SCENE II.

*Shepherds and Shepherdesses, (crown'd with garlands of Cypress and
Yew) bearing the body of* Menalcas.

1 SHEPHERD.

Here gently rest the corse.—With faultring breath
Thus spake *Menalcas* on the verge of death.
'Belov'd *Palemon*, hear a dying friend;
'See, where yon hills with craggy brows ascend,
'Low in the valley where the mountain grows,
'There first I saw her, there began my woes.
'When I am cold, may there this clay be laid;
'There often strays the dear the cruel maid,
'There as she walks, perhaps you'll hear her say,
10   '(While a kind gushing tear shall force its way)
'How could my stubborn heart relentless prove?
'Ah poor *Menalcas*—all thy fault was love!

2 SHEPHERD.

When pitying lions o'er a carcase groan,
And hungry tygers bleeding kids bemoan;
When the lean wolf laments the mangled sheep;
Then shall *Parthenia* o'er *Menalcas* weep.

1 SHEPHERD.

When famish'd panthers seek their morning food,
And monsters roar along the desart wood;
When hissing vipers rustle through the brake,
20   Or in the path-way rears the speckled snake;
The wary swain th'approaching peril spys,
And through some distant road securely flys.
Fly then, ye swains, from beauty's surer wound.
Such was the fate our poor *Menalcas* found!

2 SHEPHERD.

What shepherd does not mourn *Menalcas* slain?
Kill'd by a barbarous woman's proud disdain!
Whoe'er attempts to bend her scornful mind,
Crys to the desarts, and pursues the wind.

---

* *This and the following Scene are form'd upon the novel of* Marcella *in* Don Quixote.

1 SHEPHERD.

With ev'ry grace *Menalcas* was endow'd,
His merits dazled all the sylvan croud. 30
If you would know his pipe's melodious sound,
Ask all the ecchoes of these hills around,
For they have learnt his strains; who shall rehearse
The strength, the cadence of his tuneful verse?
Go, read those lofty poplars; there you'll find
Some tender sonnet grow on ev'ry rind.

2 SHEPHERD.

Yet what avails his skill? *Parthenia* flies.
Can merit hope success in woman's eyes?

1 SHEPHERD.

Why was *Parthenia* form'd of softest mould?
Why does her heart such savage nature hold? 40
O ye kind gods! or all her charms efface,
Or tame her heart.—so spare the shepherd race.

2 SHEPHERD.

As fade the flowers which on the grave I cast;
So may *Parthenia*'s transient beauty waste!

1 SHEPHERD.

What woman ever counts the fleeting years,
Or sees the wrinkle which her forehead wears?
Thinking her feature never shall decay,
This swain she scorns, from that she turn away.
But know, as when the rose her bud unfolds,
Awhile each breast the short-liv'd fragrance holds; 50
When the dry stalk lets drop her shrivell'd pride,
The lovely ruin's ever thrown aside.
So shall *Parthenia* be.

2 SHEPHERD.

See, she appears,
To boast her spoils, and triumph in our tears.

SCENE III.

Parthenia *appears from the mountain.*

PARTHENIA. SHEPHERDS.

1 SHEPHERD.

Why this way dost thou turn thy baneful eyes,
Pernicious Basilisk? Lo! there he lies,
There lies the youth thy cursed beauty slew;
See, at thy presence, how he bleeds anew!
Look down, enjoy thy murder.

PARTHENIA.

        Spare my fame;
I come to clear a virgin's injur'd name.
If I'm a Basilisk, the danger fly,
Shun the swift glances of my venom'd eye:
If I'm a murd'rer, why approach ye near,
10 And to the dagger lay your bosom bare?

1 SHEPHERD.

What heart is proof against that face divine?
Love is not in our power.

PARTHENIA.

       Is love in mine?
If e'er I trifled with a shepherd's pain,
Or with false hope his passion strove to gain;
Then might you justly curse my savage mind,
Then might you rank me with the serpent kind:
But I ne'er trifled with a shepherd's pain,
Nor with false hope his passion strove to gain:
'Tis to his rash pursuit he owes his fate,
20 I was not cruel; he was obstinate.

1 SHEPHERD.

Hear this, ye sighing shepherds, and despair.
Unhappy *Lycidas*, thy hour is near!
Since the same barb'rous hand hath sign'd thy doom,
We'll lay thee in our lov'd *Menalcas*' tomb.

PARTHENIA.

Why will intruding man my peace destroy?
Let me content, and solitude enjoy;
Free was I born, my freedom to maintain,
Early I sought the unambitious plain.
Most women's weak resolves like reeds, will ply,
Shake with each breath, and bend with ev'ry sigh;   30
Mine, like an oak, whose firm roots deep descend,
No breath of love can shake, no sigh can bend.
If ye unhappy *Lycidas* would save;
Go seek him, lead him to *Menalcas'* grave;
Forbid his eyes with flowing grief to rain,
Like him *Menalcas* wept, but wept in vain;
Bid him his heart-consuming groans give o'er:
Tell him, I heard such piercing groans before,
And heard unmov'd. O *Lycidas*, be wise,
Prevent thy fate.—Lo! there *Menalcas* lies.   40

1 SHEPHERD.

Now all the melancholy rites are paid,
And o'er his grave the weeping marble laid;
Let's seek our charge; the flocks dispersing wide,
Whiten with moving fleece the mountain's side.
Trust not, ye swains, the lightning of her eye,
Lest ye like him should love, despair, and dye.

> [*Exeunt* Shepherds &c. Parthenia *remains in a melan-*
> *choly posture looking on the grave of* Menalcas.
>
>   *Enter* Lycidas.

SCENE IV.

LYCIDAS. PARTHENIA.

LYCIDAS.

When shall my steps have rest? through all the wood,
And by the winding banks of *Ladon*'s flood
I sought my love. O say, ye skipping fawns,
(Who range entangled shades and daisy'd lawns)
If ye have seen her! say, ye warbling race,

---

37 heart-consuming] heart consuming *31*   46 sd *Exeunt* Shepherds,] *31*; *Ex.*
Shepherds⁀ *20*

(Who measure on swift wing th' aerial space,
And view below hills, dales, and distant shores)
Where shall I find her whom my soul adores!

SCENE V.

LYCIDAS. PARTHENIA. DIONE. LAURA.

[Dione *and* Laura *at a distance.*

LYCIDAS.

What do I see? no. Fancy mocks my eyes,
And bids the dear deluding vision rise.
'Tis she. My springing heart her presence feels.
See, prostrate *Lycidas* before thee kneels.

[*Kneeling to* Parthenia.

Why will *Parthenia* turn her face away?

PARTHENIA.

Who calls *Parthenia?* hah!

[*She starts from her melancholy; and seeing* Lycidas,
flys into the wood.

LYCIDAS.

Stay, virgin, stay.
O wing my feet, kind Love. See, see, she bounds,
Fleet as the mountain roe, when prest by hounds.

[*He pursues her.* Dione *faints in the arms of* Laura.

LAURA.

What means this trembling? all her colour flies,
And life is quite unstrung. Ah! lift thy eyes,
And answer me; speak, speak, 'tis *Laura* calls.
Speech has forsook her lips.—She faints, she falls.
Fan her, ye Zephyrs, with your balmy breath,
And bring her quickly from the shades of death:
Blow, ye cool gales. See, see, the forest shakes
With coming winds! she breaths, she moves, she wakes.

DIONE.

Ah false *Evander!*

LAURA.

Calm thy sobbing breast,
Say, what new sorrow has thy heart opprest.

DIONE.

Didst thou not hear his sighs and suppliant tone?
Didst thou not hear the pitying mountain groan?   20
Didst thou not see him bend his suppliant knee?
Thus in my happy days he knelt to me,
And pour'd forth all his soul! see how he strains,
And lessens to the sight o'er yonder plains
To keep the fair in view! run, virgin, run,
Hear not his vows; I heard, and was undone!

LAURA.

Let not imaginary terrors fright.
Some dark delusion swims before thy sight.
I saw *Parthenia* from the mountain's brow,
And *Lycidas* with prostrate duty bow;   30
Swift, as on faulcon's wing, I saw her fly,
And heard the cavern to his groans reply.
Why stream thy tears for sorrows not thy own?

DIONE.

Oh! where are honour, faith, and justice flown?
Perjur'd *Evander!*

LAURA.

Death has laid him low,
Touch not the mournful string that wakes thy woe.

DIONE.

That am'rous swain, whom *Lycidas* you name,
(Whose faithless bosom feels another flame)
Is my once kind *Evander*—yes—'twas he.
He lives.—but lives, alas! no more for me.   40

LAURA.

Let not thy frantick words confess despair.

DIONE.

What, know I not his voice, his mien, his air?
Yes, I that treach'rous voice with joy believ'd,
That voice, that mien, that air my soul deceiv'd.
If my dear shepherd love the lawns and glades,
With him I'll range the lawns and seek the shades,
With him through solitary desarts rove.

I. V. 34 are] 31; is 20

But could he leave me for another love?
O base ingratitude!

LAURA.
Suspend thy grief,
50 And let my friendly counsel bring relief
To thy desponding soul. *Parthenia*'s ear
Is barr'd for ever to the lover's prayer;
Evander courts disdain, he follows scorn,
And in the passing winds his vows are born.
Soon will he find that all in vain he strove
To tame her bosom; then his former love
Shall wake his soul, then, will he sighing blame
His heart inconstant and his perjur'd flame:
Then shall he at *Dione*'s feet implore,
60 Lament his broken faith, and change no more.

DIONE.
Perhaps this cruel nymph well knows to feign
Forbidding speech, coy looks, and cold disdain,
To raise his passion. Such are female arts,
To hold in safer snares inconstant hearts!

LAURA.
Parthenia's breast is steel'd with real scorn.

DIONE.
And dost thou think *Evander* will return?

LAURA.
Forgo thy sex, lay all thy robes aside,
Strip off these ornaments of female pride;
The shepherd's vest must hide thy graceful air,
70 With the bold manly step a swain appear;
Then with *Evander* mayst thou rove unknown,
Then let thy tender eloquence be shown;
Then the new fury of his heart controul,
And with *Dione*'s sufferings touch his soul.

DIONE.
Sweet as refreshing dews, or summer showers

48 But could] *31*; And can *20*   66 And dost thou think] *31*; Canst thou
believe *20*   67 Forgo thy sex] *31*; If thou the secrets of his heart wouldst find, /
And try to cure the fever of his mind; / If thy soft speech his passions knows to move, /
If thou canst plead *Dione*'s injur'd love, / Forgo thy sex *20*

To the long parching thirst of drooping flowers;
Grateful as fanning gales to fainting swains,
And soft as trickling balm to bleeding pains,
Such are thy words. The sex shall be resign'd,
No more shall breaded gold these tresses bind;   80
The shepherd's garb the woman shall disguise.
If he has lost all love, may friendship's tyes
Unite me to his heart!

LAURA.

Go, prosp'rous maid,
May smiling love thy faithful wishes aid.
Be now *Alexis* call'd. With thee I'll rove,
And watch thy wand'rer through the mazy grove;
Let me be honour'd with a sister's name;
For thee, I feel a more than sister's flame.

DIONE.

Perhaps my shepherd has outstript her haste.
Think'st thou, when out of sight, she flew so fast?   90
One sudden glance might turn her savage mind;
May she like *Daphne* fly, nor look behind,
Maintain her scorn, his eager flame despise,
Nor view *Evander* with *Dione*'s eyes!

ACT II. SCENE I.

Lycidas lying on the grave of Menalcas.

LYCIDAS.

WHEN shall these scalding fountains cease to flow?
How long will life sustain this load of woe?
Why glows the morn? roll back, thou source of light,
And feed my sorrows with eternal night.
Come, sable Death! give, give the welcome stroke;
The raven calls thee from yon' blasted oak.
What pious care my ghastful lid shall close?
What decent hand my frozen limbs compose?
O happy shepherd, free from anxious pains,

---

89 Perhaps my shepherd] *31*; Come then my guardian, sister, friend and guide; /
Strait let these female robes be laid aside. / Perhaps my shepherd *20*
II. i. 5 Death!] *31*; ~ ; *20*

10 Who now art wandring in the sighing plains
   Of blest *Elysium*; where in myrtle groves
   Enamour'd ghosts bemoan their former loves.
   Open, thou silent grave; for lo! I come
   To meet *Menalcas* in the fragrant gloom;
   There shall my bosom burn with friendship's flame,
   The same our passion, and our fate the same;
   There, like two nightingales on neighb'ring boughs,
   Alternate strains shall mourn our frustrate vows.
   But if cold Death should close *Parthenia*'s eye,
20 And should her beauteous form come gliding by;
   Friendship would soon in jealous fear be lost,
   And kindling hate pursue thy rival ghost.

SCENE II.

LYCIDAS. DIONE in a shepherd's habit.

LYCIDAS.

Hah! who comes here? turn hence, be timely wise;
Trust not thy safety to *Parthenia*'s eyes.
As from the bearing faulcon flies the dove,
So, wing'd with fear, *Parthenia* flies from love.

DIONE.

If in these vales the fatal beauty stray,
From the cold marble rise; let's haste away.
Why lye you panting, like the smitten deer?
Trust not the dangers which you bid me fear.

LYCIDAS.

   Bid the lur'd lark, whom tangling nets surprise,
10 On soaring pinion rove the spacious skies;
   Bid the cag'd linnet range the leafy grove;
   Then bid my captive heart get loose from love.
   The snares of death are o'er me. Hence; beware;
   Lest you should see her, and like me despair.

DIONE.

No. Let her come; and seek this vale's recess,

II. ii. 4 So,] *31*; ~ ~ *20*   7 lye you] *31*; liest thou *20*   7 deer?] *31*; ~ ; *20*
8 dangers] *31*; ~ , *20*   8 you bid] *31*; thou bid'st *20*   14 you should] *31*; thou
should'st *20*

In all the beauteous negligence of dress;
Though *Cupid* send a shaft in ev'ry glance,
Though all the Graces in her step advance,
My heart can stand it all. Be firm, my breast;
Th'ensnaring oath, the broken vow detest: 20
That flame, which other charms have power to move,
O give it not the sacred name of love!
'Tis perj'ry, fraud, and meditated lies.
Love's seated in the soul, and never dies.
What then avail her charms? my constant heart
Shall gaze secure, and mock a second dart.

LYCIDAS.

But you perhaps a happier fate have found,
And the same hand that gave, now heals the wound;
Or art thou left abandon'd and forlorn,
A wretch, like me, the sport of pride and scorn?   30

DIONE.

O tell me, shepherd, has thy faithless maid
False to her vow thy flatter'd hope betray'd?
Did her smooth speech engage thee to believe?
Did she protest and swear, and then deceive?
Such are the pangs I feel!

LYCIDAS.

                    The haughty fair
Contemns my suff'rings, and disdains to hear.
Let meaner Beauties learn'd in female snares
Entice the swain with half-consenting airs;
Such vulgar arts ne'er aid her conqu'ring eyes,
And yet, where-e'er she turns, a lover sighs.   40
Vain is the steady constancy you boast;
All other love at sight of her is lost.

DIONE.

True constancy no time no power can move.
He that hath known to change, ne'er knew to love.
Though the dear author of my hapless flame
Pursue another; still my heart's the same.

27 you] *31*; thou *20*   27 have] *31*; hast *20*   31 me,] ∼∧ *31*   40 yet,]
31; ∼∧ *20*   40 turns,] *31*; ∼∧ *20*   44 hath] *31*; has *20*   46 Pursue] *31*;
Pursues *20*

Am I for ever left? (excuse these tears)
May thy kind friendship soften all my cares!

LYCIDAS.
What comfort can a wretch, like me, bestow?

DIONE.
50 He best can pity who has felt the woe.

LYCIDAS.
Since diff'rent objects have our souls possest,
No rival fears our friendship shall molest.

DIONE.
Come, let us leave the shade of these brown hills,
And drive our flocks beside the steaming rills.
Should thy fair tyrant to these vales return,
How would thy breast with double fury burn!
Go hence, and seek thy peace.

SCENE III.

LYCIDAS. DIONE. LAURA.

LAURA.
                Fly, fly this place;
Beware of love; the proudest of her race
This way approaches: from among the pines,
Where from the steep the winding path declines,
I saw the nymph descend.

LYCIDAS.
              She comes, she comes;
From her the passing Zephyrs steal perfumes,
As from the vi'let's bank; with odours sweet
Breaths ev'ry gale; spring blooms beneath her feet.
Yes, 'tis my fairest; here she's wont to rove.

LAURA.
10 Say, by what signs I might have known thy Love?

LYCIDAS.
My Love is fairer than the snowy breast
Of the tall swan, whose proudly-swelling chest

51 objects] *31*; passions *20*
II. iii sd *LYCIDAS.*] *31*; ~ ^ *20*

Divides the wave; her tresses loose behind,
Play on her neck, and wanton in the wind;
The rising blushes, which her cheek o'erspread,
Are op'ning roses in the lilly's bed.
Know'st thou *Parthenia?*

LAURA.

Wretched is the slave
Who serves such pride! behold *Menalcas'* grave!
Yet if *Alexis* and this sighing swain
Wish to behold the Tyrant of the plain,   20
Let us behind these myrtle's twining arms
Retire unseen; from thence survey her charms.
Wild as the chaunting thrush upon the spray,
At man's approach she swiftly flies away.
Like the young hare, I've seen the panting maid
Stop, listen, run; of ev'ry wind afraid.

LYCIDAS.

And wilt thou never from thy vows depart?
Shepherd, beware—now fortifie thy heart.   [*To* Dione.
    [Lycidas, Dione, *and* Laura *retire behind the boughs.*

SCENE IV.

PARTHENIA. LYCIDAS. DIONE. LAURA.

PARTHENIA.

This melancholy scene demands a groan.
Hah! what inscription marks the weeping stone?
O pow'r of beauty! here Menalcas *lies.*
Gaze not, ye shepherds, on Parthenia's *eyes.*
Why did heav'n form me with such polish'd care?
Why cast my features in a mold so fair?
If blooming beauty was a blessing meant,
Why are my sighing hours deny'd content?
The downy peach, that glows with sunny dyes,
Feeds the black snail, and lures voracious flies;   10
The juicy pear invites the feather'd kind,
And pecking finches scoop the golden rind;
But beauty suffers more pernicious wrongs,

27 See,] ~‿ *31*

Blasted by envy, and censorious tongues.
How happy lives the nymph, whose comely face
And pleasing glances boast sufficient grace
To wound the swain she loves! no jealous fears
Shall vex her nuptial state with nightly tears,
Nor am'rous youths, to push their foul pretence,
20 Infest her days with dull impertinence.
But why talk I of love? my guarded heart
Disowns his power, and turns aside the dart.
Hark! from his hollow tomb *Menalcas* crys,
Gaze not, ye shepherds, on Parthenia's *eyes*.
Come, *Lycidas*, the mournful lay peruse,
Lest thou, like him, *Parthenia*'s eyes accuse.
   [*She stands in a melancholy posture, looking on the tomb.*

     Lycidas.
Call'd she not *Lycidas?*—I come, my fair;
See, gen'rous pity melts into a tear,
And her heart softens. Now's the tender hour,
30 Assist me, Love, exert thy sov'raign power
To tame the scornful maid.

     Dione.
       Rash swain, be wise:
'Tis not from thee or him, from love she flies.
Leave her, forget her.   [*They hold* Lycidas.

     Laura.
   Why this furious haste?

     Lycidas.
Unhand me; loose me.

     Dione.
     Sister, hold him fast.
To follow her, is, to prolong despair.
Shepherd, you must not go.

     Lycidas.
      Bold youth, forbear.
Hear me, *Parthenia*.

     Parthenia.
   From behind the shade

II. iv. 31 the scornful] *31*; th'obdurate *20*   37 shade] *31*; ~, *20*

Methought a voice some list'ning spy betray'd.
Yes, I'm observ'd.   [*She runs out.*

LYCIDAS.
Stay, nymph; thy flight suspend.
She hears me not—when will my sorrows end!   40
As over-spent with toil, my heaving breast
Beats quick. 'Tis death alone can give me rest.
                 [*He remains in a fixt melancholy.*

SCENE V.

LYCIDAS. DIONE. LAURA.

LAURA.
Recall thy scatter'd sense, bid reason wake,
Subdue thy passion.

LYCIDAS.
Shall I never speak?
She's gone, she's gone.—Kind shepherd, let me rest
My troubled head upon thy friendly breast.
The forest seems to move.—O cursed state!
I doom'd to love, and she condemn'd to hate!
Tell me, *Alexis*, art thou still the same?
Did not her brighter eyes put out the flame
Of thy first love? did not thy flutt'ring heart,
Whene'er she rais'd her look, confess the dart?   10

DIONE.
I own the nymph is fairest of her race,
Yet I unmov'd can on this beauty gaze,
Mindful of former promise; all that's dear,
My thoughts, my dreams; my ev'ry wish is there.
Since then our hopes are lost; let friendship's tye
Calm our distress, and slighted love supply;
Let us together drive our fleecy store,
And of ungrateful woman think no more.

LYCIDAS.
'Tis death alone can rase her from my breast.

II. v. 13 all. . . . hopes] *31*; though my love, / Inconstant like the bee, the meadows
rove, / And skim each beauteous flower; nor time nor place / Shall the dear image from
my breast efface. / Since all thy hopes *20*

LAURA.

20 Why shines thy Love so far above the rest?
　Nature, 'tis true, in ev'ry outward grace,
　Her nicest hand employ'd; her lovely face
　With beauteous feature stampt; with rosy dyes
　Warm'd her fair cheek; with lightning arm'd her eyes:
　But if thou search the secrets of her mind,
　Where shall thy cheated soul a virtue find?
　Sure hell with cruelty her breast supply'd.
　How did she glory when *Menalcas* dy'd!
　Pride in her bosom reigns; she's false, she's vain;
30 She first entices, then insults the swain;
　Shall female cunning lead thy heart astray?
　Shepherd, be free; and scorn for scorn repay.

LYCIDAS.

How woman talks of woman!

DIONE.

　　　　　　　　　Hence depart;
　Let a long absence cure thy love-sick heart.
　To some far grove retire, her sight disclaim,
　Nor with her charms awake the dying flame.
　Let not an hour thy happy flight suspend;
　But go not, *Lycidas*, without thy friend.
　Together let us seek the chearful plains,
40 And lead the dance among the sportive swains,
　Devoid of care.

LAURA.

　　　　　　Or else the groves disdain,
　Nor with the sylvan walk indulge thy pain.
　Haste to the town; there (I have oft' been told)
　The courtly nymph her tresses binds with gold,
　To captivate the youths; the youths appear
　In fine array; in ringlets waves their hair
　Rich with ambrosial scents, the fair to move,
　And all the business of the day is love.
　There from the gawdy train select a dame,
50 Her willing glance shall catch an equal flame.

LYCIDAS.

Name not the Court.—The thought my soul confounds,

And with *Dione*'s wrongs my bosom wounds.
Heav'n justly vindicates the faithful maid;
And now are all my broken vows repaid.
Perhaps she now laments my fancy'd death
With tears unfeign'd; and thinks my gasping breath
Sigh'd forth her name. O guilt, no more upbraid!
Yes. I fond innocence and truth betray'd.   [*Aside.*
                              [Dione *and* Laura *apart.*

DIONE.

Hark! how reflection wakes his conscious heart.
From my pale lids the trickling sorrows start;   60
How shall my breast the swelling sighs confine!

LAURA.

O smooth thy brow, conceal our just design:
Be yet awhile unknown. If grief arise,
And force a passage through thy gushing eyes,
Quickly retire, thy sorrows to compose;
Or with a look serene disguise thy woes.
                    [Dione *is going out.* Laura *walks at a distance.*

LYCIDAS.

Canst thou, *Alexis*, leave me thus distrest?
Where's now the boasted friendship of thy breast?
Hast thou not oft' survey'd the dappled deer
In social herds o'er-spread the pastures fair,   70
When op'ning hounds the warmer scent pursue,
And force the destin'd victim from the crew,
Oft' he returns, and fain would join the band,
While all their horns the panting wretch withstand?
Such is thy friendship; thus might I confide.

DIONE.

Why wilt thou censure what thou ne'er hast try'd?
Sooner shall swallows leave their callow brood,
Who with their plaintive chirpings cry for food;
Sooner shall hens expose their infant care,
When the spread kite sails wheeling in the air,   80

---

56 and thinks] *31*; thinks, how *20*   77 sooner shall swallows] *31*; Should some
lean wolf to seise thee swift descend, / And gnawing famine wide his jaws distend; /
I'd rush between, the monster to engage, / And my life's blood should glut his thirsty
rage. / Sooner shall swallows *20*

Than I forsake thee when by danger prest;
Wrong not by jealous fears a faithful breast.

LYCIDAS.

If thy fair-spoken tongue thy bosom shows,
There let the secrets of my soul repose.

DIONE.

Far be suspicion; in my truth confide.
O let my heart thy load of cares divide!

LYCIDAS.

Know then, *Alexis*, that in vain I strove
To break her chain, and free my soul from love;
On the lim'd twig thus finches beat their wings,
90 Still more entangled in the clammy strings.
The slow-pac'd days have witness'd my despair,
Upon my weary couch sits wakeful care;
Down my flush'd cheek the flowing sorrows run,
As dews descend to weep the absent sun.
O lost *Parthenia*!

DIONE.

        These wild thoughts suspend;
And in thy kind commands instruct thy friend.

LYCIDAS.

Whene'er my faultring tongue would urge my cause,
Deaf is her ear, and sullen she withdraws.
Go then, *Alexis*; seek the scornful maid,
100 In tender eloquence my suff'rings plead;
Of slighted passion you the pangs have known;
O judge my secret anguish by your own!

DIONE.

Had I the skill inconstant hearts to move,
My longing soul had never lost my Love.
My feeble tongue, in these soft arts untry'd,
Can ill support the thunder of her pride;
When she shall bid me to thy bower repair,
How shall my trembling lips her threats declare!
How shall I tell thee, that she could behold,
110 With brow serene, thy corse all pale and cold

     101 you] *31*; thou *20*   101 have] *31*; hast *20*   102 your] *31*; thy *20*

Beat on the dashing billow? shouldst thou go
Where the tall hill o'er-hangs the rocks below,
Near thee thy tyrant could unpitying stand,
Nor call thee back, nor stretch a saving hand.
Wilt thou then still persist to tempt thy fate,
To feed her pride and gratifie her hate?

LYCIDAS.
Know, unexperienc'd youth, that woman's mind
Oft' shifts her passions, like th' inconstant wind;
Sudden she rages, like the troubled main,
Now sinks the storm, and all is calm again.   120
Watch the kind moment, then my wrongs impart,
And the soft tale shall glide into her heart.

DIONE.
No. Let her wander in the lonely grove,
And never hear the tender voice of love.
Let her awhile, neglected by the swain,
Pass by, nor sighs molest the cheerful plain;
Thus shall the fury of her pride be laid;
Thus humble into love the haughty maid.

LYCIDAS.
Vain are attempts my passion to controul.
Is this the balm to cure my fainting soul?   130

DIONE.
Deep then among the green-wood shades I'll rove,
And seek with weary'd pace thy wander'd Love;
Prostrate I'll fall, and with incessant prayers
Hang on her knees, and bath her feet with tears;
If sighs of pity can her ear incline,
(O *Lycidas*, my life is wrapt in thine!)   [*Aside*
I'll charge her from thy voice to hear the tale,
Thy voice more sweet than notes along the vale
Breath'd from the warbling pipe: the moving strain
Shall stay her flight, and conquer her disdain.   140
Yet if she hear; should love the message speed,
Then dies all hope;—then must *Dione* bleed.   [*Aside.*

118 Oft'] *31*; ~^ *20*   132 weary'd] *31*; weary *20*   140 conquer her
disdain] *31*; o'er her passions gain *20*

LYCIDAS.

Haste then, dear faithful swain. Beneath those yews
Whose sable arms the brownest shade diffuse,
Where all around, to shun the fervent skie,
The panting flocks in ferny thickets lye;
There with impatience shall I wait my friend,
O'er the wide prospect frequent glances send
150 To spy thy wish'd return. As thou shalt find
A tender welcome, may thy Love be kind!

[*Exit* Lycidas.

SCENE VI.

DIONE. LAURA.

DIONE.

Methinks I'm now surrounded by despair,
And all my with'ring hopes are lost in air.
Thus the young linnet on the rocking bough
Hears through long woods autumnal tempests blow,
With hollow blasts the clashing branches bend,
And yellow show'rs of rustling leaves descend;
She sees the friendly shelter from her fly,
Nor dare her little pinions trust the sky;
But on the naked spray in wintry air,
10 All shiv'ring, hopeless, mourns the dying year.
What have I promis'd? rash, unthinking maid!
By thy own tongue thy wishes are betray'd!

[Laura *advances.*

LAURA.

Why walk'st thou thus disturb'd with frantick air?
Why roll thy eyes with madness and despair?
                    DIONE.   [*musing.*
How wilt thou bear to see her pride give way?
When thus the yielding nymph shall bid thee say,
'Let not the shepherd seek the silent grave,
'Say, that I bid him live.—if hope can save.

LAURA.

Hath he discern'd thee through the swain's disguise,
20 And now alike thy love and friendship flys?

II. vi. 19 Hath] *31*; Has *20*

DIONE.

Yes. Firm and faithful to the promise made,
I'll range each sunny hill, each lawn and glade.

LAURA.

'Tis *Laura* speaks. O calm thy troubled mind.

DIONE.

Where shall my search this envy'd Beauty find?
I'll go, my faithless shepherd's cause to plead,
And with my tears accuse the rival maid.
Yet, should her soften'd heart to love incline!

LAURA.

If those are all thy fears; *Evander*'s thine.

DIONE.

Why should we both in sorrow waste our days?
If love unfeign'd my constant bosom sways,   30
His happiness alone is all I prize,
And that is center'd in *Parthenia*'s eyes.
Haste then, with earnest zeal her love implore,
To bless his hours;—when thou shalt breathe no more.

ACT III. SCENE I.

Dione lying on the ground by the side of a Fountain.

DIONE.

HERE let me rest: and in the liquid glass
View with impartial look my fading face.
Why are *Parthenia*'s striking beauties priz'd?
And why *Dione*'s weaker glance despis'd?
Nature in various molds has beauty cast,
And form'd the feature for each different taste:
This sighs for golden locks and azure eyes;
That, for the gloss of sable tresses, dyes.
Let all mankind these locks, these eyes detest,
So I were lovely in *Evander*'s breast!   10
When o'er the garden's knot we cast our view,
While summer paints the ground with various hue;

Some praise the gaudy tulip's streaky red,
And some the silver lilly's bending head;
Some the junquil in shining yellow drest,
And some the fring'd carnation's varied vest;
Some love the sober vi'let's purple dyes.
Thus beauty fares in diff'rent lovers eyes.
But bright *Parthenia* like the rose appears,
20 She in all eyes superior lustre bears.

SCENE II.

DIONE. LAURA.

LAURA.

Why thus beneath the silver willow laid,
Weeps fair *Dione* in the pensive shade?
Hast thou yet found the over-arching bower,
Which guards *Parthenia* from the sultry hour?

DIONE.

With weary step in paths unknown I stray'd,
And sought in vain the solitary maid.

LAURA.

Seest thou the waving tops of yonder woods,
Whose aged arms imbrown the cooling floods?
The cooling floods o'er breaking pebbles flow,
10 And wash the soil from the big roots below;
From the tall rock the dashing waters bound.
Hark, o'er the fields the rushing billows sound!
There, lost in thought, and leaning on her crook,
Stood the sad nymph, nor rais'd her pensive look;
With settled eye the bubbling waves survey'd,
And watch'd the whirling eddys, as they play'd.

DIONE.

Thither to know my certain doom I speed,
For by this sentence life or death's decreed.   [*Exit.*

III. ii. 4 the sultry hour?] *31*; the sultry hour? / Has not her pride confirm'd the
youth's despair? / Or does thy passion still a rival fear? *20*

SCENE III.

LAURA. CLEANTHES.

LAURA.

But see! some hasty stranger bends this way;
His broider'd vest reflects the sunny ray:
Now through the thinner boughs I mark his mien,
Now veil'd, in thicker shades he moves unseen.
Hither he turns; I hear a mutt'ring sound;
Behind this rev'rend oak with ivie bound
Quick I'll retire; with busy thought possest,
His tongue betrays the secrets of his breast.

[*She hides her self.*

CLEANTHES.

The skillful hunter with experienc'd care
Traces the doubles of the circling hare;   10
The subtle fox (who breaths the weary hound
O'er hills and plains) in distant brakes is found;
With ease we track swift hinds and skipping roes.
But who th' inconstant ways of woman knows?
They say, she wanders with the sylvan train,
And courts the native freedoms of the plain;
Shepherds explain their wish without offence,
Nor blush the nymphs;—for Love is innocence.
O lead me where the rural youth retreat,
Where the slope hills the warbling voice repeat.   20
Perhaps on daisy'd turf reclines the maid,
And near her side some rival clown is laid.
Yet, yet I love her.—O lost nymph return,
Let not thy sire with tears incessant mourn;
Return, lost nymph; bid sorrow cease to flow,
And let *Dione* glad the house of woe.

LAURA.

Call'd he not lost *Dione*? hence I'll start,
Cross his slow steps, and sift his op'ning heart.   [*Aside.*

CLEANTHES.

Tell me, fair nymph, direct my wandring way;
Where, in close bowers, to shun the sultry ray,   30

III. iii. 9 skillful] skilful *31*

Repose the swains; whose flocks with bleating fill
The bord'ring forest and the thymy hill.
But if thou frequent join those sylvan bands,
Thy self can answer what my soul demands.

LAURA.

Seven years I trod these fields, these bowers, and glades,
And by the less'ning and the length'ning shades
Have mark'd the hours; what time my flock to lead
To sunny mountains, or the watry mead:
Train'd in the labours of the sylvan crew,
40 Their sports, retreats, their cares and loves I knew.

CLEANTHES.

Instruct me then, if late among your race,
A stranger nymph is found, of noble grace,
In rural arts unskill'd, no charge she tends;
Nor when the morn and ev'ning dew descends
Milks the big-udder'd ewe. Her mien and dress
The polish'd manners of the Court confess.

LAURA.

Each day arrive the neighb'ring nymphs and swains
To share the pastime of our jovial plains;
How can I there thy roving beauty trace,
50 Where not one nymph is bred of vulgar race?

CLEANTHES.

If yet she breath, what tortures must she find!
The curse of disobedience tears her mind.
If e'er your breast with filial duty burn'd,
If e'er you sorrow'd when a parent mourn'd;
Tell her, I charge you, with incessant groans
Her drooping sire his absent child bemoans.

LAURA.

Unhappy man!

CLEANTHES.

With storms of passion tost,
When first he learnt his vagrant child was lost,
On the cold floor his trembling limbs he flung,
60 And with thick blows his hollow bosom rung;
Then up he started, and with fixt surprise,

33 those] *31*; these *20*   42 found,] *31*; ~ ^ *20*

Upon her picture threw his frantick eyes,
While thus he cry'd. 'In her my life was bound,
'Warm in each feature is her mother found!
'Perhaps despair has been her fatal guide,
'And now she floats upon the weeping tide;
'Or on the willow hung, with head reclin'd,
'All pale and cold she wavers in the wind.
'Did I not force her hence by harsh commands?
'Did not her soul abhor the nuptial bands?   70

LAURA.

Teach not, ye sires, your daughters to rebell.
By counsel rein their wills, but ne'er compel.

CLEANTHES.

Ye duteous daughters, trust these tender guides;
Nor think a parent's breast the tyrant hides.

LAURA.

From either lid the scalding sorrows roll;
The moving tale runs thrilling to my soul.

CLEANTHES.

Perhaps she wanders in the lonely woods,
Or on the sedgy borders of the floods;
Thou know'st each cottage, forest, hill and vale,
And pebbled brook that winds along the dale.   80
Search each sequestered dell to find the fair;
And just reward shall gratifie thy care.

LAURA.

O ye kind boughs protect the virgin's flight,
And guard *Dione* from his prying sight!   [*Aside*.

CLEANTHES.

Mean while I'll seek the shepherd's cool abodes,
Point me, fair nymph, along these doubtful roads.

LAURA.

Seest thou yon' mountain rear his shaggy brow?
In the green valley graze the flocks below:
There ev'ry gale with warbling musick floats,
Shade answers shade, and breaths alternate notes.   90
[*Exit* Cleanthes.

79 know'st] *31*; knowst *20*   82 care.] ⁓^ *31*

He's gone; and to the distant vales is sent,
Nor shall his force *Dione*'s love prevent.
But see, she comes again with hasty pace,
And conscious pleasure dimples on her face.

SCENE IV.

LAURA. DIONE.

DIONE.

I found her laid beside the crystal brook,
Nor rais'd she from the stream her settled look,
Till near her side I stood; her head she rears,
Starts sudden, and her shrieks confess her fears.

LAURA.

Did not thy words her thoughtful soul surprise,
And kindle sparkling anger in her eyes?

DIONE.

Thus she reply'd, with rage and scorn possest.
'Will importuning love ne'er give me rest?
'Why am I thus in desarts wild pursu'd,
10 'Like guilty consciences when stain'd with blood?
'Sure boding ravens, from the blasted oak,
'Shall learn the name of *Lycidas* to croak,
'To sound it in my ears! As swains pass by,
'With look askance, they shake their heads and cry,
'Lo! this is she for whom the shepherd dy'd!
'Soon *Lycidas*, a victim to her pride,
'Shall seek the grave; and in the glimm'ring glade,
'With look all pale, shall glide the restless shade
'Of the poor swain; while we with haggard eye
20 'And bristled hair the fleeting phantom fly.
'Still let their curses innocence upbraid:
'Heav'n never will forsake the virtuous maid.

LAURA.

Didst thou persist to touch her haughty breast?

DIONE.

She still the more disdain'd, the more I prest.

III. iv. 21 'Still] ⌃~ *20 31; Faber's emendation*   22 'Heav'n] ⌃~ *20 31; Faber's emendation*

LAURA.

When you were gone, these walks a stranger crost,
He turn'd through ev'ry path, and wander'd lost;
To me he came; with courteous speech demands
Beneath what bowers repos'd the shepherd bands;
Then further asks me, if among that race
A shepherdess was found of courtly grace;　　　30
With proffer'd bribes my faithful tongue essays;
But for no bribe the faithful tongue betrays.
In me *Dione*'s safe. Far hence he speeds,
Where other hills resound with other reeds.

DIONE.

Should he come back; Suspicion's jealous eyes
Might trace my feature through the swain's disguise.
Now ev'ry noise and whistling wind I dread,
And in each sound approaches human tread.

LAURA.

He said, he left your house involv'd in cares,
Sighs swell'd each breast, each eye o'erflow'd with tears;　　　40
For his lost child thy pensive father mourns,
And sunk in sorrow to the dust returns.
Go back, obedient daughter; hence depart,
And still the sighs that tear his anxious heart.
Soon shall *Evander*, wearied with disdain,
Forgo these fields, and seek the town again.

DIONE.

Think, *Laura*, what thy hasty thoughts persuade.
If I return, to Love a victim made,
My wrathful Sire will force his harsh command,
And with *Cleanthes* join my trembling hand.　　　50

LAURA.

Trust a fond father; raise him from despair.

DIONE.

I fly not him; I fly a life of care.
On the high nuptials of the Court look round;
Where shall, alas, one happy pair be found!

---

51 Trust . . . despair.] *31*; Yet the kind parent soft persuasion trys, / And what his
power compells not, may advise. *20*　　　52 I fly not . . . care] *31*; *om 20*

There, marriage is for servile int'rest sought;
Is love for wealth or power or title bought?
'Tis hence domestick jars their peace destroy,
And loose adult'ry steals the shameful joy.
But search we wide o'er all the blissful plains,
60 Where love alone, devoid of int'rest, reigns.
What concord in each happy pair appears!
How fondness strengthens with the rolling years!
Superiour power ne'er thwarts their soft delights,
Nor jealous accusations wake their nights.

LAURA.

May all those blessings on *Dione* fall.

DIONE.

Grant me *Evander*, and I share them all.
Shall a fond father give perpetual strife,
And doom his child to be a wretch for life?
Though he bequeath'd me all these woods and plains,
70 And all the flocks the russet down contains;
With all the golden harvests of the year,
Far as where yonder purple mountains rear;
Can these the broils of nuptial life prevent?
Can these, without *Evander*, give content?
But see, he comes.

LAURA.

       I'll to the vales repair,
Where wanders by the stream my fleecy care.
Mayst thou the rage of this new flame controul,
And wake *Dione* in his tender soul!   [*Exit* Laura.

SCENE V.

DIONE. LYCIDAS.

LYCIDAS.

Say, my *Alexis*, can thy words impart
Kind rays of hope to cheer a doubtful heart?
How didst thou first my pangs of love disclose?
Did her disdainful brow confirm my woes?

Or did soft pity in her bosom rise,
Heave on her breast, and languish in her eyes?

DIONE.

How shall my tongue the fault'ring tale explain!
My heart drops blood to give the shepherd pain.

LYCIDAS.

Pronounce her utmost scorn; I come prepar'd
To meet my doom. Say, is my death declar'd?   10

DIONE.

Why should thy fate depend on woman's will?
Forget this tyrant, and be happy still.

LYCIDAS.

Didst thou beseech her not to speed her flight,
Nor shun with wrathful glance my hated sight?
Will she consent my sighing plaint to hear,
Nor let my piercing crys be lost in air?

DIONE.

Can mariners appease the tossing storm,
When foaming waves the yawning deep deform?
When o'er the sable cloud the thunder flies,
Say, who shall calm the terror of the skies?   20
Who shall the lion's famish'd roar asswage?
And can we still proud woman's stronger rage?
Soon as my faithful tongue pronounc'd thy name,
Sudden her glances shot resentful flame:
Be dumb, she crys, this whining love give o'er,
And vex me with the teazing theme no more.

LYCIDAS.

'Tis pride alone that keeps alive her scorn.
Can the mean swain in humble cottage born,
Can Poverty that haughty heart obtain,
Where avarice and strong ambition reign?   30
If Poverty pass by in tatter'd coat,
Curs vex his heels and stretch their barking throat;
If chance he mingle in the female croud,
Pride tosses high her head, Scorn laughs aloud;
Each nymph turns from him to her gay gallant,

And wonders at the impudence of Want.
'Tis vanity that rules all woman-kind,
Love is the weakest passion of their mind.

DIONE.

Though one is by those servile views possest,
40 O *Lycidas*, condemn not all the rest.

LYCIDAS.

Though I were bent beneath a load of years,
And seventy winters thin'd my hoary hairs;
Yet if my olive branches dropt with oil,
And crooked shares were brighten'd in my soil,
If lowing herds my fat'ning meads possest,
And my white fleece the tawny mountain drest;
Then would she lure me with love-darting glance,
And with fond mercenary smiles advance.
Though hell with ev'ry vice my soul had stain'd,
50 And froward anger in my bosom reign'd,
Though avarice my coffers cloath'd in rust,
And my joints trembled with enfeebled lust;
Yet were my ancient name with titles great,
How would she languish for the gawdy bait!
If to her love all-tempting wealth pretend,
What virtuous woman can her heart defend!

DIONE.

Conquests, thus meanly bought, men soon despise,
And justly slight the mercenary prize.

LYCIDAS.

I know these frailties in her breast reside,
60 Direct her glance and ev'ry action guide.
Still let *Alexis'* faithful friendship aid,
Once more attempt to bend the stubborn maid.
Tell her, no base-born swain provokes her scorn,
No clown, beneath the sedgy cottage born;
Tell her, for her this sylvan dress I took,
For her my name and pomp of Courts forsook;
My lofty roofs with golden sculpture shine,
And my high birth descends from ancient line.

56 defend!] ∼∧ *31*

DIONE.

Love is a sacred voluntary fire,
Gold never bought that pure, that chast desire.   70
Who thinks true love for lucre to possess,
Shall grasp false flatt'ry and the feign'd caress;
Can we believe that mean, that servile wife,
Who vilely sells her dear-bought love for life,
Would not her virtue for an hour resign,
If in her sight the proffer'd treasure shine.

LYCIDAS.

Can reason (when by winds swift fires are born
O'er waving harvests of autumnal corn)
The driving fury of the flame reprove?
Who then shall reason with a heart in love!   80

DIONE.

Yet let me speak; O may my words persuade
The noble youth to quit this sylvan maid!
Resign thy crook, no more to plains resort,
Look round on all the beauties of the Court;
There shall thy merit find a worthy flame,
Some nymph of equal wealth and equal name.
Think, if these offers should thy wish obtain,
And should the rustick beauty stoop to gain:
Thy heart could ne'er prolong th' unequal fire,
The sudden blaze would in one year expire;   90
Then thy rash folly thou too late shalt chide,
To Poverty and base-born blood ally'd;
Her vulgar tongue shall animate the strife,
And hourly discord vex thy future life.

LYCIDAS.

Such is the force thy faithful words impart,
That like the galling goad they pierce my heart!
You think fair virtue in my breast resides,
That honest truth my lips and actions guides;
Deluded shepherd, could you view my soul,
You'd see it with deceit and treach'ry foul;   100
I'm base, perfidious. E'er from Court I came,

88 gain:] *31*; ~ ; *20*   97 You think] *31*; thou think'st *20*   99 could you]
31; couldst thou *20*   100 You'd] *31*; Thou'dst *20*

Love singled from the train a beauteous dame;
The tender maid my fervent vows believ'd,
My fervent vows the tender maid deceiv'd.
Why dost thou tremble?—why thus heave thy sighs?
Why steal the silent sorrows from thy eyes?

DIONE.

Sure the soft lamb hides rage within his breast,
And cooing turtles are with hate possest;
When from so sweet a tongue flow fraud and lies,
110 And those meek looks a perjur'd heart disguise.
Ah! who shall now on faithless man depend?
The treach'rous lover proves as false a friend.

LYCIDAS.

When with *Dione*'s love my bosom glow'd,
Firm constancy and truth sincere I vow'd;
But since *Parthenia*'s brighter charms were known,
My love, my constancy and truth are flown.

DIONE.

Are not thy hours with conscious anguish stung?
Swift vengeance must o'ertake the perjur'd tongue.
The Gods the cause of injur'd love assert,
120 And arm with stubborn pride *Parthenia*'s heart.

LYCIDAS.

Go, try her; tempt her with my birth and state,
Stronger ambition will subdue her hate.

DIONE.

O rather turn thy thoughts on that lost maid,
Whose hourly sighs thy faithless oath upbraid!
Think thou behold'st her at the dead of night,
Plac'd by the glimm'ring taper's paly light,
With all your letters spread before her view,
While trickling tears the tender lines bedew;
Sobbing she reads the perj'rys o'er and o'er,
130 And her long nights know peaceful sleep no more.

LYCIDAS.

Let me forget her.

127 your] *31*; thy *20*

DIONE.

O false youth, relent;
Think should *Parthenia* to thy hopes consent;
When *Hymen* joins your hands, and musick's voice
Makes the glad ecchoes of thy domes rejoyce,
Then shall *Dione* force the crouded hall,
Kneel at thy feet and loud for justice call:
Could you behold her weltring on the ground,
The purple dagger reeking from the wound?
Could you unmov'd this dreadful sight survey?
Such fatal scenes shall stain thy bridal day.   140

LYCIDAS.

The horrid thought sinks deep into my soul,
And down my cheek unwilling sorrows roll.

DIONE.

From this new flame thou may'st as yet recede.
Or have you doom'd that guiltless maid shall bleed?

LYCIDAS.

Name her no more.—Haste, seek the sylvan Fair.

DIONE.

Should the rich proffer tempt her list'ning ear,
Bid all your peace adieu. O barb'rous youth,
Can you forgo your honour, love and truth?
Yet should *Parthenia* wealth and title slight,
Would justice then restore *Dione*'s right?   150
Would you then dry her ever-falling tears;
And bless with honest love your future years?

LYCIDAS.

I'll in yon' shade thy wish'd return attend;
Come, quickly come, and cheer thy sighing friend.
                 [*Exit* Lycidas.

DIONE.

Should her proud soul resist the tempting bait,
Should she contemn his proffer'd wealth and state,
Then I once more his perjur'd heart may move,

137, 139 Could you] *31*; Could'st thou *20*   144 have you] *31*; hast thou *20*
147 your] *31*; thy *20*   148 Can you] *31*; Canst thou *20*   148 your] *31*; thy *20*
151 Would you] *31*; Would'st thou *20*   152 honest love your] *31*; love and joy
thy *20*   154 Come,] ∽∧ *31*   154 sd Lycidas.] ∽∧ *31*

And in his bosom wake the dying love.
As the pale wretch involv'd in doubts and fears,
160 All trembling in the judgment-hall appears;
So shall I stand before *Parthenia*'s eyes,
For as she dooms, *Dione* lives or dies.

ACT IV. SCENE I.

LYCIDAS. PARTHENIA asleep in a bower.

LYCIDAS.

MAY no rude wind the rustling branches move;
Breathe soft, ye silent gales, nor wake my Love.
Ye shepherds, piping homeward on the way,
Let not the distant ecchoes learn your lay;
Strain not, ye nightingales, your warbling throat,
May no loud shake prolong the shriller note,
Lest she awake; O sleep, secure her eyes,
That I may gaze; for if she wake, she flies.
While easy dreams compose her peaceful soul,
10 What anxious cares within my bosom roll!
If tir'd with sighs beneath the beech I lye,
And languid slumber close my weeping eye,
Her lovely vision rises to my view,
Swift flys the nymph, and swift would I pursue;
I strive to call, my tongue has lost its sound;
Like rooted oaks, my feet benumm'd are bound;
Struggling I wake. Again my sorrows flow,
And not one flatt'ring dream deludes my woe.
What innocence! how meek is ev'ry grace!
20 How sweet the smile that dimples on her face,
Calm as the sleeping seas! but should my sighs
Too rudely breathe, what angry storms would rise!
Though the fair rose with beauteous blush is crown'd,
Beneath her fragrant leaves the thorn is found;
The peach, that with inviting crimson blooms,
Deep at the heart the cank'ring worm consumes;
'Tis thus, alas! those lovely features hide
Disdain and anger and resentful pride.

SCENE II.

LYCIDAS. DIONE. PARTHENIA.

LYCIDAS.

Hath proffer'd greatness yet o'ercome her hate?
And does she languish for the glitt'ring bait?
Against the swain she might her pride support.
Can she subdue her sex, and scorn a Court?
Perhaps in dreams the shining vision charms,
And the rich bracelet sparkles on her arms;
In fancy'd heaps the golden treasure glows:
Parthenia, wake; all this thy swain bestows.

DIONE.

Sleeps she in these close bowers?

LYCIDAS.

Lo! there she lies.

DIONE.

O may no startling sound unseal her eyes,   10
And drive her hence away. 'Till now, in vain
I trod the winding wood and weary plain;
Hence, *Lycidas*; beyond those shades repose,
While I thy fortune and thy birth disclose.

LYCIDAS.

May I *Parthenia* to thy friendship owe!

DIONE.

O rather think on lost *Dione*'s woe!
Must she thy broken faith for ever mourn,
And will that juster passion ne'er return?

LYCIDAS.

Upbraid me not; but go. Her slumbers chase;
And in her view the bright temptation place.   20

[*Exit* Lycidas.

IV. ii. 1 Hath] *31*; Has *20*   13 Hence, *Lycidas*] *31*; Ign'rant as yet what grandeur courts her scorn, / She thinks thee train'd in fields, and vulgar born. / Hence, *Lycidas 20*   15 May . . . owe!] *31*; May kind success upon the message wait. *20*   16 woe] *31*; fate *20*   19 Upbraid. . . . Her] *31*; I'll hear no more: go then, her *20*   19 chase;] *31*; ~, *20*

SCENE III.

DIONE. PARTHENIA.

DIONE.

Now flames the western skie with golden beams,
And the ray kindles on the quiv'ring streams;
Long flights of crows, high-croaking from their food,
Now seek the nightly covert of the wood;
The tender grass with dewy crystal bends,
And gath'ring vapour from the heath ascends.
Shake off this downy rest; wake, gentle maid,
Trust not thy charms beneath the noxious shade.
Parthenia, rise.

PARTHENIA.

What voice alarms my ear?
10 Away. Approach not. Hah! *Alexis* there!
Let us together to the vales descend,
And to the folds our bleating charge attend;
But let me hear no more that shepherd's name,
Vex not my quiet with his hateful flame.

DIONE.

Can I behold him gasping on the ground,
And seek no healing herb to stanch the wound?
For thee continual sighs consume his heart,
'Tis you alone can cure the bleeding smart.
Once more I come the moving cause to plead,
20 If still his suff'rings cannot intercede,
Yet let my friendship do his passion right,
And show thy lover in his native light.

PARTHENIA.

Why in dark myst'ry are thy words involv'd?
If *Lycidas* you mean; know, I'm resolv'd.

DIONE.

Let not thy kindling rage my words restrain.
Know then; *Parthenia* slights no vulgar swain.
For thee he bears the scrip and sylvan crook,
For thee the glories of a Court forsook.

May not thy heart the wealthy flame decline!
His honours, his possessions, all are thine.   30

PARTHENIA.

If he's a Courtier, O ye Nymphs, beware;
Those who most promise are the least sincere.
The quick-ey'd hawk shoots headlong from above,
And in his pounces bears the trembling dove;
The pilfring wolf o'er-leaps the fold's defence.
But the false Courtier preys on innocence.
If he's a Courtier; O ye Nymphs, beware:
Those who most promise are the least sincere.

DIONE.

Alas! thou ne'er hast prov'd the sweets of State,
Nor know that female pleasure, to be great.   40
'Tis for the town ripe clusters load the poles,
And all our Autumn crowns the Courtier's bowles;
For him our woods the red-ey'd pheasant breed,
And annual coveys in our harvest feed;
For him with fruit the bending branch is stor'd,
Plenty pours all her blessings on his board.
If (when the market to the city calls)
We chance to pass beside his palace walls,
Does not his hall with musick's voice resound,
And the floor tremble with the dancer's bound?   50
Such are the pleasures *Lycidas* shall give,
When thy relenting bosom bids him live.

PARTHENIA.

See yon gay goldfinch hop from spray to spray,
Who sings a farewell to the parting day;
At large he flies o'er hill and dale and down;
Is not each bush, each spreading tree his own?
And canst thou think he'll quit his native brier,
For the bright cage o'er-arch'd with golden wire?
What then are honours, pomp and gold to me?
Are those a price to purchase liberty!   60

DIONE.

Think, when the *Hymeneal* torch shall blaze,
And on the solemn rites the virgins gaze;

When thy fair locks with glitt'ring gems are grac'd,
And the bright zone shall sparkle round thy waste,
How will their hearts with envious sorrow pine,
When *Lycidas* shall join his hand to thine!

PARTHENIA.

And yet, *Alexis*, all that pomp and show
Are oft' the varnish of internal woe.
When the chast lamb is from her sisters led,
70 And interwoven garlands paint her head;
The gazing flock, all envious of her pride,
Behold her skipping by the Priestess' side;
Each hopes the flow'ry wreath with longing eyes;
While she, alas! is led to sacrifice!
Thus walks the bride in all her state array'd,
The gaze and envy of each thoughtless maid.

DIONE.

As yet her tongue resists the tempting snare,
And guards my panting bosom from despair.   [*Aside.*
Can thy strong soul this noble flame forgo?
80 Must such a lover waste his life in woe?

PARTHENIA.

Tell him, his gifts I scorn; not all his art,
Not all his flatt'ry shall seduce my heart.
Courtiers, I know, are disciplin'd to cheat,
Their infant lips are taught to lisp deceit;
To prey on easy nymphs they range the shade,
And vainly boast of innocence betray'd;
Chast hearts, unlearn'd in falsehood, they assail,
And think our ear will drink the grateful tale:
No. *Lycidas* shall ne'er my peace destroy,
90 I'll guard my virtue, and content enjoy.

DIONE.

So strong a passion in my bosom burns,
Whene'er his soul is griev'd, *Alexis* mourns!
Canst thou this importuning ardor blame?
Would not thy tongue for friendship urge the same?

---

68 Are] *31*; Is *20*   79 forgo] forego *31*   82 flatt'ry] flattery *31*

PARTHENIA.

Yes, blooming swain. You show an honest mind;
I see it, with the purest flame refin'd.
Who shall compare love's mean and gross desire
To the chast zeal of friendship's sacred fire?
By whining love our weakness is confest;
But stronger friendship shows a virtuous breast.   100
In Folly's heart the short-liv'd blaze may glow,
Wisdom alone can purer friendship know.
Love is a sudden blaze which soon decays,
Friendship is like the sun's eternal rays;
Not daily benefits exhaust the flame,
It still is giving, and still burns the same;
And could *Alexis* from his soul remove
All the low images of grosser love;
Such mild, such gentle looks thy heart declare,
Fain would my breast thy faithful friendship share.   110

DIONE.

How dare you in the diff'rent sex confide?
And seek a friendship which you ne'er have try'd?

PARTHENIA.

Yes, I to thee could give up all my heart.
From thy chast eye no wanton glances dart;
Thy modest lips convey no thought impure,
With thee may strictest virtue walk secure.

DIONE.

Yet can I safely on the nymph depend,
Whose unrelenting scorn can kill my friend!

PARTHENIA.

Accuse me not, who act a generous part;
Had I, like city maids, a fraudful heart,   120
Then had his proffers taught my soul to feign,
Then had I vilely stoopt to sordid gain,
Then had I sigh'd for honours, pomp and gold,
And for unhappy chains my freedom sold.
If thou would'st save him, bid him leave the plain,

95 You show] *31*; Thou show'st *20*   111 dare you] *31*; dar'st tho·
112 you] *31*; thou *20*   112 have] *31*; hast *20*

And to his native city turn again:
There, shall his passion find a ready cure,
There, not one dame resists the glitt'ring lure.

DIONE.

All this I frequent urg'd, but urg'd in vain.
130 Alas! thou only canst asswage his pain!

SCENE IV.

DIONE. PARTHENIA. LYCIDAS,- [*listening.*
LYCIDAS.

Why stays *Alexis*? can my bosom bear
Thus long alternate storms of hope and fear?
Yonder they walk; no frowns her brow disguise,
But love consenting sparkles in her eyes;
Here will I listen, here, impatient wait.
Spare me, *Parthenia*, and resign thy hate.   [*Aside.*

PARTHENIA.

When *Lycidas* shall to the Court repair,
Still let *Alexis* love his fleecy care;
Still let him chuse cool grots and sylvan bowers,
10 And let *Parthenia* share his peaceful hours.

LYCIDAS.

What do I hear? my friendship is betray'd;
The treach'rous rival has seduc'd the maid.   [*Aside.*

PARTHENIA.

With thee, where bearded goats descend the steep,
Or where, like winter's snow, the nibbling sheep
Cloath the slope hills; I'll pass the cheerful day,
And from thy reed my voice shall catch the lay.
But see, still Ev'ning spreads her dusky wings,
The flocks, slow-moving from the misty springs,
Now seek their fold. Come, shepherd, let's away,
20 To close the latest labours of the day.

[*Exeunt hand in hand.*

IV. iv. 2 alternate storms] *31*; th'alternate storm *20*

SCENE V.

LYCIDAS.

My troubled heart what dire disasters rend!
A scornful mistress, and a treach'rous friend!
Would ye be cozen'd, more than woman can;
Unlock your bosom to perfidious man.
One faithful woman have these eyes beheld,
And against her this perjur'd heart rebell'd:
But search as far as earth's wide bounds extend,
Where shall the wretched find one faithful friend?

SCENE VI.

LYCIDAS. DIONE.

LYCIDAS.

Why starts the swain? why turn his eyes away,
As if amidst his path the viper lay?
Did I not to thy charge my heart confide?
Did I not trust thee near *Parthenia*'s side,
As here she slept?

DIONE.

　　　　She strait my call obey'd,
And downy slumber left the lovely maid;
As in the morn awakes the folded rose,
And all around her breathing odour throws;
So wak'd *Parthenia*.

LYCIDAS.

　　　　Could thy guarded heart,
When her full beauty glow'd, put by the dart?　　　10
Yet on *Alexis* let my soul depend.
'Tis most ungen'rous to suspect a friend.
And thou, I hope, hast well that name profest.

DIONE.

O could thy piercing eye discern my breast!
Could'st thou the secrets of my bosom see,
There ev'ry thought is fill'd with cares for thee.

LYCIDAS.

Is there, against hypocrisie, defence,
Who cloaths her words and looks with innocence!   [*Aside.*
Say, shepherd, when you proffer'd wealth and state,
20 Did not her scorn and suppled pride abate?

DIONE.

As sparkling di'monds to the feather'd train,
Who scrape the winnow'd chaff in search of grain;
Such to the shepherdess the Court appears:
Content she seeks, and spurns those glitt'ring cares.

LYCIDAS.

'Tis not in woman grandeur to despise,
'Tis not from Courts, from me alone she flies.
Did not my passion suffer like disgrace,
While she believ'd me born of sylvan race?
Dost thou not think, this proudest of her kind
30 Has to some rival swain her heart resign'd?

DIONE.

No rival shepherd her disdain can move;
Her frozen bosom is averse to love.

LYCIDAS.

Say, art thou sure, that this ungrateful fair
Scorns all alike, bids all alike despair?

DIONE.

How can I know the secrets of her heart!

LYCIDAS.

Answer sincere, nor from the question start.
Say, in her glance was never love confest,
And is no swain distinguish'd from the rest?

DIONE.

O *Lycidas*, bid all thy troubles cease;
40 Let not a thought on her disturb thy peace.
May justice bid thy former passion wake;
Think how *Dione* suffers for thy sake:
Let not a broken oath thy honour stain,
Recall thy vows, and seek the town again.

IV. vi. 17 hypocrisie] hypocrisy *31*

LYCIDAS.

What means *Alexis*? where's thy friendship flown?
Why am I banish'd to the hateful town?
Has some new shepherd warm'd *Parthenia*'s breast?
And does my love her am'rous hours molest?
Is it for this thou bid'st me quit the plain?
Yes, yes, thou fondly lov'st this rival swain.   50
When first my cheated soul thy friendship woo'd,
To my warm heart I took the vip'rous brood.
O false *Alexis*!

DIONE.

Why am I accus'd?
Thy jealous mind is by weak fears abus'd.

LYCIDAS.

Was not thy bosom fraught with false design?
Didst thou not plead his cause, and give up mine?
Let not thy tongue evasive answer seek;
The conscious crimson rises on thy cheek:
Thy coward conscience, by thy guilt dismaid,
Shakes in each joint, and owns that I'm betray'd.   60

DIONE.

How my poor heart is wrong'd! O spare thy friend!

LYCIDAS.

Seek not detected falsehood to defend.

DIONE.

Beware; lest blind suspicion rashly blame.

LYCIDAS.

Own thy self then the rival of my flame.
If this be she for whom *Alexis* pin'd,
She now no more is to thy vows unkind.
Behind the thicket's twisted verdure laid,
I witness'd ev'ry tender thing she said;
I saw bright pleasure kindle in her eyes,
Love warm'd each feature at thy soft replys.   70

DIONE.

Yet hear me speak.

68 ev'ry] *31*; evry *20*

LYCIDAS.
In vain is all defence.
Did not thy treach'rous hand conduct her hence?
Haste, from my sight. Rage burns in ev'ry vein;
Never approach my just revenge again.

DIONE.
O search my heart; there injur'd truth thou'lt find.

LYCIDAS.
Talk not of Truth; long since she left mankind.
So smooth a tongue! and yet so false a heart!
Sure Courts first taught thee fawning friendship's art!
No. Thou art false by nature.

DIONE.
Let me clear
80 This heavy charge, and prove my trust sincere.

LYCIDAS.
Boast then her favours; say, what happy hour
Next calls to meet her in th'appointed bower;
Say, when and where you met.

DIONE.
Be rage supprest.
In stabbing mine, you wound *Parthenia*'s breast.
She said, she still defy'd Love's keenest dart;
Yet purer friendship might divide her heart,
Friendship's sincerer bands she wish'd to prove.

LYCIDAS.
A woman's friendship ever ends in love.
Think not these foolish tales my faith command;
90 Did not I see thee press her snowy hand?
O may her passion like thy friendship last!
May she betray thee e'er a day be past!
Hence then. Away. Thou'rt hateful to my sight,
And thus I spurn the fawning hypocrite.

[*Exit* Lycidas.

SCENE VII.
DIONE.
Was ever grief like mine! O wretched maid!

My friendship wrong'd! my constant love betray'd!
Misfortune haunts my step where-e'er I go,
And all my days are over-cast with woe.
Long have I strove th'encreasing load to bear,
Now faints my soul, and sinks into despair.
O lead me to the hanging mountain's cell,
In whose brown cliffs the fowls of darkness dwell;
Where waters, trickling down the rifted wall,
Shall lull my sorrows with the tinkling fall.   10
There, seek thy grave. How canst thou bear the light,
When banish'd ever from *Evander*'s sight!

SCENE VIII.

DIONE. LAURA.

LAURA.

Why hangs a cloud of grief upon thy brows?
Does the proud nymph accept *Evander*'s vows?

DIONE.

Can I bear life with these new pangs opprest!
Again he tears me from his faithless breast:
A perjur'd Lover first he sought these plains,
And now my friendship like my love disdains.
As I new offers to *Parthenia* made,
Conceal'd he stood behind the woodbine shade.
He says, my treach'rous tongue his heart betray'd,
That my false speeches have mis-led the maid;   10
With groundless fear he thus his soul deceives;
What frenzy dictates, jealousy believes.

LAURA.

Resign thy crook, put off this manly vest,
And let the wrong'd *Dione* stand confest;
When he shall learn what sorrows thou hast born,
And find that nought relents *Parthenia*'s scorn,
Sure he will pity thee.

DIONE.
No, *Laura*, no.
Should I, alas! the sylvan dress forgo,
Then might he think that I her pride foment,

20 That injur'd love instructs me to resent;
Our secret enterprize might fatal prove:
Man flys the plague of persecuting love.

LAURA.

Avoid *Parthenia*; lest his rage grow warm,
And jealousie resolve some fatal harm.

DIONE.

O *Laura*, if thou chance the youth to find,
Tell him what torments vex my anxious mind;
Should I once more his awful presence seek,
The silent tears would bathe my glowing cheek;
By rising sighs my fault'ring voice be stay'd,
30 And trembling fear too soon confess the maid,
Haste, *Laura*, then; his vengeful soul asswage,
Tell him, I'm guiltless; cool his blinded rage;
Tell him that truth sincere my friendship brought,
Let him not cherish one suspicious thought.
Then to convince him, his distrust was vain,
I'll never, never see that nymph again.
This way he went.

LAURA.

          See, at the call of night,
The star of ev'ning sheds his silver light
High o'er yon western hill: the cooling gales
40 Fresh odours breathe along the winding dales;
Far from their home as yet our shepherds stray,
To close with cheerful walk the sultry day.
Methinks from far I hear the piping swain;
Hark, in the breeze now swells, now sinks the strain!
Thither I'll seek him.

DIONE.

          While this length of glade
Shall lead me pensive through the sable shade;
Where on the branches murmur rushing winds,
Grateful as falling floods to love-sick minds.
O may this path to Death's dark vale descend!
50 There only, can the wretched hope a friend.

                               [*Exeunt severally.*

IV. viii. 42 cheerful] chearful *31*

ACT V. SCENE I.

A Wood.

DIONE. CLEANTHES, (who lyes wounded in a distant part of the stage)

DIONE.

The Moon serene now climbs th'aerial way;
See, at her sight ten thousand stars decay:
With trembling gleam she tips the silent grove,
While all beneath the checquer'd shadows move.
Turn back thy silver axles, downward roll,
Darkness best fits the horrors of my soul.
Rise, rise, ye clouds; the face of heav'n deform,
Veil the bright Goddess in a sable storm:
O look not down upon a wretched maid!
Let thy bright torch the happy lover aid,   10
And light his wandring footsteps to the bower,
Where the kind nymph attends th'appointed hour.
Yet thou hast seen unhappy love, like mine;
Did not thy lamp in Heav'n's blue forehead shine,
When *Thisbe* sought her Love along the glade?
Didst thou not then behold the gleaming blade,
And gild the fatal point that stabb'd her breast?
Soon I, like her, shall seek the realms of rest.
Let groves of mournful yew this wretch surround!
O sooth my ear with melancholy sound!   20
The village curs now stretch their yelling throat,
And dogs from distant cotts return the note;
The rav'nous wolf along the valley prowls,
And with his famish'd crys the mountain howls.
But hark! what sudden noise advances near?
Repeated groans alarm my frighted ear!

CLEANTHES.

Shepherd, approach; ah! fly not through the glade.
A wretch all dy'd with wounds invokes thy aid.

DIONE.

Say then, unhappy stranger, how you bled;
Collect thy spirits, raise thy drooping head.   30
             [Cleanthes *raises himself on his arm.*

O horrid sight! *Cleanthes* gasping lies;
And Death's black shadows float before his eyes.
Unknown in this disguise, I'll check my woe,
And learn what bloody hand has struck the blow.   [*Aside.*
Say, youth, ere Fate thy feeble voice confounds,
What led thee hither? whence these purple wounds?

CLEANTHES.

Stay, fleeting life; may strength a-while prevail,
Lest my clos'd lips confine th'imperfect tale.
Ere the streak'd East grew warm with amber ray,
40 I from the city took my doubtful way,
Far o'er the plains I sought a beauteous maid,
Who from the Court, in these wide forests stray'd,
Wanders unknown; as I, with weary pain,
Try'd ev'ry path, and op'ning glade in vain;
A band of thieves, forth-rushing from the wood,
Unsheath'd their daggers warm with daily blood;
Deep in my breast the barb'rous steel is dy'd
And purple hands the golden prey divide.
Hence are these mangling wounds. Say, gentle swain,
50 If thou hast known among the sylvan train
The vagrant nymph I seek?

DIONE.

What mov'd thy care,
Thus, in these pathless wilds to search the fair?

CLEANTHES.

I charge you, O ye daughters of the grove,
Ye *Naiads*, who the mossy fountains love,
Ye happy swains, who range the pastures wide,
Ye tender nymphs, who feed your flocks beside;
If my last gasping breath can pity move,
If e'er ye knew the pangs of slighted love,
Show her, I charge you, where *Cleanthes* dy'd;
60 The grass yet reeking with the sanguine tide.
A father's power to me the virgin gave,
But she disdain'd to live a nuptial slave;
So fled her native home.

v. i. 35   ere] *31*; e'er *20*   39 Ere] *31*; E'er *20*

DIONE.
'Tis then from thee
Springs the foul source of all her misery.
Could'st thou, thy selfish appetite to please,
Condemn to endless woes another's peace?

CLEANTHES.
O spare me; nor my hapless love upbraid,
While on my heart Death's frozen hand is laid!
Go, seek her, guide her where *Cleanthes* bled;
When she surveys her lover pale and dead,   70
Tell her, that since she fled my hateful sight,
Without remorse I sought the realms of night.
Methinks I see her view these poor remains,
And on her cheek indecent gladness reigns!
Full in her presence cold *Cleanthes* lies,
And not one tear stands trembling in her eyes!
O let a sigh my hapless fate deplore!
Cleanthes now controuls thy love no more.

DIONE.
How shall my lids confine these rising woes?   [*Aside.*

CLEANTHES.
O might I see her, ere Death's finger close   80
These eyes for ever! might her soften'd breast
Forgive my love with too much ardor prest!
Then I with peace could yield my latest breath.

DIONE.
Shall I not calm the sable hour of death,
And show my self before him!—Hah! he dies.
See, from his trembling lip the spirit flies!   [*Aside.*
Stay yet awhile. *Dione* stands confest.
He knows me not. He faints, he sinks to rest.

CLEANTHES.
Tell her, since all my hopes in her were lost,
That death was welcome—   [*Dies.* 90

DIONE.
What sudden gusts of grief my bosom rend!
A parent's curses o'er my head impend

80 ere] *31*; e'er *20*   91 rend!] ~? *31*

For disobedient vows; O wretched maid,
Those very vows *Evander* hath betray'd.
See, at thy feet *Cleanthes* bath'd in blood!
For love of thee he trod this lonely wood;
Thou art the cruel authress of his fate;
He falls by thine, thou, by *Evander*'s hate.
When shall my soul know rest? *Cleanthes* slain
100 No longer sighs and weeps for thy disdain.
Thou still art curst with love. Bleed, virgin, bleed.
How shall a wretch from anxious life be freed!
My troubled brain with sudden frenzy burns,
And shatter'd thought now this now that way turns.
What do I see thus glitt'ring on the plains?
Hah! the dread sword yet warm with crimson stains!

                            [*Takes up the dagger.*

SCENE II.

DIONE. PARTHENIA.

PARTHENIA.

Sweet is the walk when night has cool'd the hour.
This path directs me to my sylvan bower.   [*Aside.*

DIONE.

Why is my soul with sudden fear dismay'd!
Why drops my trembling hand the pointed blade?
O string my arm with force!   [*Aside.*

PARTHENIA.

               Methought a noise
Broke through the silent air, like human voice.   [*Aside.*

DIONE.

One well-aim'd blow shall all my pangs remove,
Grasp firm the fatal steel, and cease to love.   [*Aside.*

PARTHENIA.

Sure 'twas *Alexis*. Hah! a sword display'd!
10 The streaming lustre darts a-cross the shade.   [*Aside.*

DIONE.

May Heav'n new vigour to my soul impart,
And guide the desp'rate weapon to my heart!   [*Aside.*

       94 hath] *31*; has *20*   100 disdain.] *31*; ~, *20*

PARTHENIA.

May I the meditated death arrest!   [*Holds* Dione'*s hand.*
Strike not, rash shepherd; spare thy guiltless breast.
O give me strength to stay the threaten'd harm,
And wrench the dagger from his lifted arm!

DIONE.

What cruel hand with-holds the welcome blow?
In giving life, you but prolong my woe.
O may not thus th'expected stroke impend!
Unloose thy grasp, and let swift death descend.   20
But if yon' murder thy red hands has dy'd;
Here. Pierce me deep; let forth the vital tide.
                              [Dione *quits the dagger.*

PARTHENIA.

Wait not thy fate; but this way turn thy eyes:
My virgin hand no purple murder dyes.
Turn then, *Alexis*; and *Parthenia* know,
'Tis she protects thee from the fatal blow.

DIONE.

Must the night-watches by my sighs be told?
And must these eyes another morn behold
Through dazling floods of tears? ungen'rous maid,
The friendly stroke is by thy hand delay'd;   30
Call it not mercy to prolong my breath;
'Tis but to torture me with lingring death.

PARTHENIA.

What moves thy hand to act this bloody part?
Whence are these gnawing pangs that tear thy heart?
Is that thy friend who lies before thee slain?
Is it his wound that reeks upon the plain?
Is't *Lycidas*?

DIONE.

                No. I the stranger found,
E'er chilly death his frozen tongue had bound.
He said; as at the rosy dawn of day,
He from the city took his vagrant way,   40
A murd'ring band pour'd on him from the wood,
First seiz'd his gold, then bath'd their swords in blood.

PARTHENIA.

You, whose ambition labours to be great,
Think on the perils which on riches wait.
Safe are the shepherd's paths; when sober Even
Streaks with pale light the bending arch of heaven,
From danger free, through desarts wild he hies,
The rising smoak far o'er the mountain spies,
Which marks his distant cottage; on he fares,
50 For him no murd'rers lay their nightly snares;
They pass him by, they turn their steps away:
Safe Poverty was ne'er the villain's prey.
At home he lies secure in easy sleep,
No bars his ivie-mantled cottage keep;
No thieves in dreams the fancy'd dagger hold,
And drag him to detect the buried gold;
Nor starts he from his couch aghast and pale,
When the door murmurs with the hollow gale.
While he, whose iron coffers rust with wealth,
60 Harbours beneath his roof Deceit and Stealth;
Treach'ry with lurking pace frequents his walks,
And close behind him horrid Murder stalks.
'Tis tempting lucre makes the villain bold.
There lies a bleeding sacrifice to gold.

DIONE.

To live, is but to wake to daily cares,
And journey through a tedious vale of tears.
Had you not rush'd between, my life had flown;
And I, like him, no more had sorrow known.

PARTHENIA.

When anguish in the gloomy bosom dwells,
70 The counsel of a friend the cloud dispells.
Give thy breast vent, the secret grief impart,
And say what woe lies heavy at thy heart.
To save thy life kind Heav'n has succour sent,
The Gods by me thy threaten'd fate prevent.

DIONE.

No. To prevent it, is beyond thy power;
Thou only canst defer the welcome hour.
When you the lifted dagger turn'd aside,

Only one road to death thy force deny'd;
Still fate is in my reach. From mountains high,
Deep in whose shadow craggy ruines lie,   80
Can I not headlong fling this weight of woe,
And dash out life against the flints below?
Are there not streams, and lakes, and rivers wide,
Where my last breath may bubble on the tide?
No. Life shall never flatter me again,
Nor shall to-morrow bring new sighs and pain.

PARTHENIA.

Can I this burthen of thy soul relieve,
And calm thy grief?

DIONE.

　　　　　　　If thou wilt comfort give;
Plight me thy word, and to that word be just;
When poor *Alexis* shall be laid in dust,   90
That pride no longer shall command thy mind,
That thou wilt spare the friend I leave behind.
I know his virtue worthy of thy breast.
Long in thy love may *Lycidas* be blest!

PARTHENIA.

That swain (who would my liberty controul,
To please some short-liv'd transport of his soul)
Shows, while his importuning flame he moves,
That 'tis not me, himself alone he loves.
O live, nor leave him by misfortune prest;
'Tis shameful to desert a friend distrest.   100

DIONE.

Alas! a wretch like me no loss would prove,
Would kind *Parthenia* listen to his love.

PARTHENIA.

Why hides thy bosom this mysterious grief?
Ease thy o'erburthen'd heart and hope relief.

DIONE.

What profits it to touch thy tender breast,
With wrongs, like mine, which ne'er can be redrest?
Let in my heart the fatal secret dye,
Nor call up sorrow in another's eye!

v. ii. 80 ruines] ruins *31*   91 mind] miud *31*

SCENE III.

DIONE. PARTHENIA. LYCIDAS.

LYCIDAS.

If *Laura* right direct the darksome ways,
Along these paths the pensive shepherd strays.   [*Aside.*

DIONE.

Let not a tear for me roll down thy cheek.
O would my throbbing sighs my heart-strings break!
Why was my breast the lifted stroke deny'd?
Must then again the deathful deed by try'd?
Yes. 'Tis resolv'd.   [*Snatches the dagger from* Parthenia.

PARTHENIA.

Ah, hold; forbear, forbear!

LYCIDAS.

Methought Distress with shrieks alarm'd my ear!

PARTHENIA.

Strike not. Ye Gods, defend him from the wound!

LYCIDAS.

10 Yes. 'Tis *Parthenia*'s voice, I know the sound.
Some sylvan ravisher would force the maid,
And *Laura* sent me to her virtue's aid.
Die, villain, die; and seek the shades below.
     [Lycidas *snatches the dagger from* Dione, *and stabs*
                   her.

DIONE.

Whoe'er thou art, I bless thee for the blow.

LYCIDAS.

Since Heav'n ordain'd this arm thy life should guard,
O hear my vows! be love the just reward.

PARTHENIA.

Rather let vengeance, with her swiftest speed
O'ertake thy flight, and recompense the deed!
Why stays the thunder in the upper skie?
20 Gather, ye clouds; ye forky lightnings, fly:
On thee may all the wrath of heav'n descend,

Whose barb'rous hand hath slain a faithful friend.
Behold *Alexis*!

LYCIDAS.

Would that treach'rous boy
Have forc'd thy virtue to his brutal joy?
What rous'd his passion to this bold advance?
Did e'er thy eyes confess one willing glance?
I know, the faithless youth his trust betray'd;
And well the dagger hath my wrongs repay'd.

DIONE.   [*raising herself on her arm.*

Breaks not *Evander*'s voice along the glade?
Hah! is it he who holds the reeking blade!   30
There needed not or poyson, sword, or dart;
Thy faithless vows, alas! had broke my heart.   [*Aside.*

PARTHENIA.

O tremble, shepherd, for thy rash offence,
The sword is dy'd with murder'd innocence!
His gentle soul no brutal passion seiz'd,
Nor at my bosom was the dagger rais'd;
Self-murder was his aim; the youth I found
Whelm'd in despair, and stay'd the falling wound.

DIONE.

Into what mischiefs is the lover led,
Who calls down vengeance on his perjur'd head!   40
O may he ne'er bewail this desperate deed,
And may, unknown, unwept, *Dione* bleed!   [*Aside.*

LYCIDAS.

What horrors on the guilty mind attend!
His conscience had reveng'd an injur'd friend,
Hadst thou not held the stroke. In death he sought
To lose the heart-consuming pain of thought.
Did not the smooth-tongu'd boy perfidious prove,
Plead his own passion, and betray my love?

DIONE.

O let him ne'er this bleeding victim know;
Lest his rash transport, to revenge the blow,   50
Should in his dearer heart the dagger stain!
That wound would pierce my soul with double pain.   [*Aside.*

22, 28 hath] *31*; has *20*   28 sd *herself*] *31*; *her self 20*   42, 52 [*Aside*] ⌃∼ *31*

PARTHENIA.

How did his faithful lips (now pale and cold)
With moving eloquence thy griefs unfold!

LYCIDAS.

Was he thus faithful? thus, to friendship true?
Then I'm a wretch. All peace of mind, adieu!
If ebbing life yet beat within thy vein,
Alexis, speak: unclose those lids again.
              [*Flings himself on the ground near* Dione.
See at thy feet the barb'rous villain kneel!
60 'Tis *Lycidas* who grasps the bloody steel,
Thy once lov'd friend.—Yet e'er I cease to live,
Canst thou a wretched penitent forgive?

DIONE.

When low beneath the sable mould I rest,
May a sincerer friendship share thy breast!
Why are those heaving groans? (ah! cease to weep!)
May my lost name in dark oblivion sleep;
Let this sad tale no speaking stone declare,
From future eyes to draw a pitying tear:
Let o'er my grave the lev'ling plough-share pass,
70 Mark not the spot; forget that e'er I was.
Then may'st thou with *Parthenia*'s love be blest,
And not one thought on me thy joys molest!
My swimming eyes are over-power'd with light,
And darkning shadows fleet before my sight.
May'st thou be happy! ah! my soul is free.   [*dies.*

LYCIDAS.

O cruel shepherdess, for love of thee   [*To* Parthenia.
This fatal deed was done.

SCENE the last.

LYCIDAS. PARTHENIA. LAURA.

LAURA.
Alexis slain!

LYCIDAS.
Yes. 'Twas I did it. See this crimson stain!

My hands with blood of innocence are dy'd.
O may the Moon her silver beauty hide
In rolling clouds! my soul abhors the light;
Shade, shade the murd'rer in eternal night!

LAURA.
No rival shepherd is before thee laid;
There bled the chastest, the sincerest maid
That ever sigh'd for love. On her pale face,
Cannot thy weeping eyes the feature trace   10
Of thy once dear *Dione*? with wan care
Sunk are those eyes, and livid with despair!

LYCIDAS.
Dione!

LAURA.
There pure Constancy lies dead!

LYCIDAS.
May Heav'n shower vengeance on this perjur'd head!
As the dry branch that withers on the ground,
So, blasted be the hand that gave the wound!
Off; hold me not. This heart deserves the stroke;
'Tis black with treach'ry. Yes: the vows are broke
                                        [*Stabs himself.*
Which I so often swore. Vain world, adieu!
Though I was false in life, in death I'm true.   [*Dies.* 20

LAURA.
To morrow shall the funeral rites be paid,
And these Love victims in one grave be laid.

PARTHENIA.
There shall the yew her sable branches spread,
And mournful cypress rear her fringed head.

LAURA.
From thence shall thyme and myrtle send perfume,
And laurel ever-green o'ershade the tomb.

PARTHENIA.
Come, *Laura*; let us leave this horrid wood,
Where streams the purple grass with lovers blood;

13 Constancy] constancy *31*   28 streams] *31*; steams *20*

Come to my bower. And as we sorrowing go,
30 Let poor *Dione*'s story feed my woe
With heart-relieving tears.

                L A U R A.   [*Pointing to* Dione.
                   Unhappy maid,
Hadst thou a Parent's just command obey'd,
Thou yet hadst liv'd—But who shall Love advise?
Love scorns command, and breaks all other tyes.
Henceforth, ye swains, be true to vows profest;
For certain vengeance strikes the perjur'd breast.

FINIS.

THE

CAPTIVES.

A

TRAGEDY.

Splendidè mendax, & in omne Virgo
Nobilis ævum.   Hor.

MADAM,

THE honour I received from Your ROYAL HIGHNESS, in being permitted to read this play to you before it was acted, made me more happy than any other success that could have happen'd to me. If it had the good fortune to gain Your ROYAL HIGHNESS's approbation, I have been often reflecting to what to impute it, and I think, it must have been the Catastrophe of the fable, the rewarding virtue, and the relieving the distressed: For that could not fail to give you some pleasure in fiction, which, it is plain, gives you the greatest in reality; or else Your ROYAL HIGHNESS would not (as you always have done) make it your daily practice.

I am,
MADAM,
Your Royal Highness's
most dutiful
and most humbly devoted Servant,

John Gay.

PROLOGUE:

Spoken by Mr. *WILKS*.

I wish some author, careless of renown,
Would without formal prologue risque the town.
For what is told you by this useless ditty?
Only that tragedy should move your pity:
That when you see theatric heroes shown,
Their virtues you should strive to make your own.
What gain we by this solemn way of teaching?
Our precepts mend your lives no more than preaching.
 Since then our Bard declines this beaten path;
What if we lash'd the criticks into wrath? 10
Poets should ne'er be drones; mean, harmless things;
But guard, like bees, their labours by their stings.
That mortal sure must all ambition smother,
Who dares not hurt one man to please another.
What, sink a joke! That's but a meer pretence:
He shows most wit who gives the most offence.
But still our squeamish author satyr loaths,
As children, physick; or as women, oaths.
He knows he's at the bar, and must submit;
For ev'ry man is born a judge of wit. 20
How can you err? Plays are like paintings try'd,
You first enquire the hand, and then decide:
Yet judge him not before the curtain draws,
Lest a fair hearing should reverse the cause.

PROLOGUE:] *24a*; PROLOGUE: / Sent by an Unknown Hand. *24b*

EPILOGUE:

Spoken by Mrs. *OLDFIELD*.

SHALL authors teaze the town with tragick passion,
When we've more modern moral things in fashion?
Let poets quite exhaust the Muse's treasure;　⎫
Sure Masquerades must give more feeling pleasure,　⎬
Where we meet finer sense and better measure;　⎭
The marry'd Dame, whose business must be done,　⎫
Puts on the holy vestments of a Nun;　⎬
And brings her unprolifick spouse a son.　⎭
Coquettes, with whom no lover could succeed,
Here pay off all arrears, and love in—deed:
Ev'n conscious Prudes are so sincere and free,
They ask each man they meet—do you know me?
　　Do not our Operas unbend the mind,
Where ev'ry soul's to ecstasie refin'd?
Entranc'd with sound sits each seraphic Toast.
All Ladies love the play that moves the most.
Ev'n in this house I've known some tender fair,
Touch'd with meer sense alone, confess a tear.
But the soft voice of an Italian weather,
Makes them all languish three whole hours together.
And where's the wonder? Plays, like Mass, are sung,
(*Religious* Drama)!—in an unknown tongue.
　　Will Poets ne'er consider what they cost us?
What tragedy can take, like Doctor Faustus?
Two stages in this moral show excell,
To frighten vicious youth with scenes of hell;
Yet both these Faustuses can warn but few.
For what's a Conj'rer's fate to me or—you?
　　Yet there are wives who think heav'n worth their care,
But first they kindly send their spouses there.
When you my lover's last distress behold,
Does not each husband's thrilling blood run cold?
Some heroes only dye.—Ours finds a wife.
What's harder than captivity for life?
Yet Men, ne'er warn'd, still court their own undoing:
Who, for that circle, would but venture ruin?

Dramatis Personæ.

MEN.

Phraortes,	Mr. *Wilks*.
Sophernes,	Mr. *Booth*.
Hydarnes,	Mr. *Mills*.
Araxes,	Mr. *Williams*.
Orbasius,	Mr. *Bridgewater*.
Magi.	
Conspirators.	

WOMEN.

Astarbe,	Mrs. *Porter*.
Captive,	Mrs. *Oldfield*.
Doraspe,	Mrs. *Campbell*.

ACT I. SCENE I.

The PALACE.

Hydarnes, Conspirators.

1*st Conspirator.* Is night near spent?

2*d Conspirator.* 'Tis yet the dead of night;
And not a glimm'ring ray behind yon hills
Fore-runs the morning's dawn.

1*st Conspirator.* Thus far w'are safe.

2*d Conspirator.* Silence and Sleep throughout the Palace
reign.

1*st Conspirator.* Success is now secure.

2*d Conspirator.* Are all assembled?

1*st Conspirator.* Our number's not compleat.

2*d Conspirator.* What, not yet come!
Those two were over-zealous. It looks ill.

1*st Conspirator.* Why fear ye? I'm their pledge. I know
them brave.
They'll soon be with us and partake our glory.

Hydarnes. What mean these murmurs?

10   1*st Conspirator.* If mistrust divide us,
Our enterprize is foil'd, and we are lost.

Hydarnes. My vengeful heart pants for the glorious deed,
And my thirst quickens for *Phraortes'* blood.
Why stops the lazy night?—O morning, rise;
Call up the drowsy Priests to the day's task;
The King to day the holy hill ascends,
And prostrate falls before the rising sun.

1*st Conspirator.* The sun shall rise, but rise to him no more.
For as he passes from the royal chamber
This strikes him home.

20   2*d Conspirator.* Let each man give him death.
We cannot be too sure.

Hydarnes.   Revenge is mine.
By him my father fell, by him my brothers;
They fail'd, they perish'd in the great design:
Success and vengeance are reserv'd for me.
My father led the *Median* hosts to battle,
And all the hosts of *Media* sung his triumphs.
   1*st Conspirator*. The people's hearts were his.
   Hydarnes.   The people saw
His royal virtues. He, to please his country,
Grasp'd at the sceptre which *Phraortes* holds.
For this he suffer'd ignominious death: 30
His house was raz'd; my brave, unhappy brothers
Fell in his ruin; I alone escap'd;
In banishment I've sigh'd whole years away,
Unknown, forgot.—But now, even in his glory,
Now, while he leads the *Persian* Princes captive,
And overflows whole nations with his armies,
I'll stab him to the heart.
   2*d Conspirator*.   What sound was that?
   1*st Conspirator*. Lights pass a-cross the rooms, and hasty
     steps
Move to the King's apartment. Sleep is fled,
And all the palace lives; *Phraortes* wakes.   40
   2*d Conspirator*. Hush! hark again!
   1*st Conspirator*.   The ecchoes of the night
Catch ev'ry whisper.
   2*d Conspirator*.   Some have overheard us.
   1*st Conspirator*. It must be so. The guard have took th'
     alarm.
Our Lives, (what's worse) our enterprize is lost!
   2*d Conspirator*. Retreat, my friends; let us reserve ourselves
For some more prosp'rous hour.
   Hydarnes.   You raise up phantoms,
Then start at them your selves. Some sickly qualm
Has wak'd the King too soon. Hence spring your fears,
Hence grows this mean surprise. Are these your boasts?
Danger but whets the edge of resolution,   50
And at each noise I grasp my dagger faster.
Is every thing dispos'd to give th' alarm
Among the *Persian* captives? Hope of freedom

Will arm them on our side.
　　1st Conspirator.　　　　　　　Were the blow struck,
The rest would follow.
　　Hydarnes.　　　　　　　See a gleam of light
Darts from the King's apartment. Man your hearts,
Be firm, be ready. Let not trembling fear
Misguide your aim; let ev'ry wound be mortal.
　　1st Conspirator. This way and that way danger presses near
　　　us.
60 Where shall we fly! The tread of nimble feet
Hurries from room to room, and all the palace
Swarms as at noon.
　　2d Conspirator.　　　Let us consult our safety.
　　1st Conspirator. To stay and to be taken is despair;
And what's despair? but poor, mean cowardice.
By timely caution heroes are preserv'd
For glorious enterprize, and mighty kingdoms
Are levell'd with the dust.
　　Hydarnes.　　　　　　　Withdraw your selves.
Be still, and listen. These will best inform us
If still it may be done; or if the blow
70 Must be deferr'd. But hush, they come upon us.

SCENE II.

Orbasius, Araxes *at one door, two* Magi *at the other, servants with
lights*. Hydarnes *and* Conspirators *listning*.

　　Araxes. Whence come ye, rev'rend Fathers; why these looks
Of terror and amaze? why gaze ye back
As if the strides of Death stalk'd close behind you?
　　1st Magus. The King ev'n at this solemn hour of Night
Sent privately to call us to his presence.
Ye Gods preserve him!
　　Araxes.　　　　　　　Why this wild confusion?
In ev'ry passing face I read suspicion,
　　　　　　　　　　　　　　　[*People crossing the Stage.*
And haggard fear. His sickness seiz'd the King,
And groans he with the latest pang of death?
Speak forth your terrors.

2d *Magus.* May *Phraortes* live! 10
Orbasius. Tell us the cause. If violence or treachery,
Our duty bids us interpose our lives
Between the King and death. O Heav'n, defend him!
  1*st Magus.* The King, disturb'd by visionary dreams,
Bad the most learn'd Magicians stand before him.
We stood before the King; and the King trembled
While he declar'd his dream; and thus I spoke.
'O may the great *Phraortes* live for ever!
'Avert the dire presages of the dream!
'This night the Gods have warn'd thee to beware 20
'Of deep-laid treasons, ripe for execution;
'Assassination lurks within the palace,
'And murder grasps the dagger for the blow.
'If the King trust his steps beyond his chamber
'I see him bleed! I hear his dying groan!
'Obey the voice of Heav'n.
  2d *Magus.* The King is wise;
And therefore to the will of Heav'n assented;
Nor will he trust his life, a nation's safety,
From out the royal chamber. See the dawn
Breaks in the East, and calls us to devotion. 30
It is not Man; but 'tis the Gods he fears. [*Exeunt* Magi.

SCENE III.

Orbasius. Araxes. [Conspirators *apart*.]

Hydarnes. Let's quit the palace while retreat is safe.
The deed must be deferr'd. Revenge, be calm.
This day is his, to-morrow shall be ours.
    [*Exeunt Conspirators on one side. Enter guards on the other.*
Orbasius. See that each centinel is on strict watch.
Let all the Guards be doubled; bar the gates,
That not a man pass forth without observance.
          [*Exit a party of Soldiers.*
Go you; and with the utmost vigilance
Search ev'ry room; for treason lyes in wait.
          [*Exit a party of Soldiers.*
Araxes. Divide your selves this instant o'er the palace.

10 Think *Media* is in danger; and remember
That he who takes a traytor, saves the King.

[*Exeunt Soldiers.*

    Orbasius. Whence can these dangers threaten?
    Araxes.   From the *Persians.*
Captivity's a yoke that galls the shoulders
Of new-made slaves, and makes them bold and resty.
He that is born in chains may tamely bear them;
But he that once has breath'd the air of freedom,
Knows life is nothing when depriv'd of that.
Our lord the King has made a people slaves,
And ev'ry slave is virtuously rebellious.
I fear the *Persian* Prince.
20   *Orbasius.*   You injure him.
I know him, have convers'd with him whole days,
And ev'ry day I stronger grew in virtue.
Load not th' unhappy with unjust suspicion;
Adversity ne'er shakes the heart of honour;
He who is found a villian, in distress,
Was never virtuous.
    Araxes.   Who suspects his virtue?
'Tis not dishonest to demand our right;
And freedom is the property of man.
    Orbasius. That glorious day when *Persia* was subdu'd,
30 *Sophernes* fought amidst a host of foes,
Disdaining to survive his country's fate.
When the whole torrent of the war rush'd on,
Phraortes interpos'd his shield, and sav'd him.
And canst thou think this brave, this gen'rous Prince
Would stab the man to whom he owes his life?
    Araxes. Whoever is, must feel himself, a slave.
And 'tis worth struggling to shake off his chains.
    Orbasius. But gratitude has cool'd his soul to patience.
Ingratitude's a crime the *Persians* hate;
40 Their laws are wise, and punish it with death.

SCENE IV.

Guards with Sophernes. Orbasius. Araxes.

    Araxes. Behold, *Orbasius*; have I wrong'd your friend?

Behold a slave oblig'd by gratitude
To wear his chains with patience! This is he
Phraortes honours with his royal favours!
This is the man that I accus'd unjustly!
Soldiers, advance, and bring the prisoner near us.
 Sophernes. Why am I thus insulted? why this force?
If 'tis a crime to be unfortunate
I well deserve this usage.
 Araxes.   'Tis our duty.
If you are innocent, let justice clear you.   10
Orbasius, to your charge I leave the Prince;
Mean while I'll search the palace. On this instant
Perhaps the safety of the King depends.
Come, soldiers, there are others to be taken,
Mine be that care. I'll bring them face to face,
When each man conscious of the other's crime
Shall in his guilty look confess his own.
Guard him with strictness, as you prize your life.
       [*Exeunt* Araxes *and some Guards.*

SCENE V.

Orbasius. Sophernes.

 Orbasius. Keep off a while, and leave us to our selves.
     [*Guards retire to the back part of the stage.*
I own, I think this rash suspicion wrongs you;
For murder is the mean revenge of cowards,
And you are brave.
 Sophernes.   By whom am I accus'd?
Let him stand forth. Of murder, murder say you?
Bear I the marks of an abandon'd wretch?
How little man can search the heart of man!
 Orbasius. Our Priests are train'd up spies by education,
They pry into the secrets of the state,
And then by way of prophecy reveal them;   10
'Tis by such artifice they govern Kings.
The last night's rumour of conspiracy
Form'd the King's dream, and from that very rumour
They venture to speak out, what we but whisper'd.

'Twas they that call'd us to this early watch,
'Twas they inform'd us that assassination
Lies hid, ev'n now, within the palace walls.
And we but execute the King's command
In seizing all we find.
> *Sophernes.*   It is your duty,
20 And I submit. You cannot be too watchful
To guard the life of such a worthy prince.
I saw his prowess in the rage of battel,
I found his mercy in the flush of conquest.
Do not I share his palace, though a captive?
What can set limits to his gen'rous soul,
Or close his lib'ral hand? Am I a viper
To sting the man that warms me in his bosom?
> *Orbasius.* Why is power given into the hands of Kings,
But to distinguish virtue and protect it?
30 If then *Phraortes* loves and honours you,
Why seek you thus to nourish your misfortunes
With midnight walks and pensive solitude?
> *Sophernes.* To lose the pomp and glories of a crown,
Is not a circumstance so soon forgot!
But I have humbled me to this affliction.
To lead the flower of *Persia* forth to battel
And meet with overthrow and foul defeat,
Is no such trifle in a soldier's breast!
But I submit; for 'tis the will of Heaven.
40 To see a father bleed amidst the carnage,
Must touch the heart of filial piety.
Why was his lot not mine? His fall was glorious.
To see my brave, but now unhappy people
Bow down their necks in shameful servitude,
Is not a spectacle of slight compassion.
All these calamities I have subdu'd.
But—my dear wife! *Cylene*!
> *Orbasius.*   Still there's hope.
Can you support the load of real ills,
And sink beneath imaginary sorrows?
Perhaps she still may live.
50 *Sophernes.*   Had I that hope,
'Twou'd banish from my heart all other cares.

Perhaps she still may live! no: 'tis impossible.
When storms of arrows clatter'd on our shields,
Love arm'd her breast, and where I led she follow'd;
Then Vict'ry broke our ranks, and like a torrent
Bore my *Cylene* from my sight for ever.
But say, she did survive that fatal day;
Was she not then the spoil of some rude soldier,
Whose blood was riotous and hot with conquest?
—Who can gaze on her beauty and resist it!   60
Methinks I see her now, ev'n now before me,
The hand of Lust is tangled in her hair
And drags her to his arms:—
I see her snatch the dagger from his grasp
And resolutely plunge it in her bosom.
  Orbasius. Yet think she may have found a milder fate.
All soldiers are not of that savage temper;
May she not chance to be some brave man's captive?
And Valour ever lov'd to shield Distress.
  Sophernes. Can I think thus? I cannot be so happy.   70
  Orbasius. Is still the King a stranger to this sorrow
That day and night lies rankling in your breast?
  Sophernes. A grateful heart is all I've left to pay him.
Phraortes is as liberal as Heaven,
And daily pours new benefits upon me.
Last night he led me to the royal garden,
(His talk all bent to soften my misfortunes)
Like a fond friend he grew inquisitive,
And drew the story from me.
  Orbasius.   All his heart
Is turn'd to your relief. What further happen'd?   80
  Sophernes. The King was mov'd, and strait sent forth
    commands
That all the female captives of his triumph
Should stand before his presence. Thus (says he)
Unhappy Prince, I may retrieve your peace,
And give *Cylene* to your arms again.
O source of light! O Sun, whose piercing eye
Views all below on earth, in sea or air;
Who at one glance can comprehend the globe,
Who ev'ry where art present, point me out

90 Where my *Cylene* mourns her bitter bondage.
If she yet live!
   Orbasius.   Why will you fear the worst?
Why seek you to anticipate misfortune?
The King commands. Obedience on swift wing
Flies through his whole dominions to redress you;
From hence you soon will learn what chance befell her.
'Tis soon enough to feel our adverse fortune
When there's no room for hope. This last distress
I know must move the King to tend'rest pity.
   Sophernes. He dwelt on ev'ry little circumstance,
And as I talk'd, he sigh'd.
100   *Orbasius*.   It reach'd his heart.
A tale of love is fuel to a lover.
Phraortes dotes with such excess of fondness,
All his pursuits are lost in that of love.
Astarbe suffers him to hold the sceptre,
But she directs his hand which way to point.
The King's decrees were firm and absolute,
Not the whole earth's confederate powers could shake 'em;
But now a frown, a smile from fair *Astarbe*
Renders them light as air.
   Sophernes.   If you have lov'd,
You cannot think this strange.
110   *Orbasius*.   Yet this same woman,
To whom the King has given up all himself,
Can scarce prevail upon her haughty temper
To show dissembled love. She loves his power,
She loves his treasures; but she loaths his person:
Thus ev'ry day he buys dissimulation.
Whene'er a woman knows you in her power,
She never fails to use it.
   Sophernes.   That's a sure proof
Of cold indifference and fixt dislike.
In love both parties have the power to govern,
120 But neither claims it. Love is all compliance.
Astarbe seem'd to me of gentlest manners,
A tender softness languish'd in her eyes,
Her voice, her words bespoke an easy temper.
I thought I scarce had ever seen till then

Such beauty and humility together.
   Orbasius. How beauty can mis-lead and cheat our reason!
The Queen knows all the ways to use her charms
In their full force, and *Media* feels their power.
Whoever dares dispute her hourly will,
Wakens a busy fury in her bosom.   130
Sure, never love exerted greater sway;
For her he breaks through all the regal customs,
For she is not confin'd like former Queens,
But with controuling power enjoys full freedom.
I am to blame, to talk upon this subject.
   Sophernes. My innocence had made me quite forget
That I'm your prisoner. Load me with distresses,
They better suit my state. I've lost my kingdom,
A palace ill befits me. I'm a captive,
And captives should wear chains. My fellow soldiers   140
Now pine in dungeons, and are gall'd with irons,
And I the cause of all! Why live I thus
Amidst the pomp and honours of a court?
Why breathe I morn and ev'n in fragrant bowers?
Why am I suffer'd to behold the day?
For I am lost to ev'ry sense of pleasure.
Give me a dungeon, give me chains and darkness;
Nor courts, nor fragrant bowers, nor air, nor daylight
Give me one glimpse of joy—O lost *Cylene*!
   Orbasius. Misfortunes are the common lot of man,   150
And each man has his share of diff'rent kinds:
He who has learnt to bear them best is happiest.
But see *Araxes* comes with guards and prisoners.

SCENE VI.

Orbasius. Sophernes. Araxes. Hydarnes. Conspirators, *with*
guards.

   Araxes. Behold your leader. Where are now your hopes
                             [*To the Conspirators.*
Of murd'ring Kings and over-turning nations?
See with what stedfast eyes they gaze upon him,

As thinking him the man that has betray'd them.
Angry Suspicion frowns on ev'ry brow,
They know their guilt, and each mistrusts the other.
We seiz'd them in th' attempt to make escape,
All arm'd, all desperate, all of them unknown,
And ev'ry one is obstinately dumb.   [*To* Orbasius.
10   I charge you, speak. Know you that prisoner there?
Ay, view him well. Confess, and merit grace.
What, not a word! Will you accept of life?

                                                      [*To* Hydarnes.
Speak, and 'tis granted. Tortures shall compel you.
Will you, or you, or you, or any of you?
What, all resolv'd on death! Bring forth the chains.

                                                      [*Exit Soldier.*
   Orbasius. Be not too rash, not treat the Prince too roughly.
He may be innocent.
   Araxes.   You are too partial.
I know my duty. Justice treats alike
Those who alike offend, without regard
20   To dignity or office. Bring the chains.

                                                      [*Enter Soldiers with chains.*
   Orbasius. This over-zeal perhaps may give offence,
The Prince is treated like no common slave.
Phraortes strives to lessen his affliction,
Nor would he add a sigh to his distresses:
Astarbe too will talk to him whole hours
With all the tender manners of her sex,
To shorten the long tedious days of bondage.
I'll be his guard. My life shall answer for him.
   Araxes. My life must answer for him. He's my charge,
30   And this is not a time for courtesy.
Are you still resolute and bent on death?

                                                      [*To the Conspirators.*
Once more I offer mercy. When the torture
Cracks all your sinews and disjoints your bones,
And death grins on you arm'd with all his terrors,
'Twill loose your stubborn tongue. Know ye this man?
   Hydarnes. We know him not; nor why we wear these chains.
We ask no mercy, but appeal to justice.
Now you know all we know: lead to our dungeons.

[*Exeunt* Hydarnes *and* Conspirators *guarded.*

Orbasius. How have you wrong'd the Prince! these shame-
   ful irons
Should not disgrace the hands of innocence.   40
Let's set him free.
   Araxes.   This is all artifice,
To let their leader scape. Guards, take him hence,
And let him be confin'd till further orders.
   Sophernes. Who shall plead for me in a foreign land!
My words will find no faith; for I'm a stranger.
And who holds friendship with adversity?
So Fate may do its worst. I'm tir'd of life.   [*Exit guarded.*

SCENE VII.

Araxes. Orbasius.

Araxes. I've done my duty, and I've done no more.
Why wear you that concern upon your brow?
It misbecomes you in this time of joy.
Strait let us to the King, and learn his pleasure.
Justice is ours, but mercy's lodg'd in him.
   Orbasius. I never can believe the Prince so vile
To mix with common murderers and assassins.
I think him virtuous, and I share his suff'rings.
All generous souls must strong reluctance find,
In heaping sorrows on th' afflicted mind.   [*Exeunt.* 10

ACT II. SCENE I.

The Queen's Apartment.

Astarbe.

How expectation can prolong an hour,
And make it seem a day! a tedious day!
What not yet come! the wonted hour is past.
In vain I turn my eye from walk to walk,
Sophernes is not there.—Here, every morn
I watch his pensive steps along the garden,

And gaze and wish till I am lost in love!
What not yet come! But hark! methinks I hear
The sound of feet! How my heart pants and flutters!
10 No. 'Twas the wind that shook yon cypress boughs.
Where are my views of wealth, of power, of State? *[Rises.*
They're blotted from my mind. I've lost ambition.
O love, thou hast me all. My dreams, my thoughts,
My every wish is center'd in *Sophernes.*
Hence, Shame, thou rigid tyrant of our sex,
I throw thee off—and I'll avow my passion.
Doraspe. I can bear to think no longer.   *[Sits again.*

SCENE II.

Doraspe. Astarbe.

 Doraspe. Why sits the Queen thus overcast with thought?
Is Majesty all plac'd in outward pomp?
Is it a Queen, to have superior cares?
And to excell in sorrows and distresses?
'Tis in your power to have superior pleasures,
And feel your self a Queen.
  Astarbe.   This mighty empire
I know I do command, and him that rules it.
That was a pleasure once, but now 'tis past!
To you alone I have disclos'd my heart.
I know you faithful.
10 *Doraspe.*   What avails my service?
Can I redress you? can I calm your mind?
  Astarbe. Thou know'st, *Doraspe,* amidst all this power,
That I'm a slave, the very worst of slaves.
The yoke of bondage, and the dungeon's horrors
Are easy suff'rings, if compar'd with mine.
I am confin'd to dwell with one I hate,
Confin'd for life to suffer nauseous love,
Like a poor mercenary prostitute.
His fondness is my torture.
20 *Doraspe.* Love is a pleasure for inferior minds.
Your lot is rais'd above that vulgar passion.
Ambition is the pleasure of the great,
That fills the heart, and leaves no room for love.

Think you're a Queen, enjoy your pomp, your power,
Love is the paradise of simple shepherds.
You hold a sceptre.
   Astarbe.   O insipid greatness!
She who has never lov'd, has never liv'd.
All other views are artificial pleasures
For sluggish minds incapable of love.
My soul is form'd for this sublimer passion: 30
My heart is temper'd for the real joy;
I sigh, I pant, I burn, I'm sick of love!
Yes, *Media*, I renounce thy purple honours.   [*Rises*.
Farewell the pomp, the pageantry of state,
Farewell ambition, and the lust of empire;
I've now no passion, no desire but love.
O may my eyes have power!—I ask no more.
Where stays *Sophernes*? Were he now before me,
My tongue should own what oft my eyes have spoke,
For love has humbled pride.—Why this intrusion?   40
Who call'd you here a witness to my frailties?
Away and leave me.
   Doraspe.   I obey my Queen.
   Astarbe. *Doraspe*, stay. Excuse this start of passion,
My mind is torn with wishes, doubts and fears;
I had forgot myself.—Should fortune frown,
And tear the diadem from off my brow,
Couldst thou be follower of my adverse fortune?
I think thou couldst.
   Doraspe.   If I might give that proof,
Without your sufferings, I could wish the tryal;
So firm I know my heart.
   Astarbe.   Life, like the seasons,   50
Is intermix'd with sun-shine days and tempests.
Prosperity has many thousand friends;
They swarm around us in our summer hours,
But vanish in the storm.
   Doraspe.   What means my Queen,
To wound her faithful servant with suspicion?
   Astarbe. Whene'er my mind is vex'd and torn with troubles,
In thee I always find the balm of counsell:
And can I then mistrust thee? No, *Doraspe*,

Suspicion ne'er with-held a thought from thee,
60 Thou know'st the close recesses of my heart:
And now, ev'n now I fly to thee for comfort.
   Doraspe. How my soul longs to learn the Queen's
    commands!
   Astarbe. When conquest over-power'd my father's legions,
We were made captives of the war together;
Phraortes saw me, rais'd me to his throne,
Heav'n knows with what reluctance I consented!
For my heart loath'd him. But O curs'd ambition!
I gave my self a victim to his love,
To be a Queen, the outside of a Queen.
70 I then was, what I'm now, a wretch at heart!
Whene'er I was condemn'd to hours of dalliance,
All *Media*'s gems lay glitt'ring at my feet,
To buy a smile, and bribe me to compliance.
But what's ambition, glory, riches, empire?
The wish of misers, and old doating courtiers;
My heart is fill'd with love.—Go, my *Doraspe*,
Enquire the cause that has detain'd *Sophernes*
From his accustom'd walk.—I'm fix'd, determin'd,
To give up all for love.—A life of love.
80 With what impatience shall I wait thy coming!
   Doraspe. Happy *Sophernes!*
   Astarbe.   If you chance to meet him,
Talk of me to him, watch his words, his eyes;
Let all you say be turn'd to wake desire;
Prepare him for the happy interview,
For my heart bursts, and I must tell it all.
To what an abject state am I reduc'd?
To proffer love! Was beauty given for this?
Yes. 'Tis more gen'rous; and I'll freely give
What kneeling monarchs had implor'd in vain.
90   *Doraspe.* This well rewards him for an empire lost.   [*Exit.*

SCENE III.

Astarbe.

Have I not caught the eyes of wondring nations,
While warm desire has glow'd on ev'ry cheek,

Ev'n when I wore the pride of majesty?
When opportunity awakes desire,
Can he then gaze, insensible of beauty?
When ardent wishes speak in ev'ry glance,
When love and shame by turns in their full force,
Now pale, now red, possess my guilty cheek,
When heaving breasts, and sighs, and kindling blushes
Give the most strong assurance of consent   10
In the convincing eloquence of love;
Will he then want a proof that's less sincere?
And must I speak?—O love, direct my lips,
And give me courage in that hour of shame!

SCENE IV

Astarbe. Doraspe.

Doraspe. May the Queen never know a moment's sorrow,
Nor let my words offend!—the Prince *Sophernes*,
Leagu'd with a crew of daring desperate men,
Had meditated to destroy *Phraortes*,
And let loose war and rapine o'er the land.
But Heav'n has made their machinations vain;
And they now groan in dungeons.
    Astarbe.   Then I'm wretched,
And ev'ry pleasing view of life is lost.
Was it confirm'd? or was it only rumour?
    Doraspe. Araxes said *Sophernes* was his prisoner.   10
My haste would not allow me further question:
And this is all I learnt.
    Astarbe.   Have I not power?
I have. Why then, I'll give *Sophernes* freedom,
I'll give him life.—I think you nam'd *Araxes*;
That man to me owes all his growth of fortune;
And if I judge him right, he's very grateful.
Tell him the Queen admits him to her presence.
                             [*Exit* Doraspe.
O Heaven! I thank thee for this blest occasion.
Did ever proof of fondness equal mine?
And sure so strong a proof must find return.   20

With what excess of transport shall I go
To lead him forth from heavy chains and darkness
To liberty and love!—But see, *Araxes*.

SCENE V.

Astarbe. Doraspe. Araxes.

Araxes. All health attend the mighty Queen of *Media*.
Astrabe. I'm told, *Araxes*, that the *Persian* Prince
Hath join'd in horrid league, and hath conspir'd
The murther of my lord and king *Phraortes*.
Speak forth; say, what thou know'st.
Araxes. The hand of heaven
Protects the King; and all the black design
Is shown in open daylight. The foul traitor
Is taken in the snares of death he laid.
Sophernes is my charge. O base ingratitude,
10 That he, whom the King honour'd next himself,
That he, whom the King's mercy spar'd in battle,
Should mix with vile assassins! Justice longs
To punish the vast crime.
Astarbe. Owns he the guilt?
Araxes. No. With the calmest face of innocence,
With looks known only to hypocrisy,
He solemnly deny'd it.
Astarbe. Is he confin'd?
Araxes. Yes, with the strictest guard and heaviest irons.
The prison joining to the Queen's apartment
Lodges the horrid crew in sep'rate dungeons.
20 To-day the King will mount the judgment-seat,
And death shall be their portion.
Astarbe. Is *Sophernes*
Stubborn and sullen? made he no confession?
I often have convers'd with that vile man,
That hypocrite, whose talk was always honest.
How have I been deceiv'd!—Yet, ere his sentence,
With secresy I fain once more would see him.
Araxes. I'm happy to obey my Queen's commands.
His prison lies so close to these apartments,

That unobserv'd I can conduct him hither.
    Astarbe. I know thee faithfull, and such ready zeal   30
Shall always find reward.
    Araxes.   The Queen is gracious.

SCENE VI.

Astarbe. Doraspe.

    Astarbe. Now my design is ripe for execution.
Then let *Doraspe* well consult her heart,
If she will share with me all change of fortune.
    Doraspe. Doubt not your faithfull servant. I'm prepar'd.
I know, however heinous is his crime,
Your intercession always must prevail.
His gratitude will kindle into love,
And in possession every wish be lost.
    Astarbe. How little thou hast div'd into my thoughts!
My purposes are otherways determin'd.   10
I'll shake off bondage, and abandon empire;
For him disrobe my self of majesty;
Then to my native *Parthia* will I fly
With all my soul holds dear—my guide *Sophernes.*
    Doraspe. Let me not find my gracious Queen's displeasure
If I dissent, and offer other counsel.
Why will you quit your crown? why fly from *Media?*
Does jealousy restrain your liberty?
Your love, your empire, both are in your power.
    Astarbe. Mine's not the common passion of our sex,   20
Which ev'ry day we can command at pleasure,
And shift and vary as occasion offers.
My love is real and unchangeable,
Controuls my heart, and governs absolute.
My eyes, words, actions, are no more my own:
My ev'ry thought's *Sophernes.*—Other women,
Who have the power to practise little arts
To cheat a husband, and delude his fondness,
Ne'er knew the burning passion that I feel.
Those are the trifling wanton airs of women,   30
All vanity, and only love in name.

No. She who loves, must give up all her self;
She ne'er can be content with a stol'n minute,
Then pass whole days and nights with him she hates.
Advise no further—for I am determin'd.
    Doraspe. Araxes, with the *Persian* Prince!
    Astarbe.   Retire.

SCENE VII.

Astarbe. Araxes. Sophernes.

It is not meet, while in the royal presence,
That he should wear these irons. Take them off.
                        [Araxes *takes off the Chains.*
Now leave me; and without attend my pleasure.

SCENE VIII.

Astarbe. Sophernes.

Be not surpriz'd that I have call'd you hither,
Most noble Prince, in this your hour of trouble;
For I ev'n bear a part in your misfortunes.
Who's your accuser?—whence those shameful chains?
    Sophernes. I'm charg'd with crimes of the most heinous
        nature.
If 'tis Heav'n's will to try me with afflictions,
I will not, like a dastard, sink beneath them,
But resolutely strive to stem the torrent.
Not the dark dungeon, not the sharpest torture
10 Can ruffle the sweet calm of innocence.
My chains are grievous, but my conscience free.
    Astarbe. I long have mark'd your virtues and admir'd them.
Against a resolute and steady mind
The tempest of affliction beats in vain.
When we behold the hero's manly patience
We feel his suff'rings, and my tears have own'd
That what you bore with courage touch'd my heart.
And when compassion once has reach'd the mind,
It spurs us on to charity and kindness.
20 Instruct me then which way to cure your sorrows.

Sophernes. The Queen is gracious and delights in mercy.
Astarbe. I speak with the sincerity of friendship.
Friendship is free and open, and requires not
Such distant homage and respectful duty.
Forget that I'm a Queen: I have forgot it;
And all my thoughts are fixt on thy relief.
Draw near me then, and as from friend to friend,
Let us discharge our hearts of all their cares.
    Sophernes. How beautiful a virtue is compassion!
It gives new grace to every charm of woman!   30
When lovely features hide a tender soul,
She looks, she speaks, all harmony divine.
    Astarbe. Tell me, *Sophernes*, does not slav'ry's yoke
Gall more and more through ev'ry pace of life?
I am a slave, like you. And though a Queen
Possest of all the richest gems of *Media*,
I know no pleasure; this distasteful thought
Imbitters all my hours; the royal bed
Is loathsome, and a stranger to delight.
I'm made the drudge to serve another's pleasure.   40
O when shall I be free! take, take your empire,
And give me peace and liberty again.
    Sophernes. The strokes of fortune must be born with
        patience.
    Astarbe. But I have lost all patience.—Give me counsel,
Give me friendship, and assist a wretch
Who thirsts and pants for freedom.
    Sophernes.   Who seeks succour
From one whose hands are bound in double irons?
I am a slave, and captive of the war,
Accus'd of treason and ingratitude,
And must from hence go back to chains and darkness,   50
But had I power, such beauty might command it.
    Astarbe. But I have power, and all my power is thine.
If I had arm'd my self with resolution
To quit the pompous load of majesty,
To fly far off from this detested empire,
To seek repose within my native land,
Wouldst thou then be companion of my flight,
And share in my distresses and my fortune?

Sophernes. The Queen intends to try a wretched man
60 Whether he'd break all hospitable laws,
The strictest oaths and tyes of gratitude,
To sacrifice his honour to such beauty
That can command all hearts.
  Astarbe.   Tell me directly,
Wouldst thou accept of freedom on these terms?
  Sophernes. How shall I answer?
  Astarbe.   Is thy heart of ice?
Or are my features so contemptible
That thou disdain'st to fix thy eyes upon me?
Can you receive this offer with such coldness?
I make it from my heart; my warm heart speaks:
70 Distrust me not. What, not a word! no answer!
  Sophernes. O may the Queen excuse her prostrate servant,
And urge no more a tryal too severe.
  Astarbe. What means *Sophernes*? Why this abject posture?
'Tis I should kneel; 'tis I that want compassion.
         [Gives him her hand.
Thou art unpractis'd in the ways of women,
To judge that I could trifle on this subject.
Think how severe a conflict I have conquer'd,
To over-rule ev'n nature and my sex,
Think what confusion rises in my face
80 To ask what (to be ask'd) would kindle blushes
In ev'ry modest cheek!—where's shame? where's pride?
Sophernes has subdu'd them. Women, I own,
Are vers'd in little frauds, and sly dissemblings:
But can we rule the motions of the blood?
These eyes,—this pulse—these tremblings—this confusion
Make truth conspicuous, and disclose the soul.
Think not I fly with man for his protection;
For only you I could renounce a kingdom,
For you, ev'n in the wild and barren desart
90 Forget I was a Queen; ev'n then more happy
Than seated on a throne. Say, wilt thou chuse
Or liberty, and life, and poor *Astarbe*,
Or dungeons, chains, and ignominious death!
  Sophernes. O how I struggle in the snares of beauty!
Those eyes could warm pale elders to desire,

I feel them at my heart; the feaver rages,
And if I gaze again—how shall I answer!
   Astarbe. How is my pride brought low! how vilely treated!
The worst of scorn is cold deliberation.
   Sophernes. Cylene may be found. What, take me from her!   100
How can I go and leave my hopes for ever?
Can I renounce my love, my faith, my all?
Who can resist those eyes?—I go—I'm lost!
Cylene holds me back, and curbs desire.   [*Aside.*
   Astarbe. Resolve and answer me. For soon as night
Favours our flight I'll gather up my treasures.
Prepare thee then, lest death should intercept thee,
And murder all my quiet.
   Sophernes.   If in her sight
I've favour found, the Queen will hear me speak.
How can my heart refuse her! how obey her?   110
Can I deny such generous clemency?
Join'd with all beauties ever found in woman?
Yet think on my unhappy circumstance.
I've giv'n my word, the strictest tye of honour,
Never to pass beyond my bounds prescrib'd;
And shall I break my faith? Who holds society
With one who's branded with that infamy?
Did not *Phraortes* in the heat of battle
Stay the keen sword that o'er me menac'd death?
Do not I share his palace, and his friendship?   120
Does he not strive by daily curtesies
To banish all the bitter cares of bondage?
And shall I seise and tear his tendrest heart-string?
Shall I conspire to rob him of all peace?
For on the Queen hangs ev'ry earthly joy,
His ev'ry pleasure is compriz'd in you!
What virtue can resist such strong temptation?
O raise not thus a tempest in my bosom!
What shall I do? my soul abhors ingratitude.
Should I consent, you must detest and loath me,   130
And I should well deserve those chains and death.
   Astarbe. Is this thy best return for proffer'd love?
Such coldness, such indifference, such contempt!
Rise, all ye Furies, from th' infernal regions,

And prompt me to some great, some glorious vengeance!
Vengeance is in my power, and I'll enjoy it.
But majesty perhaps might awe his passion,
And fear forbid him to reveal his wishes.
That could not be. I heard, I saw him scorn me;
140 All his disdainful words his eyes confirm'd.
Ungrateful man! Hence, traytor, from my sight.
Revenge be ready. Slighted love invokes thee.
Of all the injuries that rack the soul,
Mine is most exquisite! Hence, to thy dungeon.
Araxes!

SCENE IX.

Astarbe. Sophernes. Araxes.

Take the villain from my presence,
His crimes are black as hell. I'll turn away,
Lest my heart melt and cool into compassion.
His sight offends me. Bind his irons fast.

       [Araxes *puts on his Irons*.
So: lead him hence; and let *Doraspe* know
The Queen permits her entrance.

SCENE X.

Astarbe. Doraspe.

Doraspe. What's the Queen's pleasure? See your servant
 ready.
Why are your eyes thus fixt upon the ground?
Why that deep sigh? and why these trembling lips?
This sudden paleness, and these starts of frenzy?
You're sick at heart.
 Astarbe.   Yes; I will be reveng'd.
 Doraspe. Lift up your eyes, and know me. 'Tis *Doraspe*.
 Astarbe. Look on me, tell me, is my beauty blighted?
And shrunk at once into deformity?

IX] VIII *24*
X] IX *24*

Slighted! despis'd! my charms all set at nought!
Yes. I will be reveng'd.—O my *Doraspe*,   10
I've met with foul contempt, and cold disdain:
And shall the wretch who gave me guilt and shame,
The wretch who's conscious of my infamy,
Out-live that crime? he must not, nay, he shall not.
   Doraspe. Let reason mitigate and quell this feaver;
The safest, surest, is the cool revenge.
Rash anger, like the hasty scorpion's fury,
Torments and wounds it self.
   Astarbe.   It is in vain.
The torrent rushes on; it swells, ferments,
And strongly bears away all opposition.   20
What means that hurry in the antichamber?
What are those crowds?
   Doraspe. The King intends to mount the judgment-seat,
And the conspirators now wait their sentence.
   Astarbe. Go tell *Araxes* (if with privacy
He could conduct him) I would see their chief;
The desp'rate instrument of this bold scheme;
This instant; ere he stands before the Presence.

SCENE XI.

Astarbe.

Revenge, I thank thee for this ready thought.
Death now shall reach *Sophernes*, shamefull death;
Thus will I satiate love. His death alone
Can raze him from my heart, and give me peace.

SCENE XII.

Araxes *conducts in* Hydarnes, *and retires.*

Astarbe. Hydarnes.

   Astarbe. The King is gracious, and delights in mercy;
And know that free confession merits life:

XI] X *24*
XII] XI *24*

I'll intercede. Know you the Prince *Sophernes*?
You are unhappy men betray'd to ruin.
And will ye suffer for another's crime?
Speak of him, as ye ought; 'twas he betray'd you.
   Hydarnes. If racks and tortures cannot tear confession
From innocence, shall woman's flattery do it?
No; my heart's firm, and I can smile on death.
10   *Astarbe*. Think not to hide what is already known.
'Tis to *Sophernes* that you owe those chains,
We've fathom'd his designs, they're all laid open;
We know him turbulent and enterprizing.
By the foul murder of my lord the King,
He meant to set his captive nation free.
Unfold this truth, and I'll insure thy pardon.
   Hydarnes. What! lead a hateful life of ignominy!
And live the bane of all society!
Shun'd like a pestilence, a curst informer!
20 Yet since the fate of kingdoms may depend
On what I speak; truth shall direct my lips.
The Queen has offer'd grace. I know the terms.
   Astarbe. By the King's life, I swear.

SCENE XIII.

Astarbe. Hydarnes. Araxes.

   Araxes.   Excuse this entrance,
The pris'ner must attend.
    Astarbe.   I'm satisfy'd.
This man seems open, and may be of service.

SCENE XIV.

Astarbe.

How my heart bleeds thus to pursue revenge
Against the man I love! But me he scorns;
And from my beauty turns his head away

XIII] XII *24*
XIV] XIII *24*

With saucy arrogance and proud contempt.
I could forgive him ev'ry other crime,
Ev'n the base murder of my dearest friend;
But slighted love no woman can forgive.
For thro' our life we feel the bitter smart,
And guilt and shame lye festring at the heart.

ACT III. SCENE I.

A Room of State with a Throne.

Hydarnes. Conspirators. Orbasius. Guards.

1st Conspirator. THE information of those two vile cowards,
Who mingled with us brave and active spirits,
Hath giv'n us death. Let those mean creatures live,
They're fitter for the world.
   2d Conspirator.   Lead us to death.
   Hydarnes. Death is pronounc'd on you, on me, on all.
Would I could take your guilt upon my self,
So to preserve some virtue in the world.
But those informers have deny'd me that;
We all must perish, and fall unreveng'd.
But since I cannot take your crimes upon me;   10
I'll live, and execute our great design,
And thus revenge your deaths.
   1st Conspirator.   Could this be done!
   Hydarnes. It can.
   1st Conspirator.   You flatter us.
   Hydarnes.   I say, I'll do it.
Soon as the King returns to sign our sentence,
Only confirm the words which I shall speak,
And I'll revenge you soon, and soon be with you.
                   [*Talks to them apart.*
   Orbasius. The guilty perish; innocence is freed.
Suspicion has not cast the smallest stain
Upon the virtuous *Persian.* Those accusers,
Who have condemn'd their fellows, know him not.   20
Of all the pleasures that a monarch tastes,

Sure mercy is most sweet! 'Tis heav'nly pleasure
To take the galling chains from off the hands
Of injur'd innocence! That privilege
O'er-ballances the cares that load a crown.

SCENE II.

Phraortes seats himself on the Throne. Magi. Orbasius. Araxes.
Sophernes. Hydarnes. *Guards and Attendants.*

    Araxes. Make room; The *Persian* Prince attends his
sentence.
    Phraortes. Most noble Prince, I grieve that you were
injur'd.
When foul conspiracy molests a state
The ear of Kings is open to suspicion,
And we grow jealous of our bosom friends.
When calumny would blast a virtuous man,
And justice has made clear his innocence;
It only throws a brighter lustre on him,
And serves to make his virtues more conspicuous.
10 Approach the throne; and let the King's embrace
Make some attonement for your shameful bonds.
I feel your suff'rings, and my heart grows fonder.
Now bring the pris'ners to receive their sentence.
Justice cries loud for vengeance on your crimes.
Say, have ye ought to plead to ward the blow,
Ere I enroll your names among the dead?
    Hydarnes. That I design'd to bath these hands in blood,
Even in thy blood, O King, I dare confess,
And glory in th' attempt. I know thy power;
20 I know that death with all his dreadful tortures
Stands ready at thy nod. Give then the signal,
For I unmov'd can face the ghastly terror.
How is thy wisdom foil'd! Prepare to follow.
Think not with us our enterprize is lost.
A King shall bleed to pacifie our ghosts.
Come, lead to death. Spend all thy wrath on us,
The raging tyger bites the shaft that wounds him,
And spares the man who threw it. I have done.

Phraortes. These are the starts and ravings of despair.
Think'st thou by threats to force me into mercy? 30
  Hydarnes. I grow impatient; lead me to my fate.
  Phraortes. Know you that I have life within my power?
  Hydarnes. I know the utmost of thy power is death.
  Magus. Ye Gods avert his words, and save the King!
  Phraortes. What said he? Speak again.
  Hydarnes.   Death is my choice.
  Phraortes. I will be satisfy'd.
  Hydarnes.   I've said too much.
  Phraortes. Say more, or torture shall extort it from you.
  Hydarnes. Let torture do its worst. You dare not try it.
  Magus. If memory can recal the solemn speech,
These were his very words, 40
A King shall bleed to pacifie our ghosts.
The raging tyger bites the shaft that wounds him,
But spares the man who threw it. Was it thus?
  Hydarnes. Now let your wisdom fathom this deep secret.
I answer no more questions.
  Phraortes.   Reverend fathers,
What may these words portend? Expound the mystery.
  Magus. Thy sacred life, O King, is still in danger.
While justice pours down vengeance on these wretches,
These mean subservient instruments of mischief,
Their leader scapes, and lives for future crimes. 50
  Hydarnes. Go on.
  Magus.   The words imply no more.
  Hydarnes.   'Tis well.
All's safe.—I'm ready.—Why is death delay'd?
  Phraortes. Thus speaks the voice of Mercy from my lips.
Th' irrevocable sentence is not sign'd,
And still there's room for hope. Attend, and live.
By this bright sceptre, by the throne of *Media*,
By yon great light that rules the rolling year,
If you lay ope the depth of this foul treason,
And point me out that undetected villain,
I swear, to grant you life and liberty. 60
Speak now, or death shall seal your lips for ever.
  Hydarnes. The royal word is giv'n, and I accept it.
The King shall live, and all his foes shall perish.

Danger stands near the throne. How blind is Justice!
The *Persian* Prince!
 Phraortes.   *Sophernes*!
 Hydarnes.   He's a traytor.
'Twas he that put the dagger in my hand.
So. Now I have betray'd. O love of life!
Where was my resolution? I'm a coward;
And cowards can endure a life of shame.
70 *Phraortes. Sophernes*!—Let strong proof confirm your charge,
I must have proof.
 Hydarnes.   Call in my fellow-prisoners.
 Sophernes. What can set bounds to man's impiety,
And where is virtue safe? Accus'd thus falsely,
With all the strongest circumstance of guilt,
By one I know not! Heav'n has then determin'd
That I must fall. Shall man contest with *Jove*?
'Tis all in vain. The will of Fate be done.
 Hydarnes. Those who accus'd us, brib'd with *Persian* gold,
Conceal'd the author of our enterprize.

SCENE III.

The Aforesaid and Conspirators.

Know ye that man?
 1st Conspirator. Would he had been unknown.
 Hydarnes. The King has trac'd our mischief to the source.
Who was it prompted you to this attempt?
Had ye not views to set a nation free?
And to restore him to his crown and kingdom?
 1st Conspirator. By him we fell, 'tis just that he fall with us.
 2d Conspirator. So, now one ruin has involv'd us all.
 Phraortes. Death is the lot of those that thirst for blood.
Conduct them hence. This hour prepare to suffer.

SCENE IV.

Phraortes. Magi. Orbasius. Araxes. Sophernes. Hydarnes.
Guards *and* Attendants.

Ungrateful Prince!

Sophernes.   Since 'tis the will of Heaven
To load me with calamities and shame,
Since the most searching eye cannot discern
The heart of man; O where shall I find justice!
I am a stranger, in adversity,
Bereft of wealth and power, without a friend.
　　Phraortes. Hence, base dissembler. Take him from my
　　　presence.
When hypocrites are stript of Virtue's plumes,
Vice then appears most hideous and deform'd.
Back to thy dungeon, to remorse and death.   10
　　Sophernes. Vain are excuse and solemn protestation;
How shall my words prevail, and truth appear,
When there's a crowd of witnesses against me!
The Guilty perish with remorse and horror,
But innocence ne'er feels the sting of death.
Death is a blessing to adversity;
Anxiety, calamity and sorrow,
And all the daily fretting cares of life
Are shook from off our shoulders; and we rest.

SCENE V.

Phraortes. Magi. Orbasius. Araxes. Hydarnes. Guards *and*
Attendants.

　　Hydarnes. Safety now guards the throne, and *Media*'s
　　　happy.
　　Phraortes. I ratifie my word, and give you life,
I give you liberty; but on conditions.
Those I shall send you soon, and then you're free.
O Sun, I thank thee; thy all-seeing eye
Has trac'd the villain through his secret ways,
And how the hand of Justice is upon him.
　　Araxes. *Media* rejoice.
　　All.   May the King live for ever!
　　Phraortes. Proclaim a festival for seven days space;
Let the Court shine in all its pomp and lustre;   10
Let all our streets resound with shouts of joy;
Let Musick's care-dispelling voice be heard;

The sumptuous banquet and the flowing goblet
Shall warm the cheek, and fill the heart with gladness.
For *Media*'s foes are put to shame and death.
Astarbe shall sit soveraign of the feast,
That Queen of beauty shall direct our pleasures.
I'll to her bower.—I would have no attendance.

SCENE VI.

Araxes. Doraspe.

Doraspe. Inform me, what has past?
Araxes.   The Queen's conjectures
The King has now confirm'd. The *Persian* Prince,
That hypocrite is known, and prov'd a traytor,
And leader of that crew of vile assassins.
But see the Queen.—The King is gone to seek her.
Excuse my haste; for Duty calls me hence.

SCENE VII.

Doraspe. Astarbe.

Astarbe. 'Twas downright arrogance. I saw his scorn.
A Lover reads the thought of every look,
And needs no comment or interpreter.
What woman can forgive that worst of insults?
Not ev'n the most deform'd of all our sex
Can bear contempt. And shall I pardon it?
To pardon it, is to insult myself,
And own that I deserve it. [*aside.*] Know you ought
Of what the King in judgment has determin'd?
Doraspe. Sophernes was accus'd.
10   *Astarbe*.   Was he found guilty?
Doraspe. Yes, prov'd a traytor.
Astarbe.   Then I'm satisfy'd.
Doraspe. How one affliction crouds upon another,
To punish this ungrateful man!
Astarbe.   What mean you?
Dorapse. It is confirm'd among the captive women

(Who now attend to pass before the presence)
His wife was slain in battle.
    Astarbe.   Would he were dead!
Yet were he dead, would he dye in my thoughts?
Talk to me, speak; leave me not to reflection. [*To* Doraspe.
Yet what will talk avail?—I've lost attention.
Were her words soft and soothing as the lyre,   20
Or strong and sprightly as th' enlivening trumpet,
I could hear nought but conscience. Would he were dead!
You shall not leave me.
    Doraspe.   See the King returns.

SCENE VIII.

Phraortes. Astarbe.

    Phraortes. Welcome, my Queen; how my heart springs to
        meet thee!
Each day, each hour thy beauty grows upon me,
Ev'n while I gaze some undiscover'd charm
Opens it self, and wounds my heart anew.
Rejoyce, *Astarbe*; *Media* is deliver'd:
The gathering storm that threaten'd desolation
Is over-blown, and all is now serene.
Then let us give our future days to pleasure;
My ev'ry pleasure is compris'd in thee.
    Astarbe. Be firm in justice, nor give way to mercy,   10
'Tis the mind's frailty, and the nurse of crimes.
Punish. And root out treason from the land.
    Phraortes. *Sophernes* was their chief.
    Astarbe.   Ungrateful villain!
    Phraortes. How he deceiv'd me!
    Astarbe.   Your too easy nature
Must always harbour mischiefs in your empire.
Does he still live?
    Phraortes.   His death is fix'd and sign'd.
    Astarbe. Each hour he lives your people doubt your justice.
Would you deter the populace from crimes,
Let punishment be sudden. That's true mercy.
    Phraortes. He never shall behold another Sun.   20

But why should cares of state intrude upon us?
   Astarbe. Why this reproof? In what have I deserv'd it?
All my concern was for the peace of *Media*,
And for your safety. I have said too much.
   Phraortes. What has *Astarbe* ask'd that I refus'd?
Thy beauty has all power. Who waits without?
Go; let the Captives be dismiss'd the palace,
                       [*Speaks at the door.*
The King resigns his privilege of choice.
Should the selected beauties of the world   [*To* Astarbe.
In full temptation stand before my presence,
Still would my heart and eye be fixt on thee.
Thy charms would (like the Sun's all-powerful rays)
Make all those little stars of beauty fade.
Why that dejected look? that thoughtful sigh?
In what have I offended? If to love,
Be to offend; *Phraortes* is most wretched.

SCENE IX.

Phraortes. Astarbe. Araxes.

   Araxes. I spoke the King's commands; when from the crowd
One of the Captives rose, and humbly pray'd
Admission to the throne.
   Phraortes.   I hear no suits.
   Araxes. She wish'd to speak a matter of importance.
   Phraortes. Dismiss them all. Let us retire, my Queen.
   Astarbe. Araxes, stay.   [Araxes *going out.*
   Phraortes.   What is *Astarbe*'s pleasure?
   Astarbe. This matter should be search'd. The fate of
    Empires
Turns often on the slightest information;
And were my counsell worthy to be heard,
I would admit her.
10   *Phraortes.*   Let her be admitted.   [*Exit* Araxes.
       [Phraortes *seats* Astarbe *on the throne, then places*
         himself by her. The Guards enter, and range themselves
                           on each side.

SCENE X.

Phraortes. Astarbe. Captive. Doraspe. Araxes. Attendants.

Phraortes. Arise, fair maid; and let thy suit be heard.
Captive. The King has done his prostrate servant justice.
　　　　　　　　　　　　　　　　[*Kneeling.*
Thus low I pay my thanks to Heaven and you.
　Phraortes. Rise from that humble posture, and speak forth.
　Captive. The *Persian* Prince, to whom we owe our bondage,
　　　　　　　　　　　　　　　　　[*Rises.*
'Tis said, is doom'd to death for horrid treachery.
　Phraortes. He well deserves it. If you fall before me,
To melt me into mercy with your tears,
Woman, your tears are frustrate. Take her hence.
　Captive. I speak for mercy! No. I sue for tortures.　　10
With rapture I could gaze upon his sufferings,
Enjoy his agonies and dying groans,
And then this hand could stab him to the heart.
　Phraortes. Whence rose this furious spirit of revenge?
　Captive. By brutal violence he slew my husband.
Excuse my tears. Love calls them from my eyes;
With him I lost all joy, all peace and comfort.
　Phraortes. What mov'd *Sophernes* to the barbarous deed?
　Captive. My husband was distinguish'd in his armies;
With him I always shar'd the toils of war,　　　　　20
The tedious marches, and the scorching suns,
For Love makes all fatigue seem light and easy.
Sophernes saw me, sigh'd, and spoke his passion.
I spurn'd his offers, and despis'd his suit.
He still persisted, and my virtue strengthen'd:
'Till on a day, inflam'd with loose desire,
He sent my Lord upon some feign'd command;
I in his tent sate waiting his return,
Then suddenly the ravisher rush'd in.　　　　[*Weeps.*
　Phraortes. Go on.　　　　　　　　　　　30
　Captive. He seiz'd me, tore me, dragg'd me to his Arms;
In vain I struggled; by resistance weaken'd,
I lost all strength, and so—he spoil'd my Honour.
O shame! O brutal force!　　　　　　　　[*Weeps.*

Phraortes. Unhappy woman!
Proceed.
    Captive. Just in the moment of my shame
My husband enter'd. Strait the villain left me,
And desperate by the stings of guilt and terror,
He stabb'd him to the heart.   [*Weeps.*
    Phraortes. Most monstrous villain!
His life's a series of the blackest crimes.
40   *Captive.* I in the hurry of the murder fled,
And 'scap'd the tyrant's power. Alone, disguis'd,
I've past away my restless hours in sorrow.
Revenge was all my wish, and all my comfort,
For that I watch'd him through long weary marches,
And Revenge gave me strength and resolution.
Why fell he not by me? His crime requir'd it.
Vengeance o'ertakes him for another guilt,
And I have lost revenge. O may he feel
The pain and horror due to both his crimes.
    Phraortes. His death is sign'd.
50   *Captive.*   That is his due for treachery.
    Phraortes. What would Revenge have more? Th' offender's
    blood
Allays its strongest thirst.
    Captive.   Most gracious King,   [*Kneels.*
Hear an unhappy woman's just petition,
And may my prayer find favour and acceptance!
Grant me to see him in his latest gasp;
Let my appearance strike him with confusion,
Let me awake fresh terrors in his conscience,
And bring my murther'd husband to his view.
Entrust the sword of justice in my hand;
The stroke shall then be sure.
60   *Phraortes.*   What fortitude
Lies hid beneath that face of softest feature!
The death of his confederates is sign'd,
And he with privacy this very evening
Shall be dispatch'd in prison. Now you're satisfy'd.
    Captive. O, were that office mine!
    Astarbe.   For such offence
He cannot feel too much; her suit is just.

Then let me intercede in her behalf;
Grant her request. Give her the fatal signet,
Give her the dagger.—Such revenge is virtue.
   Phraortes. Take this; your boon is granted. Soon my orders 70
                                  [*Gives her his dagger.*
Shall send you to revenge a husband's murther.
Let her attend without. Draw near, *Araxes.*

SCENE XI.

Phraortes. Astarbe. Doraspe. Araxes. Attendants.

                             [Phraortes *talks aside to* Araxes.
   Astarbe. What, sue to her! and when I sued disdain me!
How my disgrace grows on me! Let him perish,
And perish by that woman. My resentment
Kindles and burns to take her charge upon me.
Yet still would he relent, I could forgive him.
   Doraspe. His wife is dead, on whom his heart was fix'd:
That obstacle's remov'd.
   Astarbe.   And Death hangs o'er him.
That sight perhaps may shake his resolution.
If I could hope, I would delay his sentence.
I dread his death. What is there to be done?   10
I'll see him ere he dies. O abject thought!
Yes, I will see him, and renew my offers
In his last moments: For whene'er he dies
My mind will ne'er know peace. I will defer it.
I'll sooth the King in his soft hours of love,
When all his strongest purposes are nothing.
When 'tis deferr'd—Would I could cease from thought!
   Phraortes. Tell her as soon as justice is perform'd,
The King requires her thanks—She's wondrous fair!
You know my will; these are my last commands,   20
Let punctual care and diligence obey me.   [*Exit* Araxes.

SCENE XII.

Phraortes. Astarbe. Doraspe. Attendants.

Go, bid the priests prepare the sacrifice;
This ev'ning shall the fragrance of devotion

Smoak in our temples, and perfume the skies.
Phraortes shall attend the solemn rites,
To pay his grateful thanks in songs of joy.

                           [*Exeunt* Doraspe *and Attendants.*

Astarbe, come.—One glance of those bright eyes
Dispells all care, and empires are forgot.
In what is man superior to the brute?
Brutes eat, drink, sleep; like us, have all the senses.
10 The male and female meet, then coldly part,
Part with indifference, and desire is cloy'd.
In love alone we feel th' immortal part,
And that celestial fire refines the heart.

ACT IV. SCENE I.

A Prison.

Hydarnes. Conspirators.

  Hydarnes. I shall survive but for a little space;
Doubt not my plighted faith, and dye in peace.
What is an hour of life! an hour of torment.
Think then what I shall suffer for your sake,
How I shall long and pant to be among you!
To him who fears not death Revenge is sure,
To him who fears not death Revenge is speedy.
Soon as the chains are struck from off these hands,
I'll dye them purple in the royal blood;
10 I'll watch all time. The throne shall not secure him,
The solemn temple, ev'n that sacred ground
Shall not protect him from my resolution.
Would it were done; that we might fall together!
  1*st Conspirator.* May all success attend thy glorious purpose!
Thinking upon thy brave undaunted spirit,
I shall forget my pains, and smile in torture,
Ev'n when the sharpest pang of death is on me.
  Hydarnes. Ere you are cold my Ghost shall overtake you,
And bring the welcome news.—Impatience racks me.
20   2*d Conspirator.* We thank our bold revenger, and will dye
Like men that well deserv'd so great a chief.

3d Conspirator. Farewell. And when you lift the dagger for
　　the blow
Think on my friendship.
　　4th Conspirator.　　　　　And on mine,
　　5th Conspirator.　　　　　　　　　And mine.
　　1st Conspirator. Think of us all, and give him death for each.
　　Hydarnes. Farewell, unhappy friends; you're brave and
　　　true,
And you entrust one who deserves such friendships.
Your prayers and wishes, shall direct the dagger
Deep in his heart. And when this deed is done
I've done my task of life; and I'll resign it.

SCENE II.

Hydarnes. Conspirators. Araxes. Officers.

Araxes. Time presses on us, and your hour is come.
We must obey our orders. Lead them hence.
Torture and Death expect you.
　　1st Conspirator.　　　　　Well. Lead on.
　　Araxes. 'Tis your last moment.
　　1st Conspirator.　　　　　We're impatient for it.
　　Araxes. Stay here till my return. To you, my message
　　　　　　　　　　　　　　　　[*To* Hydarnes.
Is of a sweeter sound. 'Tis life, 'tis freedom.
I'll see them to the scaffold; then discharge you.

SCENE III.

Hydarnes.

What's death to that I feel within! 'Tis nothing.
Tortures but tear the flesh, and crush the bones,
But guilt and horror tear my restless soul,
And ev'ry thought's an arrow in my heart.
Sophernes is condemn'd, and I accus'd him.
For what?—For means to satiate my revenge,
And that's sufficient.—O Revenge, support me!
What, am I grown a coward? Does repentance,

Does vile contrition sink my boasted courage?
10 Does resolution stagger! Hence, away,
I will not hear thee, dastard, medling conscience!
No, I'll go on, I feel my spirits rise;
My heart grows harder, and I scorn remorse,
That's the poor whining refuge of a Coward.
My friends are now expiring. Hark, their groans
Start me from thought, and summon me to vengeance!
I come, my friends; in that great deed I'll fall.

SCENE IV.

Hydarnes. Araxes.

Araxes. *Phraortes* sends you life and liberty.
Twelve days are granted you to pass the confines
Of his Domains: to stay beyond that time
Annuls his pardon, and your life is forfeit.
You're now discharg'd. Be grateful for this mercy,
Pray for the peace of *Media*, and repent.
　Hydarnes. *Media*, farewell. With all the wings of speed
I fly thy bounds. Let me forget thy name;
'Twill bring to my remembrance my lost friends.

SCENE V.

Araxes. Sophernes.

Araxes. Come forth, unhappy Prince, excuse my words.
　　　　　　　　　　　[*Unlocks the dungeon.*
'Tis with reluctance that I bring the message.
Your death's at hand.
　Sophernes.　　　　　Death is the only friend
That I have left; thy message is most welcome.
My friend's at hand; O how long I to meet him!
In him is all my hope, in him my refuge,
He shall disburthen me of all misfortune,
He shall wipe off calamity and sorrow,
And give me peace and everlasting rest.
I thank thee for the news.

Araxes.   Such unconcern,   10
Such steady fortitude amidst afflictions
Was never seen till now.
    Sophernes.   My wife is dead!
And I have no attachment to the world.
What is't to live? And who counts life a blessing?
It is to see Injustice hold the scale,
And weigh with partial hand the deeds of men;
It is to see a race of servile flatterers
Worship the author of all mischief, Gold;
To see Oppression rich, and Virtue starving.
Death only closes this distasteful scene.   20
    Araxes. This scorn of death appears like innocence.
    Sophernes. All mortal justice errs. Heav'n knows the heart.
'Tis easy in my circumstance to dye,
For I have no possessions to forgo,
My kingdom is another's. Round my couch
No faithful servants stand with weeping eyes;
No darling children cling around my neck,
And with fond kisses warm my hollow cheek;
No wife, who, (worn, and wearied out with grief)
Faints in my arms. These give the pangs of death;   30
These make us covet life. But I leave nothing.
    Araxes. What manly resolution! I grieve for you.
    Sophernes. At   death's   approach   the   guilty   conscience
       trembles,
But I have not those horrors.—Hark, he knocks.
                          [*Knocking heard.*
With what impatient joy I come to meet thee!
    Araxes. Farewell, thou most unfortunate of men;
A mind so great, unshaken by distress,
Deserv'd a nobler end. Forgive my duty,
It seems severe, but 'tis the King's command.
The dungeon must confine you.
    Sophernes.   I submit.   40
                 [*Locks him in the dungeon.*

SCENE VI.

Araxes. Captive.

Captive. This letter will instruct you in your duty.
Araxes. The prisoner shall be given into your hands.
Captive. And he shall perish by an injur'd woman.
Thus has the King decreed; so shall he suffer
Both for his treason, and my murder'd lord.
To see me arm'd with such just resolution,
My husband's ghost is pleas'd, and smiles upon me.
Phraortes gave this dagger. This shall end him.
    Araxes. Within that iron gate he mourns in darkness.
[Gives the Keys.

10 This will conduct you.—'Tis the King's command,
Soon as the bloody office is perform'd,
That you present your self once more before him.
    Captive. His will shall be obey'd.
    Araxes.   He's now your charge.
    Captive. And soon my charge shall end.—Leave me to
       justice.
How will my sight dismay his guilty soul!
Ev'n while that terror preys upon his heart,
I'll hurle him to the deepest shades below.
But I delay; and justice grows impatient.
I'd be alone. You now have done your duty.

SCENE VII.

Captive. Sophernes.

Captive. Come forth, *Sophernes*.   [*Unlocks the Dungeon.*
Sophernes.   I will meet thee, Death.
Captive. Draw near.
Sophernes.   Hark! was it not a woman's voice?
That voice no more is sweet;—*Cylene*'s dead.
Yes. 'Tis the Queen. Here satiate thy revenge,
My bosom heaves, and longs to meet the dagger.
Why is thy hand so slow?
    Captive.   Look on this face,
[Lifts up her veil.

Is not thy heart acquainted with these eyes?
And is thy ear a stranger to this voice?
What, not a word!

 Sophernes.   O dear delusion!   [*Faints.*
 Cylene.   Wake.
'Tis thy *Cylene* calls, thy lost *Cylene*.   10
Cannot this bosom warm thee into life?
Cannot this voice recall thy sinking spirits?
Cannot these lips restore thee? O look up;
Thy voice, thy lips, could call me from the dead.
Look up, and give me comfort.

 Sophernes.   'Tis *Cylene*.
'Tis no delusion. Do I live to see thee?
And must I be torn from thee? cruel thought!
O tyrant Death, now thou hast made me fear thee!

 Cylene. When will misfortunes leave us?
 Sophernes.   Death must end them.
'Twas said you fell in battle; from that time 20
I lost all pleasure, and desire of life.

 Cylene. In that sad day of our adversity,
When *Persia* was made captive, every eye
Wept for the fall of my dear Lord *Sophernes*,
For you they sorrow'd, and forgot their bondage.
I lost my self in heart-consuming grief,
And lest a conqueror's arrogance and pride
Should tempt him to condemn a captive Queen
To his loose hours, industriously I spread
The rumour of my death; and by those means 30
Have sigh'd away my days obscure, unknown.

 Sophernes. How gain'd you this access? and why that
  dagger?

 Cylene. This is no time for talk; consult thy safety.
Catch at the present moment, for the next
May throw us back again into despair.

 Sophernes. What means, my love? No innocence can stand
Against the voice of perjur'd calumny.

 Cylene. This dagger was design'd to murder thee;
And I am sent upon that bloody errand.
This hand that now is thrown about thy neck 40
Was to have done the deed. O horrid thought!

Unknown, among a train of captive women,
They brought me to the palace: there I learnt
The tale of thy unhappy sufferings,
And how the King had sign'd the fatal sentence.
I fell before the throne, extoll'd his justice;
Then with feign'd tears, and well-dissembled speech
Charg'd thee with violation of my honour,
And murder of a husband. He was mov'd;
50 Pleas'd with my bold request he heard my prayer,
And for revenge and justice gave me this.   [*Shows the dagger.*
But the time flies. I come, my Lord, to save thee.
'Tis by that hope, I live.
   Sophernes.   That hope is past.
It is impossible. Resentment, power,
And perjury, all work against my life.
O how I fear to dye! for thee, I fear,
To leave thee thus expos'd, a helpless Captive,
In a strange land, and not one friend to chear thee!
   Cylene. I think thou lov'st me.
   Sophernes.   Sure thou long hast known it.
60   *Cylene.* Is there ought that I could deny *Sophernes*?
No. I have try'd my heart!
   Sophernes.   What mean these doubts?
I never gave you cause.
   Cylene.   Then promise, swear,
That you will not refuse me what I ask;
Thus on her knees *Cylene* begs it of you.
   Sophernes. Does this appear like love? speak, and 'tis
    granted.
   Cylene. I thank thee. Thou hast given me all my wishes,
For now thy life is safe; and sav'd by me.
Here, take this veil; this shall secure thy flight,
With this thou shalt deceive the watchful guard.
70 O blest occasion! fly, my Lord, with speed
I never wish'd to part till now.
   Sophernes. What, go and leave thee thus! my heart forbids
    it.
No. Death is all that I am doom'd to suffer;
But thy distress is more.
   Cylene.   Dispute it not.

Hast thou not sworn?
  Sophernes.   What never can be done.
Why wilt thou force severer torture on me?
No. Give me death; I chuse the slighter pain.
When I am dead may the just Gods relieve thee.
  Cylene. Was ever love thus obstinately cruel!
Only thy life can save me; think on that.   80
                  [Sophernes *fixes his eyes on the ground.*
Like the deaf rock he stands immoveable.
How my fears grow, and chill my shiv'ring heart!
Has then thy stubbornness resolv'd to kill me?
  Sophernes. Shall I that was her shield in every danger
Abandon her to the rude hand of power?
  Cylene. Hear me, my Lord; embrace the happy moment;
This is, perhaps, the last that is allow'd us.
  Sophernes. What! give her my disgress!
  Cylene.   Look up, and answer.
Have my words lost all int'rest in thy heart?
Hear then my purpose; and I will perform it.   90
I'll never feel the pang of that sad hour
When thou shalt suffer. No. I'll dye before thee.
How gracious was this Present of the King.
'Tis kind, 'tis merciful, 'twill give me peace,
And show me more compassion than *Sophernes.*
  Sophernes. O give me strength, ye Powers, to break my
    chains,
That I may force the lifted weapon from her!
Spare, spare thy dearer life! I grant thee all.
I will abandon thee to my distresses;
I'll fly this instant; by our loves, I will.   100
The Gods are kind. O may their mercy save her!
  Cylene. From thy dear hands I take the galling chains.
Lest danger intercept thee, haste, be gone;
And as thou valuest mine, secure thy life.
Thou hadst no hope. Who knows but my offence
May find forgiveness! 'tis a crime of love;
And love's a powerful advocate to mercy.
  Sophernes. O how I struggle to unloose my heart-strings,
That are so closely knit and twin'd with thine!
Is't possible that we may meet again?   110

That thought has fill'd my soul with resolution.
Farewell: may Heav'n support thee, and redress us!

SCENE VIII.

Cylene.

Cylene. O blessed opportunity, I thank thee.
If for this pious act of love I perish,
Let not *Sophernes* rashly follow me.
Live to revenge me, and the world shall praise thee.
Though all my hours be doom'd to chains and darkness,
The pleasing thought that I have giv'n thee safety,
Will chear me more than liberty and day-light.
Though I'm condemn'd to suffer shameful death,
Ev'n in that hour I shall forget his terrors,
10 And knowing that preserv'd thee, dye with pleasure.
But hark! what noise was that? New fears alarm me.
Is he detected?—Heaven has more compassion.
Be still, my heart. I go to take his place,
And wait th' event with steady resignation.

[*Enters the dungeon.*

SCENE IX.

Araxes. Astarbe.

[*Cylene in the Dungeon.*

Astarbe. I bring the royal mandate, read your order.
The sentence of *Sophernes* is suspended;
I'd question him in private. Guide me to him.
Araxes. He's dead.
Astarbe.   *Sophernes* dead! when? how? by whom?
Araxes. The captive woman by whose hand he fell,
Is gone before the King; just now she parted.
Astarbe. My guilt, my hate, my love, all war within,
And conscience and distraction will betray me.   [*Aside.*
Araxes. Within that dungeon lyes the breathless body.
10 *Astarbe.* Name him no more. Begone; I'd be alone.
You know my pleasure.
Araxes.   I am all Obedience.

SCENE X.

Astarbe. Cylene *in the dungeon.*

Astarbe. Who shall appease this tempest of my soul?
'Tis done. He's dead: now it will rage for ever!
Yet why? Hence, conscience. All I did was justice.
Am I the cause? I proffer'd life and love
The murder was not mine. Why then this horror?
Could a Queen bear such insolence and scorn?
Was I not injur'd? shall I not resent?
He well deserv'd his fate. Ungrateful man!
The bloody spectacle shall please revenge,
And fix eternal hatred in my heart.   [*Cylene comes forth.* 10
Hah! speak: what art?—
It moves! it comes! where shall I hide me from it?
Nature shrinks back, and shivers at the sight. [*Hides her face.*
  Cylene. See at your feet a poor unhappy captive. [*Kneeling.*
O may the Queen be gracious to her servant!
  Astarbe. Araxes said that he had let you forth,
And by command you went before the King.
Why has he thus deceiv'd me?
  Cylene.   Turn not away,
Bestow one look of pity on a wretch
Who lifts her eyes to you for grace and pardon.   20
  Astarbe. Pardon! for what? you did it by command.
Is it a crime t' obey the voice of justice?
And did not thy own wrongs demand his blood?
What has detain'd thee in that horrid place?
Was it to hear him in the pangs of death,
And taste the pleasure of his dying groan?
Stretch forth thy hands. Where are the crimson stains?
Where lies the reeking sword? Is he yet cold?
'Twas bravely done.—Go, haste, before the Throne;
Phraortes shall reward thee for this service.   30
  Cylene. When I shall stand before that awful presence,
How shall I stem the torrent of his wrath!
Then let the Queen instill soft mercy in him,
And intercede to spare a wretched wife.
  Astarbe. Make known thy crime.

    Cylene. All my offence is love.
Sophernes is my husband.
    Astarbe. Hast thou kill'd him?
    Cylene. No. I dar'd disobey. My love has sav'd him.
With lying speeches I deceiv'd the King,
Accus'd *Sophernes* of imagin'd crimes,
40 And thus have giv'n him life. My veil conceal'd him,
And brought him forth from death. This is my guilt.
If e'er your heart has felt the tender passion,
You will forgive this just, this pious fraud.
Who would not do the same for him she loves?
Consult thy heart; and Pity will plead for me.
    Astarbe. How dar'd you contradict the King's command?
    Cylene. No power on earth commands the heart but Love,
                                      [*Rises.*
And I obey'd my heart.
    Astarbe. Thy life is forfeit.
Dar'st thou avow thy crime?
    Cylene. I glory in it.
50 If 'tis a crime when innocence is wrong'd
To snatch it from the rage of credulous Power;
If 'tis a crime to succour the distrest;
If 'tis a crime to relieve injur'd virtue;
If 'tis a crime to be a faithful wife;
Those crimes are mine. For I have sav'd my husband.
    Astarbe. Is this an answer turn'd to move compassion!
Such insolence is only match'd in him.
Thine is the most consummate pitch of treason.
Who gave thee power? Are traytors at thy mercy?
60 Let not hope flatter thee. Nor prayers not tears
Shall turn away the sword of justice from thee.
Rash woman, know, thy life shall pay this ransom.
    Cylene. Alas! my life is of too little price;
Such as it is, I freely give it for him.
May safety guard his days, aud watch his nights!   [*Kneeling.*
May ev'ry sun rise happier than the last,
'Till he shall reascend his native throne!
Then think upon *Cylene.* Heaven shall aid thee
To punish *Media* for thy murder'd wife.
70   *Astarbe. Araxes.* Seize this bold presumptuous woman.

Your charge beneath her veil is fled from justice,
And she dares own the crime. I fear your duty
Will be suspected. Lead her to the dungeon.
There wait thy fate.
    Cylene.   Ye Gods, preserve *Sophernes*.
                       [She is lock'd into the dungeon.

SCENE XI.

Astarbe. Araxes.

Astarbe. If I had power, this instant she should die.
Araxes. I fear the King will soften into mercy.
Astarbe. Why that suspicion?
Araxes.   While she spoke before him,
I saw the King with the most fond attention
Hang on her words, and as she spoke he languish'd.
And ev'ry look he gave was love or pity.
    Astarbe. She shall not live an hour. Lest with each
        moment
His passion strengthen, and my power diminish.
Did beauty strike all hearts as well as eyes,
For me the rival world would be in arms;   10
Beauty's admir'd and prais'd, not always lov'd.
Some eyes are dazled with too strong a lustre,
That gaze with pleasure on a fainter object;
This homely captive then may steal his heart,
And bring disgrace upon me. I'll prevent her.
This hour I'll see her bleed, and thus remove
At once the rival of my throne and love.

ACT V. SCENE I.

A TEMPLE

Astarbe.

Doraspe knows,—and I am in her power.
Araxes was employ'd; he may suspect me.
One crime supports another—I must on.

I fear them both. How shall I lose my fear?
Their deaths must end it. But they may be honest.
I'll sift them—for my Soul has lost all rest.
But see *Doraspe*.

SCENE II.

Astarbe. Doraspe.

             Thou sometimes wert known
To miss Devotion's hours. How comes it then
Thou'rt now so soon? hast thou ought that concerns me?
Think'st thou *Araxes* honest? I have doubts.
I fear the prisoner 'scap'd by his connivance.
Are my commands obey'd?
    Doraspe.   'Tis not yet done.
He could not gain admission to the King.
    Astarbe. Does he not know a frown of mine can crush
      him?
    Doraspe. I know his heart and hand are wholy yours.
He waits the King's commands.
10   *Astarbe*.   Are mine then nothing?
And want I power to justify the deed?
Why was she not dispatch'd? He knew my pleasure.
My pleasure is his duty. 'Twas I rais'd him;
And dares he now dispute what I ordain?
Tell him, I'll have it done; that I command it.
Thou too art false. Then on her self alone
Astarbe shall depend. Away, thou flatterer.
Go hence, and tremble at the Queen's displeasure.
She shall this instant die. For see *Phraortes*.
20 *Astarbe* now has all things at her nod.
Of this day's worship I'll appoint the victim.

SCENE III.

Phraortes. Astarbe. A solemn Procession of Priests.

              [*The Queen talks apart to* Phraortes.
    Phraortes. Bid them suspend a while the sacrifice,
The Queen requires a private conference

On matters that concern the state. Withdraw.

[*Exeunt Priests.*

Now speak, my Queen; I'm ready to obey.

    Astarbe. All is not safe. Your state still harbours treason.
Ev'n now I tremble for my Lord the King;
For through the dark the traytor's arrow flies;
And which way will you turn your shield against it?

    Phraortes. What means my Queen?

    Astarbe.   Cast off all clemency;
So shall your throne stand firm to latest time.   10

    Phraortes. And has my danger giv'n *Astarbe* fear?
Where shall I find reward for so much goodness?
I swear by *Jove*, and yon wide sapphire Heaven,
Astarbe's will shall fix the King's decree.

    Astarbe. What shall be done to him, whose lying lips
Mis-lead the King from the strait paths of justice?

    Phraortes. *Media* decrees that death shall be his portion.

    Astarbe. What is ordain'd for him, who (when the King
Entrusts the royal signet in his hands)
Dares contradict the sacred mandate?

    Phraortes.   Death.   20

    Astarbe. What shall our laws inflict on that bold
      miscreant,
Who saves th' offender whom the King condemns?

    Phraortes. The fatal sentence falls upon his head.

    Astarbe. Let justice then support the throne of *Media*.
Let justice then preserve thy sacred life!
All these offences are that captive woman's,
Who with feign'd tears beg'd pity and revenge.
With lying lips she fell before the throne,
She turn'd the King from the strait paths of justice,
The royal seal was trusted in her hands;   30
Presumptuously she broke the sacred mandate,
She spar'd whom you condemn'd, and with vile treachery
Hath set *Sophernes* free. So this assassin
Shall kindle new rebellions in your Empire.

    Phraortes. These flagrant crimes demand immediate
      death.

    Astarbe. Let it be so. The King is wise and just.

    Phraortes. She shall this instant bleed. Audacious woman!

Astarbe. Let her endure the shameful pomp of death,
Expose her through the city's publick street,
40 So shall your people's shouts extol your justice;
So shall you strike your enemies with fear,
And awe them to subjection. Bring her forth;
Here let her bleed, ev'n on this holy ground,
Before the presence; *Jove* delights in justice,
The righteous sacrifice shall please the Gods.

SCENE IV.

Phraortes. Astarbe. Orbasius. Magi. Attendants.

Phraortes. Come from the croud, *Orbasius*; hear and obey.
Haste to the Prison, and bring forth that woman
(Who freed *Sophernes* from the hand of power)
To publick justice. She shall bleed before me.
Let her be led a publick spectacle.
Dispatch. Remember that the King expects you.

SCENE V.

Phraortes. Astarbe. Magi. Attendants.

The shield of Heaven has turn'd Destruction from us;
And Gratitude requires our thanks and praise.
Call up the Priests. Begin the sacred rites.
  1st Magus. Turn all your eyes to yon bright arch of
    Heaven.
  2d Magus. When *Jove* in thunder threatens impious men,
May the red lightnings scatter *Media*'s foes,
And lay their cities desolate and waste!
  1st Magus. May the vast globe of inexhausted light,
That rolls its living fires from east to west,
10 Strow all his paths with fragrant herbs and flowers,
And bless his people with perpetual spring!
  2d Magus. May the bright lamp of night, the silver moon,
And all the starry myriad that attend her,
Guard and defend his midnight couch from dangers!
  1st Magus. May everliving springs supply our fountains,
And wind in fertile rivers through the land!

2d Magus. Bless him, ye winds, with ever-prosp'rous gales!
  1st Magus. Pour not your wrath in tempests on his people.
Let your sweet breath chase dearth and pestilence,
And cool our summers with eternal health!   20

SCENE VI.

Phraortes. Astarbe. Magi. Orbasius. Attendants. Cylene *as
led to execution.*

                            [Orbasius *talks apart to the King.*
  Phraortes. Again we must defer the solemn worship.
Bid the procession move towards the Temple.
And let th' offender stand before the presence. [*To* Orbasius.
  Astarbe. *Sophernes* has expos'd me to this woman;
And while she lives, I live in fear and shame.
Shall she then triumph in a Queen's disgrace?   [*Aside.*
  Cylene. Most gracious King, consider my transgression.
                                                    [*Kneels.*
My life is forfeit; justice has condemn'd me.
I broke th' inviolable laws of *Media.*
Yet let *Phraortes* with impartial scale   10
Weigh my offence; he'll find my crime was virtue.
Sure Heaven that trys the heart will pardon me.
And Kings, who imitate the Gods in justice,
Should not forsake them in the paths of mercy.
  Phraortes. Have not thy lying lips deceiv'd the King?
How shall thy words find faith! They're air, they're
    nothing!
  Cylene. O be not rash in judgment! Hear me speak.
What mov'd my tongue to practise this deceit?
Was it ambition and the lust of power?
Was it to vex your empire with rebellion?   20
Was it the meaner views of sordid gain?
Was it to hurt the lowest of your people?
All my offence if faithful love and duty;
Sophernes is my husband, and I sav'd him.
  Phraortes. Thy husband!
  Astarbe.   Hear her not: woman, away.
Remember you have sworn.

Phraortes.   Thy husband, say'st thou?
Astarbe. Think on your oath, and spurn dissimulation.
Phraortes. Am I debarr'd the chief delight of Kings?
Have I the power to punish; not to pardon?
But I have sworn.
30 *Cylene.*   If there's no room for mercy *[Rises.*
My life is well bestow'd. My death is glorious;
I chose it; and repine not at my fate.
 Astarbe. Turn from her. Listen not to fraud and guile.
 Cylene. Think not I shudder at th' approach of death,
That the keen sword which glitters in my eyes
Makes my heart fail, and sinks me to despair.
I fear not for my self; for him I fear.
How will he bear my death?—As I could his.
 Phraortes. Why have I bound the tender hands of mercy?
              [Musing.
40 *Astarbe.* You but delay. The royal oath is sacred.
 Cylene. Well then. Lead on. His punishment is mine.
Live, live, *Sophernes*, and forget *Cylene*;
Lest grief destroy thy peace, and make thee wretched.
I'm ready.
 Phraortes. How shall I pronounce the sentence!
 Astarbe. For your oath's sake.
 Phraortes.   'Tis granted. Let her dye.
But let me first perform my due devotions,
To beg that mercy which I must refuse.
As soon as I have paid my solemn vows,
I'll make the sign. Then let the blow be given.
50 See all be ready. Now renew the rites.

SCENE VII.

The Aforesaid. Hydarnes *disguis'd.*

Hydarnes. Thus far I'm undiscover'd.—Now's my time.
The King of *Media*'s given into my hands.
And when he leaves his guards to trust the Gods,
Ev'n while he prostrate falls, and lifts his eyes
To the bright God of day, th' all-seeing sun;
This shall dispatch him first, and then *Hydarnes*.

1*st Magus.* Now let the King advance.
Phraortes.   O glorious Sun!
                                        [*Kneeling.*
        [Hydarnes *attempting to stab* Phraortes, *is stab'd by*
              Sophernes *disguis'd, who is seiz'd by the* Magi.
What means this consternation in all eyes?
Whence this alarm, and all this wild disorder?
Hah! who lies here thus weltring in his blood,   10
Gasping for life? what means this horrid murder?
Strike not till I command. [*To the Executioner.*] Who did
        this deed?
    1*st Magus.* Behold the man. What bounty can reward
        him?
What shall be done for him who sav'd the King?
    Phraortes. Say who, and whence thou art?
    Sophernes.   A wretched man
Who comes to take his sentence on him, death.
Sophernes was condemn'd; 'tis he must suffer.
Spare then that pattern of heroic virtue.
The sentence is not hers; I claim my right.
Sophernes stands before you, and demands it.   20
                        [*Throws off his disguise.*
    Cylene. O stay not for the signal. Give the blow.
Save him, ye Gods. Why is the stroke delay'd?
The King has sworn. O may my death preserve him!
    Phraortes. Suspend her sentence till my further orders.
Who slew this man? what mov'd thee to the murder?
Why hast thou stain'd this holy place with blood?
    Sophernes. That villain who lies groveling there before
        thee,
Had rais'd his arm to take thy life, O King;
And as the point descended, in the moment
I lay'd him low; and Heav'n has done me justice.   30
If favour shall reward me for this deed,
Spare my *Cylene,* grant her your protection.
I ask not life, for without her 'tis nothing.
    Astarbe. Where will this end? How are my schemes
        destroy'd!
Fear chills my heart, and guilt lies heavy on me.
Leave me not, Hell; desert not now thy cause.

I've gone too far. O blind the eyes of justice!
And sink me not in ruin and perdition.   [*Aside.*
 Phraortes. Know you this bold Assassin? View him well.
 Hydarnes. Ay, gaze upon me.
40 *Orbasius.*   Sure I've seen this man.
 Sophernes. Among the crowd I mark'd this perjur'd
  wretch,
Who charg'd me with ingratitude and treason.
With fury in his looks, and hasty strides
He stept before me; strait he rais'd his dagger:
In justice to my self and thee, I smote him.
  Astarbe. Where shall I hide me? how my fears distract
  me!
Who knows the torment of the guilty wretch,
When accusation stares him in the face?
Then all our spirits sink into despair,
50 And when we want most strength, then most it fails us.
He speaks, and I'm betray'd. Why err'd the dagger!
To bring confusion, shame and death upon me.
Where shall I fly?—for conscience will detect me,
'Twill faulter on my tongue, and stain my cheek.
O horror! O disgrace!—I fly from shame.   [*Exit.*

SCENE VIII.

Phraortes. Cylene. Sophernes. Magi. Orbasius. Araxes.
Executioner. Attendants.

 Sophernes. 'Twas I that gave thee death.
 Hydarnes.   Thou hast done justice.
 Phraortes. What sayest thou? speak again.
 Hydarnes.   He has done justice.
I barb'rously accus'd him of my crimes;
That guilt upbraids me; and I ask forgiveness.
          [*To* Sophernes.
 Phraortes. Whence art thou?—why this zealous rage
  against me?
 Hydarnes. I grieve not that I perish'd by his hand;
But that he disappointed my Revenge
I can't forgive him. Had he stay'd 'till then,

Hydarnes had faln greatly. But that's past.
Still I shall wound thee in the tenderest part. [*To* Phraortes. 10
I faint. O grant me strength to give it utterance!
Draw near, *Araxes*. Speak, inform the King;
Did not you guide me to the Queen's apartment?
You know why I was call'd. Disclose the secret.
   Araxes. What past I know not.
   Hydarnes.   What you fear to own,
I dare reveal. Hear then a dying man.
The Queen, on promise of my life and pardon,
Prevail'd upon me to accuse this Prince;
I knew him not. Yet to pursue thy life,
And gratify revenge, I undertook it. 20
   Phraortes. It is impossible. Advance, my Queen,
And let thy presence strike him with confusion.
Come forth, *Astarbe*. Hah! she's fled, she's guilty!
Haste, bring her back. I will extort confession.
What mov'd her to this perjur'd information?
                          [*Exeunt* Officers.
Whence sprung this hate and malice to *Sophernes*?
                           [*To* Hydarnes.
   Hydarnes. Ask her. I speak the truth, and know no
     further.
Look on me, Tyrant, and observe my features;
Seest thou not here the lines of brave *Lysamnes*?
He by thy power was led to shameful death, 30
His son now dyes, and never has reveng'd him.
                            [*Dyes*.

SCENE IX.

Phraortes. Astarbe *brought in by* Officers. Cylene.
Sophernes. Magi. Attendants.

   Astarbe. Bring me before the King.
   Phraortes.   Perfidious woman!
Look on that wretch, who there lyes pale and cold,
Was he not brought in private to your chamber?
Who gave instructions to accuse *Sophernes*?
Who promis'd life and pardon to *Hydarnes*?

Astarbe. All then is lost. *Astarbe* is betray'd.
But shall I stoop to lead a life of shame?
No. This shall close a scene of long remorse.   [*Stabs her self.*
Phraortes. Astarbe! hold!
Astarbe.   Forgive me!   [*Dyes.*
Phraortes.   Her foul treachery
10 My soul detests. But love will force a tear.
What mov'd her hatred thus against your life?
Sophernes. She was unhappy. Let her be forgot,
Phraortes. Draw near, *Cylene*. May heav'n bless your loves!
                              [*Gives her to* Sophernes.
Cylene. Shall he then live? My heart o'er flows with joy.
Now life is worth accepting, worth desiring,
Worth ev'ry wish, and ev'ry daily prayer.
Phraortes. By you the royal vestment shall be worn,
And next the King, all honour shall be paid
To you who sav'd him.   [*To* Sophernes.
Sophernes.   What I did was due.
20 I've only paid a debt of gratitude;
What would your bounty more?—you've giv'n me all.
For in these arms I ev'ry wish possess.
Phraortes. Life is a voyage, and we with pain and labour
Must weather many a storm to reach the port.
Sophernes. Since 'tis not giv'n to mortals to discern
Their real good and ill; let men learn patience:
Let us the toils of adverse fate sustain,
For through that rugged road our hopes we gain.

FINIS.

COMMENTARY

In the headnote to each play I give details of first performance and publication, followed by the sigla and bibliographical descriptions of the editions collated, with an indication of the copy-text used and a note of any editorial problems. In the Commentary itself, the keyed words or passages from the text for comment are printed for ease of reference entirely in italics. Definitions of single words will be found in the Glossary, p. 461. For Abbreviations, see p. xi.

The Mohocks

The Mohocks was not performed. The description on the title-page, 'As it was Acted near the Watch-house in *Covent-Garden*. By Her Majesty's Servants', is ironical, and refers only to the action of the play. *The Poetical Register* (1719), p. 115, lists 'The Mohocks; a Farce, never acted.' It was published on 10 April 1712. See *The Spectator* no. 349, Thursday 10 April 1712: 'This Day is Published The Mohocks. A Tragi-Comical Farce. As it was Acted near the Watch-house in Covent-Garden. By her Majesty's Servants. Printed for Bernard Lintott, at the Cross Keys between the two Temple Gates in Fleet Street.' Faber (p. xxxv) gives the publication date as 15 April, no doubt on the strength of a similar advertisement in *The Evening Post* no. 418, Saturday 12 April to Tuesday 15 April, or in *The Daily Courant* for April 15. Although these advertisements are not often reliable (see John Robert Moore, 'On the Use of Advertisements as Bibliographical Evidence', *Library*, 5th ser., ix, 1954, 134–5) it would seem plausible to accept the earliest notice of a book that can be found, and this is the practice followed in this edition.

Siglum: *12* THE | MOHOCKS. | A | Tragi-Comical Farce. | As it was Acted near the | Watch-house in *Covent-Garden*. | BY | Her MAJESTY's Servants. | [rule] | *Quo, quo, scelesti, ruitis? aut cur dexteris* | *Aptantur enses conditi?* Hor. | [double rule] | *LONDON:* | Printed for *Bernard Lintott*, at the *Cross-Keys* be-/tween the two *Temple-Gates*, in *Fleet-street*. 1712.

8° in half-sheets: A-D⁴ [\$2 signed (−A1)]. Press-figure 5:C2ᵇ. D4 contains notice '*Books Printed for* Bernard Lintott.' *Copies consulted*: Bodley 12. Θ. 555 (−D4); Bodley Vet. A4e. 1043; BL 11775. d. 2; Houghton *EC7. G2523. 712m (A); Houghton *EC7. G2523. 712m (B). This second Houghton copy has caused some confusion. Lester M. Beattie, *John Arbuthnot, Mathematician and Satirist* (Cambridge, Mass., 1935), p. 235, writes: 'Cibber, like Dennis, had been mocked by Gay in 1712 in a lively dialogue appended to the epilogue of *The Mohocks*, wherein Booth, Wilks, and Mrs. Oldfield were made to exchange pointed witticisms at Cibber's expense.' Irving (p. 149) virtually repeats this remark when he writes of Gay having 'made fun of Cibber also in the dialogue appended to the epilogue' of *The Mohocks*. The second Houghton copy lacks D4 and has in its place a leaf containing what appears to be Beattie's and Irving's 'dialogue'. This is tentatively attributed to Charles Johnson in the Widener Catalogue. It is, in fact, the Epilogue to Thomas Killigrew's *Chit Chat* (1719), and the made-up copy has no authority.

Copy-text: 12. The textual footnotes record editorial emendation of errors in the copy-text. Speech-prefixes are silently expanded.

The Mohocks] The name derives from the four Mohawk chiefs who had visited London in a Colonial Deputation early in 1710. See Richmond P. Bond, *Queen Anne's American Kings* (Oxford, 1952). The chiefs were of the Iroquois 'Five Nations', friendly to Britain, but other Indian tribes in alliance with the French were notorious for cruelty in warfare against the Colonists. See Trevelyan, iii. 141, for the atrocities at Deerfield in 1704.

Motto] 'Whither, whither are you rushing, wicked ones? And why are your right hands grasping hidden swords?' (Horace, *Epodes* vii. 1–2). The epode expresses horror at the prospect of some fresh outbreak of civil war.

To Mr. D***] The critic, John Dennis. Gay's ironic dedication (not so titled, but the headline in the copy-text is '*DEDICATION*') is generally considered to be a gesture of friendship towards Pope, whose feud with Dennis had been precipitated in the previous year by the gratuitous reference in *An Essay on Criticism* (585–7). Gay's 'On a Miscellany of Poems, to Bernard Lintott', with its praise of Pope, was a friendly gesture of another sort, as Pope's letter to Cromwell of 21 December 1711 shows: 'I wou'd willingly return Mr *Gay* my thanks for the favor of his *Poem*, & in particular, for his kind mention of me. I hop'd, when I heard a new Comedy had met with success upon the Stage, that it had been his, to which I really wish no less; and (had it been any way in my power) shou'd have been very glad to have contributed to its introduction into the World' (Sherburn, i. 137). Although *The Mohocks* is highly topical, Pope may here have in mind an early draft (Queen Anne's first Order in Council relating to civil disorders of this kind is dated 22 October 1711). His willingness to contribute to the introduction into the world of Gay's first play may well have extended to supplying it with a malicious dedication to delight the literati. For the Pope–Dennis feud, see E. N. Hooker, 'Pope and Dennis', *ELH*, vii (1940), 188–98.

Dedication. 3. *Horrid and Tremendous*] Examples of Dennis's critical vocabulary. In *A Comparison Between the Two Stages* (1702), p. 37, the author (Gildon?) remarks that very few people knew at the time what to make of Dennis's *Iphigenia* (1700), 'tho' there were many TREMENDOUS things in't; but if there be any thing of Tragedy in't it lies in that word, for he is so fond of it, he had rather use it in every Page, than slay his belov'd *Iphigenia*.' Sir Tremendous Longinus in *Three Hours after Marriage* was easily recognizable as Dennis.

Dedication. 8. *Appius and Virginia*] The tragedy by Dennis, produced in 1709. Nicoll (ii. 214) writes that *The Mohocks* 'seems to attack definitely *Appius and Virginia*', but the dedication's point is largely ironical. The two plays do not much resemble each other, except that the Mohocks' ceremonies are based quite closely on Lucius Icilius' vow at the end of Act I to kill Appius.

Dedication. 16. *your elegant Retreat*] Possibly an ironical reference to the Mint, where Dennis was safe from arrest for debt. The critic did, however, spend some of his time in Cobham, in Surrey. See H. G. Paul, *John Dennis, his life and criticism* (New York, 1911), pp. 59–60.

Dedication. 23. *a modern Writer*] Pope. Addison's *Spectator* no. 253, in praise of *An Essay on Criticism*, appeared on 20 December 1711.

Dedication. 24. *I am not at all concern'd . . . Reception*] That Dennis's plays were unsuccessful had already been claimed by Pope. See *The Prose Works of A. Pope*, ed. Norman Ault (1936), i. 14, for his gibe in *The Critical Specimen* about 'the success of the *What d'ye call 'um* and the *Criticks Third Night*', which I take to be a reference to Dennis's *Gibraltar: or, The Spanish Adventure*. This was produced at Drury Lane on 16 and 20 February 1705, but did not reach the third, the author's benefit night (see Nicoll, ii. 318). However, according to Nicoll, the only published dramatic work of Dennis's which was never performed was the masque *Orpheus and Eurydice* (1707), and several of his plays had respectable runs.

Dedication. 36. *April*, 1] There was a precedent for this significant dating. See George P. Mayhew, 'Swift's Bickerstaff Hoax as an April Fools' Joke', *MP*, lxi (1964), 270–80.

Dedication. 36. *W. B.*] Gay's name is not attached to the first edition of the play, but his authorship has never been disputed. It is ascribed to him on G4ᵇ of the fourth edition of *The What D'Ye Call It* (1725). In Lintot's Account Book is found the following postscript to a list of payments made to Gay: 'The Mohocks, a Farce, 2l 10s—Sold the Mohocks to him again' (see Nichols, viii, 296). Isaac D'Israeli annotates this item as follows: 'The late Isaac Reed, in the Biog. Dramatica, was uncertain whether Gay was the Author of this unacted Drama. . . . Why Gay repurchased "the Mohocks", remains to be discovered. Was it another joint production with Pope?—The literary copartnership between Pope and Gay, has never been opened to the Curious' (*Quarrels of Authors*, 1814, i. 291 n). D'Israeli goes on to suggest that the dedication is a touch from Pope's finger. The initials 'W. B.' were probably intended for William Burnaby, a friend and collaborator of Dennis's (see Hooker, ii. xviii). In the 1795 edition of Gay's *Works*, 'THE AUTHOR' is substituted for 'W. B.', and the date is omitted.

Prologue. 6. *honest Dicky*] Henry Norris (1665–1730?) was known as 'Jubilee Dicky' from playing Dicky in Farquhar's *Constant Couple, or a Trip to the Jubilee*.

Prologue. 10. *Grimace*] An obsolete use of the word without an article to mean the employment of affected looks or gestures, rather than the 'grimace' itself. Addison writes in the *Spectator* no. 305, 19 Feburary 1712, of the 'Practice of *Political Grimace*' in which the student statesmen are taught 'to nod judiciously, to shrug up their Shoulders in a dubious Case, to connive with either Eye ...'

Dramatis Personae] *Moloch* and *Abaddon*, as T. B. Stroup notes (in 'Gay's Mohocks and Milton', *JEGP*, xlvi, 1947, 164–7), are taken from Milton (*Moloch* from *Paradise Lost*, i. 392; *Abaddon* from *Paradise Regained*, iv. 624). *Whisker* is a lively young gallant. *Myrmidon* is a body-guard or hired ruffian. *Cannibal* suggests Steele's *Spectator* no. 324, 12 March 1712: '... the *Mohock Club*, a Name borrowed it seems from a sort of *Cannibals* in India ...' The title of 'The Emperor of the *Mohocks*' is provided by the same essay. For *Gogmagog*, see Revelation xx. 8. *Moonshine* appears in *A Midsummer Night's Dream*, while *Peg Firebrand* and *Jenny Cracker* are descriptive sexual names analogous to *Doll Tearsheet* in *2 Henry IV*, and distinct from the kind of name given to the prostitutes in *The Beggar's Opera*. The names of the watchmen are taken from descriptions of the weather announced by the watch in the course of duty, and also allude to their dim-wittedness.

i. 1. *Thus far, etc.*] Stroup (*op. cit.*, p. 165) writes of this first speech: 'The description of the activities of these roisterers [is] strongly suggestive of Milton's various descriptions of the battle in heaven as found in *Paradise Lost*, Book VI (see especially lines 15 ff., 99 ff., and 250 ff.).' There may be a further dimension to this parody in a mockery of Dennis's own imitations of Milton, *The Court of Death* (1695), *Britannia Triumphans* (1704), and *The Battle of Ramillia* (1706). Dennis was one of the most obvious admirers of Milton at the time (in *The Grounds of Criticism in Poetry*, 1704, he called *Paradise Lost* 'the greatest Poem that ever was written by Man') and Pope had mocked his praise in *The Critical Specimen* (1711) when he wrote: 'He held ... that they [the Muses] understood the Art of Flying, which they had communicated to himself, *Milton* and two or three others' (Ault, *Prose Works*, p. 11) and later, as a footnote to the above: 'Several Judicious *Criticks* of my Acquaintance seem here to doubt the Matter of Fact, since it cannot be sufficiently prov'd from any of his Writings, that he ever allow'd any Proficient in this Art of Flying Except himself and Milton' (Ault, *Prose Works*, p. 17). Although Stroup's article has convinced many Gay critics (e.g. Peter Lewis, 'Another look at John Gay's "The Mohocks"', *MLR*, lxiii, 1968, 790–3, and Patricia Meyer Spacks, *John Gay*, New York, 1965, p. 129) parallels here between Gay and Milton are quite difficult to find, and Stroup's are not close. It has not been noticed that the first two lines of the play are in fact a close parody of the opening lines of Dryden's *Tyrannick Love* ('Thus far my Arms have with success been crown'd; / And found no stop, or vanquish'd what they found.').

i. 5. *Watchman ... Watchman*] A commonplace device in epic. Cf. *Iliad*, xiv. 131; Furius Bibaculus (Morel, fr. 10); *Aeneid*, x. 361; Lucan, *Bellum Civile*, vii. 572–3; etc. The passage may have been more directly influenced, however, by Fenton's *Cerealia* (1706) which describes the flight of undergraduates before a '*PROCTOR* Armipotent, in stern Deport /

Resembling Turban'd *Turk*' and in which '*SOPH* Rowls on *SOPH* Promiscuous' in the town ditch. See also Pope, *The Rape of the Lock*, i. 101–2, and Gay, 'The Story of Acheloüs and Hercules', 53–4 (Dearing, i. 187).

i. 11. *While each fond Mother ... Son*] Moloch was a god to whom children especially were sacrificed (see *Paradise Lost*, i. 392). That Gay was aware of this is clear from 'The Baboon and the Poultry': 'When barb'rous Moloch was invok'd, / The blood of infants only smoak'd' (*Fables*, Second Series, no. 3, 37–8).

i. 25. *Sashes ... Rage*] Cannibal had been a 'nicker' in his youth. See *Trivia*, iii. 323–4: 'His scatter'd Pence the flying *Nicker* flings, / And with the Copper Show'r the Casement rings.' Gay's own gloss here on '*Nicker*' is: '*Gentleman, who delighted to break windows with* Half-pence.' The activity seems to have been novel a few years before. See the *Tatler* no. 77, 4–6 October 1709: 'I was lately very much surpris'd by an Account of my Maid, who enter'd my Bed-Chamber this Morning in a very great Fright, and told me, She was afraid my Parlour was haunted; for that she had found several Panes of my Windows broken, and the Floor strow'd with Half-pence. I have not yet a full Light into this new Way, but am apt to think, that it is a generous Piece of Wit that some of my Contemporaries make Use of, to break Windows, and leave Money to pay for 'em.'

i. 38. *But come ... begin the Rites*] Stroup notes: 'The last line of the Emperor's speech suggests line, and situation as well, in *Comus*: "Come let us our rights begin, / Tis onely day-light that makes Sin." (lines 124–5).'

i. 39. *By all the Elements, etc.*] This passage is modelled on Dennis's *Appius and Virginia* (1709), p. 9, where Lucius Icilius forces the conspirators to kneel and swear to kill Appius.

i. 46. *That we'll to Virtue ... Pleasure*] Stroup notes: 'This passage suggests not only Satan's famous oath in *Paradise Lost* (iv. 110), "Evil, be thou my good", but the entire role of the satanic hosts in Milton's universe.'

i. 62. *The Macedonian Youth*] Alexander the Great.

i. 69. *Come fill up the Glass*] There is no surviving music for this song.

i. 86. *The Grand Seignior*] Ruler of the Ottoman Empire. Cf. *The Beggar's Opera*, Air LXIX ('*Thus I stand like the* Turk, *with his Doxies around*') and the *Tatler* no. 50, 2–4 August 1709 ('Woman was his Mistress; the whole Sex his Seraglio').

ii. 29. *slit Noses*] See *Journal to Stella*, ii. 508.

ii. 33. *Dancing Masters*] 'Others are called the Dancing-Masters, and teach their Scholars to cut Capers by running Swords thro' their Legs; a new Invention, whether originally *French* I cannot tell' (*Spectator* no. 324, 12 March 1712).

ii. 52. *I saw them hook a Man*] Not entirely a product of Gay's imagination. A report from Dublin, dated 29 March, about the 'Mohocks' there, appeared in the *Supplement* no. 702, 7–9 April 1712: '... last Night a Woman was very ill used, and had a Fish Hook stuck in her Cheek, with a String fastened to it, and so dragg'd about, till these unmerciful Wretches thought fit to cut it out.'

ii. 56. *bleeding*] i.e. as a medical treatment.

ii. 74. *the Guildhall Giant*] Gay made this comparison elsewhere: 'Those Emblems of GOG and MAGOG at the *Guild-Hall* shall fall to the ground, and be broken asunder. With them shall perish the MOHOCKS and HAWCUBITES, and the whole world shall perish with them' (from *An Argument Proving from History, Reason, and Scripture, That the Present Mohocks and Hawkubites are the Gog and Magog mention'd in the Revelations*, a broadside, a copy of which in the British Library, 816 m. 19 (73), a contemporary hand has attributed to Gay. The figures of Gog and Magog were 'about fourteen Feet high finely carved' (*The Foreigner's Guide*, 1729, p. 66).

ii. 112. *nine Mohocks . . . six*] Cf. Falstaff's account of the Gadshill episode (*1 Henry IV*, ii. iv).

ii. 119. *Mohocks in all Reigns*] See T. S. Graves, 'Some Pre-Mohock Clansmen', *SP*, xx (1923), 395–421. This question of the ancestors of the Mohocks is raised by Justice Scruple at iii. 2: 'I am informed that there were *Mohocks* in Queen *Elizabeth*'s Days.' Graves quotes from a·sermon delivered by Gosson in May 1598, referring to 'a prophane company about this Cittie which were called *the damned Crewe*' (Collier, *Bibliographical and Critical Account of the Rarest Books in the English Language*, ii. 72–3). Graves goes on to discuss the Roaring Boys, Tityre-tues, Bugles, Hectors, and Scourers who preceded the Mohocks.

ii. 161. *make you cry . . . like an Italian*] i.e. like a castrato. That this is addressed to Cloudy himself underlines the meaning of the names of the watch.

ii. 165. *Gillian*] i.e. a woman. See Grose, p. 164: 'Every jack has his gillian, or female mate.' Cloudy's wife is called Joan.

ii. 176. *I'll be an Ass*] Cf. *Much Ado About Nothing*, iv. ii.

ii. 180 sd. *A Patch like an half Moon*] 'The President is stiled *Emperor of the Mohocks*; and his Arms are a *Turkish* Crescent, which his Imperial Majesty bears at present in a very extraordinary Manner engraven upon his Forhead' (*Spectator* no. 324).

ii. 189. *Janizary*] '. . . formerly only the Grand Signior's Foot Guard, chosen out of Tributary Christians, taken early from their Parents, and perverted to Mahumetanism, ever accounted their best Soldiers; but now any Prince's or great Man's Guards; also the Mob sometimes so called, and Bailives, Serjeants, Followers, Yeomen, Setters, and any lewd Gang depending upon others' (*Canting Crew*).

ii. 214. *full Bottom*] i.e. a full-bottomed wig. It is possible that this fear of Gentle's for his wig was prompted by the experience of Henry Davenant on Saturday 8 March 1712. According to Lady Strafford, 'coming from the opera they asalted Mr. Davenant and drew there swords upon him, but he took won of them and sent to the round house, but 'tis thought 'twas sombody that would have been known and they gave mony and made their eskape, but what was the great jest about town was they said they had cut of his head of hare' (*The Wentworth Papers, 1705–1739*, ed. James J. Cartwright, 1882, p. 277). Davenant was 'a very giddy-headed young fellow, with some wit' according to John Macky (*Journal to Stella*, ii. 509).

ii. 243. *one could not see ones Hand*] Cf. *1 Henry IV*, II. iv.

iii. 37. *tip the Lyon*] 'Some are celebrated for a happy Dexterity in Tipping the Lion upon them; which is perform'd by squeezing the Nose flat to the Face, and boring out the Eyes with their Fingers' (*Spectator* no. 324).

iii. 127. *good Huswifery*] Cf. *The Wife of Bath* (1713), IV. i. 510.

iii. 136. *how comest thee in this Pickle?*] Cf. Alonso to Trinculo in *The Tempest*, v. i.

iii. 146. *fath*] Obsolete and dialectal form of *faith*.

Epilogue I. 18. *Three days of Grace*] The third night was the author's benefit.

The Wife of Bath (1713)

The Wife of Bath was first performed at Drury Lane on 12 May 1713, and received two performances in the season. Dearing (i. 3) claims that it was produced only once, and as a favour, but there appears to be no evidence for this. It was published on 22 May 1713. See *The Guardian* no. 62, Friday 22 May 1713: 'This Day is Publish'd, The Wife of Bath, a Comedy, written by Mr. Gay, author of The Rural Sports, pr. 1s 6d.'

  Siglum: 13 THE / WIFE of BATH. / A / COMEDY. / As it is Acted at the / THEATRE-ROYAL in *Drury-Lane*, / BY / Her MAJESTY's Servants. / [rule] / By Mr. *GAY* / [rule] / —*Magicis sanos avertere Sacris* / *Experiar Sensus.* Virg. / [rule] / *LONDON:* / Printed for BERNARD LINTOTT, at the *Cross-Keys* between / the Two *Temple-Gates* in *Fleetstreet.* MDCCXIII.

  4°: *A*⁴B-I⁴ [$2 signed (−A)]. The half-title (*A*1ᵃ) reads: 'THE / WIFE of BATH. / A / COMEDY.' and the rest of the page is blank. *Copies consulted*: Bodley Malone 70 (−*A*1); Worc. Plays 6. 1 (4); BL Ashley 3251; Houghton 15460. 286. 10* (A); Houghton 15460. 286. 10* (B). Two further copies, BL 643. i. 20 (7) and Houghton 15460. 286. 5*, have a variant half-title which adds a cut in a round frame of a fat man wearing a laurel crown and holding a jug and a bowl in either hand. Lintot had used this cut before in a publication attacking Richard Bentley's edition of Horace and his conduct as Master of Trinity. See [William King], *Useful Miscellanies, Part I* (1712), p. 40: 'Some Account of HORACE his Behaviour during his Stay at *Trinity-College*, in *Cambridge*. With an ODE to Entreat his Departure thence; Together with a Copy of his Medal, taken out of *Trinity-College* Buttery, by a Well-Wisher to that SOCIETY.' This 'medal' is reproduced, the obverse being identical with the half-title cut in *The Wife of Bath* and the reverse bearing the legend: 'E PROMPTUAR COL: TRIN. CANT.'

Copy-text: 13. Speech-prefixes are silently expanded. Scenes other than the first of each act are not numbered, and I have not interfered with this arrangement. The textual footnotes record editorial emendations of errors in the copy-text and variants from three other texts of the song in Act V, 'There was a Swain full fair', for which the sigla are as follows:

S   Songsheet, BL G312 (39).

MM   In *The Musical Miscellany* (Printed by and for John Watts, 1731), vi. 206.

H   In *The Hive, A Collection of the most Celebrated Songs* (4th edn., 1732), iv. 242, entitled '*The Agreeable NEGATIVE*'.

The extensively revised version of the play published in 1730 gives authority to a number of the emendations, but the text is so different that I have not thought it advisable to refer to it in the textual footnotes.

Motto] '[so that] I may try to subvert the right senses [of my husband] with magical rites' (Virgil, *Eclogues* viii. 66-7).

Epilogue] The Epilogue is entitled simply 'EPILOGUE / Spoken by Mrs. BICKNELL.', Mrs Bicknell having played the title role in the first performance. In 1730, no part of the play was untouched by Gay's revisions save the Epilogue, which was reprinted with a new title: 'EPILOGUE / By a FRIEND.' I believe we need look no further than the obvious friend: Pope. The two had a common interest in Chaucer at this time. Pope had revised Betterton's modernizations for Lintot's *Miscellany* published in May 1712, and was at work on his own version of *The Temple of Fame* during the winter of 1712/13 (*Early Career*, pp. 50, 135); there is the reference to Chaucer in his letter to Gay of 24 December 1712 (Sherburn, i. 169); and he was to publish his translation of 'The Wife of Bath her Prologue' at the end of 1713. In these circumstances the idea itself of using Chaucerian characters and setting may have been suggested directly or indirectly by Pope.

Some of their contemporaries imagined collaboration between the two to have existed as early as this. Leonard Welsted even viewed the play as the first product of Scriblerian drama, though with hindsight and Buttonian bias at the time of the fuss over *Three Hours after Marriage*. In *Palaemon to Celia at Bath; or the Triumvirate* (1717) he wrote:

    ' 'Tis plain', Sir Fopling cry'd, ' 'Tis plainly so:
    For me, I have not writ, of late, you know:
    This province the Triumvirs only claim,
    Crown'd, by *The Wife of Bath*, with thundering fame;
    To see their first essay, the House was full;
    None fear'd a secret to make Chaucer dull:
    This damn'd, absurder projects they disclose,
    And raise preposterous mirth from human woes.'

                    (*Works*, ed. John Nichols, 1787, p. 41)

Scriblerus was not to be launched until the autumn of 1713 (see Irving, p. 96), but Gay had already made several gestures of literary friendship to Pope, including the inscription of *Rural Sports* in January 1713 (and see my comments on the Dedication to *The Mohocks*, p. 406 above). Pope must by this time have felt some reciprocal obligation. His offer to help in his letter to Cromwell of 21 December 1711 may very well have been put to the test by the impending production of Gay's first full-length play. A letter of Pope's to Caryll in February 1713 shows how much he was in demand for this sort of thing: 'I have ten different employments at once that distract me every hour: five or 6 authors have seized upon me, whose pieces of quite different natures I am obliged to consider, or falsify the trust they repose in me' (Sherburn, i. 174). It is interesting to note that of the six prologues and epilogues in the canon, three were written in 1713: 'Prologue to Mr. Addison's Tragedy of *Cato*', 'Prologue Design'd for Mr. Durfy's last Play', and 'Epilogue to *Jane Shore*' (Ault and Butt, pp. 96, 101, 113).

So, Pope was interested in Chaucer; he was interested in helping, and had reason to help, Gay; he was thought to have contributed to the play; and in the year in question wrote three similar theatrical pieces. There is, however, a small piece of purely internal evidence that also suggests Pope's authorship. We find not only that the tone of the Epilogue is like that of Pope's 'The Wife of Bath her Prologue' (after all, the speaker is the same in each case) but that at one point both poems draw directly upon a passage from the Chaucerian original. Compare the Epilogue, 25–8:

> When-ever Heav'n was pleas'd to take my Spouse,
> I never pin'd on Thought of former Vows;
> 'Tis true, I sigh'd, I wept, I sobb'd at first,
> And tore my Hair—as decent Widows—must.

with 'The Wife of Bath her Prologue', 308–10:

> It pleas'd the Lord to take my Spouse at last!
> I tore my Gown, I soil'd my Locks with Dust,
> And beat my Breasts, as wretched Widows—must.
>
> (Tillotson, pp. 71–2)

There is scarcely here the possibility that separate paraphrasers could arrive at such similar verions, for the relevant passage of the original, at lines 587–9, is as follows:

> Whan that my fourthe housbonde was on beere,
> I weep algate and made sory cheere,
> As wyves mooten, for it is usage . . .
>
> (*Works*, ed. F. N. Robinson, 2nd edn., 1957, p. 81)

If Pope is not the author of both poems, it seems unlikely that a mutual friend would borrow so openly. Although written, according to Tillotson (p. 5), about nine years earlier, 'The Wife of Bath her Prologue' was not published until 29 December 1713, in *Poetical Miscellanies . . . Publish'd by Mr. Steele* (1714), over seven months after the publication of the Epilogue to Gay's play. It would seem that, being asked for a Chaucerian epilogue, Pope found it an easy matter to derive one from a Chaucerian paraphrase conveniently to hand, cast in the same persona. It would accord with his customary caution to request anonymity for such a slight piece of work, though it may be noted that he was hardly forthcoming about his larger shares in Gay's plays. Compare the evidence for his authorship of the Prologue to *Three Hours after Marriage* (see p. 438) which has been accepted by all except one of Pope's editors since 1824 (according to Norman Ault, *New Light on Pope*, 1949, p. 221).

i. 19. *Do-puppy, I think*] Gay may be remembering an anecdote about D'Urfey and Charles II ('*my Name is not* Durfey, *but* De-Urfey. *Oh! very good,* said the King, *pray Friend* De-Urfey, *will you help me to a Slice of* De-umplin, *just by you there*', *Pasquin* no. 112, 28 February 1724).

i. 125, 209, 216. *three Midsummer-Eves, Bride Cake, St. Agnes's Night . . . Dumb-Cake*] The action of the play occurs on St. Agnes' Eve, i.e. 20 January (the first performance of the revised version was on 19 January 1730). According to the tradition used by Keats, it was required that girls who wished to know when and whom they should marry should not eat on this day (see T. F. Thiselton Dyer, *British Popular Customs Present and Past*, 1876, p. 46). The dumb-cake ceremony appears more properly to belong to St. Mark's Eve (24 April) when the cake is made and eaten in silence at midnight, the participants walking backwards to bed, hoping to see the image of their future husband hurrying after them (Dyer, p. 199). Putting the bride-cake under the pillow belongs to Midsummer Eve or St. John's Eve (23 June). Dyer (p. 312) quotes the traditional rhyme: 'Two make it, / Two bake it, / Two break it; / and the third must put it under each of their pillows . . .' Myrtilla's remark at line 209, therefore, indicates that she has not been punctilious in her observance of the ceremony.

i. 290. *that Body of yours . . . Key-hole*] The tradition that Chaucer was fat seems to have been late in gaining official currency. 'The first account of Chaucer into which statements of this nature were incorporated was that prefixed to the edition of the poet's works which was started by Urry' (Thomas A. Knott, 'A Bit of Chaucer Mythology', *MP*, viii, 1910, 135–9). John Urry's edition, though begun in 1711, was not published until 1721. The tradition is based on the *Prologue to Sir Thopas*, 696 ff, and *Lenvoy de Chaucer a Scogan*, 31, and seems to have been widely enough known for Lintot to have found it worth re-using his 'Horace' cut (see p. 411 above).

i. 374. *Then who would not be a Bride*] There is no surviving music for this song.

ii. 54. *Pitch-frog*] Antony confuses *frog = scabbard* with *pitchfork*, an implement more familiar to him.

ii. 219. *beware Head . . . throw the Stocking*] An old custom by which on a wedding night the bride's stocking was thrown among the guests: whoever it hit would be the next to be married.

ii. 327. *lend me your Apron and Cap*] Cf. *2 Henry IV*, ii. iv.

ii. 388. *Hic & Ubique*] Here, there, and everywhere.

ii. 421. *the Mairmaid . . . the Dolphin*] Every room in an inn was commonly given an individual name, but Gay here seems to have remembered one of the rooms of the Boar's Head, '. . . my Dolphin-chamber . . .' (*2 Henry IV*, ii. i. 77).

iii. 43. *the Candle burn Blue*] 'If a Candle burne blew, it is a signe there is a spirit in the house' (John Melton, *Astrologaster*, 1620, p. 46).

iii. 87. *Spirits of all Shapes*] The hauntings described by Alison may be compared with those investigated by Joseph Glanvill in *Saducismus Triumphatus* (1681). See also the *Spectator* no. 110, 6 July 1711.

III. 95. *the Headless Horse*] Cf. Gay's 'An Answer to the Sompner's Prologue of Chaucer', 23, and 'A True Story of an Apparition', 18 (Dearing, I. 198, 223).

III. 105. *The Maiden and the Batchelor*] There is no surviving music for this song.

III. 156. *Cunning-men*] Astrologers. In the *Spectator* no. 505, 9 October 1712, Addison is (perhaps jocularly) more distinct in his classification: 'It is not to be conceived how many Wizards, Gypsies and Cunning Men are dispersed through all the Countries and Market-Towns of *Great-Britain*, not to mention the Fortune-Tellers and Astrologers, who live very comfortably upon the Curiosity of several well-disposed Persons in the Cities of *London* and *Westminster*.'

IV. 38. *my Hieroglyphical Cap, etc.*] Cf. the description of the astrologer in John Melton, *Astrologaster* (1620), pp. 8–9.

IV. 77. *the Son of the seventh Son*] Proverbially a doctor. Cf. *Trivia*, ii. 541, and the *Tatler* no. 240, which mentions it as a claim made by quack doctors.

IV. 86. *Green and Hermetical Dragon*] If this is not deliberate nonsense, it may be intended to refer to sulphur in alchemical parlance. Cf. 'the *Male* and *Female Dragon*' (sulphur and mercury) referred to in Swift's *A Tale of a Tub* (in the edition of A. C. Guthkelch and D. Nichol Smith, Oxford, 1958, p. 68. For this interpretation the editors refer to H. S. Redgrove, *Journal of the Alchemical Society*, vol. iii, pt. 18, and James Campbell Brown, *A History of Chemistry*, 1913, p. 161).

IV. 87. *Female Fern-Seed*] '[the fern] was supposed at one time to have neither flower nor seed, the seed which lay on the back of the leaf being so small as to escape the sight of the hasty observer. Hence, probably, proceeding on the fantastic doctrine of signatures, our ancestors derived the notion that those who could obtain and wear this invisible seed would themselves be invisible' (Dyer, *British Popular Customs*, p. 312). See *The London and Lacedemonian Oracles* (Tom Brown, *Works*, 1707–8, iii. 144); '*Quest*. Whether the Herb which we commonly call *Fern*, bears or produces any Seed? And how, or which way, it is to be sav'd?' See also *1 Henry IV*, II. i. 82: 'wee haue the receyte of Ferneseede, wee walke inuisible.'

IV. 89. *The Philosophers Stone*] It is part of Gay's avowed purpose in this play to mock still current superstitions. Even the admired Steele was said to have toyed with the idea of turning base metal into gold. See *Town Talk* no. 4, 6 January 1716, for his 'Epilogue, Spoken at the *Censorium*, on the King's Birth-Day': 'Early in Youth, his Enemies have shewn, / How narrowly he miss'd the Chymic Stone.' See also Mrs. Manley, *Secret Memoirs and Manners of Several Persons of Quality*, [1709], pp. 188–92, and *Three Hours after Marriage*, II. 233 ff.

IV. 158. *my Necromantic Mirror*] 'What frauds may be acted with Glasses, speaking Trumpets, Ventriloquies, Ecchoes, Phosporus, Magic Lanthorns,

&c' ([John Trenchard], *The Natural History of Superstition*, [1709], in *A Collection of Scarce and Valuable Tracts*, 1748, iii. 211). The mirror-scene was popular in plays of the period. Examples may be found in Congreve's *Love for Love*, Farquhar's *The Recruiting Officer*, and Orrery's *Guzman*. Genest (ii. 514) thought that Gay borrowed his from John Wilson's *The Cheats* (1662), v. i, where Mopus arranges for Afterwit to appear in a glass to Beatrice (4th edn., 1693, p. 45). Cf. also Bacon's 'glass prospective' in Greene's *Friar Bacon and Friar Bungay* (1594), a play from which may also have come the suggestion of Doublechin's falling asleep in Act V.

IV. 189. *Zutphin, and Zephin*] A nonsense-phrase, but *Zutphen* is a Dutch town, near Arnhem, and *Zephaniah* an Old Testament prophet.

IV. 203. *hurly-burly*] Gay, writing a magical imprecation in tetrameter couplets, has probably remembered this word from the third line of *Macbeth*.

IV. 454. *Ye Gods! etc.*] Cf. Prior, 'To a Friend on his Nuptials' (*Poetical Works*, ed. H. Bunker Wright and Monroe K. Spears, Oxford, 1959, p. 213): 'When *Jove* lay blest in his *Alcmena*'s Charms, / Three Nights in one he prest her in his Arms', and Tom Brown, 'The Pleasures of Love' (*Works*, 3rd edn., 1710, p. 136): 'Happy Great *Jove*, who in *Alcmaena*'s Arms, / For three full Nights Enjoy'd Loves Charms!' Gay seems to have intended Doggrell's poem to be the quintessence of such hyperbole. For Doggrell's pedantic explication and Chaucer's equivocal comments, compare Bickerstaff and Ned Softly in the *Tatler* no. 163, 22–5 April 1710, and Horace and Crispinus in Jonson's *Poetaster*, III. i.

V. 250. *my youthful Excursions*] Gay seems here to have in mind the encounter between May and Damyan in the tree in *The Merchant's Tale*.

V. 256. *There was a Swain full fair*] Compare the refrain with that in 'Tom and Doll, or the Modest Maid's Delight' in *Wit and Mirth*, ii. 26. The setting of this song by John Barrett survives in a contemporary songsheet, BL G312 (39), and reappeared in *The Musical Miscellany* (1731), vi. 206, even though the song had been omitted from the revision of the play produced in the previous year. Barrett was music master at Christ's Hospital around 1707 and organist at the church of St. Mary-at-Hill around 1710. He composed songs for a number of plays between 1700 and 1715. His 'Ianthe the lovely' is used as Air LV in *The Beggar's Opera*.

The What D'Ye Call It

The What D'Ye Call It was first performed at Drury Lane on 23 February 1715, and received seventeen performances in the season. It was published on 19 March 1715. See *The Evening Post* no. 876, Thursday 17 March to Saturday 19 March 1715.

Sigla: 15a THE | *WHAT D'YE CALL IT :* | A | Tragi-Comi-Pastoral | FARCE. | [rule] | By Mr. *GAY.* | [rule] | —*Spirat Tragicum satis, & feliciter audet.* | Hor. | —*Locus est & pluribus Umbris.* | Hor. | [rule] |

LONDON: | *Printed for* BERNARD LINTOTT between the | two *Temple* Gates in *Fleet-street.*

8° in half-sheets: A⁴a²B-F⁴*G* [$2 signed (−A1, a2, *G*)]. An engraved frontispiece is guarded in facing the title-page (A1). *Copies consulted*: Bodley Malone B.47; Worc ZZ. 9. 42; BL Ashley 769; Houghton 15460. 285. 10; Barnstaple 680/21.

15b As *15a*, but the title-page has 'The SECOND EDITION. | [rule]' inserted between the rule after the motto and the place of publication. The text is not re-set. This 'second edition' was issued on 26 March 1715. See advertisements in *The Post Man* no. 11050, Thursday 24 March to Saturday 26 March 1715, and in *The Evening Post* no. 880, Saturday 26 March to Tuesday 29 March 1715. *Copies consulted*: Bodley Godw. Pamph. 1267; BL 1164. e. 50 (1); Houghton 15460. 285. 15.

16 THE | *WHAT D'YE CALL IT:* | A | Tragi-Comi-Pastoral | FARCE. | As it is acted at the Theatre Royal in | Drury Lane. | [rule] | By Mr. *GAY.* | [rule] | *—Spirat Tragicum satis, & feliciter audet.* | Hor. | *—Locus est & pluribus Umbris.* | Hor. | [rule] | The THIRD EDITION | *LONDON:* | Printed for BERNARD LINTOT between the | two Temple Gates in Fleet-street. 1716.

8° in half-sheets: *A*⁴B-G⁴ [$2 signed (−*A*)]. Frontispiece printed on A1ᵇ. Set from *15*. *Copies consulted*: Bodley Godw. Pamph. 61; Bodley Vet. A4. e. 1043; Magd s. 11. 30; Worc LR5. 4; BL 11775. c. 44; Houghton 15460. 285. 20; Houghton 15460. 285. 22.

20 In *Poems on Several Occasions* (1720), i. 213–68. Set from *15*. *Copies consulted*: Bodley Radcl. d. 60; BL 83. R. 21; BL Ashley 4838; a copy in my possession.

25 THE | *WHAT D'YE CALL IT:* | A | Tragi-Comi-Pastoral | FARCE. | As it is acted at the Theatre Royal in | Drury Lane. | [rule] | By Mr. *GAY.* | [rule] | *—Spirat Tragicum satis, & feliciter audet.* | Hor. | *—Locus est & pluribus Umbris.* | Hor. | [rule] | The FOURTH EDITION | *LONDON:* | Printed for BERNARD LINTOT between the | Temple Gates in Fleet-street. 1725.

8°: A-C⁸G⁴ [$4 signed (−A1, A2, G3, G4)]. Press-figures 1: A5ᵃ, G2ᵇ; 3: A5ᵇ, C1ᵇ, C2ᵇ; 6: B2ᵇ, B7ᵇ. Set from *16*. *Copies consulted*: Bodley Douce P. P. 10; Linc o. 10. 21 (c); BL 11777. aaa. 9; Houghton 15460. 285. 35; Houghton 15460. 285. 37; Barnstaple 680/23.

31 In *Poems on Several Occasions* (2nd edn., 1731), i. 209–60. Set from *20*. *Copies consulted*: Bodley 12 Θ 752; BL 11609. c. 10; a copy in my possession.

Copy-text: *15*, with the authorial emendations of *20* and *31*. Speech-prefixes are silently expanded. The textual footnotes record editorial emendations of errors in the copy-text, all substantive variants in the above editions, and readings from separate texts of the song in II. viii, ' 'Twas when the Seas were roaring', the sigla for which are as follows:

S1   Songsheet BL G. 305. 59.
S2   Songsheet BL H. 1601 (427).

M   In *The Merry Musician; or, a Cure for the Spleen* (Printed by H. Meere, for J. Walsh ... J. Hare ... A. Bettesworth and J. Brown, 1716), i. 297.

E   In *Eloisa to Abelard, written by Mr Pope* (2nd edn., 1720), p. 53.

H   In *The Hive. A Collection of the most Celebrated Songs of our best English Poets* (1724), i. 177.

MP   In *Miscellany Poems, Vol I, by Mr Pope* (5th edn., 1726), p. 225.

MM   In *The Musical Miscellany* (Printed by and for John Watts, 1729), 11. 94, entitled '*The Faithful Maid*'.

Manuscript: I have been unable to trace the present whereabouts of a MS copy of *The What D'Ye Call It* from the Heber Collection (possibly once belonging to Isaac Reed). It appears in the *Catalogue of the Library of the late Richard Heber Esq*, Part 11 (1836), p. 57, and was sold to Rodd for 6*d*. It then appeared in Thorpe's *Catalogue of upwards of fourteen hundred manuscripts* (1836), no. 497: 'Gay's What D'Ye Call It, a Tragi-Comi-Pastoral Farce, *neatly written*, 4to, 3*s*. 6*d*. Contains some passages not printed, particularly a quotation from the Pilgrim's Progress.' This note about unprinted passages is apparently written on the MS and is by James Bindley, although the MS does not appear in Bindley's *Catalogue* (1818–20). The MS was bought from Thorpe by Sir Thomas Phillipps (no. 10097 in the Phillipps Catalogue, 1837) and sold after Phillipps's death by Sotheby's on 20 June 1893. It was purchased for 6*s*. by Sotheran's, who have no records of its movements thereafter.

The Key, and its authorship: I have in my commentary quoted liberally from *A Complete Key To the last New Farce The What D'Ye Call It* (Printed for James Roberts, 1715) so that a word about the vexed question of its authorship is on order. It was published on 30 March, according to a contemporary MS note on one copy, Worc ZZ. 9. 43 (A). In a note to his 1735 *Letters*, Pope said that the *Key* was written by 'one *Griffin* a Player, assisted by *Lewis Theobald*' (Sherburn, i. 288 n). Theobald was, however, friendly to Pope at this time and it was thought that Pope himself wrote it (see Thomas Burnet in the *Grumbler* no. xiv, 3–6 May 1715: 'Another obliges the World with a *Key* to his own *Lock*, in which the *Wards* are all false ... The same Arch Wag, a little before this, gave us a *Compleat Key* to his *Farce*'). Robert Carruthers in his *Life of Alexander Pope* (2nd edn., 1857), p. 155, concurred. George Sherburn in *Early Career*, p. 138, thought that the nature of some of the *Key*'s remarks belied this tradition, but Kerby-Miller in his edition of *The Memoirs of Martinus Scriblerus* (New Haven, 1950), p. 44, argued that some of the *Key*'s identifications are so specific 'that it does not seem possible for a person who did not know what was intended to have discovered the original passages'. He ingeniously argues that it is 'largely, if not wholly, the work of Pope and Gay' and suggests that Griffin was merely used to see it through the press, concluding (p. 45 n): 'Perhaps the biters were bit and some of the reflections in the piece against the authors were slipped in by those who last had the manuscript.' Irving (p. 114) had hinted at some such possibility, but on the whole did not seem to think it unlikely that Theobald was responsible. See R. F. Jones, *Lewis Theobald* (New York, 1919), p. 17: 'In the preface the derivation of the word "burlesque" and the reference to Dr. Bentley are in Theobald's manner. In the wide and various citations from the plays of Shakespeare the author shows a knowledge of the dramatist wholly consistent with Theobald's later accomplishments. His comment on Othello's putting out the light is somewhat similar to the note on the same passage in Theobald's edition of Shakespeare. The high praise of Addison and the reference to the jealousy of Dennis are in keeping with the pronounced opinions in *The Mausoleum* and *The Censor*. Nor is the evinced knowledge of the chorus of Greek tragedy beside the point.' For myself, I find that if one makes some sort of distinction between the severe preface and the key itself, Kerby-Miller's theory seems credible. There are, however, many small details that make it difficult to expound and impossible to prove. Dearing (i. 17) firmly discountenances the idea, and the *Key* is accepted as Griffin's and Theobald's by J. V. Guerinot in *Pamphlet Attacks on Alexander Pope 1711–1744* (1969), p. 29.

The What D'Ye Call It] The title is in the tradition of Shakespeare's *As You Like It* and *Twelfth Night; or, What you Will*, but the *Key* (fol. A4ᵃ) finds a *double entendre:* '. . . *it must needs have been a merry Scene to see a Wit and Witling in deep Meditation, to fix the Name of this laborious Performance. How incontinently did they laugh at the first Thought of the* Distress'd *Damsel! But then how were they transported at the* What d'ye call it! *O dear, remote, dull Hint at Something!—It puts me in mind of the old Song at the* Gossiping, *when facetious* Dad Roger, *after much Dispute about the Babe's Name, Swears it shall be* Cunicula, *"Because there's a pretty Jest in't."* ' The phrase may still have signified a lavatory. See *As You Like It*, III. iii. 66, where Jaques ('Jakes') is so-called.

A Tragi-Comi-Pastoral Farce] Cf. *Hamlet*, II. ii. 377 ff.: 'The best actors in the world, either for tragedy, comedy, history, pastoral, pastoral-comical, historical-pastoral, tragical-historical, tragical-comical-historical-pastoral, scene individable, or poem unlimited . . .' This quotation appears on the title-page of the *Key*. Perhaps in acknowledgment of the satire on meaningless libretti in the Ghost's Song in I. iv, the play was described in a play-bill for a Covent Garden performance on 19 April 1797 as 'A Tragi-Comic, Pastoral, Operatical, Farcical Drama' (Houghton 15461. 703PF*).

Mottoes] 'He has some tragic inspiration, and is happy in his ventures' (Horace, *Epistles* ii. 1. 166). 'There is room, too, for several "shades"' (Horace, *Epistles* i. 5. 28). *Umbrae*, in this context, means the uninvited companions of some important guest. Gay is evidently referring to the five ghosts which Sir Roger had demanded for his play, though there may be a punning reference, more closely aligned to the Horatian sense, to attempts to fill the theatre on Gay's benefit night. See Pope and Gay to Caryll, 3 March 1715: 'Your epistles in Mr. Gay's behalf were sent, attended with a competence of tickets, to my Lord Waldegrave and Mr. Plowden: the effect of 'em I do not yet know' (Sherburn, i. 282).

The Preface] See Pope and Gay to Caryll, 3 March 1715, where Pope writes of the growing approval of the play: 'There are still some grave sober men who cannot be of the general opinion, but the laughers are so much the majority, that Mr. Dennis and one or two more seem determined to undeceive the town at their proper cost, by writing some critical dissertations against it: to encourage them in which laudable design, it is resolved a preface shall be prefixt to the farce in the vindication of the nature and dignity of this new way of writing' (Sherburn, i. 283). The collation of the first edition is A⁴a²B-F⁴G, with the text of the play starting on B1ᵃ. The half-sheet A seems to have been reserved for the title-page, a Preface, and the Dramatis Personae (since the preliminary matter without a Preface would not have needed so much space). Lintot therefore must have been informed of the intention to write a Preface before he began imposition (presumably at about the time of the letter quoted above) but began to print those sheets for which he had copy before he could judge the length of the Preface. The play was published on 19 March.

Hooker (ii. lviii) thinks that the Preface probably reflects upon Dennis, but Dennis, apart from two slighting references in *Remarks upon Mr. Pope's Translation of Homer* (1717), does not seem to have written against *The What D'Ye Call It*, though incidentally he treated it as Pope's work (see his letter to the *Daily Journal* of 11 May 1728, in Hooker, ii. 417). Apart from the *Key*, none of the 'critical dissertations' that Pope expected seem to have materialized. Thomas Burnet attacked the play in the *Grumbler* no. iv, 17 March, and in no. xiv, 3–6 May 1715 (not 2–3 May as Kerby-Miller, p. 43, states), prompted perhaps by Ambrose Philips who was among the writers parodied. The Preface to the *Key* reports the admonitions of '*a certain* tall, well-dress'd *Modern of great Gravity and much Politeness*' who is identified as Philips by Aline Mackenzie Taylor, *Next to Shakespeare: Otway's Venice Preserv'd and The Orphan* (Durham, N. C., 1950), p. 261. For Philips's connection with the *Grumbler*, see *The Poems of Ambrose Philips*, ed. M. G. Segar (Oxford, 1937), pp. xl–xli. Gay, in a letter with Pope to Parnell of 18 March, speaks of 'the fury of Mr. Burnet, or the German Doctor' (*Letters*, p. 21). The latter is Philip Horneck, doctor of *The High-German Doctor* (2 vols., 1719). See the issue of 15 March 1715, which refers to 'a dull *what d'ye call it* . . . under the Auspices of a *Small Wit* and a *clumsey Beau*' (ii. 186). Horneck was later satirized by both in Chapter VI of *The Memoirs of Martinus Scriblerus* (Kerby-Miller, p. 116) and in *The Dunciad* (B), iii. 152.

Preface. 25. *You all have Sense, etc.*] The last line of the play.

Preface. 44. *Tragicus, etc.*] 'In tragedy [a Telephus and Peleus] often grieve in the language of prose' (Horace, *Art of Poetry*, 95).

Preface. 48 n. *Bossu*] See *Monsieur Bossu's Treatise of the Epick Poem* (1695), p. 251: 'Chap. V. *Of* Disguis'd Sentences.' The reference is a dig at Dennis. Hooker (ii. cxxii) writes that Dennis 'approved heartily of Le Bossu'. See also Hooker's note (i. 459–60) to the *Remarks on Prince Arthur*. Dennis followed Le Bossu in feeling that sententious utterances should be short and infrequent.

Preface. 84. *Impius, etc.*] 'Is a godless soldier to hold these well-tilled fallows?' (Virgil, *Eclogues*, i. 70).

Preface. 115. Λιμναῖα, *etc.*] 'Children of the lake and the fountains' (Aristophanes, *The Frogs*, 209–11).

Preface. 118. *the Opera of Dioclesian*] [Thomas Betterton and John Dryden], *The Prophetess: or, the History of Dioclesian. Written by Francis Beaumont and John Fletcher with Alterations and Additions. After the manner of an Opera.* (1690). See its p. 36 for the scene in Act III ('*A Room, Chairs in it, the Hangings and Figures Grotesk*'): 'When they [the figures] have danc'd a while, they go to sit on the Chairs, they slip from 'em, and after joyn in the Dance with 'em.' No swans are mentioned in the printed version of the opera, so it seems likely that Gay is remembering a detail of production, perhaps that of 23 May 1705 (Avery, p. 94) which he could have seen during his first period in London. He used Purcell's melody for the song 'What shall I do to show how much I love her' in *The Prophetess* for Air VI in *The Beggar's Opera*.

Dramatis Personae] Dane Farnsworth Smith gives a perhaps over-detailed interpretation of Gay's evident indebtedness to Shakespeare in the naming of the characters: 'The relation between Peaseblossom and Dock, or Nettle, for that matter, is that of a flower to a weed and the borrowing comes by analogy. Peascod, on the contrary, seems a direct borrowing from Peaseblossom's father, the Peascod mentioned by Bottom [*Midsummer Night's Dream*, III. i. 194], or might even have been suggested by Touchstone's "wooing of a peascod" [*As You Like It*, II. iv. 51–2]. Peter Nettle, if the conjecture offered above does not please, might well be a comic degradation of Peter Quince [*Midsummer Night's Dream*]; and Kitty Carrot, though she could bear only a general relationship to Mustardseed [*Midsummer Night's Dream*] is certainly not far removed in kin from Mistress Squash, to whom Bottom wished to be commended [*Midsummer Night's Dream*, III. i. 193]. In Shakespeare, Mistress Squash is the wife of Master Peascod' (*Plays about the Theatre in England*, New York, 1936, p. 99). *Sir Roger* seems to be borrowed from the pages of the *Spectator*.

Gay wrote to Caryll on 3 March 1715: '... the Parts in general were not so well play'd, as I could have wished, and in particular the Part of Filbert, to speak in the Style of the French Gazette. Penketham did wonders; Mrs Bicknell perform'd miraculously, and there was much honour gained by Miss Younger tho' she was but a Parish Child' (*Letters*, p. 20).

Introductory Scene] Sir Roger and his Christmas play may take some inspiration from Dennis's eccentric friend Richard Norton of Southwick, who was accused of having turned his chapel into a theatre (Davies, *Dramatic Miscellanies*, 1784, iii. 410); invited the players to perform at Southwick (see Dennis's letter of 10 August 1708 in Hooker, ii. 392–3); and left his estate to the poor (Sherburn, iii. 390). The *Key* (p. 32) suggests as much, perhaps with the intention of arousing Dennis's annoyance. Norton is down for six copies in the 'meagre' subscription list to Dennis's *Grounds of Criticism* (Hooker, i. 507).

Introductory Scene. 15. *Jo-Jo-Jonas*] For Penkethman's use of the stammer, see my note to *Three Hours after Marriage*, I. 124.

Introductory Scene. 39. *The Pope's Mitre*] An effigy of the Pope was customarily burned on the anniversary of the Gunpowder Plot, 5 November 1605 (see Grose, p. 266).

Introductory Scene. 79. *old Dog*] *31*'s addition of the article misunderstands the idiom.

Introductory Scene. 83. *your Othello*] Betterton played the role for the last time on 15 September 1709 (Avery, p. 199). Steele had noted his brilliance in the handkerchief scene at some length in the *Tatler* no. 167, 2–4 May 1710. Cf. *The Rape of the Lock*, v. 105–6: 'Not fierce *Othello* in so loud a Strain / Roar'd for the Handkerchief that caus'd his Pain.'

i. i. sd. *Grandmother, Aunt*] 'These two Characters are a Mimickry of *Shakespear* in several of his Historical Plays, particularly of the old *Duchess* of *York* in *Rich.* 3d.' (*Key*, p. 4). See *Richard III*, ii. ii, for the grief of the old Duchess of York and Queen Elizabeth (Grandmother and Aunt to Clarence's children).

i. i. 1. *Here, Thomas Filbert*] 'This seems to be a Jeer on Mr. *Dryden* and other Writers for the Stage, for putting the most vulgar things in Rhyme; as for Instance, in a Passage in the 5th Act of the 2d Part of the *Conquest* of *Granada*' (*Key*, p. 3). The lines referred to are: 'Say for what end you thus in arms appear: / What are your names, and what demand you here?' (v. ii. 37–8).

i. i. 4. *To serve . . . in War*] See my note to i. iv. 1 below.

i. i. 17. *Well, if I must, I must*] 'This looks a-squint at part of a Speech of *Julius Caesar*'s in *Shakespear*, viz.
>   —Seeing Death a necessary End
>   Will come when it will come
And again, upon *Hastings* in *Jane Shore*.
>   But since what must be, must be.—' (*Key*, p. 4).
This line from Rowe is from Act IV of *Jane Shore*. The *Key* misquotes *Julius Caesar*, ii. ii. 34–7, a passage which Gay adapts in *The Distress'd Wife*, iii. iv 11. See also *Three Hours after Marriage*, iii. 550.

i. i. 33. *O Tyrant Justices, etc.*] 'This Repetition of the Misfortunes, of Relations, alludes to the 3d. Act of the *Distress'd Mother*, where *Andromache* repeats all the Misery of *Priam*'s Family:
>   "But how can I forget it? How can I
>   Forget, &c.
And then goes on with a Detail of the *Trojan* Misfortunes.' (*Key*, p. 4). See Ambrose Philips, *The Distress'd Mother*, iii. vi. Gay copied out this speech of the Aunt in a letter to Parnell of 29 January 1715 (*Letters*, p. 17–18).

i. i. 35. *He shall walk in White*] 'This seems to jeer the extravagant Rants in many of Mr. *Dryden*'s Plays particularly, whose Heroes and Heroines, when they can't be satisfied in their Life-time, threaten to become Ghosts and haunt their Enemies in the Night: As twice in the Conquest of *Granada*,
>   *Alman.*—After I am slain
>   I'll send my Ghost to fetch it back again.

But we can't forbear mentioning one more than ordinary Flight of *Melisenda* in *Aurenzebe*, where she threatens her Ghost shall haunt *Morat*'s Ghost.

> "Dying I'll follow your disdainful Soul;
> A Ghost, I'll haunt your Ghost.' (*Key*, p. 5).

See *The Conquest of Granada, Part I*, iv. ii 418 ff. and *Part II*, iii. i. 134–5; and *Aureng-Zebe*, v. i. 380–1.

i. i. 39. *o'er the Hills and far away*] See the note to *The Beggar's Opera*, i. xiii. 42.

i. i. 41. *Ten Pence*] This was the agricultural labourer's average daily wage in the West and North of England at this time. See Elizabeth W. Gilboy, *Wages in Eighteenth Century England* (Cambridge, Mass., 1934).

i. i. 45. *Nisiprises*] Nisi Prius, the trial or hearing of civil causes by judges of assize. See Francis Buller, *An Introduction to the Law relative to Trials at Nisi Prius* (2nd edn., 1775).

i. i. 53. *Behold how low*] 'This is an invidious Parodie on Mr. *Philips*'s *Andromache* in the *Distress'd Mother* where she kneeling to *Pyrrhus* says thus,

> Behold how low, you have reduc'd a Queen.' (*Key*, p. 5)

See *The Distress'd Mother*, iii. vi.

i. i. 54–5. *Thus to your Worships . . . Pew*] 'This reflects both on Mr. *Dryden* and Mr. *Southern*,

> "A Posture only known to Heav'n and you.' (*Key*, p. 5)

I have not been able to trace this quotation to either Dryden or Southerne, and suspect that it is misquoted. No doubt the *Key* has in mind the lines from Southerne's *The Disappointment*: 'Thus in this awful Posture, I invoke / Heav'n, Earth, and Men to evidence my Truth' (Thomas Southerne, *Works*, 1721, i. 119) and from *The Conquest of Granada, Part I*, v. i. 242–3: 'Forgive me; for I had not learn'd to sue / To any thing before, but Heav'n and you.'

i. i. 70. *Hold, Thomas, hold*] 'This Rivalship of *Kitty* and *Dorcas* seems copied from the Rival Queens in *Alexander*, and from *Octavia* and *Cleopatra* in All for Love' (*Key*, p. 6). See Nathaniel Lee, *The Rival Queens, or the Death of Alexander the Great* (1677).

i. i. 71. *Plain-work*] i.e. not fine embroidery. *OED* gives the earliest example of the word to Pope: 'She went, to plain-work, and to purling brooks' ('Epistle to Miss Blount, on her leaving the Town, after the Coronation', 11). The poem was written in 1714.

i. i. 73 ff. *Yes, yes, my Thomas, etc.*] 'They run still upon the *Distress'd Mother* in these two Lines

> "Yes, my Astyanax, we'll go together,
> Together to the Realms of Night we'll go.' (*Key*, p. 6)

See *The Distress'd Mother*, i. v. This couplet had been quoted by Hughes in the *Spectator* no. 541, 20 November 1712. Kitty's proposal is reminiscent of Polly Oliver. See S. Baring-Gould, *English Minstrelsie* (1895–9), vii. Cf. also

Charles Shadwell, *The Humours of the Army* (1713), where Belvedera follows
Wilmot, disguised as an officer.

1. i. 76. *This Arm ... Head*] The *Key* (p. 6) points out the similarities in this
speech to one of Belvidera's. See Thomas Otway, *Venice Preserv'd*, I. 377: 'I'l
make this Arm a Pillow for thy Head.'

1. i. 88. *Canst thou bear Hunger*] Cf. 'Can'st thou bear Cold and Hunger?'
(*Venice Preserv'd*, I. 360). This reference is made by the *Key* (p. 7) and by
Thomas Davies (*Dramatic Miscellanies*, 1785, iii. 234).

1. i. 92. *Take out that Wench, etc.*] 'This is design'd a general Ridicule on Mr.
Rowe's ill Choice of a Subject in his *Jane Shore*; as to the Words they have
allusion to *Glocester*'s in that Play.
                —Turn this Strumpet forth, &c. [Act IV]
... This ridicules the improper Distress of *Jane Shore*'s doing Penance to
move Compassion. [Act V]' (*Key*, pp. 7–8).

1. i. 94 ff. *Ah! Why does Nature, etc.*] 'This sentiment is a ridicule on several of
the like kind in many Plays, as the *Fair Penitent*, &c. but seems more
particularly to aim at *Jane Shore*'s too soft Nature and Complaint, at the
Close of the first Act.
        "Such is the Fate unhappy Women find,
        And such the Curse intail'd upon our kind,

        ——   ——   ——   ——

        While Woman, Sense, and Nature's easy Fool,
        If poor weak Woman Swerve from Virtue's Rule, &c.' (*Key*, p. 8)
The *Key* is followed in this reference by 'J. R.' in a letter printed in *The Life
of Mr. John Gay* (Printed for E. Curll, 1733), p. 34. William Coxe, however,
in his edition of the *Fables* (1798), pp. 67–8, shows that the passage is an
imitation of Guarini (*Il Pastor Fido*, III. iv):
                Se'l peccar è si dolce
                E'l non peccar si necessario, o troppo
                Imperfetta natura
                Che repugna a la legge;
                O troppo dura legge
                Che la natura offendi.
This is translated by Fanshawe as follows:
                O why, if this be such a naturall
                And powerfull passion, was it capitall?
                Nature too frail, that do'st with Law contend!
                Law too severe, that Nature do'st offend!
See *A Critical Edition of Sir Richard Fanshawe's 1647 Translation of Giovanni
Battista Guarini's Il Pastor Fido*, by Walter F. Staton, jr. and William E.
Simeone (Oxford, 1964), p. 78. The passage was often quoted. See the
Guardian no. 28, 13 April 1713: 'In the *Pastor Fido*, a Shepherdess reasons
after an abstruse Philosophical manner about the Violence of Love, and
expostulates with the Gods, *for making Laws so rigorous to restrain us, and at the
same time giving us invincible Desires.*' Pope twice imitated the passage at about

this time. Cf. 'The Universal Prayer' (1715), the suppressed stanza in Lady
Mary Wortley Montagu's autograph (Ault and Butt, p. 147):

> Can Sins of Moments claim ye Rod
> of Everlasting Fires?
> Can those be Sins wth Natures God
> wch Natures selfe inspires?

and 'Chorus of Youths and Virgins' from 'Two Chorus's to the Tragedy of
Brutus' (dated 'before 1716' in Ault and Butt, p. 154), 9–12:

> Why, virtue, doest thou blame desire,
> Which nature has imprest?
> Why, nature, dost thou soonest fire
> The mild and gen'rous breast?

I. ii. 3. *the Deserter*] Desertion could be dealt with under articles of war by
authority of the Mutiny Acts (1 William and Mary c. 5, 1 Anne st. 2 c. 20).
See the note to II. i. 3 below.

I. ii. 5. *Ah! take me, take me too*] The *Key* (p. 8) suggests *The Distress'd Mother*
(III. vi): 'Ah! Sir, recall those Words: What have you said? / If you give up
my Son, Oh give up me.'

I. ii. 12 ff. *O rueful Day! etc.*] The *Key* (p. 8) notes the parody of *Romeo and
Juliet* (the Nurse's exclamations in IV. v). Farnsworth Smith (p. 96) notes
The Shepherd's Week, 'Thursday', 6. See also Ambrose Philips, *Fourth
Pastoral*, 47.

I. ii. 18 ff. *Yet, Justices, etc.*] The *Key* (p. 9) refers to parting speeches of
Southampton to Essex (in John Banks, *The Unhappy Favourite: or, the Earl of
Essex*, 1682), and of Hastings in *Jane Shore* (Act IV).

I. ii. 19. *To break this Ninepence*] Cf. *The Shepherd's Week*, 'Friday', 130:
'Three silver pennies, and a ninepence bent'. This coin must have been one
of the lozenge-shaped Newark siege pieces of 1645 and 1646, which became
popular with Royalist supporters as keepsakes (see Peter Seaby, *The Story of
the English Coinage*, 1952, pp. 70–1). These coins are fairly thin and might
well be broken in half by someone with a strong wrist. They were often bent
up at the edges to prevent them being spent by mistake. Essex Hawker's *The
Wedding, A Tragi-Comi-Pastoral-Farcical Opera* (1729), p. 4, has a sixpence
broken as a love-token, and in some other instances derives from *The What
D'Ye Call It*. See also the milkmaid's use of the shilling whose adventures are
related by Addison in the *Tatler* no. 249, 11 November 1710.

I. ii. 21sd. *She is drawn away, etc.*] The *Key* (p. 10) refers to the separation of
Oroonoko and Imoinda (Thomas Southerne, *Oroonoko*, IV. ii. See *Works*,
1721, ii. 244), and of Artaxerxes and Amestris (Rowe, *The Ambitious Step-
Mother*, 1700, III. ii). See also Banks, *Cyrus the Great*, III. i.

I. ii. 23. *Ah!—Oh!*] The *Key* (p. 10) refers to '*Almeria*'s repeated Sighs at the
Sight of her Father's dead Body.

> Spouting Veins and mangled Flesh! Oh, Oh!—'

See William Congreve, *The Mourning Bride*, Act V.

I. iv. 1. *the Press-Act*] The first of a long series of Recruiting Acts was passed in the 1703/4 session (Sir John F. Fortescue, *A History of the British Army*, 1899, p. 566). The JPs were empowered to levy all able-bodied men without visible employment or means of sustenance, and, by 1707, the parish received £3 for every such recruit. The Acts became open to abuses. 'The Recruiting Acts were seized on as a chance to rid the countryside of poachers and suspected persons, and to pay off personal or political scores' (Trevelyan, i. 219).

i. iv. 2sd. *A Ghost rises*] The *Key* (p. 11) refers to *Richard III* (v. iii. 131 ff.) for the source of the ghosts. It also seems likely that Gay had in mind the apparitions in *Macbeth* (IV. i. 69 ff.), since the bloody child who says 'none of woman born / Shall harm Macbeth' is intended for an embryo, or, rather, a Caesarian new-born. Sir Roger parodies *Macbeth* at i. iv. 13. See the following notes.

i. iv. 8 sd. *A Ghost of an Embryo*] See preceding note. Chrysander thought the embryo was a hit at Handel's *Amadis de Gaul*: '... erscheint der Geist eines ungebornen Kindes, was auf Ritter Dardanus zielt' (*G. F. Händel*, Leipzig, 1858–67, i. 424). The passage may be by Pope: 'Mr. Pope brought some of the *What D'Ye Call It* in his own handwriting to Cibber, the part about the miscarriage in particular: not much. When it was read to the players, Mr. Pope read it though Gay was by. Gay always used to read his own plays' (Spence, i. 103. See also Colley Cibber, *A Letter from Mr. Cibber to Mr. Pope*, 1742, p. 21).

i. iv. 13. *Why do you shake, etc.*] Cf. *Macbeth*, III. iv 50–1: 'Thou canst not say, I did it: never shake / Thy gory locks at me.' The *Key* (p. 12) misquotes Shakespeare here: 'These are almost *Shakespear*'s own Words in *Mackbeth*, speaking to *Banquo*'s Ghost.

> Why dost thou shake thy goary Locks at me,
> Thou can'st not say I did it—'

This need not imply that Gay and the *Key* are alluding to a current adaptation of *Macbeth*. Davenant does not change these lines (see Christopher Spencer, *Davenant's Macbeth from the Yale Manuscript*, New Haven, 1961, p. 116).

i. iv. 16 ff. *Ye Goblins and Fairys, etc.*] This song bears a close formal similarity to the 'Ode, for Musick, on the Longitude' (*Miscellanies, The Last Volume*, 1727, p. 172), not reprinted since the editions of the *Miscellanies. The Fourth Volume. Consisting of Verses ...* (1742):

RECITATIVO
The Longitude mist on
By wicked *Will. Whiston*.
And not better hit on
By good Master *Ditton*.
RITORNELLO
So *Ditton* and *Whiston*
May both be bep-st on;
And *Whiston* and *Ditton*
May both be besh-t on.

> Sing *Ditton*,
> Besh-t on;
> And *Whiston*,
> Bep-st on.
> Sing *Ditton* and *Whiston*,
> And *Whiston* and *Ditton*,
> Besh-t and bep-st on,
> Bep-st and besh-t on.
>   *DA CAPO*

See Gay to Caryll in April 1715: 'Mr Pope owes all his skill in Astronomy & particulary in the revolution of Eclipses to him [Titcomb] and Mr Whiston, so celebrated of late for his discovery of the Longitude in an extraordinary Copy of verses which you hear'd when you were last in Town' (*Letters*, p. 23). *A New Method for discovering the Longitude both at Sea and Land* by W. Whiston and H. Ditton was published in July 1714, and a revised edition appeared in mid-April 1715. Spence's misreading of his own notes led him to ascribe the authorship of the 'Ode' to Gay, when in fact Pope had told him that Gay wrote the prose satire, 'A True and Faithful Narrative of What Passed in London', printed in the 1732 volume of Pope's and Swift's *Miscellanies* (see James M. Osborn, '"That on Whiston" by John Gay', *PBSA*, lvi, 1962, 73–8, and C. J. Rawson, *PBSA*, lvii, 1963, 91–2). The 'Ode', with its overt parody of Italian opera libretti, might be by Pope. It was attributed to him in a copy of the *Miscellanies* (1727) at Welbeck, which belonged to the Earl of Oxford's daughter. Faber (p. xxxiv) inclines towards Arbuthnot as its author, on grounds both of scatology and preoccupation with Whiston-baiting.

Identity of authorship of the song and the 'Ode' is probable. The metre, repetitions, and inversions are similar, and although the Italian musical directions have been abandoned in the song, the *Key* (pp. 12–13) has no doubt that it alludes to 'our Modern *Opera's*, where a parcel of unmeaning Words are introduc'd meerly to support the Air'. Parody of this sort was not new (see, for instance, Richard Estcourt, *Prunella*, performed 12 February 1708). The music for the song, which unfortunately does not survive, may also have been of a burlesque kind; that the only existing music for the play is attributed to Handel might lead to some curious conjectures (see note to II. viii. 22). As for the words, a reason for believing that Gay was, after all, responsible is the similarity of Orpheus's song in the Prologue to D'Urfey's *Wonders in the Sun* (1706), p. 8: 'The Thrushes / From Bushes, / And Prickets / From Thickets, / Come whisk it, / And frisk it, / And skip it, / And trip it. / In honour of Love and the Muses.' Gay's use of D'Urfey is well-known (see A. E. H. Swaen, 'The Airs and Tunes of John Gay's *Beggar's Opera*', *Anglia*, xliii, 1919, 152–90, and 'The Airs and Tunes of John Gay's *Polly*', *Anglia*, lx, 1936, 403–22, and William D. Ellis, jr., 'Thomas D'Urfey, The Pope–Philips Quarrel, and *The Shepherd's Week*', *PMLA*, lxxiv, 1959, 203–12). Gay mentions *Wonders in the Sun* in a note to line 11 of 'Wednesday' in *The Shepherd's Week* (1714), and alludes to it in the Preface to *The What D'Ye Call It* itself (line 116). The musical, scatological and anti-scientific subject-matter of the 'Ode' is thoroughly Scriblerian; the metrical and stylistic elements which it has in common with the song appear to derive from D'Urfey or another semi-popular source. If the 'Ode' is earlier than the song, then the latter acquires overtones of a private joke. If the song is earlier than the 'Ode', then the arguments for Gay's having initiated the form are slightly stronger.

II. i. 1. *Stand off there, etc.*] 'The Humour of this is nothing but a Ridicule of the general *Rhiming* Orders in our Poets, where the meanest Trifles are supported by the Pomp of the Numbers. As for Instance, that in *Otway*'s *Alcibiades* of the same Nature.

    Look that y'r Care and Diligence be great,
      See the Guards doubled, and the Cent'nels set.' (*Key* p. 13)
The reference is to a speech of the Captain of the Guards, II. 216–17.

II. i. 3. *Prime all your Firelocks*] 'Prior to the passing of the first Mutiny Act (1689) and the consequent legalisation of military modes of execution in *this country*, the punishment of death was inflicted by the rope on soldiers as on any other felons under civil law, but after that era death for military offences, not of a disgraceful character, was effected by shooting' (Clifford Walton, *History of the British Standing Army 1660 to 1700*, 1894, p. 555). Although desertion seems to have been considered 'disgraceful', after this Act there were many instances of death by shooting for desertion.

II. i. 5 ff. *O Fellow-Soldiers, etc.*] 'This pathetical *Exordium* of *Tim*'s is a debasing of those solemn beginnings commonly used by all Tragical Writers, and is not unlike making one of *Paul Lorrain*'s Saints take his leave of the World in the old *Roman* strain. *Anthony*'s Speech in *Shakespear* seems most in the Writers View.—

    Friends, Romans, Country-men—' (*Key*, p. 13).
See *Julius Caesar*, III. ii. The *Key* (pp. 13–15) continues by finding distant parallels throughout this speech of Peascod's with Banks's *The Unhappy Favourite*, Rowe's *Jane Shore* and Shakespeare's *Henry VIII*.

II. i. 23–4. *The Pilgrim's . . . Progress*] 'These Lines are the most unjust Abuse of the Famous *Cato*. A Play whose Scenary is so universally known, that 'tis almost Impertinent to remember the Reader, that in the Fifth Act thereof, preparatory to his design'd Murther of himself, the *Hero* is introduc'd reading the Treatise of *Plato* on the Immortality of the Soul, and from which he draws the finest Soliloquy, that ever appear'd on the Stage.

    It must be so, —*Plato* thou reason'st well;
The Authors had design'd to change this Verse conformable to their Thought of the *Pilgrim's Progress*, to
      —*Bunyan*, thou reason'st well:
But on a Second Deliberation they found the *Parodie* so flagrant, that they expected it would entail the Curse of an Audience, and for that reason grew more Modest' (*Key*, p. 16). The untraced manuscript of the play (see above, p. 418) contained unpublished passages, including a quotation from *The Pilgrim's Progress*.

II. i. 25. *Eighth Edi-ti-on*] *Cato* had at the time run to eight editions, all of which had appeared in 1713 (the eighth edition of Boddington's Bunyan was published in 1682). The joke was borrowed by Thomas Tickell in 'A Poem in Praise of the Hornbook' (1726), 71 ff.

II. ii. 1. *What Whining's this*] 'This alludes to *Pierre's* check of *Jaffier* in *Venice Preserv'd*, when he comes to beg pardon for having betray'd his Friend.

      Pierr. What whining Monk art thou?—' (*Key*, p. 17).
See *Venice Preserv'd*, IV. 287.

II. ii. 3. *My Friend in Ropes*] 'This is likewise a Ridicule of the generous Compassion of *Pierre*, in the same Play, when *Jaffier* is presented to him bound.

      Pierr. My Friend too bound!' (*Key*, p. 17).
See *Venice Preserv'd*, IV. 249.

II. ii. 8. *For what is Means*] 'This is design'd to rob Mr. *Phillips* of a fine Line of *Cephisa* to *Andromache* in the *Distress'd Mother*.

      Life is not worth my Care when you are gone. [IV. viii]
Only the word *Kitty* has broke into the Harmony of the Original's Monosyllables, an Indignity worthy of the resentments of so polite a Tragick Poet! Or as in Mr. *Dryden's Aurenzebe*.

      Death's Life with you; without you Death to Live. [IV. i]' (*Key*, p. 18).

II. iii. 4. *In a white Sheet*] Cf. 'Memoirs of P. P. Clerk of this Parish' (*EC*, x. 440).

II. iii. 13. *O Brother, Brother!*] 'This is an Imitation of the Scene where *Alicia* running in stops *Ratcliffe* in the Execution of her belov'd *Hastings*.

      Alic. Stand off, and let me pass.—
      ————————————————Stop, a Minute:
      O *Hastings! Hastings!*—' (*Key*, p. 19)
See *Jane Shore*, IV. i.

II. iii. 15. *The Squire betray'd me*] Cf. *The Shepherd's Week*, 'Wednesday', 75–86:

      Ah! didst thou know what Proffers I withstood,
      When late I met the *Squire* in yonder Wood!
      To me he sped, regardless of his Game,
      While all my Cheek was glowing red with Shame;
      My Lip he kiss'd, and prais'd my healthful Look,
      Then from his Purse of Silk a *Guinea* took,
      Into my Hand he forc'd the tempting Gold,
      While I with modest struggling broke his Hold.
      He swore that *Dick* in Liv'ry strip'd with Lace,
      Should wed me soon to keep me from Disgrace;
      But I nor Footman priz'd nor golden Fee,
      For what is Lace or Gold compar'd to thee?

II. iii. 19. *thy base-born Child*] Cf. 'Memoirs of P. P. Clerk of this Parish' (*EC*, x. 437).

II. iv. 3–4. *O save me, Sergeant . . . I cannot die*] 'This is another merry Specimen of *Andromache*'s tenderness for her Son; but the Wits have carried it further than the Author to raise the Ridicule; for she only says,

"Tell him, I love my Son to such excess,—

with a passionate Break, which they have supply'd with,

———————————————————— *I cannot dye.*

According to their usual Candor' (*Key*, pp. 19–20).

II. iv. 9–10. *if ever Father . . . Market-day*] Peascod was bound to provide for his bastard daughter, according to 18 Elizabeth c. 3. See Richard Burn, *The History of the Poor Laws* (1764), p. 80: 'two justices . . . shall . . . take order for the keeping of every such bastard child, by charging such mother or reputed father with the payment of money weekly, or other sustentation for the relief of such child, in such wise as they shall think meet and convenient.'

II. iv. 12. *this Badge*] '. . . the pointing to the Badge, &c. seems a jocular Imitation of *Boabdelin*'s pointing to the Scarff on *Almanzor*'s Arm, which was given him by *Almahide*. *Vid. Conq.* of *Granad.* part 2. Act. 3' (*Key*, p. 20). The badging of paupers was authorized by 8 & 9 William III c. 30. See Burn, *History of the Poor Laws*, p. 99: 'And to the end that the money raised only for the relief of such as are impotent and poor, may not be misapplied and consumed by the idle, sturdy, and disorderly beggars; every person put upon the collection, shall upon the shoulder of the right sleeve upon the uppermost garment, wear a badge of a large roman P together with the first letter of the name of the parish or place where he inhabits, cut in red or blue cloth.' It was used more and more during the eighteenth century as a deterrent, to avoid claims on parish relief (see Sir Frederic Morton Eden, *The State of the Poor*, 1928, pp. 274, 314, 343).

II. iv. 13–14. *Church-Wardens . . . Silver*] The Churchwardens, the official overseers of the poor, were meant to be accountable annually to the two justices, but clearly there was not always effective control. See Burn, *History of the Poor Laws*, p. 86.

II. iv. 17. *Worsted spun*] See Burn, *History of the Poor Laws*, pp. 81 ff.

II. iv. 21. *O that I had by Charity been bred!*] '*Peascod* is here introduc'd, as charging the Disaster of his Death on the height of his Station, *viz.*—a *Carter*: And wishing he had been brought up in meaner Circumstances. This is aim'd at the *Princes* and *Heroines* in Tragedy, who being involv'd in unexpected Misfortunes, wish they had never known the Plagues of Grandeur, but been blest in a low and peaceable Obscurity' (*Key*, p. 21).

II. iv. 24. *Sol-fa*] Cf. 'Memoirs of P. P. Clerk of this Parish' (*EC*, x. 440): 'Now was our over-abundant quaver and trilling done away, and in lieu thereof was instituted the Sol-fa, in such guise as is sung in his Majesty's Chapel.' The sol-fa system identifies each note in the scale (not pitch) by a syllable based on words in an eighth-century hymn by Paulus Diaconus. The syllables were a notation intended to facilitate sight-reading. See *A New and Easie Method to learn to Sing by Book* (1686) and W. G. McNaught, 'The History and Uses of the Sol-Fa Syllables', *PMA* (1892/3), 35–49.

II. iv. 30. *Beware of Papishes, etc.*] '...*Popery* and *Knitting* are so admirably well put together, as things of equal *Importance*, that any Man, who has but read the Celebrated *Rape of the Lock*, cannot be at a loss for the Author of these Lines' (*Key*, p. 22).

II. v. 2. *And I*] 'This is only design'd to sneer at the frequent short Breaks in some Tragick Lines; as in *Venice preserv'd*,

Pier. Again: Who's that?
Spin. 'Twas I.
The. And I.
Rev. And I.
Eli. And all.

[III. ii. 442–6, but the *Key*'s arrangement creates an alexandrine] Or as in *Dennis*'s *Appius* and *Virginia*;

L. Icil. I want not one by Heaven!
M. Icil. Nor I.
C. Num. Nor I
P. Num. Nor I. [Act I]'

(*Key*, p. 23).

II. v. 4. *When I am dead, etc.*] The *Key* (p. 23) suggests Banks as the origin of this line, but Pope annotated his own copy of the *Key* to the effect that the line is a burlesque of *Cato*, where Cato says of his son, 'When I am dead, be sure thou place his urn near mine' (see *EC*, vi. 225).

II. v. 6. *bore the Bell*] Cf. Pope, 'The Wife of Bath her Prologue' (1714), 211: 'In Country Dances still I bore the Bell.' The metaphor is from the bell-wether, leader of the flock. See also *The Wife of Bath*, IV. 66.

II. v. 7. *Say, is it fitting, etc.*] Cf. *Venice Preserv'd*, v. iii. 445–51:

Pierr. Is't fit a Souldier, who has liv'd with Honour,
       Fought Nations Quarrels, and bin Crown'd with Conquest,
       Be expos'd a common Carcass on a Wheel?
Jaff. Hah!
Pierr. Speak! is't fitting?
Jaff. Fitting?
Pierr. Yes, is't fitting?

This is remarked by the *Key* (pp. 24–5) and by 'J. R.' in *The Life of Mr. John Gay* (Printed for E. Curll, 1733), p. 34.

II. v. 11. *'Tis hard, 'tis wond'rous hard!*] The *Key* (p. 25) points out the similarity to *Othello*, I. iii: 'She swore in faith 'twas strange: 'twas passing strange, / 'Twas pittiful: 'twas wondrous pittiful.'

II. v. 13. *Take you my 'Bacco Box, etc.*] 'This is a Banter on *Mary* Queen of *Scots*, who just before her Execution disposes of her things among her Servants' (*Key*, pp. 25–6). See John Banks, *The Albion Queens, or the Death of Mary Queen of Scotland* (1704), p. 59: '. . . thou *Melvil*, take this Ring . . .' etc.

II. vi. 2. *a Reprieve*] 'This Reflection is general, and exposes the too sudden and unprepar'd *Peripetias* in most *Tragedies*. If this had been the Conduct of the *Farce Writers* throughout their *Scenes*, their Design, instead of deserving Censure, would have merited Applause' (*Key*, p. 26).

II. vii. 7. *Thus said Sir John*] Presumably Sir John Holt, Lord Chief Justice of England from 1688 to 1710, whose judgments were collected in *Modern Cases Argued and Adjudged in the Court of Queen's-Bench at Westminster, in the Second and Third Years of Queen Anne, etc* (1713) and in *A Report of Cases, etc* (1737) and *A Report of all the Cases, etc* (1738). I have not, however, been able to locate any judgment of his that bears upon the distinction between stealing a horse and a mare. The felonious stealing of horses, geldings, and mares is not so distinguished by, for example, 1 Edward VI c. 12 and 2 & 3 Edward VI c. 33, acts by which horse-stealers lost their benefit of clergy (see William Hawkins, *A Treatise of the Pleas of the Crown*, 1716, ii. 344–5, 350). It may possibly be that the theft of a mare remained a capital felony, whereas that of a horse could in practice be treated more lightly. Sir John Fortescue, for example, notes a case of flogging for horse-stealing in 1712 (*A History of the British Army*, 1899, p. 586). Gay clearly finds this equivocation (actual or invented) an outrageous piece of legal comedy. These lines may be compared with the parody of legal jargon in 'A Specimen of Scriblerus's Reports. Stradling versus Stiles' (written by Pope and William Fortescue. See *EC*, x. 430), a piece deeply concerned with horses that turn out to be mares. The Scriblerians were inclined to mount such attacks on the absurdities of the law (see Kerby-Miller, pp. 307 ff.).

II. viii. sd. *Chorus of Sighs and Groans*] 'This Chorus, it must be owned, is entirely new, design'd perhaps to laugh at the odd *Chorus's* of the Antients, and their Chiming in with the Words of the Actors' (*Key*, p. 28).

II. viii. 1. *Dear happy Fields, farewell*] Cf. Milton, *Paradise Lost*, i. 249: 'Farewel happy Fields ...' The *Key* (p. 27) mentions *Othello*, III. iii; 'Farewell the tranquil mind ...' etc. Farnsworth Smith refers to *The Shepherd's Week*, 'Wednesday', 99: 'Farewell ye woods, ye meads, ye streams that flow.'

II. viii. 22. *'Twas when the Seas were roaring*] See Cowper's letter to the Revd. W. Unwin, 4 August 1783: 'What can be prettier than Gay's ballad, or rather Swift's, Arbuthnot's, Pope's and Gay's, in the *What d'ye Call It*—"'Twas when the seas were roaring"? I have been well informed that they all contributed, and that the most celebrated association of clever fellows this country ever saw did not think it beneath them to unite their strength and abilities in the composition of a song' (*The Correspondence of William Cowper*, ed. Thomas Wright, 1904, ii. 92). Kerby-Miller (p. 43 n.) notes: 'Mr. Sherburn believes that Cowper's source may have been his aunt, Judith Cowper Madan, who was a friend and correspondent of Pope's.' Bodley MS Montagu e. 13 fol. 22, a collection of songs transcribed by Mary and John Tadwell, includes an additional stanza after stanza 4, though this is of no authority. The ballad was translated into Latin as 'Nympha Lugens' in *Poemata, partim reddita, partim scripta, a Martino Madan* (1784), p. 26. The ballad was immediately popular, and was parodied in both Jacobite and anti-Jacobite literature (see Coxe's edition of the *Fables*, p. 69 n.; *Mughouse Diversion*, 2nd edn., 1717, p. 30; Bodley Douce Ballads 4, fol. 21a). The *Key* (p. 28) suggests that the ballad is 'An Imitation of Mr. *Rowe's Collin's Complaint*, tho' not near so beautiful'. See also C. F. Burgess, 'Gay's " 'Twas when the Seas were Roaring" and Chaucer's "Franklyn's Tale"; A Borrowing', *N & Q*, ccvii (1962), 454–5.

The setting of this song has been attributed to Handel. The attribution was not made until 1729 (In John Watts's *The Musical Miscellany*, ii. 94) after the success of *The Beggar's Opera*, in which Gay re-used the setting as Air XXVIII. Although evidence that Handel was indeed the composer of this setting is lacking, the attribution has been accepted. Schultz, for instance, writes (p. 169): 'The music is by Handel', and some Handel scholars make his authorship more credible by assuming that the setting, and indeed the ballad, first appeared in the 1725 production of the play, seven years after Gay and Handel collaborated in *Acis and Galatea*. This false assumption was no doubt prompted by February 1715 seeming an impossibly early date for such a collaboration, and by the apparent absence of dated printings of the setting before 1729, when *The Musical Miscellany* made the attribution. See Otto Erich Deutsch, *Handel, A documentary biography* (1955), p. 179: 'At a revival of John Gay's farce *The What d'ye Call it*, at Drury Lane Theatre on 30th April 1725, the ballad " 'Twas when the seas were roaring", generally attributed to Handel, is sung. This "comick, tragick, pastorall Farce" was produced in 1715 at Drury Lane. The 1725 libretto does not mention Handel as the composer of the new [*sic*] ballad. It appeared, with the music, in single sheet folio editions, and in song collections. After it had been inserted into the *Beggar's Opera* (cf. 29th January 1728), Handel's name was added in 1729 in Vol. II of the *Musical Miscellany*, published by John Watts, under the title *The Faithful Maid*.' William C. Smith's dating of the two British Library songsheets of the setting (BL H. 1601. 427 as 'c. 1725' and BL G. 305. 59 as 'c. 1730') in his *Handel, A Descriptive Catalogue of the Early Editions* (1960), p. 202, seems in accord with Deutsch. There is an early edition of the setting, however, which has not previously been recorded. This is in *The Merry Musician; or, a Cure for the Spleen* (Printed by H. Meere, for J. Walsh and others, 1716), i. 297, and textual evidence suggests that it was set from a songsheet. We must presume, then, that this setting is the setting used at Drury Lane in the previous year. The question of Handel's authorship must remain undecided. It is possible, of course, that the tune was not acquired directly from Handel, or even with his acquiescence. It is possible that Gay and Handel had met by February 1715 (see Introduction, p. 32), even though collaboration at that date in a work containing parody of Italian opera (see the note to i. iv. 16 above) is not entirely easy to contemplate. William Barclay Squire, 'Handel in Contemporary Song-Books', *Musical Antiquary*, January 1913, 110-11, lists the song under 'Doubtful and spurious compositions'. In the absence of internal, or satisfactory external, evidence, I would prefer, with Faber (p. 357) and Irving (p. 116), merely to note that the attribution has been made.

New music for *The What D'Ye Call It* was composed by Johann Friedrich Lampe for a production at Covent Garden on 4 April 1745, but this music does not seem to have survived. Lampe came to London in about 1725, and began to write for the stage in 1730. He wrote the music for Henry Carey's *Amelia*, *The Dragon of Wantley*, and *Chrononhotonthologos*, and also for the opera *Dione*, based on Gay and produced at the Haymarket on 23 February 1733, less than three months after Gay's death. There is no evidence that Gay wrote any of the words for the additional songs in this opera. In about 1755 (Grove's dating), ''Twas when the Seas were roaring' appeared as no. ix of *Twelve Songs Set by William Jackson of Exeter*. Jackson's setting was used in a performance at Drury Lane on 20 April 1772 and appeared under the title 'Susanna' in *Vocal Music* (1771–2), i. 197–9. J. A. Dahmen also set the song (no. 8 in his *Twelve Canzonets*). There are, incidentally, two modern settings of the whole play as a one-act opera, by Frederick May and Frank Mumby (Leeds, 1957) and by Phyllis Tate, with a libretto adapted by V. C. Clinton-Baddeley (1966).

The popularity of ''Twas when the Seas were roaring' is well-attested. Despite the Lampe and Jackson settings mentioned above, however, it was the earliest setting that continued to appear in the song-books till late in the century, and I should here like to record all the editions of the original music that I have come across: Songsheets BL G. 305. 59 and BL H. 1601. 427; *The Merry Musician* (Walsh and Hare, 1716), i. 297; *A Collection of Sea Songs* (Walsh and Hare, [1720?]), p. 10; *Musical Miscellany* (Watts, 1729), ii. 94; *A Choice Collection of English Songs* (Walsh, [1731?]), no. 22; *British Melody, or the Musical Magazine* (1739), no. 58; *The Merry Companion: or, Universal Songster* (2nd edn., 1742); *Musical Entertainer* (n. d.), i. 53; *Universal Harmony* (n. d.), p. 54; *Calliope* (Published by John Simpson, n. d.), i. 168; *Amaryllis* (n. d.), i. 79; *Muses Delight* (n. d.), p. 176; *Vocal Music* (n. d.), i. 13 (mentioned by [W. Aikin], *Essays on Song-writing*, [1762], p. 62); *Vocal Enchantress* (1783), p. 125.

II. viii. 66sd. *Whispers and gives her a Penknife*] The *Key* (p. 28) refers to *Venice Preserv'd*, v. iii, where Pierre whispers to Jaffier to stab him and save him from a dishonourable death.

II. viii. 68. *Thus then I strike, etc.*] The *Key* (p. 28) refers again to Otway, and for the latter part of the line to Dryden and Southerne: 'And yet I cannot look on you, and kill you, / Pray turn your face' (Ventidius to Antony in *All for Love*, v. i. 326–7) and 'I'll turn my Face away, and do it so' (Oroonoko about to kill Imoinda in *Oroonoko*, Act v, *Works*, ii. 263).

II. viii. 69. *'Tis shameless, etc.*] Cf. *The Shepherd's Week*, 'Wednesday', 101–4: 'What, shall I fall as squeaking Pigs have dy'd! / No—To some Tree this Carcass I'll suspend,— / But worrying Curs find such untimely End!'

II. viii. 80. *Hah!—I am turn'd a Stream, etc.*] 'The Reader need only refer to any Tragical Madness for this Passage, if it was intended as a Banter on Mr. *Dryden's Nourmahal* in *Aurenzebe* it is witty enough. It is so very ridiculous indeed, that we can't help quoting it.

Nourmahal. I burn, I more than burn; I'm all on Fire:
See how my Mouth and Nostrils flame expire.
I'll not come near my self.—
Now I'm a burning Lake, it rowls, and flows,
I'll rush, and pour it all upon my Foes. [*Aureng-Zebe*, v. i. 640 ff.].

But in justice to the *Farce* we can't help taking notice of that delicate piece of *Smut* of a Girl being turned into a Stream, and the pretty pointing of the *Actress* when she repeats.

> —*look all below;*
> *It flows, and flows, and will for ever flow.*
> O lovely Diabetes!—' (*Key*, p. 30).

II. viii. 81. *It flows . . . flow*] Cf. Horace, *Epistles* i. 2. 42–3: 'rusticus exspectat dum defluat amnis, at ille / labitur et labetur in omne volubilis aevum.'

II. viii. 84–5. *Bagpipes in Butter, etc.*] The *Key* (pp. 30–1) refers to *Venice Preserv'd*, v. iii. 368–9: 'Murmuring streams, soft shades, and springing flowers, / Lutes, laurels, seas of milk, and ships of amber.'

Final Scene. 41. *So comes a Reck'ning, etc.*] A quotation? See *N & Q*, clxxiv (1938), p. 189, where information is required on 'Men laugh and jest till the feast is o'er; / Then the reckoning comes, and they laugh no more.' The query is answered in the same volume, p. 233, where the passage is identified as Gay's, misquoted. It may be Gay's source, however, or the source may be a similar proverb. Cf. 'The feast is good until the reck'ning come' (Quarles, *A Feast of Worms*, 1620, Sect. 6, Med. 6).

Final Scene. 50. *What a plague, am I trick'd then?*] 'At the Conclusion, the Trick of Sir *Roger*'s Son being really Married, by the Father's Consent, yet without his suspecting it, may be borrowed from the Imposition put on the *Old Knight*, thro' his own means, in the late *Farce* of the *Slip*; unless it glances at a more Modern Marriage' (*Key*, p. 32). Christopher Bullock's *The Slip*, in which Trickwell extorts money and jewels from his uncle during a play which he performs, was produced at Lincoln's Inn Fields on 3 February 1715. The trick wedding itself was a familiar enough *coûp de théâtre*. Settle's *The City Ramble; or, A Playhouse Wedding* was produced at Drury Lane on 17 August 1711, and the anonymous *The Apparition; or, The Sham Wedding* on 25 November 1713. *The What D'Ye Call It* was later sometimes performed without the framework, thus spoiling the real point.

Epilogue] This final piece of nonchalance proved especially memorable. See references to it in Edward Phillips, *Briton's, Strike Home, or The Sailor's Rehearsal* (1739), p. 24; the *Westminster Journal* for 20 March 1742; Joseph Reed, *Madrigal and Trulletta* (1758), p. 60 n. and *Saint Peter's Lodge* (1786), p. 39; *The Three Conjurors, A Political Interlude* (n. d.), p. 26.

Three Hours after Marriage

Three Hours after Marriage was first performed at Drury Lane on 16 January 1717, and received seven performances in the season. It was published on 21 January 1717. See *The Daily Courant* for 21 January 1717.

Sigla: *17   Three Hours after Marriage.* | A | COMEDY, | As it is Acted at the | *Theatre* Royal. | [rule] | *Rumpatur, quisquis rumpitur invidia.* | Mart. | [rule] | [ornament] | *LONDON:* | Printed for Bernard Lintot between the | *Temple Gates, Fleetstreet.* 1717.

8°: A^4B-F^8G^2 [$4 signed ($-A$, G)]. Press-figures 1: E1^b, F8^a; 2: E2^b, F6^b. Press-variants (in Prologue, Scene and Time indications and Epilogue) are due to the presence of uncorrected sheets in some copies. The distribution of corrected and uncorrected sheets in the copies consulted is as follows. *A* and *G* corrected: Line 0. 10. 21 (d); Worc. ZZ. 9. 42 (A); Trin. W. 10. 106 [Rothschild 918]; BL 641. f. 17; Manchester Central Library; Princeton University Library; University of Texas Library; Yale University Library. *A* only corrected: Library of Congress. *G* only corrected: Ohio State University Library. *A* and *G* uncorrected: University of Michigan Library. I have also made use of the following imperfect copies: Bodley Malone 103 (*A* uncorrected, lacks *G*); Buffalo Public Library (*A* corrected [?], lacks *A*3 and *G*); Manchester University Library (*A* corrected, lacks *G*).

58   In *A Supplement to the Works of Alexander Pope, Esq.* (Printed for W. Whitestone, Dublin, 1758), pp. 133–205. Though published after Gay's death, this edition has been consulted because of its interesting departures from *17*. Following Whitestone's 1757 edition of the same volume, it divides the text into five acts and contains a number of substantive variants, including a complete sentence not in the first edition. It also omits from the Advertisement 'for, tho' the Players in Compliance with the Taste of the Town, broke it into five Parts in the Representation; yet, as the Action pauses, and the Stage is left vacant but three times, so it properly consists but of three Acts, like the *Spanish* Comedies', and gives a revised list of actors.

In his edition of the play for the Augustan Reprint Society (Los Angeles, 1961), John Harrington Smith chose to reproduce this text as one derived from 'an authentic acting MS of the play'. His argument was largely based on Gay's Advertisement, which states that the play is 'printed exactly as it is acted'. Smith (p. 9) found this irreconcilable with the above-quoted passage omitted in *58*: '... there is a contradiction which must have puzzled any reader who has used the 1717 edition, namely that if the players broke it into five parts and the play is printed exactly as it is acted, the play that follows should be in five acts but actually is in three. The London 1757 *Supplement to Pope* merely reprints Advertisement and play as they are in 1717 and it is not until the Dublin printings that the play appears in the five acts in which Gay says it was acted. I suggest that Lintot in 1717 had two scripts of the play, one in three acts, one in five, and that Gay wrote the Advertisement under the impression that Lintot would discard the former. I judge that when W. Whitestone undertook his Dublin Supplement of 1757 he took the Advertisement from the London book that had just been published (see the title-page of the volume) but that when he re-issued his book in 1758 he deleted the lines quoted above, perceiving that they were not to the point so far as his text of the play was concerned.' Smith, however, did not see that Gay's Advertisement in *17* may well have been intended merely to reassure readers of a patently three-act play that nothing in fact had been omitted from the five-act performance they might recently have witnessed. If Gay expected Lintot to print a five-act version, he would hardly have gone out of his way to write that it consisted 'but of three Acts, like the *Spanish Comedies*'.

One might make a further objection to Smith's theory. The difference between *17* and *58* in their list of actors concerns only five minor roles, 'where', he claims, 'as rehearsals went on, substitutions would be easy' (p. 10). He therefore considers *58*'s cast list 'more probably correct' than *17*'s. But Corey (*58*'s Possum) acted Tiresias at Lincoln's Inn Fields on 22 January 1717 (Avery, i. 432) and could hardly have kept up two roles in different theatres on the same night. Furthermore, Cross, Wright, Diggs, and Watson (*58*'s remaining cast changes) are not listed in the known rosters of the companies of either theatre for the season 1716/17 (Avery, i, 414).

Smith's conclusion, 'that Whitestone in fact had got the very MS of the play that Gay thought Lintot was going to print', is therefore by no means conclusive, and without external evidence is likely to remain so. However, the presence in *58* of the Key, and the Letter giving an account of the quarrel between Cibber, Pope, and Gay, both previously unpublished, would suggest that Whitestone did have a genuine source of original material connected with the first production. If *58* was set from an annotated copy of *17* (rather, I think, than from an 'acting MS') it is conceivably of authorial or playhouse authority, and therefore I have included its substantive variants in the textual notes. *Copy consulted*: Bodley Vet A5. e. 2770.

Copy-text: 17. The textual footnotes record press-variants and editorial emendation of errors in the copy-text, together with substantive variants from *58* and from *Miscellanies. The Fourth Volume. Consisting of Verses . . .* (1742) which prints the Prologue with Pope's emendations (*siglum: M*). Speech-prefixes are silently expanded.

Motto] 'Let whoever is bursting with envy burst' (Martial, *Epigrams* ix. 97.12). 'Timothy Drub' in *A Letter to Mr. John Gay concerning His late Farce, Entituled, A Comedy* (1717), p. 4, comments: 'What! hang up your *Trophy* before you have got the *Victory?*' Jonson had appended this motto to his *Poetaster* (1601).

Advertisement. 5. *three Acts, like the Spanish Comedies*] See *The History of the renown'd Don Quixote de la Mancha, by several hands* (P. Motteux, 1700–3), ii. 614. For the respective textual claims of the five-act and the three-act version of the play, see above.

Advertisement. 8. *two of my Friends*] Pope and Arbuthnot. The identification was first made in a broadside, *The Drury-Lane Monster*, published on 22 January 1717, during the play's run.

Prologue] Normally included in the Pope canon on the grounds of lines 5–6 (later incorporated into *The Dunciad*. See following note) and of the minor emendations made by Pope after the deaths of Gay and Arbuthnot. See Ault and Butt, p. 179.

Prologue. 5–6. *Blockheads ... War*] Cf. *Dunciad* (B), iii. 175–6: 'Blockheads with reason wicked wits abhor, / But fool with fool is barb'rous civil war.' See also Dryden's Epilogue to *All for Love*, 5–7.

Prologue. 11. *Owlers*] Smugglers. See 'Mr. Joseph Gay' [John Durant Breval], *A Compleat Key to the Non-Juror* (1718): 'This Writer [Cibber] has been so long engag'd in putting a Cheat upon the World, by plundering the Works of his Betters, that it looks as if he thought he had a Privilege for it, or had been so long accustom'd to the Trade, that he thought it as lawful to run *French* Poetry, as our Owlers on the Coast do to run *French* wine or Brandy.' The conjecture that this Key was written by Pope is rejected by George Sherburn in *Manly Anniversary Studies in Language and Literature* (Chicago, 1923), pp. 176–9.

Prologue. 15. *Lopez*] Lope de Vega (1562–1635), Spanish dramatist.

Prologue. 17–22. *How shall ... a Friend*] Ault and Butt, p. 180, point out a similarity of sentiment in Pope's Prologue to *Cato*, 42–6.

Prologue. 28. *Chaps in Monmouth-Street*] Chapman (cheap salesmen) in the second-hand clothes market. See *Trivia*, ii. 548.

Prologue. 30. *Ears of Issachar*] One of Jacob's sons. See Genesis 49:14: 'Issachar is a strong ass.'

Dramatis Personae] The significance of the differences in the cast as given in the Dublin edition of 1758 is discussed above, p. 437. Bearing in mind some echoes of Jonson's *The Silent Woman* in the play (see the notes to I. 49 and 614, and III. 388) it should be pointed out that Fossile was acted by Johnson, who regularly and without a rival acted the part of Morose between 21 February 1707 and 13 February 1742. See R. G. Noyes, *Ben Jonson on the English Stage 1660–1776* (Cambridge, Mass., 1935), p. 188. Townley was acted by Mrs Oldfield, who according to Noyes (p. 189) played Epicœne most frequently and attained most fame in the role. This casting would have underlined the general similarity between the predicaments of Morose and Fossile. *Possum* is from the Latin. *Nautilus* is a fossil shell related to the Paper Nautilus, a small dibranchiate cephalopod. *Ptisan* is a medicinal drink originally based on barley-water. For the name *Plotwell*, see Aphra Behn, *The Town Fop* (1677) and the anonymous *The Apparition, or the Sham Wedding* (1713). *Clinket* is from 'clink', to make jingling rhymes. *Sarsnet* is a soft silk material, now used for linings. *Prue* is not named until Act II, though I take it that she is also Clinket's maid in Act I. I have not emended the speech-prefixes.

The play contains incidental satire on the personalities and interests of the

critic, John Dennis, and the scientist, John Woodward, in the characters of
Sir Tremendous and Dr Fossile. Though these are the only certain
impersonations in the play (and though Sir Tremendous is a fairly minor
character, and the Woodwardian aspect of Fossile less to the foreground
than his role as imaginary cuckold) there have been so many similar
identifications of other characters, and these seem to have played such an
important part in the reception of the play, that it may be convenient to
assemble the evidence for all of them here. I shall discuss (in order of
probability) Sir Tremendous, Dr Fossile, Clinket, Townley, Plotwell, and a
few of the minor and off-stage characters.

Sir Tremendous Longinus was easily identifiable by name alone. Dennis's
passion for the sublime was familiar enough. Pope in *The Narrative of Dr.
Robert Norris* had already spoken of his 'pot of half dead ale covered with a
Longinus' and made Dennis himself say: 'See Longinus in my right-hand,
and Aristotle in my left; I am the only man among the moderns that
support them' (*EC*, x. 454, 457). 'Tremendous' was a key word in his
vocabulary, Gildon (?) in *A Comparison Between the Two Stages* (1702), p. 37,
wrote of Dennis's *Iphigenia* (1700) that 'there were many TREMENDOUS
things in't; but if there be any thing of Tragedy in't it lies in that word, for
he is so fond of it, he had rather use it in every Page, then slay his belov'd
Iphigenia'. There could be no mistaking it. As if to make sure, there is a hit
in the text at the supposed originality of his *Iphigenia*, delivered by Sir
Tremendous himself at a high pitch of Dennisian pomposity in a probable
parody of the Creed (1. 421–6). Dennis was always very sensitive about
plagiarism.

Both Parker (p. 5) and the author of the 1758 *Key* (p. 211) identify Fossile
as Woodward with some certainty, and they both quote as an explanation
of his stage name an anecdote about his asking some workmen in the
Kensington gravel-pits whether they had found any fossils (cf. 1. 144). Even
without the name as a guide, however, such aspects of Woodward as his
fondness for emetics (1. 216 and note), his theory of the flood (1. 473 and note),
and his passion for spurious antiquities (Act III passim) would probably
have been enough to identify him. For his antiquities and emetics, see Pope,
'The Fourth Satire of Dr. John Donne', 28–30 and 152–3. Woodward is
also remembered as one of the founders of experimental plant physiology,
and Dr Johnson was probably right in complaining that he was 'a man not
really or justly contemptible'. But Arbuthnot's feud with him had begun as
early as 1697 (see the note to 1. 473) and there were many good scientific
reasons for his becoming a Scriblerian butt, besides his own tetchiness: in
1710 he had insulted Sloane and been expelled from the council of the
Royal Society, and his quarrel with Mead in 1719 produced a number of
squibs. See *An Account of the Sickness and Death of Dr. W--dw-rd; As also of what
appeared upon opening his body* (4 April 1719), which says that 'his writings
were the jest of the town and country, and admitted even into the farce of
Harlequin and Scaramouch [*Harlequin Hydaspes, or, The Greshamite*, a mock
opera acted at Lincoln's Inn Fields in 1719]'. See also *Tauronomachia* (1719),
a mock-heroic poem about the Woodward/Mead quarrel. The 1758 *Key*
adds a personal motivation in its report that Woodward had 'very concisely

affronted them all three in one speech, *viz.* Pope's essay in criticism, was plundered from Vida—Gay's pastoral lucubrations, were built upon Spencer, and Brown's Britania's pastorals, published in the year 1613—and Arbuthnot could never be eminent in surgery, since he never study'd at Paris or Leyden; for in Scotland, he could learn nothing, but to cure the itch' (p. 211). There is no difficulty in accepting the identification, while a MS note in a contemporary hand on a blank leaf of Manchester University Library's copy of the first edition (822.08/c. 57) reminds us that in all these cases the impersonation may have been assisted by the skill of the actor. The anecdote may well be copied from another source (see its footnote) but I have not come across it before, and it seems worth reproducing:

> Towards the beginning of this century an actor celebrated for mimicry, was to have been employed by a comic author, to take off the person, the manner, and the singularly awkward delivery of the celebrated Dr Woodward, who was intended to be introduced on the stage in a laughable character [*MS footnote*: Dr Fossile in "Three Hours after Marriage". The Players name was to the best of the Editors' recollection Griffin the anecdote was a favourite one with Dr Campbell] The mimic dressed himself as a Countryman, and waited on the Doctor with a long catalogue of ailments, which he said attended on his Wife. The Physician heard with amazement diseases and pains of the most opposite nature, repeated and redoubled on the wretched patient. For, since the actor's greatest wish was to keep Dr Woodward in his company, as long as possible, that he might make the more observations on his gestures, he loaded his poor imaginary spouse with every infirmity, which had any probable chance of prolonging the interview. At length, being become completely master of his errand, he drew from his purse a Guinea; and with a scrape, made an uncouth offer of it. "Put up thy money poor fellow" cried the Doctor "put up thy money. Thou hast need of all thy cash and all thy patience too, with such a bundle of diseases tied to thy back." The actor returned to his employer, and recounted the whole conversation, with such true feeling of the Physician's character that the Author screamed with approbration. His raptures were soon checked, for the mimic told him, with the emphasis of sensibility, that he would sooner die, than prostitute his talents to the rendering such genuine humanity a publick laughing stock.

There seems, incidentally, to be no evidence in the text or elsewhere of Fossile being acted effeminately (for Woodward as an affected homosexual, see *London in 1710, from the Travels of Zacharias Conrad von Uffenbach*, tr. and ed. W. H. Quarrell and Margaret Mare, 1934, p. 178).

Over Phoebe Clinket there has been some controversy. Parker (pp. 5–6) said that she was meant to be the Countess of Winchelsea, 'who, *Pope* says, is so much given to writing of Verses, that she keeps a Standish in every Room of her House, that she may immediately clap down her Thoughts, whether upon *Pindaric*, *Heroic*, *Pastoral* or *Dramatical* Subjects'. This interpretation was also supplied by the author of the 1758 *Key* (p. 213), who added a further anecdote: 'That unlucky lady was heard to say,—*Gays trivia show'd he was more proper to walk before a chair, than to ride in one.* This sarcasm was the cause, why the poor Countess is thrust among such a pack of motley figures on the stage.' Baker (*Biographica Dramatica*, 1764) concurred, repeating both the standish story and Lady Winchelsea's supposed remark about Gay, while in *The Learned Lady in England, 1650–1760* (Boston, 1920), p. 395, Myra Reynolds gave some detailed points of analogy, mentioning in particular Lady Winchelsea's learning, her devotion to literature, her fecundity in verse, her opposition to amatory themes, her detestation of the modern stage, and her religiosity.

This did not satisfy George Sherburn, who in 'The Fortunes and Misfortunes of *Three Hours after Marriage*', *MP*, xxiv (1926), 91–109, and again in *Early Career*, p. 194, offered a rival candidate, Mrs Centlivre. His case rested on (*a*) Lady Winchelsea's continued friendliness to Pope, her contributions to *Poems on Several Occasions* (July 1717) edited by Pope, and her commendatory verses to his *Works* in June 1717; (*b*) Pope's attack on Mrs Centlivre's similes in the *Further Account of the most Deplorable Condition of Mr. Edmund Curll* in the previous year; (*c*) the fact that Mrs Centlivre's husband was one of George I's cooks (see l. 65); (*d*) Mrs Centlivre's difficulty in getting her plays performed, as recounted in the *Tatler* no. 91, 8 November 1709, and the *Female Tatler* no. 69, 14 December 1709; and (*e*) a MS identification of Clinket as Mrs Centlivre in a copy of the play in the Wrenn Library (dated, however, 8 August 1878). Critics have not taken kindly to this view. Phoebe Fenwick Gaye in *John Gay* (1938), p. 170, and John Wilson Bowyer in *The Celebrated Mrs Centlivre* (Durham, NC, 1952), pp. 194–206, pointed to the Epilogue, 19–20, to repin the satire on Lady Winchelsea: 'Whom can our well-bred Poetess displease? / She writ like Quality—with wondrous ease.' Farnsworth Smith (p. 104) pointed out that Sherburn's evidence (*a*) and (*b*) presumed Pope's responsibility, and stressed the report of the 1758 *Key* that it was to Gay that Lady Winchelsea had given offence. Farnsworth Smith thought, however, that Townley might be a casual satire on Mrs Centlivre, taking the latter's amorous history into account. They are both called Susannah. This is a slender likeness, for the name is a common one: Townley could equally 'be', say, Mrs Manley. Of more recent scholars, Harrington Smith (p. 3 n.) supports the Winchelsea interpretation, but Morton and Peterson (p. ii) take Clinket as a generalized rather than a specific portrait, and reintroduce the hint in Parker (see the note to l. 97) that the part is also meant to suggest the Duchess of Newcastle. See Jean Elizabeth Gagen, *The New Woman: Her Emergence in English Drama, 1600–1730* (New York, 1954), p. 32, for her discussion of the Duchess's plays, which 'were all intended for the stage, yet there is no record of a single performance of any of them'. Her eccentricity was notorious (*DNB* iii, p. 1266) and the lines in the Epilogue could equally apply to her. Morton and Peterson's conclusion seems to me the most satisfactory, for the standish point of the early keys (to take a typical piece of evidence) can be made to apply to almost anybody, certainly to the Duchess of Newcastle: 'The Duchess kept a great many young ladies about her person, who occasionally wrote what she dictated. Some of them slept in a room contiguous to that in which her Grace lay, and ever ready, at the call of her bell to rise any hour of the night, to write down her conceptions, lest they should escape her memory' (Theophilus Cibber, *Lives of the Poets*, 1735, ii. 164). It could even apply to Pope himself: 'Lord Oxford's domestick . . . in the dreadful winter of Forty . . . was called from her bed by him [Pope] four times in one night, to supply him with paper, lest he should lose a thought' (Johnson, *Lives of the Poets*, 1781, iv. 155). It was obviously one of the customary hazards of being a servant in a literary household.

With the next identification we enter the more speculative realm of satire through mimicry. Townley was said to represent 'the Wife of another Eminent Physician' (Parker, p. 5). The 1758 *Key* virtually repeated this: 'They say another eminent physician's wife sat for that picture . . .' (p. 213). Breval (*The Confederates*, 1717, ii) identifies her as Mrs Mead, and says that the idea was suggested by the 'fat *Baroness*' Lady Mohun:

OLDFIELD.
    Ill-judging Beauties (tho' of high Degree)
    Why did you force this wretched Part on me?
    And thou, fat *Baroness*, with Cheeks so Red,
    Whence came this Maggot in thy ancient Head?
    Oh! that I had (with BOOTH and WILKS combin'd)
    Obdurate as at first, not chang'd my Mind!
    Or, since I could not from the Task be freed,
    Had mimick'd Lady M---N, not Mrs. M--D.

It might have been more appropriate to have mimicked Lady Mohun, for it would have been a neat inversion of the January/May match of Fossile and Townley. The widow of the Lord Mohun killed in a duel in 1711, she remarried Charles Mordaunt, the nephew of Lord Peterborough, in 1717. 'The disproportionate youth of Mr. Mordaunt, and some other circumstances of the match, do not seem to have added to Lady Mohun's respectability' (*Suffolk Corr.*, i. 7 n.). The identification has not been much favoured by critics, since Mead was Pope's doctor and friend, married for twenty years with several children. It looks too much like an effort to create trouble for the triumvirate. The accusation was elaborately reintroduced by Jonathan Smedley in his *Gulliver Decypher'd* (2nd edn., 1728). Smedley's account makes much of the Court rivalry of Arbuthnot and Mead, but gives the initiative behind the play largely to Bolingbroke, who is accused of having had a liaison with Mrs Mead, and of having resented Mead's consequent removal of her to the country: '*Johnny* [Arbuthnot], you may be sure, did not forget to set off his Antagonist in the most ridiculous light, and to *bespatter* his Wife in complaisance to the Secretary, who is said to have had reason to complain of her kindness, as well as her Husband's injuries to him' (p. 7). The 1758 *Key* had also assumed that Mrs Mead was adulterous, but this is as far as the evidence goes. Smedley claims that Mead and his party 'raised such power as to defeat their Enemies' (p. 8), but in what exactly this victory consisted he does not say. Farnsworth Smith thinks that the Epilogue corroborates the identification of Townley as Mrs Mead: 'None but a *Tar* could be so tender-hearted, / To claim a Wife that had been three Years parted' (35–6). The reference is, of course, to Lieutenant Bengall, Townley's real husband (see III. 531). He is not said to be a sailor, but may have been telescoped by mistake with Jack Capstone. Farnsworth

Smith suggests that *tar* means a doctor here, a name derived from *tar-water*, a prophylactic against smallpox. The first reference to tar-water, however, is in the *Gentleman's Magazine* for January 1739 (the real popularity of tar-water being due to Berkeley's *Siris*, 1744) and *tar* is not recorded as an abbreviation for it, nor as a word for a doctor.

Plotwell as a satire on Cibber (who played the part) has proved a hard ghost to lay. It originated with Parker (p. 7: '*Plotwell*'s fathering *Clinket*'s Play, is levell'd at *Cibber*') and was taken up by Breval, iii. In the form in which the supposed identification is usually made (e.g. 'Colley Cibber played the role of an actor-manager, and was made thus to utter lines that satirized himself' *Early Career*, p. 193; see also Gaye, p. 170, Irving, p. 149, and Ault, *New Light*, p. 307) it is patently untrue, for not only is Plotwell not an actor-manager (he only pretends to have written Clinket's play) but he says nothing, either, that could be taken to be levelled against actor-managers. The identification is thoroughly and convincingly refuted by both Morton and Peterson (pp. ii–iii) and Harrington Smith (pp. 3–4).

Again, the idea that the off-stage Countess of Hippokekoana was intended for Gay's former patroness, the Duchess of Monmouth, was originated by Parker (p. 7), but neither this, nor the Plotwell/Cibber satire, was mentioned by the less biased 1758 *Key*. The practice of taking vomits was too common to be invidious here, and it seems likely to be merely a case of making trouble for Gay. Parker is leading his readers, not expressing a common reaction. One contemporary annotated 'Dutchess of *M------h*' as 'Marlbrough' before reading on to find the Duchess of Monmouth actually named (BL 641. e. 17. 5). Some other identifications are of little importance, and almost entirely depend on what the actors made of their parts. The 1758 *Key* (p. 212) claims that 'the two players by their different manner of speaking, by those whoever convers'd with them, might be easily found to mean Wilk's and Booth'. Parker (p. 6) says that 'The *Boy*'s Stammering, is a Banter on *Durfey*'. This last is of some interest. Morton and Peterson (p. 69) consider it 'surely ludicrous', pointing out that Thomas D'Urfey was then aged 63. I am inclined to think, however, that there is good reason for Parker's claim, bizarre though it may seem, and I discuss this in the note to l. 124 below.

l. 5. *Blank Licences*] See G. S. Alleman, *Matrimonial Law and the Materials of Restoration Comedy* (Philadelphia, 1942), pp. 37–8.

l. 43. *Alcmena*] Amphitryon's wife, seduced by Jove in the shape of her husband.

l. 48. *Corroborative of Crollius*] The panacea of Oswald Croll (1580–1609). Fossile imagines that it will restore his virility.

l. 49. *Oh, for a Draught, etc.*] For Fossile's speculation that laudanum would remove their disparity of sexual appetite, cf. Morose in Jonson's *The Silent Woman*, iv. iv. 130–40: 'Haue I no friend that will make her drunke? or giue her a little *ladanum*? or *opium*?'

i. 54. *Pistachoe-Porridge*] Francis Bacon wrote that 'Pistachoes . . . joyned with Almonds in Almond Milk . . . are an excellent nourisher'. See Arbuthnot, *Rules of Diet* (1732), p. 263.

i. 62. *Procidence of the Pineal Gland*] See Stephen Blancard [Steven Blanckaert], *The Physical Dictionary* (6th edn., 1715), p. 96, where he writes of the pineal gland (the conarium): '. . . the learned F. *Boyle* doubts of its Use, when he says, *That it is not so easy to determine what its Use is*.' Normally at this time it was considered to be the seat of the soul, as Descartes asserted (*Œuvres*, ed. C. Adam and P. Tannery, Paris, 1904, xi. 352). See Elijah Fenton, 'The Fair Nun' (*Poems on Several Occasions*, 1717), 1–6:

> We sage Cartesians, who profess
> Ourselves sworn foes to emptiness,
> Assert that souls a tip-toe stand
> On what we call the pineal gland;
> As weather-cocks on spires are plac'd,
> To turn the quicker with each blast.

Fossile's diagnosis depends upon an absurd analogy with a dropped womb. Blancard (p. 281) defines *Procidentia Uteri* as the 'relaxing of Inner Tunick of the Vagina'.

i. 75. *What are the Labours . . . Brain*] ''Tis to be hop'd the Reader will observe these admirable *Puns*' (Parker, p. 6).

i. 91. *Déluge*] It is not absolutely clear from the text that Gay intended Clinket to use the French, but it would accord with her affectation.

i. 97. *conceive*] '*Conceive*, was a Word mightily us'd by the Dutchess of *Newcastle*, who writ several great Books both *Philosophical* and *Poetical*' (Parker, p. 6).

i. 99. *Whales . . . Oak*] A familiar conceit. Morton and Peterson note Ovid, *Metamorphoses*, tr. Dryden, i. 411–13: 'And wond' ring Dolphins o're the Palace glide. / On leaves and masts of mighty Oaks they brouze; / And their broad Finns, entangle in the Boughs.' See also *The Shepherd's Week*, 'Wednesday', 67 ff: 'Sooner shall cats disport in waters clear, / And speckled mackrels graze the meadows fair, etc.'

i. 105. *stiff is too short*] Breval takes this up as a *double entendre* in his Dedication: 'However, tho' I take this Liberty, I shall not abuse it, by trespassing long upon your Patience; since DEDICATIONS have something in them so Formal: And you will agree with me, That a *Stiff* Thing, of This Kind at least, cannot be too *short*.'

i. 114. *my animal Spirits . . . Civility*] A parody of Descartes. According to his theories, the mind communicates with the body through the pineal gland, which is surrounded and permeated by the animal spirits which are the medium of the communication between soul and body. The pineal gland can change the direction of the animal spirits which (through nerves and muscles) control the body. See Descartes, *Œuvres*, ed. C. Adam and P. Tannery (Paris, 1904), xi. 129. For a popularization of the Cartesian explanation of the role of the animal spirits in the contemplation of ideas, see the *Spectator* no. 417, 28 June 1712.

I. 124. *Ho-ho-house*] 'The *Boy*'s Stammering, is a Banter on *Durfey*' (Parker, p. 6). Morton and Peterson (p. 69) consider this identification 'surely ludicrous'. However, Pope is known to have mocked D'Urfey's stammer previously (in 'Verses Occasion'd by an &c. at the End of Mr. D'Urfy's Name in the Title to one of his Plays', 51–4; for dating, see Ault and Butt, pp. 89–90). W. R. Chetwood in his *General History of the Stage* (1749), pp. 153–5, has an anecdote which shows that Penkethman was known for his mimicry of D'Urfey's stammer, and it would seem likely that this role of the messenger boy was in fact taken by Penkethman (Underplot, his main role in the play, does not enter until Act II). Penkethman also had the stammering role of Jonas Dock in *The What D'Ye Call It.*

I. 144. *Spoils of Quarries*] '[Woodward] gain'd that title [Fossile] tis said, by asking a man digging in a gravel-pit—if he ever met with any Fossils?' (1758 *Key*, p. 211).

I. 173. *Shock*] The shock or shough was a kind of lap-dog. Cf. *The Rape of the Lock*, i. 115.

I. 186. *Myrtillo ... Alexis*] 'A clear allusion to Cibber's pastoral dramas' (Morton and Peterson, p. iii).

I. 191. *Mrs. Colloquintida, etc.*] Parker (p. 7) says that Fossile's patients mentioned by Ptisan are 'scurrilous Reflections upon several Persons of Worth'. *Colloquintida* is *colocynthis*, a bitter kind of cucumber: 'the Seed is also exceeding bitter; 'tis a violent Purge. We call it *Coloquintida*' (Blancard, p. 94).

I. 216. *Countess of Hippokekoana*] Ipecacuanha is an emetic. 'The Countess of *Hippokekoana* is the Dutchess of M[onmout]h. To whom *Gay* was a Serving-man, and never hop'd for any higher Preferment than holding a Plate at a *side Board*, till *Pope* took him into his Protection ... [and] whom he has thought fit to Banter, for no other Reason, but because it seems 'tis her Custom to take a Vomit once or twice a Week' (Parker, p. 7). For a true account of Gay's position in the Monmouth household, see Irving, pp. 68–72. Woodward's fondness for emetics was a standing joke. See Pope's 'The Fourth Satire of Dr. John Donne', 152–3: 'As one of *Woodward*'s Patients, sick and sore, / I puke, I nauseate,—yet he thrusts in more.'

I. 261. *my self*] The letter as read by Fossile at I. 135 ends '*and I shall have the Pleasure of putting it on the first time*'. Morton and Peterson (p. 61) suggests that 'the Triumvirate presumably nodded' and find 'no significance in the change'. However, accuracy here would have been easily sacrificed for the sake of consistency: the change enables Townley to complete her ingenious explanation of the letter with a neat absurdity.

I. 268. *poison'd my Father ... kill'd my Lap-Dog*] Cf. *The Rape of the Lock*, iii. 158: 'When Husbands or when Lap-dogs breathe their last' and iv. 120: 'Men, Monkies, Lap-dogs, Parrots, perish all!' See Drub, pp. 16–17.

l. 310. *Goût de travers*] Cf. Pope's ΠΕΡΙ ΒΑΘΟΥΣ, Ch. V: '[Whoever would excel in the profound] must ... contract the true *gout de travers*; and ... acquire a most happy, uncommon, unaccountable way of thinking' (*EC*, x. 354).

l. 312. *nauseate ... a Rose*] Cf. *An Essay on Man*, i. 200: 'Die of a rose in aromatic pain'.

l. 324. *Deucalion and Pyrrha*] Pope had once written part of an epic poem about the second Deucalion, and clearly knew this sort of mythological material well (see Spence, i. 16–18).

l. 325. *Neither our Stage nor Actors ... Sacred Story*] Milton, however, had considered writing a play about the Old Testament flood. See *Works* (New York, 1938), xviii. 232.

l. 367. *a Box on the Ear*] According to R. H. Barker, *Mr. Cibber of Drury Lane* (New York, 1939), p. 204, this alludes to the *soufflet* in Cibber's adaptation of the *Cid*.

l. 387. *to dislike what has pleased them*] Cf. Pope and Gay to Caryll, 3 March 1715, where Pope writes of the reception given *The What D'Ye Call It*: '... the laughers are so much the majority, that Mr. Dennis and one or two more seem determined to undeceive the town at their proper cost ...' (Sherburn, i. 283).

l. 391. *Ten righteous Criticks*] 'The triumvir makes a little too free with the old testament' (1758 *Key*, p. 215). See Genesis 18:32, where God promises not to destroy Sodom if ten righteous men can be found.

l. 397. *Terror ... for the Third*] The author's benefit night. Cf. *The Mohocks*, Epilogue, 18.

l. 423. *Iphigenia of Racine, etc.*] Dennis noted in the Preface to his *Iphigenia* (1700): 'The subject that I chose in order to my design has been handled by several; yet the Fable or Plot is intirely my own' (Hooker, ii. 389). Dennis was sensitive about plagiarism. This speech of Sir Tremendous was perhaps delivered as a parody of the Creed (see Drub, p. 22).

l. 441. *Penetration ... Capacity, etc.*] *Double entendre*. See Drub (p. 25). Cf. Gildon on Dennis in *Lives and Characters of the English Dramatic Poets*, [1698], p. 38: 'He has shewed himself a perfect Critick, and Master of a great deal of Penetration and Judgment.'

l. 473. *a late Philosopher*] Woodward, whose *Essay towards a Natural History of the Earth* (1695) had been criticized by Arbuthnot as early as 1697, in his *Examination of Dr. Woodward's Account of the Deluge*. Lester M. Beattie describes Woodward's theory as follows: 'At the time of the Flood—the purpose of which, in Woodward's opinion, was not merely to punish, but to conform the earth to fallen man's increased need for morally bracing labor—the contents of the abyss boiled up and covered the whole globe; the crust completely disintegrated, went into solution, and then at last, upon the withdrawal of the waters, settled down in a new form with the heaviest elements at the bottom, the undissolved animal and plant remains arranging themselves in the heavier or lighter strata according to their specific gravity' (*John Arbuthnot, Mathematician and Satirist*, Cambridge, Mass., 1935, p. 191).

i. 571. *tag of the Acts*] Last lines of each act, usually in couplets.

i. 606. *Bristol Stone*] Transparent rock-crystal found in the Clifton limestone near Bristol.

i. 614sd, 619 sd. *A flourish of Fiddles . . . Drums and Trumpets*] Cf. the musicians that Clerimont brings to Morose in *The Silent Woman*, iii. vii. See also the *Spectator* no. 364, 28 April 1712.

ii. 12sd. *Gives a Letter*] For the device of the intercepted letters, see Molière, *Le Cocu imaginaire* and the anonymous *The Apparition; or, The Sham Wedding*, Act V. The letters appear to be all from citizens ('Freeman', 'Madam Wyburn', 'Habakkuk Plumb', 'Charles Bat') and about citizens ('Merchants Ladys', 'the Alderman', 'the Grocer's Wife', 'Neighbour Pinch').

ii. 26. *Madam Wyburn*] '. . . the most noted bawd in London' (1758 *Key*, p. 215). Giles Jacob refers to her in his Preface to *The Rape of the Smock* (1717), fol. A4ᵃ. See also [Richard Morley?], *Life of the late celebrated Mrs. Elizabeth Wisebourn, Vulgarly Call'd Mother Wybourn* (1721).

ii. 48. *In You the Beautys, etc.*] Cf. Lady Mary Wortley Montagu, 'Tuesday', 78–9: 'In her all Beauties of the Spring are seen, / Her Cheeks are rosy, and her mantua Green' (pointed out by Robert Halsband and Isobel Grundy in their edition of Lady Mary's *Essays and Poems*, Oxford, 1977, p. 188 n.). This is, no doubt, Gay's revenge for his embarrassment over the publication of *Court Poems* the previous year (see Irving, pp. 137–40). However, the formula lodged itself in Gay's mind. See 'The Tea-Table', 21–2: 'Last *Masquerade* was Sylvia nymphlike seen, / Her hand a crook sustain'd, her dress was green' (Dearing, i. 234). The green dress was a traditional item of pastoral costume (see, for example, the 'New Ballad of Robin Hood', 107, in *Roxburgh Ballads*, ii. 444, or *Bartholomew Fair*, iv. v. 34) with the sexual implication of 'grass-stained' (as in 'A Ballad of Andrew and Maudlin' in *Wit and Mirth*, ii. 20: 'They laid the Girls down, and gave each a green Mantle', or *The Shepherd's Week*, 'Thursday', 135.)

ii. 68. *the Enquiry allowed only to Jews*] Morton and Peterson refer to Numbers 5:14–28, and to Kerby-Miller, p. 130.

ii. 142. *We only know, that we know nothing*] Socrates, in Plato, *Apology* 21–3. See also Milton, *Paradise Regained*, iv. 293.

ii. 215. *Hah! who is here!*] 'The Character of Dr. *Lubomirski* is copied from a Farce (or *Spanish* Comedy as *Gay* will have it) call'd the *Anatomist* or *Sham-Doctor*, but spoil'd rather than Improv'd' (Parker, p. 9). Ravenscroft's *The Anatomist: or, The Sham Doctor* (1969) had been revived in 1716 (see Avery, ii. 410, 421). In it, Crispin pretends to be a 'German, or Polish Doctor' (Act II) and later parallels Plotwell's proposed treatment of Underplot by offering to dissect the disguised gallants (Act III). See Morton and Peterson, p. viii.

II. 219. *non usus sum loquere Latinam*] Since Fossile's Latin is intended to be defective, I have not substituted *58*'s 'Latinum'. His incapacity was not shared by his model. See Uffenbach on the Royal Society in 1710: 'If one excepts Dr Woodward and one or two other Englishmen as well as the foreign members, there are none but apothecaries and other such people who know scarce a word of Latin' (*London in 1710, from the Travels of Zacharias Conrad von Uffenbach*, tr. and ed. by W. H. Quarrell and Margaret Mare, 1934, p. 99). For Woodward's high-handed treatment of visiting scholars and affected manner, see Uffenbach, pp. 172, 176.

II. 241. *By Calcination, etc.*] Cf. Jonson, *The Alchemist*, II. v. 21–4.

II. 262. *Longitudes*] See Kerby-Miller, p. 167. Fantastic methods to ascertain longitude at sea were the particular bane of Arbuthnot. See the note to *The What D'Ye Call It*, I. iv. 16 ff.

II. 265. *the grand Elixir*] Cf. Pope and Gay, *Guardian* no. 11, 24 March 1713: '... what enables me to perform this great Work, is the Use of my *Obsequium Catholicon*, or the *Grand Elixir*, to support the Spirits of Human Nature'. It could turn base metals into gold, or prolong life indefinitely.

II. 266. *Fluxion*] Plotwell is referring to Newton's form of the calculus. Fossile mistakes it for *flux* (a purge). Mercury was the cure for syphilis. Cf. *The Memoirs of Martinus Scriblerus*, Ch. x: '*A Proposal for a General Flux*, to exterminate at one blow the P-x out of this Kingdom' (Kerby-Miller, p. 130).

II. 275. *monstrous Twins*] A pair of Siamese twins from Hungary were exhibited in London in 1708. They are discussed at length in Aaron Hill's question-and-answer journal, *The British Apollo*, nos. 35, 36, 37. Gay certainly, and Arbuthnot possibly, contributed to this journal. Cf. the Siamese twins Lindamira–Indamora in Chapters xiv and xv of *The Memoirs of Martinus Scriblerus* (the 'Double Mistress' episode) which Kerby-Miller (pp. 297–9) argues were written shortly after *Three Hours after Marriage*.

II. 300. *Lapis Lydius Virginitatis*] '*Lydius Lapis, Coticula, Lapis Heracleus*, is the Stone that is found in the River *Tmolus*, and other Places; on which Gold and Silver being rub'd, the Colour is try'd. 'Tis call'd the *Touch-stone*' (Blancard, p. 215). '*Lubomirski's Liquor for the Tryal of Virginity*. Is an Incident stole out of an old Play, Printed in 1653. (somewhat applicable to these Scribblers) call'd, "The *Changling*, a Tragedy. Written by *Thomas Middleton*, assisted by Mr. *Rowley*. The Foundation of this Play may be found in the Story of *Alsemero*, and *Beatrice Joanna*, in *Reynolds*'s *God's Revenge against Murder*, Book 1, Hist. 4 (*See, Mr*. Langbaine's *Account of the Dramatick Poets*, 8vo. pag. 371.)' (Parker, pp. 9–10). See *The Changeling*, IV. i.

II. 305. *Hippomanes*] A slimy fluid excreted by mares. See Virgil, *Georgics*, iii. 280–3.

II. 314sd] For Underplot's entry in a chair like a sick man, cf. Crowne, *City Politicks* (1682).

II. 359. *intemperies*] '*Intemperies, seu Dyscrasia & Acrasia*, a Disease which consists of inconvenient Qualities of the Body, and these are either manifest or occult' (Blancard, p. 196). The disease is related to the theory of the Humours.

II. 534. *enter beneath ... this Petticoat*] Swift says of the new whale-bone petticoats: 'a woman here may hide a moderate gallant under them' (*Journal to Stella*, ii. 409). See Pope's reference to 'Oldfield's petticoat' in 'The First Epistle of the Second Book of Horace, Imitated', 331. See also Aphra Behn, *The Younger Brother* (1696), IV. ii, for the device of hiding beneath a petticoat.

III. 1. *flying Dragon*] *Draco volans*, a meteor. There was a popular belief that a shooting-star left only a jelly after hitting the earth. See S. K. Heninger, jr., *A Handbook of Renaissance Meteorology* (Durham, NC, 1960), pp. 95–6.

III. 4, 6sd. *a Mummy ... an Alligator*] Pope had advised against having a crocodile as well as a mummy. See Gay's letter to him after the production (*Letters*, p. 31). The mummy and the crocodile remained in the theatrical memory for many years. See, for example, J. P. C[ollier], 'The Poetical and Literary Character of the late John Philip Kemble', *The New Monthly Magazine and Literary Journal* (1832), p. 179, for an account of Kemble's farce *The Female Officer* performed at York in 1779, and at Drury Lane in 1786, under the title of *The Projects*. This play borrows the mummy and crocodile disguises from *Three Hours after Marriage*, as Collier notes, and there are other similarities of plot. The play may be found in the Huntington Library (MS Larpent, no. 441).

III. 27. *Thy Antony ... Cleopatra*] For the mummies of Antony and Cleopatra speaking heroic verse, see Regnard and Dufresny, *Les Momies d'Egypte* (1696).

II. 47. *Bell and the Dragon*] Babylonian idols of the Apocrypha. (The history of the destruction of Bel and the Dragon, cut off from the end of Daniel).

III. 54. *Macedonian Queen*] Olympias, mother of Alexander the Great.

III. 62. *Mantegers*] See the note to III. 118 below.

III. 79. *Glass-Trumpet*] See Kerby-Miller, p. 144.

III. 81. *Venice-Treacle*] An opiate. See John Jones, *The Mysteries of Opium Reveal'd* (1700).

III. 94. *My long Tail*] See Drub (p. 18) for the possibly phallic play with the crocodile's tail (assumed also by Welsted, *Palaemon to Celia*), and Parker (pp. 10 ff.).

III. 117. *the Bird Porphyrion*] See Kerby-Miller, p. 145.

III. 118. *your Dart of the Mantichora*] '*Mantichora*, is an Indian Animal that hath three rows of Teeth' (Blancard, p. 220). See *The Memoirs of Martinus Scriblerus*: 'That word [*manteger*] (replies Martin) is a corruption of the Mantichora of the Ancients, the most noxious Animal that ever infested the earth; who had a Sting above a cubit long, and would attack a rank of armed men at once, flinging his poisonous darts several miles around him' (Kerby-Miller, p. 145).

III. 119. *Antediluvian Trowel ∴ one of the Babel Masons*] 'This is according to our *Scotch* Author's Chronology' (Parker, p. 13). The chronology is, of course, Fossile's.

III. 149. *Asphaltion ... Pice-Asphaltus*] *Asphaltion* is Pliny's term for the bituminous clover. *Pice-Asphaltus* is pitch from the Dead Sea (Lake Asphaltites). See Blancard, p. 41.

III. 153. *Dioscorides*] The first-century herbalist.

III. 284. *Hockley in the Hole*] A place in Clerkenwell, famous for bear-baiting. See the note to *The Beggar's Opera*, I. vi. 23.

III. 293. *Nunquam satis, and so forth*] Horace, *Odes* ii. 13. 13–4: 'quid quisque vitet, numquam homini satis / cautum est in horas' ('Man never heeds enough from hour to hour what he should shun').

III. 320. *Intellects of the Infant ... Suppers of the Parents*] Cf. *The Memoirs of Martinus Scriblerus*: '... he ponder'd on the Rules of the Ancients, for the generation of Children of Wit. He ordered his diet according to the prescription of Galen, confining himself and his wife for almost the whole first year to Goat's Milk and Honey' (Kerby-Miller, p. 96). See also Arbuthnot, *An Essay concerning the Nature of Aliments, and the Choice of them, according to the Different Constitutions of Human Bodies* (1732), p. 406.

III. 388. *A Bastard!*] For Possum's discussion of bastardy, cf. Cutberd's and Otter's discussion of divorce law in *The Silent Woman*, v. iii.

III. 464. *Your Drury-Lane Friends*] i.e. actors, but since Drury Lane was the home of both the playhouse and the brothels of the period, Fossile jumps to the wrong conclusion.

III. 557. *How ridiculous is the Act it self*] See Marcus Aurelius Antoninus, *Meditations*, vi. 13. x. 19.

Epilogue 35. *Tar*] See above, p. 442.

Epilogue 42. *superior Eighteen-penny Beauties*] In the Middle-Gallery.

Acis and Galatea

Acis and Galatea may be presumed to have been privately performed at Canons in 1718. The first public performances were at Lincoln's Inn Fields on 26 March 1731 (Rochetti, one performance) and at the New Haymarket Theatre on 17 May 1732 (Arne, two performances). The libretto was first published on 11 May 1732, although excerpted settings had appeared since 1722.

    Sigla: MS Handel's autograph score (BL RM 20. a. 2).

    32 ACIS and *GALATEA:* | An ENGLISH | PASTORAL OPERA. | In THREE ACTS. | As it is Perform'd at the | New Theatre *in the* Hay-Market, | Set to MUSICK | By Mr. *HANDEL.* | [Printer's ornament] | *LONDON:* | Printed for J. Watts at the Printing-Office in | *Wild-Court* near *Lincoln's-Inn Fields.* | [rule] | MDCCXXXII. | [Price Six Pence.]

8° in half-sheets: A-C⁴ [$2 signed (−A2)]. C4ᵇ contains a book-seller's advertisement dated 11 May 1732. *Copies consulted*: Bodley Douce PP 10 (1); BL 161 d.42; BL Ashley 774; Barnstaple 680/5.

39 *ACIS* and *GALATEA.* / A / SERENATA: / OR / PASTORAL ENTERTAINMENT. / Written by Mr. *GAY.* / To which is added, / *A* SONG *for St.* CECILIA'*s Day.* / Written by Mr. *DRYDEN.* / [rule] / Both Set to Musick by Mr. *HANDEL.* / [double rule] / *LONDON*: / Printed for JOHN WATTS at the Printing-Office / in *Wild-Court* near *Lincoln's-Inn Fields.* / [rule] / MDCCXXXIX. / [Price One Shilling,] / And no more.

8° in half-sheets: *A*⁴B-C⁴ [$2 signed (−*A*2)]. *Copy consulted*: Barn-staple 680/7 (−*A*1, C4).

Copy-text: 32, with substantive emendations, the two-part structure and improved punctuation, indentation, and lineation from *39*. I have not included variants in the stage and musical directions in the textual footnotes, nor indicated the differences in indentation and lineation. Speech prefixes are silently expanded. *32* was issued in connection with the Arne production of 17 May 1732, which was unauthorized (Victor Schoelcher, *Life of Handel*, 1857, p. 115). While there is no evidence that copy was supplied or corrected by Gay (who never, in any case, acknowledged authorship), its 'Argument' and stage directions make it a useful text for the purposes of this edition. *39*, on the other hand, is a better text for the words themselves, a large number of its variants being supported by *MS*. It was issued in connection with the first public performance to be produced by Handel himself (at Lincoln's Inn Fields on 13 December 1739) and is the first edition to ascribe the words to Gay. Two arias were omitted, no doubt to accommodate the Dryden Ode and the extra symphonic material performed on that occasion. There is a large number of later editions of the libretto (see Dean, pp. 186 ff.) but in general I have not complicated matters by recording their variants. I have, however, recorded all the substantive variants of *MS* in the textual footnotes, since these in most cases must represent the original words Gay provided for Handel before they were altered during the composition of the work. The *MS* accidentals are not reliable.

The music of *Acis and Galatea* may be found in the first complete edition (Walsh and Hare, 1743), in the Händel-Gesellschaft edition, vol. iii, or, most conveniently for performers, in the edition of Sir Joseph Barnby, revised by Watkins Shaw (Novello, 1974).

Acis and Galatea] Handel's autograph score (BL RM 20. a. 2) is untitled. In a list of Canons music, signed and dated 23 August 1720 by Pepusch, the work is described as 'O the pleasures of the plain, a masque for five voices and instruments, in score' (see Dean, p. 159). It is perhaps strange that Polyphemus does not figure in the title, given his role in the story. Handel's Neapolitan serenata of 1708 was entitled *Aci, Galatea e Polifemo*, and translators of the Ovidian episode which was Gay's immediate source tend to give prominence to the Cyclops in their titles (Dryden: 'The Story of Acis, Polyphemus, and Galatea'; Pope: 'Polyphemus and Acis'). However, the title *Acis and Galatea* was in early use. The work is so called in a MS copy in the hand of J. C. Smith, sen., dated 1718 (see the *Musical Times* no. 1547, cxiii, 1972, 43) and also in various editions of selected arias published by Walsh and Hare from 1722 onwards. There is no reason to doubt the title's authenticity, despite the apparent fact that the earliest public productions were unauthorized and that Handel came to use it indiscriminately for both the Canons masque and his macaronic version of 1732. The theatrical public would have been familiar with Eccles's *Acis and Galatea*, produced in 1701, a form of title reinforced by such works as Galliard's *Calypso and Telemachus* (1712, libretto by Hughes) and Pepusch's *Venus and Adonis* (1715, libretto by Cibber) and *Apollo and Daphne* (1716, libretto by Hughes).

A Serenata, or Pastoral Entertainment] This seems as close to an accurate description of the work as any of the many alternatives, and has the virtue of probable authorization by Handel when he returned to the Canons version in 1739 (though Dean, p. 159, suggests that it was copied from the Oxford macaronic libretto of 1733). In fact, both *Aci, Galatea e Polifemo* and the macaronic version were described by Handel as 'serenatas'. The Canons version was called either a 'masque' (see Pepusch in the previous note) or an 'opera' (see Smith in the previous note). Arne's production was accompanied by the 1732 libretto, calling the work 'An English Pastoral Opera'. Arne was, no doubt, seeking to distinguish his production from the Rochetti production at Lincoln's Inn Fields in the previous year, for he stressed in his advertisements that his was 'the first Time it ever was performed in a Theatrical Way'. The 1743 score returned to the description of 'masque', which Dean favours. In the 1750s the work was sometimes described as an 'oratorio', and is today (as, for example, in the Novello edition) known as a 'serenata'.

The Argument] The Argument is borrowed word for word from the Argument to the Motteux libretto of Eccles's *Acis and Galatea*, except for the omission of two sentences referring to Motteux's introduction of a happy ending and the sub-plot of Roger and Joan. Eccles's *Acis and Galatea* was produced in 1701, and the libretto was printed by J. Roberts in 1723.

Dramatis Personae] For a discussion of the part of Corydon, not included in *MS*, *32*, or *39*, see the note to II. 49 below.

I. 12. *Vine*] The metaphor clearly cannot support the *MS* reading 'Wine'. Handel's spelling is not always reliable, and he may in this case have been unconsciously supplying a German pronunciation for the word he mistakenly wrote.

I. 23. *fierce Desire*] A thematically preferable reading to the reading of *32*, 'soft Desire'. For the erotic implications of the story, see the Introduction, p. 35.

I. 46. *Love in her Eyes sits playing*] Cf. Cowley, 'The Change' ('Love in her sunny Eyes does basking play'). Faber (p. 426) mistakenly ascribes this aria to Hughes.

The Second Part] There is no indication of a break in *MS*, but *32* ended Act I here, and the Chorus 'Happy We', first added in 1739, reinforces the contrast of mood with the opening of Part Two.

II. 6. *The Mountain nods, the Forest shakes*] Cf. Pope, *Iliad* xiii, 29–30: 'the lofty Mountains nod, / The Forests shake!' (Polyphemus's 'ample Strides' are also echoed by Pope's 'ample strides' of line 32). Pope published the fourth volume of his *Iliad* in June 1718, and Gay may have borrowed these phrases from either the printed version or Pope's MS. Ault and Butt (p. 217) conclude, however, that another echo of the *Iliad* in lines in *Haman and Mordecai*, III. i, indicates Pope's responsibility for their appearance in *Acis and Galatea*.

II. 13–14. *Bring me a hundred Reeds, etc.*] Cf. Dryden, 'The Story of Acis, Polyphemus, and Galatea, from the thirteenth book of Ovid's Metamorphoses', 58–9: 'A hundred Reeds, of a prodigious Growth, / Scarce made a Pipe, proportion'd to his Mouth'. The many details from Ovid (see the notes to II. 17, 34, 38–9, 40–3, 86–7, 105, 108 ff. below) are all from Dryden's version, which had recently been reprinted in Garth's *Ovid* (1717), p. 470. If Pope had played much of a part in the composition of *Acis and Galatea*, he might have been tempted, perhaps, to draw upon his own translation of the episode, although this was a juvenile work, written at the age of fourteen, not published until December 1749 in *The London Magazine*.

II. 17. *O ruddier than the Cherry*] R. T. Kerlin, *Theocritus in English Literature* (Lynchburg, Va., 1910), p. 59, claims that this aria derives from Theocritus (i.e. from *Idylls* xi. 19 ff.) but in fact many of its details are from Dryden's Ovid, 65 ff.

II. 34. *Palace in the Rock*] Cf. Dryden's Ovid, 103: 'My Palace, in the living Rock'.

II. 38–9. *Wildings . . . Hand*] Cf. Dryden's Ovid, 110–11: 'Red Strawberries, in Shades, expecting stand, / Proud to be gather'd by so white a Hand.' The *MS* reading shows Gay consciously deploying Dryden's details. 'Wildings' occurs in Dryden, 117.

II. 40–3. *Of Infant Limbs, etc.*] That Polyphemus's guests were likely to be eaten is made clear in Dryden's Ovid, 21–2.

II. 44. *Cease to Beauty*] *MS* shows some dissatisfaction with the words of this aria. The first version probably represents Gay's intention. Dean (p. 190) feels that it 'comes straight from the world of Motteux', but its rakish pragmatism might be expected from the creator of Macheath and is, of course, not wholly unsuitable to the sentiments of Polyphemus at this point. The second version (which Dean calls a 'feeble parody') might well be Handel's own effort to make the meaning less direct, resulting in an unacceptably unnatural syntax. Clotted syntax survives in the final version (to be quite misunderstood by *32*) but Dean (pp. 157, 190) claims that it was 'adapted' from Daphne's second air in Hughes's *Apollo and Daphne*. I find it hard to see more than a general resemblance here, but it is not impossible that Hughes revised the words at a late stage in the composition of the work, for we know that he did write the words for the following aria (see note to ii. 49 below). Presumably at this stage Gay for some reason was not immediately available. Handel's dissatisfaction with 'Cease to Beauty' continued: when cuts were needed in 1739 it was one of the items to disappear. In *MS*, immediately after Galatea's previous recitative, there is written in pencil: 'here for the Boy Would you gain the tender creature'. Watkins Shaw, in his 1974 revision of the Novello edition, thinks that this means that 'Would you gain the tender Creature' might have been considered by Handel as an alternative to 'Cease to Beauty', although the libretti usually print both. At the end of 'Cease to Beauty' in *MS* Handel has written in ink: 'NB. aria.', which shows that 'Would you gain the tender Creature' found its intended place.

ii. 45. *Ever-whining Love*] This phrase (or its earlier version, 'whining lover') may have been suggested by Creech's translation of Theocritus (2nd edn., 1713), p. 41: 'Go mind thy Harvest-work, for that will prove, / Thy Wisdom greater, than this whining Love.'

ii. 49. *Would you gain the tender Creature*] This aria appears in John Hughes's *Poems on Several Occasions* (1735), i. 145, and is therefore presumably by him. It does not appear in *MS*, but the setting was published separately in 1722. The new character in the Rochetti production of 1731 ('Corydon') probably sang this aria, since it is given to him in several later libretti. The Canons production had only one singer for each of the five voices required by the setting (STTTB), so it is possible that one motive for adding this aria was indeed to give the third tenor a solo. However, a sufficient reason for its addition may be found in Handel's evident dissatisfaction with the previous aria (see the note to ii. 44 above).

ii. 56. *hideous Love*] Originally in the *MS* 'saucy Love': the emendation is further evidence that Gay's first thoughts weighted the character of Polyphemus too much in the direction of boorishness (see the note to ii. 44 above).

ii. 64.] *32* concludes Act II at this point. The break may have been suggested by the presence of a leaf in *MS* blank except for the words: 'Segue l'Aria di Damon consider fond shepherd' ('for the boy' is added in pencil).

ii. 80–2. *Not Show'rs to Larks, etc.*] Cf. Pope, 'Autumn', 44–6: 'Not balmy Sleep to Lab'rers faint with Pain, / Not Show'rs to Larks, nor Sunshine to the Bee, / Are half so charming as thy Sight to me.' This is the second of two possible contributions by Pope to the libretto (see the note to ii. 6 above).

ii. 86–7. *Help, Galatea ... Abodes*] Taken almost word for word from Dryden's Ovid, 206–7: 'Help, *Galatea*, help, my Parent Gods, / And take me dying to your deep Abodes.'

ii. 105. *roll his Urn*] Cf. Dryden's Ovid, 212: 'And rowl, among the River Gods, his Urn'.

ii. 108 ff. *Heart, the Seat of soft Delight, etc.*] The details of the final aria and chorus are drawn from the concluding lines of Dryden's Ovid, particularly 216–17 and 222 (which is close to ii. 112).

II. 112–13. *Rock, thy hollow Womb … flows*] Bertrand Bronson claims that these lines, not found in *32*, logically belong earlier ('The True Proportions of Gay's *Acis and Galatea*', *PMLA* lxxx, 1965, 330–1). He suggests that Handel transferred them in 1764 from the previous recitative. The lines are, however, found in *MS* and were no doubt simply omitted from *32* by accident.

Dione

Dione was never performed. Nicoll (p. 275) quotes the PRO document L. C. 5/157, p. 287: Rubric 'Order for Acting / Mr. Gay's pastorall / Tragedy.' 'I do hereby Order and direct that Mr. Gays / Pastorall Tragedy be immediately Acted after Mr. / Hugh's.' Directed by Wilks, Cibber, and Booth; dated 16 Feb. 1719/20. Nicoll comments: 'This evidently refers to *Dione*, which was apparently never acted; Hughes' *The Siege of Damascus* came out at D. L. on Wed. Feb. 17.' *Dione* was published in July 1720 in Gay's *Poems on Several Occasions* (see *The Whitehall Evening-Post*, 12–14 July 1720: 'This day will be deliver'd to the Subscribers POEMS on several Occasions. By Mr. John Gay.')

  Sigla: 20 In *Poems on Several Occasions* (1720), ii. 402–4 (Prologue) and 425–546. *Copies consulted*: Bodley Radcl. d. 60; BL 83. R. 21; BL Ashley 4838; a copy in my own possession.

  31 In *Poems on Several Occasions* (2nd edn., 1731), ii. 124–5 (Prologue) and 145–260. *Copies consulted*: Bodley 12. θ. 752; BL 11609. c. 10; two copies in my possession.

  Copy-text: 20, with the authorial emendations of *31*. The textual footnotes record editorial emendations of errors in the copy-text and all variants in the above editions.

Motto] 'There are powers to guard the lover, and Love is furious when abandoned for an illicit bond' (Tibullus, *Elegies* i. 5. 57–8).

Prologue] 'PROLOGUE. Design'd for the Pastoral Tragedy of DIONE' appeared in *Poems on Several Occasions* (1720), pp. 402–4. The play itself began on p. 425.

Prologue 21. *Hemskirk boors*] Egbert van Heemskerk (1634–1704) was an immigrant Dutch artist who painted grotesque scenes of contemporary life, and was an influence on Hogarth.

Prologue 26. *Calisto*] Calisto was one of Diana's virgin handmaidens, seduced by Jupiter in the form of Diana. Their son Arcas gave his name to Arcadia. Gay refers to Calisto in *Rural Sports* (1713), 285–9, and in 'To a young Lady, with some Lampreys', 46.

Prologue 33–4. *No trumpet's clangor, etc.*] Borrowed from *Rural Sports* (1713), 367–8: 'No Trumpet's Clangor wounds the Mother's Ear, / Nor calls the Lover from his swooning Fair.' These lines were not used in the final version of *Rural Sports* revised for Gay's *Poems on Several Occasions* in 1720.

Dramatis Personae] Gay obtained the names of his characters from various sources. The two main characters have the names of deities: *Evander* was a minor god worshipped in Arcadia and *Dione* was the mother of Aphrodite, though the name was often used for Aphrodite herself. Their assumed names are found frequently in pastoral literature (e.g. *Lycidas* in Theocritus, *Idylls* vii, and Virgil, *Eclogues* ix; *Alexis* in Virgil, *Eclogues* ii). *Parthenia* derives from παρθένος, a virgin. *Cleanthes* was a Stoic philosopher.

I. i. 39. *Paphian*] Aphrodite was worshipped at Paphos in Cyprus.

I. i. 40. *myrtle*] Myrtle is a sweet-smelling evergreen traditionally held sacred to Aphrodite and used as an emblem of love.

I. i. 49. *Orchomenos*] An important town in the eastern plains of Arcadia.

I. i. 69. *twelve mornings*] R. T. Kerlin, *Theocritus in English Literature* (Lynchburg, Va., 1910), p. 58, suggests that this particular interval of absence derives from Theocritus, *Idylls* ii, 4.

I. i. 121. *Black Cypress boughs*] Cf. *The History of the renown'd Don Quixote de la Mancha* (P. Motteux, 1700–3), i. 110: '... they saw advancing towards 'em, out of a cross-path, six Shepherds clad in black Skins, their Heads crown'd with Garlands of *Cypress* and bitter *Coast-mary*, with long Holly-Staves in their hands.' See the note to Gay's stated source for I. ii. below.

I. i. 122. *Menalcas*] The name occurs in Theocritus, *Idylls* viii and ix, and in Virgil, *Eclogues* iii and v.

I. i. 124. *He saw, he sighed, etc.*] Kerlin, op. cit., p. 58, suggests a derivation from Theocritus, *Idylls* ii, 82–3. See also Gay's 'Panthea', 6: 'He saw, he swore, he conquer'd and betray'd.' The formula is found also in Virgil, *Eclogues* viii. 41 ('ut vidi, ut perii, etc.').

I. ii. Gay's note] The episode of the astrologer-turned-shepherd, Chrysostom, who has died of love for Marcella, is found in *Don Quixote*, Part I, Book II, chs. 4–6. Gay used another episode from *Don Quixote* as the basis for *The Rehearsal at Goatham* (see Vol. II, p. 394).

I. ii. 5–7. *Low in the valley ... laid*] Cf. Motteux, i. 119: '... twas in yonder Bottom that he gave charge they shou'd bury his Corps.'

I. ii. 13–16. *When pitying lions ... weep*] Cf. 'Panthea', 37–40, and *The Shepherd's Week*, 'Wednesday', 67–72. These passages all derive from Virgil, *Eclogues* I, 59–63.

I. iii. sd. *Parthenia appears from the mountain*] Cf. Motteux, i. 126: 'Twas *Marcella* herself, who appear'd at the top of the Rock, at the foot of which they were digging the Grave.'

I. iii. 1–4. *Why this way ... bleeds anew*] Cf. Motteux, i. 126: 'What mak'st thou there, thou fierce, thou cruel Basilisk of these Mountains? com'st thou to see whether the Wounds of this murther'd Wretch will bleed afresh at they presence?'

I. iii. 7. *If I'm a Basilisk, the danger fly*] Cf. Motteux, i. 129: 'In short, let him that calls me a Tygress and a Basilisk, avoid me as a dangerous Thing.'

I. iii. 20. *I was not cruel; he was obstinate*] Cf. Motteux, i. 128: ' 'twas rather his own obstinacy than my cruelty that shorten'd his life.'

I. iii. 27–8. *Free was I born, etc.*] Cf. Motteux, i. 128: 'I was born free, and that I might continue so, I retir'd to these solitary hills and plains.'

I. iii. 44. *Whiten with moving fleece*] Cf. Pope, 'Spring', 19: 'Pour'd o'er the whitening Vale their fleecy Care'.

I. iv. 3–6. *O say . . . If ye have seen her*] Cf. *Acis and Galatea*, i. 28: 'O tell me if you saw my Dear.'

II. iii. 8. *spring blooms beneath her feet*] A traditional compliment, based on the myth of flowers blooming under Aphrodite's feet when she set foot on Cyprus. Cf. Pope, 'Summer', 75.

III. iii. 10. *the circling hare*] Cf. the description in *Rural Sports* (1713), 456 ff.

III. iv. 21–2. *'Still let their curses, etc.*] I agree with Faber (p. 394) that these lines are Parthenia's as reported by Dione.

IV. iii. 35. *The pilf'ring wolf*] Borrowed from Milton, *Comus*, 504.

IV. vii. 1. *Was ever grief like mine! O wretched maid!*] This line is identical with line 71 of Gay's translation of Ariosto, 'The Story of Fiordispina'. Cf. the words of Christ in the refrain of Herbert's 'The Sacrifice'. The sense is that of Lamentations, 1:12 ('behold and see, if there be any sorow like unto my sorowe') applied to Christ for example in Handel's *Messiah*.

IV. vii. 7 ff. *O lead me, etc.*] Cf. 'Panthea', 89–94.

V. i. 15. *When Thisbe sought her Love*] i.e. Pyramus, at Ninus' tomb. See Ovid, *Metamorphoses* iv. 55 f. Pyramus found her cloak mouthed by a bloodstained lion and killed himself, supposing her dead. When she found his body she stabbed herself.

The Captives

The Captives was first performed at Drury Lane on 15 January 1724, and received seven performances in the season. It was published on 23 January 1724. See *The Whitehall Evening-Post* no. 838, 21–3 January 1724.

Sigla: *24a* THE / CAPTIVES. / A / TRAGEDY. / As it is Acted at the / THEATRE-ROYAL in *Drury-lane*, / BY / His MAJESTY'S SERVANTS. / [rule] / *Splendide mendax, & in omne Virgo / Nobilis ævum.* Hor. / [rule] / *LONDON*: / Printed for J. TONSON at *Shakespear's-Head* / in the *Strand.* MDCCXXIV.

8°: A⁶B–E⁸F² [$4 signed (−A1, A2, A4, F2)]. Press-figures 2: B1ᵇ; 4: C6ᵇ, D5ᵇ; 5: B8ᵇ, D2ᵇ; 6: C8ᵃ, E8ᵃ. *Copies consulted*: Bodley M. Adds. 108. e. 144 (2); Linc 0. 10. 25 (i); Worc. LL. 1. 10; BL 11775. f. 13; BL Ashley 3253. Of these, only Ashley 3253, which is a large-paper issue, has the half-title (A1) and a frontispiece by Kent guarded in facing the title-page. *A Catalogue of Books, The Library of the late Rev. Dr. Swift* (Dublin, 1745), p. 13, records Swift's possession of a copy of the large-paper issue.

24b as *24a*, but A4 is a cancel, with 'Sent by an Unknown Hand.' inserted after 'PROLOGUE:' on A4ᵇ. *Copy consulted*: Trin I. 4. 36 [Rothschild 923].

Copy-text: 24a. Despite the claim by Faber (p. xxxviii) followed by Gaye (p. 248) and Irving (p. 202) that there was a second edition of *The Captives*, there appears to be no evidence of its existence, and Faber does not mention a second edition in his textual note to the play on p. 433. *24b* does not appear to have been known to these scholars, nor to Ault, whose attribution of the Epilogue to Pope (in *New Light*, pp. 207–14) depends upon the latter's request for an identical insertion to be made in the case of the Epilogue by means of a cancel. I discuss my reasons for rejecting *24b* in the note to the Prologue below. The textual footnotes also record the editorial emendation of an error in the copy-text, and speech-prefixes are silently expanded.

Motto] '[She was] gloriously untruthful, and a noble maiden for all time' (Horace, *Odes* iii, 11. 35–6). The girl was lying to her perjured father. She urged her husband to escape from him, not minding that she should be imprisoned for doing so. The motto alludes to Cylene's deception of Phraortes in order to secure the escape of Sophernes.

Dedication] The Princess Caroline had taken an interest in Gay's work ever since she met him at Hanover nearly ten years previously and asked for a copy of *The Shepherd's Week* (see Gay's letter to Ford, 7 August 1714, *Letters*, p. 12). There is a tradition that on the occasion of his reading of the play to the Princess he was so nervous that he stumbled over a stool and overturned a large screen. The earliest account of this incident that connects it with Gay is found in Benjamin Victor, *The History of the Theatres of London and Dublin* (1761), ii. 155–7, although a more detailed and ludicrous account of such an incident is given in *The Adventurer* no. 52 (5 May 1753). Here a whole series of embarrassments is described in the first person by 'Drammaticus' and there is no mention of Gay. Victor's anecdote may well have been prompted as much by the probably fictional *Adventurer* story as by any certainty that such a thing had actually happened to Gay, who was no stranger to the Court. But for Gay's reputedly 'clumsie Tread', see John Durant Breval, *The Confederates* (1717), ii. 64, and Philip Horneck, *The High-German Doctor* (1719), ii. 186.

Prologue] I have not incorporated into the text the words 'Sent by an unknown Hand' found on the cancel in *24b*, since they are likely to be the result of a misunderstanding by the publisher. The following letter from Pope to Jacob Tonson (Sherburn, ii. 215) should perhaps be quoted in full:

Tuesday night.

Sir,—Mr Gay & myself think it absolutely necessary that you should cancel that Leaf in which the Epilogue is printed, or if it falls out wrong, Cancell both leaves rather than fail; It must necessarily be inserted, after the Title *EPILOGUE* [*Sent by an unknown Hand.*] Whatever charge this Cancelling will cost, shall be paid. It is yet time, I am very sure, to do it, before the general publication on Thursday. This must be done to oblige him, & / Your most humble Servant / A. Pope.

I must go out before ten & shall be glad to see you (upon the other affair) before nine.

Norman Ault (*New Light*, pp. 207–14) argues that this letter refers to the Epilogue of *The Captives* and indicates Pope's authorship. The insertion would be designed to divert attention from Pope's contribution, largely because he had been refusing to supply such pieces for other friends such as Hughes and Fenton, and did not wish to offend them by revealing that he had written one for Gay. The consequent dating of the letter was tentatively accepted by Sherburn, but John Butt clearly found the evidence less than decisive and concluded that Pope's authorship was doubtful (Ault and Butt, p. 438). Ault's argument, which includes some stylistic evidence, is by no means a weak one, however (though it may be felt that Pope's objective was unlikely to have been achieved by drawing attention to the fact that the Epilogue was not by Gay but by someone else). In the absence of a credible alternative explanation of the letter, it must be concluded that in the very short time at his disposal, Tonson made the mistake of cancelling the wrong leaf, and that some copies containing the cancel were distributed before the mistake was discovered. There seems no reason, at any rate, to conclude that Gay did not write the Prologue. It is a characteristic apologia, referring to himself in the third person as he had done in the Prologue to *Dione*. *Pasquin* no. 105, 4 February 1723/24, assumes Gay to be the author of the Prologue.

Prologue 15. *sink a joke*] i.e. avoid the opportunity for satire. Gay is perhaps still mindful of the storm over his last performed play, *Three Hours after Marriage*. The light and tentative tone of this Prologue conceals a real wish to be moving and edifying, and he wants to be judged on his merits.

Epilogue] For Pope's possible authorship, see the note to the Prologue above.

Epilogue 4. *Masquerades*] For an account of the sexual opportunities afforded by masquerades, see the *Spectator* no. 8, 9 March 1711, and *The Rape of the Lock*, i. 72.

Epilogue 27. *both these Faustuses*] *Harlequin Doctor Faustus*, produced at Drury Lane in November 1723, and *The Necromancer; or Harlequin Doctor Faustus*, produced at Lincoln's Inn Fields in December 1723. Cf. *The Dunciad*, iii. 266: 'Here shouts all Drury, there all Lincoln's-Inn.' Pope has been describing (229 ff.) the Lincoln's Inn Fields production of *The Necromancer*.

Epilogue 29–30. *Yet there are wives, etc.*] Ault (*New Light*, p. 213) writes that this couplet contains 'like a miniature, the whole plot and tone of Pope's *The Wife of Bath her Prologue* (1713)'.

Dramatis Personae] Some of the names of the characters are historical, and may be found in Herodotus. *Phraortes* (i. 102) was (in Macaulay's translation) 'not satisfied to be ruler of the Medes alone, but marched upon the Persians'. *Hydarnes* (iii. 70) was brought into the plot against the Pseudo-Smerdis. Araxes (i. 202) is the name of a river that flows into the Caspian

Sea. *Sophernes* is made up of σοφός and the Persian suffix *-phernes* (from *farna*, 'glory'). 'Sophy' was also a current term for the Shah, from the reigning dynasty's surname *Safī* or *Safavī*. *Cylene* (the 'Captive') suggests the Arcadian Mt. Cyllene, birthplace of Hermes, god of the happy lie, though *Astarbe* and *Cylene* are also reminiscent of 'Astarte' and 'Cybele', both names of goddesses.

I. iii. 25. *villian*] Faber emends to 'villain', but the spelling of the copy-text is valid in the seventeenth and eighteenth centuries.

I. iii. 39. *Ingratitude's a crime*] Cf. Xenophon, *Cyropaedia*, i. 2. 7.

I. v. 8. *Our Priests are train'd up spies*] The discovery of the Atterbury plot (see the Introduction, p. 40) was a triumph for the government's network of informers. In *Pasquin* no. 63, 6 September 1723, the government 'de-cypherers' were actually called 'dreadful Magi'.

I. v. 19–20. *It is your duty, And I submit*] Cf. Oronooko's 'I know my Fortune, and submit to it' (*The Works of Mr. Thomas Southerne*, 1713, ii, 177). For the influence of *Oroonoko* on *The Captives*, see the Introduction, p. 40).

I. v. 86–90. *O source of light ... bondage*] Cf. Oronooko's words about Imoinda (op. cit., ii. 207): 'Thou God ador'd thou ever-glorious Sun! / If she be yet on Earth, send me a Beam / Of thy All-seeing Power to light me to her.'

I. v. 97–8. *This last distress ... pity*] Cf. Blanford's comment: 'Alas! I pity you' (op. cit., ii. 207).

I. v. 140–2. *My fellow soldiers ... the cause of all*] Cf. Oronooko's 'We have been Fellow-Soldiers in the Field; / Now we are Fellow-Slaves (op. cit., ii. 198).

I. vii. 1. *I've done my duty, and I've done no more*] This line was borrowed by Tom Thumb in Fielding's *The Tragedy of Tragedies*, I. iii. 6.

II. i. 8–10. *methinks I hear ... cypress boughs*] Parodied by Fielding in *The Tragedy of Tragedies*, I. iii. 52.

II. ii. 32. *I sigh, I pant, I burn*] Cf. Polyphemus in *Acis and Galatea*, II. 9: 'I rage, I melt, I burn.'

III. i. 22–5. *mercy ... crown*] Cf. *The Merchant of Venice*, IV. i. 185.

III. v. 9–16. *Proclaim a festival ... feast*] Most of these lines are quoted in Fielding's note to *The Tragedy of Tragedies*, I. ii. 1.

IV. vii. 9sd] Cf. Imoinda's fainting in the recognition scene in *Oroonoko* (op. cit., ii. 215) or Almeria's fainting at the discovery that Osmyn is her husband Alphonso in Congreve's *The Mourning Bride*, I. ii.

v. vii. 7. *O glorious Sun!*] Gay also writes about Persian sun worship in the *Fables* (I. xxviii: 'The Persian, the Sun and the Cloud'). Cf. scenes in the Temple of the Sun in Rowe's *The Ambitious Step-mother*, and in Theobald's *The Persian Princess*.

GLOSSARY

EACH word is given in the form in which it appears in the text, a reference to which immediately follows, though not all uses in the plays of a particular word are necessarily given. The following abbreviations are used:

M = *The Mohocks*
WB = *The Wife of Bath* (1713)
W = *The What D'Ye Call It*
TH = *Three Hours after Marriage*
AG = *Acis and Galatea*
D = *Dione*
C = *The Captives*

Comm indicates that the word is also dealt with in the Commentary.

Apozems (TH II. 367): Infusions.
Arcana (TH II. 232): The supposed great secrets of nature, sought by alchemists.
Asphaltion (TH III. 149 *Comm*): Bituminous clover.
Ataxy (TH I. 52): Irregularity of the animal functions.

Bolus (TH II. 366): Large round pill.
Bone-Lace (WB v. 510): A form of knitting with linen thread from bone bobbins upon a pattern made with pins.
Boobily (M III. 122): Booby-like (the earliest *OED* example is from Mandeville, *Fable of the Bees*, 1714, i. 346).
Brimmer (TH II. 494): A brimming cup.
Bristol Stone (TH I. 606 *Comm*): Transparent rock-crystal.
Bubble (WB II. 208): Dupe.
Bulk (M II. 59): Stall, or framework projecting from the front of a shop.

Calcination (TH II. 241): Reduction by fire to a 'calx' or powder.
Catopticks (WB IV. 97): Catoptrics, that part of optics which treats of reflexion.
Cephalalgy (TH II. 338): Headache.

Chap (TH Prologue 28 *Comm*): From *chapman*, a merchant, a 'person to have to do with' (*OED*).
Chaunter (WB v. 361): A priest who sings masses in a chantry.
Chiromancy (WB IV. 96): Palmistry.
Chuff (WB II. 336): Boor.
Cinder Wench (M ii. 246): Girl occupied in raking cinders from ashes.
Clearings (TH III. 545): Balance of pay (military).
Cockard (TH Epilogue 43): Cockade, a ribbon or rosette worn in the hat as a badge of office or party.
Complexion (WB I. 169): Proportion of the humours.
Crambo (WB III. 163): Game in which one player gives a word or line of verse to which each of the others has to find a rhyme.
Cramp-ring (W II. ii. 15): Ring supposed to prevent cramp or falling sickness.
Crosses (WB I. 142): Quarrels, troubles.
Cunning-men (WB III. 156 *Comm*): Astrologers.

Diopticks (WB IV. 97): Dioptrics, that part of optics which treats of the refraction of light.
Drill (TH III. 341): Mandrill.

Dub (TH II. 121): Invest with a dignity or title (i.e. of cuckold).

Eagle-stone (TH II. 214 *Comm*): Kind of iron oxide supposed to be efficacious against abortion.
Eft (TH III. 108): Small lizard.
Exuviæ (TH III. 259): Cast skins.

Fæculencies (TH II. 374): Impurities.
Fath (M iii. 146, WB II. 130): Faith.
Fescue (W I. i. 27): Pointer for teaching children letters.
Fluxion (TH II. 266 *Comm*): Newton's form of the calculus.
Fortune-Book (WB I. 206): Book used to consult fortunes or future events.
Fortune-stealers (WB II. 60): Elopers with heiresses.
Full Bottom (M ii. 214 *Comm*): A full-bottomed wig.

Genevre (TH I. 192): Gin.
Gillian (M ii. 165 *Comm*): Woman.
Glister (TH II. 353): Clyster, enema.
Goust (M ii. 246, TH III. 493): Taste.
Grigs (WB v. 322): Crickets.

Hippomanes (TH II. 305 *Comm*): Love philtre made from a slimy fluid excreted by mares.
Hoity toity (WB I. 346): 'Ramp or rude girl' (Canting Crew).
Hydroticks (TH II. 372): Medicines which cause a discharge of water.

Intemperies (TH II. 359): A disease.

Janizary (M ii. 189 *Comm*): 'Any lewd gang depending upon others' (Canting Crew).
Jointure (WB Prologue 24): Holding of property in joint use, or the entailing of an estate on the wife after the husband's death.

Lutestring (TH III. 511): A kind of glossy silk fabric.

Manteger (TH III. 62 *Comm*): Mandrill, confused with the mythical Manticore.
Matadores (TH I. 16): Highest trumps in ombre or quadrille.

Mechlen (TH I. 562): Made of Mechlin lace.
Menstruum (TH II. 251): Solvent.

Nisiprises (W I. i. 45 *Comm*): Nisi Prius, the hearing of civil causes by judges of assize.

Obnubilated (TH I. 266): Obscured.
Ombre (M ii. 208): A card game fashionable in the seventeenth and early eighteenth centuries.
Owlers (TH Prologue 11 *Comm*): Smugglers.

Paregoricks (TH II. 373): Anodynes.
Papishes (W II. iv. 30): Papists.
Pathognomick (TH II. 63): Sign or symptom by which a disease may be known.
Pax (WB v. 420): Pox (reflecting affected pronunciation).
Pearl Cordial (TH I. 203): Cordial containing powdered pearl.
Phiz (M ii. 159): Face [physiognomy].
Pipe (WB II. 356): Wine-cask of 105 gallons.
Pitch-frog (WB II. 54 *Comm*): Scabbard.
Plain-work (W I. i. 71): Ordinary sewing.
Poach (M ii. 30): Poke.
Posset (TH II. 432): A drink of hot milk curdled with wine.
Procidence (TH I. 62 *Comm*): Relaxing.
Punctilio (WB I. 256): Petty formality.
Put (TH II. 392): 'A silly, shallow-pated Fellow' (Canting Crew).

Quatenus (TH I. 37, III. 390): In the capacity of.
Quorum (W Introductory Scene 68): Those JPs whose presence was necessary to constitute a bench.

Railly (WB III. 350): Rally, tease.
Raree-show (TH I. 73): Peep show.
Round-House (M ii. 239): Lock-up, place of detention.

Sashes (M i. 25): Sash-windows.
Scower (M i. 79): Scourge.
Shatterbrains (TH I. 592): Lack of intelligence (cf. *Wit and Mirth*, ii. 327).

Shaver (WB v. 322): 'A subtil, smart fellow' (Canting Crew).
Skip (WB iv. 140): Servant.
Slabdash (WB iv. 299): Slapdash. This form is not recorded by *OED*.
Snake-root (TH ii. 70): Root of American plant, reputedly an antidote to snake poison.
Stale (M ii. 275): Beer that has stood long enough to clear.
Stink-pot (TH ii. 368): Smoke bomb.
Stragler (M ii. 262): Camp follower.

Tipstaff (TH iii. 535): Constable or law-court official.
Toast (C Epilogue 15): One of the reigning belles of the season.
To rights (WB ii. 97): At once.
Torose (TH ii. 343): Swollen.

Touchwood (WB v. 390): Irascible person.
Trimmer (TH Epilogue 12): One who inclines to each of two sides as interest dictates.
Tympany (TH i. 202): Tumour.

Vails (TH ii. 91): Gratuitites.
Vagarys (W i. iv. 17): Frolics.
Venice-Treacle (TH iii. 81 *Comm*): An opiate.

Water-pap (TH iii. 415): Baby food.
Weather (C Epilogue 19): Wether, castrated ram.
Whipping (WB v. 510): Gathering material into a frill.
Wildings (AG ii. 38 *Comm*): Wild fruit.
Woundy (W Introductory Scene 27): Very great.